McGRAW-HILL SERIES IN GEOGRAPHY

V. C. FINCH, *Consulting Editor*

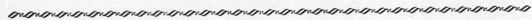

ASIA'S LANDS AND PEOPLES

McGRAW-HILL SERIES
IN GEOGRAPHY

Bennett—SOIL CONSERVATION

Cressey—ASIA'S LANDS AND PEOPLES

Finch and Trewartha—ELEMENTS OF GEOGRA-
PHY: Physical and Cultural

Finch and Trewartha—PHYSICAL ELEMENTS OF
GEOGRAPHY
(A republication of Part I of the above)

Platt—LATIN AMERICA

Raisz—GENERAL CARTOGRAPHY

Trewartha—AN INTRODUCTION TO WEATHER
AND CLIMATE

Whitbeck and Finch—ECONOMIC GEOGRAPHY

Whitbeck and Williams—ECONOMIC GEOGRA-
PHY OF SOUTH AMERICA

One-third the earth.

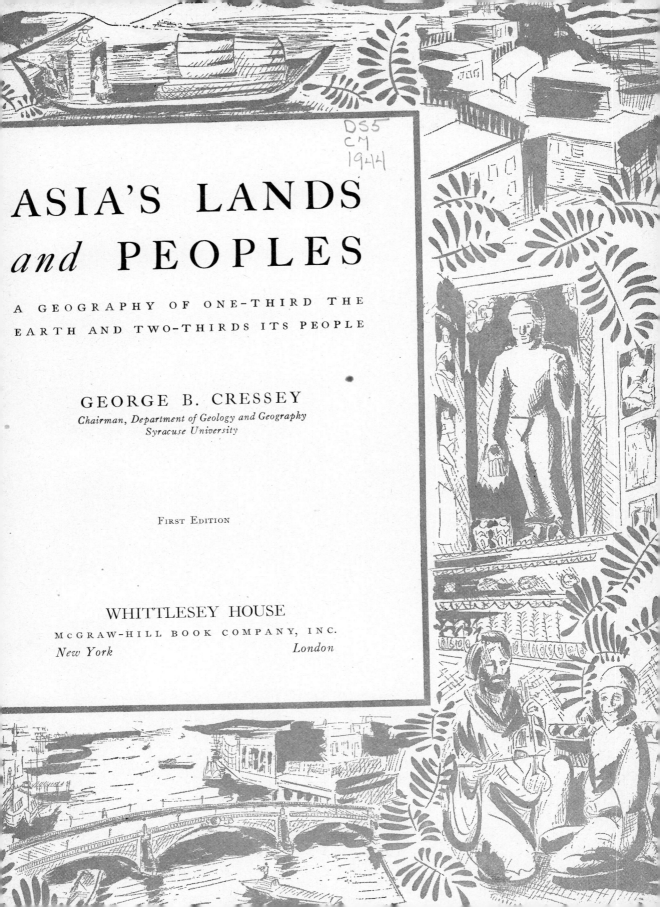

ASIA'S LANDS
and PEOPLES

A GEOGRAPHY OF ONE-THIRD THE EARTH AND TWO-THIRDS ITS PEOPLE

GEORGE B. CRESSEY

Chairman, Department of Geology and Geography
Syracuse University

FIRST EDITION

WHITTLESEY HOUSE

McGRAW-HILL BOOK COMPANY, INC.

New York   *London*

PUBLISHED BY WHITTLESEY HOUSE

A division of the McGraw-Hill Book Company, Inc.

Printed in the United States of America by the Maple Press Co., York, Pa.

Preface

This volume is a preface to world citizenship. These chapters may not be required reading for everyone, but it seems essential that many people understand many of the ideas here presented. It is not necessary to compare the relative importance of Asia with other continents, but it is obvious that one-third of the earth and two-thirds of its inhabitants command attention.

Geography deals with all the items that give personality to the face of the earth. This volume thus considers both land and people, the physical and the cultural landscapes. Too many of these pages are filled with encyclopedic facts. In themselves such facts are of little meaning except to the specialist; taken together it is hoped that they provide a basis for understanding Asia's geographic foundations. The reader will need to discern between supporting evidence and ideas, and to select the information pertinent to his interests.

Vast changes are in progress throughout Asia. The Soviet Union transformed its economic life in the period between the First and Second World Wars, and China may well duplicate this development during the second half of the twentieth century. Japan's future is uncertain, but her conspicuous achievements in the past give promise of an important place. India faces complex problems but will assuredly find a solution.

All this has significance for the United States in its role as the greatest Pacific power. On the one hand is the possibility of mutual good will, trade, and security; on the other is political and economic chaos both international and internal. Only an informed America can act intelligently in a global world.

Readers who wish to secure the highlights of the volume should examine Chapter 1 on the Pacific, Chapter 2 on Asia as a whole, Chapters 3 and 9 on China, Chapters 11 and 14 on Japan, Chapters 15 and 18 on the Soviet Union, and Chapters 30 and 33 on India. Where used as a textbook in a brief course, it should prove feasible to omit Chapters 3–5 or 6–8, 10–11 or 12–13, 15–18 or 19–21, and 29–30 or 31–32.

Acknowledgments

Asia is too large to be fully understood by any one person. The author is keenly aware of his shortcomings and of the deficiencies in this volume. The completion of the volume was made possible by two grants-in-aid from the Carnegie Corporation. Assistance from Syracuse University is also gratefully acknowledged. Almost every reference under the Suggested Readings has contributed helpful ideas. This study has evolved out of nearly 100,000 miles of travel in Asia, spread over two decades. The indebtedness to camel drivers, inn keepers, local officials, missionary hosts, and the author's students is very real.

Most of the American authorities on the geography of Asia have cooperated by

Sep '44

34416

reading portions of the manuscript. Innumerable items have been added at their suggestion. Several scholars not listed offered to assist but were prevented by other responsibilities.

The chapters on Japan have had the benefit of help from Robert B. Hall of the University of Michigan, Glenn Trewartha of the University of Wisconsin, Shannon McCune of The Ohio State University, Miriam S. Farley of the Institute of Pacific Relations, and Joseph A. Russell and Douglas Haring of Syracuse University.

Chinese chapters have profited from the criticism of James Thorp of the United States Department of Agriculture, Joseph E. Spencer of the University of California at Los Angeles, and Chi-yun Chang of the National University of Chekiang.

For assistance on the Soviet Union the author is indebted to E. C. Ropes of the United States Bureau of Foreign and Domestic Commerce, W. Elmer Ekblaw of Clark University, Harriet Moore of the American Russian Institute, and William Mandel and Andrew Grajdanzev of the Institute of Pacific Relations.

The chapters on India have greatly benefited by aid from the author's brother Paul F. Cressey of Wheaton College, Edward Groth of the United States Department of State, Wellington D. Jones of the University of Chicago, Harry P. Brown of Syracuse University, from the Institute of Pacific Relations, and from the British Library of Information.

Southeastern Asiatic chapters owe much of their value to the cooperation of Robert L. Pendleton, formerly Agricultural Adviser to the Government of Thailand; Lester Trueblood, formerly of Judson College; Samuel Van Valkenburg of Clark University; and Jan O. M. Broek of the University of California.

The maps are the work of four graduate students in the Department of Geology and Geography at Syracuse University: Rowland Illick, Walter Bailey, J. Lewis Robinson, and William Black.

Maps

In order to convey a proper sense of proportion, most of the maps are reproduced on uniform scales and a single azimuthal equal distance projection; they may be fitted together if desired. The scales are 1:75,000,000 for Asia as a whole, and 1:30,000,000 for countries and realms. A scale of 1:2,000,000 is used for the vicinity of cities. If the second of these scales unduly crowds Japan and leaves large blank areas within the Soviet Union, it is well to emphasize that just this is the case.

Lantern Slides

Lantern slides of any photographs or drawings in the book may be secured from the Syracuse University Book Store, Syracuse 10, New York.

GEORGE B. CRESSEY.

SYRACUSE UNIVERSITY
January, 1944.

Contents

Contents

ASIA'S LANDS AND PEOPLES

Chapter 1

THE PACIFIC BASIN

America Faces the Orient

The Pacific is a whale of an ocean, larger by millions of square miles than all the continents combined. From Singapore to Panama and from Bering Strait to Antarctica, lies 10,000 miles of almost empty water. Here is room for 257 states the size of Texas, or for 16 Chinas. Across this vast expanse the United States faces Asia. The largest of the oceans is an appropriate preface to the largest of continents.

What was once a barrier is now a highway; clipper planes span the Pacific in less than a week where clipper ships once took more than three months. Over the Alaska air route, one may reach Chungking from New York by plane as quickly as California by rail. The Orient has ceased to be distant, and what Europe calls the Far East is now in reality America's Near West.

Can this Pacific basin become a community? On its opposite shores have developed the oldest and the newest cultures. Diverse environments and racial contrasts need not prevent the exchange of goods and ideas. Today Japan learns from the Occident, and America may equally profit from the mature philosophy of China. Asia is a land of rich heritage and this ancient continent is rapidly assuming a new significance in the world of today.

The United States fortunately borders two oceans and faces three continents. Although physically bounded by the Atlantic and the Pacific, in too much of its thinking the country has remained an island surrounded by the Atlantic. On Oct. 12, 1492, Columbus discovered America; on Dec. 7, 1941, America discovered Asia. These two dates may come to be of comparable significance. Whatever the history of the second half of the twentieth century, we shall surely live in a world that is round. Asia may not become more important than Europe but its one-third of the earth and its two-thirds of the people will play a very large role in American affairs.

The continental pattern of North America tends to turn it toward Europe. Land, minerals, people, and history, all face east. But, even though the dominant interests have been Atlantic-ward, an increasing concern with Pacific problems is inevitable. American trade with China goes back a century and a half. The shore line of the United States along the Pacific is longer than that of any other nation, and from Seattle to Yokohama is but one hundred miles farther than from New York to Naples. Midway between Europe, Asia, and South America, the United States is indeed the "middle kingdom."

Since the fifteenth century, the riches of Cathay and the Indies have been a lodestone which has lured men around Africa or across the Atlantic. Columbus carried a letter to the Grand Khan of Cathay, John Cabot sailed from England to find Zipango or Japan, and Henry Hudson ran his boat

1

aground near Albany trying to reach Canton. The China trade came to have a significant place in the early history of the United States.

Toward the close of the Revolutionary War, an American sailor named John Ledyard deserted from the British fleet off New York City and returned to his home in Connecticut. Some years before he had been with Captain Cook in the Pacific and, while in Canton, was impressed by the excitement with which the Chinese noticed a few furs on the sailor's bunks. So eager were the Chinese that they paid $100 apiece for furs that had been bought from the Indians along the Oregon coast for sixpence worth of trinkets. Ledyard had a vision as to the importance of the Pacific Northwest in a possible fur trade with the Orient but was unable to interest the merchants of the Atlantic seaboard.

The early American states had emerged from the war for independence in serious economic straits. Many of the wealthy had fled, there were few industries and much unemployment, and foreign trade was negligible. In 1784, Robert Morris, the nearly bankrupt financier of the Revolution, determined to send the first American ship to Canton. He had heard Ledyard's story and was impressed with the market in China, but decided that it was safer to have his *Empress of China* sail via the better known African route with its established way points instead of across the Pacific. After a voyage of a year and a half, the ship returned with a profit of 25 per cent.

With this auspicious start, American trade with Asia was under way and successive vessels were invariably successful. It is not too much to say that the profits from the early China trade were a critical factor in enabling the United States to establish economic independence; without this new income from abroad it might well have remained a rural settlement.

In 1790, the vessel *Columbia* sailed from Boston by way of Cape Horn bound for Oregon, Hawaii, and Canton, and returned via the Cape of Good Hope, the first American ship to go around the world. Ginseng from the Hudson Valley for China; knives and trinkets from New England to be traded along the Oregon coast for furs, or for sandalwood in Hawaii, tea secured in Canton by trading ginseng, furs, and sandalwood; and good British cash from the sale of the tea in England—these were the items in the early round-the-world trade. By 1811, the annual commerce of the United States with China rose to $45,000,000—no small item in those days.

Furs provided a substantial part of this trade. It was an interest in the furs of the Oregon country that sent Lewis and Clark across the continent and prompted John Jacob Astor to found Astoria at the mouth of the Columbia River. Without the lure of the China trade, the United States might well have been content with less than the full span of the continent.

The war with England in 1812 nearly swept American commerce from the Pacific, but for sixty years thereafter, Yankee sealing and, later, whaling ships were supreme in their field. Unlike the trading vessels that preceded them, the whalers followed no definite course but ranged from Siberian waters to the Antarctic in quest of the sperm whale. By 1842 there were 675 vessels in the business, the majority of them in the Pacific, and the total whaling trade from 1804 to 1876 was valued at $332,000,000. Much of the wealth of present-day New England dates back to fortunes made in the Pacific during the nineteenth century.

During these wanderings, hundreds of uncharted islands were discovered and landed on for the first time. Old logbooks are still yielding records and maps. The United States did not bother to take title to these islands and they were later claimed by European powers. These whaling voyages now form the basis of revived American claims to many Pacific islands once

From the Revolution to the Civil War, the Pacific played a major role in American commerce and in the overland expansion

Clipper ships, such as the *Flying Cloud* on the right, played a large role in America's exploration of the Pacific.
(*Courtesy John Hancock Life Insurance Company.*)

ican claims to many Pacific islands once unimportant but today significant bases for transoceanic airplanes. It is fortunate for the new epoch of aviation that a century ago Yankee captains ruled the Pacific.

The era of the clipper ships began in the 1840's and, until the advent of steam, these sailing vessels broke all records for speed. The *Flying Cloud* (Captain Josiah Cressey) made two trips from New York to San Francisco in the record time of 89 days and continued to Canton in 94 days more. Scores of United States vessels traded along the China coast, and it is not surprising that it was an American, Admiral Perry, who opened Japan in 1853.

to the West Coast. With the discovery of gold in California and the settlement of the Great Plains, the United States became absorbed in internal construction, and the stars and stripes almost disappeared from the high seas.

By the time of the First World War, America had ceased to be a pioneering land devoting its energies to homesteading, new railroads, and new factories. The United States has grown up, and foreign commerce is again significant. Will the Pacific once more be a key to America's problems? Just as commerce with Asia saved the economic life of the United States in earlier years, so it is possible that trade with China may be a major factor in the immediate future. An adequate appreciation of Asia's lands and peoples provides an essential preface to an understanding of America's future.

Trans-Pacific Contacts

Trans-Pacific trade dates from the Manila galleons which sailed from 1564 to 1815. These Spanish vessels carried a fabulous cargo from the Philippines to Acapulco in Mexico, where it was shipped over the China Road to Mexico City en route to Europe. Westbound, these ships followed the trade winds south of the Hawaiian Islands; on the eastbound voyage they took a great-circle course north of the islands in order to be in the zone of the westerlies. This brought them to the California coast where Spain sought a port as a way station and for protection against such privateers as Sir Francis Drake; thus California first gained significance from its proximity to Asia.

Within the span of two and a half centuries, more than a thousand galleons moved out of the Orient. In addition to the products of the Philippines such as cigars, there were silk, porcelain, and embroidery from China; spices from the East Indies; drugs, ivory, camphor, and teak from Malaya; and gems from India. In return came Mexican silver, copper, and cacao.

This trade still continues but between different ports. Most of it moves from San Francisco, Seattle, and Vancouver to Yokohama, Osaka, Shanghai, Hongkong, Manila, and Singapore. Tokyo is today closer to San Francisco than is Salt Lake City; not in miles or time but in the cost of shipping freight. The ocean is a free highway without a roadbed to keep up or mountains to climb or taxes en route. Ocean trade has long since knit together the Atlantic basin; it will increasingly link the lands around the Pacific.

The good things of the earth are unequally distributed. Nature has seemed to play favorites, and many of the essential raw materials such as tin, oil, and rubber, or even productive soil, are highly localized. No nation has everything, and even the most fortunate countries are seriously deficient in some essentials. Some peoples have the skill or capital with which to produce complicated products; others can best specialize on basic commodities. Interdependence is the first lesson of geography.

Among the essential raw materials that America lacks are the ferroalloys—chromium, manganese, nickel, and tungsten; the nonferrous metals—aluminum, antimony, mercury, and tin; the nonmetallic minerals—mica and quartz crystal; tropical vegetable products including cocoanut oil, Manila hemp, quinine, and rubber; and also silk and wool. Political subsidies make it possible for the United States to develop low-grade domestic supplies, and synthetic products can replace some of these, but the increasing complexity of industry calls for an ever wider variety of basic resources. The United States and the Soviet Union can more nearly enjoy the luxury of self-sufficient autarchy than other countries, but no land is adequately provided with all its modern needs.

Until the Second World War, few Americans realized their vital dependence upon eastern Asia and the southwest Pacific as a source of supply. Manila hemp, quinine, rubber, silk, tin, tungsten, and cocoanut products were almost exclusively from this area; while antimony, mica, and wool were largely procured there. Thus, 10 of the 16 essentials are best obtained in Asia, while manganese, chromium, and many other less vital products are also available. No other part of the world is so essential to the normal industrial prosperity or national security of the United States. Africa contributes only chromium and manganese. To Europe it looks for mercury and manganese. Canada has nickel, while South America furnishes quartz crystal, aluminum, and antimony, plus some wool and tin. Under normal conditions, two-fifths of the tonnage required for American strategic imports comes across the Pacific. No one need ask, "Why study Asia?"

American trade with Asia has changed with the passage of time. In the early years it was a quest for the special products of the Orient, such as tea, silk, and porcelains, for which the United States had little to offer in return. In modern times there were unique products like rubber, tin, tung oil, antimony, and tungsten; with exports of simple manufactured goods, kerosene, and cotton. Asia is in the midst of her industrial revolution, and the market will call for increasing amounts of heavy machinery and producers' goods, as well as consumers' goods in great variety. Between 1926 and 1930, 29 per cent of American imports came from eastern Asia while in 1937 the figure was 30 per cent. In the same periods American exports to this area were 11 and 17 per cent. Malaya, Japan, the Philippines, and China have been the leading source of imports, in order, while Japan and the Philippines have taken the chief exports.

The items that the United States shipped to the Far East including India in 1937 were, in order of value, iron and steel products, petroleum, raw cotton, automobiles, industrial machinery, copper, paper, tobacco, cotton goods, aircraft, and lumber. These and the other products had a value of $469,123,000. From the Far East the commodities, which exceed 50 per cent of our total imports, were abacá (Manila hemp), agar-agar, bristles, camphor, cinchona (quinine), cocoanut oil and copra, jute, kapok, lac, menthol, nux vomica, oil seeds, palm oil, rubber, silk, soybeans, tapioca, tea, tin, tung oil, and tungsten.

Trade is not the only link between the East and West. Thousands of missionaries have carried a large measure of American good will to Japan, China, and India and have brought back a more intelligent understanding to their constituents in the United States. For every returned American businessman or government official who addresses a luncheon club, there are dozens of missionaries on furlough who are interpreting Asia to the United States. The mutual reservoir of good will that has resulted is incalculable.

One of the major points of weakness in American education is the lack of attention to the Orient. Children study Shakespeare but know nothing of Confucius; they understand little enough of Europe but even less of India. When China discovered the modern world, her educational program was already overcrowded but she found a place for new languages and new geography. So too must the West.

Hawaii

Two thousand four hundred and four miles west of San Francisco's Golden Gate lies Honolulu and "the loveliest fleet of islands that lies anchored in any ocean" (Mark Twain). Five jumps farther west by Pan-American clipper are Hongkong and Singapore; three flights southward bring one to New Zealand. Due north is Dutch Harbor off the tip of Alaska, and slightly south of east lies Panama.

The Hawaiian Islands are an American outpost and at the same time the crossroads of the Pacific. For the United States, their strategic significance is enormous. No other island group in Polynesia is so important in either population, products, or strategy. From the island of Midway, near the International Date Line, eastward to the big island of Hawaii is 1,500 miles. The eight major islands lie near longitude 160°W., with Oahu and the capital city of

Honolulu near the center of group; to the west are a dozen small islands and reefs.

Three dates are significant: the discovery

desire for statehood results from Congressional restrictions on sugar production in 1934 which seemed to imply that the

The crater of Halemaumau occupies the center of the down-faulted caldera of Kilauea, the most active volcano of the islands. (*Courtesy U.S. Navy.*)

by Captain Cook in 1778, the arrival of the first New England missionaries in 1820, and annexation in 1898. The islands are now a territorial possession of the United States, with their own legislature and an appointed governor from Washington. With a population of 426,654 people (1940) and an economic importance exceeding that of several western states, many interests in the Territory of Hawaii are agitating for statehood. But so long as military strategy dominates and one-third of the population is of Japanese descent, Federal control may remain. Much of the

islands were not an integral part of the United States.

Racial complexity dominates the Hawaiian Islands, and the resulting fusion has been singularly successful. Second-generation Japanese are two inches taller than their fathers and Hawaiian-born Orientals are forming a new race which insists on being called American. Since the days when Yankee fur traders en route from Oregon to China stopped for cargoes of sandalwood, immigration has brought new blood. British, Russian, and French political influence have successively been dominant and, along with Portuguese immigration, have introduced a European racial strain. Sugar plantations have called for a large labor supply, furnished by Japanese, Chinese, Korean, Puerto Rican, and Filipino migrants. Only 21,000 pure Hawaiians remain.

The Hawaiian chain is a long series of volcanic peaks. If the Pacific Ocean were drained, these would stand out as some of the highest mountains on earth, for Mauna Kea and Mauna Loa on the island of Hawaii rise 13,784 and 13,680 feet, respectively, above sea level, which in turn is 18,000 feet above the near-by ocean floor. Volcanic activity is progressively more recent toward the east, with Kilauea as the most spectacular crater under the American flag. Even within sight of Honolulu are three fresh cones, fortunately quiescent.

Several types of configuration characterize the islands. Broad lava domes surround the larger cones; deeply dissected and notably steep ridges mark old fault blocks or portions of caldera rims; elsewhere there are rough lava flows. More gentle areas include alluvial slopes, coastal plains, and weathered areas of old ash or flows. Since the islands are essentially mountain summits, it is not surprising that even approximately level land covers but a tenth of the area. Out of a total area of 6,435 square miles, considerably less than New Jersey, two-thirds is on the Island of Hawaii.

Trade-wind climate prevails for 300 days a year, with steady northeast winds and rainfall which varies according to altitude. These winds are so nearly saturated that the cooling incident to a 3,000-foot rise causes condensation; hence windward slopes have a precipitation of several hundred inches. In the lee of the mountains rainfall diminishes to less than 20 inches. Where the barrier is not too high, as on Oahu, the maximum readings may be over the crest on the southern slopes. Thus the rainfall 15 miles from Honolulu averages 240 inches while at Waikiki Beach it is but 20. Since the city extends inland several miles, one may choose his residence according to his climatic preference.

The Hawaiian Islands lie near the northern margin of the trades, and several times a year the equatorward movement of subtropical high pressure brings southern winds and rain to the previous lee slopes. These short but recurrent spells produce oppressive humidity; otherwise the islands enjoy perpetual spring with temperatures in the low seventies. The annual temperature range is so low that the maximum and minimum readings of the year may come within 24 hours.

The summit of Mt. Waialeale, 5,080 feet, appears to have the heaviest rainfall in the world, with a 20-year average, 1918 to 1938, of 460.2 inches. This exceeds the 72-year record of 451.6 inches at Cherrapunji in India. Vertical zonation of climate, and thus of land use, is conspicuous. From 2,000 to 4,000 feet, conditions resemble the tierra templada in the highlands of Central America. Snow falls only on the highest peaks.

Two crops dominate agriculture: sugar cane and pineapple. In early times taro was the chief product, and both it and rice are still important. Other products include coffee, corn, bananas, cotton, and tropical fruits. So much of the land is devoted to the two export crops that the islands do not feed themselves and import two-thirds of their food. Even fresh vegetables are shipped from California.

Sugar supplies much of the wealth. Extensive research has made production per acre the highest in the world, but the latitude is marginal for cane and the crop requires 18 to 24 months for growth in contrast to 14 months in Java and Cuba. Five to six crops are raised from each planting. Abundant moisture is essential, and if the rainfall is under 125 inches, irrigation is necessary to ensure the high yield. The cane for a ton of sugar requires 2,000 tons of the world's canned supply. The annual pack exceeds ten million cases. As with sugar, research has notably improved yields

Sugar cane and pineapples, here shown to the left and right of an irrigation ditch, are the main crops of the Hawaiian Islands. (*Courtesy U.S. Navy.*)

of water. Most plantations spend large sums for irrigation canals and pumping. Irrigated cane yields 8.6 tons of sugar in contrast to 5.5 tons on unirrigated fields.

Hawaiian sugar amounts to a million tons a year, which is 3 per cent of world output. The entire production goes to the United States and supplies one-seventh of that market. Since cane is heavy, the 38 mills are located near the fields. Plantations range from 660 to 15,000 acres, and from sea level to 2,000 feet.

Pineapples are Hawaii's most distinctive crop, and the islands furnish three-quarters

and quality. To check evaporation and prevent weeds, pineapples are planted through paper strips which give the fields a ribboned appearance. Eighteen months are required for the first crop and the plants continue to bear for six to eight years. Much of the acreage is on rolling land from 500 to 1,700 feet in elevation; irrigation is unnecessary.

Cultivated land represents 8.5 per cent of the total area. Out of 351,719 acres in 1930, sugar cane accounted for 252,128 and pineapples 78,750. Coffee covers 5,498 acres. Large areas are in pasture, notably at the Parker Ranch on the island of Hawaii with 500,000 acres and 30,000 head of cattle. The total value of all agricultural

tion has given way to centrality, and few communities can offer the wide array of visiting lecturers available in Honolulu.

The quiescent volcano of Diamond Head is Honolulu's Gibraltar. Most of the city lies out of sight to the left, but Waikiki Beach with its tourist hotels is in the central foreground. (*Courtesy U.S. Navy.*)

products is about $100,000,000, of which $60,000,000 represents sugar, $34,000,000 pineapple, $4,500,000 animal products, and $1,500,000 coffee, vegetables, and other fruits. Since exports considerably exceed imports, in both cases dominantly with the mainland, and there are large military expenditures, the islands have long enjoyed considerable prosperity.

American occupation has transformed the Hawaiian landscape. Commercial plantations have replaced subsistence farms. In earlier times all settlements were small coastal villages where fishing was important. Population has now moved inland. Grass huts have been replaced by frame houses of Oregon pine. Tapa cloth and grass skirts now appear only on days when tourists arrive in port. Mid-oceanic isola-

Honolulu with its population of 180,986 (1940) is a beautiful American city in the tropics. Ten miles to the west lies the great naval base at Pearl Harbor, with 12 square miles of deepwater anchorage, separated from the open sea by a narrow passage.

The Hawaiian Islands are the first of a series of American steppingstones, several of which are used in connection with the million miles of Pacific aviation flown annually by Pan-American Airways. Seven hundred and twenty miles southwest of Honolulu is Palmyra, 960 miles south is Johnston Island. Canton and Enderberry are other American islands in Polynesia, held jointly with Great Britain. Farther south is American Samoa with the splendid harbor of Pago Pago. Westward are Midway, Wake, and the important cable station at Guam, key to Melanesia but surrounded by the old Japanese mandated islands.

Geostrategy in the Pacific

Position is important equally in peace and in war, for it involves not only physical location but accessibility and the geographic qualities that make some places more desirable than others. These are active factors and as such bring consequences, planned or otherwise. Strategy is the application of policy and calls for a recognition of the significance of place and all that goes with it. The practical aspects of political geography are sometimes known as geopolitics but, since they cover much more than politics and the term is often misunderstood, it seems better to use the word geostrategy for the dynamic aspects of applied international geography.

America is the major Pacific power. No other nation around its shores has so much frontage, or so many resources, or such a favorable location. China is more populous and Japan has been more aggressive, but no power holds the same assets as the United States. Whether it uses these assets is another matter. These opportunities bring corresponding responsibilities. The Pacific is too vast ever to become a national lake, and any attempt to control all its waters would be impossible. The United States should map out an area within which it desires to have primary military control and recognize that economic leadership elsewhere must rest on good will and statesmanship.

Dutch Harbor, Pearl Harbor, and Panama are the Pacific fortresses for the defense of continental United States. Beyond them are the outposts of Kiska, Midway, Samoa, and other small islands. These form a natural American sphere. To go farther is to lengthen supply lines and enter areas where there are thousands of islands. To control Guam it is necessary to have all of the Marshall, Caroline, and Mariana groups. To enter the South Pacific there is no stopping till one reaches Australia and Singapore. Thus Japan took Korea to protect her islands, then Manchuria to protect Korea, later on Inner Mongolia to protect Manchuria, and she wants Eastern Siberia to protect the whole. One should beware that the appetite does not grow with the eating and exceed the capacity of the digestion.

The only possible trans-Pacific enemies of the United States for a century to come are the Soviet Union, China, and Japan. Australia and Southeastern Asia are too weak. The United States might have disagreements with a free Philippines, but the latter could scarcely attack. Whatever the future possessions of European powers in the Pacific, the United States should easily enjoy superior advantages. China will be busy with internal development for decades and has never had conspicuous maritime interests; if imperialistic her interests will turn southward. Climate and topography make it unlikely that the Soviet Union can ever be a major Pacific power, and any war would be via Alaska rather than the broad Pacific. Only Japan promises to be a future threat, and if her outer island territories are removed, she will be without offensive striking power. Hence the Dutch Harbor-Pearl Harbor defense line appears reasonably adequate.

It is clear that, when diplomacy fails and war follows, a nation must be prepared to fight whenever operations are called for, but this does not mean that it should make the whole world its castle.

So long as the islands of Micronesia were in the hands of European nations, even though powerful at home, they formed no serious threat to the United States as its own lines of communication were far shorter. Only when these islands fell into the control of a strong Asiatic naval power did they become a danger. Any arrangement that leaves them in the hands of Japan will invite future trouble. It is not necessary that the United States own them; they would be innocuous as an international or a Philippine mandate.

The primary military sphere of the United States should be limited by the 180th meridian and the equator; outside the northeastern Pacific, operations lose the advantages of proximity to the mainland. The defense of Guam is not a matter of investing hundreds of millions of dollars, it is a problem of all the surrounding islands, of great-circle routes, and of relative distances. Commerce and international cooperation will probably flourish better under a Good Neighbor Policy than with nineteenth century imperialism. A program of security that is too aggressive will imperil the trade that it seeks to develop.

The western Pacific presents problems that will be referred to in subsequent chapters. It would appear sound geostrategy that a defeated Japan should lose outlying territories which gave her offensive military power. It appears equally fair that major continental powers, such as China and the Soviet Union, should if possible be given unrestricted access to the high seas. This would suggest the retrocession of Formosa and the Liuchiu or Ryukyu Islands to China, and the transfer of Sakhalin and the Kuriles or Chishima to the U.S.S.R.

The Pacific is too big to study on a flat map; only a globe is adequately honest. Mercator maps do not show that the great-circle course from Seattle to Tokyo cuts north of the Aleutian Islands, or that the shortest route from Panama to Manila passes near Los Angeles and north of Honolulu. Nor does any merely political map emphasize the intangible aspects of friendship. American missionary and relief aid to China and the cancellation of the Boxer indemnity are worth more than a fleet of ships.

Geographic ignorance is immeasurably expensive. An understanding of geostrategy is not in itself a solution for the problems of the Pacific, but without it no sure peace can prevail. Here is a far bigger space than Americans have ever thought in terms of before. Asia and the Pacific are a new world, where stability has not yet been achieved. The Pacific is an Asiatic as well as a North American ocean.

CHAPTER 2

ASIA'S CONTINENTAL PATTERNS

The Geographic Personality

One-third of the earth is Asia and here live nearly two-thirds of all mankind; eighteen million square miles and a billion and a third people. Land and man are the essential elements in any geographical study. Empty land may be of scientific interest, and the anthropologist studies human characteristics objectively, but only as the two are put together does the face of the earth take on a meaningful personality.

Asia is not just the biggest or most continental or highest or wettest or most diverse of continents. It is interesting because it is the most human. It happens to be the home of the oldest fossil man, *Sinanthropus pekinensis*, but the earliest recorded history is in Egypt and not in Asia. More people live here than elsewhere but they do not belong to the most important nations. These superlatives are not entitled to more than passing notice. The peoples of Asia and the land from which they have sprung challenge consideration because of their unique characteristics. The Chinese have a mature and practical civilization, the people of India are philosophical, the Russians have created a new and dynamic society, and Japan has shown surprising virility.

Few common denominators unite Asia except location. High mountains and climatic barriers separate the major nations. Trade and international contacts have been outward and by sea rather than inward by land. In place of this centrifugal outlook, new highways and the air age may develop centripetal interests, with resulting continental coherence.

If it were possible to fly high enough to see all of the continent at one time, the people and the cultivated fields would be invisible. One might study the pattern of mountain and desert but the human half of geography would disappear. On the other hand we cannot know each of Asia's billion people and watch how they utilize their immediate bit of earth, and even if we did we would not understand the interrelated whole. An appreciation of Asiatic geography requires a combination of airplane reconnaissance and integration, and the analysis of individual landscapes. Those who wish to understand the regions of Asia must read both the oversimplified generalizations of this volume and some of the case studies listed under the Suggested Readings. Since so few critical detailed studies are available, many generalizations lack adequate support.

Geography is concerned with all those features which give character and personality to the face of the earth. Since they have areal distribution, they are mapable. For the most part they concern the observable objects of the landscape, but nonmaterial features are of geographic interest as well.

Much of Asia is unattractive for human settlement. Despite the pressure of population, less than ten per cent is under cultivation. Too much of the continent is too cold, too dry, too mountainous, too infertile, or too remote to be attractive to man. Vast areas face the frozen Arctic, millions of square miles are beyond the reach of much oceanic moisture, and Asia is the most rugged of all lands. Despite these handicaps, it has nearly three times the popula-

The map of land usability presents these features clearly. Ruled areas of various categories have either less than 90 days

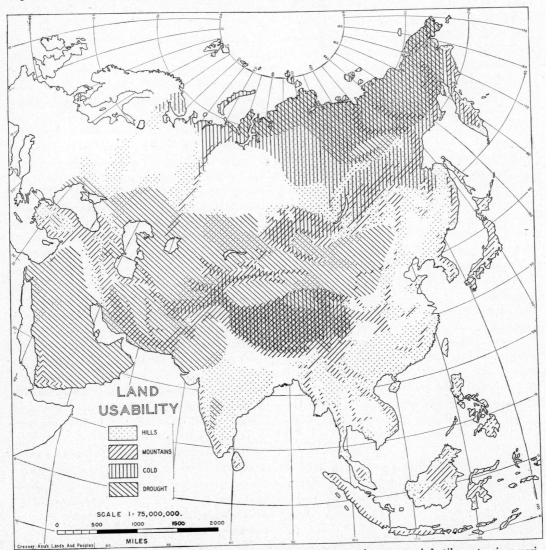

LAND
USABILITY

HILLS

MOUNTAINS

COLD

DROUGHT

SCALE 1: 75,000,000.

0   500   1000   1500   2000

MILES

Cressey: Asia's Lands And Peoples

Too much of Asia is too cold or too hot, too dry or too wet, too mountainous or too infertile, or too inaccessible to be of much use as a home for man. Compare this map with those of Population Distribution and Accessibility, pages 27 and 30.

tion density of the rest of the world, with an average of 72 people per square mile as compared with 26. For the globe as a whole, the average is exactly 40.

free from frost and are too cold for normal agriculture, or have too little rain (Koeppen *BS* symbol), or are too steep and mountainous for cultivation. Hilly land is stippled and, if not otherwise eliminated, is available for crops. Only the unshaded lands are really desirable, and parts of these have precariously short or dry summers. Irrigated oases and terraced mountain slopes add small areas. Just because Asia is large does not mean that it is all attractive. Too little is good.

Two unruled areas stand out, a triangular section in the Soviet Union which extends eastward to Lake Baikal, and a large crescent in the southeast from India to northern China. The first marks the zone of Atlantic climate and is cool; while the second is the Indo-Pacific monsoon zone, with tropical influences. Tibet is conspicuously eliminated on the basis of topography, temperature, and drought. Much of eastern Siberia is both cold and mountainous. Large parts of China and India are hilly, and thus of limited usability. Japan and Java are largely mountainous, yet support a large agricultural population.

Asia may also be divided into three great climatic realms: Monsoon Asia in the south and east, Desert Asia in the center and west including dry highlands, and Boreal Asia in the north. The monsoon realm with its summer rain and winter drought extends from the valley of the Indus to the lower Amur River and southern Kamchatka, and inland to the edge of Tibet and Mongolia. Desert Asia reaches almost to the fiftieth parallel near the headwaters of Arctic drainage; to the west it swings around the north of the Caspian Sea. Boreal Asia is the largest of the three; its western limits are formed by the wedge of maritime influence that projects eastward from Peninsular Europe as far as Moscow; within it are the tundra and taiga with some grassland.

The Pattern of Eurasia

What and where is Asia? Is the huge land mass of Eurasia one continent or two?

The common practice is to slice the Union of Soviet Socialist Republics in two parts along an arbitrary line, different on every map, and assign one part to Europe and another to Asia.

This so-called continental boundary in the general vicinity of the Ural Mountains follows no significant division of topography, drainage, climate, soils, land use, culture, or history. It accords with neither the crest of the Urals nor any political subdivisions. This conventional line is an arbitrary fiction of early map makers, without geographic validity or the sanction of those whose country it divides. Even the crest of the Urals supplies no more of a continental boundary than the Appalachians.

But if the Soviet Union cannot be divided into separate continents, is it to be classed as European or Asiatic? The old and largely untrue saying of "scratch a Russian and find a Tatar" reflects certain Mongoloid relations, but the Russians quite properly resent any exclusion from European classification to which they are clearly related in culture.

The terms Europe and Asia appear to have originated in the Aegean Sea, where the terms sunrise, Asu, and sunset, Ereb, came to be applied to Turkey and Asia, and Greece and Europe. Hence the division into the Orient and the Occident.

Europeans have looked eastward to Asia, hence the usage of Near East and Far East. These directional terms have no significance to the people of Asia itself, or to Americans. Accordingly they are seldom used in this volume.

The single mass of Eurasia has at least six major realms, not two. These divisions recognize great cultural contrasts as well as physical geography. Several of these subcontinents are more populous and more important economically or historically than any of the southern continents. One of these areas is the Soviet Union, as large as all of North America; another is China and Japan; Southeastern Asia is a third; India, officially known as a subcontinent, is fourth; and the Southwest is fifth. The Atlantic, Baltic, and Mediterranean Peninsulas in the west commonly known as Europe form the sixth major area.

This book deals with the first five of these realms. It is impossible to describe or cultural areas; they have distinct physical characteristics as well. Thus the Soviet realm has almost nothing in common with the Indian realm or with the Chinese-Japanese realm or with Southwestern Asia, each of which it borders. When one enters the Soviet Union, he is in a different world.

The chief nations of Asia with their areas and populations are as follows:

Country	Area, in square miles	Population	Year
Afghanistan	250,000	12,000,000	
British Malaya	50,880	5,174,000	1937–1938
Burma	261,610	16,000,000	1941
China	4,380,535	473,992,359	1938–1940
French Indo-China	285,800	23,030,000	1936
India	1,575,187	388,800,000	1941
Iran	628,000	15,000,000	1935
Iraq	116,600	3,560,456	1935
Japan	260,662	99,456,262	1935
Netherlands Indies	753,267	70,476,000	1940
Palestine	27,009	1,568,664	1942
Philippine Islands	115,600	16,000,313	1940
Saudi Arabia	....	4,500,000	
Soviet Union	8,176,010	170,467,186	1939
Syria	57,900	3,630,000	1935
Thailand	200,198	14,464,489	1937
Turkey	294,416	17,869,901	1940
All Asia[1]	18,523,552	1,326,000,000	1939
World total[1]	51,230,213	2,169,873,000	1939

[1] League of Nations Statistical Yearbook, 1940–1941.

Asia without including Siberia and Soviet Middle Asia, and these lands cannot be understood without reference to the balance of the U.S.S.R. But it is not imperative to consider Poland or England in describing the geography of the Soviet lands. The division lies along the western Soviet frontier rather than the Urals. The peninsular countries of Western Europe have a common culture and history and deserve separate consideration. Asia has become fixed in our vocabulary, but it is not a unit area to be described in a few easy generalizations.

These five realms are not merely political

Configuration and Drainage

Asia is unique among the continents in its mountain core and radiating ranges. Nowhere between the Aegean and the China Seas is it possible to travel from southern to northern Asia without crossing mountains. The few passes are a mile or more in height except toward either end. A complex of ranges isolates the various coastal lowlands and breaks up the continent into separate units.

The topography of Asia is determined by its geologic structure and history. Within the continent are several major structural units. In the south are the peninsulas of Arabia and India, underlain by an ancient and massive complex of highly folded Pre-Cambrian rocks. These stable positive areas are part of the ancient continent of Gondwana land; they are now locally veneered with young sediments. Northern Eurasia has two other stable areas: one the Fenno-Scandian Shield around the Baltic Sea and the other a similar block north and east of Lake Baikal known as Angara land but better divided into the Anabar and Aldan shields. Other such stable areas exist in China and elsewhere; all are composed of very ancient and metamorphosed rocks.

Between these resistant blocks are a succession of east-west folded ranges. During much of the Paleozoic and Mesozoic eras, this was the site of a great sea known as Tethys, longer and wider than the Mediterranean. Sediments accumulated in this geosyncline, and mountain building occurred at the close of the Mesozoic and especially in the Cenozoic. Pressures came from the north. The Himalaya form one of these ranges and are among the youngest mountains on earth. Similar mountains extend from Turkey to Japan.

Before considering the various mountain ranges, it is appropriate to define a few terms. The classification of land forms needs clarification. The words hill and plateau are used with no common agreement as to their slope or relief. These last two elements are the essentials in surface configuration, *e.g.*, the angular degree of slope and the vertical difference between the highest and lowest points within a given area.

Plains and plateaus are essentially flat, or have only gently rolling forms with slopes up to 5°. Depositional plains are commonly flatter than erosional plains. The difference between a plain and a plateau is that whereas the former has little or no relief, say tens or hundreds of feet at the

most, plateaus are plains that are intersected by deep valleys so that the area as a whole has noticeable relief. This may amount to hundreds or thousands of feet, but the essential feature is undissected flat land cut by steep-sided young valleys. Plains are near their base level, while plateaus are not; either may be at low or high elevations. Many areas called plateaus by geologists were once that, but have now been so dissected that only hills remain.

Hills and mountains are slope lands, whether gentle, say four to ten degrees, or steep, say over ten degrees. The distinction between hills and mountains is not in the degree of slope but in the amount of local relief. Thus hills are measured in hundreds of feet while mountains are measured in thousands. These figures do not refer to elevation above sea level, which does not enter into the definition, but to the difference between summits and valley bottoms. Some hills, such as badlands, have steep slopes while some mountains have gentle slopes.

Land forms are one thing; elevation above sea level is another. Most physical maps show only elevation, from which incorrect deductions are often drawn as to the configuration. Thus the valley of the Si River west of Canton is near sea level and commonly shown in green while interior Tibet is notably high and is conventionally mapped in dark brown or red. As a matter of fact the former is hilly while parts of the latter are a featureless plain. What we need are maps that show both elevation and configuration, and of the two the latter is the more important.

Three types of elevation deserve standard names: lowlands, from sea level to 2,000 or 3,000 feet, uplands to 6,000 or 8,000 feet, and highlands.

In this volume the regional arrangement of land forms is known as the surface configuration. This is described in terms of lowland, upland, and highland, combined with the word plain, plateau, hill, and

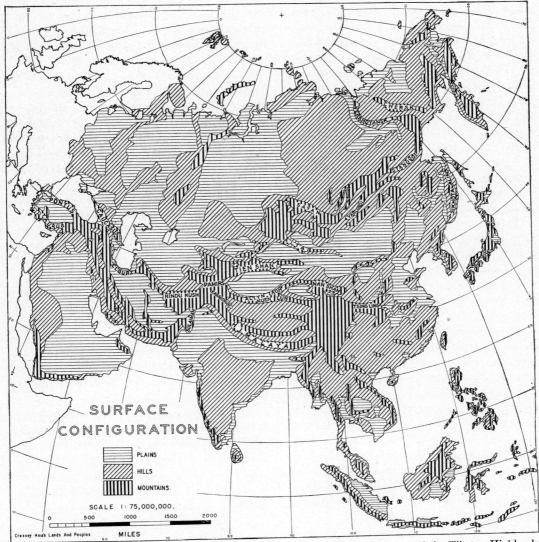

SURFACE
CONFIGURATION

PLAINS
HILLS
MOUNTAINS.

SCALE 1 : 75,000,000.

0   500   1000   1500   2000

Cressey-Asia's Lands And Peoples   MILES

Asia is a mountain-hearted continent. Great ranges spread out from both ends of the Tibetan Highlands and block easy access from north to south, and east to west. Surprisingly small areas of level land are available in the regions that are climatically usable.

ing to a knot and diverging to enclose a high plateau or intermontane basin. The

mountain. The scale of some maps does not permit this full classification.

From Turkey eastward to China there is a double series of mountain ranges, draped as festoon loops, alternately merg-

following description is in terms of topographic continuity rather than structural unity, but for the most part the mountains are geologically young and hence rugged. In Turkey the series includes the Pontus

Mountains along the Black Sea and the Taurus Mountains bordering the Mediterranean. Between them is the upland plateau of Anatolia. Eastward these ranges merge into the Armenian knot, with almost no plateau between the bordering Karabagh and Kurdistan Mountains. Parallel to this system on the north is the alpine range of the Caucasus which extends westward into Crimea and continues to the east of the Caspian in the low Kopet Dag. Iran is a second plateau basin, like Anatolia. Its eastern part is set off as the Seistan basin. To the north are the Elburz, Khoressan, and Hindu Kush mountains, while on the west and south are the Zagros, Fars, and Makran mountains.

This twin series again unites to form a knot in the Pamirs. This is the "roof of the world," a highland mostly over 12,000 feet, with mountains, deep canyons, and rolling plateaus. Mountain chains radiate from this center like arms of an octopus. To the west are the Hindu Kush; southward are the Sulaiman and their extension in the Kirthar range which continues westward into the Makran. Northwest of the Pamirs are the Alai Mountains; to the northeast are the Tien Shan. To the east are four major ranges, among the greatest in Asia. These are The Himalaya, the Karakorum, and the Altyn Tagh—Kuen Lun. These surround the great highland of Tibet with its plains and lesser ranges. In eastern Tibet there is a third knot, formed where the Kuen Lun and The Himalaya approach each other.

East of Tibet the arrangement is less clear. The Himalaya apparently turn into southeastern Asia, and may be followed topographically into the East Indian arc. Any such continuation should not be assumed to represent geologic similarity or structural unity. Other low mountains extend across southern China and turn northeast along the coast. The Kuen Lun continue into China as the Tsingling Mountains, and account for the major geographic division of China into the North and the South. The Szechwan Basin and Yunnan Plateau may be thought of as an enclosed area somewhat comparable to Iran and Anatolia. The easternmost Altyn Tagh is known as the Nan Shan; other mountains continue along the border of Mongolia east and north as far as the Khingan Range.

Northeastern Asia has an independent sequence. The Altai is a narrow range that projects into Mongolia from Siberia where it joins the Sayan Mountains on the east. The Yablonovi Mountains extend northeast from Lake Baikal and merge with the Stanovoi Mountains, incorrectly located on many maps. In the extreme northeast are the Verkhoyansk, Cherski, and Kamchatka Mountains.

No satisfactory genetic organization is available. The masterly work of Suess was written in 1901 and new data are now available. Argand's analysis of 1922 is in terms of drifting continents which are unacceptable to most English-speaking geologists. Continental generalizations had best wait until more field evidence is available.

In addition to these mountain systems, several other topographic units need to be added. The plateaus of Anatolia, Iran, and Tibet have already been listed. Other plateau or related areas are Arabia, the Deccan of peninsular India, Mongolia, and the Central Siberian Platform. Two of these plateaus, the Arabian and the Indian, are bounded on the west by bold escarpments. A comparable situation exists along the eastern and southeastern margins of Mongolia.

In the middle of Asia are three lowlands: the Tarim and Dzungarian basins of western China and the Turan Basin east of the Caspian Sea.

The principal plains are found in the valleys of the Tigris and Euphrates, Ganges and Indus, Yangtze and Yellow, Liao and as the Arabian and Syrian deserts, the Kara Kum and Kizil Kum in Soviet Middle Asia, the Takla-makan Desert in western China,

Most of Asia has a normal river pattern, but five million square miles are without drainage to the sea. Seven of the eleven longest rivers are in Asia.

Sungari, Ob, Volga, Dnieper, and Dvina, and Pechora rivers.

Desert climate prevails over many of the interior plains; thus there are such divisions

The Gobi in Mongolia, and the Thar Desert in northwest India.

No single river predominates, as in North or South America; instead a series of great rivers radiate from the interior. Five million square miles are without drainage to the ocean. Scant rainfall and excessive evaporation do not supply enough water to fill the interior basins to overflowing. During an earlier period of greater humidity, the Aral Sea expanded and overflowed to the enlarged Caspian, which in turn drained into the Black Sea.

Along the Arctic Coast are three great rivers: the Ob, Yenisei, and Lena each among the eleven longest in the world; and five smaller rivers, the Dvina, Pechora, Yana, Indigirka, and Kolyma. Pacific drainage accounts for four major rivers, again among the eleven longest: the Amur, Hwang or Yellow, Yangtze, and Mekong. Smaller streams are the Liao, Hai, Hwai, Min, Si, Red, and Menam rivers. The Indian Ocean receives three rivers large in volume but of lesser length, the Brahmaputra, Ganges, and Indus; plus smaller streams such as the Salween, Sitang, Irrawaddy, Mahanadi, Tapti, Narbada, Tigris, and Euphrates. The Black Sea receives the Dniester, Dnieper and Don rivers. Five important rivers drain into inland seas, the Volga and the Ural to the Caspian, the Amu Darya and Syr Darya to the Aral Sea, and the Ili to Lake Balkhash.

Climate and Vegetation

The continentality of Asia is best revealed in its climate. The maritime coastal areas present striking contrasts to the land-dominated interior where the seasons are accentuated. The mountain pattern adds to these contrasts. Interior Asia is nearly 2,000 miles from any ocean. Other continents extend north and south and are more exposed to the "prevailing westerlies" or to the easterly trade winds. Eurasia stretches east and west for more than half way around the earth. It has the lowest recorded temperatures for any inhabited place, and some of the highest. Rainfall also shows very great extremes. Winters in the interior are much colder than at corresponding latitudes in North America.

Almost every known climate occurs in Asia, from the equatorial rainy type of Malaya to the ice field climate of Nova Zemlya. Each of the principal Koeppen symbols is included.

The simplest explanation of Asiatic climate is that in summer the overheated interior warms the overlying air, causes it to expand, rise, and overflow aloft, and thus creates low pressure which draws in air from the surrounding relatively cooler oceans. In winter excessive radiation over the continent chills the air and develops a stationary high pressure area from which winds blow outward to the regions of low pressure over the oceans where there is still a reservoir of warmth from the preceding summer.

These to-and-fro winds are alternately moist in summer and dry in winter, and account for the seasonal distribution of rainfall. Where mountains rise in the path of incoming winds, exceptionally heavy precipitation results; in their lee are deserts. This is the seasonal monsoon, best developed in India, less conspicuous in China, and only present elsewhere as a tendency. A similar monsoon circulation develops with the other continents but is much more feeble on account of its smaller size.

Unfortunately, this simple explanation is not entirely correct, and the climatic regime of Asia becomes more and more complex as examined in detail. Thus The Himalaya are so high that they block winds from central Asia and the Indian winter monsoon is almost entirely a separate phenomenon. It will also be pointed out later that the sudden arrival of the summer monsoon over India is more than a matter of local low pressure.

Furthermore, much of southwestern Asia has a Mediterranean rather than a monsoon climate. Both have wet and dry periods but, with the Mediterranean type, rain falls during the winter months and the summers are dry.

air may be identified. Polar Arctic air masses move from Nova Zemlya to southern China, and Tropical Pacific air at times

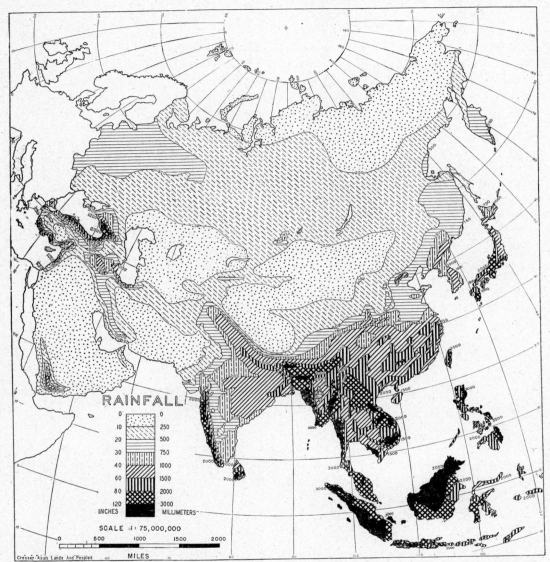

RAINFALL

0	0
10	250
20	500
30	750
40	1000
60	1500
80	2000
120	3000
INCHES	MILLIMETERS

SCALE 1 : 75,000,000

500 1000 1500 2000

MILES

Cressey "Asia's Lands And Peoples"

Asia's rainfall varies from over 450 inches to an inch or less, according to wind systems and mountain barriers. The heaviest precipitation occurs on mountains in the path of prevailing winds, as in India and Southeastern Asia, while the driest areas are behind mountains, as in western China.

Not enough is known of air mass movements over Asia to present a complete picture, but Polar, Tropical, and Equatorial air may be identified. penetrates almost to Lake Baikal. Sounding balloons show that the upper air is everywhere moving from the west.

Cyclonic and anticyclonic storms are more important in Asia than previously the Atlantic and enter Europe. Many die out in the interior. They bring with them,

CLIMATIC
REGIONS

(AFTER KOEPPEN)

SCALE 1: 75,000,000.

0   500   1000   1500   2000

MILES

Cressey: Asia's Lands And Peoples

Almost every known climate occurs in Asia. The following Koeppen symbols define the major regions. *A* climates have rain and high temperatures the year around. *B* represents dry climates, modified by *S* for steppe or *W* for desert (*wüste*). *C* and *D* are rainy temperate climates, *C* with long hot summers and mild winters and *D* with short summers and severe winters. *E* stands for polar climates, divided into *ET* for tundra and *EF* for permanent frost on snow fields.

These major groups are modified as follows: *a* hot summers, with the warmest month over 72°F., *b* cool summers, with four months above 50°F., *c* cool short summers one to three months above 50°F., *d* coldest month below −36°F., *f* no dry season, *s* dry summer, *w* dry winter.

realized. These moving lows and highs are fewer and smaller than those which cross however, the bulk of the rainfall that falls in Siberia. As they approach the Pacific, both highs and lows again become more numerous, so that China and Japan have alternations of weather several times a month. In eastern Asia the southeast quadrant of a cyclonic storm draws in moist winds from the South China Sea, which occupies a similar position as a source of moisture to the Gulf of Mexico for eastern North America. In each continent, much of the United States and much of China would be a semidesert if it were not for these tropical seas to their south. In winter weak cyclonic storms cross Palestine, Iran, and northern India, but during most of the year the main path is well to the north; in summer, even near the Arctic Circle.

Typhoons are important sources of rainfall in the southeast during the summer and fall.

The influence of the Indian Ocean is limited to the lands south of The Himalaya and east of the Indus Valley. Pacific moisture seldom penetrates beyond eastern Mongolia or occasionally to Lake Baikal. The cold Arctic Ocean contributes but little precipitation, and only along a fringe in the north. Despite the great distance to the Atlantic, it supplies such rain or snow as falls on a third of Asia. Even 4,000 miles east of the Atlantic, most rain originates in that ocean. Several million square miles are essentially without ocean-derived moisture; any precipitation that falls is derived by evaporation from rivers, swamps, and salt lakes. Since many of these areas appear to be growing drier, more moisture is blown out than comes in. As Lyde says, "This is continentality at its fiercest."

The seasonal extremes of temperature increase from the equator toward the northeastern interior. Near Singapore and Colombo the average of the warmest and coldest months differs by scarcely a degree. Along the Tropic of Cancer the figure rises to 20°F. The Moscow area shows an annual range of 45°F. Peiping and the Aral Sea have a seasonal difference of 60°F. Around Lake Baikal the figure exceeds 75°F. At the Asiatic cold pole in the vicinity of Verkhoyansk, the July average is 119°F. above that for January. Thus average annual temperatures mean little and are not a basis for mapping climatic regions.

No scheme of climatic regions is entirely satisfactory but the most widely used is that of Wladimir Koeppen. Five major types are recognized, all of them present in Asia. Tropical rainy climates with no winters form the *A* group. *B* is reserved for dry climates. Temperate rainy climates with mild winters where the coldest months average between 27 and 65°F. (*e.g.*, −3°C. and 18°C.) are classed as *C*; or *D* if the winters are boreal, with the coldest month below 27°F. and the warmest above 50°F. (10°C.). Polar climates with no warm season are named *E*.

Various modifications are introduced to indicate the season of rainfall or distribution of warmth. Thus *EF*, frost or ice cap, has no month above freezing, whereas *ET*, tundra, has temperatures up to 50°F. in its warmest month. *BS*, steppe, is less dry than *BW*, *Wüste* or desert, according to the ratios between temperature, rainfall, and season. Various lower-case letters are used to modify *A*, *C*, and *D* climates: *f*, *feucht* or moist, indicates rainfall every month or at least enough to tide over a dry period; *w* refers to a dry winter; and *s* to a dry summer; *a* indicates hot summers; *b*, cool summers; *c*, cool short summers with less than three months above 50°F.; and *d* where the coldest month is below −36°F. *B* climates are modified by *k* (*kalt*) where annual temperatures are below 65°F. (18°C.), and *h* (*heiss*) where they exceed 65°F., or they may be preceded by *C* or *D* if desired.

Tropical *A* climates characterize the peninsulas of India and Southeastern Asia, as well as the adjoining islands. This is a monsoon area with every month above 65°F. Coastal areas are *Af* while the interiors are *Aw*. Although near the equator temperatures seldom exceed 90°F.

B climates cover millions of square miles in the interior, with *BS* grassland surrounding large areas of *BW* desert. Summer temperatures are everywhere high, but winters are cold in Mongolia, Sinkiang, and Soviet Middle Asia in contrast to the year-round heat of Arabia, lowland Iran, and the Thar Desert of India.

Temperate *C* climates are present chiefly in China, Japan, northern India, and parts of Southwestern Asia. All these except the last have summer monsoon rain and winter drought, *Cw*, but in southern Japan and the Yangtze Valley the symbol is *Cfa*. Some of the chief disadvantages of the Koeppen system occur with the *C* group in China and in India. In the former it fails to stress the important climatic division into the North and the South between the Yangtze and Hwang, while in India the *Cw-Aw* boundary, as usually drawn, does not correspond with vegetation, agriculture, or land use. In the accompanying map these problems are partly adjusted.

The most characteristic climate of Asia is *D*, present throughout most of the U.S.S.R., except in Soviet Middle Asia and beyond the Arctic, and also in Manchuria and Turkey. Where Atlantic influences penetrate the continent in the west and bring year-round rain and mild summers, the symbol is *Dfb*. The northern area is *Dfc*, moist but with short summers. Eastern Siberia has only summer rain and is *Dwc* or *Dwd*, according to temperature.

Polar *E* climates occur in three situations: the ice cap of Nova Zemlya is *EF*, most of the lowland coast is covered with tundra and has an *ET* climate, while higher mountains in both northeastern Siberia and in Tibet are also *ET*, or *EB* where especially arid.

Natural vegetation is the best single summary of the physical environment, for it reflects temperature, rainfall, drainage, elevation, and soil. Parts of Asia have been cultivated so long that no trace of the undisturbed cover remains; elsewhere studies of ecological botany are incomplete. The general distribution shows many resemblances to the Koeppen map of climatic regions. The vegetation is here described by the same letters used in the legend of the map.

A belt of tundra, *A*, extends along the entire Arctic coastal plain and inland along higher elevations between the valleys. The subsoil is permanently frozen and plant growth is limited to less than three months. Swamps and lakes are very numerous, many of them associated with Pleistocene glaciation. Mosses, lichens, brush, and dwarf trees form the vegetation. The mountain flora of The Himalaya, Tien Shan, and other high areas is a specialized subtype.

Temperate coniferous forests, *B*, cover millions of square miles where the summers are short and the winters continentally cold. This is the Siberian taiga, a boreal forest of conifers such as larch, fir, and pine with some deciduous whitewoods such as birch and aspen. Commercial timber is limited to the southern portions. The soils are acid podsols.

Splendid forests of mixed conifers and deciduous trees, *C*, occur where milder climate prevails, both in the extreme east and west. Brown forest soils are the prevailing type.

Tropical and subtropical mixed forests, *D*, once covered southern China and Japan and still remain in the mountains. They include broadleaf evergreen trees, pine, fir, oak, and bamboo. Soils are yellow to red.

Prairie, steppe, and semidesert vegetation, *E*, corresponds roughly to the distribution of cool *BS* climate. Dry grasses

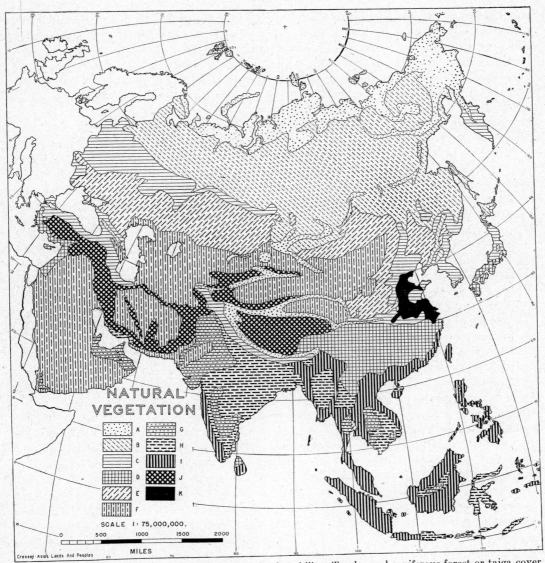

NATURAL
VEGETATION

SCALE 1 : 75,000,000.

0   500   1000   1500   2000

MILES

Cressey Asia's Lands And Peoples

Natural vegetation is the best single guide to land usability. Tundra and coniferous forest or taiga cover the cold lands of the north, tropical rain forest lies near the equator, with desert and mountain flora over the interior. The divisions are as follows:

A. Tundra and mountain vegetation
B. Temperate coniferous forest
C. Temperate mixed coniferous and deciduous forest
D. Tropical and subtropical mixed evergreen and coniferous forests
E. Prairie, steppe, and semidesert

F. Desert vegetation
G. Savanna and tropical scrub-woodland
H. Tropical deciduous forest
I. Tropical and subtropical rain forest
J. High plateau vegetation
K. Original vegetation unknown

(*Data from "Great Soviet World Atlas," Buck, Champion, and elsewhere.*)

and low brush reflect the aridity and provide pasturage for nomads. Where the temperature is low and evaporation moderate, excellent grasslands may develop even with 12 inches of rainfall. These regions have exceptionally fertile chernozem soil.

Deserts, *F*, are not necessarily lifeless, but plants are so scattered that bare ground is exposed between them.

Savanna and tropical scrub woodland, *G*, is a result of seasonal rainfall, high temperatures, and excessive evaporation. It is found in the drier parts of India and is the proper jungle. Laterite is the end product of soil leaching on level areas.

Tropical deciduous forests, *H*, are characteristic of the moist monsoon lands of southern Asia with 40 to 80 inches of rain. Teak is one of the best known trees.

Where the rainfall is heaviest, a dense rain forest results, *I*. This is a lofty evergreen forest, composed of a great variety of hardwoods, often 200 feet high. Mangrove coastal swamps are a special type. Soils are seriously leached and invariably infertile.

The high barren plains of Tibet have their distinctive vegetation, *J*.

The deltas of the Hwang and Yangtze appear to have been occupied by man almost since the time of their formation so that natural vegetation never had an opportunity to develop. Similar conditions may have prevailed in parts of the Ganges Delta. These are shown by the symbol *K*.

People

One billion, three hundred and twenty-six million people in Asia present the most challenging of all geographic problems. Who are they, where do they live, what do they do, and what of their future?

The anthropological relationships and the cultural history are not clear. Two maps show the distribution of racial groups and population density. Hundreds of ethnic groups live here, no less than 169 in the Soviet Union alone. In India there are over 200 languages, of which 20 are spoken by at least a million people each. China is supposed to have a homogeneous culture, but in the single province of Fukien there are 108 dialects.

The conventional grouping into Mongolians in the east and Caucasians in the west lacks validity. Olive-skinned, light-brown, and dark-brown people live in both areas. Head indexes show no differentiation, nor does stature. Cultural history likewise indicates no such separation, for time and again peoples and cultures have moved between the east and the west of Asia. Climatic fluctuations in the heart of the continent have repeatedly sent waves of migration into Europe, India, and China. Griffith Taylor has thus proposed the term Alpine-Mongolian to indicate that the Mongol type is only a variation of the fairly homogeneous group of peoples who occupy the main bulk of Eurasia. These people are all broad-headed. Three major language groups prevail in Eurasia: Aryan in the west, Altaic in the north, and Tibeto-Chinese in the southeast.

The principal features on the map of racial groups are the wedge of Russians in the north, the block of Chinese in the east, and the Indic people in the south. What the map fails to indicate is that almost every group shown may be divided and subdivided. What we need is an unfolding moving picture to show the evolution, migration, and mixture of these peoples during the past hundred thousand years. History is a sequence, of which geography merely shows a momentary scene.

The map of population density equally presents a challenge. When Confucius said that "one look is worth a thousand words" he might well have been thinking of a picture such as this. Asia has many places where people are few, and a few places where people are very many. No map in all the book is so important as this one of population, for it clearly shows where people live and in what numbers, and raises the

Geostrategy in Asia

The vast spaces of Asia have been a favorite field for writers in geopolitics. Un-

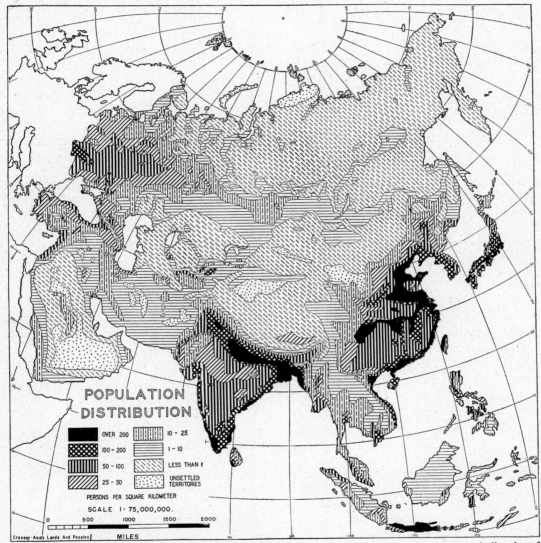

POPULATION DISTRIBUTION

OVER 200	10 - 25
100 - 200	1 - 10
50 - 100	LESS THAN 1
25 - 50	UNSETTLED TERRITORIES

PERSONS PER SQUARE KILOMETER

SCALE 1: 75,000,000.

0   500   1000   1500   2000

Cressey–Asia's Lands And Peoples   MILES

A chart of population distribution is the most significant of all maps, for it presents the most challenging of geographic questions, "Why do people live here, and what do they do?" Asia's people live in the good land, and there are vast areas that offer little attraction for settlement. (*Data from "Great Soviet World Atlas," I, 47–48.*)

question of why they do not live elsewhere. Subsequent chapters should be read in terms of this map of population distribution.

fortunately many of them have too little understood the geography of the continent which they have utilized, and have failed

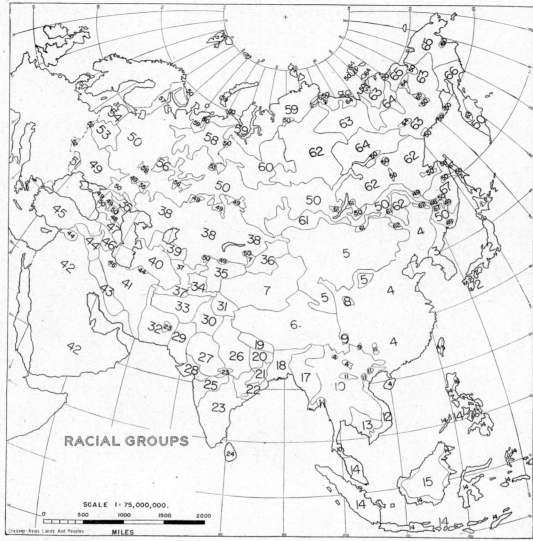

RACIAL GROUPS

SCALE 1 : 75,000,000.

0   500   1000   1500   2000

Cressey·Asias Lands And Peoples   MILES

The largest of continents is also the most ethnographically complex. Even with much simplification 68 nationalities must be recognized:

1. Ainu	21. Mundan	41. Persian
2. Japanese	22. Uriya	42. Arab
3. Korean	23. Dravidian	43. Kashkai and Luri
4. Chinese	24. Ceylonese	44. Kurd
5. Mongol	25. Maratha	45. Turk
6. Tibetan	26. Hindustani	46. Armenian and Persian-Turk
7. Yuigur	27. Rajput	47. Georgian, Azerbaijani, and Avar
8. Dungan	28. Gujarat	48. Other Trans-Caucasians (Ossetian, Abkhasian, Kumiki, etc.)
9. Nosu	29. Sindhi	
10. Thai	30. Punjabi	
11. Mon	31. Kashirian	
12. Anamite	32. Beluchi	49. Ukrainian
13. Cambodian	33. Afghan	50. Great Russian
14. Malayan and Javanese	34. Tajik	51. Moldavian and Magyar
15. Dyak	35. Kirghiz	52. Pole
16. Aeta	36. Kalmuck	53. White Russian
17. Burmese	37. Uzbek	54. Lithuanian, Latvian, and Esthonian
18. Bengalese and Assami	38. Kazakh	55. Volga-German
19. Nepalese	39. Karakalpak	56. Mordovian, Udmurt (Vot-
20. Bihar	40. Turkmen	

yak), Chuvash and Bashkir
57. Finn, Karelian, and Saami (Lapp)
58. Komi (Ziryan) and Nansi (Vogul)
59. Nenetse (Gold) and Dolgan
60. Khante, (Ostiyak); Kyeti, and Syelkupe
61. Oriot, Khakasian, and Buriat-Mongol
62. Evenki
63. Eveni (Lamut)
64. Yakut
65. Odul (Yukagir), and Luoravetlan (Chukchi)
66. Nimilan (Koryak)
67. Hebrew
68. Nonai (Goldi), Ude, and Nivkhi (Gilyak)

adequately to think in terms of the round earth.

German theories of geopolitics visualize the state as an organism and as such in need of living room; only as it grows and expands can it live. Under Karl Haushofer at Munich there developed the Institut für Geopolitik which studied the political geography of the world and formulated dynamic plans for action by which Germany might achieve her place in the sun. Relatively little attention was given the New World, and since advance westward against France and Britain appeared difficult, the natural direction of expansion was thought to lie in the east, toward and into the Soviet Union. Many of these ideas are echoed in Adolf Hitler's "Mein Kampf."

Behind the plans of Haushofer lies the volume by the distinguished British geographer, Halford Mackinder, "Democratic Ideals and Reality." This was written at the close of the First World War as a warning to the peacemakers concerning the necessity of securely enclosing Germany on the east. Mackinder viewed history as a contest between land power and sea power. The latter can outflank land power and draw on distant supplies through command of the ocean, but it needs an adequate base. Land power can win in the long run if it has resources, size, and location.

Mackinder contended that the World Island of Europe, Asia, and Africa is dominant, and that the Heartland of interior Asia is the key to security. This core lies behind mountains and deserts and is immune to sea-launched attack. Only on the west is it vulnerable, and only through the effort of advanced European technique and capital can it be developed. Hence his famous statement: "Who rules eastern Europe commands the Heartland. Who rules the Heartland commands the World-Island. Who rules the World-Island commands the World." To prevent German access to the gates of the Heartland, Mackinder favored a corridor of buffer states such as Poland and Czechoslovakia whose security was imperative for the peace of the world.

This Asiatic Heartland includes all of the Soviet Union except the part drained by the Pacific and that west of the Volga, plus Mongolia, Sinkiang, Tibet, and Iran. The area is large and well supplied with raw materials but not with agricultural possibilities; the population is not likely ever to be numerous in comparison with the rest of the world.

Strategic position, whether in war or peace, involves the favorable disposition of at least nine geographic elements: (1) size, (2) shape, (3) accessibility, (4) location, (5) boundaries, (6) relation to the ocean, (7) topography, (8) minerals, and (9) climate.

The importance of size was dramatically demonstrated during the Second World War, when the Soviet Union and China were able to retreat and thereby gain time for further resistance, in contrast to Belgium and Poland which lacked defense in depth. But mere size is not enough. No large army could withdraw into Mongolia or Tibet or northern Siberia and survive, for there are inadequate productive facilities. Too great an area may be a handicap unless well united. The Heartland is large and remote but it is devoid of the possibilities for major economic strength. No existing country anywhere will have sufficient size to be immune to air attack tomorrow, or to furnish an adequate base for world conquest. Nor could a combination of neighboring nations, such as the Soviet Union and China or the Soviet Union and Germany, be secure on the basis of size alone. Mackinder overlooked the fact that his Heartland is just over the top of the world from North America. With the air age, there are no longer any inaccessible countries or continental cores.

Form or shape is a second element in geostrategy. A nation like Chile is so

factory gross shape, the distribution of good land and people and communica-

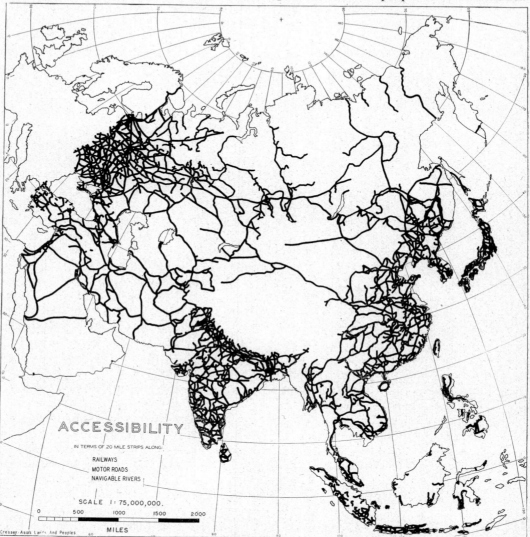

ACCESSIBILITY

IN TERMS OF 20 MILE STRIPS ALONG

RAILWAYS
MOTOR ROADS
NAVIGABLE RIVERS

SCALE 1:75,000,000.

0   500   1000   1500   2000

MILES

Cressey·Asia's Lands And Peoples

Areas that are more than ten miles from railways, navigable rivers, or automobile roads usually find it difficult to engage in trade or to share in the circulation of ideas. The Soviet Union and India are well supplied with railways; in China many of the above lines represent automobile roads.

drawn out that while her area equals that of Germany, economic unity is made difficult. Canada appears compact on the map, but her population is as attenuated as that of Chile, no more than a fringe along the boundary of the United States. While Mackinder's Heartland has a satis-

tions is so eccentric that the form lacks coherence.

Accessibility is of great importance in economic geography. Anything beyond subsistence livelihood requires trade and communications. The accompanying map presents the picture for Asia. All areas within ten miles of a railway, navigable river, or automobile road are shown in black. Elsewhere travel is by camels or mules, carts, sedan chairs, or wheelbarrows. Three dark areas stand out clearly: the western Soviet Union and India, both well supplied with a network of railways, and China where many of the lines represent new automobile roads. Interior Asia is nearly inaccessible in terms of modern communications. Northern Siberia has only its rivers, ice-bound for much of the year. No road links Burma and India, and only one leads from Burma to China. No railway and only one road connects India with Southwestern Asia. The coherence and invulnerability of a Heartland need to be considered in terms of a map such as this. Certainly other parts of the continent have better communications.

Location is the prime question in all of geography, not "where" in terms of latitude and longitude, but "where" in terms of good land and markets and world highways. Shanghai owes its importance not to latitude, but to the hinterland of the Yangtze Valley. The mouths of the great Siberian rivers lack good harbors, but the productivity of the interior is forcing port developments. Throughout history, the Russian Bear has sought warm water, an outlet to the unfrozen ocean. Position is inescapably important in political policy and economic orientation. The Heartland represents the climax of continentality, but few nations have achieved cultural or any other progress without external contacts. China may have wished that she did not have such an exposed coast line, but the peacetime assets greatly outweigh the military liabilities. Japan has an excellent position in the western Pacific but lacks a secure home base. Her defeat became so difficult during the Second World War because of her newly enlarged size and the central position of Japan within this temporary empire.

The significance of location can change. Thus Rome was once the center of the civilized world but the Mediterranean is now a minor body of water. Interior Asia is increasing its population, but there is no likelihood that it will ever hold the controlling part of mankind. Nor is it likely that a developed Heartland could be dominated by a Germany or any other alien power far from the center of gravity. We live in a North Atlantic world, and it appears probable that Europe and North America will continue to lead; this ocean may even become an Anglo-Saxon lake.

Boundaries frequently present problems; here is the fifth component of geostrategy. Mackinder has followed deserts and mountains in defining the Heartland. These form natural obstacles to ground travel but not to the airplane. If such barriers keep armies from trespassing they equally keep out goods, people, and ideas. No civilization can progress without stimulating contacts. Thus China has empty interior frontiers, but she is open to world ideas on the east.

The ocean is still the cheapest highway; without free access to it, a nation suffers. The history of civilization may be traced in terms of progressively larger and larger water bodies, from the Nile to the Aegean and Mediterranean and Atlantic, and in some measure in the future to the Pacific. Oceans are highways, not barriers. The Heartland has a long border next to the Arctic Ocean, but that is frozen for much of the year. Under whatever form of government, Russia will inevitably continue its quest for a harbor on the Persian Gulf, along the Scandinavian coast, and on the Yellow Sea.

Topography is the seventh element in geostrategy. Here Asia suffers, for rugged ranges isolate its various realms. The Himalaya would assuredly provide the Heartland with security from invasion on the south, but they also block trade. China benefited during the Japanese invasion by having poor roads in her hill country so that the mechanized equipment of the conqueror could not be used but, if there had been better communications for a decade previously, China might have been strong enough to resist more effectively.

Raw materials, both mineral and agricultural, are vital in our modern world. Other nations in other times have achieved conspicuous success in art or philosophy, but in the twentieth century national greatness rests, perhaps too much, on coal, oil, iron, copper, and aluminum. Lord Curzon remarked that, during the First World War, the Allies "floated to victory on a sea of oil." During the Second War they flew to victory on a cloud of gasoline. The following chapters consider the distribution of mineral resources in some detail. Nature has unfortunately played favorites and has distributed the good things of the earth unevenly. The Soviet Union is exceptionally rich in many of these, China has coal in abundance and India has large amounts of iron ore, but no nation is fully self-sufficient. It is not apparent that interior Asia will ever lead the world in industry. Trade is inevitable.

Climate is the last but far from the least of these factors. Health and progress are directly related to it. It is not likely that a League of Nations will ever have its capital in Singapore or in Yakutsk. Nor will exceptionally energetic people live in these areas. Maps of climatic energy give lower rank to most of Asia than to Europe or North America. The long period of winter inactivity in the Heartland is certainly a disadvantage. Agriculture is as vitally affected as is man.

This somewhat lengthy analysis of some components of geostrategy not only is directed to a consideration of the Heartland, but serves as a check list for the detailed consideration of each country that follows. No deterministic approach is possible, for human factors may reverse the totality of the physical environment. Thus language, nationality, religion, population density, and occupations are each of geographic concern.

In place of the Heartland concept, it would appear more in line with geographic realities to suggest that the interior core will remain of minor importance and that the great nations of Asia will be China, the Soviet Union, and perhaps India. The U.S.S.R. is not the same as the Heartland, for as a nation it has important outlets on the Pacific and is in contact with Europe and the Atlantic world. Each of these countries has genuine assets of which geographic security is not the least. Peace and prosperity lie not in withdrawal into the interior but in active participation in a world society.

The function of geostrategy is to understand a nation's problems and potential and to suggest a program of internal development and international cooperation that will be of mutual value. And if wars are to recur, it may indicate the wisest course of action in emergency. This is nothing more than applied geography.

If there is anywhere a world citadel or Heartland, it may well lie in North America rather than in Asia. Twice in the twentieth century it has been demonstrated that no war can be fought without becoming a world war, and that no world war can be won without the aid of the United States. This New World continent has adequate size, compact shape, internal accessibility, a central location, good boundaries, access to two oceans, favorable topography, rich minerals, excellent climate, and a dynamic spirit. Its citizens thus need to be particularly aware of their place in the global air age. The shortest route from New York to Chungking is due north over the Pole. The closest overseas neighbor of the U.S.A. is the U.S.S.R.

The Regional Framework

This volume deals with the 94 geographic regions in Asia. These are grouped into 22 provinces, some of which are also regions areas, generalizations become more valid; thus one may describe the geography of China more clearly than that of Asia as a whole, or the Yellow Plain with more detail

The continent of Eurasia contains six major realms, of which the five in Asia are divided into 22 provinces and 94 geographic regions. China-Japan includes North China, South China, Outer China, Old Japan, and Outer Japan. Within the Soviet Union is Soviet Europe, Soviet Middle Asia, and Soviet Siberia. Southwestern Asia may be broken down into the various political divisions, each of which is a geographic province. India includes Northern India and Peninsular India. The provinces of Southeastern Asia realm follow political lines.

in themselves, and 5 realms. As the continent is divided into successively smaller than for all of North China. Regions do not represent the end of subdivision, but they do have sufficient geographic unity and coherence to make them understandable.

The major realms are five: China-Japan, the Soviet Union, Southwestern Asia, India, and Southeastern Asia. They are divided into provinces and regions in the accompanying list. More than a third of the regions are merely designated by their political place name, for these adequately define the geographic area. Topographic words such as plains, mountains, or uplands are frequently employed, or in some cases the more general term of valley. Some regions are typified by their natural vegetation or land use. Geographic regions are based on the total geographic landscape. Other lists in subsequent chapters deal with surface configuration, climate, or similar single elements.

For reasons already indicated, it will be noticed that the terms Far East and Near East are seldom used in this volume. Neither is easily defined, and in any case they represent an outside approach to Asia rather than an evaluation of the continent itself.

Realms, Provinces, and Regions of Asia
China and Japan

North China
Yellow Plain
Shantung Peninsula
Loessland
Manchurian Plain
East Manchurian Uplands
Khingan Mountains
Jehol Mountains

South China
Yangtze Plain
Szechwan Basin
Central Mountain Belt
South Yangtze Hills
Southeastern Coast
Canton Hinterland
Southwestern Uplands

Outer China
Mongolia
Sinkiang
Tibet

Old Japan
Kwanto Plain
Central Honshu
Western Honshu and the Inland Sea
Shikoku
Kyushu
Northern Honshu

Outer Japan
Hokkaido
Karafuto
Kuriles (Chishima)
Korea (Chosen)
Formosa (Taiwan)
South Seas

Soviet Union

Soviet Europe
Ukrainia
White Russia
Baltic States
Metropolitan Leningrad
Kola-Karelian Taiga
Dvina-Pechora Taiga
Central Agricultural Plain
Metropolitan Moscow
Southern Agricultural Plain
Ural Mountains

Soviet Siberia
West Siberian Agricultural Plain
Altai-Sayan Mountains
Ob Taiga
Yenisei Taiga
Arctic Fringe
Baikalia
Lena Taiga
Northeastern Mountains
The Far East

Soviet Middle Asia
Caucasia
Caspian Deserts
Pamirs and Associated Ranges
Oases of Southern Turan
Aral-Balkhash Desert

Southwestern Asia

Turkey
Marmara Lowlands
Black Sea Fringe
Mediterranean Fringe
Anatolian Uplands
Armenian Uplands

Syria and Palestine
Arabia
Iraq
Iran
Afghanistan

India

Northern India
Bengal—Orissa Plain
Ganges Valley
Brahmaputra Valley
Assam Hills
Himalayan Highlands
Indus Valley
Thar Desert
Western Frontier

Peninsular India
West Coast
Black Soil Uplands
Northern Uplands
Eastern Uplands
Southern Peninsula
Ceylon

Southeastern Asia

Burma
Irrawaddy Valley
Burma Mountains
Shan Plateau
Tenasserim Coast

Thailand
Central Thailand
Northern Thailand
Northeastern Thailand
Southern Thailand

Indo-China
Red Plain
Indo-China Mountains
Mekong Plain

Malaya
Netherlands Indies
Java
Outer Provinces

Philippine Islands
Luzon
Viseyan Islands
Mindanao

CHAPTER 3

THE CHINESE LANDSCAPE

Human Heritage

China is more than a place on the map. Here is a unique phenomenon. Other lands are older and others more beautiful, but nowhere else have so many people lived so close to nature and with such cultural continuity as in China. The landscape everywhere reflects the intensity of man's occupance. The culture of the ages has permeated all levels of society so that even the ricksha coolie quotes Confucius. No land on earth is so mature.

The Chinese landscape is vast in time as well as in area and in numbers. More human beings have lived on this good earth than on any similar area in the world. Almost everywhere man has long ago utilized the resources of nature up to the limit of the tools at his command. The present is thus the product of a long and very rich heritage. The problems of today arise from the sudden impact of the western world and the reorientation of her pattern of life. Only those who understand China's history and geography as a whole can properly evaluate the events of the twentieth century. This is not a typical period in her history, for the maturity of her social adjustments has been upset by the sudden discovery of an outside world order.

The roots of the Chinese go deep into the earth. The carefully tilled gardens, the hand-plucked harvest, and the earthen homes all tell the story of man's intimate association with nature. On every hand a substantial peasantry labors industriously to wrest a meager livelihood from the tiny fields. Innumerable groups of farm buildings, half hidden in clumps of bamboo or willow, suggest the intensity of man's quest for food, and the ever-present grave mounds serve as reminders of the heritage of this venerable land.

The most significant element in the Chinese landscape is thus not the soil or vegetation or the climate, but the people. Everywhere there are human beings. In this old, old land, one can scarcely find a spot unmodified by man and his activities. Whereas life has been profoundly influenced by the environment, it is equally true that man has reshaped and modified nature and given it a human stamp. The Chinese landscape is a biophysical unity, knit together as intimately as a tree and the soil from which it grows. So deeply is man rooted in the earth that there is but one all-inclusive unity—not man and nature as separate phenomena but a single organic whole. The cheerful peasants at work in the fields are as much a part of nature as the very hills themselves. So, too, the carefully tended rice fields are an inescapable element in the human panorama.

No mere photographic portrayal of China can reveal all the varied ties that bind man and the soil together. Crisscross through the visible scene run innumerable threads of relationship. The landscape is a mosaic of many diverse elements, some dependent upon the vagaries of a none-too-certain rainfall, some conditioned by the limitations of the soil, still others molded by the force of tradition. All of these are linked together into a synthetic, animated picture. It is the task of geography to describe and understand these relationships, to draw information from widely scattered sources,

Whereas the United States and the Soviet Union extend from east to west, China trends north and south. From the far

The Temple of Heaven at Peiping was built during the thirteenth century. Here the Emperor worshipped on behalf of the country at midnight during the winter solstice. (*De Cou, from Ewing Galloway.*)

and to give it a new significance as applied to the understanding of specific areas. This living panorama forms the cultural landscape.

China is not only rich in her culture, she is diverse in her physical environment. Few countries have greater contrasts. Rainfall varies from an inch a year in the desert to nearly a hundred inches along the coastal mountains. Extensive forests stand in contrast to denuded hillsides. Rice is eaten three times a day in the South, but is a once-a-year luxury elsewhere. Shanghai may be a cosmopolitan city of the world, but one has to go only a few hundred yards beyond its borders to find a primitive countryside.

south of Hainan to the northernmost bend of the Amur River is 2,500 miles. These extremes reach from well inside the tropics to within 13° from the Arctic Circle. Thus agricultural possibilities and means of livelihood vary notably. If superimposed on North America, China would spread from Puerto Rico to Hudson Bay, with the Yangtze Valley in the latitude of New Orleans.

Few large countries have such a large percentage of hilly or otherwise uncultivable land. Only through prodigious effort and painstaking care have the Chinese been able to support so large a population. This topographic diversity has divided China into many regions, each with its personality and often with rivalries with other regions. The Chinese of the various provinces differ in physical appearance, in language, and in distinct geographic realm because the physical and the cultural geography are interwoven in a uniquely mature whole.

The Chinese are among the most friendly and democratic of all peoples. (*Courtesy China Famine Relief.*)

psychology. For example, the development of the "almond eye" characterizes 36 per cent of the people around Canton, 23 per cent near Shanghai, and only 11 to 21 per cent in the north.

Despite these contrasts, China has a distinct homogeneity. Dialects may differ but the written language is the same. The degree of modernization may vary but everywhere is a coherent ideology, in large measure the heritage of Confucius and the sages. It is this way of life, of getting along with each other and with nature, that makes the Chinese so genuine. Here is a

History

The history of China begins with *Sinanthropus pekinensis*, the Peking man. Since the first discoveries near Peiping in 1928, the skeletal material has increased so that by 1943 there were 13 skulls and bones representing at least 45 individuals. No other primitive man is so well authenticated or dated. *Sinanthropus* lived in the early Pleistocene and is roughly contemporaneous with *Pithecanthropus* in Java. The links with modern man are uncertain, but many features connect *Sinanthropus* with present-day Mongoloids. So far as is known, the Chinese have always lived in China; suggestions as to a central Asian nomadic ancestry have no foundation.

The earliest written records date from 1200 B.C., and earlier dates are known to be fictitious. The first nationwide dynasty is the Han, 206 B.C. to A.D. 220. Later came the Tang, 618 to 907, the Sung, 960 to 1280, the Ming or Mongol, 1368 to 1644, and the Ching or Manchu, 1644 to 1911. Most of these major dynasties have been times of stability and progress; between them have been intervals of chaos and confusion. It is unfortunate that we of the Occident should be learning of China during one of these transition intervals, unrepresentative of the country at its best.

As Latourette has pointed out,[1] " . . . seldom has any large group of mankind been so prosperous and so nearly contented as were the Chinese under this governmental machinery when it was dominated by the ablest of the monarchs of the Han, the T'ang, the Sung, the Ming, and the Ch'ing. It was due largely to their government, moreover, that the Chinese achieved and maintained so remarkable a cultural unity and displayed such skill—all the more notable because they were partly unconscious of it—in assimilating invaders. When one recalls how Western Europe, no larger than China proper and with no more serious internal barriers of geography, failed, both to its great profit and infinite distress, to win either political or cultural unity, the achievement of the Chinese becomes little short of phenomenal."

The present political era dates from the Revolution of 1911 which overthrew the Manchus, and the subsequent establishment of the Nationalist Government under Chiang Kai-shek in 1928. With the estab-

lishment of that government, the capital was removed from Peking to Nanking. Later on, during the Japanese invasion, it was temporarily located at Chungking. Although the rest of the world failed to appreciate the situation at the time, it is now clear that the Second World War began with the Mukden Incident of Sept. 18, 1931, when Manchuria was overrun by the Japanese. The second phase of the Sino-Japanese War dates from July 7, 1937.

China's history is a by-product of her geography. Southeastern Asia is almost an oasis, largely self-sufficient and isolated from the rest of mankind. Until the era of modern travel, the most perfect barriers surrounded China on all sides. Towering plateaus, arid deserts, tropical forests, and the widest of the oceans all helped to preserve the unity of China. Nowhere near by was there an equal neighbor, except in India which was months away. It is but natural that the Chinese thought of themselves as living in the "Middle Kingdom."

The most dangerous of these frontiers was in the north, for the Mongols gave the Chinese more trouble than all other "barbarians" put together. Hence the Great Wall was built, linked together out of earlier parts by the Emperor Chin Shih about 220 B.C. Unfortunately this rampart failed to achieve the desired result. In times of greater rainfall, the Chinese farmers were not willing to stay on their side of the fence and pushed cultivation into the grasslands to the north, while, during decades of drought, the wandering Mongol shepherds sought pasturage in the more humid lands within the Wall.

Only a few travelers reached China from Europe, notably Marco Polo and the Jesuit missionaries. Only occasional Chinese pilgrims went westward, but even in 128 B.C. the explorer Chang Chien crossed the Pamirs and reached Bukhara. The first Chinese to visit India was Fa Hsien in

[1] LATOURETTE, KENNETH SCOTT, "The Chinese, Their History and Culture," New York: Macmillan (1934), II, 21.

A.D. 413; like other pilgrims in quest of Buddhism he traveled via Sinkiang. Most of this contact with the west was overland, these seaports became the new front doors of China. Instead of being a barrier, the ocean is now a highway. The Jade Gate

The Great Wall, here seen near Nankow Pass west of Peiping, marks China's attempt to fix the frontier between the wandering nomads of The Gobi and the settled farmers of Agricultural China. (*Courtesy Canadian Pacific Steamship Co.*)

but a few Arab vessels came to Canton and Hangchow, even as early as A.D. 300.

Insofar as China had a front door, it was the Jade Gate at the Tibetan end of the Great Wall, named from the caravans that brought jade, properly nephrite, from the Kuen Lun Mountains. Out through it passed other caravans carrying silk and porcelains, some of which were carried as far as Roman Britain. China thus faced toward Inner Asia, and Japan was only of incidental concern. With the arrival of Europeans and the development of Canton, Shanghai, and Tientsin a century ago,

faded into a poetic memory. Through the new coastal cities has flowed a tide of ideas which have altered the superficial life of many Chinese. Large countries do not easily change their cultural momentum or orientation, hence the reconstruction of a nation as big and numerous and ancient as China has created major problems.

During the Second World War when the seacoast was occupied by Japan, China was again obliged to reorient her internal activities. Foreign contacts were again via the west, and a new type of freight moved in through the Jade Gate.

China has had few years of normal opportunity since the Revolution of 1911, but the resiliency of trade and the cultural progress

China's assets proved to be an unsuspected patriotism and defense in depth. With plenty of room into which to retire, China

Some of the finest buildings in Asia line the Shanghai Bund along the Whangpoo River. The building in the far distance is a 24-story apartment hotel. (*Ewing Galloway*.)

in times of peace have been amazing. Japan doubtless invaded China when she did because of the realization that another decade of internal development might make conquest impossible. From the beginning of the Manchurian conquest in 1931, it was clear that China was not yet strong enough to defeat Japan; what did not become evident until later was the fact that Japan could not conquer and develop China. Until outside aid arrived, the situation is aptly described by the Chinese proverb of a man riding a tiger; the tiger could not get at the man but the rider was afraid to get off.

could afford to sell space in order to buy time.

Political Pattern

China's international boundaries have never remained fixed for more than a few centuries at a time. Some Chinese dynasties on occasion have included areas west of the Pamirs, on the south slopes of The Himalaya, in northern Indo-China, along the left bank of the Amur River, as well as Korea, Formosa, and the Liuchiu Islands.

Under the last or Ching Dynasty, China was divided into 18 provinces and four

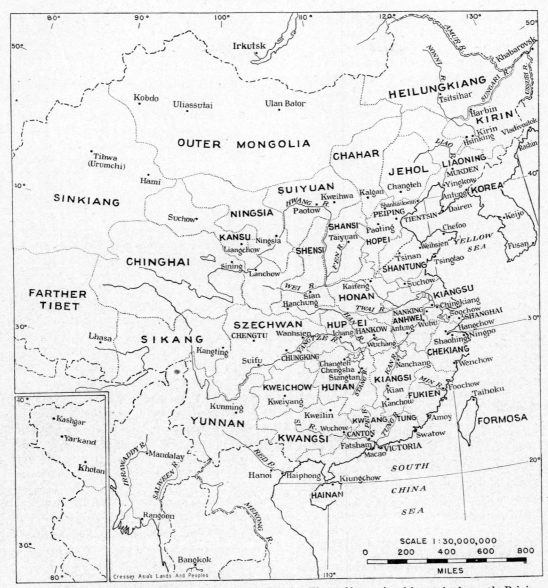

China is composed of 28 provinces and 2 outer territories. Three of her major cities are in the north: Peiping, Tientsin, and Mukden; five are in the Yangtze Valley: Shanghai, Nanking, Hankow, Chungking, and Chengtu; while two others are in the south: Canton, and Victoria on the island of Hongkong.

dependencies. Several of the provinces were united at times, but it is customary for the Chinese to refer to the traditional part of their country south of the Great Wall as "the Eighteen Provinces." Today there are 28 provinces and two territories. The original provinces, with their present areas and capitals are as follows.[1] Areas are those given in the Chinese yearbook.

Province	Capital	Area in square miles
Anhwei	Anking	51,888
Chekiang	Hangchow	39,780
Fukien	Foochow	61,258
Honan	Kaifeng	66,676
Hopei (Chihli)	Peiping (Peking)	59,321
Hunan	Changsha	105,767
Hupei	Wuchang	80,169
Kansu	Lanchow (Kaolan)	145,930
Kiangsi	Nanchang	77,280
Kiangsu	Chinkiang	41,818
Kwangsi	Kweilin	83,985
Kwangtung	Canton	83,917
Kweichow	Kweiyang	69,278
Shansi	Taiyuan	60,190
Shantung	Tsinan	69,197
Shensi	Sian (Changan)	72,334
Szechwan	Chengtu	166,485
Yunnan	Kunming	123,539

The nineteenth province was created in 1878 when Sinkiang was raised from territorial status.

Sinkiang (Chinese Turkestan)	Tihwa (Urumchi)	705,769

Manchuria was divided into three provinces in 1903 and was rearranged by the Japanese into 19 administrative districts during the period of "Manchoukuo."

[1] A few Chinese geographical terms are as follows: north—*pei*, south—*nan*, east—*tung*, west—*si*, mountain—*shan*, sea—*hai*, lake—*hu*, river—*ho* or *kiang*.

Liaoning (Fengtien)	Mukden	124,223
Kirin	Kirin	109,384
Heilungkiang	Tsitsihar	173,554

Mongolia has two parts: Inner Mongolia next to the Great Wall and thus closer to Peiping, and Outer Mongolia. In 1912 the former was divided into four provinces.

Chahar	Changchiakow (Kalgan)	107,677
Jehol	Chengteh (Jehol)	74,277
Ningsia	Ningsia	106,115
Suiyuan	Kweihwa (Kweisui)	112,492

Outer Mongolia has been independent since 1921, and is made up of two states under the protection of the Soviet Union, not recognized by China or by other foreign powers. One is the Mongolian People's Republic, with its capital at Ulan Bator, formerly Urga, and the other is the Tuvinian People's Republic, whose capital is Kizil Khoto. Their areas are 580,150 and 64,000 square miles, respectively.

Tibet is also made up of two sections: Nearer Tibet and Farther Tibet. The latter is a semiindependent territory with its capital at Lhasa and an area of 349,419 square miles. The former is divided into two provinces, thus bringing the total to 28.

Chinghai	Sining	271,116
Sikang	Kangting (Tatsienlu)	143,437

Greater China thus has an area of 4,380,535 square miles, of which 3,386,966 lies within the provinces.

Population Problems

Two of China's major problems concern people and transportation, and it is appropriate to consider them in this first chapter. No one can travel across the country without being impressed by the pressure of people on the arable land. Even in remote and inhospitable areas where one journeys for miles without seeing a house, as soon as one comes to a bit of good land

of famine and invasion and political strife and population increase have pushed the

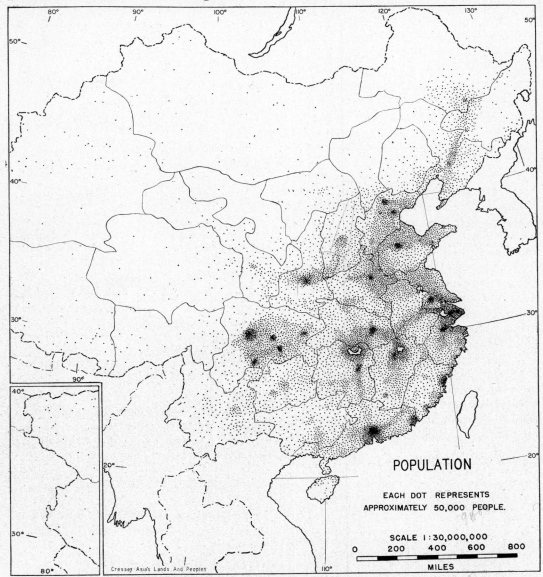

POPULATION

EACH DOT REPRESENTS
APPROXIMATELY 50,000 PEOPLE.

SCALE 1 : 30,000,000
0   200   400   600   800
MILES

Cressey Asia's Lands And Peoples

Centuries of famine, invasion, and normal population increase have pushed the 450,000,000 Chinese into every area that will possibly support life. This population map is at the same time a guide to agricultural possibilities and level land. The dark areas are densely populated because there people can live, the lightly dotted areas have been demonstrated to have a low population-supporting capacity. No conspicuous changes are possible.

there painstaking farmers have crowded the soil to its maximum capacity. Centuries

Chinese into every corner that will support life. No more good unused land remains.

One glance at the accompanying population map will show how unevenly these people are distributed, but the answer to overcrowding does not lie in redistribution. The sparsely settled areas merely have less population-supporting capacity and are already as crowded as the others. The dense areas are dense because conditions of livelihood are more attractive. China's population map is at the same time a map of agricultural productivity; change the legend and one would almost pass for the other.

A line drawn from southernmost Yunnan to northernmost Heilungkiang divides China into two parts. To the west are 2½ million square miles and 17 million people, while to the east are 1¾ million square miles and a population of 457 million. The first question of geography is: How many people live where, and why?

Although China is not an urban land, there are six cities with over 1,000,000 people: Shanghai, Peiping, Tientsin, Hankow, Mukden, Canton, and Hongkong, and as many others between 500,000 and 1,000,000. No satisfactory census returns are available, and all figures are computed from doubtful sources. The Ministry of the Interior published figures in May, 1938, for 23 of the provinces, as follows:

Data in the Far Eastern Yearbook for 1941, with population figures on Manchuria provinces for October, 1940, and the Kwantung Leased Territory for 1938, are as follows:

Heilungkiang......
Jehol............
Kirin............ } ... 43,233,954 (or 31,008,600[1])
Liaoning (Fengtien)
Kwantung Leased Territory................. 1,255,570

The remaining areas of China are as follows:

Outer Mongolia (Mongolian People's Republic).. 840,000 (or 2,077,669[1])
Tannu Tuva (Tuvinian People's Republic)...... 90,000
Sinkiang................. 4,360,020[1] (or 2,577,724)
Farther Tibet............ 1,500,000 (or 3,722,011[1])
Kowloon Leased Territory. 97,781
Shanghai International Settlement
Shanghai French Concession } 1,552,000
Hankow Foreign Settlements................. 30,935
Kwangchowwan Leased Territory............. 300,000

[1] 1936 figures from Ministry of the Interior.

This gives a total of 472,580,216 as the best figure now available. Two other figures need to be added to cover Greater China, bringing the grand total to 473,992,369.

Hongkong (British)......... 1,071,893
Macao (Portugese)........ 340,260

Other estimates differ widely. Among them is the 1926 figure of the Post Office, compiled by hsien, or counties, which totals 485,508,838 for the 28 provinces, but omits Outer Mongolia and Farther Tibet. The most detailed sample census was in connection with the land utilization studies of J. Lossing Buck of the University of Nanking. Although this provides no totals, it appears that the total population within his eight agricultural regions, largely south

Province	Population	Province	Population
Anhwei.......	23,354,188	Kwangsi......	13,385,215
Chahar.......	2,035,957	Kwangtung...	32,452,811
Chekiang.....	21,230,749	Kweichow.....	9,918,794
Chinghai.....	1,196,054	Ninghsia......	978,391
Fukien.......	11,755,625	Shansi........	11,601,026
Honan.......	34,289,848	Shantung.....	38,099,741
Hopei........	28,644,437	Shensi........	9,779,924
Hunan.......	28,293,735	Sikang.......	968,187
Hupei........	25,515,855	Suiyuan......	2,083,693
Kansu........	6,716,405	Szechwan.....	52,703,210
Kiangsi.......	15,804,623	Yunnan.......	12,042,157
Kiangsu......	36,469,321		

of the Great Wall, is between 400 and 600 million. Manchuria, Mongolia, Sinkiang, and Tibet are to be added. From 75 to 80 per cent of these are farmers. Even though the loss of life in recent decades has been large, the total population has undoubtedly increased.

The natural rate of increase is also impressive. Buck's figures give 38.3 births per 1,000 and 27.1 deaths. This net increase of 11.2 per 1,000 means an additional four or five million people a year. If the rate were continued, the population would double in 65 years. Among large nations only the Soviet Union and Japan appear to have a higher rate of increase.

If it were suddenly possible to introduce modern sanitation, check infant mortality, eliminate famines, and reduce the death rate to western standards without lowering the birth rate, a tremendous increase in population would occur within a generation. Large sections of the population, already at subsistence levels, would be driven into desperate economic straits.

If one divides China's population by the total area, there is an average of 120 per square mile. This does not represent undue crowding, for it is but the average of Indiana and Illinois. On the other hand, if the eastern and more crowded part of the country, already referred to above, were considered, the density is nearly tripled. Only when specific areas are considered does a representative picture emerge. Thus the Yellow Plain of the Hwang River has an average of 647 people per square mile, or 978 per square mile of cultivated land. For China as a whole, there are no less than 1,485 people for each square mile of agricultural land. This gives an average of 0.45 acre of cultivated land per capita.

China has certainly been overpopulated in the past; whether this situation must continue depends on the possibility that technological changes can provide increased income. The Malthusian checks of starvation, disease, and war have operated cruelly over the centuries. Flood and

Shan tribesmen are among the various non-Chinese people of southwestern Yunnan. (*Courtesy American Museum of Natural History.*)

drought have caught people without any reserve of food or money. Perhaps a hundred million have died of famine in the past century.

Within the total population are many races other than the Han or Chinese proper. Nearly twenty million "aborigines" live in the southwest, a mixture of Shan, Thai, Mon-khmer, Lolos, and many others. Mongol, Turkish, and Tungan people each number about two million. More than a million Manchus and a million Koreans live in the northeastern provinces, and there are over half a million Japanese. Large numbers of Chinese live overseas, especially in Thailand, Malaya, Indo-China, and the East Indies. The total is at least seven million, or possibly eleven million if all categories of citizenship and racial mixtures are included.

No more important problem confronts the new China. Too many people now live on a dangerously low standard. The greatness of a nation depends not upon its total numbers, but upon the quality of their life. China has a rich culture, but its material foundations are weak. Any lowering of the death rate without a corresponding decrease in the birth rate will be serious. The cultivation of marginal land and increased crop yields will help for a while. Industrialization offers other possibilities, of uncertain value. In terms of the present and near future it appears clear that China has too many people.

Communications

In terms of area, China is second only to the Union of Soviet Socialist Republics. But miles are not the proper unit in which to understand areas or distances in this country; travel is a matter of time. The Chinese have come to adjust their unit of space, the li which is roughly a third of a mile, in terms of uphill or downhill, in the city or through the country, so that distance depends on good roads or bad. Until recent years, 20 miles a day was a fair average for cross-country travel.

Poor communications have handicapped China for centuries and have helped to develop a sectionalism that makes it difficult to unify public opinion. Each valley and province has tended to become its own self-sufficient world. Considerable trade has moved over the rivers and canals, and a coarse net of imperial highways linked the provincial capitals, but few people could afford the time and expense of travel.

Railways date from 1876, but by 1940 the total length amounted to less than 15,000 miles. Half of this lies in the Man-

churian provinces to the northeast where there is an adequate coverage. The Peiping-Tientsin area has five radial lines, but no other city farther south has more than two railways. The western provinces and outer territories are entirely without railway connection. Only a few lines penetrate the south. Nine provinces of the 28 are entirely without railways, and several others have but a single line. Wherever lines have been built, they have carried a capacity business from the start. All lines are built on the American standard gauge, 4 feet 8½ inches. The construction of new railways and the rehabilitation of existing lines will be one of the major projects of the period following the Second World War. In 1922, Dr. Sun Yat-sen wrote his "International Development of China," in which he stressed the importance of transportation and mapped out routes for 100,000 miles of railway. Many of his proposed lines might be changed by a study of economic geography, but the proposal is important.

The unification of China calls for main lines linking the interior provinces with the seaboard, such as Canton to Kunming, Shanghai to Chungking, and Tientsin to Outer Mongolia. Two of the major needs are a new trans-Asia railway via Sinkiang to the Soviet Union, and an outlet through Burma to the Indian Ocean.

Automobile highways are of equal importance. Spectacular developments shortly prior to the Japanese invasion led to the completion of some 75,000 miles of road, almost none of it adequately paved but nevertheless of great service. Petroleum apparently does not occur in large quantities, and the costs of imported automobiles and fuel make private cars prohibitively expensive.

Overland travel has been confined to cart roads and flagstone trails, roughly characteristic of the North and the South, respectively. Two-wheeled springless carts

Graceful stone arch bridges span the canals in the Yangtze delta. Canalboats are propelled by a single oar at the stern used as a scull. (*Ato.*)

Where streams become too shallow for boats, the use of bamboo rafts enables shipments of cloth, kerosene, and matches to reach far into the interior.

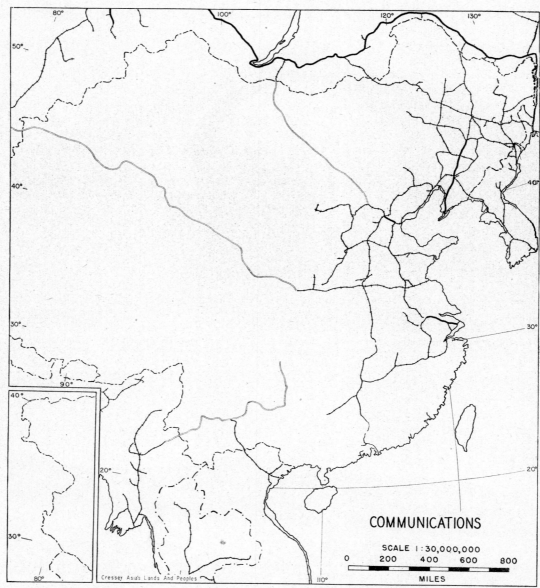

COMMUNICATIONS

SCALE 1:30,000,000

0   200   400   600   800

MILES

Cressey Asia's Lands And Peoples

Railway development is limited to eastern China. The lines that radiate from Peking were built under government influence when the capital was in the north, while those in Manchuria were constructed through the initiative of Russian, Japanese, and Chinese interests. Double-tracked railways are shown in a thick line. Three highways link China with the outer world: through Outer Mongolia, through Sinkiang, and to Burma. The extensive net of automobile roads is not shown.

with narrow iron-studded wheels grind the earth into dusty ruts in the dry season and churn it into deep mud after the rains. Under such conditions one does not travel for pleasure. Sedan chairs are scarcely more comfortable. Where animals are not available, long lines of coolies carry salt, tea, cloth, or kerosene.

Since the means of travel are slow and inefficient, commerce requires an abnormally large number of people. Where man is so numerous and lives so close to the minimum, coolie carriers work for a pittance. It is thus cheaper to wear men down than to keep roads up. Such is the value of human life where man overcrowds the land.

Great credit must be given to the Post Office. Couriers travel day and night, and the service has been remarkably dependable despite war and other interruptions.

It is notable that each of the cities with over a million people is a seaport, except Peiping and Mukden, and that all of the major inland cities are large almost in proportion to their transportation facilities.

CHAPTER 4

CHINA'S PHYSICAL ENVIRONMENT

The four million square miles of Greater China present wide contrasts in physical environment. In climatic terms, and thus in natural vegetation and soils, eastern China is a rough equivalent of eastern North America. Both areas lie to the leeward of a great continent. But in complexity of topography, eastern Asia is much more hilly. Sixty per cent exceeds 6,000 feet in height.

If China were superimposed on North America, it would reach from Cuba to central Quebec, and inland to the Rockies and the Great Basin. Canton and Hongkong are within the tropics in the latitude of Havana. Shanghai is on the parallel of Savannah, while Chungking farther west corresponds with San Antonio. Tientsin and Peiping are in the latitude of Washington, D. C. Mukden matches Albany and Harbin parallels Montreal. The northern part of Manchuria is but 13° from the Arctic Circle, while the southern island of Hainan is not unlike Puerto Rico. The more important areas of China are somewhat farther south than the most populous parts of the United States.

The physical features that characterize the geography of China grow out of the vast size of Asia with its pronounced seasonal climates and its complex mountain pattern. Considered as a whole, China has much less level land than the United States, especially in the south and west where on a clear day one is never out of sight of hills or mountains. The plateau of Tibet averages three miles in elevation, with numerous peaks to five miles. In Sinkiang the oasis of Turfan descends to 928 feet below sea level. Rainfall varies from almost nothing in the deserts to at least 100 inches on coastal mountains exposed to the typhoon. Temperatures also show wide extremes. This chapter considers these environmental foundations.

Geological Foundations

The visible Chinese landscape rests on a framework established in the Pre-Cambrian, although the present topography is much younger. Three old land masses formed buttresses between which the younger sedimentary formations accumulated and were subsequently folded. These shields or massifs are Tibetia in the west, Gobia in the north, and Cathaysia in the southeast. In each area there is an ancient complex of granites and metamorphic formations which have tended to remain above sea level during most of earth history.

During the Paleozoic and Mesozoic, repeated marine invasions spread across central China, leaving thousands of feet of limestones, sandstones, and shales which form a nearly continuous record from the Upper Proterozoic through the Jurassic. Extensive coal beds formed during the Carboniferous and also in the Jurassic. Continental formations accumulated during the Cretaceous in Mongolia, Shansi, Shensi, Kansu, and in Szechwan, at the same time as widespread lava flows spread over the southeast.

The structure of eastern Asia is exceptionally complex. Near the Pacific the major trend is from northeast to southwest, parallel to the coast. Toward the interior are several east-west tectonic zones, while further inland are great mountain chains of uncertain relationships.

From Hongkong northeast to Ningpo and southern Korea are a series of old massifs and modern geanticlines which formed part of ancient Cathaysia. This structure continues, *en échelon*, from Shantung and Liaotung through the Sikhota Alin of Siberia to the mouth of the Amur River. To the west and parallel to these uplands are a series of geosynclines shown in the sedimentary basins of the Manchurian Plain, the Yellow Plain, and the central Yangtze Plain.

West of these lowlands is another discontinuous geanticlinal axis, which extends from the Great Khingan Mountains in Manchuria south to the Taihang and Luliang anticlines of Shansi, the Gorge Mountains of Szechwan, the eastern edge of the Kweichow Plateau, and into Kwangsi. Although more strongly developed and accompanied by greater igneous intrusions in the north, the system is homogeneous. This is the innermost series of the northeast-southwest Cathaysian system. The folding of these various structures took place toward the close of the Mesozoic.

These parallel zones are continued to the east of China by a series of depressions in the Sea of Japan and the East China Sea, the elevated arcs of the Japanese Islands including the Ryukyu (or Liuchiu) and Chishima groups, and the Japan trough and Tuscarora deep. Thus in all, there are three major anticlines and three synclines, of which at least those in China have been defined and active since the late Proterozoic. Pressures were apparently directed from the Pacific.

Farther inland, this Cathaysian pattern is replaced by four equally spaced east-west structures which lie between the Siberian frontier and the South China Sea. To the north of the Gobi massif are the Tannu Ola, Khangai, and Kentai ranges in Outer Mongolia. Another mountain chain is the Taching and In Shan of Inner Mongolia, the third and largest is the Tsingling Range between the Hwang and Yangtze rivers, an eastward continuation of the Kuen Lun, while the fourth are the low Nanling Mountains in southern China. Like Cathaysian structures, these east-west mountains have maintained their integrity since the Proterozoic.

The highest and most complex of Chinese mountains are those which encircle the borders of Tibet. The Himalayan system, as young as any great range on earth, is made up of three ranges which end near the Brahmaputra. North of them are Nyenchen Tang La or Trans-Himalaya. To the east of the Tibetan Highlands are a series of north-south mountains which continue to the Great Snowy Range facing the Szechwan Basin. Farther north, the highlands are bordered by the Kuen Lun and Altyn Tagh ranges, while beyond them are the Tien Shan and Altai ranges. Geological studies have but partly organized the baffling structural pattern.

Although most mountains of eastern China have mature rather than rugged topography, diastrophism is still under way. Destructive earthquakes have been recorded in Kansu, Szechwan, and Yunnan, as well as in the Kuen Lun, Altyn Tagh, Nan Shan, and Altai ranges. Smaller shocks have also occurred in Shantung. The province of Kansu was intensely shaken in 1920 and 1927. In 1556 an earthquake in central Shensi and the resulting famine are said to have taken 830,000 lives.

No continental glaciation spread over China during the Pleistocene, for the south was too warm and the far north too dry. Small glaciers developed in a few of the higher mountains. In place of ice, the geological record closes with widespread dust deposits, the famous loess. Deposits

Along the border between Korea and China lies a little-known volcano with a crater lake, known in Chinese as Paitou Shan and in Korean as Hakuto San. (*Courtesy North China Daily News.*)

of this wind-blown silt exceed 100,000 square miles south of the Great Wall, plus other areas in Sinkiang. Over extensive areas the thickness exceeds 100 feet, so that the original bedrock topography is buried; locally the thickness may reach 300 feet.

Most loess occurs in the semiarid grasslands of northwest China. The bulk of the material is derived from river and lake deposits of the Hwang River spread out in the Ordos Desert, with lesser amounts as the product of weathering in the Gobi Desert. Local deposits have their source in river flood plains, as along the Yangtze near Nanking and in Szechwan. Dust storms today indicate that accumulation is still under way.

The only area of recent volcanic activity is along the Korean border where there is a large crater lake at the summit of Paitou Shan.

River Patterns

All of China's great rivers flow eastward to the Pacific. However, more than a million square miles in Mongolia and Tibet is without drainage to the sea.

The Heilung Kiang or Amur River together with its tributary the Ussuri forms the northern and eastern boundaries of Manchuria next to Siberia. The chief tributary within China is the Sungari. Each of these is navigable for river steamers. The Liao Ho drains southern Manchuria.

The Hai Ho or Pei Ho empties into the Gulf of Chihli 40 miles below Tientsin, where it is formed by the confluence of several tributaries, chief of which is the Yungting or Hun Ho.

The great river of North China is the Hwang Ho or Yellow River, 2,700 miles in length. As it enters the province of Kansu from Tibet, the Hwang is a torrential stream 75 yards wide, across which fragile ferryboats maneuver with the greatest difficulty. Where it crosses the Great Wall for its swing northward to Mongolia, the river widens to half a mile and has a gentle current and numerous sand bars. The Hwang's chief tributaries are the Fen Ho in Shansi and the Wei Ho, classical river of Chinese history, which flows across Shensi. After the river enters its delta, the Yellow Plain, the average slope is one foot per mile, but it is so overloaded with loessial silt that extensive deposition follows. Since this accumulation is confined between dikes, the bed of the river in many places has come to be above the level of the surrounding countryside so that the Hwang River flows on an artificial ridge. No part of the river is navigable for steamships. Between 1191 and 1852 it entered the ocean south of Shantung, but in 1852 its course was diverted 250 miles to the north. During the Japanese invasion of 1938, the Chinese cut the dikes west of Kaifeng, turning the stream across the path of the advancing Japanese into an old channel which continues southward to the Hwai Ho.

The Hwai is the largest river between the Hwang and the Yangtze, draining the southern margin of the Yellow Plain. When the Hwang River followed a southerly course prior to 1852, it usurped the channel of the Hwai and deposited so much sediment that the latter was no longer able to follow its natural course to the sea. As a result, the stream discharges into a series of fluctuating lakes in northern Kiangsu. In time of flood these enlarge and spread over thousands of square miles. A part of the water from the combined Hwang and Hwai now follows the Grand Canal south to the Yangtze, another portion flows eastward to the sea through an artificial channel.

The Yangtze Kiang, 3,200 miles in length, is the sixth longest river in the world and by far the most important waterway in China. Navigation extends to Pingshan near Suifu in western Szechwan, 1,630 miles from the sea. In the Yangtze gorges the current reaches 14 knots and makes this section one of the most difficult stretches of river navigation in the world. Ten-thousand-ton ocean steamships reach Hankow during the summer, 630 miles from the sea. The chief tributaries are the Min Kiang in Szechwan, the Han Kiang which gives its name to Hankow, and two large tributaries from the south, the Siang and Kan. These latter flow through the Tungting and Poyang Lakes which serve as storage reservoirs for the surplus flood waters of the Yangtze. The delta around Shanghai is interlaced by a network of canals; deposition is pushing the land seaward at the rate of one mile in 70 years.

In southern China three rivers converge upon the Canton Delta: the Tung Kiang or East River, Pei Kiang or North River, and the more important Si Kiang or West River. The latter is readily navigable for river steamers as far as Woochow in Kwangsi, 200 miles inland.

Surface Configuration

Topography sets the stage on which the Chinese drama unfolds but, for much

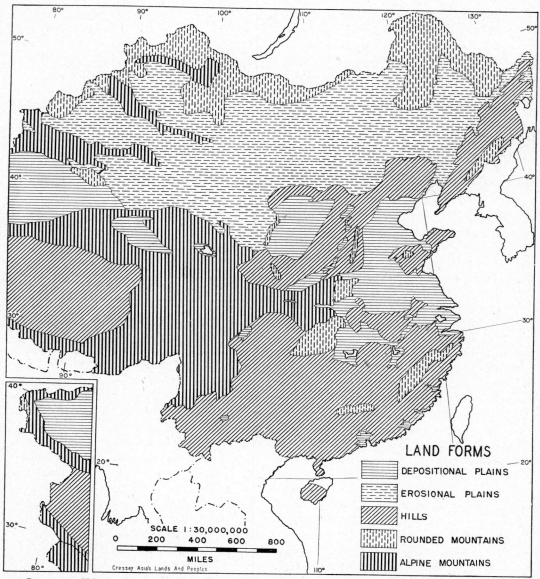

LAND FORMS

☰	DEPOSITIONAL PLAINS
┄	EROSIONAL PLAINS
⫽	HILLS
▨	ROUNDED MOUNTAINS
‖	ALPINE MOUNTAINS

SCALE 1:30,000,000

0   200   400   600   800

MILES

Cressey Asia's Lands And Peoples

In eastern China, where most of the people live, level land is limited to the alluvial plains of the Hwang and Yangtze. Rolling erosional plains are present in Manchuria and the arid Gobi. South China is largely a land of hills. Rugged mountains encircle Tibet, while more gently sloping mountains are widely scattered.

of China, slopes are so steep that normal agriculture is impossible. Wherever there is level land, no matter how inaccessible, it is used as intensively as climate permits.

Large areas are not properly mapped, and in many areas land form analysis rests on the accounts of chance travelers. Extensive plains are found only in the deltas of the Yangtze and Hwang, the rolling lowland of central Manchuria, and the deserts of Mongolia and Sinkiang. Level land may represent no more than one-fifth of the total area.

Diverse mountain structures and erosional history divide China into 11 topographic regions and 60 subregions.

LAND FORM REGIONS OF CHINA

A. Tibetan Highlands
   1. Pamirs
   2. The Himalaya
   3. Karakorum Mountains
   4. Interior Tibetan mountains and basins
   5. Altyn Tagh—Nan Shan Ranges
   6. Kuen Lun Range
   7. Tsaidam—Koko Nor Basins
   8. Land of the Great Corrosions (Kam)
   9. Great Snowy Mountains (Szechwan Alps)
B. Tien Shan Highlands
   10. Tien Shan Range
   11. Dzungarian Alatau Mountains
   12. Bogda Ola Mountains
   13. Kuruk Tagh Hills
C. Altai-Sayan Highlands
   14. Tarbagatai Mountains
   15. Altai Mountains
   16. Tannu Ola Mountains
   17. Khangai Mountains
   18. Kentai Hills
   19. Tannu Tuva Hills
   20. Eastern Sayan Mountains
D. Mongolian—Sinkiang Uplands
   21. Gobi Plain
   22. Ordos Plain
   23. Valley of the Lakes
   24. Dzungarian Plain
   25. Tarim Plain
E. Mongolian Border Uplands
   26. Great Khingan Mountains
   27. Jehol Mountains
   28. Taching—In Mountains
   29. Holan Mountains (Ala Shan)

   30. Loess Hills
   31. Liupan Mountains
   32. Shansi Mountains
     a. Taihang Mountains
     b. Wutai Shan
   33. Shensi—Shansi Plains (Wei—Fen)
F. Eastern Uplands
   34. East Manchurian Hills
   35. Long White Mountains
   36. Little Khingan Hills
   37. Shantung Hills
     a. Tai Shan
G. Eastern Lowlands
   38. Amur—Ussuri River Plains
   39. Manchurian Plain (Liao—Sungari)
   40. Yellow Plain (Hwang)
   41. Yangtze Delta Plain
   42. Mid-Yangtze Lake Plains (Poyang—Tungting)
   43. Han River Plain
H. Central Uplands
   44. Tsingling Range
   45. Tapa Mountains
   46. Gorge Mountains
   47. Tapei Hills (Hwaiyang)
I. Szechwan Lowland
   48. Red Basin Hills
   49. Chengtu Plain
J. Southern Uplands
   50. South Yangtze Hills
   51. Wuyi—Tayu Mountains
   52. Nanling Mountains
   53. Southeastern hills and deltas
   54. Canton Delta Plain
   55. East-North-West River Hills (Tung, Pei, Si)
   56. Luichow—Hainan Plain
   57. Hainan Mountains
K. Southwestern Uplands
   58. Kweichow Hills
   59. Yunnan Plateau
   60. Kunming Plain

A. The Tibetan Highlands comprise a rim of lofty mountains and an enclosed plateau-basin, much of it without external drainage. In the far west is the mountain core of the Pamirs, from which radiate most of the great ranges of Asia. The Himalayan system extends in an arc for 1,500 miles and is made up of three ranges. Fifty summits exceed 25,000 feet in The Himalaya and the Karakorum, of which only Kamet and Nanda Devi have been climbed. Mt.

Everest, 29,141 feet high, lies on the border between Tibet and Nepal.

Within Farther Tibet is a series of mountains and basins. In the south is the valley of the Tsang Po, the local name for the Brahmaputra, with the city of Lhasa and the only cultivated part of Tibet. To the north is the Nyenchen Tang La or Trans-Himalaya Range which in turn forms the southern boundary of the Chang Tang plains and mountains. This is an area of desert playas and massive mountains, all at elevations over 16,000 feet. There are many lakes, both fresh and salt, of which the largest is Tengri Nor.

Northern Tibet has two great ranges, the Altyn Tagh and Nan Shan system, as a rampart overlooking Sinkiang and Mongolia, and the Kuen Lun farther south. Both have numerous peaks of 20,000 feet. Between them are the enclosed basins of the Tsaidam and Koko Nor (Ching Hai) at elevations of 9,000 and 10,500 feet, respectively. Koko Nor is the largest lake in Tibet.

Eastern Tibet, east of 95°E., is a land of great canyons and intervening high ranges, with a general northwest to southeast orientation. This area is known to the Tibetans as Kam, or as the Land of the Great Corrosions. Here flow the Hwang, Yangtze, Mekong, and Salween. Part of this area lies in Nearer Tibet within the new provinces of Sikang and Chinghai, but the political boundary is vague. The easternmost mountains, bordering Szechwan and Yunnan, are the Tahsueh Shan or Great Snowy Mountains. The highest peak is Minya Gongkar, 25,200 feet, climbed by a party of Harvard students in 1932.

B. The Tien Shan Highlands lie in Sinkiang between the Tarim and Dzungarian basins. The Tien Shan or Heavenly Range extends into Soviet Middle Asia to join the Pamirs. It has a length of 1,000 miles in China, with peaks over 20,000 feet.

The northernmost component is the Dzungarian Alatau. In the east, the main range is the Bogdo Ola, while in the southeast are the Kuruk Tagh Hills.

C. The Altai-Sayan Highlands include the mountain complex along the frontier between northwestern Mongolia and the Soviet Union. The Altai Mountains are a long, narrow, and steep-sided range, largely barren. The highest elevations are in the west. North of them, the Tannu Ola Mountains form the southern rim of Tannu Tuva, whose northern limit next to Siberia lies along the Sayan Mountains. The Khangai Mountains and the Kentai Hills, on either side of the Selenga Valley, differ chiefly in altitude; each is an irregularly dissected upland rather than a linear range.

D. The Mongolian—Sinkiang Uplands cover a million square miles in Inner and Outer Mongolia, and in the Dzungarian and Tarim basins of Sinkiang. The largest subregion is the Gobi Plain, which occupies a broad basinlike depression, approached over a mountain rim from every side. Long erosion has worn ancient mountains to a featureless peneplain, subsequently warped to form numerous shallow basins which are now filled with younger sediments. These in turn are partly excavated by wind work. Monotonous desert plains continue for hundreds of miles, often so flat that one may drive an automobile in any direction. Within the Gobi Plain are several major depressions or tala. In the northeast is the Dalai tala, in the center is the Iren tala, while in the southwest is the Gashuin tala. The Ordos Plain lies within the loop of the Hwang River. Northwestern Mongolia includes an extension of The Gobi known as the Valley of the Lakes, which lies between the Altai and the Tannu Ola. The Dzungarian Plain is a lowland corridor from Mongolia to Soviet Middle Asia between the Altai and the Tien Shan. Farther south, the Tarim Basin lies between the Tien Shan and the Altyn Tagh; this is the Takla-makan Desert, the driest area in Asia.

E. The Mongolian Border Uplands lie between The Gobi and the lowland plains of eastern China, and extend in an arc from Kansu to Heilungkiang. The northernmost subregion, the Great Khingan Mountains, is the upturned edge of the Mongolian Upland. From the east these appear as high dissected mountains; seen from the west they are merely low hills. Toward the south, the Great Khingan become lower and there is an easy passage to Mongolia. Most of the province of Jehol is a hill and mountain land with conspicuously steep soilless slopes. Elevations reach 5,000 feet. To the west of the Jehol Mountains is a series of low mountains along the southern margin of the Mongolian Uplands. These are collectively known as the Taching and In Mountains. Although barren and rocky, their elevations are not great. Since the range is not continuous, there are several gateways to The Gobi. To the west of the Hwang River are the 10,000-foot Holan Mountains, often known as the Ala Shan.

The largest part of the Mongolian Border Upland is made up of the Loess Hills, a region where fine silt, blown outward from the Ordos Plain, has formed a veneer over the entire landscape. Two mountain areas rise above the loess, the Liupan Mountains in Kansu and the Shansi Mountains farther east. Two portions of the latter deserve special names, the Taihang next to the Yellow Plain in southern Shansi, and the Wutai farther north. Within the Loess Hills is a series of alluvial basins known as the Shensi-Shansi Plains. The most important of these is drained by the Wei River and dominated by the historic city of Sian. The second is that along the Fen River in Shansi where there are areas of alluvium around Taiyuan as well as near the mouth. The plains of the Wei and Fen lie in a structural graben which reappears farther north to form the plain around the city of Tatung.

F. The Eastern Highlands extend from Shantung to Heilungkiang. In the latter province and in Kirin are the East Manchurian Hills, a rounded and forested region with only pioneer agricultural settlement. The highest portion of this region, along the Korean frontier, has the name of the Changpai Shan or Long White Mountains. The Little Khingan Hills lie south of the Amur River and may be placed either in this region or with the preceding one. The Shantung Hills were formerly an island in the Yellow Sea but are now half surrounded by the encroaching delta of the Hwang River. An important corridor north of Tsingtao divides the region into two subdivisions and provides an avenue for the railway to Tsinan. The highest point is the sacred peak of Tai Shan, 5,056 feet, made famous by Confucius.

G. The Eastern Lowlands include by far the larger part of China's level land which has adequate rainfall for agricultural settlement. In the far north the Amur-Ussuri Plains, largely within Soviet Siberia, provide flat land along the respective rivers. There are considerable areas of swamp, and part of the area is underlain by permanently frozen subsoil. The Manchurian Plain, largely the result of erosion, covers 137,000 square miles in the provinces of Heilungkiang, Liaoning, and Kirin. The northern portion is drained by the Sungari River while in the south there is the Liao Ho. The Manchurian Plain is surrounded by hills with only three lowland gateways. One of these is to the northwest along the narrow valley of the Sungari. The second is a broad saddle in the southern Great Khingan near the upper sources of the Liao, leading to Mongolia. The third and most important is the narrow coastal plain at Shanhaikwan where the Jehol Mountains almost reach the Gulf of Chihli. This point, where the Great Wall reaches the sea, has been the scene of repeated Manchu invasions.

The Yangtze Delta Plain merges imperceptibly with the Yellow Plain in northern Kiangsu. Important climatic, soil, and crop

Rows of trees surround many temple courtyards in the mountains of China. This scene is from the Chien Shan in Manchuria. (*Ato.*)

The Yellow Plain is the largest alluvial area in China, covering 125,000 square miles. This remarkably flat plain is the compound delta of the Hwang and other streams that flow out of the encircling hills. Widespread floods have resulted from the breaking of the dikes. On account of poor drainage and the high water table, extensive areas have salty soil. All of the region is below 500 feet elevation. Peiping lies at the northern margin of the plain in close proximity to two important gateways through the Great Wall, Nankou and Kupeikou passes, and not far from the equally important corridor at Shanhaikwan.

boundaries mark the transition along the line of the Hwai River. Unlike the delta of the Hwang, the lower Yangtze Plain is cut by innumerable canals. Shanghai, Hangchow, and Nanking are the principal cities. The Mid-Yangtze Lake Plains surround numerous lakes, chief of which are the Poyang and Tungting. Unlike the flat delta, this region is studded with low rocky hills. Northwest of Hankow is a nearly enclosed alluvial area drained by the Han River and termed the Han Plain.

H. The Central Uplands are a spur of the Tibetan Highlands which continue the Kuen Lun structures eastward to the vicinity of Nanking. Elevations decrease from 20,000 feet in the west to mere hills in the east where the Uplands disappear beneath coastal alluvium. The Tsingling Range is the greatest mountain system of eastern China and forms a lofty and rugged barrier from Kansu to Honan. South of Sian peaks reach 12,000 feet in elevation. The Tsingling are a series of parallel ridges, all trending a little south of east, with canyons whose walls often rise sheer to a height of 1,000 feet above the streams. The eastern extension of the range is known as the Sung Shan and the Funiu Shan. These mountains are an effective barrier to monsoon rainfall from the south and serve to define the most important geographic boundary of the country. On one side is the dry, brown, dust-blown wheat country of the north while on the other are the green, humid, ricelands of the south. These mountains have also been of political significance, for in 1860 they prevented the Taiping rebels from coming north, and in 1875 they similarly limited the southward advance of the Mohammedan Rebellion. The Tsingling lie north of the Han River, whose valley locally widens to a plain. To the south are the slightly lower Tapa Mountains, also with an east-west trend. These join the Gorge Mountains, so named from their development across the Yangtze River above Ichang. The easternmost extension of the Central Uplands is variously known as the Tapei Hills or the Hwaiyang Hills. Elevations here are largely under 3,000 feet, and the whole character of the physical landscape is more gentle with rounded mountains and open valleys.

I. The Szechwan Lowland is an island in the heart of west China. Most of it is known as the Red Basin Hills, from the red or purplish color of the underlying sandstones. Hilltops rise to 3,000 or 4,000 feet, with valley bottoms at half these elevations. Chungking dominates this thoroughly hilly region. The Chengtu Plain is a small but intensively utilized alluvial fan along the western margin of the Szechwan Lowland, next to the Great Snowy Mountains.

J. The Southern Uplands include a large area of southern China. Level land is nowhere more than a few miles in extent, and hills or mountains are always in sight. In the region as a whole, flat areas cover less than 15 per cent and are largely confined to flood plains. The South Yangtze Hills lie in Hunan, Kiangsi, Chekiang, and southern Anhwei, largely within the drainage basin of the Yangtze River. Numerous valleys lead into the area from the Mid-Yangtze Lake Plains. To the east are the Wuyi and Tayu mountains, while on the south are the Nanling Mountains. These have trends parallel to the coast, with peaks that rise to 6,000 feet. North of Canton are two famous passes across the Nanling. The first is the old imperial highway to Nanchang by way of the Meiling Pass. The second leads to Changsha over the Cheling Pass, and is the route of the Canton-Hankow Railway. The hinterland of Canton is drained by the East, North, and West Rivers which give their name to an area of hills and scattered alluvial basins between the Nanling and the sea. These rivers have formed the compound Canton Delta Plain. In western and northern Kwangsi, in Yunnan, and in Kweichow are remarkable areas of almost vertical-sided hills of limestone, representing an advanced stage of solution or karst topography. In southern Kwangtung is the Luichow Peninsula, a rolling plain linked with that in the northern part of Hainan Island. Hainan itself is largely mountainous, with elevations to over a mile.

K. The Southwestern Uplands lie in Kweichow and Yunnan. These uplands are a subdued continuation of the Tibetan Highlands, with plateau remnants cut by deep valleys and crossed by rugged moun-

tains. The only part of the region which is
level is the Kunming Plain where there are
several lake basins. Dissection has been
most extensive in the Kweichow Hills,
where many rivers flow in valleys 2,000 feet
in depth. Elevations in the Yunnan Plateau
average 6,000 feet, while the Kweichow
Hills are about 4,000 feet. Level land probably amounts to less than 5 per cent of the
entire region.

Within the province of Yunnan, plateau
characteristics are found east of the Red
River and the city of Tali, and south of the
Yangtze River. Northwestern Yunnan lies
in the Great Snowy Mountains while the
southwest is part of the Shan Plateau along
the border of Burma.

Climate

The Chinese live close to nature and are
thus vitally dependent upon the weather.
Climatic averages seldom tell the whole
story, for rain often comes too early or too
late, or in exceptional amounts. Flood and
drought are equally serious. Honan has received 18 inches in a day, while a Kwangsi
station with a yearly average of 50 inches
once dropped to 8 inches for 12 months.
Mountains exposed to typhoons from the
South China Sea receive around 100 inches,
while the Tarim Basin is nearly rainless.

In North China, June is the critical
month for summer planting, but a Tientsin
June rainfall of over eight inches in two
successive years, three times the average,
was preceded and followed by years with
half an inch in the same month. The resulting crop uncertainties are especially
serious in a land as crowded as this.

China lies on the east coast of the largest
continent and thus has a seasonal monsoon
tendency. As a result of its location, the
climate is alternately continental and Asiatic in winter, and maritime or Pacific in
summer. On this monsoon circulation are
superimposed air mass movements, cyclonic

storms, and typhoons. Unlike India, where
summer with its inblowing air is the dominant period, winter continental winds provide the most powerful circulation in China.
Thus southern China has unusually cool
winters for its latitude.

Like the United States, China is a contest
zone for invading air masses from polar and
tropical latitudes, with frequent weather
changes as one or the other becomes
dominant.

Cold dry air masses push into China during all months except July, to a total of
29 a year. Many of these first appear in the
Arctic near Nova Zemlya. After crossing
Soviet Middle Asia they enter China via
Dzungaria and Mongolia and come to the
Wei Valley where the Tsingling Mountains
protect Szechwan. The air masses are then
turned eastward to the Yellow Plain and
continue southward along the coast. Since
the advancing wedge of a cold wave is less
than 1,000 feet thick, it is stopped by
moderate relief, but farther back from the
front the thickness of the air mass increases
to a mile so that cold air may overtop peaks
such as Tai Shan in Shantung.

These cold waves travel from Dzungaria
to the southern extremity of China in about
a week. Their speed reflects temperature
contrasts, which are most pronounced in
winter. Across Mongolia the average velocity is but 5 miles per hour, in the Yellow
Plain it reaches 30 miles, and over the
central Yangtze the wind blows as much
as 60 miles per hour. This diminishes to
5 miles per hour along the southern coast.
A few cold waves come into China from
eastern Siberia and Manchuria; if they pass
over the Sea of Japan en route, they acquire
a limited amount of moisture.

In their source areas both air masses are
dry but, as the waves advance, evaporation
from the ground adds some moisture to the
lower layers, so that only Modified Polar
Continental air masses reach China. Dust

storms rather than rainfall are brought by these winds. Such dust clouds are common throughout North China during winter months. Visibility is notably reduced, and impalpable dust finds its way even into closed rooms.

Where a cold front encounters moist tropical air, the latter is lifted and precipitation results. This wedge action accounts for three-quarters of China's rainfall and operates at all seasons.

Southern air masses invade China throughout the year from both the South China Sea and the Southwestern Uplands. The number and strength are less than those from the north. They are often altered in their passage over southern and eastern China so that the air that reaches the Yangtze Valley is characteristically known as Modified Tropical Marine or Continental air. Occasional winter outbursts of Polar air reach the equator, but South China is so well protected by the Tsingling Range that Tropical Marine winds are important even in mid-winter.

During summer months, China is bathed by repeated invasions of hot humid air from the ocean, which push as far as Mongolia. Since this air is light and buoyant, it easily passes over the Southern Uplands, and equally overrides any cold air masses in its path. As the Tropical Maritime air rises, it is cooled and rain falls. Without the lifting and cooling action of mountains or a cold front, Tropical air masses yield no rain even though their relative humidity is high.

The summer monsoon is thus the time when successive Tropical air masses are strong enough to push back the Polar air and shift the front to northern China. There is no continuous seasonal monsoon wind. Although there is an obvious correlation between the period of maximum rainfall and the time of the summer monsoon, rain seldom occurs with strong southerly winds. When they blow constantly, drought may even follow. Rain occurs principally when there is a northerly wind at the surface to underrun and lift the southeast monsoon sufficiently high to cool it and cause condensation.

Cyclonic or anticyclonic storms and typhoons introduce further variability. When the knowledge of Chinese meteorology was limited to stations along the coast, it was assumed that few cyclonic storms crossed Asia; this is now known to be incorrect. Observations in the Soviet Union and interior China show that numerous highs and lows from Europe cross Siberia and Mongolia to enter northern China on their way to Japan and Alaska. Others, especially in winter, follow a route from Europe south of Tibet into southern China. Still others may originate in the interior, especially in the upper Yangtze Valley, by the interaction of opposing warm- and cold-air masses. From 1921 to 1930, there were, on an average, 84 cyclonic storms per year. The cyclones of China have an average diameter along the major axis of 905 miles and are thus considerably smaller than those of the United States whose corresponding dimensions are 1,550 miles. Although their individual extent is limited, they follow various paths so that almost all of China feels their effect at one time or another.

The cyclonic storms of China may be grouped according to their paths into six types. One appears from Siberia and moves southeastward across southern Manchuria. Many of these storms are known to come from Europe. Two North China types first appear in the vicinity of the Ordos Desert and move either eastward across southern Manchuria or southward to the mouth of the Yangtze. Three types pass down the Yangtze Valley; the more important traverse the provinces just south of the river from Kweichow and Hunan. Two other types are known as the Eastern Sea and

Northeastern types from their place of occurrence. The numerical importance of lows along these various paths from 1921 to 1930 is as follows: Siberian type, 181; North China types, 265; Yangtze types, 277; Eastern Sea type, 71; and Northeastern type, 47.

Where the direction of the cyclonic counterclockwise circulation coincides with the monsoon gradient, the resulting wind is intensified. Thus, winds on the back side of a low reinforce the winter monsoon invasion, producing unusually strong northwest winds. Since cyclonic storms are fewer and less developed during the summer, and invading Tropical air moves more slowly than Polar air masses, the coincidence of southerly summer winds gives lower velocities. Nevertheless great quantities of moist marine air are drawn into China, and heavy precipitation frequently results. During the 1935 floods, low pressure areas from Indo-China stagnated over the Han Valley and brought 14 cubic miles of rain in six days.

The typhoons of the western Pacific originate east of the Philippine Islands in the vicinity of the Marshall and Caroline groups along the equatorial front where Tropical air undercuts unstable Equatorial air and thus releases the large amounts of energy needed for typhoons. They move west and then northeast, either striking the southeastern coast of China or recurving toward Japan before reaching the mainland. When they occasionally recurve after entering the continent, they travel twice as fast as when moving westward and, after reaching the ocean, their intensity is greatly increased. Since typhoons follow more or less regular paths, it is often possible to predict something of their movement and issue appropriate warnings to shipping. Between 1893 and 1924 there were 263 typhoons in the vicinity of China, or an average of 8.5 per year.

No part of the year is entirely free from typhoons, but they are especially abundant during the late summer. Typhoons visit Kwangtung during May, but by June the track of most storms has moved northward to Formosa. July and August are the most destructive months along the central coast, and by October the increasing pressure of the Siberian high appears to be sufficient to keep typhoons away from the continent.

Typhoons always have a succession of heavy rain squalls. The wind blows with velocities up to 150 miles per hour and carries the rain horizontally with such violence that severe damage is often done to ships and coastal districts. Pressures against vertical surfaces reach 100 pounds per square foot. Much of the summer rainfall of the southeastern provinces is derived from these tropical storms, in contrast to the gentle spring rains which are associated with cyclonic areas.

Seasons are well differentiated. Winter temperatures show great contrast with latitude, for the January average in northern Manchuria is −13°F. as compared with 68°F. in Hainan in the south. During July, temperatures are more uniform and these extreme locations average 70°F. and 84°F., respectively. Summers everywhere have oppressive heat and humidity. Peiping regularly experiences temperatures over 100°F., and may even be warmer than Shanghai or Canton. The duration of the warm period increases southward so that in Canton Europeans wear white clothing for 11 months.

Rainfall shows even greater regional contrasts and is the major item in differentiating North China and South China. South of the Tsingling barrier which lies midway between the Hwang and Yangtze rivers, rainfall is from 40 to 75 inches; to the north it ranges from 25 inches in the Yellow Plain to less than 10 inches outside the Great Wall. In North China rainfall occurs exclusively during the summer, and winters have bright sunshine; in South China summer is also the wet season but all months have some rain.

Contrasting climates divide China into seven regions, each with its regime of rainfall and temperature. The Koeppen classification does not give meaningful boundaries in this part of Asia, and the following regions are based on the work of Chu and Tu.[1]

CLIMATIC PROVINCES OF CHINA

A. Mongolian type
  1. Desert
  2. Desert-steppe
  3. Pasture-steppe
  4. Agriculture-steppe
  5. Boreal climate of the mountains
B. Manchurian type
  6. Khingan Mountains
  7. Manchurian Plain
  8. East Manchurian Hills
C. North China type
  9. Great Plain
  10. Loess Hills
  11. Jehol Mountains
D. Central China type
  12. Lower Yangtze Plain
  13. Mid-Yangtze Plain
  14. Szechwan Basin
  15. Gulf of Hangchow
E. South China type
  16. Southeastern Coast
  17. Si Kiang Valley
  18. Hainan
F. West China type
  19. Tsingling Ranges
  20. Sikang Mountains
  21. Southwestern Uplands
G. Tibetan type
  22. Northern Tibet
  23. Southwestern Tibet
  24. Koko Nor
  25. Southeast Tibet

A. Mongolia and Sinkiang have an arid and semiarid climate, with less than 10 inches of rainfall and long severe winters.

[1] Tu, CHANG-WANG, Climatic Provinces of China, *Journal*, Geographical Society of China III, no. 3 (September, 1936), in Chinese with English abstract.

The steppe type is subdivided on the basis of local variations in moisture. Koeppen maps classify the area as BW (desert) or BS (steppe), with the mountains of the northwest as Dwc.

B. Manchuria forms another unit, subdivided by its three topographic regions. Five months have averages below freezing, and the growing season is under 150 days. The rainfall decreases from 40 inches in the east to 15 inches in the west. In Koeppen symbols, it has a Dwb climate.

C. The North China climatic regions include the Great Plain of the Hwang, the Loess Hills, and the Jehol Mountains, each with many similarities to Mongolia. The rainfall average is 25 inches or less but varies widely. Winters are dry, and crops can grow for more than 240 days. This region extends south to the Tsingling Range and the Hwai Valley. Koeppen symbols are less satisfactory here, for they destroy the regional unity by breaking it up into Dw and Cw.

D. The Yangtze Valley is called the Central China type. It has 40 to 60 inches of rainfall and a growing season of 300 days. Conditions somewhat resemble the southeastern United States, where the Koeppen symbols are $Cfa;$ farther inland in China, winter drought changes the letters to Cw.

E. The South China type covers the West River Basin and the coastal areas on either side of the Tropic of Cancer. Even in the coldest month temperature averages are above 50°F. so that the growing season is nearly a year long. Rainfall exceeds 80 inches on exposed mountain slopes. Although Koeppen groups this with Shantung as Cw, the higher rainfall and the absence of a severe winter in the south make conditions quite distinct.

F. Between the lowlands of the Yangtze Valley and the Tibetan Highlands is the West China climatic type, all of it at considerable elevation. The wide ranges in latitude and altitude prevent much unity. The Tsingling is the major dividing range are the Great Snowy Mountains; while in the southwest is the Yunnan Plateau.

G. Tibetan climates cover the highland,

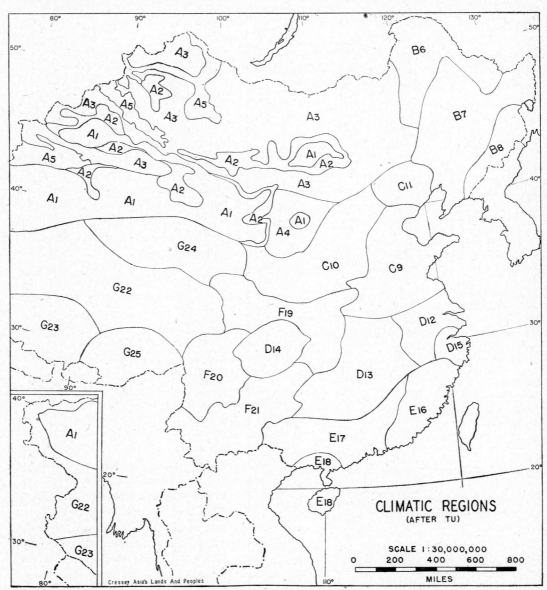

CLIMATIC REGIONS
(AFTER TU)

SCALE 1:30,000,000

0   200   400   600   800

MILES

Cressey Asia's Lands And Peoples

These seven climatic types (see page 63), as defined by Tu, describe Chinese conditions better than do the Koeppen symbols.

between humid and semiarid China; along the borders of Tibet in Sikang province with a separate division for the vicinity of Lhasa where mild temperatures and heavy precipitation produce a Koeppen *Cw* climate in contrast to *ET* elsewhere.

Natural Vegetation

There are few areas in China where the original cover of natural vegetation is still preserved. For the most part these are in localities where climate, as in the desert, or topography, as in rugged mountains, provides barriers to agricultural operations. Such areas are restricted to the steppe and desert vegetation of Mongolia, Sinkiang, and Tibet, to some of the forest regions and dry grasslands of Manchuria, and to relatively small forested areas in the mountains of central and southern China.

Villages and farmsteads are usually surrounded by planted trees even in the dry north. Farm wood lots are entirely absent on the cultivated plains, so that forests are restricted to hillsides too steep for other crops.

The popular conception of China as a deforested land is only partly correct. South China with its heavier rainfall produces large though inadequate amounts of lumber, and there has long been systematic replanting in many districts. North China has many planted trees. In the drier areas it is questionable whether there ever was a natural forest cover.

It seems probable that much of the delta plain of northern China and the flood plains of the Yangtze and other rivers of central and southern China have been occupied by man since the deposition of their present surface, so that they have never had a cover of natural vegetation.

Although adequate ecological studies are not available, the following description, based largely on studies by James Thorp,[1] presents the characteristics of ten major vegetation regions.

[1] THORP, JAMES, "Geography of the Soils of China," Nanking: National Geological Survey (1936).

VEGETATION REGIONS OF CHINA
A. Cultivated river plains
B. Desert flora
  1. Barren sands
  2. Salt-tolerant plants
  3. Xerophytic plants
C. Steppe grasslands
  1. Short-grass steppe
  2. Tall-grass steppe
    a. Tall bunch and short grass
    b. Tall and short grass with patches of forests
D. Semiarid brush
E. Dry mountain flora
F. Upland forests
  1. Deciduous and coniferous forests, dry type of the Mongolian Border Uplands.
  2. Deciduous and coniferous forests, moist type of the Central Uplands.
  3. Dense coniferous and deciduous forests, humid type of the Southwestern Uplands.
G. Szechwan lowland flora
H. High mountain flora
I. Subtropical forests
J. Tropical broadleaf forests

A. In the cultivated river plains of the Yellow, Hwai, Yangtze, and West rivers, soils are more or less constantly renewed and have never had a chance to develop a natural vegetation because they are under cultivation. In the north, pines, poplars, and willows have been planted on grave plots and in the villages, and groves of willows and poplars are common along the streams. On the plains of central and southern China many different species of trees common to those regions have been transplanted along roads and waterways and on grave plots.

On the newly forming delta lands in Tungting and Poyang lakes, and on the alluvial soils bordering small lakes of the central basins, there are large areas of reeds. This type of growth was probably characteristic of alluvial lands in the south prior to their cultivation.

B. Barren sands with scattered dunes cover relatively small parts of the Gobi and Ordos deserts, perhaps no more than 10 per cent, but are widespread in the Takla-makan

Desert. Sandy areas are known to be more extensive than indicated on the map but tamarisk is common. There is much stony land, and many small saline and alkali

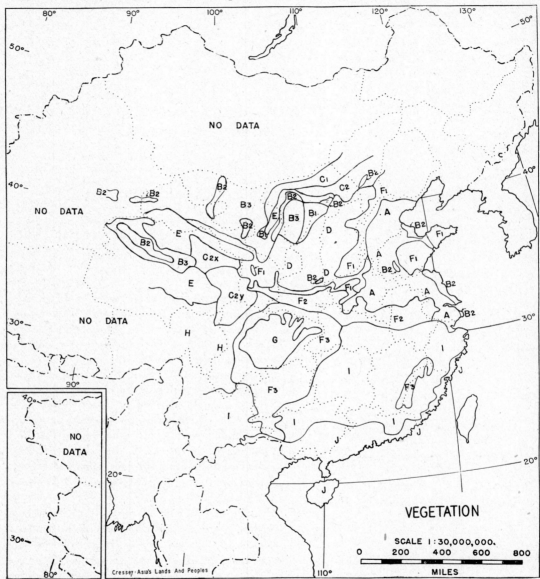

The original cover of natural vegetation over eastern China has largely disappeared, but this reconstruction (see page 65) supplies a guide to the potential land use. No information is available for outlying areas.

their exact location is uncertain. On the sand dunes, vegetation is either very sparse or entirely lacking. In intervening low areas where the water table is relatively high,

areas with their appropriate types of specialized vegetation.

Salt-tolerant species and halophytes scarcely form a distinct region but occur in scattered areas of saline and alkali soils. They are found in poorly drained parts of the desert and semiarid regions; smaller areas are present along the seacoast from Hopei to southeast of Shanghai. Two general groups of plants occur on them. One of these comprises the true halophytes or salt lovers, the second group are salt-tolerant and grow not only on the saline soils but on neighboring nonsaline lands as well.

Considerable parts of The Gobi, Takla-makan, and other deserts of northwestern and far western China have dry xerophytic plants. The vegetation mainly comprises shrubs, some short grass, and many small flowering plants that spring up rapidly following sporadic summer rains, quickly reach maturity, and disappear with the return of drought.

C. The short-grass steppe is largely confined to northwestern Suiyuan and Chahar provinces in Inner Mongolia, although it occurs in Farther Tibet, Sinkiang, and Outer Mongolia. Moisture increases toward the southeast from The Gobi region and there is a corresponding increase in the density and variety of vegetation. Near the border of the true desert the clumps of grass are a foot or two apart, while along the southeastern border of the short-grass steppe the vegetation forms a continuous cover and includes clumps of tall grasses. In places where the water table is close to the surface, soils are more or less saline or alkali, and the vegetation is halophytic. In moist areas that are not saline, there is a rich growth of tall grasses. Many flowering plants and small shrubs are included.

The tall-grass steppe lies southeastward and eastward from the short-grass steppes of Inner Mongolia, without a sharp boundary. In addition to the grasses there are many flowering plants and shrubs including licorice and several species of sage. Within the tall-grass region where there is the same

variation of density of growth as in the short-grass region, associations of species also follow topographic differences. On some of the hills one finds a few elms and pines but most of the scattered trees of the region were cut long ago.

Parts of eastern Chinghai and Kansu form subregions. Tall bunch grass, short grasses, and shrubs occur around Koko Nor. Farther south there are both tall and short grasslands on southerly slopes and flat areas, with spruce and fir on some of the northern slopes.

D. Semiarid grasses and brush form the natural cover over the greater part of the loess deposits in Shensi and Kansu. Most of these soils have been cultivated or over-grazed for so long that natural ecological associations have been seriously disturbed. On steep hillsides and in gullies too rough to be cultivated, there is a mixture of thorny shrubs and many species of both tall and short grasses. Around protected temples are groves of trees that thrive fairly well. These include the arborvitae, the pagoda tree, poplars, pines, and occasional cedars. These trees are sometimes assumed to be an indication that the Loess Hills were once forested, but there is no valid reason for supposing that this was the case except on the higher mountains which extend above the general level of the loess. The magnificent trees growing on the loess around some of the temples were all planted.

Within this region are many areas above the general level of loess deposition. On these there was once a fairly dense forest of mixed deciduous and coniferous types, with many remnants today. In the valleys, farmers have planted groves of poplars. These grow quickly on irrigated lands and in five or ten years can produce timbers for building purposes. Willows have also been planted on the sandy flood plains for stream control, timber, fuel, and material for baskets, and they line the ancient highways of the region. It seems probable that willows formed a natural feature of the landscape in ancient times.

hills and valleys have a mixed short- and tall-grass association, and many of the shady slopes have a dense cover of bushes.

Serious erosion quickly follows removal of the forest cover in the higher mountains of the northwest. (*W. C. Lowdermilk, courtesy University of Nanking.*)

A prominent feature in western China, and especially in Regions *D*, *E*, and *H*, is the difference in vegetation between the adret, or sunny, side and the ubac, or shady, side of the hills. The southward-facing adret slopes receive much greater insolation than the ubac, or northward-facing, slopes. As a consequence the latter soils are cooler and more moist. Where sunny slopes are covered by short-grass vegetation, corresponding shady slopes have tall grass and brush; where the sunny slopes are covered by tall grass and brush, shady slopes usually are in a forest.

E. Much of Chinghai, parts of northwestern Kansu, and possibly a small area in northern Sikang have a dry mountain vegetation of trees and grass. The greater part of the valley lands and lower mountain slopes is covered by grassy vegetation. The

In scattered areas at altitudes approaching 10,000 feet, shady slopes are covered by forests of poplar, spruce, and fir. At greater heights, patches of forests are more common on the sunny slopes while the shady slopes and high peaks are too cold for trees of any kind. Above 14,000 feet, and still higher on the southern slopes, is an alpine vegetation of short grasses, "cushion plants," and small flowers.

The heights of the Kuen Lun Range and the high alpine meadows of the Hwang River headwaters form a subregion. The landscape is barren and desolate.

F. Mixed deciduous and coniferous forests were the original cover over the Mongolian Border Uplands. At present the area is largely a land of grassy eroded hills and barren stony mountains, with occasional forest remnants as reminders of former conditions. Among the trees still standing are oaks, elms, chestnuts, maples, and coniferous types such as pines and junipers. In second growth thickets the jujube tree is very common and is usually interspersed with grass.

Deciduous trees grow more commonly on the deeper soils of the low hills and alluvial fans. Pines occupy the thin soils and crags of the more or less barren eroded mountains but have been planted on some of the foothills and alluvial fans.

In the valleys, groves of poplars, willows, locusts, and elms have been planted as a source of wood and as a means of controlling river erosion. Some of these groves tend to reproduce themselves and so might be considered as a seminatural vegetation.

Forests probably dominated the Central Uplands before they were settled by man. From remnants in the Tsingling Range and southern Honan it seems evident that this forest was somewhat more dense than that of the drier Mongolian Border Uplands, and dominantly of deciduous types. In the southern part there are occasional evergreen broad-leaved trees. On the shallow soils of the high mountains and on poor acid soils of the low hills in the south, pines are common.

Practically all of this original forest has been destroyed, but new growth springs up readily on the better soils. In much of Honan and Anhwei, grass has taken the place of forest and is cut every year for fuel, along with young bushes and trees. Fuel gatherers not only cut off the tops of young trees but dig up the roots as well.

Dense coniferous and deciduous forests cover the rolling to mountainous Southwestern Uplands, the mountains surrounding the Szechwan Lowland, and the higher mountain peaks of western Fukien and eastern Kiangsi. There are probably small areas in other mountains of southern China. The vegetation owes its character to the heavy rainfall and high humidity. Areas of undisturbed growth are rare, but natural reproduction takes place readily. In the Tapa Mountains of the Szechwan-Hupei-Shensi border, and in the mountain complex south of the Yangtze River, the original forest cover comprised a large number of different conifers and deciduous trees. Spruce, fir including *Cunninghamia*, and hemlock are common on the higher mountains, and are interspersed with many different deciduous trees on the rolling and hilly lands, such as oak, chestnut, and sweet gum. In the Kweichow Hills a large part of the hilly land has been partly or entirely deforested and is now covered by tall grasses. Many temples are surrounded by small areas of forest. Evergreen broad-leaved trees with thick and leathery leaves of dark green color occur in the south.

In western Fukien and eastern Kiangsi, the forests are largely of *Cunninghamia* and pines. Large plantations of bamboo are very common, especially along the streams. *Cunninghamia* forests are not natural but have been planted by the villagers as a regular tree crop.

Within most of this humid subregion the forests consist of large trees and a more or less dense undergrowth. In a few places, such as the mountains of northeastern Kweichow and northwestern Kwangsi, there are patches of tropical selva or rain forest. In this type of forest large trees of the evergreen broad-leaved type form a dense canopy of leaves 40 or 50 feet above the forest floor and make so dense a shade that there is relatively little undergrowth.

G. Pine, bamboo, and cyprus are characteristic of the Szechwan Lowland. Practically all of the valley lands and a large part of the hills are now used for cultivated crops, and much of the remainder is devoted to planted forests of pine and cypress. On the higher hills are many deciduous trees mixed with the pines. In some places oaks dominate. In the hills at the western edge of the region the nanmu, a valuable evergreen broad-leaved hardwood, is common. There are a few species of palms.

One of the most noticeable trees of Szechwan is the common banyan which was probably introduced into the region a long time ago. Banyans are evergreen broad-leaved trees used for ornamentation and shade, and as objects of worship.

H. This region comprises the high mountain flora of the borderland between the Szechwan Lowland and the Tibetan Highlands. Along the headwaters of the Min River and beyond the so-called "rain screen" mountains of western Szechwan, the tops of the mountains are covered with coniferous forests, while the intermediate slopes are in grass. Still farther northwest, grass grows on the south slopes and forests on the northerly slopes. To the west is a series of deep canyons and high rolling uplands. The gorges are either bare or covered with spruce, fir, and pine, while the smoother parts of the uplands have a thick sod of avena and festuca.

I. Subtropical evergreen broad-leaved trees, pine, *Cunninghamia* fir, and bamboo characterize much of China south of the Yangtze. Approximately virgin conditions exist only in some of the more remote and thinly settled regions and on sacred mountains. The original cover was probably a mixture of coniferous and deciduous trees, with pines and oaks important on the old red and yellow soils, and broad-leaved evergreen trees playing a subordinate role. The latter become dominant on the more fertile brown and gray soils of the region.

At present these regions are used for the production of regular crops of *Cunninghamia* and bamboo, as well as pine, deciduous and broad-leaved evergreen trees. Most of the lower hills have been cleared again and again by fuel gatherers, and in many places the work of these people has been so intensive that the soil has become entirely bare and severely eroded.

Over a large part of the region it is a common practice to burn the grass and brush of the hills every year. In Chekiang, Fukien, and parts of other provinces, young trees sprout up from the roots of the old ones after the land has been burned, but on the poorer soils a continued practice of this kind ultimately results in the complete destruction of the forest growth and its replacement by tall, coarse grasses. Much of central and southern Kwangsi has been almost entirely deforested in this manner. The present vegetation comprises various grasses whose chief value is for fuel except that during the younger stages they furnish a fair pasturage for water buffalo and other cattle. On some of the strongly acid and deforested red soils of South China, especially in Kwangtung and Kwangsi, coarse ferns entirely cover the land and are used as fuel.

Many grave plots are partly covered by shade trees, among which sweet gums and camphor are common. Camphors, also common around village sites, are often held in veneration and so protected for centuries. The camphor trees of Kiangsi and Hunan are among the most magnificent trees that exist in China today.

The northern limit of the subtropical forest region approximately coincides with the northern limit of palm and citrus trees.

J. Tropical semideciduous forests are present in the far south along the southeastern coast, and in Hainan. Broad-leaved evergreens dominate but are mixed with pines, deciduous trees, and bamboo. On the older red earths and on some of the poor thin soils of mountain sides, pine trees are more plentiful. On denuded hills coarse grasses or ferns have monopolized the soil. Some of the grasslands of this region resemble the cogonals of the Philippines and other parts of the tropics. Citrus trees, sugar cane, bananas, and other tropical and subtropical fruits are grown in addition to the dominant crop of rice. In many parts of Kwangtung and Kwangsi, crops of trees and bamboo are raised on the hills, especially near navigable rivers.

Soils

Just as vegetation summarizes climate, land forms, and elevation, so the soils of China in turn are largely a by-product of the natural vegetation. Geological parent materials place their initial stamp on young soils but, as time goes on, the composition, texture, and profile of mature soils take on environmental characteristics that increasingly reflect climate and vegetation.

Thus each of the great soil groups has a personality acquired from its environment. This is shown in their profile with its *A*, *B*, and *C* horizons, of which the lower is unmodified parent material while the upper two are zones of organic accumulation and leaching, the *A* horizon; and of clay accumulation, the *B* horizon. Intensive cultivation has further altered these natural soils through depletion or increase of fertility, erosion, and the modification of internal characteristics.

In classifying the infinite complexity of Chinese soils, two great groups appear. These result from the major physical contrasts between the North and the South and lie back of the agricultural and cultural differences of these same major regions. To the north of the Hwai River, where rainfall diminishes, soils tend to be rich in lime and soluble plant nutrients, porous and friable and easily permeated by water. In the Yangtze Valley and south, many soils are leached, heavy textured, more or less stiff, and less fertile except where renewed by flood deposits. Throughout China they tend to be low in organic

matter and many are deficient in plant nutrients.

The soils of North China are chiefly pedocals, or calcium carbonate-accumulating types, hence the "cal" of their name. Where well developed on the uplands, they include chernozems, chestnut-brown soils, and light-colored desert soils. Lowland soils of mature characteristics include shachiang and saline soils. Young alluvial soils lack a textural profile but many are calcareous and some are also saline.

South China has pedalfer or nonlimeforming soils, named from their aluminum and iron, "al" and "fe." Upland welldeveloped varieties include podzol and podzolic soils, and red and yellow earths. On lowlands with poor drainage, various rice paddy soils are formed, either with or without podzolization. Recent alluvium forms still another type.

Chernozems occur chiefly in the grasslands of northern Manchuria, Inner Mongolia, and northeastern Tibet. The thick black *A* horizons of these soils get their color from the organic residues of the tallgrass steppe. Lime concretions or soft lime carbonates occur in the *B* horizon. Typical chernozems are not extensive in semiarid eastern Asia but, if present, they are notably better developed on the shady and more moist slopes of hills where the grass cover is more abundant. Elsewhere in subhumid areas are degraded chernozems where partial podzolization has modified the profile; these are similar to the black prairie soils of the United States since they are without lime accumulation. Chernozems are among the most fertile soils in the world, but in China they occur in regions where rainfall is barely adequate for agriculture, and where latitude or altitude makes the frost-free season precariously short. Much of the colder land remains in pasture. Where the land is cultivated, soybeans are an excellent crop, also wheat, millet, and the grain sorghum kaoliang.

Chestnut-colored soils have an *A* horizon which varies from dark to light brown, largely in terms of the humus content. They are found along the drier margins of the chernozems in Inner Mongolia, eastern Tibet, northwestern Manchuria, and in the more moist parts of Outer Mongolia and Sinkiang. Short grass is the typical vegetation. Although the soil is fertile, rainfall is inadequate for normal crops and dry-farming techniques are necessary. Colonization of these areas, not unlike the American dust bowl, is sure to involve occasional disaster. Inner Mongolia is full of evidence of alternating settlement and abandonment. Since dry climates are notably variable, deserts expand and contract with the centuries. Remnants of three ancient great walls north of the present one reflect the shifting boundary between farmer and pastoralist.

The soils of the loessial parts of Shansi, Shensi, Honan, and Kansu require a special classification since they are derived from parent material of high lime content and are subject to constant renewal by wind work. They are low in organic matter but rich in plant nutrients. In general they represent imperfectly developed very light colored chestnut earths. Some soils in the drier areas of scanty vegetation are yellow-gray earths. On more humid mountain slopes chernozems and dark chestnut soils have developed. Beneath the loess are reddish shales which have given rise to local areas of red soils, so immature that their classification is uncertain. A considerable part of this area is under cultivation, although serious erosion restricts land use. In years of adequate and properly distributed rainfall crops are bountiful, but unfortunately good years are not the rule.

Gray and yellow-gray desert soils are common in the short-grass and brush areas of Mongolia and Sinkiang, the former representing the driest phase. Evaporation of capillary moisture forms a crust of lime and salts, which may partly cement the surface during times of drought. Where red soils occur, the color reflects the local parent material rather than desert processes. Sandy surfaces, known in Chinese as shamo, are so porous that little or no profile develops. Agricultural development is limited to oases whose area is insignificant in relation to the whole desert. The chief use of the desert is for pasture, but drinking water is inaccessible in large areas.

Shachiang soils are unique, although apparently related to some on the Indo-Gangetic Plain and in Texas. They occupy large parts of the Eastern Lowlands in Shantung, Honan, Anhwei, and Hopei. These soils are poorly drained and have a subsoil horizon of lime and iron-manganese concretions. Unlike proper pedocals, the lime is not all derived from the leaching of an *A* horizon but probably comes from the ground water whose fluctuating level corresponds to the zone of concretions. Flat topography is a prerequisite and, in the interstream areas, extensive sections are flooded almost every season; when the dikes of the Hwang, Hwai, or Hai are breached, shallow lakes develop and remain for a year or more. In wet weather the soil is heavy and sticky, while in dry weather it becomes very hard. Crop yields are moderate.

Recent calcareous alluvium covers the flood plains of North China and may range from sand to clay in composition. The silty soils are usually the most productive for agriculture. The coarser deposits lie closer to the rivers and make up the natural levees. Local sand dunes have developed from these deposits. During the 1935 flood in Shantung some of the Hwang River deposits were six feet thick; farms that had had poor sandy soil were covered with productive silt, and the reverse. These alluvial soils lie in the winter wheat and kaoliang area, with important amounts of corn, cotton, and tobacco.

Saline and alkali soils are widespread in North China, even in the Hwang River delta. In their technical classification they belong to solonchak and solonetz types. Evaporation of capillary water from a high water table develops a surface concentration of soluble salts. The wet season is too short to flush out the accumulation of the dry period. Such soils are found from Shanghai to northern Manchuria, and northwest to Mongolia and Sinkiang. True alkali soils contain sodium or potassium carbonate and are not very common in China, but concentrations of sodium chloride with some sodium sulphate and sodium bicarbonate are common. Where these soils are too saline for cultivation, salt-tolerant plants are harvested for fuel. Even where saline soils have not yet developed, the introduction of irrigation, as along the Mongolian bend of the Hwang River, raises the water table, increases capillary activity and evaporation, and may quickly ruin the soil. Adequate subsoil drainage must be provided to keep the water table at a low level.

Three other soils are either limy or about neutral. One is the Shantung brown soil, much eroded but resembling the brown forest soils of Mediterranean Europe. Tree crops of pears, persimmons, and other fruits supplement the common grains. Purple-brown soils are common in Szechwan and Yunnan, and in parts of Hupei, Kiangsi, and Hunan. These are derived from highly colored Cretaceous and Triassic formations, some of which may in turn be fossil pedocals. Since the erosion of these soft rocks is rapid, the soils are relatively immature. In some ways they are related to the gray-brown podzolic soil type. Rice is the dominant crop, but there is also a diversified production of corn, wheat, sweet potatoes, beans, and tobacco. This is the area of tung oil trees. Agricultural usability varies considerably. The third type is the rendzina, best developed in Kwangsi and Kweichow but found even in Manchuria. Rendzinas are dark-colored warm-climate soils with imperfect profiles, which in color and humus somewhat resemble temperature chernozems and chestnut soils. Where uncultivated, they are now covered with grass but may have had forests at one time. In addition to raising rice, these soils are used for upland crops such as corn or are allowed to produce coarse grass for fuel.

Pedalfers of South China include forms which in North America lie in the east. True podzols are a leached forest soil with a thin raw humus layer over an ash-gray sandy soil and a dense enriched B horizon. Although originally described from cool forest regions of the Soviet Union, it is now recognized that under special conditions they also occur in warm climates. Very few areas of virgin podzols remain in China, but there are occurrences in the mountains from northern Manchuria to Indo-China. Where true podzols are absent, the same or related processes may produce podzolic types. Two of these are the brown and gray-brown leached podzolic soils which are widespread in the hills on either side of the lower Yangtze River, with patches throughout the south. These soils are related to the Shantung brown soils. There is a wide variety of environmental conditions, both hot and cool, steep slope and flat land, and moderate to excessive rainfall. Soils of the clay-pan variety, similar to planosols of the United States, occur where the B horizon is especially compact. They are usually associated with old wind-laid deposits derived from flood and lake plains in central China. Normal brown and gray-brown podzolic soils are well suited to cultivation if they do not occur on slopes that are too steep. Although their native fertility is low, their colloids are capable of absorbing fertilizers. Rice is the chief crop on the clay pans, where the dense *B* horizon is an asset in allowing the fields to be kept flooded. Wheat is a winter crop.

Red and yellow soils are developed in areas of over 40 inches of rainfall and little or no freezing weather. Red soils involve lower humidity and usually higher temperatures than yellow soils. Each was developed in a topography where erosion was at a minimum. Where derived from limestone, the red soils are called "terra rosa." Some of the red soils have been developed from lateritic rocks which in turn are but fossil red soils. The resulting soil is of little agricultural value, for the colloids have no ability to retain plant nutrients. Sheet erosion and gullying are severe where the land has been cleared. The red soils have been used for tea, tung oil trees, and as a source of fuel. Yellow soils are somewhat better agriculturally and can be utilized for the foregoing crops and for rice, but they are largely in forest or wild grass. True laterite like that of India occurs in only a few places in China.

Rice paddy soils are a specialized type on the plains and terraced hillsides of the south where irrigation has developed an artificial clay pan. Both podzolic and nonpodzolic types are present.

Recent deposits of noncalcareous alluvium occur in the South as well as the North, although flood plains and deltas are smaller. Dike construction prevents accumulation except when floods break through the dikes. At the same time heavy rains remove fine material from the terraced hillsides and change the otherwise clear rivers to reddish or purplish mud.

Each of these soils has its characteristic crops, with varying productivity according to climate, fertility, etc. Only through intensive use of manures have the Chinese been able to secure so many thousand harvests from the same fields. This is especially true in South China where the original fertility is low and hillside erosion has been severe.

The most important fertilizer is human waste or night soil, carried from the cities to the farms and there either allowed to ferment or composted with earth and waste organic matter. Animal manures are available in only small quantity. Oil cake from cotton seeds, soybeans, peanuts, and sesame is also used. In areas of canals and ponds, bottom mud is spread over the fields. One of the difficulties of preparing compost fertilizers is the shortage of organic waste material to absorb properly the nitrogen liberated in the decay of the manures. Wheat and rice straw are too valuable for roofing purposes, making rope or sandals, or as a fuel to be used in compost. Commercial fertilizers are used only near the larger cities. Mineral fertilizers such as potash, phosphates, and nitrates appear to be of limited occurrence in China, although phosphates have been discovered in Yunnan.

Since the cities are the chief source of fertilizing night soil, Thorp has pointed out that each is surrounded by a ring of fertile and more productive soils which extends about as far as a man may go and come in a day with a load. Immediately outside the city wall, vegetable gardeners use enormous quantities of night soil, ashes, and city waste. In places these artificial soils are as black and rich as chernozems. Thorp adds,[1] "In riding by train across the North China Plain just before the time of wheat harvest one can always tell when the train is approaching a large city by the improved appearance of the wheat

[1] Thorp, James, "Geography of the Soils of China." 432–433.

crop. As one approaches nearer and nearer any large railway station the wheat plants become more and more luxuriant and the ears larger and more filled with seed."

Because Chinese agriculture has continued for many centuries, it should not be inferred that natural soil fertility is high or that permanent productivity is simple. Thousands of square miles have been abandoned because of reduced crop yields or severe erosion. Large areas of alluvial soils are periodically replenished by sedimentation, but production is maintained only through great care and conservation of organic waste.

Chinese soils have about the same range in character and productiveness as other parts of the world in the same latitudes. Some are naturally rich and intensively cultivated; others are poor and little used. With adequate care, China may continue to support her present size of population indefinitely, but it is clear that there are no large areas of unused good land awaiting colonization. Neither do irrigation and reclamation offer much promise. Increased harvests must come largely from better farm practices and improved plants rather than from new acreage.

Mineral Resources

The future material prosperity and political strength of China are closely related to the availability of raw materials for industry. China may remain an agricultural nation and still preserve her classical culture, but without mineral wealth there is not enough good farm land to provide an adequately improved livelihood for her people. Agricultural raw materials may furnish a basis for plastics and other synthetic products, but minerals are essential.

For two thousand years the Chinese have known something about the common metals and have searched the more accessible parts of their country for the easily smelted ores.

European travelers during the Middle Ages brought back strange stories about the wealth of Cathay, and Marco Polo was able to report to his fellow Venetians that the Chinese excelled them in the use of coal and iron.

The National Geological Survey, founded in 1916, is recognized throughout the world as the government's leading scientific agency. Although its task is far from completion, the general picture is now reasonably clear. Major discoveries will probably be confined to remote areas or to resources whose geology is less predictable.

To summarize her resources in a paragraph, China is bountifully supplied with coal and has major reserves of antimony and tungsten. Tin and iron are available in moderate amounts, and there are small quantities of a wide variety of minerals. Copper, sulphur, petroleum, and other essentials appear very limited. China has the mineral basis for a modest industrialization, but in terms of her population she ranks well down the list of the great powers. Nevertheless, no other area on the Pacific side of Asia is better supplied.

The Sino-Japanese War seriously changed the production picture. Mines in Manchuria have been enlarged, although production has not always reached the expected goals. In the occupied areas south of the Great Wall, many mines were destroyed and production further restricted by transportation shortages and guerilla activity. Although most of the coal and iron lies in areas invaded by Japan, many of the lesser metals occur in southern and western Free China where the war introduced different complications. Conspicuous mining developments occurred in Szechwan.

SOURCES OF ENERGY

Coal is China's great source of natural power, and the country ranks fourth among the nations. Out of a world total of some

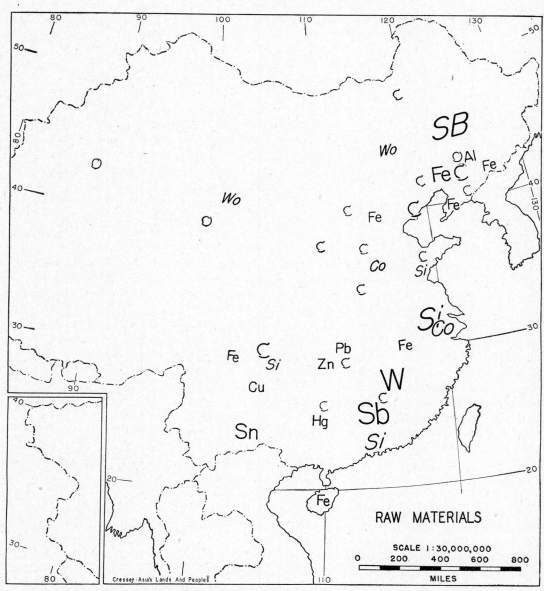

China's raw materials are diversified but inadequate in amount for a nation of its size. This map, and those for subsequent areas, deal with production rather than reserves. Most of the letters represent chemical symbols. The size suggests the relative importance in world production.

Fuels are shown in shadow letters, C for coal and O for oil. Minerals are in vertical block letters as follows: Al—bauxite or other aluminum ore, Cu—copper, Fe—iron, Hg—mercury, Pb—lead, Sb—antimony, Sn—tin, W—tungsten, Zn—zinc. Industrial agricultural products are in italics: *Co*—cotton, *Si*—silk, *Wo*—wool.

COAL RESOURCES AND PRODUCTION IN CHINA
(Reserves in Millions of Metric Tons, 1936 Estimates[1])

Province	Coal			Total reserves	Production	Year
	Anthracite	Bituminous	Lignite			
Anhwei....................	60	287	.....	347	633,000	1934
Chahar....................	17	487	.....	504	202,000	1934
Chekiang..................	20	81	.....	101	250,000	1934
Fukien....................	351	149	.....	500		
Heilungkiang..............	6	619	392	1,017	405,000	1934
Honan....................	4,630	1,994	.....	6,624	2,130,000	1934
Hopei....................	981	2,088	2	3,071	7,739,000	1934
Hunan....................	455	1,338	.....	,793	1,050,000	1940
Hupei....................	160	280	.....	440	458,000	1934
Jehol....................	2	573	39	614	356,000	1934
Kansu....................	......	1,500	.....	,500	98,245	1940
Kiangsi...................	204	765	.....	969	340,500	1940
Kiangsu..................	25	192	.....	217	267,000	1934
Kirin....................	2	986	155	1,143	411,000	1934
Kwangsi..................	150	150	.....	300	30,000	1940
Kwangtung................	50	371	.....	421	338,000	1934
Kweichow.................	774	775	.....	1,549	360,750	1940
Liaoning..................	187	1,649	.....	1,836	10,656,000	1934
Ninghsia..................	166	322	.....	488	15,000	1934
Shansi....................	36,471	87,985	2,671	127,127	2,700,000	1934
Shantung.................	26	1,613	.....	1,639	3,504,000	1934
Shensi....................	750	71,200	.....	71,950	322,450	1940
Sikang...................	......	......	.....	....	32,000	1940
Sinkiang..................	......	....	.....	....	100,000	1930
Suiyuan..................	58	337	22	417	58,000	1934
Szechwan.................	64	9,810	.....	9,874	3,280,324	1940
Yunnan...................	11	1,485	131	1,627	202,000	1940
Total....................	45,620	187,036	3,412	236,068	32,379,000	1934

[1] National Geological Survey of China: Coal and Oil Resources of China, Washington: Third World Power Conference *Transactions* (1938), II, 97–103.

seven trillion metric tons, the United States comes first with three and a half trillion, the Soviet Union has over one and a half trillion tons, Canada has one trillion although much of it is of low quality, while China has a quarter of a trillion tons.

Careful estimates of the Geological Survey are now available for 25 of the 28 provinces. The areas omitted are Sikang, Chinghai, Farther Tibet, Sinkiang, and Outer Mongolia, none of which have large deposits. The 1936 estimate of reserves amounts to 236,068,000,000 metric tons. This is a conservative figure, somewhat smaller than previous government estimates and only a quarter of the figure presented to the Twelfth International Geological Congress in 1913 amounting to 996,613,000,000 metric tons.

Although every province has some coal, the major reserves are significantly concentrated. Four-fifths are in Shansi and Shensi, and make this one of the major coal fields of the world. The only coastal provinces that are well supplied are Shantung, Hopei, and Liaoning.

Coal production has developed in the more accessible areas of the northeast rather than in the richest provinces. The total output for all China reached 30 million tons in normal years between the First and

million tons and Luta in Shantung; Chinghsing and Mentoukou in Hopei; Chungyuan with over a million tons, and Liuhokou

The open-cut coal mines at Fushun operate on the thickest bed of bituminous coal in the world. (*Courtesy South Manchuria Railway.*)

Second World Wars, or a per capita use of about 150 pounds a year. This compares with 1,000 pounds per person in Japan and 8,000 pounds in the United States. Since China's reserves exceed a million pounds per capita, there is adequate coal for several centuries.

The two leading mines are the great open cut at Fushun, southeast of Mukden, and the Kailan works north of Tientsin. The former has a capacity of over ten million tons a year while the latter can produce six million. Among the other more important mines are those at Penchihu and Sian in Liaoning, Muleng in Kirin, Peipiao in Jehol, all in Manchuria; Chunghsing with over a

in Honan; Tatung and Paochiu in Shansi; and a new group of mines near Chungking in Szechwan.

Petroleum appears to be absent over most of China, and geological factors make the discovery of major fields unlikely. The most attractive possibilities are around the eastern and northern margins of the Tibetan Plateau, especially south of Sichang in Sikang and near Chiayukwan (Yumen) in northwestern Kansu. Oil is also known along the Tien Shan at Wusu in Sinkiang and near Yenchang in Shensi. Production in Kansu was expected to reach 100,000 barrels in 1942; elsewhere the yield is negligible.

Oil shale is distilled in southern Manchuria at Fushun and elsewhere, but the oil content is low. If further search fails to

High-grade contact metamorphic ores are mined along the Yangtze River at Tayeh in Hupei and in Anhwei. For several

The Anshan Steel Works receive their ore from Taku Shan, a mountain of low-grade siliceous hematite. (*Courtesy South Manchuria Railway.*)

find natural oil, China fortunately has large quantities of coal from which to make synthetic gasoline.

The potential water power of China lies largely in the south and west, where there are swift rivers and high rainfall. It is estimated that the resources available 95 per cent of the time amount to 21,995,000 horsepower, while those available but 50 per cent of the time, owing to seasonal rainfall, total 40,873,000 horsepower. Almost no hydroelectric power is in operation.

IRON AND THE FERROALLOYS

China is relatively deficient in iron ore. Small deposits are widespread, but only a few occurrences are large and of high quality. Even these are remote from coking coal.

decades the entire output has been shipped to blast furnaces in Japan. The 1936 export was 542,000 tons, but earlier figures approached a million tons. The Tayeh ore was shipped to the now idle Hanyehping furnaces opposite Hankow prior to 1925, and during the 1930's the Nanking government proposed to build new steel mills along the central Yangtze.

Excellent sedimentary hematite occurs in the Hsuanhua-Lungyen district 150 miles northwest of Peiping, reopened in 1941 for shipment to Japan. The nearby Shihchingshan blast furnace has been little used because of the expense of transporting coke.

Scattered deposits in Szechwan and elsewhere in the southwest were developed during the Sino-Japanese War, with a total output for 1940 of 320,360 metric tons of ore in all of Free China.

By far the largest iron ore deposits are those of southern Manchuria, but the metallic content is low and there are numerous metallurgical problems. The largest deposit is at Anshan, with other mines near Penhsihu. Japanese interests have built important steel mills at each locality. The Showa Steel Works at Anshan have several times been enlarged, and were to reach a capacity of 3,600,000 metric tons of pig iron in 1942. If this ambitious program were reached, Anshan would rank among the dozen leading iron and steel centers of the world. At the same time the Penhsihu plant was to produce 500,000 tons. Shortages of coking coal are serious problems in each case. Recent discoveries of high-grade ore have been made near the Korean frontier.

The total known ore reserves for all of China as given by the Geological Survey amount to 1,302,600,000 tons. This is a very modest reserve for a country of this size and population, and places a serious limit on the future of industrialization. Conspicuous centers of heavy industry will assuredly develop, but in total production they cannot compare with the major powers. Equally serious is the distance between iron ore and coal suitable for metallurgical coke.

The level of industrial development prior to the Second World War is suggested by the total consumption of iron in China, which amounted to about 600,000 tons per year, including imports. This is a per capita average of about 3 pounds, and compares with 150 pounds per person in Japan and 1,000 pounds in the United States.

China's production of iron ore reached a top of 2,630,176 gross tons in 1929, but declined to 1,302,704 in 1936 and 551,000 metric tons in 1940 outside Manchuria.

Only one of the ferroalloys is conspicuously abundant, namely, tungsten. There is a small production of manganese, but deposits of nickel, chromium, molybdenum, and vanadium appear to be lacking.

IRON ORE RESOURCES AND PRODUCTION IN CHINA
(Data in Metric Tons, from Various Sources)

Province and Locality	Reserves	Iron content	Production	Year
Chahar:				
Hsuanhua-Lungyen	91,645,000	High	Resumed	1941
Hupei	45,000,000	High	452,000	1934
Tayeh	26,000,000	High	600,000	1940
Anhwei	20,000,000	High	480,000	1934
Liaoning:	872,200,000	Low		
Anshan	....	Low	950,000	1934
Miaoerkou	....	Low	235,000	1934
Tungpientao	100,000,000	High		
Kwangtung:				
Hainan	400,000,000	?		
Szechwan	11,600,000	Low	122,500	1940
Sikang	66,000,000	High	17,500	1940
Yunnan	15,600,000	?	18,750	1940
All China	1,302,600,000	Fair	2,595,000	1934
Free China	....	....	320,000	1940

Tungsten, derived from the mineral wolfram, is found in southern Kiangsi, and there is also a small production in Hunan, Kwangtung, and Kwangsi. The ore reserves are estimated at 1,647,500 metric tons, and at times China has supplied the major part of the world market. Although it still holds first place, the percentage of world output dropped to 22 per cent in 1940, when the production of Free China amounted to 8,757 metric tons. Burma is the second producer.

Manganese ore occurs in Kwangsi, where the 1938 exports totaled 1,246 metric tons. There is also production in Hunan, Kiangsi, and Liaoning. In 1930 the production amounted to 70,722 tons. Reserves are adequate for domestic needs.

OTHER MINERALS

Copper has been used in China for 2,500 years, but the deposits are small and scattered. Szechwan, especially at Penghsien, and Yunnan, near Tungchwan (now Hweicheh), are almost the only provinces that contributed to the 1940 production of 1,078 metric tons in Free China. This is the largest ever recorded. Areas occupied by the Japanese in that year had little output, except for a few hundred tons in Manchuria where deposits have been found. Newly discovered reserves in Sikang are reported to contain 1,824,000 metric tons of copper in rich 18 per cent ore, as compared with 216,000 in Yunnan and 131,000 in Kweichow. Sikang is expected to produce 3,000 tons of copper a year by 1944.

Aluminum production is limited to Japanese developments of alunite in Liaoning and Hopei, and bauxite in Shantung. Bauxite is reported from various provinces but the amounts appear modest. Chekiang has clays high in aluminum.

Lead and zinc are mined at Shuikoushan in Hunan and elsewhere in the southwest. The 1940 Free China output of lead was approximately 1,800 metric tons while that of zinc amounted to 250 metric tons. This is a large reduction from previous years.

Tin is China's most valuable metal next to iron. Yunnan is the major producer, with 13,340 metric tons in 1940 out of a total of 17,278 metric tons for Free China. This is about seven per cent of the world's total. Yunnan's reserves of tin are placed at 1,000,000 metric tons of metal, with 417,000 additional tons in Kwangsi, Kiangsi, and elsewhere. The chief production is from the Kochiu district in southern Yunnan, where there are both surface residual deposits and shaft mines.

Mercury is obtained in Kweichow and Hunan, with a total Free China output for 1940 of about 225 metric tons.

Antimony is one of China's conspicuous metals. The 1940 yield was 7,137 metric tons of antimony regulus (99 per cent metal) and 389 metric tons of crude antimony (70 per cent metal). These totals compare with 19,058 tons of regulus in 1925. The average yield represents 20 per cent of world production and places China behind Bolivia and Mexico. Except for a very small yield in Yunnan, all this was from the Hsikwangshan area in southern Hunan. Since the ore reserves here amount to 1,415,500 tons, with further amounts in Kweichow and Yunnan, production may continue for a long period.

Sulphur is widely produced both as a by-product in Hunan and from pyrite in Shansi, southwestern Hupei, Kweichow, and elsewhere. The official output in 1940 reached 10,000 metric tons, but the actual total may have been several times that figure.

Salt is produced extensively for domestic consumption, and there is an increasing export to Japan for industry. Most of China's salt is obtained from the solar evaporation of sea water, largely along the coast north of the Yangtze where the

Washing tin ore at Kochiu in Yunnan. Production is limited by the available water supply. (*Ato.*)

The salt wells of Tzeliutsing in Szechwan reach to depths of 3,000 feet although drilled by native methods. (*Ewing Galloway.*)

humidity is low. Salt lakes in western Manchuria, Inner Mongolia, and southern Shansi yield a small output. Szechwan has numerous salt wells. The normal production for all China amounts to 2,550,000 metric tons, with the leading provinces as follows: Kiangsu 560,000, Szechwan 425,000, Shantung 420,000, and Hopei 330,000 metric tons.

Gold is secured along the borders of Tibet and in northern Manchuria from low-grade stream gravels. The Free China production in 1940 amounted to 478,188 ounces, with Szechwan and Hunan as the leading provinces. Silver production is limited to a by-product from lead.

A Geographic Forecast

China's mineral wealth lies in two areas. Coal and iron are in the north, largely in the basin of the Hwang River and beyond. The nonferrous metals such as tin, antimony, tungsten, and such copper and lead as are present occur in metalliferous zones south of the Yangtze. Although there is no shortage of suitable coking coal in China as a whole, smelting problems are everywhere complicated by the distance between metallurgical coke and ore.

The location of future industry will reflect the distribution of raw materials, transport facilities, access to markets, and political considerations of security. The enormous coal deposits of Shansi will undoubtedly attract major industrialization. Hankow and other Yangtze centers are well located as far as transport is concerned. Seaports such as Shanghai are accessible to imported materials and skills but lack local raw materials. The mineralized areas of the far west and south have important ores but lack adequate coal and are remote from peacetime needs. Transport will everywhere be a critical economic factor.

Few areas in the world present the basic industrial opportunities that China will seek to develop during the remainder of the twentieth century. Many of these problems rest on heavy industry and in turn upon geology. The situation is somewhat comparable to the problems of the Soviet Five-year Plans, but unlike the U.S.S.R., China is only modestly endowed with natural wealth. It is fortunate that coal is superabundant for it is the key to power and to chemical industry, but the shortage in iron will be serious before many decades. These problems will be considered again in Chapter 9.

Chapter 5

FARMING IN CHINA

The Chinese live very close to nature. Their culture is a product of the soil, but the "good earth" is not everywhere or always good. Only through the most painstaking care has it been possible for the same fields to yield thousands of harvests.

Two major crop areas stand out, the North and the South. The North is a dry dust-blown land of wheat and millet, under the influence of the Mongolian Desert. The South is green and humid, a land of rice and canals and of forests. So intimate is the relation between man and nature that his cultivated crops represent a mature or climax adjustment to the environment. Both are a part of the natural landscape.

The average Chinese farm household consists of 6.2 people who cultivate 4.2 acres of land; in the United States, farm families average 4.2 persons and cultivate 157 acres.

The Agricultural Landscape

China is a land of farmers, and Chinese culture is a product of the soil. Agriculture forms the foundation of the social and economic structure, involves several times as many people and far more capital, and is much more fundamental to the national welfare than all other occupations put together. Many factors influence its success—some human, some physical. The preceding chapters have traced the background of topography, climate, natural vegetation, and soil, and those to follow will expand the cultural aspects of regional agriculture in more detail.

In describing the Chinese landscape it is important to keep specific locations in mind, for few characterizations can fit four million square miles. Land use and land usability vary widely throughout China. The oases of Sinkiang, the mountain valleys of Tibet, and the pioneer lands of Manchuria are all part of the same country, but they are very different from what may be termed Agricultural China in the east. Even within the area of the traditional 18 provinces, crops in the vicinity of Peiping and Canton have little in common.

With all this in mind, certain generalizations are valid. Chinese agriculture is intensive in its use of human labor, with relatively few draft animals. Large yields are obtained through painstaking care from farms that are divided into microscopic fields. Everywhere there are industrious people. One simply cannot escape from this teeming population. At least three-quarters of the Chinese obtain their livelihood directly from the soil, so that agriculture forms the fabric of their culture.

In few other large countries do people live so close to Mother Earth, and the density of rural population closely parallels the productivity of the land. In several places there are over 2,000 people per square mile, and the average density for the whole country in terms of cultivated land is 1,485 people per square mile. Despite the greatest care, distress and famine have often resulted from environmental uncertainties or the hazards of war, banditry, and taxation.

Chinese agriculture has had a long and honored history. For at least 30 centuries, farmers have been able to till the same fields. The patience and industry of the Chinese have become proverbial. Long experience has shown the best crops

garden plots, while hillside fields wind along the contours. Throughout the coun-

Spinning thread in the cotton areas near Shanghai. (*Mactavish.*)

for different areas, and agricultural practices have endeavored to maintain the fertility of the soil rather than to rob its productivity.

A part of the modern population growth is related to the introduction of new crops, such as sweet potatoes, corn, and peanuts from the Americas. These have given the land an increased population-supporting capacity, as in Szechwan where sweet potatoes are grown on dry hilltops unsuited for rice.

As one flies over Agricultural China, the landscape everywhere reflects the intensity of man's quest for food. Wherever crops can be raised, the land is under cultivation. River plains are divided into tiny geometric

try there is a superabundance of people and an undersupply of arable land.

Grains supply 90 per cent of the diet, with only a small part of the energy derived from meat, fruit, and nuts. The diet of the North is more diversified, for in the Hwang River Delta wheat, kaoliang, millet, corn, sweet potatoes, and soybeans each supply at least 5 per cent of the total calories. In the hills south of the Yangtze no crop other than rice supplies more than that proportion.

In a countryside so densely crowded as China, there is little land that can be spared for pasture. More food can be obtained by the direct consumption of crops rather than through feeding them to livestock. Pigs and chickens live on the household refuse. Fish are an important part of the diet near the seashore and in the canal areas.

tive surveys show that the typical holding is divided into six pieces, each made up of two unfenced fields. These have been sub-

Weaving cloth in North China. Despite modern industry there is still a large home production. (*Ato.*)

Domestic fuel is also a by-product of agriculture, for rice and wheat straw, kaoliang and cornstalks, and other plants are gathered for use in cookstoves. Supplies of firewood or coal are seldom available, but villages near the hills commonly have uncultivated areas from which brush and roots are gathered. In the northwestern provinces and in Mongolia, dried animal dung is widely used for fuel, and this use is often in direct competition with the needs for fertilizer.

About three-quarters of the cultivated land is owned by the farmers, with a larger percentage of ownership in the north than in the south. Not only are the farms small, averaging about four acres, but representa-

divided by inheritance and are scattered over a radius of as much as a mile from the farmstead.[1]

While Chinese agriculture produces good yields per acre, such production is a result of laborious and wasteful use of man power. Excessive care is bestowed upon tiny fields, and production is secured only through concentration on a small per capita area.

[1] BUCK, J. LOSSING, "Land Utilization in China," Chicago: University of Chicago Press (1937), 3 volumes. This work is based upon sample studies of 16,786 farms in 168 localities in 22 provinces of China from 1929–1933. Because of the Japanese invasion of Manchuria, it was impossible to carry on field work in that area. There are likewise no data from Outer Mongolia, Sinkiang, or Farther Tibet.

In terms of national welfare it is not the yield per acre but the yield per person that brings prosperity.

Large amounts of human labor are used in place of machines to produce crops. The man equivalent required for 1 acre of wheat in China is 26 days compared with 1.2 days in the United States. For cotton the comparison is 53 and 14 days; 1 acre of corn in China requires 23 days but only 2.5 days in the United States. On the basis of yield per farmer, China produces but 3,080 pounds a year as compared with 44,000 pounds in the United States. "A farmer who produces little cannot expect to have very much of this world's goods."

Most of China is an old land of stabilized agriculture where the soil is so intensively cultivated that increased yields are difficult to secure without uneconomic expenditures for fertilizers, machinery, or reclamation. Few opportunities for pioneering exist and are largely in areas of precarious climate. One of China's most pressing problems concerns the relation between expanding population and limited agricultural productivity.

The most detailed study of Chinese agriculture is that by J. Lossing Buck of the University of Nanking, undertaken with the support of the Institute of Pacific Relations. In summarizing his studies, Buck makes several recommendations, the first of which is that the present individual farm units should be continued rather than attempting major changes in the form of collectivization or large-scale farming. Among the policies recommended in his studies are conservation projects to check erosion and minimize flood hazards, the irrigation and drainage of new land, consolidation of farm holdings, agricultural research and education, larger crop yields through better seeds and insect control, farm credit, and improved transportation.

Land Use in China

China's greatest resources are the land and the people, but we know neither the exact size nor the population. The accompanying table presents data on the percentage of cultivated land and cultivated land per person.[1]

CULTIVATED LAND IN CHINA

Province	Percentage of total area cultivated	Area of cultivated land per person in acres
Anhwei	22.7	0.38
Chahar	4.1	1.30
Chekiang	26.3	0.30
Chinghai		
Fukien	11.4	0.35
Heilungkiang	5.2	1.84
Honan	37.6	0.55
Hopei	46.0	0.51
Hunan	12.9	0.26
Hupei	19.5	0.31
Jehol	6.1	0.83
Kansu	3.7	0.66
Kiangsi	14.1	0.26
Kiangsu	52.4	0.39
Kirin	14.4	1.19
Kwangsi		
Kwangtung	11.5	0.21
Kweichow	8.1	0.38
Liaoning	16.8	0.76
Ningshia	0.5	0.79
Shansi	21.7	0.77
Shantung	46.5	0.45
Shensi	11.0	0.48
Sikang		
Sinkiang	0.5	0.84
Suiyuan	3.7	1.40
Szechuan	15.0	0.39
Yunnan	4.2	0.41
Agricultural China	27.	0.45
Provincial China	12.	0.45
Greater China	10.	0.45

Estimates of cultivated areas are uncertain. Sample measurements under the direction of Buck showed that the actual

[1] CHANG, C. C., "An Estimate of China's Lands and Crops," Nanking: University of Nanking (1932).

cultivated land was from one-tenth to one-third greater than reported for tax purposes. On the basis of corrected figures, the total cultivated land within his eight agricultural regions, excluding Manchuria, Outer Mongolia, Sinkiang, and Farther Tibet, is placed at 362,082 square miles or 27 per cent. By allowing for those areas omitted in Buck's surveys, the total crop area may be 425,000 square miles, or nearly 10 per cent of Greater China. Whatever the figures, they represent nearly the maximum that is profitable under present economic conditions.

place this at 0.45 acre, but, allowing for incorrect data, it may be as much as 0.5 acre per capita for farmer and city dweller together. This means that an average farm family of 6.2 persons must obtain its entire livelihood from a farm of 4.18 acres, of which but 3.76 acres are actually in crops. And, in China, farming is the one great source of income; only minor contributions to the national income are derived from mining, lumbering, fishing, or grazing.

About one-fifth of the land is in forest, much of it of noncommercial types, and

This Manchurian farm near Chinchow indicates the diversity of crops grown in this rich area. (*Courtesy South Manchuria Railway*).

Other countries report cultivated land as follows: Japan 17 per cent, British India 46 per cent, the Soviet Union 8 per cent, Great Britain 23 per cent, and the United States 23 per cent.

The most significant fact is the amount of cultivated land per person. Official statistics

nearly another fifth in pasture, largely in Mongolia, Sinkiang, and Tibet. Large areas are so seriously eroded that they are now useless. The greatest contrast between Chinese and western agriculture is the negligible percentage of farm area in pasture or wood lots. Graves, farm buildings, and other nonproductive uses account for 7.6 per cent of the average farm.

Nearly half the cultivated land is irri-

the great investment of labor that has been necessary to make China productive.

Many and various crops are grown, and

The Yangtze Delta is an intensively cultivated land, cut by innumerable canals and ponds which surround microscopic fields. This aerial view near Kiangyin was taken in June just after the wheat harvest; the white fields are flooded preparatory to transplanting rice. (*Aero-Survey Nanking, courtesy J. Lossing Buck.*)

gated, in almost all cases for rice; and the areas where drainage or flood protection is developed are nearly as great. Terraced land amounts to about a quarter of the cultivated area and is common in both the irrigated ricelands of the South and the dry wheat area of the North. This suggests

Chinese agriculture differs from that elsewhere less in the varieties of things grown than in the methods used. The most important food grains are rice and wheat, with cotton as the chief textile crop. Other important products are millet, soybeans, the grain sorghum kaoliang, barley, corn, sweet potatoes, rapeseed, broad beans, and peanuts in decreasing importance of acreage. Distinctive crops are opium poppy, mulberry whose leaves are fed to the silkworm, tea, oranges, and tobacco. Hay and fodder are notably lacking.

Two-thirds of the cultivated area produces two or more crops a year. Rotation is common.

The range of yields is wide. Thus Buck found wheat harvests of 5 to 67 bushels per acre, rice from 22 to 169 bushels, and corn 8 to 82 bushels. The Chinese averages, with comparisons for other countries, are shown on the accompanying table.

CROP YIELDS

(In Bushels per Acre, except Cotton in Kilograms)

	China	Japan	India	Soviet Union	U.S.A.
Rice...........	67	68	29	...	47
Wheat.........	16	25	11	10	14
Corn..........	21	22	15	15	25
Barley.........	19	36	..	16	22
Irish potatoes..	87	139	..	128	108
Cotton lint.....	168	199	80	188	177

It seems probable that China leads the world in total agricultural production, with first place in rice, wheat, sweet potatoes, kaoliang, soybeans, millet, barley, peanuts, tea, and probably silk.

The prospects of agricultural expansion are summarized by Buck.[1] "Certain facts as regards land in China are now clear. In the first place, no great increase in the amount of farm land can be expected. The removal of graves from farm land, the elimination of land in boundaries by the consolidation of the fragmented holdings, the profitable cultivation of arable lands not now cultivated, and an economic size of farm which would lessen the proportion of area in farmsteads would probably make

[1] BUCK, J. LOSSING, "Land Utilization in China," I, 202–203.

available an additional ten per cent of the present area in farms."

"In the second place, farm land in China is already intensively used. A very large proportion of the land is in crops used directly for human food, an extremely small amount in pasture, and a comparatively small amount in forest or in other fuel crops. Not only is the type of use intensive, but the modification of the physical conditions of the land by irrigation, drainage, terracing, and to a smaller extent by fertilization, also tends to bring about a higher degree of utilization. It is, however, through the still more intensive use of the present farm land of China that the greatest increase in food production is to be expected, not only by modifying the physical conditions themselves, but through improvements in the technique of crop and animal production, independent of the physical factor of the land itself. Perhaps a 25 per cent increase in total production by more intensive methods and by modern techniques would be a conservative estimate of the possible increase economically, in China's agricultural production with the known methods of agricultural production."

The decades following the Second World War will doubtless see notable changes in agriculture. Transportation will open markets to the isolated interior producer, and new skills will improve production. But whether all the needed changes are feasible and adequate is an open question. Although an increased production of 25 per cent would be of conspicuous value, what China needs in order to take her place as a world power is an increase in her per capita income of several hundred per cent. It does not appear that agriculture holds the key to such a change.

Agricultural Regions

No one can travel more than a few hundred miles without being impressed by differences in crops and farm practices. Some of these grow out of custom, as where related to climate and soil; still other differences reflect markets. Taken together the

Agricultural conditions divide China into eight regions: three in the wheat areas of the North and five in the rice areas of the South. Drought and cold eliminate cultivation in the west. (*After J. Lossing Buck.*)

immigrants of centuries ago have brought their crops with them; others are directly pattern of agriculture forms a mosaic that has broad regional characteristics.

The most conspicuous boundary is the northern limit of continuous rice cultivation with its flooded fields, canals, and Yellow Plain, and the Winter Wheat–Millet region in the Loess Hills. Beyond the limits of Buck's surveys is the Man-

CHARACTERISTICS OF CHINA'S

	Precipitation, in inches	Growing season, in days	Cultivated area, in square miles	Percentage of total area cultivated	Percentage of cultivated land irrigated	Percentage of farmers who are tenants	Crop area per farm, in acres	Farm population per square mile of crop area
Agricultural China (without Manchuria).......	..	.....	339,644[2]	25[2]	47	17	3.8	1,485
Wheat Province (without Manchuria).........	..	.....	172,916	39	18	6	5.1	1,128
1. Winter Wheat–Kaoliang region..........	24	241	118,993	68	10	5	5.1	1,165
2. Winter Wheat–Millet region.............	17	(225)	31,869	22	10	9	3.7	1,234
3. Spring Wheat region....................	14	196	22,054	18	13	6	7.3	858
4. Manchurian Soybean–Kaoliang region....	25	150	50,000	20	5	..	8.0	800
Rice Province.................................	..	.....	166,728	18	62	25	2.8	1,746
5. Yangtze Rice–Wheat region.............	42	293	40,328	35	61	25	3.5	1,360
6. Rice–Tea region........................	59	308	42,624	18	78	19	2.2	1,788
7. Szechwan Rice region....................	39	334	47,579	32	70	43	3.1	1,610
8. Double Cropping Rice region............	69	365	19,155	13	69	28	2.3	2,072
9. Southwestern Rice region..............	46	360	17,042	7	82	21	2.0	2,636

[1] All data are from Buck, "Land Utilization in China," I, pp. 30–38, except for the Manchurian Soybean–Kaoliang area which lay
[2] Buck elsewhere gives 362,082 square miles and 27 per cent as a better figure for the area and percentage of cultivated land within

water buffalo, near latitude 33°N., shown on the accompanying map of agricultural regions. This line lies midway between the Yangtze and Hwang rivers along the crest of the Tsingling in the west and near the Hwai River in the east. South China is a green, humid, and subtropical riceland, while the north is a dry brown wheatland under the influence of the desert. Wheat extends well into the Yangtze Valley as a winter crop, but it is not a conspicuous source of food in the south.

Within the Wheat province of the north, Buck has described three agricultural regions: the Spring Wheat region along the Mongolian frontier and into Manchuria, the Winter Wheat–Kaoliang region in the churian Soybean–Kaoliang region. The Rice province of the south is similarly divided into the Yangtze Rice–Wheat region, the Szechwan Rice region, the Rice–Tea region in the hills south of the Yangtze, the Double Cropping Rice region in the far south, and the Southwestern Rice region. Scattered oases in Sinkiang, sheltered valleys in Tibet, and a fringe of cultivation in northern Mongolia are to be added.

Some of the distinguishing features are shown in tabular form on these two pages and deserve careful study. Since the detailed surveys of Buck did not extend into Manchuria, approximate figures are added from "China's Geographic Foundations" for the Manchurian Spring Wheat–

Soybean region, but are not included in the averages.

Major contrasts appear between the

AGRICULTURAL REGIONS[1]

Distribution of crop area, in per cent							Distribution of livestock, in per cent						Localities having each transport method, in per cent					Typical fruits or other products
Rice	Wheat	Millet	Corn	Cotton	Rapeseed	Others	Oxen	Water buffalo	Hogs	Donkeys	Sheep	Mules	Human carriers	Wheelbarrows	Pack animals	Carts	Boats	
33	29	..	..	7	..	.....	34	22	13									
..	40	27	..	8	..	Kaoliang, 15	37	..	..	20	11	14						Persimmons
..	46	23	16	9	..	Kaoliang, 19	40	..	..	21	..	16	32	36	21	60		Apricots
..	40	31	..	9	..	......	37	..	..	21	14	13	60	..	40	20		Jujubes
..	18	34	..	..	..	Irish potatoes, 10	21	..	..	15	28	11	..	..	76	38	13	Grapes
..	10	15	..	..	..	Soybeans, 25 Kaoliang, 25												Walnuts Pears
68	..	..	..	..	..	.....	31	38	17									Mulberry
58	31	..	..	13	..	Barley, 19	24	42	15	..	..	..	41	22	..	..	33	Bamboo
73	..	..	..	..	13	......	43	32	20	..	..	..	71	17	..	..	25	Tea
41	19	..	14	..	13	Opium, 11	53	12	31	..	..	..	100	..	..	..	22	Oranges
90	..	..	..	..	..	Sugar cane, 6 Sweet potatoes, 12	32	44	15	..	..	..	75	..	..	..	33	Tea oil Wood oil
60	..	..	..	14	..	Opium, 19 Broad beans, 17	14	49	14	..	..	..	75	..	25	13		

outside his surveys. These figures are from Cressey, "China's Geographic Foundations," p. 394, and are only approximations. the part of Agricultural China covered by his surveys.

Wheat and Rice provinces. Thus the growing season in North China is five to eight months while in South China it is ten months to a year, so that double cropping is more widespread and the same land can support more people. Rainfall is over twice as heavy in the south. The gross area of the South is larger but the presence of extensive plains in the North gives it a greater cultivated area. Nevertheless, the higher productivity of the ricelands enables them to support nearly twice the total population of the wheat-producing section.

Rice and wheat are the outstanding Chinese crops. Although the former is largely limited to the south, scattered cultivation extends into Manchuria. Winter wheat is a conspicuous crop in the Yangtze Valley and almost as far north as the Great Wall, beyond which spring wheat is common. If Manchuria is included, the wheat acreage exceeds that in rice. Water buffalo go with rice, but oxen, known to the Chinese as yellow cows, are widespread. Farms in the Wheat province are twice the size of those in the Rice province, but land value per acre in the latter is nearly twice that in the former. No column in the table on agriculture is so important as that in the center which gives the farm population per square mile of cultivated land. With an average of 1,485 people who must secure their livelihood from one square mile, China faces her greatest problem.

The intensity of farming in the South is shown by 50 per cent greater farm population per square mile of crop area, and their individual wealth is greater as measured by more clothing, furniture, and the value of farm buildings. Tenancy is more conspicuous in the South, but the figures cited do not tell the entire story, for there are numerous part owners in both areas. During the inflationary period of the Second World War, many farmers were able to pay off their indebtedness so that the percentage of tenants has decreased.

It should be remembered that these figures deal with Agricultural China which covers but 1,660,000 square miles, or only a third of Greater China.

The Winter Wheat–Kaoliang region is the most important of the Wheat regions, and includes a third of all cropland south of the Great Wall. It covers the Yellow Plain with its concentrated population of 80,000,000 people, and in addition reaches into the Shantung Hills. The chief provinces are Hopei, Shantung, and Honan. Although the rainfall is only 24 inches, it falls during the hot summer. Soils are calcareous, except in uplands near the coast. In areas of high water table, saline soils occur. Irrigation is uncommon and usually limited to vegetable gardens near hand-operated wells. Vegetables are grown in a wide variety. Winter wheat with summer millet and kaoliang are the chief crops. Corn, cotton, soybeans, and sweet potatoes also cover a considerable area in the summer. Barley is a minor winter crop. No other agricultural area has so much diversification. Farms are relatively large for China, with an average of 5.1 acres in crops. Flood and drought present recurrent hazards.

The Winter Wheat–Millet region lies to the west in the Loess Hills, with fertile soils, steep slopes, excessive erosion, and marginal rainfall. The chief plains are along the Fen and Wei rivers in Shansi and Shensi. More than a third of the cropland is terraced, not for flooded fields but to enable steep hillsides to be cultivated. Winter wheat, millet, cotton, kaoliang, and corn are the crops. Cotton is grown in the warmer Fen and Wei valleys; kaoliang and wheat are confined to the plains and valleys; while millet is grown on the higher and drier hillsides. Double cropping is practiced on 18 per cent of the land as compared with 39 per cent in the Winter Wheat–Kaoliang region.

The Spring Wheat region forms a fringe along the Mongolian frontier, lying on either side of the Great Wall. Elevations in this hilly area range from 3,000 to 8,000 feet. The rainfall is so low that normal cultivation is unsafe without irrigation, but available water is limited to the Hwang and its few tributaries and to streams from northeastern Tibet. Elsewhere dry-farming techniques must be used. Only five months are free from frost. Considerable areas are used for pasture, and it would be wise if many hillsides now plowed were put back into grass. Instead of being a prospective zone for pioneer settlement, most of the Spring Wheat region already has more people than it can safely support. The crops are all summer grown, and include spring wheat, millet, Irish potatoes, oats, kaoliang, barley, corn, rice, and formerly opium poppy which was raised on the frontier because of poor transport facilities for more bulky crops. Crop yields per acre are 16 per cent below the national average. Famine is more severe here than elsewhere. Standards of living are low.

The Manchurian Soybean–Kaoliang region spreads over the Manchurian Plains and the East Manchurian Hills, and is larger than any other agricultural area. During the early decades of the twentieth century, this new land was the goal of millions of Chinese immigrants, but by 1940 the population had reached 40,000,000 and little good land remained except along the cold northern and dry western margins. In the central portion, rainfall is adequate for successful agriculture, and soils are fertile.

The area of cultivated land per person is the largest in all China, and there is the beginning of mechanized agriculture. Draft animals are more numerous than elsewhere. The chief crops are kaoliang in the south and soybeans in the north, each with an estimated 25 per cent of the acreage. Other crops are millet, spring wheat, corn, barley, and some rice grown by Koreans along the frontier.

In the Rice province of South China, the Yangtze Rice–Wheat region is the smallest of all the agricultural areas, but its economic importance as the hinterland of Shanghai is very great. Most of the region is a low flood plain, cut by a network of rivers, canals, and lakes, and all of it is intensively utilized. Grass-covered hills account for most uncultivated land. The rainfall is abundant and the growing season long. As elsewhere in South China, most of the soils are noncalcareous. Rice is the main crop and supplies four times the total food energy derived from wheat. Winter crops occupy a larger percentage of land than elsewhere, and two-thirds of the land is double-cropped. In order to provide better drainage for dry winter crops, the fields are laboriously spaded into ridges a foot or more in height. Crops include wheat, barley, rapeseed, and broad beans. Other summer crops are cotton, soybeans, and corn. Mulberry for silkworms is distinctive.

The Rice–Tea region lies in the South Yangtze Hills in Chekiang, Kiangsi, and Hunan, with only small areas of level land. Cultivated land amounts to but 18 per cent, but three-fourths of it is irrigated and one-third terraced. Only a quarter of the farmers own their land, the smallest fraction in all China. Rapeseed, wheat, and barley are grown in the winter, followed by rice in the summer. Intertillage is common in Chekiang, with alternate rows of early and late rice. Tea is a hillside crop, as are corn, soybeans, wood oil, and sweet potatoes.

In the Szechwan Rice region the lowlands raise rice in the summer, and wheat, rapeseed, and opium poppy in winter. On the hills the crops are sweet potatoes, corn, kaoliang, sugar cane, sesame, soybeans, tobacco, and wood oil. Yields are 8 per cent above the all-China average, and the grain production per capita is also the highest. This is one of the most productive areas in the country, with crops representative of both north and south. Crops are closely adjusted to the available water, so that the upper dry fields and lower flooded terraces each have their specialized use. Rice is sown in seed beds during April or May and transplanted to the fields early in June; the harvest occurs in September. During the winter, beans may be interplanted with wheat.

The Double Cropping Rice region lies in the hills of subtropical China where there is but limited level land. Thus only 12 per cent of Kwangtung is cultivated. The growing season continues practically throughout the year, and the rainfall averages 69 inches, highest in China. Most soils were initially poor and are now badly eroded by both gulleys and sheet wash, so much so that extensive areas of rolling hills are covered with wild grass and are unused except for fuel. Over three-fourths of the land is double-cropped between spring and fall, but 92 per cent remains idle in winter. Two crops of rice are common, planted in March and August with harvests in June or July and November. Whereas the yield of 42 bushels is low, double cropping yields a total of 84 bushels per acre. Rice supplies over three-quarters of the food energy. There are considerable areas of sweet potatoes, sugar cane, tobacco, tea, mulberry, and oranges. Famines are rare.

In the Southwestern Rice region, dissected topography and mile-high elevations introduce regional contrasts. In the few valleys, rice is the summer crop followed by opium poppy (when grown), broad beans, or wheat. In the mountains the chief crops are corn, barley, and millet, and these form the staple diet of the non-Chinese tribespeople. Excellent fruit is grown. This is the second largest of the agricultural regions, next to Manchuria, but the proportion in cultivation is the lowest. Nowhere is there so much crowding, for the farm population reaches a density of 2,636 people per square mile of cropland.

CHAPTER 6

REGIONS OF NORTH CHINA

Introduction

The face of the earth may be likened to a mosaic picture made up of a myriad number of fragments. Each bit of colored tile has its own features, but they bear little resemblance to the whole. If one's eye is within a few inches of the mosaic, no pattern is revealed; stand back a few feet and the microscopic detail is lost but the picture takes on meaning.

So too with the earth. Each field or hillside has its unique features, of interest to the individual who lives thereon but of little significance to the state as a whole. Geography is interested in this micropattern chiefly as it reveals the personality of the larger whole. Airplane panoramas are more meaningful than a worm's-eye view, provided that they are oriented and interpreted in terms of reality. Regional generalizations are valid only as they rest upon demonstrated relations within the smaller mosaic, and the latter acquire meaningfulness only as oriented in their larger setting.

The function of geography is to give character and meaning to the face of the earth and to differentiate the personality of one region from that of another. This is the geographic landscape, the totality of land and water and air and people in their mutual interrelations. In pioneer lands, where man comes as an exotic intruder, these correlations are imperfectly developed; in mature lands such as China the organic unity of man and the earth is markedly obvious.

Each geographic region is an entity. In some areas the dominant feature is climate, as with a desert; elsewhere a crop or a coastal position is characteristic; still other regions are unified by a mode of livelihood. Boundaries are seldom precise, but it is usually possible to block out major landscape areas each of which is different from its neighbor.

China is too large and diverse to fit into any single mold. Few common denominators are everywhere present, unless it be a unique way of life and a common history. Climate and thus vegetation and soil differ strikingly from north to south. So too do the people. The major geographic division of China is into three provinces: the dry, brown, wheat-growing North; the wet, green, rice-growing South; and the arid nomadic steppes and mountains of Mongolia, Sinkiang, and Tibet. The geographic provinces and regions of China are shown on page 98. Although the map also shows surface configuration, there are many other factors that determine geographic boundaries.

China proper is an improper name, for in a political sense the claim of the central government to Manchuria is as valid as to the provinces south of the Great Wall. If a term is desired for the area of normal agricultural settlement and classical history east of Mongolia and Tibet, one might speak of Agricultural China or better of Cultural China, in contrast to Outer or Nomadic China to the west. No single criterion of political boundary, rainfall, or elevation separates the two, but the traveler who leaves the settled area of Chinese agriculture for the more arid or former lies in the valleys of the Hwang, Liao, and Sungari; the latter is drained by the Yangtze and the Si. Environment,

The geographic regions and land forms of China. Although these regions consider both the cultural and physical landscape, there is a close correspondence with the surface configuration. Within China are 3 geographic provinces and 17 regions as follows: North China includes the Yellow Plain, the Shantung Peninsula, Loessland, the Manchurian Plain, the Eastern Manchurian Uplands, the Khingan Mountains, and the Jehol Mountains. South China is divided into the Yangtze Plain, the Szechwan Basin, the Central Mountain Belt, the South Yangtze Hills, the Southeastern Coast, the Canton Hinterland, and the Southwestern Uplands. Outer China is made up of Mongolia, Sinkiang, and Tibet. (*Base map by Erwin Raisz, courtesy Harvard-Yenching Institute, adapted by Rowland Illick.*)

more mountainous lands of the nomad is conscious of an abrupt transition in culture.

The major division of Cultural China is twofold: the North and the South. The temperament, and history combine to make these differences so distinct that there are two Chinas, almost as unlike as two nations.

South China comprises seven major regions, each with its own geographic personality. In general, the rainfall is so abundant that the landscape is always green. Marine climatic influences predominate. Hills and mountains are the principal land form. Level land is limited to deltas and flood plains. Forests cover most uncultivated hillsides. Where the land is in crops, rice is dominant. A snowless climate provides a growing season of nine months to a year. Famine is uncommon. The people are shorter in stature than those of the North, with a more restless temperament and a distinct psychology.

North China is an area of limited and variable rainfall, under the influence of the desert. Only four to six months are free from frost. Level land is much more abundant than in the South. Crops are varied but include wheat and a variety of dry grains. Draft animals, two-wheeled carts, and wheelbarrows replace canalboats and sedan chairs. North China speaks a uniform dialect, the kuan hua or Mandarin, in contrast to the variations of the South. Famine has been recurrent. Whereas the people of South China have emigrated overseas, those in the North have gone overland to Manchuria.

The boundary between the North and the South lies midway between the Yangtze and the Hwang, near the thirty-third parallel. In the west the line corresponds with the crest of the Tsingling Mountains; farther east it follows the Hwai River.

Within the North China province are seven geographic regions: the Yellow Plain, the Shantung Peninsula, Loessland, the Manchurian Plain, the Eastern Manchurian Uplands, the Khingan Mountains, and the Jehol Mountains.[1]

[1] Many types of regions are considered in this volume, some climatic, some topographic, others geographic. In the classification of topography, a locational name is linked with a major category of

Yellow Plain

No other region has played such a large role in Chinese history, nor has any other given birth to so many people, as the Yellow Plain. During the 30 centuries of recorded history at least a trillion people have lived on this good earth. The very dust is alive with their heritage. Here is the heart of classical China.

This is the most important area of level land in the country, and it includes all the essential features of the North China landscape. Few other geographic regions are so well defined. It seems appropriate to call it the Yellow Plain not only because it is the gift of the Hwang Ho or Yellow River, but because of the color of its soil and the imperial yellow of its ancient rulers.

The Yellow Plain covers 125,000 square miles, with a population of 80,000,000. This would be equivalent to two-thirds of the people of the United States living in the area of Iowa and Oklahoma. Parts of five provinces are involved. Two of these take their name from the Hwang Ho, Honan to the south of the river and Hopei to the north. Half of Shantung is included and smaller parts of Anhwei and Kiangsu.

The plain of the Hwang is an enormous alluvial fan and delta, built into a crescentic embayment once occupied by the Yellow Sea. Other streams have contributed to the growth of the plain, notably those which converge to form the Hai at Tientsin and the Hwai in the south, but the Hwang is dominant. Where these rivers leave the encircling loess-covered mountains they are heavily burdened with sediment. As they enter the plain their gradient and

elevation: lowland, upland, and highland, and is further broken down into the land form units of plain, plateau, hill, and mountain. Geographic regions are described by their dominant characteristic whether it be topography as in a plain, location as with a coast, climate such as a desert, or a political area.

velocity decrease, hence their transporting power is lessened and deposition occurs.

The deposition of this excess silt raises from the stream, so that it is a major engineering feat to close the gap and persuade the river again to flow on top of a

Wheelbarrows are widely used for transportation in North China. When the load is particularly heavy a coolie or donkey may help out the man between the shafts. These reeds are probably destined for fence or house construction. (*Courtesy American President Steamship Lines.*)

the bed of the stream. If the river were unrestricted, the channel would repeatedly shift to lower ground on either side. To prevent this periodic flooding of fertile farm land, the Chinese have built confining dikes since at least the tenth century. As a result of continued sedimentation within the dikes, the bed of the river is now in many places above the level of the surrounding countryside and dikes progressively need to be raised. Rivers of the Yellow Plain flow on ridges rather than in valleys. One may thus look up at the sails of passing boats. Since bedrock is lacking, dikes are built of local earth and are easily eroded at times of flood. Once the dikes are breached, the river shifts to the lower land on either side. This usually slopes away

ridge. When breaks occur, flood waters spread to the horizon and disaster follows. Millions of people have drowned or have died of starvation from the resulting crop failures.

The Hwang has repeatedly shifted its course, first to the north and then to the south of Shantung. A century ago when Great Britain wished to bring pressure on the Chinese government, she decided to blockade the mouth of the river. After her fleet had anchored off the coast for several months without seeing any native shipping, it was learned that the river had moved 250 miles farther north. This was in 1852.

In 1938, when the Japanese army was pressing back the Chinese troops east of Chengchow, the Chinese cut the dikes in the path of the invaders and diverted the Hwang into a new passageway southeast to the Hwai River along channels used in 1289

Since the Hwang flows above the level of its plain, it receives no tributaries in the lower 400 miles, except where it borders the

Springless Peking carts have been the principal means of travel throughout North China.

and 1887, rather than along the channel of 1852. The Hwai in turn had lost its normal route to the sea when its original bed was usurped by an earlier diversion of the Hwang prior to 1852, thus the Hwai discharges into a series of shallow fluctuating basins, chiefly the Hungtze Lake. The drainage of the present Hwang-Hwai system reaches the sea through artificial channels, one directly eastward and the other via the Grand Canal which discharges southward into the Yangtze. The mouth of the Hwang River is now thus 500 miles south of its position from 1852 to 1938.

The flow of the Hwang varies from 10,000 cubic feet per second at low-water stage to a recorded 350,000 cubic feet per second during the 1923 flood. During freshets, the river carries a measured load of up to 40 per cent by weight. In one dike break, 18 inches of sediment was deposited 60 miles south of the river.

Shantung Hills. Thus rainfall in adjacent areas accumulates in shallow lakes. No part of the Hwang, old or new, is navigable for steamers; only a few sections are deep enough for launches.

Floods on the smaller rivers above Tientsin occur every six or seven years. In 1924 the flooded area covered 11,500 square miles and 1½ million people were driven from their homes. As is the case with Hwang River floods, the waters cannot drain back into the rivers and so remain until evaporated.

Climate in the Yellow Plain is as unpredictable as the river. The annual rainfall decreases from 30 inches in the south to 20 inches in the north, but seasonal variations in time and amount are wide. Thus Tientsin with a 20-inch average varies from 10 to 31 inches a year. Winters have only a light snowfall, and the summer rains do not begin until mid-June. Inadequate rainfall brings famine through drought, just as surplus rainfall results in famine from flood.

Strong winter winds from Mongolia lower temperatures to 0°F. and bring clear skies but no moisture. Dust storms are common. Summer temperatures rise to 100°F., with high humidity borne by ocean winds. Peiping experiences higher temperatures than Canton. The frost-free period is about 200 to 240 days.

Soil is almost the only resource. Few minerals or fuels occur beneath the plain, except for coal at Kailan in the far north and in Honan. Much of the region is underlain by recent calcareous alluvium, in places with such strongly saline characteristics as to render it unfit for agriculture. This may produce a white efflorescence. All of North China has moderately alkaline soils. On account of the repeated flooding and high ground water, many soils belong to the unique shachiang type, with an extensive development of concretions at the water table. The natural fertility is moderately high and has been maintained through intensive fertilization.

Wheat, the distinctive crop, does not have the dominance characteristic of rice in South China. Rice can be grown but the water supply is usually inadequate. No other region in China raises such a variety of crops. The grain sorghum kaoliang and a variety of millets are important summer crops. Cotton and hemp are locally significant. Corn is surprisingly widespread. Soybeans and many vegetables are widely grown. Winter crops include wheat, barley, and soybeans.

The agricultural studies of Dr. J. Lossing Buck of the University of Nanking give the following figures for this region: Over 60 per cent of the land in most districts is in cultivation. Irrigation is uncommon, generally under 10 per cent. Farmers who own their land exceed 60 per cent. Thirty-nine per cent of the cultivated land bears two crops a year. The crop area per farm amounts to 5.1 acres, and there are 6.1 people per farm family. The farm population, excluding city dwellers, amounts to 1,165 per square mile of crop area. Such data reflect the intensity of man's quest for food.

It is the people who everywhere give character to the plain. No landscape is devoid of their presence, and there is no square inch of earth but has its impress of repeated toil. One cannot separate man and the environment; they belong together as intimately as a tree and the soil from which it grows.

When crops are normal few farmers on earth are more cheerful or contented, but too often the good earth is not good. Famines, excessive taxation, or civil unrest makes it difficult to accumulate a reserve against distress, so that acute suffering is periodic. The fact of all facts for the Yellow Plain is excessive population.

Numerous cities dot the plain, some mere market villages, others railway junctions and industrial centers. The largest and finest is the ancient capital of Peiping, formerly known as Peking, or the northern capital, but renamed "northern peace" in 1928. The city was founded in 920 under the name of Yenching, but the present city pattern dates from Kublai Khan. Over the centuries the court at Peiping attracted the finest craftsmen and artists, the leading scholars, merchants, and politicians. Their heritage remains, so that Peiping still represents the finest in classical Chinese culture. Beautiful temples and palaces, quiet courtyards with a profusion of flowers, and a rich history supply a setting for a quality of life which is China at its best.

Peiping occupies the logical position for the capital of an invading Mongol dynasty, and equally so for purely Chinese rulers who are concerned with holding Mongolia.

The immediate site offers no particular advantages, but the city lies in a corner of the Yellow Plain and commands Nankow Pass, the easiest gateway through the mountains to the Mongolian Plateau.

High walls divide Peiping into five parts. The innermost was the Forbidden City of the Emperor; around it was the Imperial City for his Manchu retainers. These are enclosed by the 50-foot walls of the Tatar or Manchu City, within which is also the former Legation Quarter. Immediately to the south is the Chinese wall, built when Chinese were not permitted to live in the main part of the city. The population of Peiping numbered 1,561,027 in 1940.

The Yellow Plain lacks a satisfactory seaport. Except for the outer portions of the Shantung and Liaotung peninsulas, the seacoast of North China is a mud flat bordered by shallow water. River mouths all have submerged bars. Tientsin is by far the leading port, but it is 40 miles from the sea on the winding Hai River. Farther north is the artificial harbor of Chinwangtao, while in the southeast is the partly developed port of Haichow.

Tientsin has grown to be a city of 1,209,-696 (1940) not because of its advantageous site but owing to the compelling needs of its hinterland. Several rivers focus on Tientsin, joining to form the Hai. Alternately one or the other is in flood and brings so much sediment that the navigable channel is choked for months. A sand bar at the mouth forces medium-sized ocean vessels to anchor out of sight of land. The river freezes in winter but is usually kept open by ice breakers. By 1936, 16 million cubic yards had been dredged from the river and an equal amount from the bar. Yet in a few days of flood deposition the bed has been raised 5½ feet, and 9 feet of sediment was once deposited on the bar in 48 hours. The year 1933 was the best one for shipping, when 2,302 vessels crossed

the bar and 1,008 reached Tientsin. Of the latter only 139 had a draft of over 13 feet. The exports of Tientsin include wool from

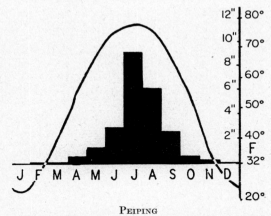

PEIPING

Elevation, 131 feet; average temperature, 53.1°F.; total precipitation, 24.9 inches. All climatic diagrams in the book are drawn on the same scale. Since the base line for rainfall corresponds to 32°F., that part of the year which is normally below freezing and receives snow rather than rain can be noticed at a glance.

Mongolia, hides and skins, raw cotton, eggs and egg products, and manufactured articles such as rugs.

Other cities of the plain are Tsinan, capital of Shantung, and Kaifeng, the capital of Honan and once a capital of China.

No other region south of the Great Wall is so well supplied with railways, largely built while the capital was in the north. Lines radiate in four directions from the Peiping-Tientsin area; south to Hankow and Canton, west to Kalgan and Paotow, north to Mukden and Siberia, and southeast to Nanking and Shanghai. The difficulty of railway construction across the plain is shown in the latter line; since no rock was available for ballast, brick kilns were built and fired with straw, and the roadbed was ballasted with broken brick. Cart roads connect most towns, and dirt automobile roads are numerous.

China's most famous line of communication was the Grand Canal. The section across the Yellow Plain was built in the

land. The latter was once an island in the Yellow Sea but has now been half surrounded by the advancing delta of the

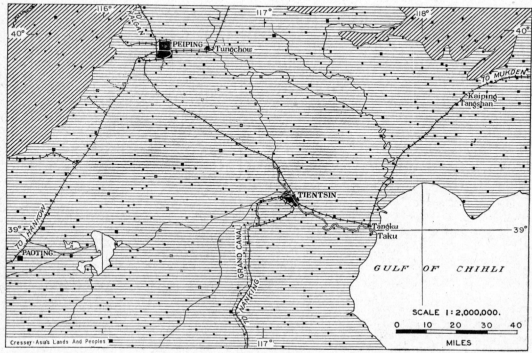

Peiping and Tientsin are the leading cities of the Yellow Plain and are surrounded by countless farm villages.

thirteenth century, more than a thousand years after the part in the Yangtze Plain. On account of seasonal rainfall, it was difficult to keep the canal full of water, and many sections have been out of commission for decades. South of Tientsin the Grand Canal is partly a canalized river which diverts water to the Hai which would otherwise flow directly to the sea, thus adding to the flood problem. The canal was built to bring tribute rice to the court at Peiping.

Shantung Peninsula

The province of Shantung is about equally divided between lowland and up-

Hwang River. The peninsula is a region of hills and mountains where level land is limited.

The geography of the Shantung Peninsula resembles that of the Yellow Plain as to crops and way of life, but with modifications due to unfavorable topography and slightly greater rainfall. Many of the steeper slopes are denuded of their original soil cover, and forests are uncommon. Settlements lie chiefly in valley bottoms, or where valleys open onto the plain.

Confucius lived in Shantung so that much history is associated with the province. The seventy-seventh generation of his descendants still live here, under the name of Kung.

Ancient sedimentary rocks, now altered, and complex igneous formations underlie the peninsula. Excellent bituminous coal

characteristic buildings with their red-tiled roofs still betray this bit of history. It has a splendid harbor on Kiaochow Bay.

Scattered villages marked by clumps of trees on the rolling hills of Shantung near Itu. (*Courtesy James Thorp.*)

occurs in abundance. Elevations reach 5,056 feet in the sacred mountain of Tai Shan, but summits are generally under half that figure elsewhere. A lowland cuts across the center of the peninsula and provides a level route from the seaport of Tsingtao to the capital at Tsinan.

Shantung owes some of its importance to the possession of excellent harbors at Chefoo and Tsingtao. The latter is the rail terminus for a hinterland which includes much of the central Yellow Plain. Tsingtao was once a German outpost, and many

The population in 1935 amounted to 524,415.

Loessland

To the west of the Yellow Plain lies a region of hills and mountains whose dominant characteristic is the widespread occurrence of yellow wind-laid silt, known as loess.

Loess is so fine a powder that when rubbed between one's fingers it has no gritty feel. It is thus easily blown by the wind and has been spread over the underlying bedrock as though by a giant flour sifter. True loess is by definition a wind deposit; subsequent erosion and redeposi-

estimated at 2,852 cubic miles. This is the largest accumulation anywhere.

The source of this loess appears to lie in

Agriculture in Kansu is divided between the intensive utilization of irrigated valley bottoms and precarious cultivation on the dry terraced hillsides where harvests depend on the variable rainfall. (*Courtesy James Thorp.*)

tion by streams has resulted in accumulations of water-laid silts which resemble loess but which must be called redeposited loess.

The thickness of the loess ranges from nothing on steep mountain slopes to a maximum of some 300 feet. Over wide areas the average is 100 or 200 feet. Similar deposits occur over the Yellow Plain, where they are mixed with stream alluvium, and in Sinkiang, but do not equal the development in Loessland where loess covers 119,090 square miles and has a volume

the Ordos Desert, outside the Great Wall and within the loop of the Hwang, where repeated deposition by the river has supplied large quantities of lake and river sediments. These are an easy prey to the winter monsoon winds as they blow outward from central Asia. Sand and coarser materials lag behind, but the silt is lifted aloft and comes to rest in the bordering grasslands of slightly greater rainfall. It is sometimes supposed that Chinese loess originated from wind scour on the Mongolian Plateau, but its distribution gives no suggestion of such an origin. Most of the loess is strongly calcareous.

Loessland occupies the middle valley of

continue opposite Peiping as the Western Hills. The highest elevation in eastern Shansi is the sacred peak of Wutai Shan,

Many of the people in Loessland live in caves, warm in winter and cool in summer but disastrous whenever earthquakes occur. Adequate timber for normal house construction is not available. (*Ato.*)

the Hwang, with its two major tributaries, the Fen and the Wei. It includes all of Shansi, much of Shensi and Kansu, and smaller parts of Chahar, Suiyuan, Ningsia, Honan, and Hopei. Loessland has an area of 203,000 square miles and a population of 44,000,000. This gives an average density of 211 per square mile, in contrast to 647 for the Yellow Plain.

Mountains and broad plains divide Loessland into numerous subdivisions. Level land is present in central Shansi along the Fen River and continues southwestward up the valley of the Wei. Other basins occur in northern Shansi around Tatung and near Kweihwa in Suiyuan. Along the eastern margin rise the Taihang Mountains, which

9,971 feet high. In western Shansi, midway between the Fen and the Hwang, are the Luliang Mountains.

The adjoining province of Shensi is a structural basin but topographically a dissected plateau, buried in loess. Beneath it lie vast reserves of high-grade coal. Eastern Kansu is marked by the Liupan Mountains, with another loess-filled basin to the west. The southern limits of Loessland border the towering Tsingling Mountains, while the north faces the desert plains of the Ordos and The Gobi.

Earthquakes have been particularly severe, as in 1920 when great landslides occurred on the loess hills of Kansu and caused the loss of 246,000 lives.

In climate, Loessland is intermediate between the aridity of Mongolia and the barely adequate rainfall of the Yellow fall is adequate for normal hillside agriculture but more commonly partial crop failure is the rule. Moisture-conserving

Cultivated fields utilize every available portion of this eroded loessland near Loyang, Honan.
(*Courtesy James Thorp.*)

Plain. Rainfall in most areas is about 15 inches; less next to the desert and considerably more on the highest mountains. A few forests remain in inaccessible areas, elsewhere the original vegetation was a steppe grassland. Almost all of the precipitation occurs in summer, with half the total in July and August. Summer temperatures seldom exceed 85°F., but winter winds from Mongolia bring three months with averages below freezing. Wide fluctuations occur from year to year. In some seasons the rain-

techniques of dry farming are necessary. About 175 to 200 days are frost free.

Millet leads kaoliang as the chief summer grain. Wheat is a winter crop except near the Great Wall where it is planted in the spring. Cash crops include cotton, tobacco, and considerable amounts of opium. Each of these latter requires irrigation. Lanchow grows exceptionally fine apricots.

Cultivated land amounts to 22 per cent of Buck's Winter Wheat-Millet area and 18 per cent in the Spring Wheat area, both in

Loessland, in contrast to 68 per cent in his Winter Wheat-Kaoliang Area on the Yellow Plain. In the plains of the Wei and the Fen even higher than in the Yellow Plain, 1,234 as compared with 1,165, despite a much less favorable environment. In place of

Unirrigated terraces in the loess hills of central Shensi. Erosion is rapidly reducing the land available for cultivation. (*Aero-Survey, courtesy J. Lossing Buck.*)

the intensity of cultivation equals that of the Yellow Plain.

Few regions in China have such acute population pressure. Unfortunately some have assumed that this and other regions in the northwest might be areas for colonization. On the contrary, the farm population per square mile of cultivated land is room for settlement, emigration is called for, or at least a considerably increased means of livelihood. Irrigation holds local promise but is not possible on a large scale. Saline soils are common where the water table is high.

Some of the earliest traces of Chinese culture are found here, notably around the city of Sian in Shensi, which was the capital of the Han dynasty, 206 B.C. to A.D. 220. Here was found the Nestorian Tablet, erected in 781 to record the early penetration of Christianity. Several million Mohammedans, of Persian and Turki descent, live in Kansu.

The chief cities are each provincial capitals: Taiyuan in Shansi, 139,000 in 1934, Sian in Shensi with a population of 209,000 in 1939, Lanchow in Kansu with 178,000 in 1942, Ningsia, capital of the province of the same name, and Kweihwa in Suiyuan. Two other cities command important gateways, Kalgan in the north next to Mongolia, and Tungkwan on the Hwang along the route to the Yellow Plain.

Travel is restricted, for the dissected topography makes road construction difficult. Most of the area is linked only by trails. From Sian to Lanchow extends the famous ancient highway which led from Peiping westward to Europe, and over which moved silk and porcelain in early times. An automobile road now follows it, crossing the Liupan Mountains by a 9,000-foot pass. Two railways penetrate the area: one in the north extends to Paotow west of Kweihwa, while in the south the line to Sian has been extended to Tienshui in Kansu. One of these will some day reach Sinkiang and provide a new trans-Asia route. A modern automobile road leads southward to Szechwan, crossing the Tsingling Mountains.

Manchurian Plain

In 1644 Manchu tribesmen invaded the area south of the Great Wall and established the Manchu dynasty which ruled China until 1911. The area from which they came is known today to Chinese as the three eastern provinces—Liaoning, Kirin, and Heilungkiang—but to foreigners as Manchuria. Chinese merchants and farmers have long lived in southern Manchuria but under the Manchu dynasty immigration was periodically restricted. With the establishment of the republic all regulations on colonization were removed and a great tide of migration followed.

Because of political developments since 1931, it is well to point out that this area has been an integral part of greater China during most of the past 2,000 years. In fact China once held land north of the Amur River. Although once administered as a territory, the three divisions listed above have had provincial status since 1907. To the southwest is the province of Jehol, originally a part of Inner Mongolia but grouped with "Manchoukuo" by the Japanese when that puppet state was inaugurated in 1932.

Manchuria has been a cradle of conflict since the end of the nineteenth century. In 1896 an agreement was signed with Russia for the construction of the Chinese Eastern Railway as a short cut for the Trans-Siberian line to Vladivostok. This was later amended to include a branch southward to Port Arthur. The activities of the Russians in this area provoked the Russo-Japanese War of 1904–1905, after which Japan took over the southern part of the line and renamed it the South Manchuria Railway. In 1935 the Soviet Union sold its rights in the Chinese Eastern to Japan.

Both corporations were much more than railways, for they policed zones several miles wide along the line, owned mines and factories, built cities, operated postal systems, and were in effect sovereign spearheads for their respective countries.

In addition to Russian and Japanese activity, many Chinese railways have been built, so that the region is better supplied with transportation than any other area in China. The railway total reached 6,600 miles in 1940, more than all the rest of the country together.

On Sept. 18, 1931, Japanese forces seized the city of Mukden and the next year set up the deposed Manchu emperor as ruler northeastern provinces, it is urgently needed by the Chinese themselves.

If a Japanese Empire is to achieve com-

Road building has been an important Japanese activity in the central plains of Manchuria. This hand-made highway connects Hsinking with Kirin. (*Courtesy Manchoukuo Department of Foreign Affairs.*)

of the kingdom of "Manchoukuo." Since this puppet state was not recognized by the United States or by the League of Nations, the area is here referred to as Manchuria and regarded as under Chinese suzerainty. These northeastern provinces are overwhelmingly Chinese in race and culture and occupy a significant place in China's national consciousness. A sovereign China will assuredly not rest until her political control is secure.

It is clear that Japan's interests are commercial and strategic rather than an outlet for surplus population. Despite extensive efforts at colonization, the total number of Japanese on Manchurian farms is only 100,000. China's population problem is quite as acute as that of Japan, and insofar as undeveloped land still remains in the

plete geostrategic security with defense in depth, she cannot rest until Siberia east of Lake Baikal is hers. Manchuria is thus an essential step in this direction. During the period of Japanese occupation of Manchuria, new railway construction was designed to enable her to cut the encircling Trans-Siberian Railway. Thus nine lines, old and new, point toward Soviet territory.

The Manchurian Plain differs from the Yellow Plain in that the latter is of depositional origin and thus amazingly flat, while the former is an erosional plain with rolling topography. Two river systems, those of the Liao and the Sungari, divide it into a southern and northern half. From north to south the plain measures 600 miles, while from east to west it is 400 miles. The area of the region is 138,000 square miles.

Except for three narrow gaps, the Manchurian Plain is everywhere surrounded by mountains. On the east are the Long White

of the river. To the west, a low portion of the Great Khingan Range gives easy access to Mongolia; in fact on old maps a part of

Piles of soybeans along the Sungari River at Harbin. The bridge of the Chinese Eastern Railway is in the background with its fortress tower to the right.

Mountains, to the north is the Little Khingan Range, in the west are the Great Khingan, while to the southwest are the mountains of Jehol. Between these uplands are corridors to the outside world.

The valley of the Liao in the south has a 75-mile frontage on the Gulf of Liaotung. A narrow strip of coastal lowland leads to the Yellow Plain at Shanhaikwan where the Great Wall reaches the sea. This coastal avenue of invasion may be likened to Thermopolae in Greece. In the northeast the Sungari enters the Amur lowland along a valley where hills close in on either side

the western and more arid Manchurian Plain is labeled the Eastern Gobi. Within this enclosure, nature has provided a most favorable environment and man in turn has developed one of the most spectacular pioneer lands of the twentieth century.

Manchuria lies in the latitudes of the northern United States and southern Canada. Dairen corresponds to Baltimore, Mukden is on the parallel of Albany, Harbin matches Montreal, and the northern border along the Amur River reaches the latitude of southern Hudson Bay. This suggests similar climatic conditions, but the greater continentality of Asia brings sharper seasonal contrasts. Winters are long and bitterly cold, summers short and hot. Snow

becomes precarious in the western plain. Fortunately the rains occur during the growing season.

The Anshan ironworks south of Mukden were developed by Japan as their principal base of heavy industry on the continent. Successive enlargements raised Anshan to an important place among world steel centers. (*Courtesy South Manchuria Railway*.)

begins to fall in the north in late September and in the south a month later; it continues until mid-April in the south and mid-May in the north. Monthly averages are below freezing from November through March. Central Manchuria often has January minimum temperatures of −30°F., while August maxima rise to 95°F. Frequent weather changes are related to the passage of cyclonic storms. Thus winter months characteristically have "three cold and four mild" days in succession. Only 150 to 175 days are frost free.

Precipitation is seasonal, with light winter snowfall, a dry spring and fall, and concentrated rain in July and August. The amount decreases from 25 inches in the east to 15 inches in the west, so that agriculture

Owing to the natural cover of grass, soils are the most fertile of any area in China, with an extensive development of chernozem and chestnut-brown soils. Some saline and alkali soils appear in the drier areas.

Good empty land has brought tens of millions of farmers, often a million a year. Thus the population of the three provinces and the Japanese leased areas amounting to 14,917,000 in 1910 rose to 25,266,000 in 1926, and to 44,459,524 in 1940 (including Jehol). Many of these settlers have gone to the pioneer fringe where they have plowed new land, formerly the home of the nomad.

Crops resemble those grown elsewhere in North China but are raised in larger fields and with a surplus for export. Nowhere else is the yield so large per person; hence living standards are higher. In the north, wheat and soybeans predominate; in the south the

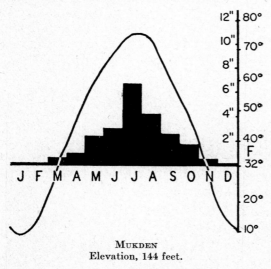

MUKDEN
Elevation, 144 feet.

crops are more diversified with kaoliang, millet, soybeans, corn, and wheat the most important. In 1929, Manchuria grew 60 per cent of the world's soybeans, and their export supplied the basis for considerable prosperity.

Large areas remain uncultivated, but they are in the far north where the growing season is short or in the extreme west where aridity creates a peril. Another undeveloped area lies in the extreme northeast in the Amur Valley along the lower Sungari and Ussuri. This area resembles the Amur lowland of Siberia rather than the Manchurian Plain, with swamp and meadowland and a rigorous climate.

The mineral wealth of Manchuria is inferior to that of the rest of China, but superior to that of Japan. Estimates of coal reserves have been increased to 20,000,-000,000 tons, and production in 1941 amounted to approximately 20,000,000. Most of this comes from the Fushun deposits, near Mukden, which have the thickest bed of bituminous coal in the world, no

less than 417 feet. Fuel oil is obtained from associated oil shales, with a projected capacity of 1,000,000 tons in 1941.

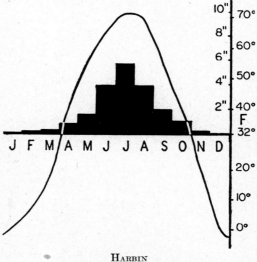

HARBIN
Average temperature, 37.15°F.

Iron ore is available at Anshan, where the Showa Steel Works has several blast furnaces reported to have a 1941 capacity of 1,750,000 tons of pig iron and 1,000,000 tons of steel. In the Eastern Manchurian Uplands, two furnaces are located at Penhsihu, and new rich deposits have been located near the Korean border at Tungpientao. Liaoning Province contains nearly three-fourths of China's known iron ore deposits.

As part of her program of a Greater East Asia Co-prosperity Sphere, Japanese investments in Manchuria amounted to five billion yen by 1941. These have brought few financial dividends but have had strategic value.

All the cities are of recent growth. The only seaport in the plain is Yingkow at the mouth of the shallow Liao, whose population numbered 180,871 in 1940. Whereas this was the largest port of Manchuria prior to 1907, it is now greatly outdistanced by Dairen on the Liaotung peninsula, and may some day be surpassed by the new port of Hulutao on the western shore of the Gulf of Liaotung.

a line eastward to the new port of Rashin in northern Korea. Harbin lies at the crossing of the Chinese Eastern Railway and the

The Changpai Shan in eastern Manchuria along the line of the railway from Hsinking to Rashin. These mountains are largely covered with splendid mixed forests. (*Courtesy South Manchuria Railway.*)

The three chief cities of the Plain lie along the main railway, Mukden, Hsinking, and Harbin. Mukden is at the junction of the lines to Peiping and to Korea. It is the capital of Liaoning Province and includes an old walled city and a newer area around the South Manchuria Railway station in the Japanese zone. The 1940 population was 1,135,801, double that of 1936 on account of the development of light industry. One-tenth of the population was Japanese. Hsinking, known to the Chinese as Changchun, was made the capital of Manchoukuo and has grown rapidly. It had a 1940 population of 544,202, of whom 100,000 were Japanese. Hsinking is the rail junction for

Sungari River and is the junction of the line south to Dairen. Streamlined express trains link these cities in 12½ hours. The population in 1940 was 661,984, of whom some 35,000 were Russians. The coal city of Fushun had 269,919 people in 1940, while the steel city of Anshan had 213,865.

Eastern Manchurian Uplands

Uplands border the Manchurian Plain on almost all sides. Those on the east, north, and southwest are forested, while aridity gives rise to a grass cover in the west. Agricultural settlement has penetrated well into the eastern and southern mountains but those in the west are still the home of the nomad and resemble Mongolia in their geographic characteristics.

Since the Eastern Manchurian Uplands

Three important railways cross the region from west to east; in the south there is the branch of the South Manchuria from

The railway between Mukden and Antung cuts through the southern part of the mountains of Eastern Manchuria. (*Courtesy South Manchuria Railway.*)

extend 850 miles from the Liaotung Peninsula northeast nearly to the junction of the Amur and the Ussuri and are but 200 miles wide, conditions naturally differ. The south has a mild climate, all level land is intensively utilized, and the forests are deciduous, while the north is an undeveloped coniferous wilderness.

The Eastern Manchurian Uplands have the finest forests in China with large reserves of excellent Korean pine, spruce, larch, elm, birch, oak, and fir. This timber is rafted southward along the Yalu River to the port of Antung or westward on the Sungari to Kirin. Fur-bearing animals are trapped in the more mountainous areas.

Mukden to Korea, in the center is the line from Hsinking via Kirin to the new port of Rashin in northern Korea, while farther north is the Chinese Eastern from Harbin to Vladivostok. Several other railways provide good access.

The rainfall is more abundant than in the Manchurian Plain, with as much as 40 inches of rain and snow in the higher areas. Where the land is sufficiently level for cultivation, agriculture is thus more favorable. Soybeans, millet, wheat, and kaoliang are the crops. Many Koreans have pushed across the border and are engaged in raising rice, especially in the Chientao or Yenki district.

Coal is present all along the western margin of the region, and large iron reserves occur in the south and in the east. Prospects was leased to Japan in 1905 as the Kwantung Leased Territory.

Antung lies near the mouth of the Yalu,

The Tumen River forms the frontier between Manchuria and Korea. (*Courtesy South Manchuria Railway.*)

are especially favorable in the Tungpientao district near Korea where the Japanese have developed an important iron and steel industry with an 800,000-ton capacity.

The highest elevations occur in the Long White Mountains or Changpai Shan along the Korean frontier, where the volcanic peak of Paitou Shan with a crater lake rises to 8,990 feet.

The leading city is Dairen at the tip of the Liaotung peninsula, the major seaport for all of northeastern China. When the Russians first came to the area, Port Arthur was their chief base but the Japanese emphasized Dairen and made it into a splendid port. The population in 1939 numbered 555,562. The surrounding area

opposite Korea; it had a 1940 population of 315,242. Kirin is the capital of the province of the same name, with a population which numbered 173,624 in 1940. The only other center of importance is the coal and steel town of Penhsihu.

Khingan Mountains

Although the uplands that border the Manchurian Plain on the north and west cover 168,000 square miles, their economic importance is slight. The elevations are commonly under a mile but the local relief is less than 1,000 feet. Along a north-south axis is an area known as the Great Khingan Range, sometimes spelled Hsingan. Toward the south this is largely the upturned edge of the Mongolian Plateau; farther north the region widens and is less perfectly known. The Little Khingan Range parallels the Amur River from the Sungari to its tributary, the Nonni.

North of the Chinese Eastern Railway the Khingan Mountains have a Siberian-type larch and birch forest; to the south is a Mongolian-type steppe. There is little agriculture, and the few settlers are lumbermen, hunters, or pastoralists.

Jehol Mountains

The province of Jehol is at the easternmost end of what was once Inner Mongolia. Although it lies outside the Great Wall, it is essentially Chinese in culture, and its proximity to Manchuria has given it less and less of a Mongolian orientation. Nomadic tribes and Lama temples persist in the west.

The geographic region here described includes the hills and mountains that make up most of the province. These resemble Shantung in their ruggedness but have a more continental climate with Mongolian winters. The higher areas were once forested and formed an imperial hunting ground, but the timber has now been cut from most accessible areas. Forests are noticeably more abundant on the shady north slopes.

The topography is so unfavorable that the only access to most areas was by trail. New automobile roads and a railway from Manchuria to Peiping via the capital at Chengteh have changed this.

Coal and some oil are produced along the eastern margin. The crops include millet, kaoliang, and spring wheat. Opium is widely grown, as is common in the less accessible areas of interior China where expensive transportation makes it necessary to grow cash crops that are easily shipped.

CHAPTER 7

REGIONS OF SOUTH CHINA

South China belongs to the humid sub-tropics, with summer monsoon rainfall. Winters are short and cool rather than cold; smaller and cultivation more intensive so that the net income per farm family is only slightly higher.

The farmhouses of South China are generally more substantial than those of the North; heavier rainfall calls for tile roofs rather than thatch.

snow is almost unknown. The amount of rainfall is 40 to 80 inches, so that the landscape is always green. Flood, drought, and famines are uncommon. This is a land of rice, with much less diversification than in the wheat-millet-kaoliang region of North China. Along with rice culture go flooded fields, often terraced, and water buffalo. Two crops are raised a year, but farms are

For all of Agricultural China, the surveys of J. Lossing Buck show an average of 0.45 acre of crop area per farm person; for his Rice Province of the South the figure is 0.37 while in the Wheat Province of North China the acreage is 0.56 acre. If all crops are converted into the equivalent of grain and if all laborers are put on a uniform work basis, the average annual yield for South

119

China is 1,520 kilograms per person in contrast with 1,231 for North China. The average for all China is 1,393, as compared with 20,000 kilograms for the United States with its mechanized farming.

The boundary between the North and the South is clearly marked by climate, natural vegetation, soil, crops, and culture. In general, it follows the crest of the Tsingling Mountains and their eastern extension; near the coast it lies along the Hwai River whose southern tributaries drain riceland while the northern tributaries flow through fields of kaoliang and millet.

Both the North and the South are dominantly rural, and the cities in each region exist for commerce rather than for modern industry. On the whole, South China has larger and more modern cities.

Seven regions are present in the South, the Yangtze Plain, the Szechwan Basin, the Central Mountain Belt, the South Yangtze Hills, the Southeastern Coast, the Canton Hinterland, and the Southwestern Uplands.

Yangtze Plain

Water is the key to the geography of the Yangtze Plain. On either side of the river is a network of canals, and in several areas there are large lakes. Transport is by river steamer and junk, or by launches and canalboats. Since rice is the characteristic crop, most fields are flooded for half the year. This is a green world, very different from the brown landscapes of North China.

The Yangtze Plain has 900 people per square mile, and 70 per cent of the area is in cultivation. Both these figures are the highest of any region in China, and betray the intensity with which man crowds this fertile lowland. The region lacks compactness, but it has coherence. The shape is irregular since boundaries follow the flood plain. From east to west the distance is 600

miles, but from north to south the width varies from 20 to 200 miles. The area is 75,000 square miles and the population numbers some 68,000,000.

Whereas many characteristics are common throughout, the region may be subdivided into the delta below Wuhu and the flood plains and lakelands of the middle Yangtze. The delta occupies most of the province of Kiangsu and part of Chekiang. The middle Yangtze lies in Anhwei, Kiangsu, and the twin provinces of Hupei and Hunan. These latter take their name from the Tungting Hu, or Lake, with respect to which they lie north and south.

Although the Yangtze is comparable in length to the Hwang, it flows through a region of three times the rainfall and carries much more water. During the 1931 flood the Yangtze sent a volume of 2,800,000 cubic feet per second past Hankow, as compared with a mean annual discharge of 1,047,500 cubic feet per second at Wuhu. This flood inundated 34,000 square miles, as compared with an area of 25,000 square miles flooded by the Mississippi in 1927. Fortunately disastrous floods are rare. This is in part because of the storage capacity provided by the marginal lakes such as the Tungting, Poyang, and Tai, and the network of smaller waterways. Unlike the Hwang, the Yangtze is not overloaded and is able to carry its burden of sediment to the sea. This load amounts to 600,000,000 tons a year, and its deposition in the delta is advancing the shore line one mile every 70 years.

Much of the Yangtze Plain is geologically so young that the land is not yet much above sea level. Even at Ichang in the far west, the elevation of the river is but 295 feet. The river gauge zero at Hankow is only 11.94 feet above that at Woosung outside Shanghai, 630 miles to the east. The mean annual variation at Hankow is 34.7 feet. On the seaward margin, man has built dikes to reclaim the land as soon as it appeared above the level of low tide. The large lakes that lie on either side of the river represent unfilled parts of the original lowland. When the Yangtze rises in summer, often 50 feet or more, these lakes are filled by back water from the river. The Tungting Lake then has a size of 50 by 75 miles and the Poyang is nearly as large. During the winter the basins become almost dry. The Tai Lake in the delta varies less in size and is roughly 40 by 40 miles. Comparable lakes are present along the lower Hwai River.

The Yangtze provides a splendid avenue of communications. Next to the Rhine it may be the busiest river in the world. Where islands divide the river, there are a few troublesome sand bars; elsewhere the channel is sufficiently deep for ocean steamers of 4,000 tons to reach Hankow, 630 miles upstream, at all seasons, and for 10,000-ton boats in summer. This inland port normally handles 5 per cent of China's foreign trade. River boats easily reach Ichang at the foot of the gorges, 1,000 miles from Shanghai.

Three major tributaries join the Yangtze within the region. On the north there is the Han, at whose mouth is Hankow. On the south there are the Siang, which flows through Tungting Lake, and the Kan, which reaches the Yangtze via the Poyang Lake. Each of these has its own lowland plain which forms further subdivisions of the region as a whole.

No area in the world has such a network of canals. Most of them are navigable for small boats, and these waterways are the roads of the region. Their total length has been variously guessed but greatly underestimated. They are especially abundant south of the Yangtze and east of the Tai Lake. In one measured square mile, which appears representative, they have a total length of 27.8 miles, with an average spac-

ing of 380 feet. Many of these are navigable for small farm boats. The mileage in this small part of the delta may thus approxi-

Scores of villages in the Yangtze Delta are intersected by canals. These waterways provide for transportation, irrigation, waste disposal, and domestic water supplies. (*Courtesy U.S. Bureau of Agricultural Economics.*)

mate 150,000 miles, and for the region as a whole there may be a quarter to half a million miles of navigable waterways.

Climatic conditions provide a growing season of 300 days free from frost, so that at least two crops a year may be raised. Since rainfall lines in this part of China extend nearly east and west, the region has a fairly uniform rainfall of 40 to 50 inches. From March through August the rainfall amounts to 5 inches a month, with a maximum in June. January and December are the only months with less than 2 inches. Fall and winter are the most pleasant seasons with clear skies and average temperatures below 50°F. from October through February. Summers are oppressively hot and humid. Shanghai

lowlands of Java, and the lower Ganges Plain.

Tiny fields are the rule, the result of

Farmhouses of the poorer type in Kiangsu. In this district the principal crops are wheat, cotton, and barley.
(*Courtesy James Thorp.*)

observations give a July temperature mean of 98°F. and a humidity of 84 per cent. During the summer of 1934, Shanghai experienced 21 consecutive days each with a maximum over 100°F., while for 60 days the daily maximum averaged 97°F.

Although the Yangtze Plain has a larger number of important cities than elsewhere, three-quarters of the people are farmers. Nowhere in the world is the land more intensively utilized. Many districts have a farm population in excess of 2,500 per square mile. Only five areas in Asia duplicate this congestion: the Chengtu Plain in Szechwan, the area around Canton, the Kwanto Plain centering on Tokyo, the

repeated subdivision through inheritance. Because of the meticulous care, crop yields are large per acre, but on account of the excessive labor required the return is low per person. China's agricultural problem is not so much to increase the total harvest as to raise the per capita yield. Rice is the standard summer crop, with wheat, beans, and barley as the chief winter crops. Winter crops are more common than elsewhere in South China, with 62 per cent according to Buck's surveys in the Yangtze Rice–Wheat region. Vegetables are widely raised. Water buffalo and oxen are the characteristic farm animals.

The two distinctive crops are cotton and silk, both produced more extensively here than in any other part of China. Cotton is modernize her methods, but the domestic production probably leads the world.

The Yangtze Plain has at least eight

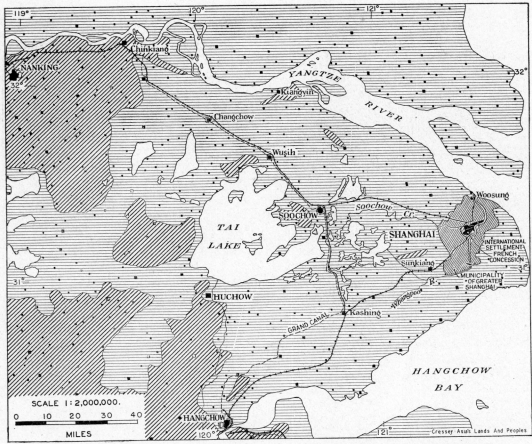

Shanghai dominates the Yangtze Delta. Nanking, Soochow, and Hangchow are also of importance.

increasingly important in the delta, with large mills in Shanghai. Fully a third of China's cotton is grown in this region. Some of the finest silk in the world is produced in the immediate hinterland of Shanghai where a quarter of the land is locally devoted to mulberry cultivation. Silk is obtained from cocoons spun by the silkworm which in turn is fed on mulberry leaves. China has lost most of her export market for silk through unwillingness to

cities whose population exceeds 500,000, and at least a dozen more of over 100,000. More than elsewhere these are semi-modernized cities with extensive world contacts.

Shanghai is great because in its hinterland lives one-tenth of the human race. No other city dominates such a market, nor is it apt to have a rival. Shanghai is the entrepôt for the Yangtze and occupies the only feasible site for a modern port near its mouth. Even though new outlets develop via Indo-China, Burma, or Canton, the trade of Shanghai will doubtless up the winding Whangpoo River. Extensive dredging has provided a 31-foot channel up the Whangpoo, but enormous

Industrial Shanghai receives its electric power from this 200,000-kilowatt plant, operated on coal from north China and elsewhere. (*Courtesy Shanghai Power Co.*)

increase even faster than any diversion. No other Chinese port is so close to Japan, and the location midway along the coast is a commercial advantage. The population of 3,703,430 in 1940 is over twice the size of her closest rival, Peiping. Shanghai ranks next to Tokyo as the largest center in Asia, and holds seventh place among world cities.

When the city was opened to foreign trade in 1843, it was already one of the busiest ports of China, although entirely devoted to domestic commerce. Since then its growth has been phenomenal. Shanghai has prospered, owing in part to geography and in part to the economic security provided by the International Settlement. When trade flourished in the interior, it brought business to Shanghai or, when civil warfare gripped the country, people and wealth sought refuge here.

The wide mouth of the Yangtze does not provide a suitable location for a harbor. Instead Shanghai lies 14 miles to the south

sand bars in the estuary of the Yangtze, known as the Fairy Flats, have a low-water depth of only 18 feet. The site of the city is a mud flat, barely above high tide, with no bedrock for at least 1,000 feet down. On this foundation have been built 24-story buildings, some of the tallest outside the Americas.

Metropolitan Shanghai is made up of three areas: the commercial area of the International Settlement, the largely residential French Concession, and the surrounding Chinese areas including the old once-walled native city. As the city grows, it will probably gravitate northward toward the Yangtze.

Shanghai is primarily a commercial city, with industry dependent upon foreign contacts rather than local raw materials. Cotton and silk are the only resources produced in the immediate hinterland. Nearly half of China's imports and exports pass through Shanghai each year and, despite the absence of near-by resources, the city has accounted for almost half of all China's industry. Among world ports, Shanghai is exceeded in tonnage of ships

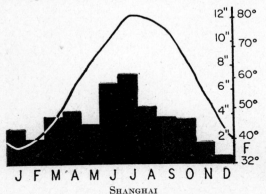

SHANGHAI

Elevation, 33 feet; average temperature, 59°F.; total precipitation, 45.8 inches.

entering only by New York, London, Kobe, San Francisco, Liverpool, Los Angeles, Hongkong, Antwerp, Hamburg, and Rotterdam (1935). No other port in China has such extensive steamship connections. The city is thus China's cultural front door. During the period prior to the Second World War, the foreign population of Shanghai included some 75,000 foreigners among whom were nearly 5,000 Americans.

Five hours southwest of Shanghai by rail is Hangchow, while two hours to the west is Soochow, linked in the Chinese expression "Heaven above, Soochow and Hangchow below." Hangchow is famous for its beautiful scenery and Soochow for its beautiful women. Their populations are 576,000 (1935) and 389,000 (1936), respectively. To the east of Hangchow are Shaohing and Ningpo, each with over a quarter of a million people.

Nanking became the capital in 1928, in response to the earlier suggestions of Sun Yat-sen. It was also the seat of government during the Sung and Ming dynasties before 1416, but most signs of its former magnificence are gone except the name, "southern capital." New boulevards and modern

government buildings were beginning to modernize the city prior to the Japanese occupation in 1937, when its population

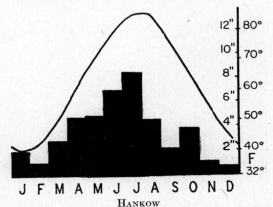

HANKOW

Elevation, 118 feet, average temperature, 63.3°F.; total precipitation, 43.8 inches.

exceeded a million. The city lies on the Yangtze 200 miles northwest of Shanghai with railroad connections to Shanghai, Tientsin, and westward.

Hankow and its twin city of Wuchang across the Yangtze dominate central China. Railways lead north to Peiping and south to Canton. Hankow's water traffic not only follows the Yangtze east and west but also leads northwestward up the Han and southwestward through Tungting Lake to the Siang River. Hankow is the more modern city, with buildings along the water front, or Bund, that rival those of Shanghai. Wuchang is the capital of Hupei province. In 1940 the population of Hankow amounted to 804,526, while Wuchang had about half that number. Together with nearby Hanyang, the three cities are collectively known as Wu-Han.

The Szechwan Basin

The tragic war with Japan had the advantage of compelling China to rediscover its own west. Until the arrival of Europeans along the coast a century ago, China had faced toward inner Asia, and the interior provinces were of major importance. Owing to the lack of modern transportation, Szechwan, Kansu, and the rest of western lation density within the region is thus 580 per square mile, highest of any region that is not a plain.

A bamboo suspension bridge across the Min River in western Szechwan. (*Courtesy Robert F. Fitch.*)

China did not share in the modernization that has characterized Shanghai, Tientsin, Canton, and their coastal provinces. The land behind the gorges remained as it had been. When the seaboard was overrun by the Japanese, Free China emerged in the Far West. The basin of Szechwan is the most notable of these revitalized areas.

Szechwan is the most populous of China's provinces, with a 1939 total of 52,706,210 people. Of this number, some 43,000,000 live within the geographic basin. In area, this is one of the largest provinces, exceeded only by Kansu among the original 18 south of the Great Wall. Out of a total area of 156,675 square miles the Szechwan Basin occupies about 75,000 square miles; the remainder is mountainous. The average popu-

The Szechwan Basin is a land of hills and low mountains, cut by swift rivers flowing through steep-sided valleys. Beneath the region are soft shales and sandstones of Cretaceous age which are purple or in some places red in color. It is these which led von Richtofen to call this the Red Basin.

Central Szechwan is a structural basin with numerous sharp anticlines and gentle synclines, trending roughly northeast to southwest. Much of the area was once a peneplain at a height near the present hilltops. As streams became entrenched, harder anticlinal areas of limestone and sandstone remained as ridges. Falls and rapids mark the outcrop of these formations along the streams and account for the gorges that characterize many tribu- taries. Several terrace levels are present in

north, and there is a January average of 50°F. and a July average of 80°F. The

Terrace lands along the streams of Szechwan are irrigated by water wheels turned by the force of the current.

most valleys. The only level area is the alluvial fan around Chengtu.

Elevations with the river gauge zero along the Yangtze decrease from 820 feet at Pingshan in the west to 590 feet at Wanh- sien in the east. Elsewhere the region is generally under 2,000 feet in height. Szechwan takes its name from the "four rivers" that drain into the Yangtze. These are the Min which enters the Yangtze at Suifu, the Lu at Luchow, the Chialing at Chungking, and the Wu from Kweichow.

The climate of Szechwan has numerous surprising features. Although far in the interior and surrounded by imposing moun- tains, the rainfall is nearly 40 inches and the seasonal extremes are small. Winters rarely have snow or frost, except in the

frost-free period is 325 days. Cold Mongol- ian air is kept out by the barrier of the Tsingling Mountains to the north. The province has a great deal of cloud and mist, so that the humidity is high. Rain may fall gently for several days in winter yet the amount be too little to record; summer months have thundershowers. After the summer rains the level of the Yangtze may rise 75 feet, and twice that in the gorges. Sacred Mt. Omei, 10,145 feet, at the western edge of the region recorded 311 inches from August, 1932, to September, 1933. Despite its location, 600 miles from the ocean, this is the heaviest precipitation of any station in the country.

Agriculture is thus carried on under favorable circumstances, although the thoroughly hilly topography requires extensive terracing. Forty per cent of the region is population density per square mile of cultivated land is 1,610 people. Rice supplies

The soft sandstone hills of the Szechwan Basin are extensively terraced for the cultivation of rice. (*Courtesy China International Famine Relief Commission.*)

cultivated. The Szechwan Basin grows a greater variety of crops than elsewhere, with both the wheat, millet, and corn of the North, and the rice, rapeseed, and sugar cane of the South. Rice is the usual summer crop wherever water is available for irrigation; it is planted in April or May and harvested in September. Sweet potatoes are important on the dry hilltops. Wheat is a winter crop. Silk and tea are widely produced, together with some cotton, tobacco, and opium before 1941. Tung oil is a major export to the United States, where it is used as a quick drier in varnish. Citrus fruits are grown south of the Yangtze.

Buck found in his Szechwan Rice Area, which includes more than the basin, that crop yields were 8 per cent above the national average, with 75 bushels of rice and 23 bushels of wheat per acre. The farm

more than half the food energy, with one-seventh from corn.

The landscape of the Szechwan Basin is made distinctive by the widespread terracing. Other regions are as green and intensively developed, but nowhere else is so much land terraced. In fact, nowhere else except in Loessland is it so easy to construct terraces, for the bedrock is horizontal and soft. Variations in hardness produce many natural terraces. Even 45° slopes have tiny steps of level land. Water wheels line the swifter streams and lift irrigation water to the fields as they are turned by the current. Elsewhere water is obtained by chain pumps, often operated by water buffalo. Clusters of trees and bamboo surround the houses, with many banyan, cypress, pines, and some oaks and palms. Few parts of China are so highly praised for their beauty.

Beneath the surface occur extensive deposits of salt and coal, together with some iron ore. Natural gas is also present. During the war with Japan coal production was greatly increased, so that the 1940 output amounted to 3,280,324 metric tons, largely from the basins of the Chialing, Min, and To rivers. Pig iron similarly rose to about 50,000 metric tons. Copper was produced to the extent of 500 tons, and gold amounted to nearly 100,000 ounces. Modern industry is largely confined to the vicinity of Chungking.

The most spectacular aspect of Free China's development was the removal of the capital from Nanking to Chungking, and the subsequent rebuilding and repeated bombing of that city. Chungking is nearly 1,400 miles up the Yangtze. The city occupies a strategic site on a high hill where the Chialing River joins the Yangtze. The original city wall dates from 320 B.C., and the city is sometimes referred to by its early name of Pahsien. Suburbs have spread outside the wall, as well as across both rivers. The population of the municipality amounted to 882,480 in 1943. Since the city itself covers only four square miles, there are at least 70,000 per square mile within the wall. New roads have been cut through the old city and modern buildings up to seven stories in height have taken the place of the old. Prior to 1927 there was not a wheeled vehicle inside the city wall and not many streets wide enough for them; today there are busses and taxicabs as well as rickshas.

Chungking is the commercial center of the province, and its geographic setting will make it continue to grow after the capital is moved back to Nanking.

The second city of the Szechwan Basin is Chengtu in the far west, within sight of the Great Snowy Mountains of Tibet. Chengtu is on the alluvial plain of the Min, near where it leaves the "Azure Wall"

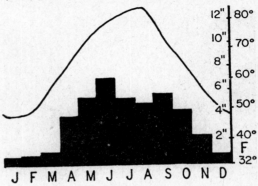

CHUNGKING
Average temperature, 64.84°F.

of mountains. This plain has an area of 1,730 square miles and a population of 3,700,000, a density of 2,150 people per square mile. Few other spots on earth are so fertile and productive, in part owing to a remarkable irrigation system. Chengtu is rich in history and culture, but with limited modern developments. Its population was about 600,000 in 1942.

The great problem of the Szechwan Basin has been difficult transportation, both internally and especially to the rest of China. Steamships on the Yangtze date from 1898 but freight rates are very high. Automobile roads now lead north to Shensi and Kansu, and south to Kweichow. Most domestic freight still moves by river boat.

Central Mountain Belt

Between the Yangtze and the Hwang is a mountain zone which accounts for the abrupt contrasts between dry North China and the humid South. Toward the west the mountains are Tibetan in character; near the latitude of Nanking where they die out they have become mere hills. The northern slopes are dry but once the crest is reached monsoon rains result in forests and rice culture. This is the southern limit of loess and the northern boundary of extensive rice, tea, mulberry, and bamboo.

This region is part of the Kuen Lun Mountain system which originates far to the west in the Pamirs. Where the range

A canyon in the Tsingling Mountains of southern Shensi. This range is the major dividing line between the North and the South. (*Bayley Willis, courtesy Carnegie Institution.*)

enters China in southern Kansu it is known as the Min Mountains and rises to 20,000 feet; farther east in Shensi elevations are over 10,000 feet and are called the Tsingling, a name which is often used for the whole range east of Tibet. In Honan are the 6,000-foot Funiu Mountains, while in Anhwei the hills are but 3,000 feet in height and are termed the Tapei Mountains; the name Hwai-Yang also appears on some maps.

In addition to this sequence along the northern margin of the Central Mountain Belt, there is a parallel chain of mountains to the south of the Han River. In northern Szechwan these are called the Tapa, while farther east they cross the Yangtze as the Gorge Mountains.

This region separates the wheat-eating Chinese of the north from the rice-eating population of the south. It also marks important cultural and historic boundaries, for revolutions have commonly been limited to one side or the other.

Since the western half is rugged, most of the people live in the eastern hills where level land amounts to 5 or 10 per cent. The chief city is Hanchung on the Han River, amid a miniature Chengtu Plain.

Not only does the Central Mountain Belt separate the north and the south, it also isolates the basin of Szechwan from the Yangtze Plain. The Yangtze Gorges provide some of the finest scenery and most difficult navigation in China. The river descends 300 feet in the 200 miles from Wanhsien to Ichang, and the current flows as much as 14 knots. The principal gorges occur where the Yangtze cuts across anticlines of hard limestone. Vessels up to 1,400 tons are used during the high-water period in summer, but so much power is required and the risks are so great that freight rates remain high. Smaller boats operate throughout the year.

South Yangtze Hills

The Yangtze River drains four regions after it leaves Tibet: the Szechwan Basin, the Central Mountain Belt, the Yangtze Plain, and the South Yangtze Hills. The latter includes a large area south to the watershed. The region lacks internal coherence as a geographic entity, but conditions of life are surprisingly uniform.

Four north-flowing streams, all but the easternmost of which are tributary to the Yangtze, guide the economic life. These are the Yuan and Siang in Hunan which reach the Yangtze via the Tungting Lake, the Kan in Kiangsi which flows via the Poyang Lake, and the Chientang River in Chekiang province. In each instance the major city of the valley lies in or near the

Yangtze Plain to the north. These are, respectively, Changteh, Changsha, Nanchang, and Hangchow.

to river flood plains and to the rolling topography on summit levels, elsewhere slopes are fairly steep. Terracing is widespread.

The Wushan Gorge in the Yangtze. Through this gateway has passed virtually all the traffic between Szechwan and the lower Yangtze Valley. (*Asia.*)

These rivers and their tributaries carry a great volume of traffic on native junks but are of limited value for steam navigation. Where streams become too shallow for even the smallest boats, bamboo rafts extend the navigable distance. Thus almost every city is served by some water transport. Modern automobile roads have revolutionized the accessibility of the region. Journeys that once required days are now simply a matter of hours.

Hills of reddish sandstone are characteristic. Except for mountains along the various provincial borders, elevations are under 2,000 feet. Level land is restricted

Surprisingly large remote areas are in forest. Fir, pine, and bamboo are systematically grown for export to cities along the Yangtze. The most extensive of these forest areas are in western and southern Hunan in the basin of the Yuan River. Where the original vegetation has been cleared from the hillsides, whether for lumber or for temporary cultivation, excessive erosion has occurred. After the land is abandoned it becomes covered with wild grass rather than returning to forest.

Several uplands lie within the region, such as the Lu Mountains in northern Kiangsi with the summer resort of Kuling, the Hung Mountains in southern Hunan, and the Nanling next to Kwangtung. Each exceeds 4,000 feet.

ever irrigation is feasible. Shortly before the harvest, a second planting is often put into the same fields in alternate rows with

The river plains of Chekiang, devoted to rice, fail to provide enough livelihood for the dense population so that the cultivation of sweet potatoes and tung oil trees has spread up the hillsides despite serious erosion.

This is the warmest and wettest part of the Yangtze Valley. Rainfall everywhere exceeds 50 inches, and in the higher areas is as much as 70 inches. Temperatures are not excessively high or low, with frost only rarely, but the average annual relative humidity exceeds 80 per cent. It is this high moisture content which keeps the landscape always green. Whereas prolonged drought may turn the Yangtze Plain brown, such conditions seldom occur here. At least 325 consecutive days are frost free. Oranges, palms, tung oil trees, and bamboo reveal the subtropical nature of the climate. Soils are red podsols and much leached.

Rice is the universal summer crop wher-

the first crop, but the growing season is not long enough for two successive crops. Uplands are unirrigated and devoted to tea, rapeseed, and sweet potatoes. Winter crops include beans, oil seeds, and wheat.

Tea is a distinctive crop, with characteristic flavors in each valley. Nearly a million acres in China are devoted to tea plants, of which two-thirds are in the South Yangtze Hills. Siangtan in central Hunan is especially famous. Hunan and Kiangsi commonly cure the leaves in such a way as to make black tea, while green tea is produced in Chekiang and Fukien.

Cultivated land amounts to 18 per cent, of which 78 per cent is irrigated. Buck's surveys for the Rice–Tea Region show

1,788 farm people per square mile of cultivated land. This is the highest of any region yet considered but is surpassed by widespread and is produced especially at Pingsiang in Kiangsi. Iron ore is mined at Tayeh and elsewhere along the Yangtze.

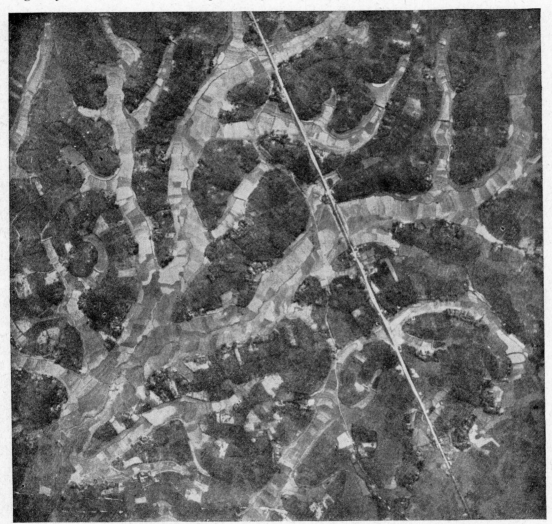

Terraced rice fields follow up each valley between uncultivated hilltops. This aerial photograph is from Hunan. *(Aero-Survey, courtesy J. Lossing Buck.)*

those farther south. The total population amounts to some 65,000,000 in an area of 155,000 square miles, or an average including city dwellers and farmers alike of 420 per square mile.

The South Yangtze Hills fortunately have conspicuous mineral wealth. Coal is

The nonferrous metals are distinctive, and include antimony from central Hunan and tungsten from southern Kiangsi. Zinc and lead have been mined for many years. In 1940 the coal output of Hunan amounted to 1,050,000 metric tons while Kiangsi produced 340,500 tons. The same provinces mined about 970 and 5,800 metric tons of tungsten ore, respectively, and 380 and 1,000 metric tons of tin. Kiangsi produced extensive maritime interests and skill as sailors. Typhoons are recurrent and yield heavy rainfall. Race and language are

Hundreds of thousands make their home on boats in the coastal cities between Shanghai and Canton. Many of these people are non-Chinese groups who emigrated from the South Seas centuries ago. (*Ato.*)

7,100 metric tons of antimony regulus and 400 tons of crude antimony. Almost all the industry arising from this mineral wealth has developed outside the region. National planning will doubtless lay stress upon the development of these resources.

The completion of the Canton-Hankow Railway, and of the east-west line linking Hangchow with Nanchang, Changsha, and Kwangsi has opened up the region to modern trade.

Southeastern Coast

A variety of factors give geographic personality to the Southeastern Coast. The coast line is embayed and has led to complex. No other region is so oriented to the sea, nor so detached from interior China. Millions of overseas Chinese count this as their ancestral home.

This is a subsiding shore line with drowned valleys and offshore islands that once were hilltops. Hundreds of sheltered harbors provide havens for native junks, but only in a few localities is there sufficient access to the hinterland to give rise to a commercial port.

The irregular coast reflects the rugged topography of the interior. This is a hard and rocky land, largely underlain by granite, rhyolite-porphyry, and other resistant formations. Only in sheltered basins are there softer formations, and these in turn give rise to rounded hills rather than rugged mountains.

An analysis of the land forms of that part of Chekiang province which lies within this region shows that about 5 per cent are coastal flatlands, 1 per cent are interior lowlands, less than 1 per cent are rolling hills (with 4 to 10° average slopes), 90 per cent are mountain lands (10 to 25° slopes), and 3 per cent are steep lands (with slopes over 20°). Topographic conditions in Fukien are probably comparable, but in eastern Kwantung there are more level land and more gentle slopes.

Along the western border is a line of mountains that rise to 4,000 and 6,000 feet. Those in southern Fukien are the Taching Mountains, while farther north are the Wuyi Mountains, sometimes romanized as Bohea.

This is a hot and very wet region, with 60 inches of rainfall on the lower coastal areas and over 80 inches on the interior mountains. All months have some rain, but from May through September the monthly average is over six inches. Typhoons are most common during the late summer and bring torrential rains. The destructive force of the wind is limited to the immediate coast, but heavy rains extend throughout the region. Fukien is somewhat drier than the other provinces since it lies in the rain shadow of Formosa.

Except for a short railway behind Swatow, this region and the Szechwan Basin are the only ones in the country without railway facilities. Overland roads leading to the rest of China are also nearly absent except in the far north and south. Contact with the other provinces has been by sea. The same problem of isolation is true within the Southeastern Coast. Each river-mouth city has its independent hinterland. Thus Wenchow, Foochow, Amoy, and Swatow dominate subregions of their own; and each valley has its own

unique customs and speech. In the days of clipper ships, Foochow shipped 65 million pounds of tea a year.

The lingual and psychological confusion that makes China so difficult to unify is not characteristic of the bulk of the interior but of the coastal zone from Shanghai to Canton. Yunnan and the southwest have even greater racial differences but they relate to "tribespeople" rather than to nominal Chinese stock as along the coast. Fortunately the radio and standardized school pronunciations will make people mutually intelligible; but cultural contrasts will persist.

Since the land offers so little, many people have turned to the sea. Fishing boats dot the coastal waters, and seagoing junks sail north to Tientsin and south as far as Singapore. Modern Chinese steamships draw many of their crew from this coastal school for seamen. Emigrants from Amoy, Swatow, and elsewhere have gone to Indo-China, Malaya, and the East Indies by the millions. Their remittances to relatives at home amount to large sums.

With an area of only 70,000 square miles, the region supports nearly 30,000,000 people. Only 15 per cent of the area is in cultivation, and the crop area per person averages but 0.23 acre.

Canton Hinterland

If Canton and the Cantonese are what many foreigners imagine all China to be like, it may be due to two factors. This was the first port for foreign trade and has had the longest contact with westerners, and it is also the home of most of the Chinese who now live in the United States and Europe. Arab and Persian traders came to Canton in the fourth century and were followed by the Portuguese in 1516 and later by the Dutch. When modern trade began early in the nineteenth century, this was the only port at which foreign vessels might call. Here also came the first Protestant missionary, Robert Morrison, in along the northern border are the wettest area in China, although isolated stations elsewhere may have more precipitation.

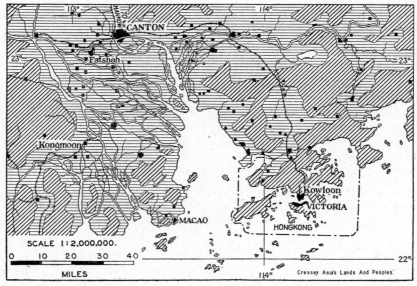

Canton, and Victoria on Hongkong Island, are the leading cities of the Si River Delta.

1807. Millions of Cantonese have gone overseas and have brought back money and ideas which have helped to make their region one of the most progressive.

This is tropical China, for most of the Canton Hinterland lies within 25 degrees of the equator. There is a long wet summer with excessive humidity and high temperatures from mid-April till mid-October, then follows a relatively cool and dry winter till mid-February, after which there are two months of transition with fog and muggy weather. This region is almost as wet as the southeastern coast, with 65 inches or more along the coast and less in the interior. The maximum precipitation occurs in August with nearly 12 inches, but June and July are nearly as wet. Even winter months have 1 or 2 inches. Snow falls only on the highest mountains, and there but rarely. The Nanling Mountains

Temperatures are high, since the sun is vertically overhead in June, but the cloudiness keeps maximum summer temperatures in the 90's rather than around 100°F. as in Shanghai or Peiping. Europeans wear white clothing for 11 months in the year. Occasional frosts kill banana plants and other tropical vegetation.

These climatic conditions are reflected in the soils and natural vegetation. Except on river flood plains and deltas, soils are red in color with lateritic tendencies. They are low in humus and so badly leached that their fertility is very low. The colloid content is of such character that they erode badly. Heavy and repeated fertilization is essential. Most hillsides should have been kept in the original forest. Where this has been destroyed, cogonal grasses have taken possession of the surface. Such rank grass covers about a third of the region.

The fruits of the area further suggest the low latitude for they include oranges, and six-tenths to mulberry fields. Part of the fish food is supplied by residual ma-

Unusually good roads characterize the landscape of the Kowloon Leased Territory across from Hongkong. Numerous ponds and canals make fish and ducks an important item in the farm economy.

bananas, pineapples, lichees, olives, and figs. Sugar cane is also grown.

The Canton Hinterland is a region of two successive rice crops. Although the yield for each harvest is the lowest in the country, the double harvest returns 84 bushels per acre. Over three-quarters of the cropland is double-cropped in summer, but only 8 per cent carries a third winter crop. Sweet potatoes are more common than elsewhere but are grown far less than rice; they are often raised on drier areas as they do not require irrigation. Poorer people may eat dried shredded sweet potatoes as a substitute for rice.

Silk is important in the delta south of Canton. Many farmers also raise fish, devoting four-tenths of their farm to ponds

terials from the raising of silkworms, and the fertile mud from the pond bottoms is used in turn to enrich the mulberry fields.

Cultivated land in the entire region amounts to some 13 per cent of the total area. Land values are the highest in the country, according to Buck, with a price of 53 Chinese dollars per acre; this is twice the national average. No less than 2,072 farm people occupy each square mile of cultivated land. By far the most intensive utilization occurs in the plain around Canton.

Three major streams drain the area, each one converging on a common delta. In the east is the Tung or East River, in the center is the Pei or North River, while the third and longest is the Si or West

River. The latter carries six-foot draft steamers as far as Wuchow, 200 miles from the sea, at all seasons. Each river is exten-

from 100 to 600 feet above the plain, with the picturesque effects which characterize Chinese landscape paintings. They are

Typical karst hills in Kwangsi. (*Courtesy James Thorp.*)

sively served by motor launches and native junks. These rivers flow through very hilly topography. Fully 85 per cent of the region is in hills and mountains, considerably more if the delta is excluded.

Where these streams reach the sea, they have built a compound delta. Unlike those of the Hwang and Yangtze this is not a broad plain, but rather a fragmented area of alluvium which surrounds many hills and is cut by wide distributaries. Its area is 2,890 square miles, and the population nearly 9,000,000. This gives a density of 3,100 people per square mile. A shorter stream in the delta is the Chu or Pearl River, on which lies Canton.

The province of Kwangsi has unique karst topography, nowhere surpassed though equaled in Yugoslavia and Puerto Rico. Isolated vertical-walled hills rise

remnants left by ground-water solution and are associated with features such as caves, underground drainage ways, and sinkholes where the roofs have collapsed and only occasional pillars remain. The area is in an old-age stage of the ground-water erosion cycle; such limestone hills are known as hums.

Hainan Island is a detached subregion, more tropical and less developed. The area is 14,000 square miles and the population numbers 2,500,000, many of whom are Lois tribesmen rather than Chinese. Elevations reach 4,428 feet in the Five Finger Mountains. Extensive deposits of iron ore are present.

Canton, and Victoria on the island of Hongkong, are the major cities, each in the million class of population. The city of Canton was founded in 1053 when the

Chinese settled Kwangtung. It was one of the first cities to tear down its city wall and open wide streets, and the city is now part

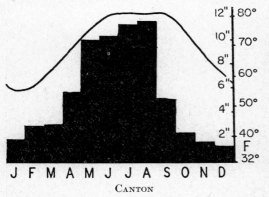

J F M A M J J A S O N D
CANTON

modern and in part old style. Canton dominates all of China south of the Yangtze, commercially and intellectually. The city serves a rich hinterland, both up the three rivers as well as along the coast. Unfortunately, the Pearl River is shallow, and it is necessary for West River steamers to go out around the delta to reach the city. Deep water is available nine miles downstream at Whampoa, but much dredging will be necessary in order to create a modern ocean port.

The island of Hongkong was ceded to Great Britain in 1842, and additional territory was leased later on the mainland. Its advantages have been both geographic and political. The harbor is excellent, and the proximity to major shipping lines to Europe and to America made it an important port of call. Hongkong has served as an entrepôt for smaller ports from Foochow to Haiphong, but as trade and facilities developed at these lesser ports the need for Hongkong diminished. The city of Victoria, often called by the name of the island, is picturesquely situated at the foot of an 1,825-foot peak. Across the bay is Kowloon, with rail connections to Canton and central China, and for that matter with Europe. Hongkong was established as a free port,

so that trade has flourished. If Canton should develop an adequate harbor, Hongkong might lose much of its significance.

A typical street in the crowded Chinese section of Hongkong. (*Courtesy Canadian Pacific Steamships.*)

Portuguese Macao was settled in 1557 and is the oldest foreign possession along the China coast. Two hundred thousand people live in its dozen square miles.

The Canton Hinterland lacks adequate railway facilities. The line to Hankow was not completed until 1936, and the only other railways are the line to Hongkong and short sections in the delta.

Southwestern Uplands

Yunnan and Kweichow lie in the far southwest, 2,000 miles from the old capital at Peiping, yet the Chinese speak some of the best Mandarin heard outside the Yellow Plain. More than half the people are of non-Chinese stock. Conspicuous changes in transportation and industry arise out of the westward orientation of Free China following the late 1930's.

The topography of this region may be subdivided into three areas, each a much-dissected plateau, which form a giant set of topography resembling that of Kwangsi. In Yunnan the few plains all lie on undissected interstream uplands, and the valleys

Most Chinese cities have an even sky line broken only by temples, pagodas, and gate towers. This is the main street in the city of Tali, Yunnan. (*Ato.*)

stairs from the lowlands of the Canton Hinterland to the highlands of Tibet. Western Kwangsi has a general level of 2,000 feet. Kweichow lies about 4,000 feet, while most of eastern Yunnan is above 6,000 feet. Toward the east few traces of summit levels remain, and most settlements lie in open valleys. Central Kweichow is so extensively cut by deep valleys that agricultural possibilities are very limited, and the hard limestone hills are not easily terraced. Soil erosion has been very destructive and has so depleted the hillsides that terracing is less extensive than formerly; this is one reason for the poverty of the province. Kweichow has some karst

are narrow and deep. There are several lakes and old lake basins on the Yunnan Plateau, notably near the cities of Kunming and Tali. The general topographic trend is from northwest to southeast, so that travel at right angles involves crossing a series of mountains and valleys. Level land in the region as a whole is between 5 and 10 per cent. Earthquakes have been severe in western Yunnan.

Although subtropical in latitude, the altitude is a moderating factor so that temperatures are mild and the seasonal range low. Conditions vary according to local elevation. At Kunming the January average is 50°F., and in July it is 70°F.;

extremes have never exceeded 90°F. or dropped below 29°F. The rainfall average is 42 inches, with only minor variations.

the good land and raise rice, while the tribesmen live on the hills and raise corn, millet, and barley. Expensive transporta-

A Shan house in southwestern Yunnan. (*Courtesy American Museum of Natural History.*)

Half the total falls in July and August. The growing season is some 325 days but permits only one summer crop of rice. Two-fifths of the fields raise a winter crop.

The Southwestern Uplands have a great variety of native peoples. Chinese have lived here for 2,000 years, but the area has remained semicolonial in government and the Chinese have pushed the aborigines or tribesmen into the hills or steeper valleys rather than assimilating them. Non-Chinese people include the Miao, Lolo, Chungchia, and many others, each with distinct languages and culture. In many areas Chinese control is only a matter of the past century.

These racial contrasts are reflected in the agricultural pattern. The Chinese occupy

tion doubles the cost of rice if carried two days' journey, so that cash crops are needed if agricultural products are to be exported. Opium once supplied this need but thereby preempted much of the best land. New cash crops might be found in lumbering, livestock, fruit, sugar cane, cotton, or tung oil. All these must wait upon improved access to outside markets.

This region is the largest in Agricultural China, but the percentage of cultivated land is among the lowest. This is estimated by the writer at 4 per cent, and by Buck at 7 per cent of his Southwestern Rice Area. Nowhere else are there so many people per square mile of cultivated land. Buck reports a farm population of 2,636 per square mile of crop area. Even allowing for possible errors in computation, this is an extraordinarily high average. Since so much of the land is naturally poor, it must

Kunming is a city of nearly 100,000 at the terminus for a narrow-gauge railway from Haiphong in Indo-China, built late in

Rice fields in the central plateau of Yunnan where ancient lakes have left a fertile plain. (*Courtesy China International Famine Relief Commission.*)

represent intensive effort and low standards of living. The average farm has but two acres.

These uplands have a variety of mineral wealth, although in no case do the reserves appear to be extensive. In 1940, Yunnan produced 202,000 metric tons of coal, 7,500 metric tons of pig iron, 13,340 metric tons of tin, enough to be of world importance, 485 tons of copper, largest in China, and some gold, mercury, and antimony. Kweichow in the same year yielded 360,750 metric tons of coal, 3,400 metric tons of pig iron, and some 150 metric tons of mercury, highest in the country.

the nineteenth century. This line suddenly became important when Japan occupied China's seaports, and Yunnan was for a time the major side door into Free China. When the railway was cut, the famous Burma Road was available partly to take its place. This automobile road crosses extremely difficult country in the gorges of the Salween and Mekong rivers. A network of automobile roads now links the region with the rest of China.

The migration of colleges, factories, and millions of refugees from the eastern provinces has been of great significance in the modernization of these backward areas.

CHAPTER 8

REGIONS OF OUTER CHINA

Interior Asia has two large areas with less than ten inches of rainfall: one lies northwest of the Pamirs in Soviet Middle Asia, the other is to the east in Outer China. Except for oases along mountain-fed streams or favored areas with slightly higher rainfall, this is the home of the pastorialist rather than the farmer. Nomadic encampments replace fixed settlements. Although grazing utilizes far more land than does farming, most of the population is sedentary.

Outer China covers some two million square miles, but the population is under ten million people. Two-thirds of the area is a rolling upland plain, one-third highland plateau and mountains. Everywhere the dominant note is aridity. Most of this dry heart of Asia is without drainage to the sea. The few withering streams are centripetal rather than centrifugal, and basins are not filled to overflowing as in humid lands where precipitation exceeds evaporation.

Three areas are involved, each with somewhat confused political status. Mongolia may be divided into Inner and Outer Mongolia, named from their position with respect to the rest of China. Since 1911, Inner Mongolia has been grouped into Jehol, Chahar, Suiyuan, and Ningsia. Outer Mongolia has been independent of effective Chinese rule since 1913 and is now divided into the Mongolian People's Republic and the Tuvinian People's Republic, both of them satellites of the Soviet Union.

Sinkiang has had full provincial status since 1878, but its remoteness from the capital has rendered political control diffi-

cult. The province has increasingly been oriented toward the Soviet Union, especially since the construction of the Turk-Sib Railway near the frontier.

Tibet is also divided into two parts. Nearer Tibet lies closer to Cultural China, and is administered as the provinces of Chinghai and Sikang. Farther Tibet includes the bulk of the great plateau, but its boundaries next to Sinkiang and Nearer Tibet are vague. Conventional lines as shown on maps have no validity with the local inhabitants. Chinese authority was negligible between the Revolution of 1911 and the removal of the capital to Chungking in 1938. During that period British influence was strong.

These major political districts roughly form geographic regions; if not entirely homogeneous in their physical pattern, at least they are a unit in cultural coherence. Mongolia includes the Gobi Desert and encircling steppelands, with arid mountains in the northwest. Sinkiang has three parts: the Tarim Basin, the Tien Shan Range, and the Dzungarian Basin, each inhabited largely by Mohammedans. Tibet is the great plateau from The Himalaya to the Altyn Tagh.

Half of Greater China lies here in the interior. Its economic influence is negligible, but politically it has had profound significance since the earliest dynasties. Time after time migrations that started in this arid interior have swept south across China and westward into Europe. This is the "Pulse of Asia," as Ellsworth Huntington has titled his book, and many of the secrets of Old World history will be better understood as we learn the story of fluctuating rainfall in Outer China. Two thousand

12 days from the nearest Soviet railway. The 675 miles from Kalgan just inside the Great Wall to Ulan Bator can be covered

Lama shrines dot the boundless plains of Mongolia. (*Courtesy American Museum of Natural History.*)

years ago under the Han Dynasty, Chinese rule extended west of the Pamirs into the basin of the Aral Sea. Under Genghis Khan and his grandson Kublai, the Mongols built up the largest continuous land empire ever known.

Overland travel is a major problem. Railroads are lacking, and automobile roads few and poor. Caravans of two-humped Bactrian camels or ox carts are the chief means of communication. Distances are measured in days rather than in miles. Thus the trip from Kashgar in western Sinkiang to Paotow at the railhead west of Peiping normally requires 125 days for 2,500 miles, while an additional 50 days are needed to reach Hailar in northeastern Mongolia. In contrast, Kashgar is but

in three days by car but require 30 to 45 days by camel. Two months are involved in the journey from Koko Nor in northeastern Tibet to Lhasa in the south. Effective political control is difficult under such handicaps.

Mongolia

Mongolia is a land where all of life depends on grass. Agriculture is rarely possible, mining is largely undeveloped, there are few trees for forestry and no water bodies for fishing, industry is almost lacking, and the chief means of livelihood is in animal husbandry and in hunting. In the central Gobi the rainfall is under eight inches and the desert surface is nearly barren. Around the margins of the true desert the rainfall rises to 12 inches and it is in this steppe that the nomad finds his home. Higher elevations in the northwest

Within the Mongolian People's Republic there were reported in 1937 to be 576,000 camels, 1,909,000 horses, 2,410,000 cattle,

Mongol encampments in summer use cloth tents as well as the round felt-covered winter yurts.

intercept more rainfall and have local forests. The only agricultural possibilities are in the extreme south and north.

Flocks of sheep, cattle, horses, and camels are pastured on this grassland. Since the grass seldom grows tall enough to be harvested, the animals must go where it is. Inner Asia is the home of nomadic people who are continually on the move. Their felt-covered yurts are found from the valley of the Volga to that of the Amur. From their animals come food, clothing, shelter, transportation, fuel, and wealth. When the rains fail, the grass withers, and life is impossible. In few environments does man live so close to nature. Centuries of rigorous life in an exacting environment have long since weeded out the unfit.

4,000,000 goats, and 14,370,000 sheep. Wool and hides are the chief export, formerly moving to the North China cities of Kweihwa, Kalgan, and Hailar, but currently sold to the Soviet Union.

Sheep are the most useful of these animals. They provide wool for the felts that cover the yurts, sheepskins for clothing, milk in summer plus cheese and butter which may be stored for winter, mutton in winter, and dung for fuel. Since they do not provide transport, the Mongols also keep horses, cattle, and camels.

The food of the Mongols is largely derived from their flocks. A little barley, millet, flour, and brick tea are bought from passing caravans. Milk, butter, cheese, and mutton are the chief items in the diet.

Since water is scarce, dishes are seldom washed. Sour milk is the basis of the staple drink, a concoction of tea, salt, and rancid

It was formerly customary for one son from every family to become a lama so that the number of priests in Mongolia was a guide to the total population. (*Courtesy American Museum of Natural History.*)

butter, often with parched barley and bits of cheese. This is drunk piping hot from a wooden bowl.

The Mongols are all believers in the Lama variety of Buddhism, similar to that of Tibet. Monastaries receive one monk from every family and are the chief centers of fixed settlement. Many lamaseries possess considerable wealth, in herds, as well as in buildings and money. The Lama heirarchy once exercised much temporal as well as spiritual power.

The Mongols are organized into banners and khans. The Tsetsen khan occupies an area in the east, the Tushetu khan lives in the center, the Sain-noin khan controls

the northwest, while in the far west is the Jassektu (Sassaktu) khan.

Geographic Mongolia is enclosed by the Siberian frontier, largely mountainous and forested, the Great Khingan Mountains, Jehol, and the vicinity of the Great Wall next to Loessland. Only in the west adjoining Sinkiang is the boundary uncertain. The distance from north to south is 600 miles, while from east to west it is more than 1,000. The region covers nearly 1,000,000 square miles. Population estimates are highly uncertain, with a possible total of 3,000,000, two-thirds of whom are Chinese colonists in the far south. The Mongolian People's Republic is credited with an area of 580,150 square miles, and a population of 840,000, ten per cent of whom are Russians and Chinese.

The chief city is Ulan Bator, formerly known as Urga, with a population of 70,000. This is an important center of Lamaism, and the capital of the Mongolian People's Republic. Near-by brown coal mines produced about 100,000 metric tons in 1937. North of Ulan Bator and opposite the Soviet city of Kyakhta is the trade entrepôt of Altan-Bulag with 20,000 people. Other settlements are usually monasteries or trading villages such as Uliassutai and Kobdo, both in the northwest, or Pailing-miao in the south.

Nomadic life is progressively diminishing, especially since 1924 under Soviet attempts to collectivize herding. During the Manchu dynasty, the various tribes and banners were assigned specific grazing areas. Trade was introduced and, through the manipulation of Chinese merchants, whole tribes became in debt for large amounts. This tended further to fix groups of people in specific areas.

After 1923, Outer Mongolia became almost a closed land. The Mongolian People's Republic and the Tuvinian People's Republic are protectorates of the

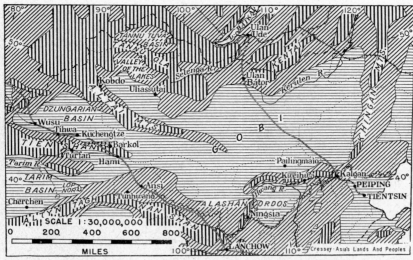

The pattern of Mongolia. Plains are shown in horizontal lines, hills in diagonal lines, and mountains in vertical lines.

The ancient city of Urga has become modernized since its name was changed to Ulan Bator under Soviet influence. (*Sovfoto.*)

Soviet Union, and few foreigners have been able to secure passports. Important changes have occurred in the place of Lamaism and

between the lands of adequate and inadequate rainfall. But since deserts are areas of fluctuating precipitation, the arable

The women of each Mongol tribe have their characteristic headdress commonly made of silver, turquoise, and coral. Since surplus wealth cannot be invested in fixed property and it is hazardous to increase the size of one's flocks beyond the local grazing resources, jewelry is the chief method of accumulating wealth among the nomads. (*Ato.*)

in the economic life, and the countries are regarded as in a state preparatory toward socialism. Inner Mongolia came increasingly under Japanese influence after 1938.

The strategic significance of Soviet interests in eastern Mongolia with respect to those of Japan in Manchuria should be obvious. Japanese railways in northern Manchuria were built to cut the Trans-Siberian Railway in time of war, while Soviet activity in Mongolia has been aimed at a possible drive eastward across central Manchuria toward Korea.

The Great Wall was China's attempt to set a limit between farmer and shepherd;

limits expand and contract with passing decades. Time after time throughout Chinese history, rainfall outside the Wall has increased to the point where it has been sufficient for crops, and Chinese colonists have pressed 100 miles or more into Mongolia. The nomads in turn were able to retreat toward the then wetter core of the usual desert area. Later on in drier cycles when the rains failed, dust bowl conditions developed along the fringe of cultivation and the farmers were obliged to retreat southward. The nomads in turn moved outward, eventually invading the cultivated areas within the Wall. The Great

Wall was an attempt to stabilize a shifting climatic boundary. It failed because, like all deserts, The Gobi did not stay put. Similar to-and-fro migrations are known to have taken place around the eastern and northern limits of Mongolia.

Inner Mongolia has been the scene of considerable Chinese colonization within recent decades, reaching to latitude 42°N. outside the Great Wall north of Kalgan. Soils are fertile but rainfall is precarious; no large possibilities for settlement are present. Similar colonization has occurred in the north where Russian and Buriat settlers have pushed into the Selenga Valley.

The Gobi is the most northern of all deserts, and the most continental. Other parts of Asia have drier climates, but none experience a greater range of temperatures. In winter the thermometer regularly drops to −30 and even −40°F. Summer days often record 90°F. in the shade, and exposed rock surfaces may be heated to 150°F. Nights are always cool. The annual day and night average for Ulan Bator is 35°F.

Winters and spring have only a light snowfall, seldom covering the ground to a depth of more than a few inches. Herds may thus graze on dried grass throughout the winter. Summer is the rainy period. Ulan Bator reports eight inches and the rainfall decreases southward and westward, so that the central and western Gobi is the driest area.

Unlike tropical deserts, rainfall occurs in showers or a protracted drizzle rather than in torrential downpours. Such showers may be local in distribution, so that nomads in quest of grass find it necessary to be frequently on the move. Some precipitation is convectional, but much of it is cyclonic or due to the frontal action of moving air masses.

In the absence of instrumental records, climatic characteristics must be determined in terms of vegetation. Most of The Gobi has a *BS* (Koeppen symbol) climate, that of a dry steppe rather than a true desert.

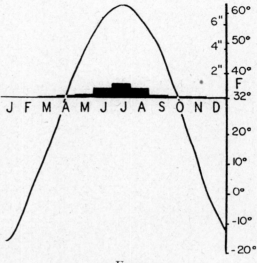

URGA
Elevation, 3,800 feet.

Patches of *BW*, true desert, are usually mapped in the south and southwest where there is an almost complete absence of vegetation and extensive sand dunes. The northern hills and mountains appear to be *Dw*, a cold temperate climate with a dry winter.

Two-thirds of Mongolia lies in the flat Gobi; the other third is made up of barren mountains to the north and west. From every side The Gobi is approached over a mountain rim, inside which the surface gradually descends. Within these encircling mountains, the monotony of boundless desert plains continues for hundreds of miles, broken here and there by rugged mountains or dissected badlands.

The ancient rock floor is a complex of hard formations, much folded, faulted, and locally injected with igneous rocks. In some cases the original sedimentary rocks have been altered to crystalline gneiss and schist. Granite is present in many areas.

The soil cover is thin and vegetation is nearly absent so that the rocks are directly exposed on the surface.

smooth erosion surface known as the Gobi peneplain. Although the elevation varies considerably, it commonly lies around

Most of the undrained hollows of the Pang Kiang erosion surface are bordered by badland topography. In this arid landscape vegetation is almost completely absent. (*Courtesy American Museum of Natural History.*)

Despite wide differences in age, hardness, and structure, these ancient rocks have been worn down to an essentially flat surface, known as the Mongolian peneplain. Across it one may drive an automobile for miles without obstruction. Few areas on earth have been eroded to such flatness, and one passes across rocks of notably different resistance to erosion with scarcely a topographic break. Here and there are residual monadnocks. This nearly perfect plain lies at an elevation of 5,300 feet in southern Mongolia and at over 6,000 feet near the Arctic Divide, with lower elevations in the center.

At altitudes lower than the Mongolian peneplain there is another remarkably

4,000 feet. This surface is developed on the softer sediments, Cretaceous and younger, which have accumulated in down-warped basins. It also is extraordinarily level, with little relation to the resistance to erosion or structure of the underlying rocks.

From place to place, the Gobi surface is interrupted by shallow undrained hollows that range in size from 200 yards to 10 miles in length, and from 20 to 400 feet in depth. These are known as the Pang Kiang erosion surface, not sufficiently perfect or widespread to be a peneplain. Whereas these hollows have relatively flat floors, they are never so perfectly level as the Gobi upland. In most cases they contain intermittent playa lakes. The bluffs that descend from the Gobi plain to the Pang Kiang floor are here and there carved into badlands by innumerable gullies. Although the rainfall is low, the runoff from occasional showers, perhaps years apart, does considerable work. Depressions of the Pang Kiang type appear to be largely excavated by wind work in the softer and less cemented recent sediments. As a result of this deflation a veneer of shifting sand covers the adjoining uplands, especially around their southern and eastern sides.

Sand dunes are not extensively developed in Mongolia or in any other part of central Asia except the Takla-makan Desert. For The Gobi as a whole, they probably cover less than five per cent of the desert, chiefly in the southwest.

The larger part of The Gobi is covered with a thin veneer of gravel or small stones, forming a desert pavement. During the passage of time, all surface sand and silt have quite generally been removed by wind and water, and these residual pebbles remain to armor the underlying rocks or soil. All finer material has been swept out of the desert; loess is entirely absent.

Within the plains of Mongolia, Berkey and Morris of the American Museum of Natural History have defined several major basins or broad depressions, known as tala. In the northeast, extending into northwestern Manchuria, is the Dalai tala, roughly parallel to the Great Khingan Mountains. Its northern part is occupied by a chain of lakes, some of them in the Amur drainage system; to the south is rougher country with lava flows and recent volcanoes. The Iren tala lies in the central Gobi, on the direct route between Kalgan and Ulan Bator. It is a broad open country, which rises from the center at 2,930 feet to 5,000 and 6,000 feet in the broad swell that surrounds it; within it are at least seven minor basins. The Gashuin tala lies in the southwest, between the Gurbun Saikhan

Mountains and the Nan Shan Range; its chief stream is the Edsin Gol. The eastern part is known as the Alashan Desert. The Ordos Desert inside the great loop of the Hwang River represents a fourth basin.

In northwest Mongolia are a series of basins, bounded by faulted mountains and much smaller than the warped talas just described. These are known collectively as the Valley of the Lakes.

Most of the mountains of Outer Mongolia are associated with the great system of ranges that extends north into Siberia. From west to east these are as follows: Next to Sinkiang are the narrow Altai, which rise to 13,553 feet at the Siberian border and continue southeastward 900 miles to the Gurbun Saikhan in the middle of Mongolia. North of the Valley of the Lakes is the Tannu Ola, which forms the southern boundary of Tannu Tuva or the Tuvinian People's Republic. Farther north are the Sayan Mountains, and these in turn mark the Mongolian frontier east to the Selenga River. East of the Tannu Ola and south of the Sayan is a confused mountainous area known as the Khangai Mountains, a dissected dome rather than a range. East of the Selenga Valley are the Kentai Hills, in part mountainous.

In the extreme northwest is Tannu Tuva, currently known as the Tuvinian People's Republic, under Soviet patronage. The country occupies an enclosed basin in the Yenisei Valley, and thus within Siberian drainage. The people are of Finno-Turki stock rather than pure Mongols; part are steppe nomads with cattle, others are forest dwellers with reindeer. The capital is Kyzyl.

Sinkiang

Sinkiang commands the only low-level gateways between Oriental and Occidental Eurasia. Highways have crossed the province since the dawn of history, to link ancient China with the Roman World or to carry military supplies from the Soviet Union during the Second World War. This

The present road strikes north from Ansi across the barren desert to Hami at the foot of the Tien Shan or "Heavenly

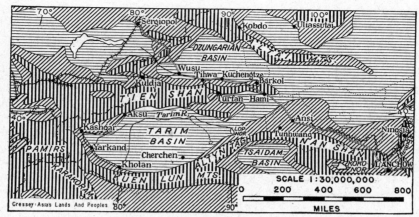

The pattern of Sinkiang. Plains are shown in horizontal lines, hills in diagonal lines, and mountains in vertical lines.

was the route of Marco Polo and of the monks who brought Buddhism from India. Into China came jade from the Kuen Lun, while westward moved silks and porcelain. Strategy even more than wealth or colonization has been China's territorial interest.

The great highway of central Asia leads west from Sian, one of China's former capitals in Shensi, to Lanchow and then follows the long arm of Kansu through the oases of Liangchow, Kanchow, Suchow, past China's ancient front door at the Jade Gate near the end of the Great Wall, to Ansi. The road follows the base of the Nan Shan Range, stepping from one irrigated area to another along the edge of Mongolia.

West of Ansi the original Silk Road entered Sinkiang and followed the southern edge of the Tarim Basin past Lop Nor to Yarkand, but the oases are now largely in ruins and the route crosses extremely desolate country. From Yarkand a difficult trail leads over the Karakorum Pass to India. This abandonment appears to be associated with climatic changes.

Mountains." Here the trail divides. One route leads along the oases south of the mountains through the Turfan Depression to Kashgar, where the 12,700-foot Terek Pass crosses the Pamirs to Soviet Fergana. The other and currently more important road lies north of the Tien Shan through Kuchengtze to Tihwa, or Urumchi, capital of Sinkiang. Three roads lead west from Tihwa to the Turk-Sib Railway in Soviet territory; one via Kuldja and the Ili Valley, another through the famous Dzungarian Gate, while the most used crosses the frontier near Chuguchak.

This Imperial Highway required 18 days each from Sian to Lanchow, to Suchow, to Hami, to Tihwa, and to Ili. Three more series of 18 stages each led from Tihwa to Kashgar.

Automobiles now travel from Chuguchak to Tihwa, Hami, and Lanchow over fair desert roads. This became the principal back door to China after the Burma Road was cut during the Second World War. Modest sources of gasoline in the Tien

Shan and western Kansu are of local importance. A trans-Asiatic railway will surely one day parallel these ancient lines of history.

None of these routes offered much attraction to early nomadic wanderers, as long stretches of pastureless country intervene between oases. Farther north, along the base of the Altai, the grassland is continuous and provides an easy avenue to western Asia along the valley of the Black Irtysh.

Political Sinkiang covers some 600,000 square miles, with a population of 4,360,-000. Of these only 500,000 are nomads, and no more than ten per cent Chinese. Most of the people are Turki or others of Persian stock and Mohammedan religion. Unlike Mongolia and Tibet where Chinese influence is a matter of recent centuries, Sinkiang has been under Chinese control off and on since the Han Dynasty in 200 B.C. At distant Kashgar, however, China has exercised complete control for only 425 out of 2,000 years. In contrast to Manchuria where the Chinese have occupied the land as agricultural settlers, in Sinkiang they were merely traders in the oases. Chinese control has been less since Mohammedanism replaced Buddhism in the fourteenth century. Serious civil war has occurred several times during the twentieth century. Soviet influence is strong and the control of the central Chinese government is only nominal.

Despite its remoteness, notable changes have taken place since the inauguration of reconstruction plans in 1936. In 1939 there were 330,000 students in various schools. Stations for the improvement of agricultural and animal husbandry have been established. Mining and industry are undergoing development, and major improvements have taken place in communications.

Geographic Sinkiang is somewhat smaller than the political province, for it does not include the large section of the Tibetan Plateau shown within the political boundary on most maps. Three major subregions are involved, the desolate Tarim Basin in the south, the rugged Tien Shan Range in the center, and the semiarid Dzungarian Basin to the north. The Tarim Basin is drier than any other desert in China, but Dzungaria is comparable to the moister parts of The Gobi. The prevalence of Turkish and Mohammedan culture creates resemblances to Soviet Middle Asia, so that Sinkiang is sometimes known as Eastern or Chinese Turkestan.

Sinkiang is a land of oases. Most of the plains are too arid for grazing and the mountains are too rugged. Wherever semipermanent streams descend from the highlands, irrigation ditches spread the water over their alluvial fan. Each such oasis commands a bit of desert, an irrigated area with the principal city, barren foothills, and well-watered mountain valleys upstream. Each settlement is largely independent of its neighbors along the highway.

The only important oases along the south of the Tarim Basin next to the Altyn Tagh are Yarkand, with an area of 810 square miles and a city population of 60,000, and Khotan, with an irrigated area of 620 square miles and a city of 26,000. The most important settlements lie at the southern base of the Tien Shan. In the west is Kashgar with 1,000 square miles under cultivation and a city population of 35,000. Farther east is the Aksu-Ust Turfan oasis with 600 square miles and 20,000 people in Aksu. Other centers are Maralbashi, Kucha, Karashar, Korla, Turfan, and Hami. The population of these oases averages 300 people per square mile.

The oases of Dzungaria are less noteworthy. None of importance line the Altai where the more abundant grassland changes the economy from irrigated agriculture to that of pastoralism. At the northern foot of the Tien Shan are Hsihu, Manass, Tihwa, Kuchengtze, and Barkol.

Safe agriculture is largely limited to these areas of dependable water. Wheat, kaoliang, millet, beans, rice, excellent fruit, tobacco, and cotton are the chief crops. Widespread ruins of abandoned cities and ancient irrigation systems suggest a larger population in the past, presumably owing to more abundant rainfall. Not all such evidence has this interpretation, however, for some settlements are known to have been abandoned because of diversion of water upstream, the development of alkali or saline soils, or political troubles. Any expansion of crop acreage is tied up with reorganization of the water supply. Dry farming may offer some possibilities in Dzungaria.

Many oases are supplied by underground tunnels, known as karez from their Persian name, often several miles in length, which bring water down alluvial slopes. These tunnels prevent evaporation losses and are close enough to the water table to check seepage. Where they collapse, an oasis may be abandoned.

The great mountain system of Sinkiang is the Tien Shan which has a length of 1,000 miles in China plus its westward continuation into the Soviet Union. This is the highest range in Asia north of Tibet. Elevations within Sinkiang reach 23,616 feet in Khan Tengri in the west and 17,712 feet in the Bogda Ola north of Turfan in the east. Numerous long glaciers descend from extensive snow fields. Part of the topography is very rugged; elsewhere there are uplifted peneplains and broad valleys covered with alpine meadows.

To the west the Tien Shan system divides to surround the broad and fertile Ili Valley, which drains to Lake Balkhash. Ili is famed in Chinese history as the most remote place of banishment.

The other mountains of Sinkiang are the narrow Altai in the north, largely in Mongolia, and the Altyn Tagh on the south, outermost rampart of the Tibetan highland with elevations over 20,000 feet. Along the Soviet frontier in the west is a series of ranges which completely close in the Tarim Basin and almost block passage from the Dzungarian Basin. The only lowland gaps are those referred to earlier in connection with travel. In the far north is the valley of the Black Irtysh at a height of about 1,500 feet between the Altai and the Tarbagatai, with elevations of 13,553 and 11,910 feet near the frontier, respectively. Farther south is another corridor near Chuguchak, not so low but most used. The classic Dzungarian Gate at 1,060 feet elevation is a graben between the Tarbagatai and the Dzungarian Alatau which here forms the northern spurs of the Tien Shan. This is the lowest pass in all central Asia and famous for its strong winds.

The main river of Sinkiang is the Tarim. All streams that descend from the encircling mountains seek to reach it but many evaporate, sink into the earth, or are used up for irrigation en route. There is almost no cultivation along its banks. The Tarim gives its name to the entire basin, the central part of which is the nearly rainless Takla-makan Desert. Only one stream from the south persists across the desert. Much of the Takla-makan is filled with great sand dunes, more developed here than anywhere else in Asia except possibly southern Arabia. Travel across the central desert is virtually impossible. Fine dust derived from the beds of withering streams and the deflation of soft sediments has been blown into accumulations of loess on the encircling mountain slopes.

Lop Nor is the terminal lake for the Tarim River. This salt lake in southeastern Sinkiang has had a unique history. Two thousand years ago it occupied a site near

90°E. and 41°N., with the now ruined trade city of Loulan on its banks. Later the river was diverted southward and a new lake developed near 88°E. and 39°N., leaving the original Lop Nor a salt-encrusted flat. Sven Hedin has recently shown that the Tarim has now returned to its earlier course and that the original site of Lop Nor is again a lake. The alternation from basin to basin appears to be the result of sedimentation, raising the level of first one then the other higher than the first. When dry, wind deflation excavates a part of the silt.

In addition to the main basin there is the famous Turfan Depression, 928 feet below sea level.

To the north of the Tien Shan is Dzungaria, unlike the Tarim in several particulars. Its plain is open on both east and west, there is no unifying river, and sand dunes are less developed. The longest stream is the Manass which sometimes reaches its terminal lake of Telli Nor at an elevation of 951 feet. In 1928 the lake was completely dry, for the basin had become so full of silt that the river had been diverted to the east.

No area in the world is so remote from the ocean, so that Sinkiang is almost entirely cut off from the moisture and the moderating influences of the sea. Few air masses ever reach it from the Indian, Pacific, or Arctic oceans. The Atlantic is even more distant, and westerly winds from that ocean must first cross the mountains of Europe and nearly 4,000 miles of Asia, but such rainfall as Sinkiang receives appears to be largely of Atlantic origin.

Whereas all of Sinkiang is arid, the Tien Shan separate an exceptionally dry south from a slightly less arid north. Thus the north slopes of the Tien Shan facing Dzungaria, and the Atlantic, are more humid than those on the south facing the Taklamakan. An important fringe of poor grazing

land follows the northern edge of the Tien Shan, and a much richer belt of steppe borders the southern Altai. These grass-

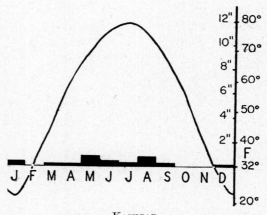

KASHGAR
Elevation, 4,255 feet; average temperature, 54.6°F.; total precipitation, 3.5 inches.

lands make it possible for nomads to migrate east and west with their flocks. They were the routes used by the Mongols in invading western Asia under Genghis and Kublai Khan. The Tarim Basin has no such continuous grasslands, and the population is limited to fixed oases, tens of miles apart.

There are few meteorological stations, but Kashgar reports 3.5 inches and Yarkand 0.5 inch of rain a year, based on short observations. Precipitation fluctuates widely from year to year and includes both winter snow and summer rain. On mountain slopes, the amount may reach 20 or 30 inches, with the maximum at intermediate elevations and drought above and below. Thus forests grow on the middle slopes of the Tien Shan from 5,000 to 9,000 feet, above which are upland meadows. Sheep and cattle from the lowlands are pastured on these grasslands during the summer. The snow line lies higher than three miles. Nomads are able to pasture their flocks on the upper Tien Shan and Pamirs throughout the year.

In this arid landscape, temperatures from season to season and from day to night differ sharply. Few deserts in the

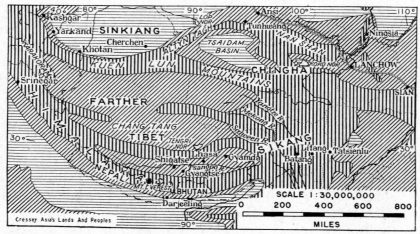

The pattern of Tibet. Plains are shown in horizontal lines, hills in diagonal lines, and mountains in vertical lines.

world have greater extremes. Summer temperatures often exceed 100°F., with a July average of 80°F. or more. The Turfan Depression has recorded a maximum of 118°F. and a July mean of 90°F. January averages are considerably below freezing, with several stations reporting less than 22°F., so that the few lakes and rivers freeze over. Hedin has measured −25°F. at the beginning of January in the central Takla-makan.

Tibet

There is nothing in Asia quite like Tibet. Three-fourths of its million square miles lie above 10,000 feet, and in large areas all elevations exceed 16,000 feet. Within the Himalayan and Karakorum ranges alone there are 50 summits over 25,000 feet high. Much of the country is a desolate highland plain without vegetation or nomadic possibilities. Elsewhere a milder climate and adequate rainfall permit some agriculture.

Tibet is so variously defined that it is well to compare the extent of topographic and geographic Tibet, the great highland

between the Tarim Basin and the plains of India, with the various political divisions involved. In the far west is the Indian native state of Kashmir, while parts of the Punjab and United Provinces reach into The Himalaya. Nepal and Bhutan are independent kingdoms, now related to Britain but once tributary to China.

The eastern part of Tibet lies in the Chinese provinces of Chinghai and Sikang set up in 1928, plus corners of Kansu and Szechwan. A large area in the northwest is theoretically within Sinkiang. This leaves less than half of the plateau for Farther Tibet, the semiindependent Chinese outer territory governed from Lhasa. Farther Tibet is credited with 349,419 square miles and about 1,500,000 people. The entire plateau of geographic Tibet may have twice that number.

Within Tibet are seven physical regions, as follows:

A. The Himalayan System in the south, made up of three parallel ranges.

B. The Karakorum Mountains in the west, between The Himalaya and the Altyn Tagh.

C. The Tsang Po Valley north of The Himalaya.

D. The Chang Tang Plateau, covering much of northern Tibet.

E. The Altyn Tagh and Kuen Lun systems in the north.

F. The Tsaidam and Koko Nor basins between the Altyn Tagh and the Kuen Lun in the northeast.

G. The "Land of Great Corrosions" in eastern Tibet, often known as Kam.

A. The Himalaya extend 1,500 miles in a great arc. The southernmost range, termed the Siwaliks, rises abruptly from the plain of the Indus and the Ganges. Although elevations reach 5,000 feet, these Outer Himalaya are known as foothills. To the north are the Lesser Himalaya, 7,000 to 15,000 feet. The Great Himalaya, still farther north, have an average crest line of 20,000 feet. In this range are most of the giant peaks, such as Nanda Devi in the United Provinces, 25,645 feet, Mt. Everest in Nepal, 29,141 feet, and Kinchinjunga in Nepal, 28,146 feet.

B. The Karakorum Mountains in the west are said to be the whitest, snowiest, and iciest range outside polar regions. They include the world's second highest peak, K², with an elevation of 28,250 feet. Within this area are numerous glaciers 30 and 40 miles long. The famed Karakorum Pass, 18,270 feet in elevation, lies to the northeast outside the Karakorum Mountains. Further details on The Himalaya and Karakorum will be considered in the chapters on India.

C. The Tsang Po is the local name for the upper Brahmaputra River where it flows eastward across southern Tibet. Since this area contains the central or U province with Lhasa as the capital, it is sometimes known as Central Tibet. Within this region are several other important towns, such as Shigatse and Gyangtse. This is the lowest part of Farther Tibet and the most populous. The Tsang Po flows at an elevation of 12,000 feet and is more or less navigable by native craft for 400 miles.

Although the peaks of The Himalaya rise 10,000 to 15,000 feet above the Tsang Po lowland, the passes from India are no more than 3,000 feet and in several cases only a few hundred feet above the floor of the valley.

D. The largest part of Tibet lies in the region of Chang Tang, extending from 80 to 92°E., and from 31 to 36°N. This part of the plateau is a series of desert playa basins and massive but low mountains, all at elevations over 16,000 feet. Scoured by the wind, baked by the sun, and cracked by frost, these desolate uplands have a grandeur of their own but are not a feasible home for man.

Within Chang Tang are hundreds of lakes, both fresh and salt, and many square miles are whitened by a surface crust of salt or alkali. Some salt lakes are known not as lakes but as salt pits; potash, soda, and borax are found around their margins. The largest lake of the region is Tengri Nor, with an area of 950 square miles. The Chang Tang is too cold and dry for grass, trees, or cultivated crops. For eight months or more the ground is frozen, but in summer large areas become swampy, especially where external drainage is lacking.

Scores of partly explored mountains trend roughly east and west. The southernmost range is a massive chain, variously known as the Kailas or Nyenchen Tang La, and described by Sven Hedin as the Trans-Himalaya. The average elevation is greater than The Himalaya, as are also the passes, but the peaks are lower. Other important ranges farther north are the Tang La, the Dungbura, and the Kokoshili.

E. The Altyn Tagh and Kuen Lun systems are the northern counterpart to The Himalaya. The Altyn Tagh rises directly from the Tarim Basin of Sinkiang to heights of 17,000 feet. Its eastward extension in

Kansu is called the Nan Shan, of which the Richthofen Mountains form the outer range with elevations touching 20,000 feet.

Towering mountains and precipitous canyons separate the Szechwan Basin from the highlands of Tibet. This is the tea route from Yachow to Tatsienlu and Lhasa. (*Courtesy Robert F. Fitch.*)

The Kuen Lun lies close to the Altyn Tagh where they join the Pamirs in the west, but diverges eastward. There is a fairly continuous series of peaks of 20,000 feet and over in the west. Toward the east, elevations are somewhat less and the chain is known as the Amne Machin, which continues into China as the Tsingling.

F. The Tsaidam and Koko Nor basins are enclosed within the eastern Altyn Tagh and Nan Shan. The former is a vast desert swamp at an elevation of 9,000 feet, while the latter holds a beautiful lake at a height of 10,500 feet in the midst of a mountain-rimmed basin. Koko Nor has an area variously given as 1,600 to 1,800 square miles and is the largest in Tibet; like most others it is salty. Both areas are semidesert with very meager pastoral possibilities.

G. Eastern Tibet is a land of great canyons and intervening high ranges, with a general northwest to southeast orientation. It is known to the Tibetans as Kam, or as the "Land of Great Corrosions." Here are the Hwang, Yangtze, Mekong, Salween, Irrawaddy, and their tributaries. Although the rivers flow at elevations of slightly over a mile, there is so little level land in the valleys that most people live at altitudes between 9,000 and 13,000 feet. Because of the more abundant rainfall, extensive forests cover the lower slopes.

In southeastern Tibet these rivers plus the Brahmaputra approach within 400 miles of each other, but on leaving the plateau they diverge so that their mouths are 2,000 miles apart. Since each river is in a deep gorge and intervening ridges are sharp crested, cross-country travel between India and China is very difficult.

The easternmost mountains, bordering Szechwan and Yunnan, are known to the Chinese as the Tahsueh Shan, or Great Snowy Mountains. Numerous peaks exceed 20,000 feet and are glacier clad. As an expression of decreasing moisture northward toward the heart of Asia, the snow line rises from 13,500 feet in Yunnan to 18,000 feet in Kansu. The highest peak is Minya Gongkar, southwest of Tatsienlu. The elevation is 25,250 feet.

The climate of Tibet is conditioned by its great elevation and by the encircling mountains. High altitudes and thin air join with intense insolation and strong radiation to produce sharp temperature contrasts between day and night as well as from the dry winter to the somewhat moist summer. Conditions differ widely, for whereas the vicinity of Lhasa has a mild *Cwb* climate (Koeppen symbols), the northern plains are a cold desert, *EBw*, and the windward slopes of The Himalaya have subtropical conditions.

Most of Tibet is cut off from the summer Indian monsoon by the Himalayan barrier, especially in the west where pressure gradients and winds parallel the mountain front. In the southeast, moisture-bearing winds blow up the valleys of the Brahmaputra, Salween, Mekong, and Yangtze and bring summer rain to the Tsang Po lowland. Almost none of this moisture crosses the Nyenchen Tang La Range.

The difference between temperatures during the day and at night may exceed 80°F. In the short summer the thermometer may reach 90°F., while in winter travelers have recorded −40°F. The winter cold is intensified by strong winds.

In the southern agricultural districts seed cannot be sown till April. Autumn comes early, and the crops must be gathered by the middle of September, for night frosts then become very severe even as low as 12,000 feet above the sea.

A climatological station has been established at Lhasa since 1935, and the available records to 1938 indicate a more mild climate than was previously recognized, certainly unrepresentative of most of Tibet. The city lies at 12,243 feet elevation and is surrounded by mountains that rise 3,000 and 4,000 feet above the smooth floor of the Lhasa River. The climate of Lhasa consists of two distinct seasons, the rainy or growing season from May to September, and the dry or cold season of the remaining months. Spring and autumn are brief. Local topography obscures wind directions, but the southeast monsoon is clearly developed in summer. In winter the westerly winds tend to be stronger and last longer. Mean temperatures range from 32°F. in January to 64°F. in June, with an annual average of 48°F. The latter is exceptionally mild for the latitude and altitude. The highest temperatures are in May, before the heavy

rain, as in the Ganges Valley. Frost occurs on 225 days a year. The annual rainfall average for 1935, 1937, and 1938 was

A Tibetan pilgrim on his way to the monastery at Kumbum in Chinghai. Although this photograph was taken in July, felt clothing is worn even in summer.

18 inches, but the rainfall was raised to 198 inches in 1936. There is plenty of sunshine at Lhasa, and even in the rainy season it is unusual not to have patches of blue sky for two days in succession.

The shortage of water causes most of Tibet to be uninhabited and makes travel hazardous. Most of the population lives in the south and east, where lower elevations provide meager agricultural and grazing possibilities. The chief food is parched barley or tsamba and a tea made from sour milk and brick tea as in Mongolia.

The yak is the typical draft animal, a long-haired form of cattle whose shaggy appearance exaggerates his massive proportions. Both yak and mules carry about 170 pounds but, while loaded mules travel 20 to 25 miles a day, and donkeys 10 to

15 miles, yaks cover even less. The yak needs a longer period for grazing than the other animals since he is fed no grain, but

mountains and deep valleys via Gyamda, Chamdo, Batang, and Litang to Tatsienlu west of Chengtu. Since this leads at right

The Potala at Lhasa is the headquarters of Lamaism and the home of the Dalai Lama. Few structures in all Asia are more imposing. (*Ewing Galloway*.)

no other animal is so well adapted to Tibetan travel. Sheep and goats are used for transport purposes in western Tibet and carry 20 to 25 pounds each.

The main highways focus on Lhasa. The Northern Road leads northeast across mountains nearly 20,000 feet high past Koko Nor to Tangar west of Lanchow. Caravans take about 50 days for the journey, usually traveling in summer on account of the more abundant grass and water as well as the warmer weather. Yaks are used across the Chang Tang in summer, and camels in winter.

The Chinese Road, also known as the Tea Road, runs east from Lhasa over high

angles to the trend of the mountains, the route presents great difficulties but is used extensively.

The South Road from Lhasa leads to Gyangtse, whence roads continue to Sikkim, or to the very important trade center of Kalimpong near Darjeeling. Mail covers the 330 miles from Lhasa to Gangtok in India in eight to ten days.

The main West Road runs up the valley of the Tsang Po past Lake Manasarowar to Gartok on the upper Indus and continues to Leh, the capital of Ladakh, 900 miles from Lhasa.

In the far west are trails that connect India and Sinkiang, either across the Burzil and Hunza passes from Srinagar to Kashgar, or farther east over the Karakorum Pass.

Lhasa is the Mecca of Tibet and the dream city of explorers throughout the world. The city lies in a sheltered valley where it is possible to raise vegetables, apples, and peaches, and many flowers. Bamboo and trees grow well, but the hillsides have been denuded for fuel. The city has electric lights and telephones. The crowning feature of the city is the monastery palace of the Dalai Lama, known as the Potala. This is the climax of Tibetan architecture and one of the most majestic buildings in the world.

Lamaism governs many aspects of Tibetan life, political as well as spiritual. Control is divided between the Panchan Lama at Tashilumpo, the traditional spiritual head, and the more politically powerful Dalai Lama at Lhasa. The fourteenth Dalai Lama was installed in 1932. Monasteries serve as centers of industry and learning, as well as for religious pilgrimage.

Chinese interest in Tibet dates from 650 when a Chinese expedition entered Lhasa. In 1209 Tibet was conquered by Genghis Khan, and in 1270 Kublai Khan became a convert to Lamaism and set up the rule of priest-kings. Chinese control continued intermittently until 1911 when the Amban in Lhasa was killed and all Chinese expelled. Only since 1932 has it been possible for Chinese again to send representatives to Lhasa. British influence developed late in the nineteenth century and has continued to be effective, with a telegraph line to India, a Tibetan army trained by Indian officers, and frequent British missions in Lhasa.

CHAPTER 9

CHINA IN THE NEW WORLD

Nationalism

From the beginning of the war with Japan in 1931, the issue was whether China was to be colonial or independent. That question is settled but the consequences remain. Until the Revolution of 1911, government was a function of the Emperor, organized patriotism scarcely existed, and public opinion was apathetic. Only with the establishment of the Nationalist Government in 1928 did a tide of national consciousness sweep over the country. Few aspects of wartime China so surprised her foreign friends as the depth of patriotism and unity. China has now demonstrated her right to a place in the forefront of the United Nations.

But what kind of China is emerging? Will she follow the socialist formula of the Soviet Union with detachment from world trade, will she pattern after the democratic United States, or will China relapse into civil war and chaos?

The key to enduring peace in eastern Asia is a strong China, so strong that no foreign nation will again be tempted to seek special privilege. If any residue of alien power remains on Chinese soil, its presence will provoke further trouble. China must be so powerful in economics and in government and in spirit that she is completely master in her own house. Japanese imperialism failed just as did that of Europe; and it is inconceivable that any other country can succeed in keeping China in bondage. China has always been the dominant nation in her part of the world,

and it appears probable that she will so continue.

In terms of territory, this means that China insists upon the complete restoration of foreign concessions at Shanghai, Hankow, and Tientsin, and of territory ceded or leased under duress such as Hongkong and Kowloon (to Britain), Macao (to Portugal), and Kwangchowwan (to France). Manchuria must unquestionably be restored, and the transfer of Japanese investments there may in some measure serve as indemnity. Outer Mongolia presents a special problem, for its population is non-Chinese and the interests of the Soviet Union are strong. Other territorial changes will be considered in a later section.

During the period of twentieth century unification, an antiforeign nationalism was used as a rallying cry to rouse the people. In the postwar decades, an intense patriotism will continue, in part to assert a fully regained sovereignty and in part to unify public opinion in the tasks of reconstruction. To the extent that this may make China unwilling to invite foreign assistance, it will be unfortunate both for China and for the world.

Just as China was unprepared for war, so she is not ready for the demands of peace. The needs for industry, transport, and public utilities greatly exceed the available capital and technological skill. Unless China should decide to spend decades in lifting herself by her own bootstraps, outside assistance is essential. But it need not carry imperialist restrictions as heretofore.

It seems probable that during the second half of the twentieth century, China will experience a great and spectacular renaissance, comparable to that of the Soviet Union between the First and Second World Wars and of the United States after the Civil War. Geographic factors all point to China's leadership in eastern Asia and to her place as one of the major world powers. Problems of social transition and political organization lie outside geography, but a nation cannot utilize its resources without coherence and purpose. It will be regrettable if China's nationalism should lead her to a self-sufficient autarchy rather than cooperative internationalism. This issue will determine whether China is to be reoriented toward her seaports or will seek self-sufficiency in the interior.

Sun Yat-sen, founder of the Republic, recognized China's need for external aid in his volume entitled "The International Development of China." It seems probable that his attitude toward foreign assistance will guide postwar developments.

China's Economic Potential

The three great geographic assets of China are coal, man power, and location. Minerals are present in only modest amounts and the soil is good but so inadequate in terms of population that there is little room for industrial crops or export surplus. Extensive forests may be grown on hillsides. The country almost lacks petroleum, and where water power is available it is also seasonal. Despite such shortages, China can look forward to a far greater industrial future. Certainly no other country in eastern Asia is so well endowed as a nation; per capita possibilities are more modest.

The mineral resources of China are varied, and their exploitation is a matter of metallurgy, economics, and political policy. Location and world prices are quite as important as geological origin. It is possible that China has enough of most metals to supply all the industries that can be built for several decades. Coal without iron ore is better than iron without coal, for coal is the key to chemical industries, to cement, and to power. China's coal supply is very great and well distributed, though not all is of metallurgical quality.

China's millions provide the world's largest source of labor. At present they are inefficient, but there is no reason why two generations of training may not make labor as skilled as in Europe. A limited diet and a somewhat enervating climate are handicaps, but the sheer bulk of China's man power is impressive. The new China has an enormous amount of work to be done in building roads, controlling rivers, improving agriculture, developing forests, operating factories, and improving housing. The people to do the job are available.

Location is a geographic resource, for the possession of material assets is of little value in Antarctica or central Africa. Most of China's economic potential lies in areas accessible to the seacoast, which in turn is at the meeting point on the main sea routes from Europe and from North America. In the territory between India, Australia, and Soviet Siberia, China has no possible rival except Japan, which is dynamic but poor.

Starting with the early 1930's, China was experiencing spectacular developments in road building, city rehabilitation, and education, all of which were arrested by the Japanese invasion. Postwar China faces exceedingly urgent economic needs that touch all of her life. To list some of them alphabetically, they include agriculture, consumer goods, export products, housing and sanitation, hydroelectric power, industry both heavy and light, land reclamation and resettlement, military defense, mining, reforestation, river conservancy, roads and railways, shipping and port facilities, and urban reconstruction.

Some plan is essential. When the Soviet Union started its five-year programs it ruthlessly postponed the manufacture of consumer goods and started at the bottom with mining, transportation, heavy industry, and defense. Some such emphasis is needed in China, but other needs will not wait. Nor is it possible to duplicate the Soviet program here, even with comparable political and social ideology, for China lacks the mineral wealth of the U.S.S.R. and does not possess even the initial tools.

At the close of the First World War, Dr. Sun Yat-sen proposed a huge scheme of internal development and invited the outside world to participate. This envisioned the establishment of three great new ports, near Tientsin, Shanghai, and Canton, with an extensive network of railways radiating from each. Along with improved communications there was to be emphasis on water power, mining and industry, agriculture, irrigation, colonization, and reforestation. This program overlooked the momentum of established ports such as Shanghai, gave inadequate attention to the location and amounts of raw materials and of markets, ignored topographic barriers to communications, and greatly overestimated the settlement possibilities of Outer China. All these essential geographic items are basic to planning.

China's first need is inventory. Few major developments are justified until the possibilities are all clear. This was illustrated in the Soviet Union by the creation of steel mills in the Kuznets coal basin prior to the discovery of Karaganda coal much closer to the iron ore. China should not plan for heavy industry until the location of all available resources is known. Does China have unused land with soil and climate suitable for crops? Is the flow of certain rivers dependable enough to justify large hydroelectric installations? Can the metal of various ores be extracted economically? What population trends may be counted on? What areas if any will be strategically safe from invasion during the next war?

Within the first decade of peace, China must catch up with a century of progress in the west. For this she needs vast amounts of capital. As of 1937 and excluding the Manchurian provinces, the total modern industrial capital of China amounted to 3,807 million Chinese dollars, of which 74 per cent represented foreign investments.[1] Japanese investments in Manchuria reached five billion yen by 1941. This averaged less than $2 per capita accumulated by Chinese themselves. In contrast to this, the figure in the United States in 1930 was U.S. $430 or $1,433 in Chinese currency. Or if machinery per inhabitant is considered, prewar northwestern Europe has an index figure of 100, the United States 405, and China less than 1.

The industrial centers of prewar China were as follows:

A. Mukden-Dairen, with coal, iron, chemicals, soybean products, cement, and railway equipment.

B. Tientsin-Chinwangtao, with coal, salt, cement, glass, and cotton textiles.

C. Tsingtao-Tsinan, with coal and cotton textiles.

D. Shanghai-Hangchow-Nanking, with cotton and silk textiles, flour mills, cigarettes, shipbuilding, and miscellaneous light industries.

E. Hankow, with iron and agricultural products for export.

F. Hongkong-Canton, with shipbuilding, silk, and miscellaneous industries.

To these were added in wartime the small but impressive developments in Free China,

[1] FONG, H. D., K. Y. LIN, and TSO-FAN KOH, "Problems of Economic Reconstruction in China," Mount Tremblant, Canada: China Council, Institute of Pacific Relations (1942).

notably the Chungking area with coal and iron, and the vicinity of Kunming with tin, copper, and machine shops.

All these will continue to be important. New centers of industry should arise in the Shansi coal basin and in the mineralized belt across south central China. For strategic reasons, early attention may be concentrated on heavy industries in the southwest, notably near Siangtan in central Hunan, and around Chungking and Kiating in Szechwan. Although the lower Yangtze Valley does not have the largest resources, it has superior water transport for both river and ocean steamers and is fed by numerous rail lines. Here is the largest market, the greatest head start, and the easiest contact with imported materials and skills. Should China, like Japan, desire to import iron ore from the Philippines and Malaya, neither of which has proper coal, the Yangtze provides a good setting for steel mills. The Yangtze Valley is also the source of important agricultural exports. The center of this new industrial area may well be Hankow.

The new China must plan regionally, with balanced attention to the problems of all areas and adequate appreciation of geographic conditions. It should be clear from the preceding chapters that the possibilities of Sinkiang and of the Southeastern Coast are unlike, but each has its needs. Only a balanced China can be a strong China.

Foreign Trade

All figures on China's foreign trade since 1928 have been confused by changing tariffs, fluctuating exchange rates, and political developments. Every year since 1877 has shown a visible excess of imports over exports, but invisible items such as remittances from overseas Chinese and expenditures by foreign legations and missions probably bring the total trade into balance. Despite all handicaps, foreign business has grown, increasing sevenfold between 1900 and 1930.

Notable changes have occurred in the character of this trade. China was once self-sufficient and importers found it difficult to offer anything in exchange for tea and silk. Later on, there developed a large market for cotton cloth and thread, kerosene, cigarettes, matches, sugar, rice, and manufactured goods. China in turn exported unprocessed agricultural products. Between the First and Second World Wars the country came to weave much of its own cloth and make many of its simple factory needs. Owing to the cheapness of labor these articles were exportable to the markets of Southeastern Asia, where they successfully competed with products from Japan where efficiency was higher but where labor costs were also higher.

The new China will undoubtedly offer a large market, particularly to the United States. It is possible that the needs of Asia will be a significant factor in maintaining the industrial productivity of America. Trade with the Orient after the Revolutionary War and the War of 1812 was a major item in enabling the United States to keep going economically; this may again be true following the Second World War.

The China market has hitherto called for consumer goods which could be sold at very low prices, and Japan has been able to undersell other nations. Once China develops its own industrial capacity, the need for cheaper imports will diminish. Even a modest amount of planning will call for a great supply of producer goods, and it is in these that the United States excels. This includes mining equipment; smelters and refineries; factories for automobiles, paper, cement, and chemicals; railroad and highway equipment; and electric power plants. In addition there will be need for materials largely unobtainable in China such as gasoline, rubber, and some metals.

The development of an industrial system will bring large dividends, but only after decades. China will be hard pressed to pay for essential imports and will doubtless discourage the importation of luxury goods and of as many consumer products as possible.

If the western world desires to sell to China, it must buy in return. China will naturally make strenuous efforts to find markets for her goods, and these must largely be the product of her agriculture, mines, and cheap labor. Before the Second World War, the chief exports were soybeans and bean cake, raw silk, wool, hides, furs, egg products, tin, antimony, tungsten, and tung oil. Not all of these will regain their former prominence. Manchuria no longer has a monopoly in the world supply of soybeans; silk is partly replaced by synthetic substitutes but China might recapture the market from Japan; and wool and hides of better quality are available elsewhere. China's unique metals will continue to find a ready market. China once supplied the world's tea and might regain some of the market. Artistic items such as embroideries and lace, novelties, and products in which unskilled labor is important will increase.

China's trade has been concentrated with a few countries, but it is difficult to determine their proper rank on account of transshipment through the free port of Hongkong. Japan has probably led in the past but was closely followed by the United States. Great Britain was third, followed by Germany and France. A large trade also exists with the areas to which Chinese have emigrated, such as Indo-China, Thailand, Malaya, the Netherlands Indies, and the Philippine Islands. Taken together they surpass Britain.

The new China will have two chief areas of overseas trade interest: the United States and Southeastern Asia. From the latter will come petroleum, rubber, cocoanut oil, sugar, hemp, lumber, aluminum, nickel, chromium, manganese, and iron. To these areas China will ship cheap manufactured goods such as textiles, cigarettes, novelties, and articles requiring moderate skill. The United States will supply the tools for heavy industry, complicated machinery, some consumer goods, technological aid, and certain raw materials such as copper. In return China will export silk, hides and wool, tung oil, other agricultural raw materials, antimony and tungsten, and cheap labor goods. Unfortunately these do not appear likely to equal the value of essential imports.

A modernized China will have all it can do for decades to meet its internal needs and balance its foreign trade. The best market for Chinese products is at home. Instead of being a threat to world commerce, it offers a great market and a supply house. The industrialization of the Orient provides one of the best prospects for the prosperity of the West. China will dominate its corner of Asia, but it lacks the basic iron and associated materials ever to achieve first rank as an exporter.

Geostrategy

China emerges from the Second World War as one of the Big Four of the United Nations, weakest in actual achievement but with a very great potential in area and position. Before the end of the twentieth century she will probably have caught up with the West and regained her historic leadership in the East, provided that civil war does not retard her progress.

In this era of material civilization and power politics, China is well endowed with the essentials of political geography. These include large size, compact shape, advantageous location, natural boundaries, access to the ocean, reasonably satisfactory land forms, diversified if none too abundant minerals, and an agriculturally productive climate. Few nations are more fortunate in their geopolitical picture.

If China had not been huge, she might not have survived the Japanese invasion. One of a nation's greatest military assets is defense in depth. Without the ability to trade space for time, China could scarcely have held out. Even omitting the sparsely populated areas of Mongolia, Sinkiang, and Tibet, two million square miles remain. Large size is not synonymous with self-sufficiency, but within the diverse environments of Greater China there is a wide variety of resources. A large size at the same time brings problems in communications and the welding together of diverse peoples.

China's location is not of first rank for world commerce, but she is well situated with respect to a large trade area within which as a whole are exceedingly great resources and attractive markets. Her location is both continental and maritime. Two great ocean highways meet along the China coast; one from Europe via Singapore, the other from North America. Overland communications with the Soviet Union and India are inadequate but can be improved.

Many international disputes arise from unsatisfactory boundaries. China's frontier with India along The Himalaya is easily defined and defended. Next to Soviet Siberia the broad Gobi Desert interposes a different environment but there is no sharply defined boundary. A strong China pushes her control to the north of the desert, a strong U.S.S.R. pushes her influence to the southern margin in the form of the Mongolian People's Republic. The only part of China across which a foreign power might legitimately wish a transit route is in the far northeast where Manchuria projects into Soviet territory and blocks the normal avenue from Lake Baikal to Vladivostok.

China has a coast line 4,000 miles in length, without measuring irregularities. In comparison, the land frontier is 9,500 miles. The delta sections are deficient in good harbors, but on the whole there are adequate port possibilities and good access to the hinterland. The coastal Chinese have a long record of maritime interests, with native junks reaching Ceylon early in the Christian era. Nevertheless, China as a whole has been continental minded, and one of her current problems is to reorient her economic and social interests.

Whereas China has a long coast line, she does not enjoy unrestricted access to the sea. Korea and the Maritime Provinces of the Soviet Union block access to the Sea of Japan, hence the importance of the new Korean gateway at Rashin. To the east of Shanghai are the Liuchiu or Ryukyu Islands, once a Chinese dependency but taken over by the Japanese late in the nineteenth century. Formosa screens the Fukien coast, while the Philippines lie to the southeast. It is but natural that as large a power as China with historic claims to Formosa and the Liuchius should demand their retrocession.

The strategic advantages and disadvantages of topography were repeatedly illustrated during the war with Japan. Invasion was blocked by mountains, but internal strength is also handicapped. Towering mountains to the west and a broad desert to the north provide buffer zones. Except for the Central Mountain Belt, eastern China has no mountains higher or more rugged than the Appalachians, nor hills more difficult of access and utilization than the Appalachian Plateaus.

The mineral picture has already been considered in detail. With superabundant coal and passable iron ore, China is moderately well equipped for industrialization.

Southeast Asia as a whole, including the adjoining islands, is exceptionally rich. A strong China will presumably wish assured access to the South Seas, from where she will have to draw numerous mineral and agricultural products.

Too little attention is given to the importance of climate. It is clear that agriculture is intimately related to temperature and rainfall, but human health and energy are also tied up with climatic stimulus. World maps of climatic energy give intermediate rank to China, which in turn rates above the lands to the south where Chinese immigrants have captured much of the retail business.

Leadership in any part of the world depends partly upon factors such as these. China has a large and secure home base, and a commanding position in her larger region. Japan's location is as good but she lacks the security, the resources, the number of people, and the psychology of leadership.

China's immediate neighbors are Japan, the Soviet Union, India, and the countries of Southeastern Asia. With Japan, China has fought two wars in modern times, and even with victory in the second very large problems remain. Japan will be considered in subsequent chapters, but the problem transcends geography. As neighbors, these lands must learn to live together. A defeated Japan without her outlying possessions which gave her offensive military power should not again threaten China for a generation. An independent Korea, possibly under China's protection, will offer further security. Japan has enjoyed the advantages of a head start, but she does not have the geographic requirements in her homeland to hold a place among Class A powers. Her program for an East Asia Co-prosperity Sphere was motivated by her lack of domestic resources and need for markets,

but this dream has now disappeared. Neither India nor Southeastern Asia constitutes a conceivable military threat to China.

The future foreign program of the Soviet Union is not clear, but her policy toward China will presumably be social and economic rather than military. Overland communications are not adequate at present for sizable trade, and the rail haul is uneconomically long; return shipments are lacking. Outer Mongolia and Tannu Tuva present special problems. China will not willingly part with northern Manchuria, but the Soviet Union might with considerable justice ask for transit rights over the old Chinese Eastern Railway to Vladivostok.

Europe and North America are farther away but even more important for trade than these near neighbors. It is unlikely that either area will ever again be able to achieve imperialistic control in the Orient. German trade came back strongly between the First and Second World Wars and may do so again, but adequate capital and plant facilities are lacking. England is the chief rival of the United States but is farther away and has smaller resources. If the British Commonwealth should act as a unit, the situation would be different.

The external aspects of China's geostrategy which call for attention are fourfold. They involve economic access to the resources and markets of Southeastern Asia; colonization possibilities in the same area; transit corridors through northern Korea from Manchuria to the Sea of Japan, via northern Indo-China from Yunnan to the South China Sea, and across Burma for a window to the Indian Ocean; and military security through possession of Formosa and the Liuchius. The political status of the Paracel Islands south of Hongkong is not clear, but their ownership would add to

China's security. This points to a southern orientation of foreign policy, whereas internal policy looks westward.

These problems are of concern to a strong China; they are equally important to the United Nations. Although it is impossible to foresee distant centuries, it does not appear likely that China will become a threat to the rest of the world. The Chinese have a peaceful and democratic tradition and, whereas they will be supreme in their own realm, their country lacks the geographic factors that might make for world dominance. Under able leadership, China will find that she has the geographic resources with which to meet her geographic needs, provided her population remains within bounds.

CHAPTER 10

JAPAN'S NATURAL FOUNDATIONS

In Japan's quest for empire, she originally had but few assets; chiefly location and a virile and dynamic people. Although the homeland is poor, surrounding areas add important resources. At the height of her conquests in 1942, Japan was more nearly self-sufficient than the United States. Her conquered territory extended from the Aleutians 4,500 miles south to the Solomon Islands, and from Wake Island 5,000 miles west to Burma. This involved a land area of 3,250,000 square miles and a population of 300,000,000. Time was temporarily on Japan's side, for no other nation ever conquered so much territory with such riches so quickly or so easily.

Prior to Dec. 7, 1941, the Western World failed to appreciate Japan's economic and military potential, for they thought only in terms of the limited agricultural and mineral possibilities within Japan proper. Nor did America or Europe understand the enormous size and geostrategy of the Pacific. Japan's world position will be considered in Chapter 14, but her place can be evaluated only after the basic elements in her geography are clear.

Land Forms

The Japanese Empire is both insular and mountainous. Land and water are everywhere near each other, and the few plains are so small that one is almost always within sight of mountains. The encircling seas have such a large role that the geography of Japan is nearly as much hydrography as topography.

Four large islands make up Japan proper. The largest is Honshu in the center. This is the mainland and economic core of the country. In the southwest lie Shikoku and Kyushu, and to the north is the newer frontier island of Hokkaido. Hundreds of smaller islands cluster around these larger lands. The Empire also includes Karafuto and the Kurile or Chishima Islands in the north; the peninsula of Korea or Chosen to the west; and Formosa or Taiwan, the Liuchiu or Ryukyu Islands, and the mandated islands southward to the equator. "Manchoukuo" has been closely associated with Japan but has already been considered in connection with China. The term Old Japan is here used for Honshu, Kyushu, and Shikoku, leaving the balance of the Empire as Outer Japan. Unless otherwise indicated, most generalizations in these chapters deal with Old Japan. Japan proper covers 147,707 square miles, about the size of California, while the Empire has an area of 263,050 square miles including the Mandated Islands.

The Pacific Ocean is encircled by a series of rugged Tertiary mountains from Cape Horn through Alaska to Australia. Along the coast of Asia these form a festoon of mountainous island arcs, each with its ends curving inward toward the continent. Japan proper occupies one of these arcs, while the island possessions of the Chishima and the Ryukyu are similar arcs to the north and south. From north to south these arcs enclose the Sea of Okhotsk, the Sea of Japan, and the East China Sea.

If we could take away the encircling ocean, the Japanese archipelago would stand out as a great mountain range, with of which 60 have been active within historic times. Symmetrical Fujiyama, now officially spelled Huzizan, is the most famous of the

The summit crater of Fujiyama is the goal of more than 50,000 pilgrims a year. (*Germaine Kellerman, courtesy Japan Reference Library.*)

peaks rising five and six miles above their base. And if we could change geological history to moving-picture speed, we might observe the frequency with which volcanoes and block faulting and crustal folding have disturbed the configuration of Japan. Scattered sedimentary rocks reveal that the islands have been submerged at various times since the Pre-Cambrian, while widespread lava flows, ash deposits, and intrusions betray repeated igneous activity. In tectonics and topography, Japan is so young that there has not been time to round off the edges. Slopes are unusually steep and summits jagged.

Within this mountainous framework, the Japanese Empire has over 500 volcanoes, active peaks, although it has not erupted since 1707. Since many of the volcanoes are high and isolated, they are significant elements of the landscape. Earthquakes are common, with about 1,500 shocks a year. There are seven principal seismic zones: offshore along the margin of the continental shelf and the Japan deep, along the coast of the Sea of Japan, the western Inland Sea, from Osaka past Lake Biwa to Tsuruga, the Fossa Magna and Fuji zone, the Nasu volcanic chain in northern Kyushu, and the Ishikari depression in Hokkaido. Where the earthquake epicenters are near large cities, great damage results, as at Tokyo and Yokohama on Sept. 1, 1923. The destruction is especially devastating on unconsolidated rock, such as underlies many cities.

Within Japan proper is an infinite com-

Alluvial lowlands lie near the water table and are utilized for rice fields whereas the upper diluvial terraces cannot be flooded and are devoted to dry crops in larger plots. Youthful valleys cut into the terrace lands.

plex of topography, and yet an essential repetition of associated land forms. Insular Japan has intricate patterns of microdetail rather than the gross structures of China. According to Oseki, 73½ per cent of the slopes are over 15°,[1] and less than 15 per cent of the land is flat.

Land that is even approximately level is limited to discontinuous fragments of up-lifted sea floor, interior basins filled with debris, alluvial flood plains and deltas, and the dissected terraces of earlier streams or marine plains. Valley floors have a notice-

[1] Oseki, K., The Economic Geography of Japan, *Scottish Geographical Magazine*, XXXI (1915), 452.

able slope, and down them during the rainy season flow turbulent yet overloaded mountain streams, whose braided courses are strewn with sand and cobbles. On either side dikes guard the adjoining fields, for so much deposition has occurred that the bed of the stream may be level with or above the surrounding countryside.

Not all of the nearly level land is usable. Coastal swamps and stony river beds almost defy reclamation. The largest areas of unused level land are the old flood plains and coastal plains which now stand as terraces a few tens or even hundreds of feet above present stream levels. These former surfaces, graded to sea level when the land was lower but now uplifted and dissected, are known as diluvial terraces, in contrast to the present-day undissected surfaces called alluvial. In some plains they cover a quarter to a half the lowland area. Since within Japan proper. The total level area does not exceed 20,000 square miles, no larger than half the state of Ohio. The four

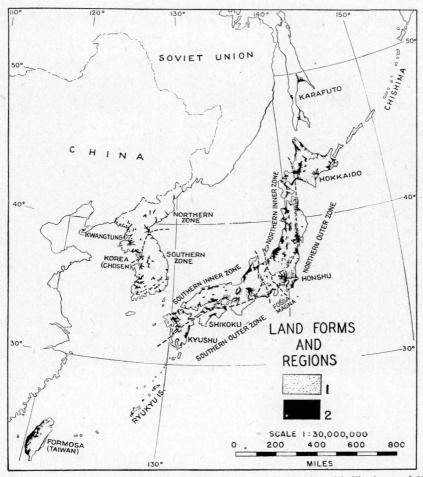

Level land covers but 15 per cent of Japan proper and may be divided into (1) diluvium and (2) alluvium. The major geomorphic regions of Japan proper are the outer and inner zones, each divided into southern and northern halves; between them lies the Fossa Magna. Korea likewise has a southern and a northern half.

diluvial terraces are built of sand and gravel and have a low water table, they are of limited use for Japan's great crop, rice. Irrigation is difficult.

These isolated and discontinuous plains, peripheral and interior, form the principal home for the 70 million Japanese who live

main islands contain about three dozen lowland areas large enough to identify, ranging from the Kwanto Plain near Tokyo, with an area of about 2,500 square miles, of which more than half is diluvial, to strips a few hundred yards in width and a few miles in length. In addition to the Kwanto

Plain, the principal lowlands are the Kinai Plain around Osaka and Kyoto, the Nobi Plain near Nagoya, the Echigo Plain near

other low and often swampy and usually near the mouth of a short torrential stream. The coast is highly irregular and has numer-

The Japanese Alps in central Honshu are a favorite summer resort for many Japanese mountain climbers.
(*Ewing Galloway.*)

Niigata on the western coast of northern Honshu, the Sendai Plain in the northeast, and the Ishikari, Tokachi, Nemuro, and Central plains in Hokkaido.

Japanese rivers are short, with the longest but 229 miles. Few of them are suitable for navigation, owing to their swiftness as well as to the variation in seasonal flow. There are many possibilities for hydro-electric power development, but sites for adequate reservoir storage are seldom available. Lake Biwa near Kyoto is the largest fresh-water body.

Fringing the sea are two types of coast line, one with cliffs and offshore islands, the

ous large embayments on the Pacific side. The ratio of 1 mile of coast line to 8.5 square miles of area, in contrast to 1 to 13 for Great Britain, reflects the nearness with which the Japanese live to the sea.

The geomorphic pattern of Japan proper may be grouped in either of two twofold divisions. The north differs from the southwest, and even more so the Pacific side differs from that next to the Sea of Japan. These four areas meet west of Tokyo in the Central Mountain Knot, or Japanese Alps, known to the Japanese as the Hida Range. To the east is the downfaulted Fossa Magna. Between the young Pacific folded mountains that form the Outer Zone, and the Inner Zone of block mountains lies a linear series of faults and tectonic depressions. From the island of Kyushu in the southwest to Hokkaido in the north, this boundary is marked by bold fault scarps and grabens. Contrasts between Pacific and Asiatic sides are especially marked in the southwest.

The Outer Zone along the Pacific has well-developed parallel ridges and depressions. The mountains are high and rugged, with few plains, and are underlain by a regular arrangement of crystalline schists and of Paleozoic and Mesozoic sedimentaries. Volcanic rocks are rare in the south but abundant to the north, especially in Hokkaido. The Inner Zone is a series of fault block plateaus, dissected into steep-sided hills and mountains. The geological structure is that of elongated domes with ancient sedimentary rocks and granitic intrusions greatly disturbed but without regular folding. Faulting and volcanic activity are widespread. The Inland Sea lies between the Inner and Outer Zones and occupies a series of submerged fault blocks, whose former mountain peaks now project as islands. Whereas few summits in the Outer Zone exceed 3,500 feet, altitudes of 6,000 feet are common in the Inner Zone.

Central Japan is cut by a transverse lowland which extends from the Pacific to the Sea of Japan, known as the Fossa Magna. Along the western margin of this depression is a fault scarp over 6,000 feet high, and at its base is a series of grabens. Great volcanoes have been poured out along this zone, notably Mt. Fujiyama, 12,461 feet high. The highest elevations and most alpine topography of the country are found just west of the Fossa Magna, with several peaks in excess of 10,000 feet.

Vertical zonation dominates the Japanese scene. Delta plains are bordered by diluvial terraces. Above them rise low foothills of weak Tertiary formations which merge with mountains carved in crystallines or old sedimentary rocks. Enclosed within these mountains are numerous alluvial basins at various elevations. Alpine land forms are found near the highest summits. Throughout the geographic story to follow, the greatest contrasts are up and down rather than between north and south. Climate, forests, agriculture, land use, and settlement all reflect this layering with altitude.

Land forms are thus basic in the understanding of how people live in Japan. With only one-seventh of the land approximately level, and much of the rest too steep to be terraced or otherwise utilized except for forests, the Japanese face inescapable problems. Viewed from the sea, Japan rises hill upon hill; seen from the land the panorama is water, water everywhere. The two dominant aspects of her physical setting are thus the restricted extent of level land and insularity. Over large areas the Japanese are plainsmen enveloped in mountains; elsewhere they became fishermen.

Climate

Japan's climate cannot be judged by latitude and solar insolation alone. It is warmer than comparable parts of China to the west, yet cooler than Mediterranean lands on the same parallel. Since the islands lie off the east coast of a great land mass, powerful continental influences are modified by marine conditions.

No simple summary can give an adequate picture of Japanese climate. The main islands have a latitudinal extent of a thousand miles, and the irregularities of topography introduce sharp vertical contrasts. If placed along the Atlantic seaboard, Japan proper would reach from Maine to Georgia, while the Empire would extend from Labrador to Brazil. Although summer conditions in Japan closely correspond to those in the northeastern United States, Japanese winters are colder. At both seasons Japan has higher humidity. The most populous part of Japan lies in the latitude of the Carolinas, 400 miles south of the American center of population.

During the summer, a flow of hot moist air moves over Japan from the Pacific. In winter months conditions are reversed with strong winds, cold and dry, from Siberia. Thus Tropical Pacific air masses dominate one season, while Polar Continental air masses rule the other; of these the latter are the more dynamic.

Several centers of action account for this basic circulation. During the winter the semipermanent anticyclone south of Lake Baikal pours great quantities of very cold dry air over Eastern Asia. Two main streams of this air cross the Japanese Empire; one moves eastward to the winter Aleutian low pressure area, the other and stronger is drawn southward to the equatorial low beyond the China Sea. This merging of clockwise winds from the continental high pressure area with oceanic low pressure counterclockwise circulation develops the winter monsoon.

With the arrival of summer, conditions are reversed. The high temperatures of northern China and Mongolia give rise to an area of low pressure. At the same time, high pressure over the north Pacific is intensified, producing an outblowing anticyclone. This results in the summer monsoon.

The winter monsoon blows from the west in Karafuto, from the northwest over Old Japan, from the north over the Ryukyu Islands, and northeast in Formosa. The summer monsoon has weak winds which are less dependable. They come from the southwest in Formosa, south and east over Japan proper, and east in Karafuto. Although the winter circulation produces

marked temperature contrasts from north to south, summer conditions are more nearly uniform throughout. Thus the January gradient is 2.6°F. per degree of latitude while in the summer it is 1°F.

Superimposed on this monsoon tendency is a parade of cyclonic and anticyclonic storms, moving northeastward out of China. These introduce a nonperiodic element, especially during the winter and spring. During winter months most of the disturbances come from the Yangtze Valley; at other seasons the sources are both central China and farther north, including even Siberia. These traveling storms move the length of the Japanese islands and continue via the Aleutians and Alaska to the United States.

During June and July weak tropical lows cross Japan and bring warm sultry weather. The rains of this period occur during the time of the plum blossoms and are known as the "Plum blossom rains" or Bai-u. This is a time of cloudiness, high humidity, protracted gentle rain, and high sensible temperatures. Convectional showers occur during the summer months, often in the warm sector of cyclonic storms.

When cyclonic whirls cross Japan during the time of Polar Continental air movements from Asia, the back side of each cyclonic storm with its northern circulation combines with the winter monsoon from the same direction to produce powerful northwest winds, while on the front side the two wind tendencies are in opposition. The reverse tends to be true in summer, with the southerly component of the cyclonic storm supplementing the southern monsoon, except that neither cyclonic storms nor the movements of Tropical Pacific air masses are so well developed at this season. Thus, at all times, the front and back of each cyclonic whirl tend alternately to augment or to cancel the monsoon tendency.

A third factor, typhoons, still further influences this circulation. These storms are apt to occur several times a month in the this warm current enters the Japan Sea, where it is known as the Tsushima Current. Thus summer winds from the Pacific are

Western Hokkaido has heavy snowfall for six months of the year although special plows keep the railway open for traffic. (*Pix.*)

late summer and fall. Although less severe than along the shores of China, serious damage may result. Destructiveness from typhoon winds is limited to the southern coasts, but torrential rain may be widespread with resulting floods from mountain streams.

The principal oceanic circulation in the western Pacific is the Kuroshio or Japan Current, the largest current in any ocean, with a volume 5,000 times that of the Mississippi. This bathes the southeastern shores of Japan, but turns eastward away from the coast near Tokyo. A branch of

warmed. The winter winds from Asia are moderated in temperature and given an increased moisture content as they cross the Japan Sea, while the warm offshore Kuroshio lies to windward of the islands and is scarcely effective. A minor cold current from the north, the Oyeshio or Okhotsk Current, hugs the eastern coast of Hokkaido and northern Honshu and produces lower summer temperatures and considerable fog. The situation is somewhat comparable to the Gulf Stream and Labrador Current in the Atlantic.

All parts of the four main islands have adequate precipitation, but the pattern is very patchy, owing to relief. Several sta- in a few localities. Except along the west coast, the precipitation maximum occurs at most stations of Old Japan during the

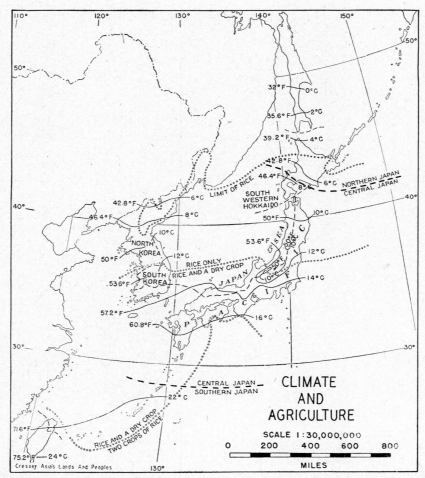

CLIMATE AND AGRICULTURE

SCALE 1:30,000,000

0   200   400   600   800

MILES

Cressey Asia's Lands And Peoples

Three major types of climate are present in the Japanese Empire, that of (*a*) Northern Japan, chiefly Hokkaido, Karafuto, and the Kuriles; (*b*) Central Japan which may be divided into the subregions of Southwestern Hokkaido, the Japan Sea side of Honshu, North Korea, South Korea, and the Pacific subregion which extends from Kyushu to the tip of Korea; and (*c*) Southern Japan which includes the Ryukyu and Formosa.

The major agricultural regions are fourfold. The first is in the south with two crops of rice a year, largely in Formosa but with small areas in Old Japan. To the north of it is a region of one rice and one dry crop. Northern Honshu and northern Korea raise one crop of rice only. The fourth region lies north of the limit of rice.

tions in the south along the Pacific receive over 125 inches and there is a similar precipitation maximum along the central part of the Japan Sea side. Rainfall in interior basins only drops below 40 inches summer, a result of the monsoon plus Bai-u and typhoon rains. Winter winds are dry as they blow out from the interior of Asia, but in crossing the Japan Sea they acquire some moisture and yield heavy snowfall on the western slopes of Honshu and Hokkaido. Snow remains on the ground along the west coast as far south as central Honshu; on the Pacific side, in contrast, only the northern end of the island has a snow cover.

August is the hottest month except in Formosa where July temperatures reach the maximum. Tropical clothing is worn everywhere during the summer even in Hokkaido, and the high humidity and sultry air are enervating. South of Tokyo, books, shoes, and clothing are quickly covered with mildew in summer. Mosquito nets are required almost the year around in southern Japan. The July temperature difference from southern Kyushu to central Hokkaido is but 9°F., whereas in January the range is 29°F.

Since the populous part of Japan is toward the south, many people spend some time in mountain or seaside resorts. For one not accustomed to it, it is particularly desirable to avoid the period of the "Plum blossom" rains from mid-June to mid-July.

The frost-free period, essentially equivalent to the growing season, ranges from 120 days in the interior of Hokkaido and 160 days in mountainous Honshu to 240 days along the southeastern coast. Thus two crops of rice may be grown in parts of Kyushu, Shikoku, and the southern peninsulas of Honshu.

Various attempts have been made to subdivide the Japanese Empire into climatic divisions. In the Koeppen classification, all of Old Japan except the highlands of northern Honshu belongs to the *Cfa* (mild winter, always humid, hot summer) type, while Hokkaido and Karafuto are classed as *Dfb* (severe winter, humid, cool summers). Most of Korea is *Dwb* (severe winter, summer rain, cool summer).

In terms of climatic conditions as they distinctly apply to Japan itself, Fukui has prepared a new classification in which the Empire is divided into three major divi-

sions.[1] These are shown on page 178. The first is northern Japan which includes the Karafuto and Hokkaido provinces, the former with five months with mean temperatures below freezing and the latter with four. Precipitation on the lowlands ranges from 25 to 40 inches, decreasing toward the north. Central Japan is the second division, characterized by moderate climates and a mean annual temperature below 68°F. It has five provinces: southwest Hokkaido, somewhat warmer than the rest of the island; north Korea with cold winters as in northern Japan but warmer summers and 25 inches of rainfall, the lowest precipitation in the Empire; south Korea, also dry but warmer than the north; the Japan Sea province with abundant winter snow which exceeds the summer precipitation; and the Pacific province, characterized by a summer precipitation maximum and mild sunshiny winters. This includes all of eastern and southern Honshu, Shikoku, Kyushu, and the tip of Korea. A third climatic division is southern Japan, with mean annual temperatures of more than 68°F. Separate provinces provide for the Liuchiu or Ryukyu Islands, the Ogasawara Islands, and Formosa.

There is a noticeable contrast between the cloudy and cool Japan seacoast, known as the shady side, and the warm Pacific coast, known as the sunny side.

Despite the wide contrasts within the Empire, all lowland areas except in the far north have adequate warmth and rainfall for agriculture. Slight differences in altitude result in marked differences in land use. Variations in orographic rainfall, temperature gradients, air drainage, and the length of critical growing periods restrict certain crops to certain elevations. This vertical zonation brings together within a few miles

[1] FUKUI, E., Climatic Division of Japan, *Geographical Review of Japan*, IX (1933), 1–19, 109–127, 195–219, 271–300 (in Japanese with English summary).

horizontally the climatic zones that would otherwise lie a thousand miles apart. Bamboo and rice are within sight of snow fields and the tree line. Japan's climate is as micropatterned as its topography.

Forests and Soils

Half of Japan is still covered with forests, though little of it is virgin growth. An additional 15 per cent is in brush or coarse grass. Almost all of this is in mountainous areas. Except for a few alpine meadows above the tree line, trees are almost everywhere the climax vegetation. Thanks to the absence of Pleistocene glaciation, the flora is exceptionally rich and diversified with a range from palms and orchids to maples and pines. Hillsides are clothed in rich verdure, in striking contrast to Chinese provinces in the same latitudes.

Fall foliage is especially glorious. Japan, Manchuria, and the northeastern United States are the finest areas in the world for brilliant yellow and red leaves of maple, oaks, and other deciduous trees, with the arrival of autumn. In the spring, flowering plum and cherry trees are renowned. Magnificent stands of ancient cryptomeria around temples, shrines, and old castles attest to Japanese appreciation of trees.

The vertical zonation of vegetation is especially noticeable in a country so mountainous as this. One may stand on the deck of a vessel along the shores of Japan and see this stratification rising from subtropical forms at sea level through successive climatic zones to boreal forests at heights of a mile or so. On the higher peaks there are tundra zones next to summer snow fields. Climate paves the way for this zonation of vegetation, which in turn influences soil types and thus land use. The beauty of travel in Japan is the wide variety of landscapes which are accessible in a short horizontal distance. These transitions, plus the mingling of relict forms of vegetation, make mapping of forest types difficult.

Bamboo, properly a grass rather than a tree, is widespread as far as northern Honshu. In general, a subtropical forest extends north to central Honshu near latitude 37°N., with broad-leaved evergreens such as camphor and some oaks. This is the northward limit of tropical forms.

Temperate mixed forests in northern Honshu and western Hokkaido are economically the most important for lumber. Maple, birch, beech, poplar, and oak mingle with fir, pine, hemlock, and cedar. Cryptomaria and pine are the chief commercial timbers. As one goes southward, these forms rise above sea level. In central Japan the boundary lies at 1,800 feet on Fujiyama and above 3,000 feet in Kyushu. Boreal forests cover the summits of the higher mountains in northern Honshu and the lowlands in eastern Hokkaido; fir and spruce predominate. Temperatures in the subtropical forest zone range from 55 to 70°F.; in the temperate forest zone, the mean annual temperature varies between 43 and 55°F.; while in the boreal forests averages are below 43°F.

Creditable progress has been made in reforestation, both for future timber and for flood control. On eroded slopes and the headwaters of streams, large areas have been planted as protective forests, and the traveler cannot fail to be impressed with the care that has been used.

Charcoal is an important forest product and the chief household fuel. Its value is almost equal to all timber. Many villages have their communal areas where it is produced for domestic needs, and it is a common sight to see lines of people coming out of the woods laden with bundles of charcoal. The annual value of charcoal is three-fourths the value of sawn timber.

Whereas the latter is largely from conifers, hardwoods are preferred for the former.

Despite improvements in all aspects of forestry, the supply is inadequate, so that both timber and wood pulp are imported. Oregon, Washington, and British Columbia are a large source of supply, and Manchuria is increasingly important. Hokkaido and Korea have the largest domestic reserves.

Soil studies in Japan have dealt with texture and underlying rock rather than climatic influences or profiles. Flood plain and delta sediments form the best agricultural land, with the sandy, recent alluvium favored over the coarser diluvium. Volcanic soils are generally infertile as they are derived from acidic lavas or ash. Many soils are so fresh that mature profiles have not developed.

Podsolized soils of various types cover Sakhalin, much of Hokkaido, and are present on higher elevations in northern Honshu and northern Korea. This roughly corresponds to the area of boreal forests. Northern Honshu is a region of brown forest soils, some of them slightly podsolized, and likewise of temperate forests. Similar soils and forests occur in central and southern Korea. The southern part of Old Japan and the tip of Korea have yellow and red forest soils with lateritic tendencies. Red tropical soils are limited to the lowlands of Formosa.

Mineral Resources

The story of Japan's mineral wealth is easily told. There is a wide variety of natural resources within Old Japan, but practically none of them is adequate for current industrial needs. Only coal, copper, gold, silver, and sulphur are present in large quantities, and of these only sulphur and gold are available for export. In normal years the Japanese Empire as a whole pro-duces but two-thirds of her copper, one-third of her zinc, one-third of her salt, one-fourth of her tin, one-twelfth of her lead, one-sixth of her iron, and one-tenth of her consumption of petroleum. Nickel, aluminum, and magnesium are entirely lacking. Even the domestic production of coal is but nine-tenths of the consumption, largely because of the necessity of importing special coking coals.

These shortages were almost all relieved by the conquests during the Second World War, when her mineral position became strong. The acquisition of Manchuria and other parts of China added important minerals, but Japan was economically vulnerable until she acquired Southeastern Asia. Raw materials were available in abundance, but problems of mining, refining, transportation, and fabrication required time for development.

Three commodities accounted for the overwhelming share of the total mineral output in 1936. Coal represented about 60 per cent, gold 13 per cent, and copper 11 per cent. Despite her material handicaps at home, Japan has achieved a great industrial development on the basis of imported raw materials, such as oil and scrap steel from the United States, and iron ore from the South Seas. The following paragraphs will consider power resources, the metals, and the nonmetallic minerals.

Japan is comfortably supplied with coal and hydroelectricity but has very little oil and no natural gas. Coal is widely distributed and predominantly bituminous of only fair quality. Almost none is suitable for high-grade metallurgical coke. Deposits are found in Paleozoic, Mesozoic, and Tertiary rocks, with the latter by far the most important. The official reserves as estimated in 1932[1] are as follows:

[1] The Japan-Manchoukuo Yearbook, Tokyo (1940), 355.

	Metric Tons
Proved reserves	5,960,000,000
Probable reserves	4,045,000,000
Possible reserves	6,685,000,000
Total reserves	16,690,000,000

These are distributed between Hokkaido, with 8,000,000,000 metric tons chiefly in the Ishikari Plain, Kyushu with 6,000,000,-000, and Honshu with 2,500,000,000. Reserves elsewhere in the Empire account for 2,500,000,000, giving a total for all Japan of something over 19,000,000,000 metric tons. Because of difficulties of mining, no more than half of this is economically usable.

Since the development of modern coal mining 60 years ago, the leading area of production has been northwestern Kyushu which supplies about two-thirds the output. Most of this comes from the Chikuho field south of Moji. The production of Japan proper reached 20,000,000 metric tons in 1912 and has been above 30,000,000 metric tons since 1933, except for two depression years. In 1941 production probably amounted to 55,500,000 metric tons within the Empire, which includes imports amounting to 5,000,000 metric tons from Korea, 2,500,000 each from Formosa and Sakhalin, and 4,000,000 metric tons from outside the Empire, largely China and Indo-China. Japanese coal is well suited for steamship boilers, so that Nagasaki has long been an important bunkering point for steamers from Europe and across the Pacific. Since domestic coal is generally unfit for metallurgical coke, it is necessary to import suitable coal from Penhsihu in Manchuria, Kaiping in north China, and Hongay in Indo-China.

Japan's per capita reserves, even including all possible deposits, amount to but 238 tons per capita as compared with 4,070 for the United Kingdom and 27,500 for the United States. Although production may be expected to continue for many years and should prove adequate for domestic needs in time of peace, there is no likelihood that Japan can increase her production of this basic source of power so as to compete in heavy industries with the leading countries of the world. Any great industralization must rest on imported coal.

The second great source of modern power is petroleum. Japan's two dozen producing districts extend from Karafuto in the north to Formosa in the south, with the principal area in the Niigata and Akita prefectures on the Japan Sea side of Honshu. There are about 4,000 wells, yielding an average production of less than two barrels per day. The 1941 production in Japan proper of 2,659,000 barrels is approximately equal to the daily yield in the United States, and represents but 0.1 per cent of the world production. An additional 1,000,000 barrels is secured from Formosa and concessions in Soviet Sakhalin. Despite strenuous governmental efforts over the past decade, there is little geological prospect that the output can be materially increased. Whereas imports in 1931 were seven times domestic yield, by 1939 imports had increased to over eight times domestic production.

In addition to large imports from the United States and the Netherlands Indies prior to the Second World War, fuel oil for the navy was distilled from oil shale in Manchuria. In 1939 the consumption of oil products in Japan amounted to 25,400,000 barrels. No commercial supplies of natural gas are reported.

The rugged topography and heavy precipitation of the central mountainous area lend themselves to the development of water power. In 1936 the total consumption of hydroelectric power amounted to nearly 20 billion kilowatt-hours as compared with yearly 5 billion kilowatt-hours of electricity produced by coal. Despite the 50 per cent growth of hydroelectric power in the previous five years, it was not possible to meet the demands, so that the use of thermal-electric power increased by 250 per cent. Japan still has undeveloped

three load centers around the Japanese Alps: Tokyo and Yokohama; Kyoto, Osaka, and Kobe; and Nagoya.

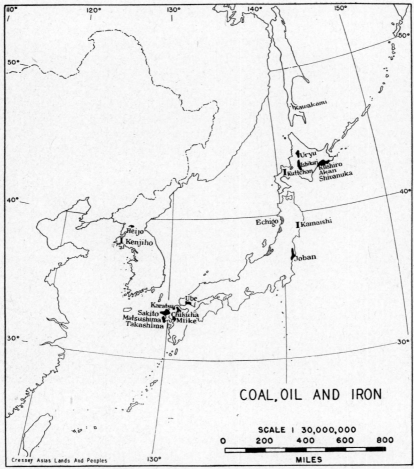

COAL, OIL AND IRON

SCALE 1 30,000,000

0   200   400   600   800

MILES

Cressey Asias Lands And Peoples

Japan's limited coal districts are shown in black, the oil regions are in ruled lines, and the sources of iron ore are indicated by a capital *I*. Only the coal is adequate for domestic needs.

water-power sites, but they are mostly small in size and lack adequate reservoir storage to equalize the highly seasonal flow. Out of an ultimate theoretical production of 10 million kilowatts, half is already in use. In 1936 there were 12,176,098 customers, but the number of lamps was but 3.6 apiece. The major use of electricity is in

Japan's resources of iron ore are especially insufficient. Reserves for the entire Empire are estimated at 90,000,000 metric tons, of which 10,000,000 are in Korea. This compares with some 5,000,000,000 tons in the United States. Less than a dozen deposits are in commercial production in Japan proper. Domestic output of iron ore in Japan proper for 1941 amounted to 935,000 metric tons largely in Hokkaido, which was but 13 per cent of the require-

Although Japan imported 35 per cent of her pig iron, the use of large quantities of imported scrap enabled her to carry on a

The hydroelectric plant on the Kiso River northeast of Nagoya has a capacity of 40,000 kilowatts. (*Ewing Galloway.*)

ments. The fivefold increase in the preceding decade reflects strenuous mining efforts rather than large reserves. The deficiency was met by importations from Korea, Tayeh in the central Yangtze Valley amounting to nearly 500,000 metric tons in 1940, Johore and elsewhere in Malaya to the extent of 1,874,000 metric tons in 1940, and the Philippine Islands which supplied 1,236,000 metric tons in the same year. British India has supplied as much as 1,000,000 tons annually plus 300,000 tons of pig iron. Australia has shipped several hundred thousand tons a year.

slight export of steel, chiefly to her colonies and to Manchuria.

Copper was the second most important mineral product in Japan until 1935, and the country ranks seventh in world production. At one time Japan had a large surplus for export, but prior to the Second World War she found it necessary to import substantial quantities of copper, largely from the United States. The 1941 production was 118,000 metric tons, plus 4,000 tons each in Korea and Formosa.

The production of gold and silver has long been of nominal importance, but in the 1930's the output grew rapidly, so that the value of gold production passed that of copper in 1936. Korea has overtaken

duction of tin and chromium. There are no domestic ores of aluminum in Japan proper, but bauxite has been discovered in the

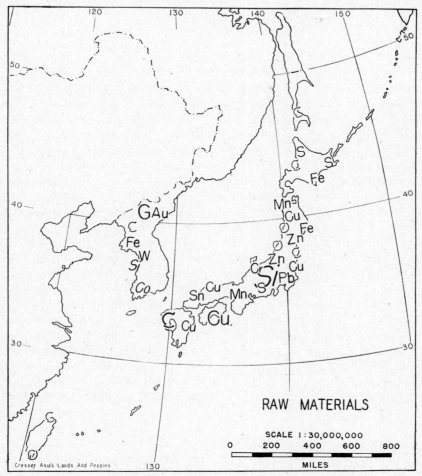

RAW MATERIALS

SCALE 1 : 30,000,000

0   200   400   600   800

Cressey Asia's Lands And Peoples

MILES

Japan's raw materials are diversified but for the most part are of limited quantity. Fuels are shown by shadow letters; C for coal and O for oil. Minerals are in vertical letters: Au—gold, Cu—copper, Fe—iron ore, G—graphite, Mn—manganese, Pb—lead, Sn—tin, S—sulphur, W—tungsten, Zn—zinc. Industrial agricultural products of significance are shown in italics: *Si*—silk, *Co*—cotton.

Japan proper in gold mining. By 1940 the gold production within the Empire was valued at $85,000,000. Three-fourths of the silver output is obtained as a by-product in the smelting of copper.

Zinc is much more plentiful than lead, amounting to about 60,000 and 15,000 tons, respectively. There is also some pro-

Palu group of the Mandated Islands. Less than half Japan's manganese is obtained at home. Korea contributes nearly 80,000 tons of graphite.

The most noteworthy nonmetallic resource of the islands is sulphur, one of the basic tonnage materials needed for industry. High-grade deposits are widely distributed, usually in association with volcanic rocks. The production in 1940 amounted to as shown by the figures in the accompanying table.[1]

Area	1913	1919	1931	1936
Japan proper............................	146,849,000	641,128,200	241,826,000	589,400,000
Korea...................................	8,204,000	25,415,000	21,742,000	110,430,000
Empire total............................	159,186,000	677,864,000	283,282,000	746,089,000

240,000 metric tons. The availability of sulphur furnishes a basis for the growth of such industries as paper, celluloid, and rayon. About a third of the production is available for export. Phosphate rock is mined in the Mandated Islands.

Salt is obtained from sea water, but the high humidity does not favor solar evaporation. Production around the Inland Sea is barely sufficient for salt in foodstuffs, and most of the industrial needs, which are twice those of foodstuff salt, are secured from East Africa and the North China coast.

Despite strenuous efforts for many years to increase the home supply of minerals, the percentage of import remains high. Thus in 1931 production of natural resources within the Empire amounted to 283,000,000 yen, with supplementary imports of 220,000,000 yen, a total sufficiency of 60 per cent. In 1936 the internal supply was valued at 746,000,000 yen which accounted for 61 per cent of the total with net imports amounting to 660,000,000 yen. The production of minerals within greater Japan has fluctuated widely since 1913,

It may be of interest to compare the production of certain basic resources in the Japanese Empire with those in the United States. America's output of copper is 7 times that of Japan; coal 10 times; iron 40 times; and oil 432 times. In comparing these figures, it should of course be borne in mind that the population of the United States is 25 per cent greater than that of the Japanese Empire.

The geology of Japan and her possessions is now well enough known to make it abundantly clear that there is no likelihood of great industrial developments in terms of her own mineral resources. There is not even enough for domestic needs, let alone world trade. Fortunately, Japan does have coal, although it lacks coking qualities. Economic or political conditions may make it feasible to import ores from the mainland, but it does not seem likely that Japan can permanently enjoy a dominant position in the mineral industry of eastern Asia. Her industrial future would appear to rely upon such resources as cheap labor, limited agricultural products, and skill.

[1] The Japan-Manchoukuo Yearbook, Tokyo (1940), 337.

CHAPTER 11

THE HUMAN RESPONSE IN JAPAN

The People

Japan's greatest assets, and likewise her greatest problems, concern people. Over 70 million live on the main islands and 30 million more elsewhere in the Empire. Within Japan proper the net annual increase has been over a million people in some years. Where can these islanders live, what can they do, how shall they be fed? Population pressure is no mere abstraction; it is an inescapable and increasing problem.

Japanese origins go back into obscurity. The earliest authenticated records date from the first century A.D., although legendary history places the first Emperor Jimmu in 660 B.C. Several racial elements have contributed to the people and culture of today. Some strains came from the south and are Indonesian, Malayo-Polynesian, and southern coastal Mongoloid; others are northern Mongoloid from within Asia. In terms of physical ethnography the southerly contribution is slightly dominant; culturally Asiatic influences are stronger.

Most of this blending preceded the beginnings of the Christian era and can be deciphered only by archeological evidence. The Japanese adoption of Tang dynasty civilization, Confucianism, many Chinese arts, and Buddhism is well known. On the other hand, house types and short stature point southward. One illustration will suffice. The Japanese custom of eating raw fish is found also in the East Indies, in Ceylon, and in Madagascar, but almost nowhere on the continent. A few alien tribes of boat people in southern China eat uncooked fish, but not the Chinese themselves.

Within the islands are three ancient culture centers. In southern Kyushu is the Satsuma area, which received racial and cultural contributions from the coast of south China prior to the arrival of the Chinese, from the South Seas, and possibly Oceania by way of the Liuchiu archipelago. On the west coast of Honshu was the local Izumo culture, closely allied to Korea and the Amur Valley tribes. The Yamato culture flourished in central Honshu and gave rise to the present civilization of Japan; it is in part a fusion of Satsuma and Izumo types. Its early contacts were with central and northern China, Korea, and even India. Each of these was to some extent superimposed on the indigenous Ainu culture, a very early human type which once covered most of the islands but is now pushed northward to Hokkaido.

Thus from the beginning, the Japanese have been a mixed group, influenced by imported cultures. Unlike self-sufficient China, Japan has been accustomed to cultural borrowing and adaptation. Other peoples were not necessarily barbarians without civilization. Such a historical frame of mind with its willingness to learn may help to explain the rapidity with which modern Japan has accepted ideas from the European world. Perhaps too, ethnography may suggest some of Japan's difficulties in understanding Chinese mentality and point to the South Seas as a more logical path of expansion.

The beginnings of Japanese life were all in the southwest, in Kyushu and western Honshu. As time progressed the in 1876–1879. Formosa was seized in 1895, the Kuriles taken over in 1875, and a beginning toward mainland possessions

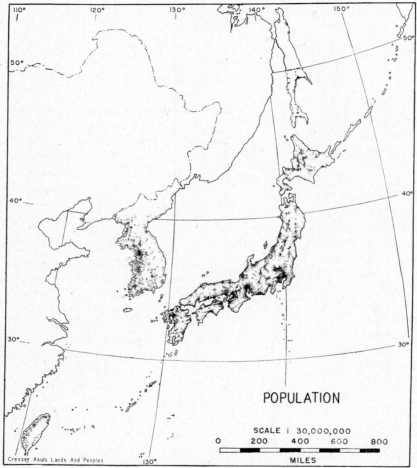

POPULATION

SCALE I 30,000,000

0   200   400   600   800

MILES

Cressey Asia's Lands And Peoples

Japan's population is strikingly concentrated in the coastal lowlands and interior valleys. The densest belt of population of Old Japan extends through the Inland Sea eastward to the Kwanto Plain in Tokyo.

Ainus were driven northward, but only with much difficulty. Lake Biwa marked an important boundary in early historic times, and the main island was not completely conquered until the close of the tenth century. Japan's imperial expansion is not a matter of the twentieth century alone. Much of the Liuchiu or Ryukyu chain was acquired in 1609 and the rest

was made in the Sino-Japanese War of 1894–1895. Korea was occupied during part of the seventeenth century.

The seventy million people of the main islands are distributed in close agreement with land forms. Wherever there are level land and fertile soil, no matter how surrounded by mountains, there are people. Modern urbanization but emphasizes this pattern. So close is the correspondence, that a map of population is at the same time a good representation of land forms, or Fragmentation and microdetail are as true of population patterns as of surface configuration.

Japanese rooms are separated by sliding partitions and the floors are covered with matting which is kept clean since shoes are removed upon entering a home. The maid is carrying a tub of rice. (*Germaine Kellerman, courtesy Japan Reference Library.*)

equally of cultivated land. Vertical zonation is obvious, for the areas of population concentration are all lowlands, and the density decreases with altitude. The Japanese live near sea level, and the good land is already filled to capacity and more.

Few regions have even population distributions. Even the pattern of the Kwanto Plain around Tokyo is highly irregular, owing to the distribution of alluvium and diluvium. Everywhere mountains interrupt settlement, so that isolation and difficulty of access characterize the human scene.

Population figures for the two centuries of the Tokugawa Shogunate (1602–1867) appear to be remarkably uniform, with little variation from twenty-six million. After the restoration of the Emperor Meiji in 1868, the population rapidly increased. By 1925, the population had doubled, and even the rate of increase was rising. In some measure, these additional millions are the responsibility of Admiral Perry, who opened Japan in 1853 and brought in the disrupting influences of the western world.

In 1940, the population of Japan proper numbered 73,114,308. That of the chief cities follows:

City	Population
Tokyo	6,778,804
Osaka	3,252,340
Nagoya	1,328,084
Kyoto	1,089,726
Yokohama	868,091
Kobe	967,234
Hiroshima	343,968

tion density in 1938 was 393 per square mile for the Empire or 490 in Japan proper. Such figures become meaningful only when seen in the light of cultivated area. In such a comparison, Japan has 3,116 people for each square mile of tilled land.

The crude birth rate stood at 30.3 per 1,000 in 1936, while deaths numbered 17.5. The net increase reached 1,028,623 in 1935 but declined to 653,000 in 1939 and

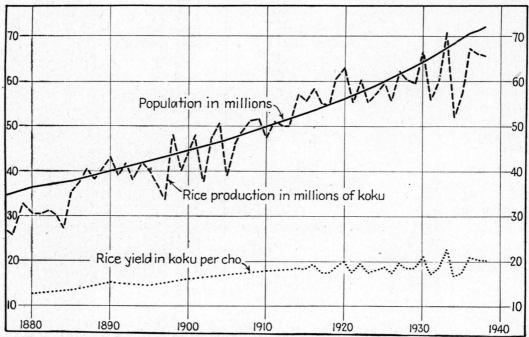

The population of Japan has shown a steady increase from 1880 to 1938, which has been matched by an increase in the total rice production (1 koku equals 4.96 bushels). Some of this increased rice has been derived from greater yields per acre (1 cho equals 2.45 acres); some from additional acreage. (*After Orchard, "Japan's Economic Position."*)

For 1938 in the dependencies of Korea, Formosa, and Karafuto there were 24,-327,326, 5,746,959, and 339,357, respectively; the leased territory of Kwantung in southern Manchuria, the South Manchuria Railway zone, and the mandated South Sea Islands accounted for an additional 1,339,-123, giving a grand total of 105,226,101 (1940). In terms of total area, the popula-

239,000 in 1940. Among large countries, Japan's birth rate stood next to India (34.9) and was nearly twice that of the United States (16.7).

With four babies born every minute, and no room for more agriculture, Japan faces her greatest difficulty. Fortunately each new mouth provides a pair of hands. So long as foreign trade flourishes or there is a war boom, there is a job for them in a factory or the army. Emigration has failed to care for the surplus, since the Japanese have shown little inclination to colonize either in their own Hokkaido or in Manchuria, or in subtropical areas such as Brazil. Immigration barriers keep them out of many countries.

Faced with agricultural overpopulation, the country has turned to industry; but without an adequate base of supplies or market at home, industrial Japan must first import raw materials and then export manufactured goods. A policy of international good will would thus seem imperative, but instead the nation turned to the gamble of war. Without a clear military victory and the subsequent economic exploitation of Asia, Japan may experience a serious decline. Her skills and resources should easily make her an excellent second-class nation, but they scarcely qualify her for the domination of the western Pacific and eastern Asia.

Malthusian principles are still effective. No nation has a moral right to allow its population to exceed the productive capacity of its domain unless it is willing to accept a lower standard of living. Mere population pressure does not entitle a country to seize the land of its neighbor, especially when that neighbor is equally pressed. The world is now full, and the regulation of population has become one of the most essential of international problems. Reckless increase without corresponding technological advance can lead only to chaos.

Agriculture

Japan is still a nation of farmers. Despite current urbanization and industrialization, 43 per cent of all households were occupied in farming in 1940. This proportion has declined from 64 per cent in 1903. Even factory workers are closely tied to the land, for many of them were born on a farm where their parents still live. Serious difficulties of increased costs of operation, rising taxes, and uncertain cash income make agrarian problems acute.

The area under cultivation in 1937 was 14,940,000 acres. This is 15.8 per cent of the total area of Japan proper, and compares with 10,615,000 acres or 40 per cent in Ohio, and 12,881,000 acres and 21 per cent of the United Kingdom. The ratio of cultivated land has increased slowly, rising from 11.8 per cent in 1887 to 13.7 per cent in 1902, 14.4 per cent in 1912, and 15.7 per cent in 1919. In 1929 the figure dropped to 15.4 per cent. Apparently the economic maximum has been reached. Any further addition to the present cultivated acreage will depend upon expensive irrigation, drainage, or fertilization. Large areas of diluvial upland areas remain uncultivated, seemingly because they are unusable for rice culture.

Farm households number 5,374,897, so that the tilled area per family is but 2.67 acres; in comparison, the United States averages 155 acres. This average size is quadrupled in Hokkaido and reduced to less than two acres in the southwest. Not only are the farms everywhere small, but 70 per cent are below the average size and 34 per cent are under $1\frac{1}{4}$ acres. As a result of generations of feudal subdivision, each farm has come to embrace several widely scattered plots, which are in turn divided into tiny unfenced fields, a sixth to a tenth of an acre in size. In some localities, governmental action has caused a consolidation with some resulting increase in yields. The uneconomic fragmentation has its minor advantages, for a flood or crop failure in some fields still leaves the farmer with a yield elsewhere.

Irrigated fields, universally in rice, account for 54 per cent of the crop area while unirrigated upland farms, usually on diluvium, represent 46 per cent. Rice is the master crop and the characteristic food

Two successive harvests of rice per year are found only in Formosa and the extreme south coast of Shikoku and Kyushu. As

The scarcity of level land makes it necessary to terrace every hillside that can be flooded. (*Germaine Kellerman, courtesy Japan Reference Library.*)

from the extreme south almost to the north. As elsewhere in the Orient, it is generally sown in seedbeds and transplanted by hand in flooded fields. Skillful cultivation, fertilization, and scientific seed development have raised the yield to 43 bushels per acre (1936).

Japanese canals, unlike those in China, are used for irrigation only and are thus mere ditches. In order to keep the land flooded, ridges a foot or so wide and high separate individual fields, and the surplus water is led from one level to another. Narrow paths follow the tops of some of these miniature dikes, or they may be planted to a row of mulberry trees, soybeans, or other dry crops.

far north as Sendai two crops are interplanted, one maturing several weeks in advance of the other. Sixty per cent of the rice fields are left fallow during the winter; many remain flooded since they are too low to be properly drained. Winter cropping is negligible north of Sendai, but common in the south. This idle land in a country so pressed for food as Japan is puzzling, but its fallow character apparently reflects an inability to grow a crop. Where rice fields are planted to fall crops, these are wheat, barley, rapeseed, or radishes. Because of wet soil the earth is heaped into ridges on which seeds are sown. Intervening depressions are often flooded by the winter rains.

The domestic supply of rice is inadequate for the expanding population, so that nearly a fifth of the needs must be obtained from Formosa and Korea. The available supplies in these areas are apparently used to the limit, so that further population increase must be fed from abroad. The export of rice from Korea is made possible only by the importation of cheaper millet from Manchuria for the Koreans.

Wheat, rye, barley, oats, and rapeseed account for about half the area devoted to rice. They are grown as spring crops in Hokkaido, or as fall crops in Old Japan either on paddy fields after the rice harvest or on uplands after a crop of beans or vegetables. With the introduction of western culture, there is an increasing consumption of bread, so that wheat production has risen 60 per cent since 1932, making Japan almost self-sufficient. Sweet potatoes are a large crop in the south, with some white potatoes in the north. Carbohydrates represent an overabundant proportion of Japanese diet.

Despite the widespread use of tea, less than half of one per cent of all cropland is devoted to its production. Diluvial uplands and steep terraced hill slopes are usually selected, especially in the vicinity of Shizuoka.

Silk is the great cash crop of the Japanese farmer and mulberry leaves for feeding the silkworms are raised everywhere south of Sendai. A quarter of all the upland fields in crops is given over to mulberry, notably in central Honshu in the hinterland of Yokohama. In several interior basins, such as Suwa, mulberry occupies over half of the cultivated area. Many rice farmers in the lowlands have a small patch of mulberry, or scattered trees around the house or fields.

Other cash crops are flax and hemp, pyrethrum, tobacco, peppermint, and camphor. Common vegetables include the giant radish known as daikon for pickles; soy, kidney, and red beans; peas; and taro. Interculture is common, and several crops a year may be grown on the same field.

Fruit is extensively and increasingly grown. Mandarin oranges lead, followed by persimmons, apples, pears, grapes, and peaches. Apples are raised in the highlands of Honshu and Korea, and in Hokkaido. Oranges grow best in southern Japan.

The animal industry is conspicuously undeveloped, and the few horses or cattle are largely kept for draft purposes on the farm. Dairy cows amount to 40 per cent of all animals in Hokkaido but are uncommon to the south. Pigs are even less abundant than horses, and sheep are rare. The scarcity of animals reflects the pressure of human population for food and may also be accounted for by the lack of good pasture, the poor native grasses, the long hot summers, and the reluctance of the Japanese rice farmer to keep animals. From the earliest times, fish has taken the place of meat in the diet. The total protein diet for the Japanese is 11 per cent, as compared with 45 per cent for Americans and Europeans.

Food for seventy million people living on islands requires that crop yields be at a maximum. Unfortunately Japanese soils are poor. The diluvium is usually sandy and sterile, uplands are leached, and soils developed on volcanic parent materials are infertile. Only by the most painstaking and repeated fertilization can adequate crops be grown. In the production of rice, the expense of fertilizer stands next to wages in the average cost distribution. Commercial fertilizers such as bean or other oil cake, waste from fish or from silk cocoons, and prepared minerals are valued at three-fourths the consumption of farm-supplied manure which includes compost, human excrement or night soil, and green manure. Little barnyard manure is available, so

Rice is started in seedbeds and later transplanted to flooded fields where it grows for three months in standing water.

After the harvest, sheaves of rice are hung on racks to dry.

The top of the rice is separated from the stalk by drawing it through a comb. (*Courtesy Presbyterian Board of Foreign Missions.*)

Rice is polished by pounding in a hollow log.

that the farmer must make an extensive cash outlay.

Modern science has added little to Japa-

enterprises still require support and few bring much income to the government.

Mounting fiscal requirements have

Silkworms are raised in the home and the cocoons are spun in nests of straw. These women are preparing the cocoons for shipment to a filature.

nese agriculture other than commercial fertilizer, seed improvement, and protection from crop diseases. Machinery is impractical in the tiny fields, so that the spade and hoe and, to some extent, the plow remain the traditional tools. Power for pumping irrigation water is usually too expensive.

Agriculture has carried the burden of modernization in Japan. When the country set out to industrialize, farmers provided the chief available source of taxation. Through rising taxes on farm land, the government was able to subsidize railroads, shipping, and industry of all sorts, and to build up an army and navy. Many of these

brought increased taxes. The farmer in turn was forced to find a cash income, and for many years this was supplied by Japan's great export, raw silk. With the proceeds from American purchases of silk, the farmer paid the government and it in turn continued to aid industry. With the collapse of the silk market in the early 1930's, the farmer was obliged to mortgage his holdings in order to meet tax payments. World-wide depression accompanied by difficulties in Japan's export sales of cotton textiles and other manufactured goods, plus war in China and with the United States, has added to the internal problem.

In 1911 the average indebtedness of the farmer amounted to 135 yen per household (the yen had a par value of $0.50). By 1937 it had risen to 1,000 yen, and the total farm debt was some 6 billion yen. This compares with a net annual income, after deducting farm and household expenses, of 132.7 yen per family. Many readjustment plans have been proposed, but the problem remains unsolved. Political attempts to raise the price of rice and silk have met with little success. Interest rates are exorbitant, and marketing systems monopolistic.

The situation is further aggravated by preferential income taxes. "In the annual income group of 300 yen, peasant proprietors paid 35 per cent in taxes while manufacturers paid 1.5 and traders 12.5 per cent. In the 500 yen group, landlords paid 51, peasant proprietors 31.5, manufacturers 18, and traders 14 per cent, approximately."[1] A farmer or rural landowner with an income of 5,000 yen had an income tax of 1,395 yen while if he lived in a city the amount would be 701 yen. These figures were compiled by the Imperial Agricultural Association which protests the continued subsidization of industry by agriculture.

Wide variations in agriculture exist from place to place within Japan. These will be discussed in the subsequent regional chapters.

Fishing

Crowded Japan looks out on a friendly sea. Typhoons occasionally devastate the shores, but there are innumerable harbors. Sheltered waters such as the Inland Sea invite the fisherman and trader. The waters around Japan comprise the greatest fishing grounds of the world. Both in tonnage and value, the catch exceeds that of

[1] HOLLAND, WILLIAM L., The Plight of Japanese Agriculture, *Far Eastern Survey*, V (1936), 4.

any other country. Japan is responsible for half the world's catch, and fish are the seventh most important basic export from

Japan is the leading fishing nation of the world, with great numbers of near-shore craft such as these, as well as modern deep-sea boats. (*Germaine Kellerman, courtesy Japan Reference Library.*)

Japan. These pastures of the sea furnish a considerable part of the Japanese diet, for fish is an integral part of every meal.

Fishing interests characterize all shores of Japan. The calm Inland Sea, the stormy Chishima or Kurile Islands, and the coasts of Honshu each has its fishing villages. In many instances, these settlements fringe a narrow gravel beach for a mile or more, backed by mountains so that virtually no level land is available for agriculture. Houses line the shore just above high-tide mark, often clinging to the cliffs. The beach is strewn with boats, nets, and drying fish. Contact with the rest of Japan may be exclusively by boat. Many of these villages reflect the poverty of those who engage in the industry, for the more important fishing activities are in the hands of large corporations and the operators are but hired hands.

seasonal fishermen. The total catch credited to those living in Japan proper was valued at 358,500,000 yen in 1938, about a tenth

Most of the diving for culture pearls is carried on by Japanese girls. The oysters are planted in sheltered bays. (*Germaine Kellerman, courtesy Japan Reference Library.*)

Off the east coast flows the warm Kuroshio or Japan Current with a branch that enters the Japan Sea, while cold currents circulate in both the Sea of Okhotsk and the Japan Sea. Thus varied environments offer a habitat for many kinds of aquatic life. The limited supplies of food on the land, the coastal character of the population, and the highly indented shore line all tend to push people to the sea. Within the present century, fishing has expanded from a littoral and small-boat industry to one that ranges from the sub-Arctic to Antarctica.

Over a million and a half people are engaged in fishing, nearly half of whom are

the value of agriculture. An additional 122,000,000 yen in Korea, Formosa, Karafuto, and the South Seas raises the Empire total to 480,000,000 yen.

Coastwise and near-shore fishing account for 61 per cent, with the leading items of the catch in order as follows: sardines; seaweeds for food, fertilizer, fodder, or iodine; salmon; cuttle fish; yellow tail; and shellfish. Out of the total of 364,260 boats only one-fifth have engines, so that most of the near-shore catch is obtained in picturesque sail or rowboats which return home each night.

Deep-sea fishing represents 28 per cent of the total industry, with the balance covered by whaling, coral and pearl collection, and aquiculture on the land. Sardine, cod, bonito, shark, mackerel, and tuna are

newal of leases for these concessions have been a recurrent source of international friction. Whereas Soviet-operated fisheries

Seaweeds provide a considerable part of the Japanese diet. Thin pieces are spread on frames to dry. (*H. Suito.*)

the leading fish. Modern refrigeration has made it possible for Japanese vessels to operate in the far north, even along the coasts of Alaska. Floating canneries prepare large amounts of crab and salmon for export. In 1938 these factory ships canned 204,000 cases of crab meat and 370,300 cases of salmon. Four Japanese whaling ships were in Antarctic waters in 1938.

Under the Treaty of Portsmouth (1905), which closed the Russo-Japanese War, Japanese fishermen were given certain rights along the coasts of the Soviet Maritime Provinces, Kamchatka and Sakhalin. Specified fishing "lots" are provided on lease, and agreements concerning the re-

along these coasts once represented but a tenth of the total production, they now exceed the Japanese catch. On account of population increases in Siberia and for strategic reasons as well, the U.S.S.R. would like to terminate the agreement, but the 20,000 Japanese workers and the annual catch of 50 million yen represent a vital interest for Japan.

Since Japan's emergence toward the close of the nineteenth century, she has built a merchant marine that ranked third among world powers at the beginning of the Second World War. Furthermore her navy dominated the western Pacific. This rapid maritime expansion reflects the intimate familiarity with the sea and its ways which is a feature of Japan. Even though isolation characterized earlier centuries, fishing has limited to a few areas. The typical factory is a family workshop employing members of the household and two or three relatives.

Swift-flowing canals run through many Japanese villages. This water wheel provides a source of power for a roadside mill. (*De Cou, from Ewing Galloway.*)

always been important. Fisheries are schools of seamanship, for those who live on the water learn to read the clouds and find their way over horizonless seas.

Industry

In the statistical analysis of twentieth-century Japan, few items are more spectacular than the rise of industry. Although most of the modern industry is in the larger cities, even rural landscapes are changed. Modern factories literally pop out of the rice fields. Cities have grown enormously and have cosmopolitan cores, but residential sections are still old style. Towering factories with their smoke and noise are uncommon, and western-style industry is

Current population increases cannot be absorbed on the farms; hence there is a large labor surplus available to industry at nominal cost. Wages, which were once very low, have been considerably raised, but costs of urban living have increased even faster so that the lot of factory employees is still marginal. Rising costs of labor within Japan have led some Japanese industrialists to move their plants to China with its reservoir of cheap labor.

Japanese industry is highly monopolistic and subsidized by the government. Most of it is in the hands of a few great families, such as the Mitsui, Mitsubishi, of Sumitomo. Through various corporations, these houses own banks, shipping lines, textile mills, heavy industries, import and export firms, and even control much of the handicraft. The activity of these giant combines has extended Japan's trade to the corners of the world. Wherever there is a market for goods that Japan is able to produce, these firms have made her a serious competitor. The foundation of Japan's newer export industry is the fabrication of other peoples' raw materials into articles to fit the tastes and pocketbooks of overseas customers.

Small-sized factories are characteristic; in fact the gradation from family handicraft to small shops is imperceptible. Nearly two-thirds of the workers are in establishments using five employees or less, and another quarter in plants with between five and ten. Over one-third of all employees are women, chiefly in cotton mills and silk filatures.

In the decade from 1927 to 1937, manufacturing increased two and a half fold, reaching 16,412,000,000 yen. This is three times the value of agriculture, although the number of workers is but one-third. Textiles have long been first, but the relative percentage has declined from 41.4 in 1926 to 23.8 in 1937. Metallic industries rose from 6.4 per cent in 1926 to 20.5 in 1937. Chemicals accounted for 18.6 per cent, and machines and tools for 14.5 per cent in 1937.

The distribution of industry corresponds with the belt of densest population with its labor supply and markets; the availability of silk, electric power, and coal; and adequate harbors for overseas raw materials and markets.

The Inland Sea plus an extension eastward to Tokyo marks the industrial core of Japan. From Nagasaki to Tokyo is 600 miles, and along this line is a discontinuous collection of factory towns. Four areas stand out: the Osaka-Kobe-Kyoto region is first, followed by Tokyo-Yokohama, Nagoya, and northern Kyushu.

The outstanding Osaka area specializes in Japan's leading product, cotton textiles. More than with most Japanese cities, Osaka industry is housed in large structures. Iron and steel fabrication and shipbuilding are important. Osaka lies at the head of a shallow bay that has been dredged for ocean vessels. Previously all larger ships were obliged to dock at near-by Kobe. Both cities are now ports, with Kobe taking first place in the nation and Osaka third. Shipbuilding is important in each. Whereas Osaka has ample level land, Kobe unfortunately lies on a narrow alluvial fan with inadequate room for industry. Inland Kyoto, the old imperial capital, is in marked contrast as an industrial center. It is not a modern city, and specializes in artistic crafts such as silk weaving, pottery, cloisonné, lacquer, bamboo, bronzes, and toys. The Osaka-Kobe-Kyoto region lacks both cheap power and raw materials. It does have abundant labor and a central market.

Tokyo and Yokohama have more industrial diversification than Osaka. Like Osaka, Tokyo lies at the head of a shallow bay but, unlike Osaka, the harbor has not been adequately dredged so that most shipping must stop at Yokohama. In the hinterland lies the chief silk area, and Yokohama is the closest port of shipment for the American market. Silk reeling and weaving, machinery, electrical goods, printing, and a wide variety of labor-consuming industries center here. Electrical power is available from the near-by mountains. Small workshop factories predominate.

Nagoya is a replica of Osaka in location and products. It lies on a delta at the head of a shallow bay with a dredged harbor. Its port ranks fourth, preceded by Kobe, Yokohama, and Osaka. Silk reeling, cotton cloth, cotton spinning, and wool weaving account for 60 per cent of Nagoya's output.

There are no metal industries, but cheap pottery is centered here.

The fourth center lies between Moji and Nagasaki in northern Kyushu. This is the base for heavy industry, and the blast furnaces, rolling mills, shipyards, cement plants, glass works, and related factories make this region unique in Japan. Coal is king. Level land is at a premium so that there is an irregular succession of industrial towns along the coast for miles.

Kyushu has had European contacts longer than any other port in Japan, chiefly with the Portuguese and Dutch at Nagasaki, who introduced shipbuilding. This city was an early coaling port for European steamers, but most of them now call at Moji instead. The district is well situated for the importation of iron ore from the mainland and accounts for three-quarters of the pig iron of Japan. Chinese coal from the Kailan mines is available to mix with the local product for making coke. The chief steel center is at Yawata near Moji, where the government has large plants.

There are three other areas of pig-iron production. The oldest is near ore at Kamaishi in northeastern Honshu, and others are at Muroran in Hokkaido where there is coal, and at Yokohama where neither coal nor ore is present. The steel production of the Empire together with "Manchoukuo" in 1940 amounted to 6,455,000 metric tons. Almost all of the raw materials came from outside Japan proper, and 55 per cent came from areas outside Japanese control, including scrap iron from the United States. American steel production is over ten times that of Japan.

In 1937 northern Kyushu produced about 2,900,000 metric tons of steel, which placed her in eleventh place among world steel districts. Osaka-Kobe and Tokyo-Yokohama each accounted for 1,000,000 metric tons.

The Japanese steel industry is unique in that it turns out twice as much open-hearth steel as blast-furnace pig iron, owing to the use of scrap and imported pig.

Japan has not been able to solve her problem of population or to secure a better economic livelihood through industry. During the decade of the 1930's the standard of living fell, even from the low point of the world depression. Real wages declined, especially among textile and small shop employees. This was in part a result of Japan's shortage in raw materials but was also related to increasing trade restrictions in foreign markets. The relation of economic distress to war should be clear.

Communications

The compactness of Japan has aided the development of transportation facilities on land and by sea. Unfavorable topography handicaps railway construction, but hundreds of harbors aid coastwise shipping. Thus heavy freight moves by water, and railways derive more revenue from passengers than from freight.

Medieval Japan was linked together by a series of imperial highways during the seventeenth, eighteenth, and early nineteenth centuries. These connected government centers and various shrines and were used by great numbers of officials, merchants, and pilgrims.

Greatest of these highways was the Tokaido which connected the imperial capital, then at Kyoto, with the feudal capital at Tokyo, 300 miles distant. Other roads from Kyoto led to the western end of Honshu, one along the northern or shady side and the other skirting the Inland Sea along the sunny southern side. Still other roads led north. Many of these ancient highways are now paralleled by modern railroads. The ancient roads still exist but for the most part are narrow pine-bordered lanes ill-suited to automobile traffic.

Cross-country automobile roads are little developed. Out of a total of 621,400 miles of roads in Japan, only one-ninth are outside Yokohama and Kobe in half an hour. In these areas electric interurban facilities are popular.

Railways have played a large part in the modernization of Japan. To the right are the railway yards near Iidabashi; to the left is the elevated electrified belt line around Tokyo. (*Frederick L. Hamilton, from Three Lions.*)

of cities and towns, and most are narrow and poorly paved. Automobiles and imported gasoline are too expensive for the common man, but bus lines are very popular.

The present system of railroads, three-fourths under government ownership, provides a dense rail net reaching all parts of the islands. The total mileage within Japan proper is 13,581 (1938). More than a billion passengers are carried annually, but the average journey is only 15.4 miles. The usual gauge is 3 feet 6 inches in contrast to the American standard of 4 feet 8½ inches, so that speeds are reduced. Two per cent of the lines are electrified, chiefly in the vicinity of Tokyo and Osaka where frequent services reach the respective seaports of

Express trains from Tokyo to Aomori at the northern end of the island require 13 hours for the 457 miles. From Tokyo to Shimonoseki in the extreme west is a distance of 682 miles, which requires 16½ hours by express. Aomori and Shimonoseki are the termini for railway-operated ferry services which connect with Hokkaido and Korea, respectively. The principal line in Korea starts at Fusan in the south, and runs through Seoul to Manchuria, while another important route extends from Seoul northward to Rashin. A tunnel beneath the Straits of Shimonoseki links Honshu and Kyushu.

Water transport has always been important in Japanese commerce. Prior to the opening of the country at the time of

Perry's visit in 1853, the policy of non-intercourse with foreign nations under the Tokugawa regime prohibited the construction of ocean vessels, so that navigation was limited to coastal regions. The first modern shipyards were built in 1891 and, from this time on, the construction of steel vessels has increased rapidly.

Japanese steamers of over 100 tons represent an aggregate registered tonnage of 5,007,000 tons, of which 1,198,000 tons were built in 1936–1938. This placed the country in third rank among maritime powers, truly a remarkable record for so short a time. Older vessels have been systematically scrapped, so that the fleet is modern and efficient. Despite Japan's lack of petroleum, many of the newer vessels are oil burning.

Japan has 758 seaports, of which 38 are open to foreign ships, but only three are of major international significance: Kobe, Yokohama, and Osaka. These stand third, fourth, and eighth in net registered tonnage entered among the ports of the world. Coal from Moji to Osaka and Yokohama, and timber from Karafuto account for three-quarters of all domestic cargoes; bean cake from Dairen to Yokohama, sugar, rice, wheat, raw cotton, salt, and ores follow in importance.

Two great ocean highways lead out from Japan. One extends eastward across the Pacific either along the great-circle route to Vancouver and Seattle or, as is more common, stopping at Honolulu en route to San Francisco and the Panama Canal. The other leads south along the China coast to Europe or the East Indies.

Regular passenger and freight services under the Japanese flag link her ports with all the world. From Kobe and Yokohama there are frequent sailings to San Francisco and Seattle, to the east and west coasts of South America, to Batavia, to Melbourne, to Cape Town, and to London. Other lines provide extensive facilities along the China coast and up the Yangtze River, while the coastwise classification is most important of all. The fastest services from Yokohama to Seattle require ten days, and about a month to Europe.

Prior to the Second World War, an extensive network of airlines linked all parts of the Empire from Karafuto to the Mandated Islands near the equator. Japanese international services reached Manchuria, China south of the Great Wall, and Thailand.

The Japanese Landscape

Few countries have the charm of Japan. Verdant hillsides, painstaking cultivation, artistic gardens, and courteous people combine to create a delightful landscape. Wherever the land permits, miniature rice fields crowd so closely that there is scarcely room for roads or villages. It is this intricate field pattern, in varying shades of green or brown according to the maturity of the crop, which gives the dominant note to the landscape. Tea and mulberry climb the slopes, while forests and clumps of bamboo partly hide the shrines and temples among the hills.

If all Japanese landscapes were merged into a single scene, one might look down upon a maze of hills and mountains interlaced by winding ribbons of alluvium. At one side would be the inescapable sea, fringed by rocky cliffs and tiny deltas. Rice culture leads to agglomerated settlement with innumerable clusters of farmhouses surrounded by fruit or mulberry trees. Many of these villages are elongated along highways, river levees, or the seacoast. Larger settlements cluster about feudal castles or shrines. Automobile highways are few, but the inevitable hydroelectric transmission lines introduce a modern note to the rural scene.

Nature has exercised a closely guiding hand, for the correspondence between the cultural pattern and the physical surroundings is intimate. The Japanese landscape is still dominantly rural. Large cities are not numerous, and villages are but slightly westernized. Agriculture shows a mature adjustment to land forms, and population distribution follows food possibilities from both land and sea. Vertical differences in climate and soils bring modifications from place to place but do not greatly disturb the ensemble within Honshu, Kyushu, and Shikoku. Hokkaido is new and different, and the outer dependencies are each unique.

Most of Japan is wooded but, if seen from the air, the importance of reforested tracts and erosion-control projects with their regular spacing of trees is evident. Despite the pressure for food, surprisingly large areas of unused land are to be seen. Some of this is wild bamboo grass or brushland on mountain slopes, fit neither for grazing nor for tree crops. Elsewhere this idle land represents diluvial terraces with excessively coarse soils where cultivation is impractical. Other areas of sandy flood plains or coastal swamps are unfit for agriculture. The government is well aware of the problem, and the failure to find a use for these areas suggests that they are economically submarginal.

Field patterns are best seen at the time of rice transplanting when the tiny flooded fields stand out like broken mirrors. There are no fences, and only low dikes separate each plot. Where the slope is gentle, rectilinear patterns prevail; on hillsides the dike system follows the contours. Unless irrigation water is easily available, rice fields seldom rise much above the valley floor. Above the irrigated fields may be sloping terraces for tea or mulberry or fruit. Almost everywhere the micropattern of surface configuration determines the land use. In the new agricultural districts of Hokkaido the farms average 11.25 acres and were laid out along American lines, but in

Old Japan farms of about 2.52 acres are the rule. This acreage is split up by scattered holdings.

The exteriors of Japanese houses tend to be drab and monotonous to western eyes, except for the lattice windows. Walls are of unpainted thin wooden siding, or mud and straw plaster on a wattle foundation. Roofs in the country are characteristically covered with thatch, or with tile in the cities where the fire hazard is greater. One- and two-story structures are the rule. There are no stoves for heating, although on the colder west coast, houses are built with the Korean device of allowing smoke from the kitchen fire to circulate through a brick baffle which extends under the earthen floors of several rooms. Elsewhere a charcoal brazier supplies enough heat to warm one's hands before writing or doing fine work.

The charm of Japanese houses lies not in the exterior, but in the enclosed courtyards with their formal gardens. Even the better village residences are often entered through a low gateway crowded between shops along the street. Only temples and inns have attractive exteriors. Sliding lattice partitions with translucent paper in place of glass are artistic and well adapted to the subtropical climate, but they are ill suited to the cold and snowy winters of the north.

Japan has 107 cities with over 25,000 people, but only 6 exceed 500,000. Unlike towns of the West, these show but limited functional zoning. One- and two-story houses produce a flat urban profile, interrupted perhaps by the feudal castle or shrine that served as the original nucleus. Both village and metropolitan streets are surprisingly similar in structures, types of business, and general character. Shops open directly on the narrow street, without doors or windows, and are boarded up at night. Many business places have the residence of the owner in the rear or upstairs.

In parts of Tokyo the westernization is striking. Modern subways, hundreds of neon lights, excellent department stores, businessman wears western clothing, and the few schoolboys who think they speak English have never heard it spoken by a

The urban core of Tokyo, rebuilt since the earthquake of 1923, contains many splendid buildings such as this office of the First Life Insurance Company seen across the inner moat of the Tokyo Castle. (*Germaine Keller-man, courtesy Japan Reference Library.*)

and three-quarters of the men in European dress give a cosmopolitan air. Tokyo is in tune with cities the world over; it is the most modern city in all Asia. An American will have little difficulty in finding someone along the downtown streets who speaks or at least reads English. The central parts of Osaka, Kobe, and Yokohama are somewhat similar.

Provincial cities are entirely different. There may be a few semimodern buildings and other new externals, but life is still thoroughly Japanese. Only an occasional

foreigner. Whereas an occasional Japanese woman in Tokyo may be seen in western dress, the kimono is worn universally in smaller places. Sidewalk shops are lighted with a few unshaded electric bulbs, and display thermos bottles, enameled ware, and umbrellas, but the customers still wear wooden clog shoes.

Contrasts and contradictions mark the rapid transition from centuries of seclusion to world awareness. No nation has ever so transformed its national life as has Japan since 1868 when the Emperor Meiji ascended the throne. Many of these adjustments are psychological and social, but the material evidences are widespread. Rural landscapes have changed less than the urban, but everywhere there are signs of the new. Nevertheless, Japan is not becoming westernized; rather she is skillfully remolding her own life to be in tune with the world. Acceptance of some western techniques is not mere copying; instead the Japanese are grafting some branches of material civilization onto the parent stock of their indigenous culture.

CHAPTER 12

REGIONS OF OLD JAPAN

Within the Japanese Empire are wide variations in environment and life. This

Six regions make up Old Japan: the Kwanto Plain, Central Honshu, Western

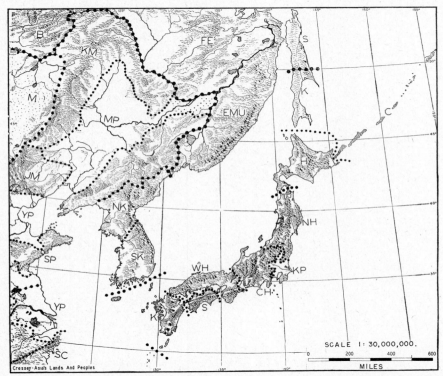

The geographic regions and land forms of Japan. Two geographic provinces and 10 regions are shown above. Old Japan includes Honshu, Shikoku, and Kyushu. Outer Japan embraces Hokkaido, Karafuto, the Kuriles or Chishima, Korea or Chosen divided into a northern and southern half, Formosa or Taiwan, and the South Seas. (*Base map by Erwin Raisz, courtesy Harvard-Yenching Institute.*)

chapter deals with regional characteristics in the main islands of Honshu, Shikoku, and Kyushu which form the traditional home of Japanese culture. Although Hokkaido is administratively a part of Japan proper, its geography is so different that it is considered with the other portions of Outer Japan in the next chapter.

Honshu and the Inland Sea, Shikoku, Kyushu, and Northern Honshu.

Kwanto Plain

On almost any kind of map of Japan, the Kwanto Plain around Tokyo is conspicuous. Whether because of its geology, surface forms, land use, or population concentration, this is an outstanding region. Nowhere else is there so much approxi-

Portions of the region near the seacoast to the east are occupied by coastal swamps

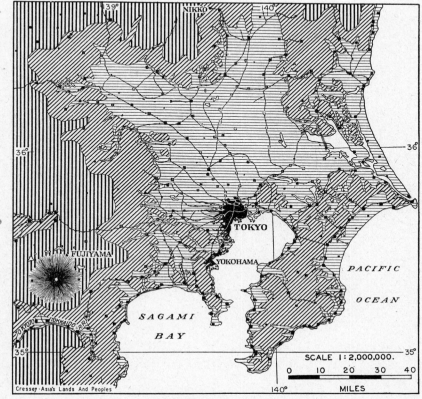

The Kwanto Plain is the largest area of level land in Japan; part is an alluvial lowland, part of it is covered with diluvial terraces. Plains are shown by horizontal ruled lines, hills by diagonal lines, and mountains by vertical ruling.

mately flat land, yet even here the surface is far from level. Most of the region is a compound alluvial fan built by the many rivers that pour out of the central Honshu mountains. Uplift has rejuvenated the streams which now have flood plains graded to a lower base level. Thus, dissected diluvial terraces alternate with alluvial lowlands. Elsewhere is uplifted coastal plain. Many of the rivers flow between dikes; when these are overtopped by flood waters, wide areas of farm land are inundated. Sand, coarse sediments, and volcanic ash predominate.

and unfilled lakes. In this section a few hard rock hills rise above the general level.

In many respects the Kwanto Plain is representative of Old Japan. Midway between north and south, the climate is a fair sample of humid subtropical conditions in the main islands. Rainfall amounts to 63 inches in Tokyo with a maximum in September that is over eight times the December minimum. Snow falls during two or three weeks of the mild winter but does not remain long on the ground. As the growing season lasts 220 days, multiple cropping is feasible during the hot summers.

Within an area of 5,000 square miles lives a population of over 12,000,000, half of them in Tokyo. This is the largest unit of grown in the Kwanto. Rice fields generally lie fallow during the winter or are planted to a crop of green manure. Near many of the

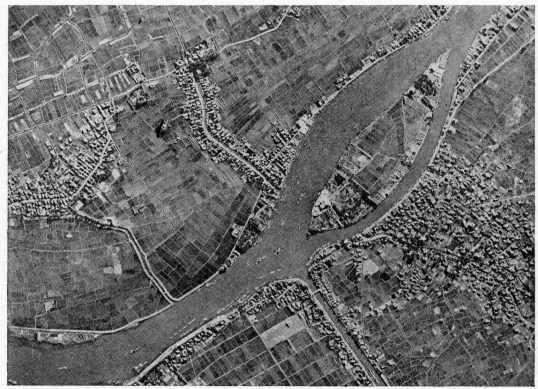

The Kwanto Plain in the suburbs of Tokyo is intensively utilized for rice culture, with numerous canals for irrigation. Many of the villages are strung along the streams and canals.

compact settlement and contains one-sixth the population of Japan proper. The Kwanto Plain is the most modernized of all regions, and its great port, Yokohama, is the principal front door to the United States.

Arable land within the Kwanto district amounts to 2,356,200 acres. This means that about two-thirds of the area is actually under cultivation.

Irrigated rice dominates the low alluvial-filled valleys and coastal plains and occupies 42 per cent of all arable land. One-seventh of the rice in Japan proper is

farmhouses are clumps of mulberry. Tea, dry grains, and tobacco are also raised.

Upland agriculture on the flat-topped diluvial terraces is less continuous than on the lowlands. Irrigated rice is uncommon; instead there are fields of vegetables, beans, peas, sweet potatoes, millet, or buckwheat. Extensive areas are planted to mulberry trees, which are trimmed back near the ground, so that the leaves may be more easily gathered. A quarter of all Japan's silk is produced on the Kwanto Plain, with even larger amounts in the near-by mountains. In some upland districts from 30 to 50 per cent of the cultivated land is in mulberry. In addition, these uplands are the center of Japan's limited production of tobacco. Tea is widely raised. Where fall crops are to be planted, wheat and barley are sown.

Terrace margins facing the lowlands are steep and usually in forest. Large areas of flattish diluvium are still in wild grass or woods. This is the northern limit of broadleaved evergreen hardwoods.

Population densities are high on the lowlands, ranging from 1,000 to 3,000 people per square mile. On the uplands the crowding is half to a quarter of these figures. Tiny villages are always in sight and, within the plain, there are 80 cities and towns with populations over 10,000.

The great metropolitan center is the twin city of Tokyo and Yokohama. Although separate politically, they function as one. From center to center is but 18 miles, and the intervening area is almost solidly built

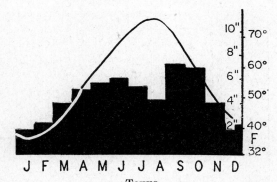

TOKYO

Elevation, 69 feet; average temperature, 56.8°F.; total precipitation 57.9 inches.

up with residential and industrial suburbs. This urban area serves not only the Kwanto

A village street near Tokyo. (*Frederick L. Hamilton, from Three Lions.*)

Plain but all of northern Honshu, and in a real sense the Empire as well.

The southern shore of Honshu is charac-

registered tonnage of all vessels entering Tokyo rose from 300,000 in 1922 to 7,865,000 in 1937. This compares with

The entrance gate to the Asakusa Temple in Tokyo. (*De Cou, from Ewing Galloway.*)

terized by a series of long bays, usually of tectonic origin and now in the process of being filled by delta growth. The easternmost of these is the Sagami-Tokyo embayment, locus of the great 1923 earthquake. The city of Tokyo lies at the head of the bay on the compound delta of the small streams that drain the Kwanto Plain. The bay is too shallow for ocean vessels so that Yokohama, halfway to the open sea, has become the port of call. Tokyo is not yet open to foreign vessels without permission, but dredging operations have made a harbor for vessels up to 6,000 tons. The

26,785,000 net tons entered at Yokohama during 1935.

Despite the early handicaps of Tokyo as a shallow-water port, the volume of its barge and lighter freight is now equal to the entire tonnage entering Tokyo by rail. Most of this represents transshipments from Yokohama.

But Tokyo does not owe its greatness to the sea only. It has been important since the sixteenth century, when it became the capital of the Tokugawa Shoguns and their feudal Daimos. After the Emperor Meiji was restored in 1868 the imperial capital was moved here from Kyoto. Tokyo is today the political, social, educational, cultural, and commercial center of the lesser chiefs also have their radiating streets so that the city pattern is complicated. Since the great fire following the

The Imperial Palace lies within this ancient enclosure with its castle walls and towers, built in a day of bows and arrows. (*Germaine Kellerman, courtesy Japan Reference Library.*)

Empire. Here are the head offices of the great industrial houses of Mitsui and Mitsubishi, the center of government, the leading universities, and the greatest wealth.

The eastern part of the city lies on a low river flood plain with canals that serve commerce and industry. The western and residential section is on a dissected terrace. On a spur of this upland is the old Shogun castle, now the imperial palace. From it streets radiate in a cobweb pattern, cut by two concentric moats now largely filled in to make roads. Subsidiary castles of

earthquake of Sept. 1, 1923, when half the city was destroyed, wide avenues have replaced many narrow streets or have cut through traffic barriers. The area devoted to streets has thus risen from 12 to 25 per cent. Reconstruction was officially completed in 1930, and downtown Tokyo is marked by splendid department stores, banks, and office buildings. These are of concrete and steel, designed to be earthquake resistant; few are over eight stories in height as they are limited by law to 100 feet.

Industry in the Tokyo-Yokohama area is diversified, with small workshops more important than large factories. Textiles, machinery, electrical goods, food, chemicals, novelties, rubber, glass, paper, and

777,500. In 1940 the ports of Tokyo and Yokohama were officially united under the name of Keihin.

The outer moat of Tokyo Castle leads through the present Ginza shopping district. The buildings to the left are part of Tokyo's newspaper row. (*Germaine Kellerman, courtesy Japan Reference Library.*)

printing are each important. Shipbuilding and ship repair are significant along the waterfront. The only local raw material is silk, and most of the filatures for reeling silk are in villages outside the city. Coal, iron, raw cotton, and other supplies are all imported. Electric power is abundant.

In 1932, Tokyo covered 31 square miles and had a population of 2,070,000. By the annexation of surrounding cities and some purely rural land, the area rose to 223 square miles with a population of 6,778,804 in 1940. There are five miles of subway lines.

Yokohama is a newer city than Tokyo, and its growth is largely the product of industry and foreign commerce. Splendid wharves accommodate the largest vessels in the Pacific. The population in 1938 was

Industrial operations in the Kwanto Plain are largely for domestic consumption, except for silk as the chief export. Since the earthquake, Yokohama has yielded first place as a port to Kobe.

Excellent rail services lead out from Tokyo and make it the chief railway center of the nation. There are several hundred miles of railway within the Kwanto itself.

Central Honshu[1]

The central portion of Honshu is the most mountainous region of all Japan. Numerous peaks approximate 10,000 feet, and level land is restricted to isolated basins

[1] Central Honshu and the Kwanto Plain are collectively the equivalent of the Chubu Region as defined by Trewartha, and the Kwanto, Tosan, Tokai, and southern Hokuroku regions as described by Hall.

or coastal margins. Giant volcanoes and fault scarps give parts of the area a rugged and inhospitable topography. These mountains are often known as the Japanese Alps. Unfavorable land forms create a blank on the population map. On the other hand, wherever level land is present, so is man.

The central mountain knot has always been a barrier to travel along the Tokaido from Kyoto to Tokyo. South of Fujiyama there was once a gateway, and this gave rise to the names Kwanto, meaning east of the barrier, and Kwansai, the region around Kyoto and Osaka, to the west of the gate.

Lowland climates are not very different from the Kwanto Plain, but sharp differences in altitude and exposure introduce pronounced climatic variations. On the shady Japan Sea side, rainfall amounts to 80 and 100 inches with a winter maximum. Winters are cool and long, with cloudy weather and considerable snow in the mountains. Along the sunny Pacific side, the 60 to 80 inches of rain occur largely in the summer, partly associated with typhoons and Bai-u rains. Interior basins with 40 to 50 inches are among the driest parts of Japan proper. Frosts are an agricultural hazard at higher elevations.

Some portions of the area are progressive and prosperous; others more isolated are poor and backward. This is especially true on the west coast which is Japan's back door, where there are no large cities or ports, little industry, and landless farmers who are a holdover from feudal times. These conditions have given rise to emigration to Hokkaido and to Brazil.

The outstanding geologic feature is a lowland that cuts across the island from north to south. This great graben, known as the Fossa Magna, is bordered by towering ramparts, especially on the west. Along the fault lines numerous volcanoes have built huge cones of lava and cinders, in some places entirely filling the transverse

lowland. Minor faulting has produced local basins, now deeply filled with steep-sloping alluvial fans and diluvium, often terraced.

Tokyo's theater for the classical drama is appropriately designed in modified Japanese architecture. (*Germaine Kellerman, courtesy Japan Reference Library.*)

The greatest of the volcanoes is Fujiyama, variously written as Fuji or Fujisan, now romanized as Huzizan. Its symmetrical cone is 12,461 feet high and has a slope up to 37°, the angle of rest for loose cinders. The last eruption was in 1707. Fuji is surrounded by a series of five lovely lakes, in which artists delight to mirror the mountain. Over fifty thousand pilgrims a year climb to the summit.

Northwestern and southeastern shores both have discontinuous narrow strips of arable land along steep alluvial fans or terraces.

Rice is the dominant crop almost everywhere but is handicapped in the mountains by coarse soil, limited rainfall, and cooler summers. Along the north coast there is a surplus for shipment to other parts of Japan. Where double cropping is possible, wheat or barley follow rice.

grapes are taking their place. Nearly one-third the silk of Japan is produced in the region of Central Honshu.

The symmetrical cone of Fujiyama, seen through cherry blossoms, graces the background of many Japanese villages. (*Germaine Kellerman, courtesy Japan Reference Library.*)

Several specialized crops are important. Chief of these is the growing of mulberry leaves in interior basins where rice does not do well. Cheap land and cheap labor favor mulberry. The trees are tolerant of poor soil and do not require irrigation. The Suwa Basin is the most important sericultural center in the world, with 40 to 60 per cent of all cultivated land in mulberry. When the silk market in the United States expanded, mulberry cultivation in the Suwa area climbed higher and higher up the slopes; with the decline in silk export, mulberry gardens are receding, and apples or

Central Honshu also supplies half the crop of green tea, chiefly in the hinterland of Shizuoka from where it is exported to the United States, the Soviet Union, and Canada. This is the northern limit of Mandarin oranges which are raised extensively along the south coast. More daikon pickle is grown around Nagoya than elsewhere.

Landscapes usually show a dominance of rice on the irrigated valley floors, surrounded by variable amounts of mulberry, both on lowlands and rising up the slopes, and tea on terraced hillsides. Villages tend to lie next to the hills, often at the mouths of valleys. Unused hillsides are clothed with forest.

Small mines in the mountains produce

of Nikko, just north of the Kwanto Plain. Beautiful pagodas and shrines, surrounded by giant cryptomeria trees, provide the

Tea on the hillsides and rice in the lowlands, near Shizuoka. (*Germaine Kellerman, courtesy Japan Reference Library.*)

copper, lead, zinc, and silver. Fishing is significant along both coasts.

A few places deserve mention. On the north coast is the city of Kanazawa with a population of 157,300. This is the largest city on this side of Honshu, but the chief port is Fushiki, 25 miles to the north. Within the mountains at an elevation of 3,180 feet is the well-known summer resort of Karuizawa.

Many places in Japan compete for the greatest charm, but probably no interior spot is more lovely than the temple city

background for Japanese culture at its best.

The one great metropolis is Nagoya, at the head of Ise Bay and on the Nobi Plain, second largest in Japan proper. The Nobi Plain, with a population of 2,750,000, is comparable to the Kwanto Plain, except that on the flat alluvium the population is even denser, from 1,500 to 3,000 per square mile, and on the much-dissected diluvium somewhat more sparse.

The city of Nagoya lies on a low terrace four miles from the head of the shallow bay, but its port of Yokkaichi is much inferior to Tokyo's Yokohama or Osaka's Kobe. Port improvements at Nagoya make

the Inland Sea. Here is the richest culture and the most perfected land use. Before modern industry invaded the area, agri-

A mountain valley near Tokyo with its diked streams and patchwork of rice fields and farmhouses. (*Germaine Kellerman, courtesy Japan Reference Library.*)

it possible for 10,000-ton vessels to enter, and the city ranks a poor fourth among Japan's ports. The population rose to 1,224,000 in 1937, so that Nagoya is the third largest center of the Empire. Imports include wool from Australia, raw cotton from British India, lumber from the United States, and soybeans and cake from Manchuria. Exports are cotton cloth and cheap chinaware, as well as industrial goods to other parts of Japan. Nagoya is one of the modern industrial centers.

Western Honshu and the Inland Sea

No part of Japan has the same maturity and intensity of occupance as the shores of

culture had reached a climax adjustment with complete utilization of all available fields. This is the heart of Old Japan. Ancient cultural forms reflect the long history. Population crowds the land even more than in the regions already considered. Western Honshu is a region of great industrial importance.

The Inland Sea is Japan's Mediterranean. Through it moves both internal and external commerce. Sheltered waters and countless harbors make it a fishing region of significance. Thousands of vessels, with sail or engine, transport cargo from one port to another. Through the Inland Sea pass all trans-Pacific steamers, as well as those bound from Yokohama for Europe or the South Seas. It is possible that as many vessels use the Inland Sea as the precipitation of 40 inches or less in the plains must be amplified by an elaborate system of wells, ponds, and irrigation

This farm building near Nara houses a silk cocoon plant for a farmer who raises his own mulberry leaves and silkworms and operates his own filature. (*R. Moulin, from Ewing Galloway.*)

English Channel. Clear blue skies, mirror-like water, and countless islands with forests or rice terraces make this one of the most picturesque spots in the world.

Although western Honshu lies in the latitudes of Italy and Greece and has comparable temperatures, there is twice the rainfall and no dry summer as in the European Mediterranean. Monsoon winds bring a summer rainfall maximum to the sunny south coast, but the bordering mountains keep back some of the moisture so that the canals. On the shady north coast there is a winter maximum with some snow. Fortunately the mountains have twice and three times the lowland rainfall, but the runoff is seasonal and of limited value for irrigation or hydroelectric power.

The frost-free period averages 220 days near the Inland Sea and somewhat less along the Japan Sea. Temperature contrasts within the region are not pronounced, for elevations seldom exceed half a mile. Summers are uncomfortably hot, with high humidities till September. Winters are mild and snow is rare. Winter cropping is common, except on the north shore. The high coastal plain alluvium, diluvial terraces only partly dissected, and older and higher diluvial terraces often made of very coarse

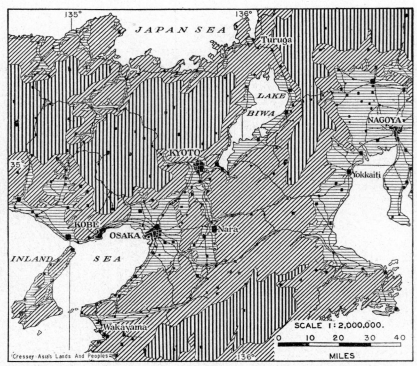

The Kinki district of western Honshu includes the great cities of Kobe, Osaka, and Kyoto at the eastern end of the Inland Sea. Farther east lies Nagoya. The narrow width of Honshu is illustrated by the presence of both the Pacific and the Japan Sea.

productivity of the land does not mean greater farm income, but rather smaller farms, with the average under two acres.

Unlike the mountains of Central Honshu, the western part of Honshu is merely hilly. There are large areas of granite, eroded into rounded hills. Interior basins are not numerous. A complicated system of block faulting furnishes the pattern for streams, and the Inland Sea itself is a series of dropped blocks, the islands being remnants of a dissected peneplain. Wherever approximately level land occurs, there is the usual association of flattish swampy delta or

material and much eroded. Artificial terracing is more abundant than elsewhere, with steps to the top of the hills in some locations. The largest areas of level land are in the vicinity of Osaka and Kyoto.

Rice is everywhere the principal crop, with the highest yields in the nation, 45 bushels per acre. Mulberry and tea are widespread on the slopes. On account of the prevalence of winter cropping, this is the most significant area for wheat and barley. Rye, rapeseed, and legumes are of some importance. Citrus fruits and apples are common. Near the cities are large areas of vegetables, fruit, and flowers. Local specialization has made some localities famous for watermelons, peaches, and

tion of salt from sea water. The final evaporation is over coal fires.

Within the region is Japan's greatest

The temple at Kyoto with its giant cryptomeria trees.

strawberries. The tea grown near Uji, south of Kyoto, is especially well known. Along the south shore of Honshu are raised the reeds that are woven into the tatami mats that invariably cover the floors of Japanese homes.

Many farmers supplement their income from crops by fish culture in the ponds and moats that surround the villages. A large number of those who live near the northern or southern shore are part-time fishermen. The abundant sunshine and high temperatures along the Inland Sea make it a favored coast for the extrac-

industrial area, that around Osaka and Kobe. Textiles, metal industries, and ship-building are outstanding. Natural resources are lacking, but plentiful labor and favorable location stimulate industry. In western Honshu too are the old crafts and arts for which Japan is famous. Communications by water and rail are excellent throughout the region, although the north coast is much less favored.

Western Honshu and the Inland Sea include three subregions: the Kinki district in the east around the great cities of Kobe, Osaka, and Kyoto; the sunny south side of Honshu with the offshore islands; and the shady Japan Sea side. Whereas all share most of the characteristics just de-

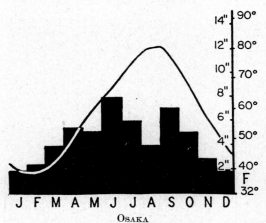

OSAKA

Average temperature 59°F.; total precipitation, 55.4 inches.

scribed, each has its personality. In fact, one never stops subdividing Japan, for successive generalizations each have their exceptions when applied to smaller and smaller areas.

Kinki takes first place in history and culture. Kyoto was the imperial capital for eleven centuries. Near-by Nara with its temples and natural beauties is visited by three million tourists a year. Osaka is Japan's second city and was on a par with Tokyo in population before the latter enlarged its boundaries.

The Kinki district includes five fault basins, separated by unimportant mountain barriers. Each is in part swampy, and some have unfilled lakes. To the northeast is Lake Biwa, Japan's largest lake, surrounded by only a limited area of level land. West of it is Kyoto Basin, south of which is the Nara or Yamato Basin. Only two of these lowlands reach the sea: the delta around Osaka and the unimportant Kino graben to the south.

Rice fields are often too low and poorly drained to be planted to a winter crop, but

nearly three-fourths of the upland fields raise a second crop, and a few even a third. Intertillage is common, and one may find combinations such as alternating rows of mulberry, persimmon, and tea. A thousand years of population pressure have pushed cultivation to its limits.

The rivers of the Kinki subregion are diked to protect adjoining fields and, as a result, deposition is confined to the channel so that dikes must be raised repeatedly. Near Lake Biwa this process has gone so far that the beds of some streams are 20 feet above the surrounding plain. In a few places, railroads and highways are carried under the river by tunnels rather than over them by bridges. When the dikes break, disaster follows.

Many rural areas are laid out according to a rectangular pattern known as the Han den brought from China during 645-655 A.D. Roads and canals conform to this scheme, which is restricted to the Kinki area.

For centuries, Kyoto was the imperial capital and thus the center of arts and crafts. The city is still the home of craftsmen who produce lacquer, porcelain, cloisonné, bronze, and silk textiles. There is almost no modern-style industry, but weaving and dyeing are important occupations. Kyoto has its own personality of dignity and charm, without the noisy and dirty modernity of the other large cities. The city is laid out with wide streets in a rectangular pattern around the old palaces and temples, in the style of Peiping. The population in 1938 was 1,159,800, fourth among Japanese cities.

Osaka is Japan's premier industrial center, with cotton yarn and cloth as the dominant production. Osaka's unlovely factories and narrow residential streets are the opposite of lovely Kyoto. A quarter of the nation's factory workers are here, and they produce a third of the manufactured goods. In 1936 industrial production reached a billion and a half yen. The city lies at the head of a shallow bay, with

trade, Osaka was already the most important domestic trading center, owing to its nearness to Kyoto.

The main-line railway from Osaka to Shimonoseki, with the characteristic landscape of western Honshu. (*Frederick L. Hamilton, from Three Lions.*)

adequate room for expansion. Numerous canals and rivers simplify barge transportation but require 1,600 bridges within the city.

Within recent years, the harbor has been dredged so that 20,000-ton ocean vessels may be accommodated. The absence of port facilities in the early years led to the development of Kobe, 16 miles to the west. Kobe still serves as Osaka's chief entrepôt for overseas trade, but the foreign shipping of Osaka itself now ranks third, next to Kobe and Yokohama. If domestic and overseas commerce are combined, Osaka is first. When Japan was opened to foreign

The Osaka area produces a wide variety of goods. Only cotton is manufactured in large factories and, out of the 30,000 manufacturing establishments in 1932, only 5,676 employed over five workers. Although there are no blast furnaces, the fabrication of steel is important. Smoke, slums, and smells are characteristic. The 1938 population amounted to 3,321,200.

Kobe lies on an alluvial fan at the base of mountains that restrict its inland growth and cause it to expand along the shore toward Osaka. Since Kobe is the chief port of call for foreign shipping, it is but natural that it should have many western influences. The harbor has facilities for the largest ocean vessels in the Pacific, and there is a heavy movement of freight. Kobe is doubly fortunate in its maritime position. All ships from Canada, the United States, or the Panama Canal include Kobe en route to Asia. Likewise all ships from Europe to the Far East, together with those from Australia and the East Indies, invariably proceed to Kobe. Japan thus lies on two of the major ocean highways. The 27,000 vessels with a total of 28,334,000 registered tons that enter Kobe annually place it next to New York and London in world ports. If Osaka is included, the district ranks second. The population of Kobe was 989,100 in 1938; of these 8,900 were foreigners, the largest number in any city.

The Japanese have always differentiated between the shady Japan Sea and the sunny Pacific sides of their islands. The northwest shore of Honshu is known as the San-in, since it is darker, stormier, and snowier. In contrast, the southeast margin is the San-yo, bright and sunny. The San-in coast receives the winter continental monsoon from across the Japan Sea, with resulting snow. The San-yo coast is under the influence of the summer oceanic monsoon. Salt may be evaporated and citrus fruits grown on the south, but not on the north.

In western Honshu, neither shore has much arable land, although the margins of the Inland Sea are more hospitable. The northern coast is less indented and has fewer harbors. Despite the lack of shelter, or perhaps owing to the scarcity of farm land, fishing is important along the Japan Sea. Korean influences are noticeable in this San-in area.

The western entrance to the Inland Sea is guarded by the twin cities of Shimonoseki, population 132,737 in 1935, and Moji, on either sides of the mile-wide straits. In 1940, these two ports were combined under the name of Kammon. Shipping prefers Moji on account of its coal and steel, but Shimonoseki became important as it was the rail terminus for the larger island. A railway tunnel now links Moji and Shimonoseki. Many cities lie along the San-yo between Shimonoseki and Kobe, chief of which are Hiroshima, population 310,118 in 1935, and Okayama, population 166,144 in 1935.

Shikoku

The island of Shikoku is the smallest of the main Japanese group, and the least important. The topography is maturely dissected, with high mountains and steep slopes which strictly limit agriculture and handicap communications. A major geologic boundary runs east and west through the island, marked by the great fault scarp which separates the Inner and Outer Zones of Japan. To the south is a series of parallel ridges and valleys underlain by ancient folded rocks; to the north is granite eroded into hills similar to the topography across the Inland Sea.

Both geologically and geographically, southern Shikoku is similar to southern Kyushu and to the Kii peninsula south of Osaka.

In the north, agricultural conditions closely correspond with those in Honshu, just described. On the south shore a more nearly tropical climate with 300 days free from frost permits palms, camphor, and wax trees, and two successive crops of rice. The summer monsoon brings heavy rainfall to the mountains of Shikoku, so that precipitation on the south slopes exceeds 75 inches. In the lee of the mountains near the Inland Sea the rainfall is but half. In addition to rice, there are the usual dry crops of rye, barley, buckwheat, sweet potatoes, and mulberry.

Lumbering and fishing are important occupations, and the island is Japan's most specialized paper area. In the mountains near the Inland Sea is a large copper mine at Besshi. Shikoku has no volcanoes.

There are few cities, little industry, limited railroad service, and considerable area with but sparse population.

Kyushu

Although Kyushu lies at a corner of Old Japan, it has an important history and is one of the ancient centers of Japanese life. The island is closest to China and has long had contacts with the South Seas through the steppingstones of the Ryukyu Islands. The highly indented coast line is an aid to fishing activities, so that people from Kyushu are accustomed to life on the sea. The old Satsuma culture was based on these overseas contacts. Customs and dialects still differ from Honshu. Modern cities are few, and interests are still peripheral.

More than elsewhere, volcanic landscapes are dominant with several active craters, but even in Kyushu less than half the island is occupied by lava flows or ash deposits. There are two separate areas of vulcanism, one around Mt. Aso in the center, the other the volcano of Sakurajima in the south. Even in this peripheral island, population pressure is so great that rice terraces and dry fields have been pushed far up the slopes, and 70,000 people live within the supercrater or caldera of temporarily quiescent Mt. Aso. The island is divided into two equal parts by the same structural boundary that cuts Shikoku.

This is the warmest part of subtropical Japan. Summer temperatures are higher and much more oppressive because of the humidity. There is no protection against the winter monsoon, but in these latitudes it brings no snow or low temperatures. Agriculture is intensive but not unusual. Double cropping is common, with rice often planted as the second crop in mid-July, following dry grains. Sweet potato is widely grown as it is a dependable crop and

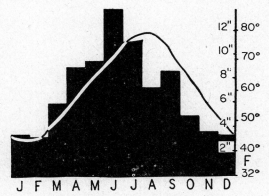

KAGOSHIMA (southwestern Kyushu)
Elevation, 394 feet; average temperature, 61.5°F.; total precipitation 84.7 inches.

the poor man's food. Originally raised in China, it moved from there to the Ryukyu Islands and thence to southern Kyushu and eventually to the rest of Japan. Each successive area refers to it by a name that indicates its importation from the adjoining region. Much of the island is forested, so that lumber and paper mills are important.

Southern Kyushu is more distinctly tropical than the north with rural houses covered by simple thatched roofs, dense vegetation, and abundant bamboo, bananas, and oranges. Tobacco and sweet potatoes along with sugar cane, beans, taro, and vegetables supplement rice culture, which covers but a third of the arable land. This is the lowest fraction in Old Japan and both yields and quality are poor. Kyushu has small specialized horse-breeding areas utilizing the wild grasses of the uplands.

The city of Nagasaki, north of the dividing escarpment, has been a significant port for foreign trade for several centuries, and for a long time was the only gateway for occidental culture. Dutch and Portuguese traders have made Nagasaki conscious of the outside world since the middle of the sixteenth century. The city is closest of all Japanese ports to China, and express steamers leave several times a week for

lurgical coke. There are several dozen large mines, but operations are complicated by faulting. The region supplies the Japanese

The Mikki coal mine in northwestern Kyushu is the largest in Japan. Fifteen tons of water must be pumped from the workings for each ton of coal that is mined. (*Ewing Galloway*.)

Shanghai, 500 miles distant. Nagasaki's modern foreign contacts were aided by the presence of near-by coal suitable for steamship use and, prior to the substitution of fuel oil, it was customary for many steamers from Europe or North America to take on supplies here. Nagasaki has lost much of its commercial importance and ranks but eighth among Japanese ports. It is still the second largest shipbuilding center. The population in 1938 was 211,702.

About half of the nation's coal is mined in the Chikuho basin in the extreme northern part of the island. This coal, of Tertiary age, is subbituminous and must be mixed with imported coal in order to make metal-

market as far north as Nagoya, beyond which supplies come from Hokkaido and the Joban district near Sendai.

Coal from Chikuho and adjacent fields has given rise to a great concentration of heavy industry on the southern side of the Straits of Shimonoseki. In a belt some 20 miles long and usually less than a mile wide from Moji west to Yawata, there is a continuous succession of coal docks, ore piles, blast furnaces and steel mills, cement works, flour mills, sugar refineries, paper mills, oil refineries, glass works, machine shops, and unattractive factory towns. The industrial area has an aggregate population of over half a million. The government-owned Yawata plant and its subsidiaries produce three-fourths of Japan's pig iron and one-half of the steel.

Level land is limited, so that many of the factories are directly on tide water. The area is well situated midway between supplies of coking coal and ore from the continent or the South Seas, and the domestic markets for its products. The straits are a converging point for all Far Eastern traffic, but neither Moji nor Shimonoseki is an important port for passengers. Rail facilities are well developed.

Kyushu exhibits wide contrasts. Heavy industry dominates a small corner of the landscape, but isolation affords the key to most rural areas, especially south of the dividing escarpment. Southern Kyushu has important gold and copper mines.

Northern Honshu[1]

Despite the essential unity of the Japanese islands, it is at once evident that there is marked variation from place to place. Few countries, certainly none in Asia, have so much detail in land pattern or land use within so small an area. In his "Reconnaissance Geography of Japan," Trewartha recognizes over 100 distinct subdivisions, of which 27 are in Northern Honshu. The generalizations necessary in the present study cannot do justice to this diversity.

This is the largest of all regions in Old Japan, the most recently developed, and the least densely populated. Parts of the area have been cultivated but a century, and expansion is still under way. Subtropical conditions merge into a temperate climate, and the growing season ranges from 160 to a maximum of 200 days, according to latitude and altitude. Tea, sweet potatoes, and bamboo drop out, double cropping is uncommon, and mulberry is

[1] Northern Honshu corresponds to the region of Ou as described by Trewartha, and Ou plus northern Hokuroku as defined by Hall.

only locally important. Winters are longer and cooler, and many localities have snow on the ground for four months. The original

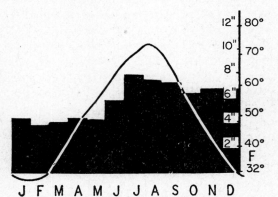

AKITA (west coast of northern Honshu)
Elevation, 20 feet; average temperature, 50.5°F.; total precipitation, 71.4 inches.

forest consisted of maple, birch, chestnut, poplar, and oak. These climatic and vegetation conditions have given rise to brown forest soils.

Three north-south mountain ranges with intervening lowlands give a parallel arrangement to the topography, which is reflected in maps of cultivated land and population distribution. Each of these zones has its interruptions, so that the feasible sites for settlements are isolated. The central range is the highest and is crowned by a number of volcanoes, several of which reach a mile; elsewhere elevations are but half that figure. Structurally, the eastern range is the dividing line between Inner and Outer Japan. There are a few coastal plains, especially in the west, and several of the interior lowlands reach the sea through breaks in the mountains, elsewhere level land is absent along the shore.

Along the Pacific side flows a cool current, and as the summer monsoon blows over it, condensation produces considerable fog. As a result, summers along the east coast are cooler and drier than on the west.

The Japan Sea side has a slight winter precipitation maximum due to the very heavy snowfall. The heaviest snowfall is on the west coast in the vicinity of latitude 37°N. in central Honshu rather than farther north where average temperatures and hence precipitation are lower. Railroads have built many miles of snow sheds, but service may be interrupted for days at a time. In many towns along the Japan Sea and in the mountains, covered sidewalks and wide eaves known as gangi are necessary to permit winter access when the snow is deep. Strong winter gales make it necessary to weight house shingles with large stones.

There are few harbors along either coast, but the cooler waters provide a favorable habitat for sardines so that fishing is important.

Farms average 3½ to 4 acres, twice the size farther south where double cropping is feasible. Rice is grown wherever it may be irrigated, but other crops are favored by cooler conditions. White potatoes and beans do well, as do millet, buckwheat, and barley. Three quarters of Japan's apples are raised here, and have a flavor superior to those grown in the south. Cherries are another new fruit. Horse raising is a thriving industry. Serious agricultural distress prevailed during the 1930's.

Northern Honshu has a number of relatively important natural resources. Copper is mined at Kosaki, Hitachi, and elsewhere. The coal mines at Joban south of Sendai are the third ranking producer. North of Sendai there are blast furnaces at Kamaishi, also of third rank in the nation. Along the Sea of Japan are the country's leading petroleum fields, especially near Niigata in the Echigo hills. Reserves are limited, and intensive developments have failed to yield satisfactory production. Gold, silver, sulphur, and hydroelectric power are also developed in the central mountains.

The small percentage of level land has restricted population. Cities are few and industries lacking. There is little overseas trade, and Yokohama serves as the chief port. The two urban centers of Northern Honshu are Sendai on the east coast, population 219,547 in 1935, and Niigata on the west, population 134,992 in 1935. Each lies in a small plain along the sea.

CHAPTER 13

REGIONS OF OUTER JAPAN

Surrounding the homeland of Old Japan is a series of newer regions. Hokkaido is politically a part of Japan proper; Karafuto, the Chishima or Kurile Islands, Korea or Chosen, Formosa or Taiwan, and the Liuchiu or Ryukyu Islands were ruled as dependencies; while the Marshall, Caroline, and Mariana Islands were acquired as mandates. Manchuria or "Manchoukuo" was increasingly within the Japanese orbit after 1931 but has already been described under China. Although sometimes referred to as Japan's life line, its importance prior to the war with the United States was largely strategic. More capital was poured into Manchuria than the economic dividends warranted.

Outer Japan includes the regions of Hokkaido, Karafuto, Kuriles, Korea, Formosa, and the South Seas.

Hokkaido

Hokkaido is Japan's northland, a frontier of settlement with a population density but one-sixth that of Honshu. Since this is the newest part of Japan proper, much of it has a pioneer landscape. This is the remaining home of the aboriginal Ainu, of whom only 16,000 remain. These non-Japanese peoples once occupied most of Old Japan.

Sixty per cent of the island is still covered with boreal forests, underlain by peaty or podsolic soils. The land that is potentially arable amounts to 14 per cent and resembles that of Old Japan, but restrictions of short growing season and peripheral location will permanently handicap development.

This northern island, lying almost in the latitude of Nova Scotia, has a marine phase of the Asiatic climate with severe winters. Rainfall on the agricultural lowlands approximates 40 inches. Along the east coast, cool offshore currents from the north bring fogs as in Nova Scotia. There is little winter sunshine in the west and one interior station reports but 44 hours for the entire month of January. The two largest cities of Hakodate and Sapporo average but 84 hours each. Daily average temperatures during the winter remain continuously below freezing for four months. Asahizawa has reported a minimum temperature of −41°F., and in Sapporo the thermometer has dropped to −16°F.

The frost-free period is generally less than 150 days, and in the north drops below 90, which is the minimum growing period for the most rapidly maturing varieties of rice. Unfortunately these averages vary widely from year to year. Hazards of unseasonable frost and occasional drought make agriculture somewhat precarious.

The winter monsoon begins at the end of September or early in October and continues until late in March. Strong northwest winds, occasionally of gale strength, bring snowstorms of unusual intensity. A snow cover of several feet is common in the west, occasionally reaching a depth of six feet. The summer southeast monsoon from May to September is intermittent and weak. As this warm air passes over the cold water of the Oya Siwa, chilled by melting sea ice from the Bering Sea, considerable fog results in June and

The extractive industries of mining, forestry, and fishing are relatively more important than elsewhere in Japan. The

The Ainu who now live in Hokkaido are a non-Japanese race who once occupied most of the islands. (*Burton Holmes, from Ewing Galloway.*)

July in the east. Late summer is the most pleasant period.

Although many aspects of Hokkaido's geography differ from Old Japan to the south, there is a similarity in the association of mountains and lowlands. The lowest plains represent alluvial deposits, often poorly drained. The most important of these is the Ishikari Plain which contains a large share of the population. Diluvial terraces and ash fields are widespread. Two north-south mountain ranges cross the island, intersected by an east-west series of volcanoes. Where they meet, elevations exceed a mile.

island contains the largest coal reserves, but they are unfortunately much disturbed by faulting and folding. A dozen mines produce a fair quality of bituminous coal that makes a poor but usable coke. Deposits of iron ore supplemented by imported supplies are the basis for the steel and iron industry at Muroran which ranks as the second center in Japan. Copper, gold, silver, and sulphur are also secured. Hokkaido produces one-sixth of Japan's timber, some of which is made into paper on the island; reserves are excellent. About a fifth of the fish catch is accounted for here, and numerous canneries have long been established. Dismal fishing settlements line the coast. The resources of Hokkaido

crop with exports to the United States and Europe.

The American-style barns of Hokkaido are a reminder of the initial assistance provided by agricultural experts from the United States. (*Germaine Kellerman, courtesy Japan Reference Library.*)

are remote from the chief centers of Japanese population.

With the development of railroads in the decade following 1880, farmers began to come into the Ishikari Plain. Most of the island was then an unoccupied wilderness. As the result of extensive agricultural experimentation, the Japanese have learned how to grow rice in this northern climate, but it occupies only 24 per cent of the cultivated land, less than half the average in Old Japan. If all varieties of beans are considered together, they take first place in acreage. Apples, white potatoes, sugar beets, cherries, and bay replace tea and mulberry as cash crops. Hokkaido and Korea are the only places where oats are important. Peppermint is a specialized

Hokkaido has some 12,000 milk cows and the most extensive dairy industry in the country, shipping considerable quantities of canned milk and butter. Some of the cattle are kept in American-style barns and fed from corn-filled silos, a reflection of the early agricultural advice supplied by American experts. Horses are seven or eight times as numerous as on the farms of Old Japan, with a total of over 200,000 in Hokkaido. Another reflection of early American influence is seen in the use of "giddap," "whoa," "gee," and "haw."

Despite the differences in climate, Japanese immigrants have transplanted their conventional subtropical house types without much modification for the severe winter conditions. Farms average 11 acres in size, usually in one continuous unfenced plot. Roads are laid out in accordance with rectangular land surveys, drawn prior to settlement, and fields conform to the road pattern. In contrast to the clustered settlements of Old Japan, individual disseminated farmsteads dot the landscape.

Life in Hokkaido is not attractive to the average Japanese farmer, and colonization is largely the result of government subsidies. Now that the best land has been occupied, there is an increasing unwillingness of Japanese to settle in the island. In 1914 some 320,000 people went to the northland, a considerable increase in view of the fact that the total population was then under 2,000,000. But in the years from 1916 to 1921, there was an average of only 77,000 incoming residents. During the next five-year period, the average fell to 28,000 and in 1933 it declined to 22,000.

The agricultural population numbers about 2,000,000, and colonization authorities believe that there will be room for an additional 1,000,000 farmers, although expensive irrigation and drainage will be required to bring more land into cultivation. The urban population amounts to 800,000 and it is thought that this may be increased by approximately 2,000,000. The chief cities are the capital Sapporo in the Ishikari Plain, population 196,541 in 1935, and the principal seaport and rail terminus Hakodate, population 207,480 in 1935.

The presence of undeveloped settlement possibilities within this island of Japan proper raises serious questions as to Japan's justification in seeking lands elsewhere outside the Empire, particularly at comparable latitudes on the mainland. It emphasizes too the essentially subtropical character of Japanese culture and the unwillingness of the people to leave their homeland and settle in lands where rice is not easily raised. Thus the total number of

Japanese settlers throughout the world outside of the Empire numbers a million, of whom half are accounted for by those in Manchuria. This compares with seven million Chinese who have left China, in addition to twice that number who moved into Manchuria when it became open to settlement. Japanese emigrants living in Brazil number 200,000 while there are 126,947 in the United States and another 157,905 in Hawaii, and but 3,000 in all Europe.

Karafuto

Thirty miles north of Hokkaido lies the elongated island of Sakhalin, owned half and half by Japan and the Soviet Union since 1905. Prior to that time there was a period of Russian control and, still earlier, informal Japanese and Russian claims that date back to the seventeenth century. In 1875 Japan agreed to give up Sakhalin while Russia in turn withdrew from the Kuriles. The Japanese have given the southern half of the island its old Ainu name of Karafuto.

Karafuto is cold. Winter lasts six months, and snow covers the island to an average depth of three feet, so that dog sleds are in common use. Summer is the more moist season, but the total precipitation is only 25 inches. Records of the seven meteorological stations show rain or snow every day in the year except for 22 to 53 days. Most ports are icebound for long periods, and the loading of oil tankers in the northern half of the island is impossible for eight months. At some ports occasional winter steamers tie up at the ice margin offshore and transport goods to the land by sleds.

Two mountain chains limit level land to narrow coastal fragments and a central lowland. Soils are podsolic and of low fertility.

The wealth of the island is its timber, fish, oil, and coal. Agriculture is expanding, but only slowly. In 1937 there were 10,811 agricultural families in Karafuto, including 623 arrivals. In 1932, the new agricultural colonists numbered 1,341. The cultivated area amounts to only 86,175 acres. Optimistic estimates suggest that the potentially arable land is many times this acreage, but poor soil, short growing seasons, and limited sunshine restrict agricultural possibilities. Government-sponsored immigrants from Old Japan, accustomed to rice and intensive cultivation, find great difficulty in adjusting to these new conditions. The more adjustable colonists come from Hokkaido. Each new settler is allotted 12½ to 25 acres and a log house of Russian style. Chief crops are oats, fodder, potatoes, and peas in order. Rice experiments are partly successful.

Fishing is the oldest occupation and conditions resemble those in Hokkaido at the turn of the century. Squalid fishing villages border many bays. Each summer 10,000 fishermen and other workers come from the islands to the south to supplement those who live there. Herring, sea trout, salmon, cod, and crab are the chief catch, in order. Many of the fish are processed for fertilizer or oil, or are dried and salted for shipment as food. Canned crab meat is an important export to the United States.

Many of those who fish during the summer months work as lumbermen in the winter. Coniferous forests with dense undergrowth cover many of the mountains, interspersed with patches of tundra. Trees are usually small, and forest fires serious. Spruce is cut for pulpwood and paper, and there are also fir, larch, birch, elm, and willow. Mine props, railroad ties, and charcoal are each important, but pulp is by far the most valuable product. At Shiretori is what is reported to be the largest and most modern pulp plant in eastern Asia. The total value of lumbering exceeds fishing.

Coal reserves are moderate, but the production is mainly used on the island for railroads and other needs. Soft bituminous coal is Eocene in age, and there is also Pliocene lignite. Beds occur on both flanks of the western range. Some oil is secured in Karafuto, but the output is disappointing. The northern half of the island, under Soviet control, contains extensive oil deposits, and since 1925 Japanese interests have had concessions in ten fields, in each of which their operations are limited to alternate checkerboard plots. In 1934 there were 159 Japanese wells, whose yield accounted for a quarter of Japan's total output. The Soviet government is also vitally interested in its 166 wells, for this is the chief production east of the Urals, and it is doubtful whether the Japanese concession will be extended indefinitely.

The population of Japanese Karafuto in 1930 numbered 295,000, in contrast to some 15,000 in Soviet Sakhalin. The distribution is very uneven, and two-thirds live in the eleven towns which have over 4,000 each. Most settlements are along the coast or in the Suzuya Plain in the south where Otomari and Toyohara are the chief cities.

The Kuriles

Japan's northernmost possession is a chain of islands from Hokkaido northeastward to the tip of Soviet Kamchatka at latitude 51°N. These are the Chishima or thousand islands, better known to foreigners by their Russian names of Kuriles which means "smoke." Actually there are but 32 islands, mostly volcanic. Precipitous cliffs fringe the shores and there is virtually no agricultural land. Snow falls from mid-September to June, and there is much fog in the summer.

The Kuriles are surrounded by valuable fishing grounds which attract a large number of boats in summer. Salmon, cod, and crab are important. On the islands are large bears, fox, and sable. Fur seals and sea otter have been protected since the 1911 treaty between Japan, Russia, Great Britain, and the United States.

The North Pacific great-circle route lies near both the Kuriles and Aleutian Islands, but steamers avoid each group on account of fog. This is the closest contact between the Japanese Empire and the United States. Unfavorable flying conditions make both groups ill-suited for trans-Pacific aviation.

Korea[1]

Korea presents a series of problems: political, agricultural, and cultural. The Koreans are ethnographically a distinct people. Throughout their history there has been a constant struggle to maintain their national entity. Situated on the borderlands of China, Korea has been alternately independent and subject in varying degree to China. Culturally she owes much to her continental neighbor, although there were independent or concurrent developments within the peninsula. Koreans have their own language, literature, and customs. It was by way of the peninsula that Japan gained much of its culture.

For centuries the country was so beset and ravaged by invasions of Chinese, Mongols, Manchus, and Japanese that she sought to maintain isolation and thus gained the title of "the Hermit Nation." The weakened position of the people was not much improved during the isolation period because of bitter internal political strife, so that Korea was but a weak pawn in the struggle associated with Japan's rise to power. One of the avowed objectives of the Sino-Japanese War of 1894–1895 and again of the Russo-Japanese War of 1904–

1905 was to give the peninsula its independence, but since that time Japanese influence has been on the increase. After a short protectorate, Korea was formally annexed in 1910. Koreans have not welcomed Japanese rule and there have been uprisings, such as that of 1919. Independence following the Second World War was one of the early objectives of the United Nations. The official Japanese name of the country is Chosen, romanized as Tyosen.

Japan's exploitation brought widespread material improvements in communications, agricultural yields, and mining, but the relative livelihood of the Korean farmer appears to be declining. A good example is education where a strong policy of Japanization was developed. A high official epitomized the objectives when he stated that "Koreans should be taught to follow, not to know." There are school facilities for only about 18 per cent of the children, contrasted with 99.5 per cent in Japan. The economic lot of Korea seems to be worsening, for with the bettering of material conditions there has been a disproportionate increase in population, in tenancy, in debt, and in imports over exports. Owing to this economic pressure many Koreans have engaged in the shadier aspects of Japanese exploitation, not only in Korea but in other lands and thus have sadly brought discredit on their name. Many people believe that this moral degradation is one of the most tragic aspects of Japan's influence on Korea.

In the life of modern Japan, Korea became a source of food and raw materials such as rice, cotton, fish, iron ore, coal, and gold; a market for manufactured goods; an outlet for nonagricultural colonists; and a strategic approach to the mainland. At one time it was a bulwark against Russian advance, but later, except for the extreme northeast, Manchuria took that place. Although it is predominantly an

---

[1] The author is particularly indebted to Shannon McCune for assistance in preparing this section.

asset to the capitalists of Japan, there are many liabilities as well.

Korea is a land of mountains. From the and generally forms highlands; granite may be eroded to more rounded forms and to lower elevations.

Rugged topography characterizes the Konga San or Diamond Mountains of eastern Korea.

air they seem to be without number; range after range extend to the horizon so that the land resembles a sea in a heavy gale. High mountains are lacking; it is their profusion that impresses one. No plain is so extensive that the encircling mountains cannot be seen on a fair day. Although mostly small, these plains are vital, for it is in this one-fifth of the 86,000 square miles that the 23,000,000 people are crowded.

Beneath the surface is a complex of granite, gneiss, and early Paleozoic and late Proterozoic limestones and metamorphics. Patches of Carboniferous and Cretaceous formations occur, especially in the southeast. Recent deposits are confined to small areas. The distinction between older and younger alluvium is not emphasized as in Japan. Neither volcanoes nor earthquakes are active. The gneiss is resistant

The Manchurian frontier is marked by two rivers and a mountain range. The Yalu flows southwestward and marks a very strong cultural boundary. The Tumen drains northeast, but across it Koreans have migrated for centuries. Between the headwaters lies the volcanic Hakuto San, or Paitou Shan in Chinese, with a maximum elevation of 9,020 feet. At the summit is a large crater lake comparable to that in Oregon. There are few open valleys, and much of the northern frontier is an uninhabited land with magnificent forests of spruce, fir, larch, and pine. The geologic development and erosional history have given rise to the Kaima Plateau, a rolling upland in some places lava-capped, dissected by deeply entrenched rivers, and disrupted by some minor ranges. There is abrupt transition to the east from this interior upland, marked by sharp fault escarpments. To the southwest, the descent

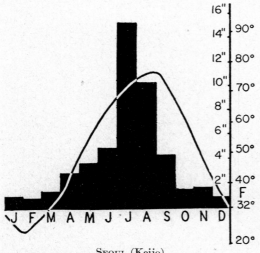

SEOUL (Keijo)
Average temperature 51°F.; total precipitation, 50.5 inches.

is more gradual to the mountains, valleys, and plains of northwestern Korea.

Northern and Southern Korea are separated by a graben which cuts the peninsula along a northeast-southwest line followed by the railroad from Genzan to Keijo, or Seoul. This is the major geographic boundary of the country. South and east of this line, Korea is dominated by the Taihaku Mountain range which parallels the east coast. This is a maturely dissected block, a mile in height, which slopes gently to the west but descends abruptly to the Japan Sea. The most picturesque scenery occurs in the Kongo San, or Diamond Mountains. The Rakuto Basin of the southeast is divided from the rest of the peninsula by a range, the Syohaku, trending southwest from the southern Taihaku. There are many other ranges caused by old earth folds or recent tectonic activity which confuse the structure of southern Korea.

Most rivers rise in the mountains near the Japan Sea and flow into the Yalu and Tumen systems or westward to the Yellow Sea. None of them is long. Thus the widest plains are on the west, and the economic life of these areas might tend to move toward the continent were it not for Japanese occupation. There are few harbors on the east, while the western and southern embayed coast lines with their many islands provide better shelter for fishing vessels or modern steamers, although the high tides are a handicap.

The climatic characteristics of Korea more nearly resemble those of central and north China than Japan. There are considerable contrasts between winter and summer in the different regions. Because of the location of the peninsula on the margins of the Asiatic winter high pressure area, there are monsoonal drifts of cold dry air coming from the north and west during the cold season. The passage of cyclonic storms, especially strong in the spring and fall, brings periodic variations to the winter weather. There is more precipitation due to these storms in the south than in the north; even so it is slight compared with the summer rains. Snow may stay long on the ground in the north but it melts quickly in the mild temperatures of the south. The northern interior has bitterly cold winters; only the extreme southern fringe has mean January temperatures above freezing. For example, the frost-free period varies from 130 days in the northern interior (Tyokotin), to 178 days in the center (Keijo), to 226 in the south (Fusan).

Summers are hot and humid with a marked concentration of the annual rainfall. Regional temperature contrasts are not so sharp in summer as in winter, although the northern interior and northeastern littoral are cooler than the south. Within Korea precipitation varies mainly with orographic position; the highest amounts are over 60 inches along the Syohaku range, in the south; and the least are in the sheltered Tumen basin, less than 25 inches. Since most of the precipitation occurs during the growing season, agriculture is in Japan itself. The population density of 190 per square mile in 1937 is less than half that of Japan but this fails to give a true

Threshing with a flail in a farm courtyard of Korea. (*Courtesy Presbyterian Board of Foreign Missions.*)

normally well supplied. Occasional torrential storms, caused by typhoons or convection, may do much damage but are rare.

Sharp seasonal contrasts are characteristic, as shown by extremes at Keijo, where the maximum is over 100°F. and the minimum −10°F. The proximity to the continental interior makes these extremes normal. Naturally they are greater in the north and in the interior rather than in the south or along the coast.

Although the area of Korea is but slightly over half that of Japan proper, cultivated land totaled 11,034,342 acres in 1936 as compared with 14,907,973 acres picture. Eighty per cent of all Koreans live on the soil, and there is little profit to them from mining, forestry, or industry. Centuries of intensive cultivation have impoverished the soil, so that crop yields are low. Fertilization would help, but povery-stricken farmers are in no position to make the necessary adjustments.

Korean agriculture is characterized by the intensity of human labor. Only the simplest tools are available, and there is neither capital nor experience for the use of machinery. Crops are similar to those described in Japan, although yields per acre are often but half. Since the annexation of Korea in 1910, agricultural experimentation has materially increased yields and quality. The average holding per farm family is 3.6 acres, but most of the farms

southeast has a figure of 192, in contrast to 109 in the northeast.

The economy of Korea is tuned to the

A farm landscape on the outskirts of Kosyu. This December scene shows barley planted in the rice fields.
(*Courtesy of Shannon McCune.*)

are smaller and are diminishing in size while the large holdings of Japanese-financed companies are increasing in number and area.

Double cropping is somewhat more common than in Japan proper, and the average for the whole country, in terms of 100 as representing single-crop utilization, is estimated by Lee[1] at 134. Corresponding figures for Japan are 128 (Nasu) and China, 147 (Buck). These figures are for the entire country; actually most of the double cropping is concentrated in the southern portions where climatic conditions are favorable. For example, the extreme

cultivation of rice which is the major crop, although occupying only a third of the cultivated land. Almost all of the rice is irrigated, but two-thirds of the flooded fields are precariously dependent for water upon fortunate rainfall; one-fortieth of the rice is sown as a dry crop. Japanese government supervision conspicuously increased the acreage of rice by 25.3 per cent from 1910 to 1935 and the yield by 71.6 per cent. The yield and acreage fluctuate considerably from year to year; price fluctuations are also pronounced and work adversely to the tenant farmers. Official estimates of yields are 17 bushels per acre while other figures are 28 bushels, in either case far below the Japanese average of 43 bushels. Over two-fifths of the rice crop

[1] Lee, Hoon K., "Land Utilization and Rural Economy in Korea," Institute of Pacific Relations, Shanghai: Kelley and Walsh (1936), 113.

is shipped to the Japanese Islands to meet the deficiency there. This leaves an inadequate food supply for Korea which is especially in the northwest; wheat is grown in the same area. Other crops include grain sorghum, oats, buckwheat, corn, white and

A farmstead in an isolated mountain valley, with cultivated fields on the steep hillside. (*Courtesy of Shannon McCune.*)

partly corrected by imports of millet from Manchuria.

Barley represents the second most important crop and is the principal food for the mass of the people. It occupied an acreage just over three-fifths that of rice, had just under three-fifths of the yield, but only one-fifth of the value in 1935. In southern Korea barley is planted during October or November in the drained rice fields or on dry fields and harvested in June or July. In the north, where winters are more severe, it is sown in the spring. Soy and other varieties of beans occupied similar positions in acreage and value as barley, but fit into the agricultural economy quite differently. Millet is also important

sweet potatoes. There are many vegetables especially turnips and cabbage used in kimchi, the Korean pickle. Excellent pears and apples are grown, but no citrus fruits.

Southern Korea is well suited for the growing of American varieties of cotton; native varieties are grown in the northwest. Virtually all of Japan's production is obtained there. Increasing acreages and better yields have resulted from government pressure. The growth of mulberry and the production of silk are widespread subsidiary agricultural occupations, but are of minor importance in comparison with Japan proper.

Korean cattle are of good quality and the total number of oxen and cows exceeds that of all Japan proper. There is an average of one to every two farm houses; most of the cattle actually are used communally. There are many more swine than in Japan.

Climatic conditions divide Korea into two major agricultural regions, the northern and southern. Unlike the geomorphic boundary which is a northeast-southwest line, the climatic and agricultural boundary tends to run from southeast to northwest, deflected southward by the mountains along the Japan Sea. Although the regions are roughly equal in size, more than three-fourths of the rice is grown in the south together with almost all of the cotton, barley, and sweet potatoes. Northern Korea specializes in the hardier grains in addition to rice. Although double cropping is characteristic of the south, severe winter conditions make it impractical in the north.

One of the unfortunate features of farming in the northern interior and in the central mountain sections is the practice of "fire-field" agriculture, or burning the hillsides in preparation for planting a temporary crop. There are extensive areas of state forest land, and squatters quasi-illegally burn the brush or grass in order to fertilize the soil preparatory to planting crops of millet, oats, or potatoes. After one or two years, fertility diminishes and erosion becomes serious, so that the fields may be abandoned. The government is striving to regularize these practices. After almost static conditions from 1919 to 1928 there was slight increase to 1932; then the fire-cleared acreage more than doubled by 1934 and remained almost the same in 1935 with a figure of a million acres, a tenth of the cultivated area.

Throughout Korea, especially in the south, tenancy and debt are of tragic concern and intimately affect land utilization and rural landscapes. Japanese authorities do not publicize these aspects, so that one must turn to the study that Lee made in 1931 and 1932. Undoubtedly conditions have become much worse since that time. According to Lee, 48.4 per cent of the farm households are tenants, and 29.6 per cent are part tenants; in other words "almost four out of every five Korean farmers are tenants." The most prevalent rent is about one-half of the yield; it may be as high as nine-tenths. Since most of the leasing is for only one year, the land is exploited as much as possible. There are many other undesirable conditions and customs of tenancy. In addition, three out of four farmers are heavily in debt for amounts averaging almost twice their average total yearly income. Interest rates are about 30 per cent but they go as high as 70 to 80 per cent. Although figures are unavailable, there is a great increase of land in the hands of Japanese capitalists. Some of the developments in the south during the late 1930's of large well-irrigated tracts by Japanese companies, including the notorious Oriental Development Company, are very striking.

About 73 per cent of Korea is forest land. In the densely settled areas most of the commercial timber has long since been removed, so that there is only a cover of scrub trees and grass. The best timber resource is along the Manchurian border where there are excellent stands of spruce, fir, larch, and pine. The remaining forests, mainly in the mountain lands of the south, are dominantly pine with some oak and elm. The chief use of these forest lands is for domestic firewood. A little bamboo is grown in protected patches in the extreme south and is almost a crop rather than natural forest.

The peninsula of Korea has several minerals that Japan finds of value. Mineral production and associated industries were greatly expanded during the Second World War. These included aluminum works, chemicals, nonferrous refining, machinery, and munitions. Gold has been known for many decades, and there were American concessions even before the period of

The cities, which in the past existed largely for administrative or market functions, are the centers for increasing modern

The harbor of Rashin in northern Korea provides a new gateway to Manchuria. These apartment houses were built for workers during the construction of the port that lies to the left of the photograph.

Japanese occupation. With the increased price of gold in 1934 and Japan's growing need for foreign exchange, production was increased greatly, from an output of 199,483 troy ounces in 1930 to an estimated yield of 838,709 troy ounces in 1937. Both placer and lode deposits are widely scattered.

The second most important mineral is iron ore, mined in the western peninsula. Most of it is shipped to Japan, but there are blast furnaces and steel mills at Kenjiho; Chinnampo, southwest of Heijo, or Pyengyang; and the far north. Another new development is just across the border in Manchuria at Tungpientao. Coal is the third most important mineral product with an output of 2,282,000 metric tons in 1936. Two-thirds of the reserves are anthracite, with mines near Heijo; the remainder is poor lignite. Copper, silver, and tungsten are mined. Graphite is one of the more unusual resources, but competition with deposits in Ceylon makes the yield fluctuate, although the quality is excellent.

Among power resources are hydroelectric projects, especially those which utilize the Yalu and its tributaries.

industrialization. The largest city, Keijo, or Seoul, is the governmental, financial, and cultural center of the peninsula, with a population of 706,396 in 1937; it has growing industrial suburbs. The major city of the northwest, Heijo, or Pyengyang, 185,-419, and Taikyu in the southeast, 110,866, are also becoming industrial centers. The two important seaports are Fusan at the railway terminus opposite Japan, 213,142, and Jinsen or Chemulpo, 102,473, the gateway of Keijo on the west coast. In the far northeast the developing ports of Yuki and Rashin serve as outlets for central Manchuria.

Out of a total population of 22,355,485 in 1937, there are 629,000 Japanese. Few of these are farmers, although many subsidized efforts have been made to attract colonists. Most of the Japanese are in government service, including railways; others are merchants. Most of the industry, of which cotton textiles is the chief, is likewise in Japanese hands. Four-fifths of all Korea's foreign trade is with Japan proper, and an excess of imports is gradually draining the country of its limited wealth.

Whereas it is true that Japanese occupation has tended to impoverish the average Korean, it is also true that possession of Korea has not been a blessing to the average Japanese. Korean laborers are able to underlive the Japanese. In fact, the Korean farmer is the only one in the world who has been able to compete successfully with the Chinese. Large numbers of Korean laborers have migrated to the industrial districts of Japan, often upon solicitation of Japanese factories, because of the their lower wage scale. This cheap labor displaces Japanese workers and adds to the labor difficulties at home. The number of Koreans in Japan proper rose from 40,775 in 1920 to 419,009 in 1930. Figures for 1940 would show actually more Koreans in Japan than Japanese in Korea.

Korea does not look like Japan. Volcanic landscapes are absent, hills are covered with scrub and are eroded, and cultivation is less intensive. It is particularly in the cultural element that contrasts are most noticeable. Houses are substantially built with mud walls, and their floors are heated by passages underneath which circulate smoke from kitchen fires. Rural settlement is commonly in villages, often located at the edge of the hills; but in the northern interior isolated, wooden-shingled farmhouses are common. Neither roads nor irrigation canals are so numerous as in the islands. Green fertilizer and compost replace the human manure of Japan and China. Most noticeable is the difference in racial appearance and dress, although the white clothing of the Koreans of a decade ago is being changed to darker colors.

Korea has been subjected to tremendous changes since 1910. How many of these transformations are products of the times or the result of Japanese initiative is difficult to judge rightly. Nevertheless, Korea offers a laboratory to study Japanese colonial policies and their effects. The fact that there are still so many problems, both old and new, is significant. Independence has been increasingly demanded and will doubtless occur with the defeat of Japan. Some years of tutelage will be needed, and Korea may need to come within the sphere of influence of some other great power, presumably China.

Formosa

The island of Formosa or Taiwan represents one of the major areas of expanding agriculture within the Empire. Rapid and ambitious exploitation is under way, and large shipments of sugar, rice, bananas, and pineapple supplement the food supply of Old Japan.

The name Formosa is a Portuguese word meaning beautiful and dates back to the seventeenth century when the Portuguese contested with the Dutch and Spanish for possession. Taiwan is the ancient native name, as well as the legal Japanese term. Chinese control became effective in 1683 and lasted until the Sino-Japanese War of 1894–1895. Chinese influence still persists, for nine-tenths of the population of 5,212,426 (1935) are Chinese from the near-by provinces of Fukien and Kwantung. Japanese number less than 300,000, practically none of them agriculturalists. The population of Formosa has doubled since the beginning of the century.

The general configuration of the island is that of a tilted fault block, sloping to the west from a range of two-mile-high mountains along the eastern axis. The highest peak in the island, and for that matter in the Empire, is Niitaka, known to foreigners as Mt. Morrison, 12,956 feet. This peak gives its name to the entire range. Slopes on the east descend precipitously to the sea, but between the central Niitaka Range and the Pacific are the Taito lowland and mountains. Fertile coastal plains border the western shore.

Formosa lies astride the Tropic of Cancer in a position comparable to that of Cuba. Its shores are bathed by the warm Kuroshio. Tropical conditions prevail except in the mountains where there is alpine vegetation. Lowland temperatures never reach freezing and seldom approach 100°F. The island is exposed to the monsoons, that of the winter being especially important. The northeastern monsoon lasts from early October till late March and, since its direction coincides with the trade winds, to be expected at these latitudes, strong winds result. Steamers along the China coast barely make headway at times. These winds bring copious precipitation, particularly to the north where heavy orographic rainfall results.

The southwest summer monsoon from early May to late August is weaker, since it is masked by the trade-wind tendency. Occasional summer typhoons bring concentrated rainfall to the abrupt eastern slopes. The annual precipitation in the lowland varies from 40 inches in the west to double that amount near the mountains. Within the mountains rainfall is among the heaviest in the world, with a recorded maximum of 289 inches at Kashoryo.

Seventy per cent of Formosa is in forest. Where the land has not been cleared, there is a tropical cover of camphor, cypress, bamboo, and other forms, many of them of commercial value. Mangroves border the shallow western coast.

Agriculture resembles the Chinese pattern, with rice terraces, water buffalos, pigs, two-wheeled carts, ducks, and Chinese implements. The cultivated area is 2,116,-174 acres (1937), so that the population density in terms of cropland alone is 1,576 per square mile.

Rice is the dominant food crop, but exports to Japan slightly exceed domestic consumption and amounted to 28 per cent of Formosa's outgoing business in 1937. Two

harvests a year are common. Sweet potatoes, introduced long ago from China, are the main food of the poorer folk. The most

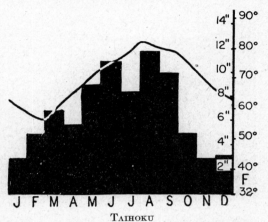

Taihoku
Average temperature, 69°F.; total precipitation, 83.6 inches.

spectacular increase is the production of sugar cane, grown especially in the west and north. Despite the world surplus, Japanese interests have expanded its production manyfold in Formosa in order to make the Empire self-sufficient. The shipment of raw sugar to Japan was 42 per cent of the island's export trade in 1937. Yields and costs are still less satisfactory than in Java. Sugar consumption in Japan increased from 15 pounds per capita in 1918 to 30 pounds in 1928. Bananas and canned pineapple are significant exports to Japan. Oolong tea, widely grown in the north, is consumed by the United States and Great Britain.

Formosa supplies three-fourths of the world's natural camphor, but synthetic substitutes are available so that the natural product has lost its monopoly. Jute and ramie are local fibers.

Good steamship coal is mined in the north. Salt is evaporated along the western coast for shipment to Japan. Some petroleum and a variety of metals are mined, but production is small.

There are two cities of importance. Taihoku in the extreme north is the capital and is 18 miles south of its port of

ment remain, but increased efficiency has greatly improved crops and yields. The place of the Japanese appears to be the

The mountains of eastern Formosa are inhabited by primitive peoples who have been head-hunters until recently. (*Frederick L. Hamilton, from Three Lions.*)

Keelung. In 1935 the population was 278,-446. Tainan is the center for the south, population 111,959 (1935). The only satisfactory harbors are at the two ends of the island. Several times a week there are steamer connections with Kobe and Yokohama, and less frequently with Hongkong.

Formosa has failed to provide an outlet for surplus Japanese farmers. Subsidized attempts at colonization have not met with success, as the native Chinese are willing to live on a lower standard than the Japanese. Few unoccupied areas for settle-

same as in Korea—administrators and exploiters but not permanent settlers.

South Seas

After the First World War, greater Japan extended to within 1° of the equator, for the Empire was given a mandate over the former German possessions in the Marshall, Caroline, and Mariana or Ladrone islands. Three other island groups lie south of Old Japan. Directly south of Kyushu are the Izu Shichito, politically a part of Japan proper, while farther south are the Ogasawara or Bonin Islands. Between Kyushu and Formosa are the Ryukyu, often known by their Chinese name of Liuchiu.

As a whole, the groups have a tropical climate with heavy rainfall and low seasonal range of temperature. Destructive typhoons visit the area during the summer.

Sweet potatoes are everywhere more important than rice. Important developments in sugar-cane production have characterized recent years. Cocoanuts, tapioca, and taro reflect the low latitude.

The Ryukyu group includes 55 small islands near the edge of the continental shelf with a total area of 935 square miles. Several are volcanic and level land is limited on each. Coral reefs fringe the shore. Overpopulation has led to emigration to Japan proper and to Hawaii.

Within the mandated region are 1,458 islands and reefs, many of them quite insignificant since the total area is but 830 square miles. The population has grown rapidly, owing to migration from Japan. The 1938 figures show 121,128 people of whom 70,141 are Japanese. Most of the latter live on Saipan in the Mariana group and are engaged in sugar production. Phosphate rock is mined on two islands. The largest of the Marianas is Guam, directly south of Saipan, and the property of the United States. With this exception, all islands north of the equator between the Philippines and Wake were under Japanese control.

CHAPTER 14

JAPAN'S WORLD POSITION

Foreign Trade

It is doubtful whether any other nation has so transformed its economic life in a similar period. Since the opening of Japan in 1853, the country has made enormous strides in its international position. Internal and external expansion was especially noticeable between the First and Second World Wars. In the 50 years ending with 1938, overseas trade grew from 144 million to 5,331 million yen. Japan's share of total world trade was still but 3.7 per cent in 1938, as compared with 13.7 per cent for the United Kingdom and 11.8 per cent for the United States.

In the international market, Japan's great assets are cheap labor, a considerable measure of skill and efficiency, and nearness to Asiatic consumers. Essential raw materials are scarce, so that exports must rest on imports. As long as Japan can add enough secondary value to basic raw commodities through manufacturing, she can command a market. Japanese labor costs are rising so that this initial advantage is nearly over. It is already profitable for Japanese cotton mills to move to Shanghai and there use cheap Chinese labor and then undersell the native product in the homeland. If Japanese export prices become too high, it is possible for her customers to install factories of their own since textile and other machinery is available to any country. The real test is comparative inventiveness and commercial skill; political advantage is temporary. Japan can hold her markets only so long as she makes a cheaper or better product than her competitors, and enjoys international good will. The old statement about the Japanese being merely "copyists" no longer has much meaning.

The first economic contacts with Europe came with the arrival of the Portuguese and Dutch at Nagasaki in the middle of the sixteenth century, but this trade was shortly suppressed and later restricted to one Dutch ship a year. Not until the treaties arranged by Admiral Perry in 1853 were foreigners permitted to carry on commerce, and the conspicuous developments date from the Meiji Restoration in 1868.

The First World War presented great commercial opportunities to Japan, and the war years were one of the few periods when exports exceeded imports. The resumption of normal world trade in 1918 brought a sharp drop in Japanese overseas sales, but her foreign trade continued to be of large proportions. The depression of the 1930's presented new problems as nation after nation imposed tariff restrictions and endeavored to develop national self-sufficiency. Japan is a poor country where a closed economy is impossible. Agriculture has proved incapable of caring for the expanding population and the expense of modernization, so that the nation is committed to industrialization and foreign trade.

It is imperative for Japan to import if she is to maintain anything approaching her present standards. Food is nearly adequate within the Empire, but many overseas products such as cotton, wool, petroleum, iron, and machinery are indispensable. This is true even though all exports should cease. But to pay for these indispensable materials, silk, sea foods, and art goods are the only native export products. Foreign sales of manufactured imports must be expanded, no matter whether at a profit or not, but each expansion of exports requires added imports. Unfortunately, Japan's major exports are either luxury goods, such as silk, or items like cotton cloth which are available elsewhere. Japan's trade problem is thus the necessity of securing markets. This has required skill but has been generally successful.

It is always difficult to determine the exact international balance of payments for a country as there are so many invisible items. Between the beginning of the First and Second World Wars, total imports of merchandise exceeded exports by over a billion yen. This was more than offset by income from shipping, tourists, dividends, and other foreign services, so that the international balance of trade and services was favorable. On the other hand, large exports of capital and gold shipments give the total picture a negative aspect. The investments in Manchuria and elsewhere may someday return a profit, but the immediate prospects are unfavorable.

During the past half century the character of Japanese trade has undergone several changes. An early concentration on manufactured imports is changing to the purchase of raw materials; likewise in exports the emphasis has shifted from raw silk to cotton textiles and simple manufactures. Thus, finished goods accounted for 29 per cent of the sales in 1913, and 59 per cent in 1938.

The leading export is now cotton cloth. Raw silk is second but declining, and in its place Japan produces rayon. Sales of sea foods and lumber are significant, as is a large miscellaneous group of variety goods.

Imported materials include raw cotton and wool, iron ore, pig iron, scrap steel, minerals, petroleum products, bean cake, chemicals, and machine tools.

Because of her dependence upon essential imports, Japan suffers when her currency is depreciated or when world prices rise. On the other hand, she profits greatly at times of world surplus when many nations are willing to dump their products at prices below costs. It is an open question as to whether Japan is seriously handicapped by not having her own basic commodities; military strategy is another matter.

In order to solve the financial aspects of her import needs, Japan endeavored to set up a closed financial system in eastern Asia known as the yen bloc. But neither Manchuria nor China proper supplied Japan's material deficiencies. Cotton might be grown, but boycotts and disrupted economics have handicapped the supply. Coal, iron, and salt are available, but the war with China restricted production. Only after her conquests in southeastern Asia following 1941 did the "Greater East Asia Co-prosperity Sphere" include a self-sufficient economic realm.

In normal times, China is Japan's best customer. The United States is second in total trade, largely on account of Japanese purchases of raw cotton, oil, iron, and automobiles; prewar sales to America declined owing to the decrease in silk. Statistics for the British Empire are complicated by the inclusion of Hongkong which is merely a transshipment point for China; otherwise, Britain ranks third, largely because of increasing trade with India.

In 1936, Japan stood fifth among all nations in the value of her foreign trade, with a total of $1,183,000,000 or $28.10 per capita. The leaders were the United Kingdom, United States, Germany, and France.

Japan's great market lies in eastern and southern Asia, and there too may be found many of her basic needs. But whether this American-made consumer goods, but as her standard of living increases, Japan will be a better customer.

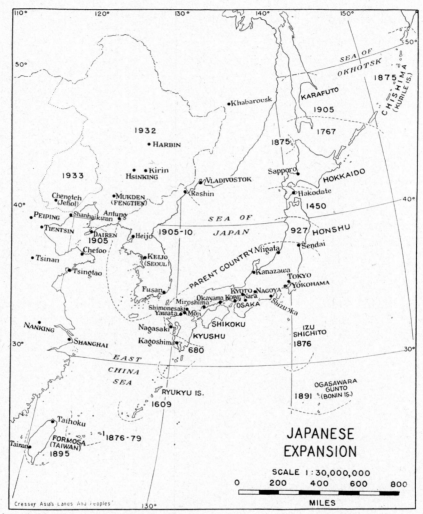

The expansion of the Japanese Empire began in the seventh century when the Ainus were gradually pushed northward. Further attempts at expansion since 1937 extend beyond the limits of this map.

trade is to be captured by Japan or China is a major question. For some decades Japan's chemicals, machines, and the products of skill will have to come from Europe and America. At present, the ultimate consumer in Japan can seldom afford

Expansion by Land and Sea

Japan is insular and her people ambitious. Emigration is unpopular, industry insecure, and foreign trade unpredictable; territorial expansion is thus sought as a panacea. With overseas political control it is hoped that raw materials and markets may be assured, but unfortunately little consideration has been given to international good will by those in authority.

The earliest expansion within what is now Japan proper was due to the pressure for riceland. From the old centers of Satsuma, Izumo, and Yamato culture in the southwest, the Japanese pushed back the Ainu and gradually occupied all of the main islands.

Modern imperialism started with the first Sino-Japanese War in 1894–1895, fought ostensibly to give Korea its independence from China. With the treaty of peace, Japan acquired Formosa but, in place of securing the Liaotung Peninsula in southern Manchuria, she yielded to pressure from Russia, Germany, and France and accepted instead an indemnity from China. A few years later, Russia built the Chinese Eastern Railway across Manchuria to Vladivostok with a branch south to Port Arthur in the Liaotung Peninsula. Thus Russia became established in the same area that Japan had sought previously. This led to the Russo-Japanese War of 1904–1905 from which Japan secured certain economic concessions, often termed "treaty rights" in southern Manchuria. In 1910, Korea was formally annexed. Throughout the opening decades of the century, territorial security was the chief military motive.

During the First World War, Japan seized German concessions in Shantung which were not returned to China until the Washington Conference of 1922. At the end of the war, Japan was awarded a mandate over the German islands in the Pacific north of the equator. With the Russian Revolution of 1917, Japan and the United States joined in sending an expedition into Siberia as far as Lake Baikal. Each country agreed to send 7,500 soldiers, but Japan sent 72,500 and withdrew only on strong diplomatic pressure.[1] At the same period she took over northern Sakhalin, but had to return it later.

Manchuria became the puppet state of "Manchoukuo" after the "Mukden incident" of Sept. 18, 1931, and fighting spread south of the Great Wall in 1937. This was the beginning of the Second World War. The attack on Pearl Harbor of Dec. 7, 1941, offered still further opportunities for expansion on the mainland and to the south. Japanese patriots describe these continental moves as an altruistic attempt to rid China of her internal troubles and bring Japanese enlightenment. In the face of increasing trade restrictions and with a sense of heaven-sent mission, Japan has sought an adequate empire from which she might challenge the West. These are continuing goals which temporary defeat will not eliminate. They are as basic as the quest of the Russian bear for warm-water ports.

Japanese imperialists have had two territorial goals. One group, led by the army, has favored expansion on the continent; the other, dominated by the navy, has pointed to the South Seas. China offers a market and certain raw materials. Action in the northwest also provides a buffer against the Soviet Union and its ideology. One of the reasons for acquiring Korea was to secure protection against Russia; to render Korea secure, Manchuria was desirable, and in turn Mongolia; eastern Siberia would similarly be a safeguard; hence the appetite grows with the eating. So far as colonization is concerned, assuming that the Japanese can be persuaded to migrate at all, Manchuria is too cold and China too full already. Programs of conquest relate to military strategy and trade rather than settlement.

[1] DOUGLAS, HENRY H., A Bit of American History—Successful Embargo Against Japan in 1918, *Amerasia* (1940), IV, 258–260.

The South Seas refer vaguely to the Philippines, the Netherlands Indies, Malaya, Thailand, and French Indo-China. Here are important resources of iron ore and many other minerals, petroleum, rubber, lumber, rice, vegetable oils and fibers, and potentially of cotton. The markets are large, and of equal significance there is room for colonization in warm rice-growing lands. Southward expansion was blocked, for most areas were colonies of Europe or the United States, and not until Europe was involved in war did Japan venture to attack.

All of this is part of a geopolitical Greater East Asia program, by which Japan would like to obtain military security and economic self-sufficiency. Unlike the Monroe Doctrine, Japanese plans did not call for internal independence of the satellite countries concerned, nor for an open-door trade policy. Can Japan succeed? It is one thing to secure advantages while the rest of the world is upset; it is another to hold and exploit them during times of peace. It may well be that all of Japan's legitimate objectives can be more economically satisfied by normal trade relations. And it is obvious that imperialism is not welcomed by countries that are conquered.

Much has been said about Manchuria as Japan's "life line," but trade statistics fail to bear out the assertion. It may even be that so much ill will has been created in China that Manchuria will prove to be a millstone rather than a life line. Attempts at agricultural colonization by the Japanese have repeatedly failed; mining is expanding but most of the coal and iron ore are consumed locally; the market for goods is considerable but requires large capital expenditures which may never yield a profit. Manchuria's place in the larger Japanese economy before 1941 was still a minor one; during the war, however, a great expansion

of heavy defense industry took place on the mainland.

Japan seeks more adequate "living room." Just how large a place in the sun is she entitled to? Do her location and resources and abilities entitle her to leadership in eastern Asia? National greatness is sometimes measured in size or wealth or statistics, hence bigness is assumed to be an asset, but the quality of individual life is more significant.

Japan is geographically well endowed to be an important second-class power, but not more. Her island position, like that of England, gives her advantages of accessibility and maritime interests, but unlike England she is poor in the things that made England industrial: coal, iron, tin, and a head start in world markets. On the other hand, Japan's empire is compact and commands the western Pacific in a way that makes overseas invasion by Europe or America very difficult. Economic strength is quite another matter. Japan's future is assured if she is willing to pattern her life in terms of her notable cultural achievements and geographic environment, but only misfortune can accompany overexpansion.

Relations with the United States

The Pacific is a wide ocean and the relations between its margins are still immature. Commerce has grown, but cultural understanding lags. Political and military rivalries present still other problems. No community similar to that around the Atlantic has yet fully developed, but as contacts increase so must understanding.

American political interests in the western Pacific have involved the Philippines, the Open-door Policy in China, and the general problem of world peace. The Open-door Policy was announced in a series of notes in 1899 which emphasized that no country should obtain exclusive rights in Chinese territory, and was expanded in 1922 when the Nine-power Treaty pledged to China full liberty in working out her internal development.

In addition to political geostrategy, economic considerations are significant. Without relative freedom of commerce, neither Japan nor the United States can carry on a satisfactory internal economy. Pacific relations are especially important to America because of the many strategic materials that Asia alone can supply.

In the absence of world-wide collective security, it is desirable for the United States to maintain a balance of power, and China is our traditional ally. One of the ways to check an aggressive Japan is to ensure a strong China.

The United States has benefited greatly through Japanese trade. Annual sales by the United States have often been double the imports from Japan so that the financial balance is favorable to America. Japan is one of America's largest buyers of raw cotton, and there are important sales of petroleum, steel, automobiles, and industrial machinery. These are all indispensable to Japan, although poorer qualities of cotton and gasoline are available elsewhere. Among minor purchases are copper, chemicals, wood and pulp, tobacco, hides, phosphate rock, and paint.

Japanese exports to the United States are dominated by raw silk, which accounts for half the total. Other items have small totals; they include pottery, vegetable oils, toys, rags, floor coverings, cotton cloth, and canned sea food. If the United States wishes to enlarge its trade to Japan, it is obvious that it should buy more in return. Japanese-American commerce should grow in significance, both as to actual volume and in ratio to other areas, for commercial possibilities are supplementary rather than conflicting.

Postwar relations with the United States call for unusual consideration on the part of America since Japan is an especially sensitive nation. The peace must be just and provide for the recovery of face. There will always be a Japan, and she will continue to be America's neighbor across the Pacific. Two essentials are called for, the removal of Japan's offensive power through the loss of outlying territories and recognition of her legitimate economic and psychological needs.

American interests in the Aleutians will be more secure and the Soviet Union will have the freer access to the open Pacific which she deserves if the Kuriles and Karafuto are returned to the U.S.S.R. Korea unquestionably deserves her independence although she may need the political protection of the new China. Manchuria is of course the first item in China's legitimate claims, followed by Formosa and the Liuchiu Islands. Japan's possession of the Mandated Islands near the equator enabled her to attack Pearl Harbor, so that their status will surely be changed to an American, Philippine, or International Mandate.

Japan proper will suffer but minor economic hardship through the loss of these islands, though the relations with Korea and Manchuria are more intimate. The total Japanese population in the territories is small and trade may still be carried on. Japan will continue to be an important nation, but her offensive power must be taken away.

In return, the United States and the world should by treaty guarantee to Japan that she will have the same access to raw materials and to markets enjoyed by other powers, without discrimination or excessive tariffs. This will make possible all the international trade that Japan can properly earn. Furthermore, the Japanese must be fully received into world society as individuals through the removal of racial laws that reflect on their standing. Without such concessions and mutual understanding, Japan will assuredly again attempt to seek an empire by military means.

The Japanese Outlook on Life

Japan's place in the world cannot be understood without an appreciation of her history and ideology. During the centuries when she shut herself from intercourse with the outside world, even from China, it was but natural that there should have developed an attitude of superiority. Knowing no outside power, Japan regarded her culture as the most desirable. When Western civilization suddenly broke in during the nineteenth century, the Japanese were keenly disappointed that Europe did not grant equality to the arts and achievements of the Orient. What had been a feeling of superiority was suddenly changed to one of inferiority. Only when the Japanese had demonstrated competence in the Western art of war in 1904–1905 did the country begin to receive recognition. The Anglo-Japanese alliance was another acknowledgment of her importance by the West.

Underlying much of Japan's foreign program is this desire for cultural respect and political equality. Japan wants desperately to be understood, to acquire face through appreciation by the West. If she cannot receive this recognition from the United States or another of the great powers, a resentment of everything western follows.

When the first Japanese went overseas, there was a tendency for commercial representatives and naval officers to visit England. Army men went to Germany, while thousands of students came to the United States. These early relations have continued, and there are now many influential Japanese who once studied in American universities. No country enjoys a larger measure of basic good will and admiration, although momentary differences may reverse the picture. Japan's own culture is secure, but many ideas from her neighbor across the Pacific find their way into life and thought.

The most distinctive aspect of Japanese politics is the unique place of the Emperor. Other nations have autocratic rulers, but in Japan the Emperor is a direct descendant of the Sun Goddess and hence is an object of worship himself. Coupled with the loyalty given to a divine ruler are the messianic aspects of Shintoism. Many Japanese feel that they have a commission to bring their way of life to the rest of the world.

No one can understand Japanese geographic imperialism without an appreciation of this cultural and spiritual urge which lies behind it. Expansion in Asia is not merely a search for food, livelihood, and security. Behind the lure of empire is the goal of what to the Japanese appears a better society.

Chapter 15

THE SOVIET REALM

Significance and Location

Within the Union of Soviet Socialist Republics lies one-sixth of the land on earth. From the Baltic to the Pacific, the country spreads across 160° of longitude, nearly halfway around the globe. But mere size, even though it exceeds eight million square miles, is not a country's most striking geographic characteristic. The human drama is always more challenging than material aspects. Whether one is sympathetic or opposed to Soviet ideology, the U.S.S.R. is a development of unquestionable interest, among the most challenging in our time.

Geography deals with the environment and resources that give character to the Soviet landscape, but it must also objectively consider the social, economic, and political developments that characterize this part of Eurasia. Where controversial issues are involved, these chapters should enable one to bring his prejudices up to date.[1]

[1] The Soviet Union has been neglected by writers on both European and Asiatic geography. The regional sections of four standard volumes on the geography of Europe devote space to the U.S.S.R. as follows: (a) 22 out of 317 pp.; (b) 32 out of 520 pp.; (c) 41 out of 390 pp.; and (d) 122 out of 778 pp. The consideration given the country in textbooks on the geography of Asia is even more scanty. Thus in the regional portion of three leading volumes, the U.S.S.R. receives space as follows: (e) 39 out of 620 pp.; (f) 31 out of 530 pp.; and (g) 49 out of 560 pp. No one would contend that countries should receive consideration in proportion to their area or even to their population, but it seems clear that the geographic treatment of Eurasia has lacked balance.

The key word in Soviet geography is continentality. Within the Union is room for all of the United States, Alaska, Canada, and Mexico. From Leningrad to Vladivostok is as far as from San Francisco to London—nine and a half days by the Trans-Siberian Express. There are continental extremes in temperature, rainfall, natural vegetation, usability, and accessibility.

Too much of the land is too cold, or too dry, or too wet, or too infertile, or too mountainous, or too inaccessible, or too something else. Good agricultural land covers no more than a million square miles, largely within a narrow triangle or wedge bounded in the west by Leningrad and the Black Sea and tapering eastward toward Lake Baikal. Elsewhere there may be the attraction of minerals or timber or local oases, but climatic barriers have restricted normal settlement over vast areas.

Although landlocked continentality is obvious, the Soviet Union at the same time has the longest coast line of any country, and the most useless. Frozen seas bar access for most of the year. Even the rivers flow in the wrong direction. The Volga ends in the isolated Caspian, and the Ob, Yenisei, and Lena point to the Arctic Ocean. Even the Amur bends north before joining the Pacific. The Don and the Dnieper enter the Black Sea but it too is enclosed. Nowhere does the country border an open ice-free ocean except at Murmansk in the extreme northwest. How different might have been the country's history and economics if her continental position had been modified by easy access to the ocean!

The challenging pioneer spirit of the Soviet Union is typified by the statue atop the Soviet Pavilion at the Paris Exposition in 1937.

Russian geographers have long lamented this frozen sea. The *czarist* regime made feeble efforts to navigate the Arctic, but the Soviets are actively developing the Northern Sea Route. Scores of steamers call at Siberian ports during the brief summer period of open water, and a few dozen make the complete transit from Murmansk to Vladivostok, aided by ice-breakers and scouting planes. If Arctic navigation proves dependable in linking the Atlantic and Pacific coasts of the Union, it may compare in significance with the Panama Canal for the United States.

Like the United States, the U.S.S.R. faces two ways and has interests in both Europe and Asia. America's neighbors are across the seas, while those of the Soviet Union, on all frontiers except the west, lie across deserts and mountains. The country is influenced by its position in an isolated part of Asia and the climatically least desirable portion of Europe, remote from the Atlantic. This position would be a disadvantage were not the Union's economy largely self-sufficient because of the abundant resources within the country.

Custom has divided Russia into European and Asiatic sections, but this tradition has little geographic validity. Various maps disagree as to the continental limits and do not even consistently follow the crest of the Urals. These mountains are no more of a continental barrier than the Appalachians. No political boundary has followed the Urals for centuries; neither do they mark any conspicuous change in climate, crops, nationalities, or economic activities. Ancient Greek geographers drew their dividing line at the Don River, and properly, since for centuries Asiatic nomads roamed across the plains northwest of the Caspian. In some instances it may be convenient to separate the eastern and western parts of the Union, but any use of the terms Europe or Asia in this connection is apt to be misleading. What we conventionally mean by European culture lies in the peninsular areas of western Eurasia, not in the vast plains of the Volga. The Soviet Union is a single geographic realm; in culture she is knit to Europe, but by nature she stands between two worlds, the Orient and the Occident.

The factors that give the Soviet Union its geographic coherence are its great expanse of level land; its isolation by oceans, deserts, and mountains; the pioneering achievements in agriculture and industry which are transforming the landscape; and its unique political structure. These all make it a phenomenon as well as a Middle Asia, conditions resemble Nebraska and Utah. The exceptions are the cotton and fig country of the southern oases,

The statue of Peter the Great and the Admiralty Building on the bank of the Neva at Leningrad. (*Sovfoto.*)

place. This unity is offset by the diversity of nationalities, by the wide contrasts in climate and usability, and by the difficulty of communications. Such diversity is implicit in the fact that this is the most continental of all countries, compact yet diffuse. No one could expect that Russia would have duplicated the history of a maritime power such as Britain.

It is well to remember that the geography of much of the U.S.S.R. is more easily comparable with that of Canada than with the United States. Climatic conditions place severe limitations on agricultural possibilities in each continent. Almost all of the Soviet Union lies north of the United States, for the Black and Caspian Seas are in the latitude of the Great Lakes. Fortunately no Rocky Mountains keep out moderating Atlantic influences. Where the Union extends farthest south in

the citrus and tea east of the Black Sea, and the rice of the Pacific Maritime Province.

History

The beginnings of Russia as a political unit go back to a series of independent Slavic principalities in the ninth century, united by adventuresome Varangian princes from Sweden. Conflicts between these principalities were interrupted by the Mongol invasions from 1238 to 1462, when the Golden Horde established its capital on the lower Volga.

With the Czardom of Muscovy under Ivan III (1462–1505) came a succession of autocratic rulers who enlarged the territory to its present limits. Notable among them was Ivan the Terrible (1533–1584), who pushed back the Tatars through Cossack colonists and pressed westward into Lithuania and Poland. Under subsequent rulers, the Ukraine, or Little Russia, was frequently a battle-

cow in 1812. Alexander II (1855–1881) instituted extensive reforms, in contrast to the repressive measures of previous

The Red Square in Moscow lies next to the walled Kremlin, in front of which is the tomb of Lenin. The Cathedral of St. Basil is to the left. (*Sovfoto.*)

ground with Poland. In 1580 the Cossack bandit Yermak crossed the Urals and captured the town of Sibir on the Irtysh. This started the conquest of Siberia which brought Russia to the Pacific in 1639. Following Bering's discovery of Alaska in 1741, colonists pushed south to within 40 miles of San Francisco in 1812, and Russia retained a foothold in North America until the sale of Alaska in 1867.

Peter the Great (1689–1725) was the unifier of the country. So great was his contribution to the expansion and westernization of Russia that the Soviets have now accepted him as the first revolutionary leader. As happened so often in Russia, this strong ruler was followed by a period of weakness and war, which continued until the progressive and expansionist reign of the German princess Catherine II (1762–1796). Under Alexander I (1801–1825) occurred Napoleon's march on Mos-

czars, but the economic condition of the peasantry was only slightly improved and revolutionary propaganda grew through secret societies until he was assassinated by terrorists. Then followed a frankly reactionary period under Alexander III (1881–1894) and Nicholas II (1894–1917). Southward expansion was marked by the conquest of Bessarabia in 1812, the Caucasus in 1864, and Turkestan in 1881.

Russia did not share in the intellectual stimulus of the Renaissance, nor was she influenced by the Reformation.

Revolutionary movements in Russia are of long standing. In 1825 came the Decembrist outbreak. The revolution of 1905 was premature but resulted in the formation of a parliamentary Duma. Following the reverses of the First World War, victory went to the Bolshevik party. After a series of revolutionary governments, the Russian Soviet Socialist Republic was established on Nov. 7, 1917, under Lenin, followed in 1923 by the Union of Soviet Socialist Republics.

Since the days of Peter the Great, Russia has sought to break her landlocked limitations and reach the open sea. Much of the country's subsequent evolution is understandable in terms of the quest of the Russian Bear for warm water. After Peter gave Russia a "window to Europe" on the Baltic, there were successive outward thrusts to the Black Sea under Catherine II, toward the Persian Gulf by Nicholas I (1825–1855), across Siberia to Vladivostok under Alexander II, and on to Port Arthur under Nicholas II. Intrigue in Persia, Afghanistan, Tibet, Mongolia, and China proper are parts of the same story. This expansionist tendency brought Russia into conflict with Britain in the Crimean War, and along the northwestern approaches to India. Completion of the Chinese Eastern Railway to Vladivostok and Port Arthur in Manchuria produced the Russo-Japanese War of 1904–1905.

Free access to the sea is an indispensable requisite for modern nations, so that the quest for an ice-free port was an inevitable part of Russia's foreign policy. Soviet economy, on the other hand, was compelled to be largely self-sufficient and the natural wealth of the Union made this to a large degree possible.

Just as Russia has grown externally, so population has shifted internally. For the middle of the nineteenth century, Vernadsky[1] placed the center of population near Kaluga, 36°E.; by 1897 it had shifted southwest to Tambov, 41°E., while today it is near Saratov on the Volga, 46°E. The progressive eastward shift reflects the settlement of Siberia, while the southward component is due to the growth of popula-

tion in Middle Asia. With the development of Siberia it should gradually approach the Urals. The center of area is near Tomsk.

Through the course of Russian history settlement has pushed into Asia as an advancing wedge. To the north of the occupied land lies the great coniferous forest with acid podsol soils; to the south is the steppe, fertile but precariously dry. Each eastward advance of the wedge of settlement brings a corresponding expansion to the north and to the south. Population pressure and pioneering lure combine to press cultivation eastward, and at the same time north and south. The northward course of agriculture has already moved the frontier into lands of precariously short growing season, while southward expansion is at the expense of drought. Both movements involve the hazard of famine. The southward thrust is more attractive since there are no forests to be cleared and the soils are exceptionally fertile; in good years, rainfall is adequate but, too often, a limited amount or poor distribution results in widespread starvation.

Siberia has been Russia's pioneer east, just as Anglo-Saxon settlement pressed westward into the New World. The dates are comparable since Tomsk was founded in 1604 and Jamestown in 1607. Siberia was occupied rapidly but thinly, with Yakutsk on the Lena dating from 1632, whereas Hartford was not founded until 1638. On the other hand, the Trans-Siberian Railway was not completed until thirty years after the Union Pacific.

Russian explorations in the Pacific are more extensive than usually appreciated. They include not only voyages in the vicinity of Alaska, but also exploration along the northern coasts of Japan. In early days the supplies for colonists in Russian-occupied America had to be carried across Siberia to Okhotsk. This led to a round-the-world voyage in 1803–1805

[1] VERNADSKY, GEORGE, The Expansion of Russia, *Transactions of the Connecticut Academy of Science,* (1933), XXXI, 391–425.

via Cape Horn, which brought the discovery of numerous islands in the mid-Pacific. Subsequent trips led to extensive explorations in the central and north Pacific and included Bellingshausen's notable discoveries in the Antarctic.

With the defeat of the Russian navy by Japan in 1905, her influence almost disappeared from the Pacific. At the same time, the U.S.S.R. borders the Pacific for 5,000 miles and cannot be ignored in Eastern Asiatic affairs. Many of the developments in Siberian railways, industries, agricultural colonization, and city expansion are designed to strengthen the Soviets' hold in the east.

Pioneering Economy

When the Soviet Union emerged from the disorder of the First World War and the civil war that followed, her industrial structure was chaotic. Railway equipment was in disrepair, factories had been destroyed, and mines lay in disuse. Consumer goods were seriously inadequate. A severe drought had brought widespread agricultural suffering. Further, the revolutionary shift from czarism and capitalism to soviet socialism introduced profound governmental complications.

In order to rebuild and expand the economic structure, the First Five-year Plan was inaugurated in 1928, followed by two others. In each there was a series of objectives as to industrial and agricultural output, usually involving a doubling of production within the period. In this program of reconstruction, heavy industry came first. New mines must precede the expansion of steel mills, and the construction of new locomotives and railway facilities must precede tractor factories. Military defense took first precedence. Consumer goods largely had to wait, even though desperately lacking. With the Third Five-year Plan, starting in 1938, it was possible to shift some of the emphasis from coal, steel, oil, electricity, and chemicals to clothing and food.

It is characteristic of soviet totalitarianism that it visualizes Utopian goals. The leaders propose to create the world's first socialized state, and this end appears so desirable that any means are justifiable. Where the development of the state is the goal, individuals must be prepared to suffer. Only time can demonstrate the validity of such a philosophy, but it should be pointed out that the government leaders regard themselves as humanitarians. The spectacular success of the Soviet Union during the Second World War is evidence that the five-year programs did succeed.

When the First Five-year Plan was introduced, the Union was in no position to rebuild through its own efforts. Machinery and engineering aid had to be brought from abroad. Thus steel mills and automobile plants were built under technical aid contracts with American, British, or German companies. Foreign experts supervised the expansion of mines and railroads. To finance these basic essentials, the country's exportable products were limited to lumber, grain, manganese, and gold.

It is now clear that the Union of Soviet Socialist Republics is one of the richest countries in the world. Her coal reserves exceed a trillion and a half tons, second only to the United States. Petroleum reserves are more difficult to estimate, but Soviet geologists credit their country with more oil than any other. Hydroelectric possibilities are great. Iron ore deposits are huge, and within the country are manganese, copper, lead, zinc, gold, platinum, aluminum, and even nickel. Commercial timber covers a million square miles, and there is four times as much rich chernozem soil as in the United States. Here is one land where a self-sufficient national economy is almost feasible.

Socialism is characterized by planning, and in this geographers play a large role. State planning bureaus function for the U.S.S.R. as a whole and also in the constituent republics. These organizations not only deal with the development of industries and transport but allocate raw materials to factories and manufactured products to retail outlets. Even the probable demand for clothing or nails is mapped out in advance and correlated into the national scheme.

With pressing needs of many types, the procedure has been to select a few for thorough attention and let the others drift. Thus the Moscow subway is unquestionably the most beautiful in the world, the Kuznets and Magnitogorsk steel plants employ the most modern techniques, the Northern Sea Route Administration has had unlimited resources, and child welfare is everywhere favored. The Great Soviet World Atlas is without a rival.

It is probable that no nation has ever transformed its economic life so rapidly as has the U.S.S.R. since 1928. The goal is nothing short of overtaking and surpassing all other nations. As a result, millions of people have been moved from farms into factories. Illiterate peasants whose mechanical experience was limited to a plow and a hoe now operate complex machinery. Thousands of miles of new railways have been laid down, thousands of new locomotives built, factory cities of 200,000 people replace tiny villages, and large areas of virgin steppe have been plowed for the first time in history.

If continentality is the basic geographic note, pioneering developments characterize the economic life. No one can travel across the country without being impressed by the material results of the Five-year Plans. The capacity of the government to achieve is obvious. The pioneering spirit that typifies all parts of the Union is unique. Nowhere else in temperate lands is there so much good undeveloped farm land. Nowhere else is the rural or urban landscape in such transformation.

All this must be viewed in relative terms and properly adjusted for the social factor. In comparison with czarist times, the changes are stupendous. Yet in comparison with western Europe, the country still has a long way to go. Prior to the Second World War, the Union boasted that within Europe it had become the second producer of steel, occupied third place in coal, and led in oil. This did not mean that there were as many automobiles on the streets, or that the trains were adequate or clean, or that people were dressed as in Berlin or London.

To the outside world, the Soviet Union has variously appeared as a "big bad wolf" about to devour the rest of civilization, a Utopia that may solve all our ills, or an incomprehensible riddle. In reality it is none of these, and yet in some measure all. Climate, soil, and topography impose permanent restrictions in some respects, but in other ways it is evident that the land of the Soviets has become one of the major world powers.

Political Structure

The term Russia should be used only historically or in a very loose sense. Russian people live in most of the country, but alongside them are Ukrainians, Georgians, and other national groups, each in its separate republic. Where racial minorities were suppressed under the czar, each culture is now encouraged.

The Union of Soviet Socialist Republics is a federation of republics, some of which also include autonomous republics. The fundamental basis of political regionalization is twofold: economic and racial. On these bases, sometimes conflicting, the local *okrugs* (districts), *oblasts* (regions), *rayons* (subdistricts), and autonomous areas are grouped into larger *krais* (territories) and republics, and they in turn into union republics. One of the latter is very large and complex, others small and with few subdivisions. Boundaries are fluid so that changes in economic developments may be quickly reflected in the political structure.

Prior to the Second World War, there had come to be 11 union republics as follows:

Republic	Area, square miles	Population, 1939
1. Russian Soviet Federated Socialist Republic.........	6,375,000	109,278,614
2. Ukrainian Soviet Socialist Republic.................	171,950	30,960,221
3. White Russian (Belorussian) Soviet Socialist Republic.................	48,960	5,567,976
4. Georgian (Gruzian) Soviet Socialist Republic.........	26,875	3,542,289
5. Azerbaidzhanian Soviet Socialist Republic...........	33,200	3,209,727
6. Armenian Soviet Socialist Republic.................	11,580	1,281,599
7. Kazakh Soviet Socialist Republic.................	1,059,700	6,145,937
8. Turkmenian Soviet Socialist Republic..............	171,250	1,253,985
9. Uzbek Soviet Socialist Republic...................	146,000	6,282,446
10. Tadzhik Soviet Socialist Republic................	55,545	1,485,091
11. Kirghiz Soviet Socialist Republic...............	75,950	1,459,301
	8,176,010	170,467,186

During 1940, territorial changes on the western frontier resulted in the addition of five republics:

12. Karelo-Finnish Soviet Socialist Republic
13. Estonian Soviet Socialist Republic
14. Latvian Soviet Socialist Republic
15. Lithuanian Soviet Socialist Republic
16. Moldavian Soviet Socialist Republic

At the same time, portions of Poland allocated to Russia by the Treaty of Brest-Litovsk, but seized by Poland during the troubled years of the civil war, were reoccupied and added to the Ukrainian and White Russian Republics because of the nationalities involved. With minor exceptions, these newly acquired areas had been parts of czarist Russia.

The first of these republics, the Russian S.F.S.R., is by far the largest and most powerful. Within it are five krais and more than fifty oblasts, autonomous oblasts, national okrugs, and autonomous soviet socialist republics. It occupies three-quarters of the area and dominates the political life of the U.S.S.R. This is the only part of the Union to which the term Russia might properly be applied.

Moscow, or more correctly Moskva, is the capital of both the U.S.S.R. and the R.S.F.S.R. and had a population in 1939 of 4,137,018. It is at the center of the old industrial area, and the focus of 11 railway lines. Four hundred miles to the northwest is the port of Leningrad, with a 1939 population of 3,191,304. Within the European portion of the Russian Soviet Federated Socialist Republic are a score of roughly equal-sized oblasts, each dominated by a city such as Moscow, Gorki, formerly Nizhni-Novgorod (644,116 in 1939), Rostov-on-Don (510,253 in 1939), or Stalingrad, (445,476 in 1939). There are also a dozen autonomous soviet socialist republics set up because of their non-Russian population, including the Bashkir, Daghestan, and Tatar A.S.S.R. East of the Urals the political units are larger and more complicated. They include oblasts with capital cities such as Sverdlovsk (425,544 in 1939), and Novosibirsk (405,589 in 1939); large krais such as the Krasnoyarsk and Far Eastern Krai, and the huge Yakut Autonomous Soviet Socialist Republic.

The Ukrainian Soviet Socialist Republic includes two large cities, the capital at Kiev (846,293 in 1939), and industrial

R.S.F.S.R., the White Russians, and the Little Russians in the Ukraine.

The Caucasus is a region of diverse

The interior of a home on a collective farm near Stalingrad. (*Sovfoto*.)

Kharkov (833,432 in 1939). There are a score of oblasts, reaching into former Polish territory around Lwow. Within the republic are the great coal and iron areas of Donets and Krivoi Rog.

The White Russian S.S.R. occupies an area west of Moscow, extending into former eastern Poland. The capital is Minsk (238,772 in 1939). The name apparently results from the characteristic white clothing formerly worn by the peasants. To avoid confusion between the political implications of whites and reds, it is better to use the Russian name of Belorussia. In national terms, the eastern Slavs have long been divided into the Great Russians, characteristically living in the

nationalities. What was once the Transcaucasian S.S.R. is now divided into three union republics, the Georgian or Gruzian S.S.R. with its capital at Tbilisi, formerly Tiflis (519,175 in 1939), the Azerbaidzhanian S.S.R. with its capital at Baku (809,347 in 1939), and the Armenian S.S.R. with the capital at Erevan, (200,031 in 1939).

The large area east of the Caspian and south of Siberia was once known as Turkestan, but the name is no longer applicable since the Turkmenian Soviet Socialist Republic occupies only a small part of the desert. Its capital is Ashkhabad (126,580 in 1939). East of it is the Uzbek S.S.R. centered at Tashkent (585,005 in 1939); farther on is the Tadzhik S.S.R. whose capital is Stalinabad. The short-grass area next to Siberia was once known as the Kirghiz Steppe, but the name is no longer applicable since the Kirghiz S.S.R. is located in the southeastern corner of Soviet Middle Asia, with its capital at Frunze. Covering the former Kirghiz Steppe is now the huge Kazakh Soviet Socialist Republic, whose center is Alma-Ata (230,528 in 1939).

Under the constitution of 1936, the highest governing body is the Supreme Soviet. One chamber is called the Soviet of the Union, with one deputy elected directly from each 300,000 citizens, and the other is the Soviet of Nationalities, also elected directly but apportioned among the various republics and national areas. Each local area has considerable autonomy in its internal affairs.

Adjoining the Union are two satellite countries which have not yet achieved full socialism but are under the tutelage of the U.S.S.R. These are the Mongolian People's Republic and Tannu Tuva or the Tuvinian People's Republic.

People

The original home of the Slavic peoples appears to lie northeast of the Carpathians, from whence they began to migrate during the first century. The present Bulgars and Serbs represent a southern group, the Poles and Czechs a northwestern division, while the eastern group is divided among the Great Russians, White Russians, and Little Russians or Ukrainians. Little is known of the eastern Slavs until their unification under the leaders from Rus in Scandinavia.

But, although the Russians are clearly of European origin, two centuries of Mongol domination and the later Siberian expansion brought in an Asiatic element. The plains of Russia were a melting pot akin to those of North America. The genealogical register

of the sixteenth century shows that 17 per cent of the noble families were of Tatar and Oriental origin while 25 per cent were of German and west European extraction. To speak of the Russians as Asiatics with a European veneer is surely incorrect; one cannot "scratch a Russian and find a Tatar." Their alphabet is from the Greeks, but in their mid-continental environment they have acquired a mixed culture. The Russians are at the same time the most eastern of European peoples and the most western of Asiatic.

No less than 169 ethnic groups are recognized within the Union, although only 50 number more than 20,000 representatives. Slavs account for three-quarters of the population, while most of the remainder are Mongoloid, Persian, or Turkic divisions. Where formerly these minorities were subject peoples of the Russians, there is today a peaceful symbiosis. The accompanying table indicates those nationalities which numbered a million or more in 1939.

Nationality	Population	Percentage
Great Russians	99,019,929	58
Ukrainians	28,070,404	17
White Russians	5,267,431	3
Uzbeks	4,844,021	3
Tatars	4,300,336	3
Kazakhs	3,098,764	2
Hebrews	3,020,141	2
Azerbaidzhanians	2,274,805	1
Georgians	2,248,566	1
Armenians	2,151,884	1
Mordvinians	1,451,429	1
Germans	1,423,534	1
Chuvash	1,367,930	1
Tadzhiks	1,228,964	1

Slavs occupy the bulk of eastern Europe and have spread across Siberia along railways and rivers. Turkic peoples are concentrated in Middle Asia with extensions into the Tatar Republic and Bashkiria in the Volga Valley, and in Yakutia. Mongol peoples live around Lake Baikal, and along the lower Volga. In the extreme

have grown enormously. In fact, it is hard to find a center that did not double in the period between the First and Second

This kindergarten in Sverdlovsk, in the Urals, suggests the great attention given to child welfare throughout the Union.

north and northwest are relic races such as the Finns and Nentsi, while the northeast has Paleo-Asiatics and Tungus.

Only three census enumerations have ever been made. In 1897, the total was found to be 129,200,200, while in 1926 it was 146,989,460. These figures are not comparable as to area, for after the Revolution the country lost 27,000,000 people in Finland, Poland, and the other frontiers, and there was great loss of life during the First World War and the ensuing years. The 1939 total was 170,467,186. Population data for the last two returns are given in the table shown on page 266, with the distribution between urban and rural inhabitants.

As a result of the five-year plans, cities

World Wars. Moscow and Leningrad are the two giant cities, but no others exceed a million. Between the latter figure and half a million came Kiev, Kharkov, Baku, Gorki, Odessa, Tashkent, Tbilisi, Rostov-on-Don, and Dniepropetrovsk. In 1939 the Union had 82 cities in excess of 100,000 population as against 31 in 1926 and 14 in 1897.

This is a nation of young people, most of them born since the Revolution and therefore with no memories of czarism. In 1939, 63 per cent were under 30 years of age.

The distribution of people is clearly shown in the accompanying population

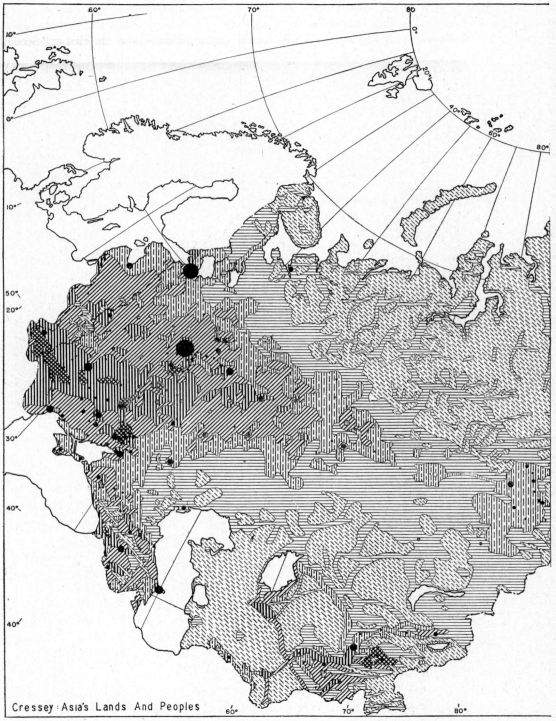

Cressey: Asia's Lands And Peoples

The distribution of population closely corresponds to that of cultivated land and reflects the wedgelike
tionate to the population. (*Data from "Great*

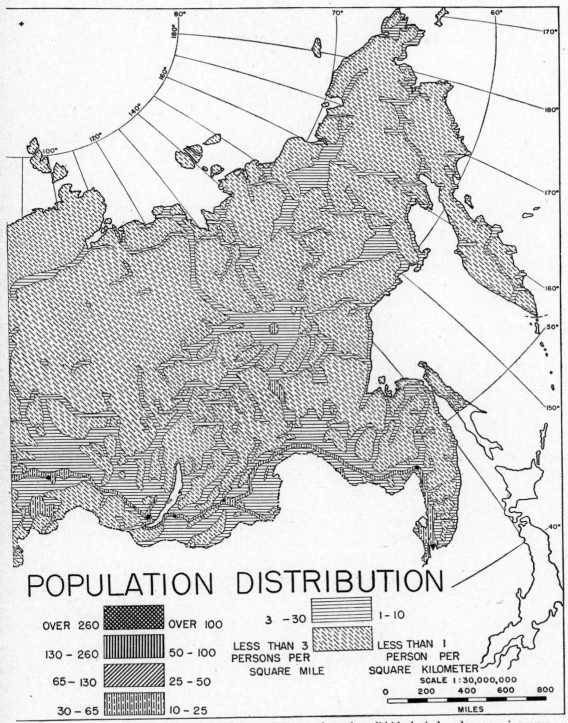

POPULATION DISTRIBUTION

	OVER 260		OVER 100
	130 – 260		50 – 100
	65 – 130		25 – 50
	30 – 65		10 – 25

3 – 30   1 – 10

LESS THAN 3   LESS THAN 1
PERSONS PER   PERSON PER
SQUARE MILE   SQUARE KILOMETER

SCALE 1:30,000,000

0   200   400   600   800

MILES

extension into Siberia from the European frontier. Cities are shown by solid black circles whose area is propor-
Soviet World Atlas," II, *Plates* 11-12.)

THE POPULATION OF THE SOVIET UNION

Republic	Dec. 17, 1926			Jan. 17, 1939		
	Urban	Rural	Total	Urban	Rural	Total
Russian S.F.S.R.	16,785,189	76,672,807	93,457,996	36,658,008	72,620,606	109,278,614
Ukrainian S.S.R.	5,373,553	23,669,381	29,042,934	11,195,620	19,764,601	30,960,221
White Russian S.S.R.	847,830	4,135,410	4,983,240	1,372,522	4,195,454	5,567,976
Azerbaidzhanian S.S.R.	649,557	1,664,187	2,313,744	1,160,723	2,049,004	3,209,727
Georgian S.S.R.	594,221	2,083,012	2,677,233	1,066,560	2,475,729	3,542,289
Armenian S.S.R.	167,098	714,192	881,290	366,416	915,183	1,281,599
Turkmenian S.S.R.	136,982	861,172	998,154	416,376	837,609	1,253,985
Uzbek S.S.R.	1,012,274	3,553,158	4,565,432	1,445,064	4,837,382	6,282,446
Tadzhik S.S.R.	160,003	926,213	1,032,216	251,882	1,233,209	1,485,091
Kazakh S.S.R.	519,074	5,554,905	6,073,979	1,706,150	4,439,787	6,145,937
Kirghiz S.S.R.	122,333	879,364	1,001,697	270,587	1,188,714	1,459,301
U.S.S.R.	26,314,114	120,713,801	147,027,915	55,909,908	114,557,278	170,467,186

map. As the features of climate, soil, and agriculture are developed in subsequent chapters, the reasons for this concentration will be apparent, for most settlement rests on natural factors. The general shape of the fertile triangle or wedge is obvious, with scattered extensions east of Lake Baikal to the Pacific and outliers in the fertile valleys of the Caucasus and Soviet Middle Asia.

With the increased emphasis on industry, new centers of concentrated population have arisen in the mining districts of the Urals, the Kuznets Basin, and the Kola Peninsula. Improved irrigation has added to the population in the oases of Central Asia and along the left bank of the Volga. Old industrial areas such as the Donets Basin and the Moscow area have grown. Everywhere urban expansion is conspicu-ous. Agricultural colonization is especially important in the Soviet Far East.

It is probable that the general pattern of occupance is well defined. The center of population lies west of the Volga, but with the development of Siberia, it should gradually approach the Urals.

Settlement patterns conform to types of land use. Where hunting, fishing, and lumbering predominate in the north, people live in compact clearings along rivers, for the watersheds are swampy and over-land travel difficult. In the cleared conif-erous forest lands devoted to cereals and flax, villages are apt to be on morainic hills away from the damp valleys. In the fertile black soil lands of the south, settlements are larger and typically on high stream banks. Russian villages often extend for a mile or more along a single street. Scattered farmsteads are uncommon.

CHAPTER 16

ENVIRONMENTAL FACTORS IN THE SOVIET UNION

Geology

The geography of the Soviet Union begins with its most ancient geology. In four corners of the country are pre-Cambrian massifs around which younger mountains have been folded and within which lie great plates of undisturbed Paleozoic sediments. Each buttress or shield is a positive area that has tended to remain above sea level and so has been deeply eroded. In their geology and topography they resemble the Canadian Shield.

The best known of these shields is in the northwest where much of Scandinavia is occupied by a complex of granite, gneiss, and metamorphic rocks of Archeozoic and Proterozoic age. This is termed the Fenno-Scandian or Baltic Shield, but the only part within the U.S.S.R. is Karelia and the Kola Peninsula.

In the Ukraine are scattered windows into a partly buried shield that extends from the Sea of Azov northwest to the Carpathian foothills. Its central portions are thinly buried beneath Tertiary sediments. This is the Azov-Podolian Shield. Whereas Karelia and Kola rise 3,000 feet above sea level, the Ukrainian crystalline block lies below 900 feet. Somewhat north of the main Azov-Podolian mass is the smaller Voronezh block. These southwestern outcrops are linked with the Fenno-Scandian Shield through buried connections that follow the western frontiers of the Union.

The eastern corners of the quadrilateral are in central Siberia; one near the Arctic, the other near Lake Baikal. Between the mouth of the Yenisei and Lena is an outcrop of typical pre-Cambrian schist and gneiss along the Anabar River, from which the shield derives its name. Farther south is a larger and more irregular exposure, partly southwest of Lake Baikal but largely to the east near the Aldan River.

Three of these windows into the pre-Cambrian are mining regions of significance. The Kola Peninsula has very large deposits of apatite, the Ukrainian area has iron and manganese, and the Aldan Shield is rich in gold.

Four regions of sedimentary rocks lie within these shields. Soviet Europe is largely underlain by a great platform of essentially undisturbed upper Paleozoic formations. Across the folded Urals the West Siberian Lowland is floored with young marine deposits and glacial sands. Beyond the Yenisei are the Central Siberian Uplands, covered by late Paleozoic sediments and considerably more hilly than the platform in Europe. Except for the narrow Urals, there is no major disturbance in the 3,000 miles from the Baltic to the Lena. East of the Caspian Sea is the fourth lowland where Quaternary sands mask Tertiary and Mesozoic formations.

Surrounding these lowlands are a continuous series of high, rugged mountains. The outermost of these are the youngest and of Tertiary age, such as those in Crimea, the Caucasus, the Hindu Kush, Kamchatka, and Sakhalin. Mesozoic mountains occupy the area from the Sea of Okhotsk to the Lena. The Urals and the structures of Kazakhstan date from the Permian.

Earthquakes and volcanoes are limited to the marginal zones. Except for two small quakes in the central Urals, no epicenters have ever been recorded outside the limits of young mountains. The areas of greatest intensity are the Caucasus, the mountains of Middle Asia, Lake Baikal, and southeastern Kamchatka. Current vulcanism is restricted to the Caucasus and Kamchatka.

The last chapter in geology is often more important than the first. During the Pleistocene, the northeastern quarter of the Union was glaciated, while the eastern third acquired permanently frozen ground.

At least three continental ice sheets invaded the area. The earliest stage was the Mindel, corresponding to the Kansan in North America. The most widespread was the Riis, equivalent to the Illinoian, when a lobe of ice followed the valley of the Dnieper to latitude 48°N., its southernmost limit in Europe, as compared with 37°N. in North America. The uplands south of Moscow blocked this ice and formed a reentrant, but a second lobe occupied the Don Valley, limited on the east by hills along the Volga. Ice crossed the Urals near latitude 60°N., and the boundary continued eastward irregularly to the Yenisei, east of which it swung sharply to the north and reached the Arctic Ocean just east of the Taimyr Peninsula.

Local glaciers spread out from the mountains in the Caucasus, Pamirs, Tien Shan, Altai-Sayan, Baikal, and Verkhoyansk areas, but it is certain that there were no continental ice sheets in eastern Siberia.

The last stage was the Wurm or Wisconsin, but the advance did not reach Moscow, and the Asiatic portion was limited to the Ob estuary and the Taimyr Peninsula. Eurasian ice radiated from three centers, Scandinavia, Nova Zemlya, and the Taimyr Peninsula.

These glacial invasions left a record of morainic deposits, swamps, and deranged drainage, but the effects were not confined to the ice limits. Increased precipitation and decreased evaporation greatly enlarged the Caspian and Aral seas, so that they overflowed westward into the Black Sea. Ice blocked the mouths of the north-flowing Ob and Yenisei, and a vast lake developed in southwestern Siberia, which in turn found its outlet south to the enlarged Caspian. This proglacial lake exceeded the size of glacial Lake Agassiz in North America and was evidently the largest fresh-water lake ever known. The amazing flatness of western Siberia is partly due to the silt deposited by this huge lake.

Much of Siberia now has an average annual temperature below freezing. Only the absence of an adequate snowfall prevents continental glaciers today. During the rigorous climate of glacial times, the absence of blanketing snow or ice permitted excessive radiation so that the ground became permanently frozen. Extensive research, spread over 400 localities, has traced the characteristics of this frozen ground. In many areas it extends to depths of 100 feet and reaches a maximum of 920 feet. The total area underlain by permanently frozen earth amounts to 3,728,900 square miles. The construction of buildings and railroads presents special engineering problems.

Land Form Regions

The major physical divisions of the Soviet Union are shown in the accompanying table and map, which should be studied along with the text that follows. The regions are geomorphic as they present land forms and structural history. Contour maps are unavailable for the bulk of the area, hence many details remain obscure.

A. Fenno-Scandian Uplands
- Karelian Hills
- Kola Hills

B. Central European Lowlands
- Baltic Galcial Plain
- Upper Dnieper Plain
- Pripet Marshes

C. Central Russian Uplands
- Valdai Hills
- Smolensk-Moscow Hills
- Kursk Hills

D. Ukrainian Uplands
- Don Hills
- Donets Hills
- Dnieper Hills
- Bug Hills
- Podolian Hills
- Dniester Hills

E. Central Russian Lowlands
- Oka-Don Plain
- Upper Volga Plain
- Trans-Volga Plain
- Dvina Plain
- Pechora Plain

F. Volga Uplands
- Pre-Volga Hills
- Ergeni Hills

G. Black Sea Lowlands
- Lower Dnieper Plain
- Crimean Plain
- Kuban-Manych Plain

H. Ural Uplands
- Ural Mountains
- Mogudjar Hills
- Nova Zemlya Hills
- Ufa Hills
- Timan Hills
- Ural Piedmont

I. Caucasian Highlands
- Stavropol Foothills
- Greater Caucasus Mountains
- Mid-Caucasian Valleys
- Lesser Caucasus Mountains
- Crimean Mountains

J. Turan Lowlands
- Caspian Depression
- Ust Urt Plateau
- Kara Kum Plain
- Kizil Kum Plain
- Hunger Plain
- Balkhash Basin
- Turgai Plain

K. Central Asiatic Highlands
- Pamir Ranges
- Fergana Basin
- Tien Shan Ranges

L. Kazakh Upland

M. Altai-Sayan Highlands
- Tarbagatai Mountains
- Siberian Altai Mountains
- Salair Mountains
- Kuznets Basin
- Kuznets Alatau Mountains
- Minusinsk Basin
- Western Sayan Mountains
- Eastern Sayan Mountains

N. West Siberian Lowland
- Yamal and Gydan Peninsulas
- Ob Glacial Plain
- Vasyugan Swamp
- Ob Plain
- Khatanga Plain

O. Central Siberian Uplands
- Anabar Hills
- Taimyr Peninsula
- Tunguska Hills
- Yenisei Ridge
- Vilui Plain
- Aldan Hills
- Patom Plateau
- Lena Hills

P. Baikal-Stanovoi Highlands
- Baikal Mountains
- Vitim Plateau
- Yablonovi Mountains
- Olekminsk-Stanovik Mountains
- Stanovoi Mountains

Q. Far Eastern Uplands
- Amur Basins
- Northern Amur Hills
- Sikhota Alin Mountains
- Sakhalin Island

R. Northeastern Mountain Complex
- Verkhoyansk Range
- Yana-Oimekon Lowlands
- Cherski Range
- Kolyma Lowlands
- Okhotsk-Chaun Uplands
- Anadyr Mountains
- Anadyr Lowlands
- Kamchatka-Koryak Ranges

A. That part of the Fenno-Scandian Upland within the U.S.S.R. is a land of low hills developed on a pre-Cambrian shield of great complexity. Glacial erosion has scoured and smoothed the surface, disrupted drainage, and produced innumerable lakes. Karelia resembles Finland. The Kola Peninsula is nearly detached and more mountainous. Along the eastern and southern margins are a series of depressions between the crystallines and bordering sedimentaries, partly due to glacial scour, represented by the Gulf of Finland and the White Sea at either ends and Lakes Ladoga and Onega in the center.

B. The Central European Lowlands include large areas west of the Soviet Union, into Germany and France, but

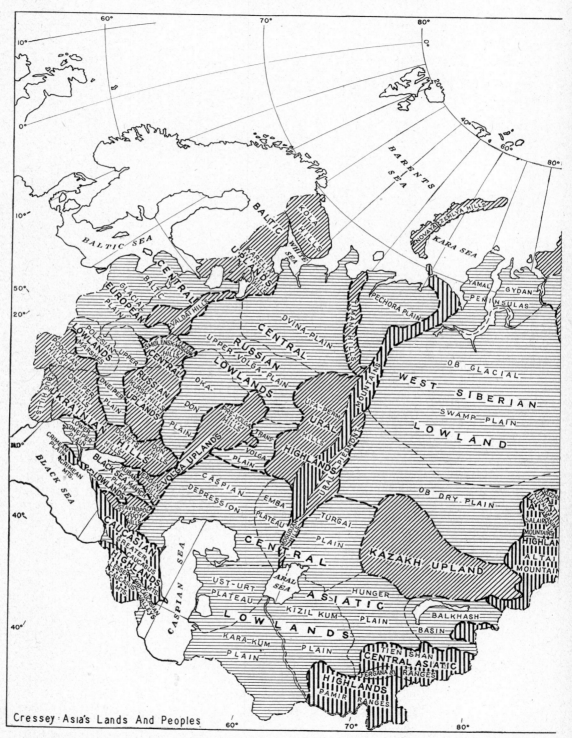

Cressey: Asia's Lands And Peoples

Within the eight million square miles of the Soviet Union are 18 major land form regions and 82 subdivisions.

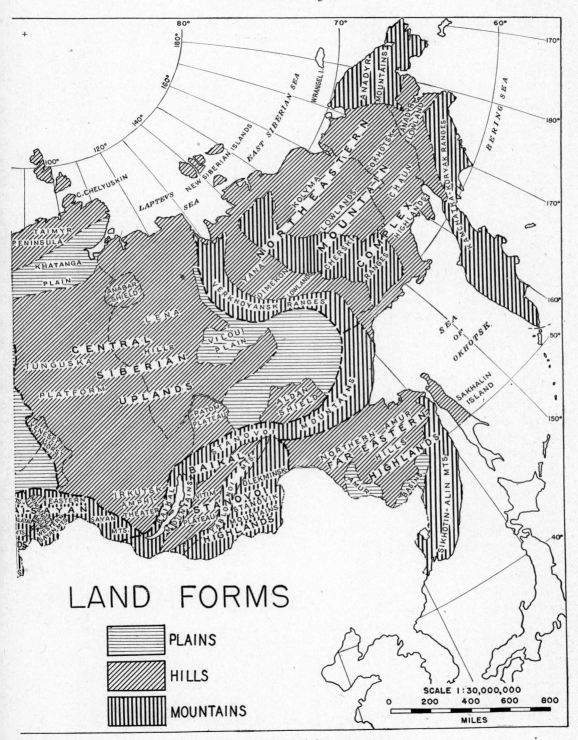

LAND FORMS

	PLAINS
	HILLS
	MOUNTAINS

SCALE 1:30,000,000

0   200   400   600   800

MILES

Rugged mountains are limited to the southern frontiers and the extreme east.

within its limits are three separate regions. The Baltic Plain is the result of glacial deposition in a region of early Paleozoic sedimentaries. This region roughly coincides with the limits of Baltic drainage and the extent of the latest glacial invasion, the Wurm. It is crossed by a series of recessional moraines. The Upper Dnieper Plain was also glaciated but is a southward sloping surface without lakes. The Pripet or Polesian Marshes spread over western White Russia into former Poland. The large extent of uncultivable land is reflected in the map of population density.

C. The Central Russian Uplands are a linear region of low hills. In the north the Valdai Hills are formed by a west-facing Devonian escarpment. The transverse Smolensk-Moscow Hills, which die out just north of Moscow, are in part a morainic belt. The southern and largest region is named the Kursk Hills from its principal city, better known for the presence of extensive iron ore deposits in the buried Voronezh crystalline block.

D. Beneath the Ukrainian Uplands is a partly exposed pre-Cambrian Shield, but the topography is related to southward-dipping sedimentary formations of the late Paleozoic. These form a series of northwest-southeast cuestas arranged *en échelon.* Several Ukrainian rivers flow southeast, parallel to these escarpments, then turn and cut through them in antecedent valleys. Hence reading from the east, the regions may be termed the Don Hills, the Donets Hills, famous for their coal, the Dnieper Hills, and the Bug Hills. Farther west are the Podolian Hills along the base of the Carpathains; these also have a north-facing escarpment overlooking the Pripet Marshes. Bessarabia might be included as the Dniester Hills, though the structural parallel does not hold.

E. The Central Russian Lowlands spread from the Arctic tundra to the southern

black-soil steppes. The most representative region is the rolling hill and valley country south of Moscow drained by the headwaters of the Oka and Don. The Upper Volga Plain is slightly more hilly but still in its gross aspects a nearly featureless plain. Russians have long named various areas with relation to their position as regards Moscow, as for example the Trans-Volga Plain on the left bank below the junction of the Kama. This is a dry steppe which gradually rises to the Urals. Two regions of Arctic drainage complete the division, the Dvina Plain and the Pechora Plain. Both have a veneer of glacial deposits and postglacial marine sands. The Pechora area is underlain by coal and oil.

F. The Volga Uplands comprise the Pre-Volga Hills along the right bank, including the low Jiguli Mountains in the Samara Bend. The Ergeni Hills form the southern end of the area.

G. The Black Sea Lowlands include the Lower Dnieper Plain, extending from the Dniester to the Sea of Azov, the Crimean Plain in the northern two-thirds of the peninsula, and the extensive region between the Don and the Caucasus drained by the Kuban and Manych Rivers. This was once an outlet for the enlarged Caspian Sea.

H. The Ural Uplands are an old mountain range, largely reduced to rounded hills. In history, structure, and relief they somewhat resemble the Appalachians. On the east is an abraded crystalline platform termed the Ural Piedmont. In the center are the narrow Ural Mountains proper, composed of folded geosynclines on either side of a granite core, deformed at the end of the Paleozoic. The southern projection is the Mogudjar Hills, and the northern extension is found in the islands of Nova Zemlya. The Timan Hills to the northwest are a peneplained anticline of late Paleozoic rocks, bordered by Mesozoic synclines. To the west of the Ural Mountains is a broad dissected plateau carved in Permian formations, the Ufa Hills.

embraces the area north of the sea, partly below ocean level, which was covered when the enlarged Caspian overflowed westward.

The snow-clad summit of Mt. Elbrus, highest mountain in all Europe. (*Sovfoto.*)

I. The Caucasus presents great topographic variety, and the division here suggested is an oversimplification. On the north the Stavropol Foothills project into the Kuban-Manych Plain. Next is the main range of the Greater Caucasus, with rugged land forms and elevations to 18,468 feet. South of the mountains are valleys draining toward the Black and Caspian Seas, and beyond them rise the Lesser Caucasus Mountains followed by portions of the high Armenian Plateau. The structure of the Greater Caucasus is continued in the mountains of southern Crimea.

J. The Turan Lowlands are a series of desert plains. The Caspian Depression

East of the Caspian is the Ust Urt Plateau. Three desert plains lie between and on either side of the Amu Darya and Syr Darya. Between the former and the Caspian is the Kara Kum, sometimes romanized as Qara Qum; between the rivers is the Kizil Kum or Qizil Qum, and to the east of the Syr Darya is the Hunger Plain or Bedpak Dala. The Balkhash Basin farther east commands the entrances to China. The Turgai Plain in the north is a corridor into Siberia and once carried drainage from glacial lakes to the north.

K. The Central Asiatic Highlands mark the structural core of the continent and extend into Afghanistan, India, and China.

The Pamir region includes numerous other mountains such as the Alai, Turkestan, and Gissar. Here are the highest elevations in the Soviet Union: Mt. Stalin, 24,584 feet, and Mt. Lenin, 22,377 feet. North of these ranges is the Fergana Basin in the upper valley of the Syr Darya. Beyond it is the western end of the Tien Shan with numerous subregions.

L. The Kazakh Upland is an ancient mountain range, worn down to rolling hills and plains so that only the roots of the mountains remain. Coal and copper are important. This area has sometimes been called the Kirghiz Steppe.

M. The southern and eastern borders of Siberia are fringed with high mountains, from the Altai to the Verkhoyansk. The Altai-Sayan Highlands are made up of numerous structures with a general northwest-southeast trend. At the western end are the Tarbagatai Mountains, and next to them the Siberian Altai which continue into Mongolia. The Salair and Kuznets Alatau extend northward on either side of the Kuznets Basin, famous for its coal. East of the Kuznets Alatau is the Minusinsk Basin along the upper Yenisei, surrounded on the south side by the Western Sayan and on the north by the Eastern Sayan. The latter extends to near Lake Baikal.

N. The West Siberian Lowland occupies the vast plain of the Ob and Irtysh, one of the largest and flattest lands on earth. Two peninsulas characterize the Arctic portion, the Yamal and Gydan. The northern Ob Plain is veneered with glacial and recent marine deposits; south of it is the Vasyugan Swamp. Along the Trans-Siberian Railway is a dry plain, pitted with innumerable deflation hollows. It is drained by the Tobol, Ishim, Irtysh, and Ob Rivers. The Khatanga Plain is a northeast continuation of the Lowland. The Lowland extends a short distance to the east of the Yenisei.

O. The Central Siberian Uplands reach from the Yenisei to the Lena and are sometimes called Angaraland. The core is the Anabar Shield, southwest of which are the Tunguska Hills, a dissected platform of late Paleozoic formations with extensive coal beds and widespread lava flows. The Taimyr Peninsula projects into the Arctic beyond the Khatanga Plain. In the southwest, the ridge formed by the Yenisei horst combines with the Eastern Sayan and Baikal Mountains to enclose the amphitheater of Irkutsk, a southern subdivision of the Tunguska platform. The geomorphic characteristics of the Lena Valley are less apparent. A large basin in the center may be termed the Vilui Plain, and in the south are the Patom and Aldan plateaus. The remainder of the valley is grouped as the Lena Hills; part of the region is a plain.

P. The Baikal-Stanovoi Highlands continue the mountainous relief described in the Altai-Sayan Highlands. The Baikal Mountains rise on either side of the graben that holds the lake. To the east is the Vitim Plateau, part of the ancient shield of southeastern Siberia, and beyond it are the Yablonovi Mountains. These have a southwest-northeast trend and extend from the Mongolian border to the Olekma River. East of them is an area of low mountains and basins known as the Olekminsk-Stanovik Mountains. Much uncertainty has surrounded the use of the word Stanovoi, but it is now clear that it embraces a series of mountains from near the upper end of Lake Baikal eastward and northward along the Okhotsk Sea to latitude 60°.

Q. The Far Eastern Uplands include but one well-defined mountain chain, the Sikhota Alin, and the remaining geomorphology is obscure. A series of basins along the Amur and its tributaries, notably the Zeya, Bureya, and Ussuri, form the chief plains. The island of Sakhalin may be included.

R. The Northeastern Mountain Complex is adequately characterized by its title. The line of the Stanovoi is continued by the curving Verkhoyansk Range along the right bank of the Lena. Between it and the high Cherski Range are the Yana and Oimekon lowlands; air drainage into these basins makes them the coldest inhabited places on earth. The Kolyma Lowlands comprise the swampy Kolyma Plain in the north, the Alazeya Plateau on the west, and the Yukagir Plateau on the south. Farther east and south is a series of uplands, chief of which is the Gydan Range bordering the northern Sea of Okhotsk and continuing through the Anyui Mountains to the Arctic. The Anadyr Mountains cover the Chukchee or Chukotsk Peninsula opposite Alaska, and the Anadyr Lowlands lie between the Anadyr and Gydan Mountains and the Koryak Mountains. The peninsula of Kamchatka contains volcanoes whose size and activity parallel those of Java.

Climate

Despite the vast extent of the Soviet Union, climatic conditions over a large part of the country have much in common. The situation is different near the Black Sea, across the Caspian, and in the Far East, but elsewhere long winters and low precipitation dominate.

Millions of square miles are eliminated from normal settlement because of too short a growing season or too little rainfall. Elsewhere, occasional frosts that extend into the summer or come early in the fall, the lack of adequate spring rainfall or ground moisture from melting snow, or drying winds introduce crop uncertainties that do not appear in the annual averages. It has long been a recognized climatic rule that the lower the annual rainfall, the greater the variability from year to year; it appears to be equally true that the lower the annual temperature, the greater the variation in the period between spring and fall frosts. Thus climatic hazards compress the central fertile triangle on both north and south.

Only a few areas in the west and in the higher mountains receive more than 20 inches of rainfall. If it were not for the low summer temperatures and limited evaporation, almost none of the country would be safe for agriculture. Middle Asia and northeastern Siberia each have under eight inches, but where the former is hot and a desert, the other is cold and a tundra. Fortunately precipitation in the cultivated areas comes during the summer when it is most needed, although the spring rains necessary for planting are often seriously delayed. Severe famines have resulted from this cause in the steppes of the Ukraine, Don, and Volga. During dry seasons the Emba does not reach the Caspian Sea, and streams in Kazakhstan run salty.

Although surrounded by seas, the country receives surprisingly little marine benefit. On the south, mountain barriers and great distances effectively bar any influence from the Indian Ocean. The Pacific lies to leeward on the wrong side of the continent, and mountains limit the penetration of summer monsoon moisture to Lake Baikal. For much of the year the Arctic Ocean is frozen, and the area of ice-free water as a source for evaporation is never large. Its low temperatures at all seasons make it an unimportant source of moisture or ameliorating warmth. Only the Atlantic remains, and it lies across the width of peninsular Europe; yet even in central Siberia more than three-quarters of the rain must be of Atlantic origin. While lowlands are dry, mountains such as the Sayan are unexpectedly moist,

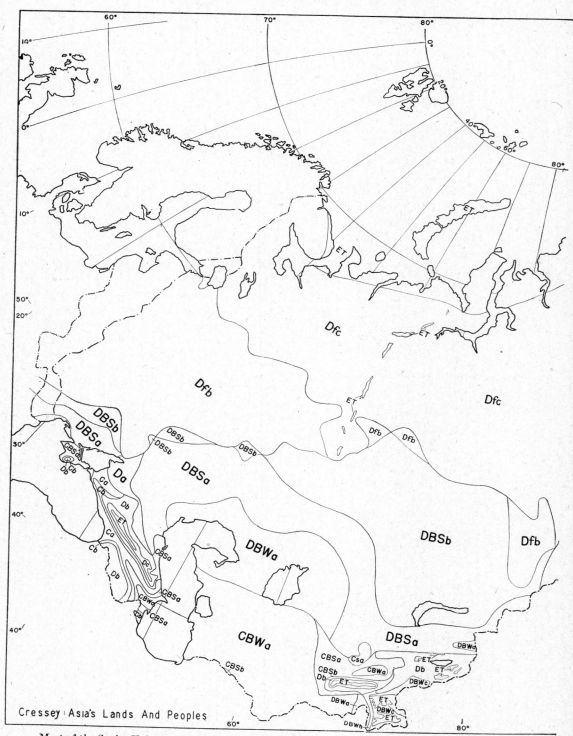

Cressey: Asia's Lands And Peoples

Most of the Soviet Union is a cold temperate land with Koeppen *D* symbols. *E* climate prevails in the far refers to steppe and *BW* to desert. These small letters are used as follows: *a*, hot summers, with the warmest above 50°F.; *d*, coldest month below −36°F.; *f*, no dry season; *s*, dry summer; *w*, dry winter. (*After Voznesenski*.)

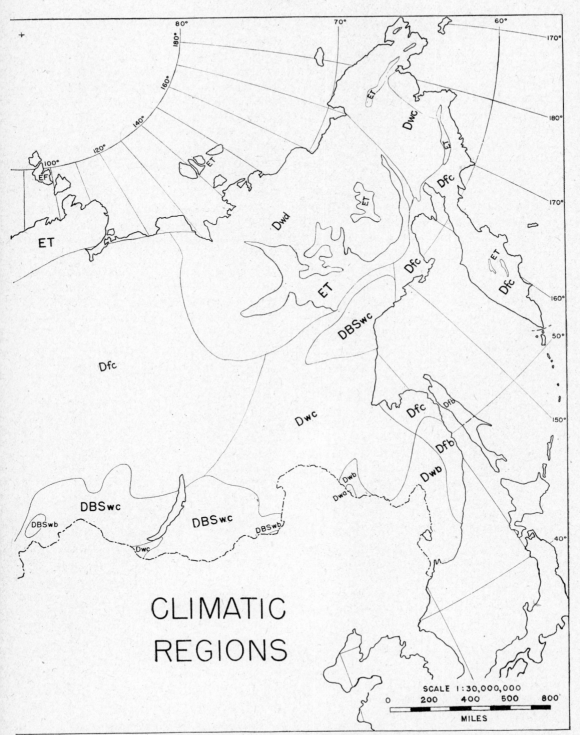

CLIMATIC
REGIONS

SCALE 1:30,000,000

0   200   400   500   800

MILES

north and warm temperate *C* types are present in the south. *ET* or tundra is present in the extreme north. *BS* month over 72°F.; *b*, cool summers, with four months above 50°F.; *c*, cool short summers one to three months with a yearly precipitation of 47 inches. Apparently this moisture has come overland 4,000 miles from the Atlantic. This is all the more surprising since the only low altitude path from the Atlantic lies through the 900-mile gap between the Alps and the Scandinavian Highlands.

Changes of latitude and altitude do not always bring the normal results found elsewhere. The yearly average at Moscow is 3°F. lower than Leningrad, though 300 miles to the south, and winters in the deltas of the Volga and Syr Darya are colder than the Gulf of Finland. Likewise, the New Siberian Islands in the Arctic Ocean are warmer than the coast of Siberia, which in turn is warmer than the interior. In the same manner, the lowest recorded temperatures in the Yenisei Valley lie near the Mongolian border instead of at the mouth, 1,300 miles to the north.

Air drainage in the mountains introduces further inversions. Intense winter radiation, especially in windless northeastern Siberia, causes cold air to flow into the valleys which become colder than surrounding mountains. The extremely low temperatures at Verkhoyansk and Oimekon are well known with a January average of −58°F. and an extreme minimum of −90°F. at the former station. Even lower temperatures have been reported from Oimekon, where there is an unconfirmed reading of −103°F. and the annual average is apparently lower than at Verkhoyansk. These are the coldest towns in the world.

Winter is the dominant season. The frost-free period is less than 60 days in the Siberian Arctic and only 90 to 120 days in the northern half of Soviet Europe and central Siberia. In the central European area and the Ukraine and in southwestern Siberia, the frost-free time is between 120 and 180 days, and exceeds 200 days only in Middle Asia. Snowfall is not heavy but,

since thaws are rare in winter, it accumulates and may be blown into formidable drifts. Throughout Siberia snow lies on the ground for 160 to 260 days, and in the European part of the Union it persists for 100 to 200 days except in the Ukraine.

The severity and duration of the winter season affect man in many ways. Daylight hours are short. Outdoor farm activities and general construction are obviously restricted. Blizzards block communications and cause the loss of unprotected cattle even as far south as the Ukraine. Fresh foods are lacking and the winter diet is characteristically monotonous and deficient in vitamins.

Seasonal contrasts are intensified toward the east, and the range from January to July averages increases from 54°F. at Moscow to 119°F. at Verkhoyansk. This is shown in the accompanying table.[1]

Station	January temperatures, °F.		July temperatures, °F.	
	Mean	Minimum	Mean	Maximum
Batumi................	43	18	74	95
Tashkent.............	30	−15	81	109
Leningrad............	15	−35	64	97
Moscow..............	12	−44	66	99
Tomsk...............	−3	−60	66	95
Yakutsk.............	−46	−84	66	102
Verkhoyansk.........	−59	−90	60	93

Summers are almost everywhere warm, with July isotherms extending east and west. Along the Arctic Coast long hours of sunshine raise the day and night monthly average to 50°F.; from Arkhangelsk and Igarka south to Kiev and Irkutsk, July temperatures are 60 to 68°F.; in the steppes temperatures increase to 75°F. and exceed that in the deserts.

January conditions show no east-west uniformity; instead the isotherms are from

[1] KENDREW, W. G., "The Climates of the Continents," Oxford: Clarendon Press (1927), 176.

northwest to southeast. Monthly averages in Soviet Europe are from 25 to 5°F., while Siberian stations drop to −5°F. or even −40°F. Soviet Middle Asia has averages of 32 to 14°F.

During winter, great masses of cold air develop in the vicinity of Lake Baikal and westward along latitude 50°N., with a high averaging 30.5 inches. This stationary center of Subpolar Continental air is the dominant factor in winter climate, with outblowing winds over most of Asia. Winter winds over western Siberia and Europe, however, tend to blow from the south and southwest. Summer conditions are not entirely reversed, for solar insolation moves the center of low pressure to Mongolia and northwestern India. Summer circulation is irregular, but in general there are inblowing winds from the west and northwest from the Atlantic.

Cyclonic storms introduce variations at all seasons. Their paths across western Europe are well known, but less information has been available concerning their movements into Asia. Meteorological stations are now widespread in Siberia, and the Soviets issue daily weather maps of the entire Northern Hemisphere. Examination of the maps for February, 1936, shows that eleven highs and seven lows moved eastward across the Yenisei between the Mongolian border and the North Pole. In August, 1936, the same area was crossed by seven highs and five lows. Although their intensity is less, this is no fewer than the number of cyclonic and anticyclonic storms that cross Europe. Siberian weather is less monotonous than sometimes regarded.

Natural Vegetation

The major pattern of natural vegetation is both simple and significant. No other regional picture is so expressive of land usability, for natural vegetation sums up many of the items of temperature, rainfall, surface configuration, drainage, and soils. In long-settled lands such as China, man has so changed the landscape that the original cover of vegetation is gone, but in undeveloped areas like Siberia it still dominates.

Most of the Soviet Union is a forest land, a fifth of that on earth. Many of the trees are conifers such as pine, spruce, or larch; and broad-leaved forms are in many places softwoods like birch and aspen. Oak and other hardwood forests were never extensive and are now largely cut over. Most furniture is perforce made of softwoods. Pine railroad ties deteriorate within five years unless treated.

The distribution of vegetation is best understood if lowland landscapes with their horizontal zones are distinguished from vertical zonation in the mountains. They are accordingly considered first.

The tundra has a severe winter with frosts even in summer. From north to south are four subzones, the first of which is the Arctic tundra with moss and lichens but without trees or bushes. Second is the typical bush tundra with dwarf birch and willow, widespread lichens, and moss. Next is the south tundra with low fir, birch, and larch trees along river valleys, and well-developed sphagnum peat bogs. The wooded tundra, the fourth subzone, forms a transition to the true forest. Patches of tundra are present almost to the southern limit of the taiga, but in general the tundra zone lies north of the Arctic Circle and within 250 miles of the ocean. The southern limit corresponds with the July isotherm of 50°F.

Tundra vegetation is exclusively perennial. Many forms spread over the ground to secure the maximum insolation. Dwarf growths are typical. Bright flowers and green grass suddenly come to life during the long summer days. Remains of trees in peat bogs more than 100 miles north of the present wooded tundra suggest a

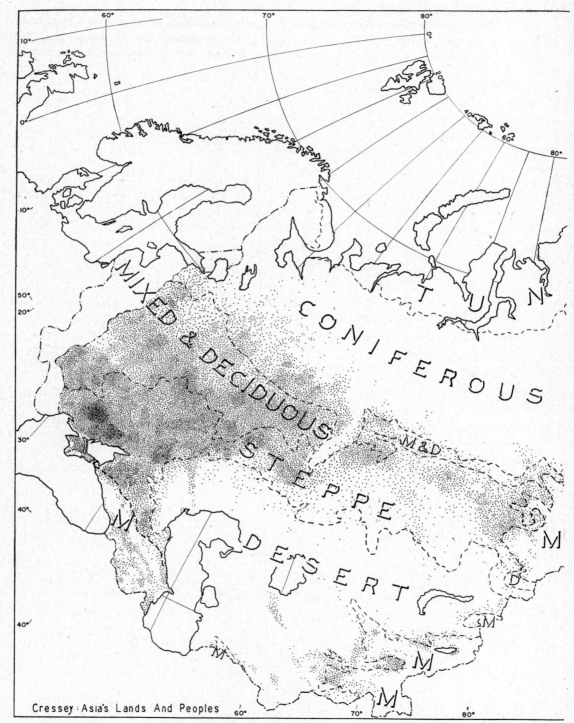

The major vegetation pattern of the Soviet lowlands is fivefold: tundra, coniferous forest, mixed and vated triangle is strikingly concentrated in the areas of mixed and deciduous forest and steppe. (*Data from*

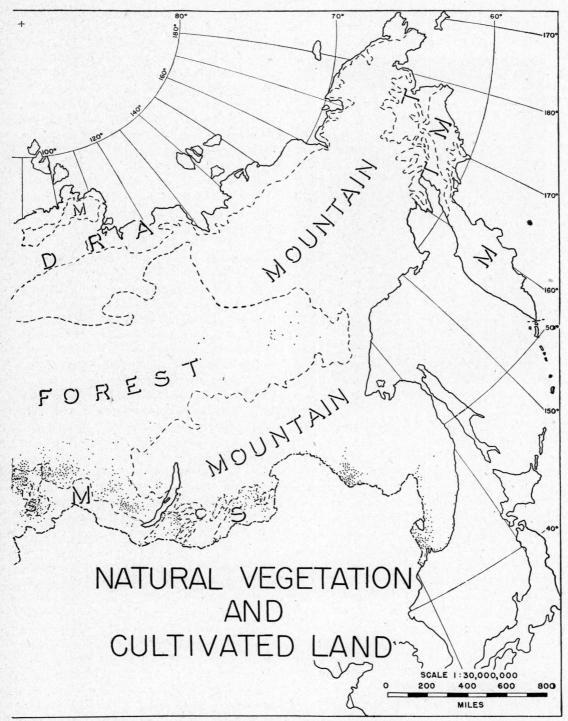

NATURAL VEGETATION
AND
CULTIVATED LAND

SCALE 1:30,000,000

0   200   400   600   800

MILES

deciduous forest, steppe, and desert. Mountainous areas combine these forms according to altitude. The culti-
"*Great Soviet World Atlas*," I, *Plates* 121–122, 155–156.)

warmer and drier postglacial climate. Since frozen subsoil prevents ground-water drainage, widespread swamps develop during the

The Angara River below Irkutsk flows through splendid coniferous forests. (*Courtesy Intourist.*)

summer and become breeding grounds for swarms of mosquitoes.

Farther from the ocean is the taiga, a cool temperate forest, dominantly coniferous. Winters are severe, but summer months have average temperatures between 50 and 68°F. The usual trees are pine, fir, larch, and cedar, with subordinate but locally important areas of birch, aspen, and alder. There are scattered meadows on river flood plains and open watersheds.

East of Lake Baikal, Daurian larch replaces the Siberian larch which grows to the west and is especially adapted to growth above frozen ground. Where the soil is sandy and the blanket of vegetation is thin, summer thaw may reach a depth of six to ten feet. When the forest is burned, birch and whitewoods precede conifers in order of natural restoration. Peat bogs and marsh,

widespread in western Siberia and northern Europe, are rare east of the Yenisei where relief is greater, the summers have less rainfall, and the air is dry. Much of the northern taiga has no commercial value, but trees are taller and larger in diameter toward the south. Large mammals such as elk, reindeer, bear, and lynx were formerly abundant, but the chief taiga animals are now rodents like squirrel, rabbit, and fox.

The mixed forest zone of the western Soviet Union lies in a milder climate where fir and oak are found together. The warmest month exceeds 68°F. Along river valleys such as the Volga, oak extends north to 57°N. The distribution of deciduous trees is somewhat conformable with the wedge of population and cultivated land. Oak forests spread from Leningrad almost to the Black Sea and east to the Ural and Kama rivers, bordering the Ural Mountains. Maple has about the same distribution; ash covers a smaller area; linden spreads farther north and east than oak, while hornbeam is confined to the middle Dnieper Valley. In the Far East, another mixed forest zone reappears in the basin of the Amur with oak, maple, ash, linden, and elm. Considerable areas of splendid timber remain. Bright summer greens and brilliant fall foliage distinguish these mixed forests from the somber taiga. The fauna includes wild boars, reindeer, leopard, and Manchurian tigers.

South of the continuous forest lies a transition zone termed the wooded steppe, where solid stands of trees alternate with open grassland. Local factors of soil, relief, or vegetation history cause islands of steppe to lie within the mixed forest, and forest outliers are present within the continuous steppe to the south. In the European areas, oak is dominant; in Siberia birch is the typical tree. In the west, the northern and southern boundaries are Kiev and Kharkov, respectively; along the Volga they are Kazan and Kuibyshev. East of the Urals the center of the wooded steppe follows the

Trans-Siberian Railway from Chelyabinsk to Omsk and Novosibirsk.

The steppe is a treeless expanse with a

The steppe zone continues from the Black Sea and northern Caucasus east to the Altai Mountains. Prominent steppe cities

Large amounts of lumber are floated down the Suna River to Petrozavodsk, in Karelia. (*Sovfoto.*)

continuous cover of short grass, often developed on loessial soils. Summers are dry and warm, with the July average above 68°F.; the yearly rainfall is 12 to 16 inches. Only near the forest is the grass luxuriant enough to be termed a meadow, elsewhere cereal grass and feather grass are typical. The presence of chernozem soil shows that the absence of trees is not due to deforestation by man. Instead, the prolonged dry period, low summer humidity, and deep ground-water surface make natural forest growth unlikely. Shelter-belt planting has long been practiced in the European steppe, but the forests do not reproduce themselves.[1] In the Rostov oblast alone, these cover 75,000 acres.

[1] VYSSOTSKY, G. N., Shelterbelts in the Steppes of Russia, *Journal of Forestry*, (1935), XXXIII, 781–788.

MIROV, N. T., Two Centuries of Afforestation and Shelterbelt Planting on the Russian Steppes, *Journal of Forestry*, (1935), XXXIII, 971–973.

are Odessa, Rostov, Chkalov, formerly Orenburg, and Semipalatinsk. These grasslands are the traditional home of the Cossacks, especially in the valleys of the Don and Volga, and were once overrun by the Mongol hordes. The steppe has so stamped its personality on the southern third of the country that one author has facetiously entitled a volume "Across Russia, Steppe by Steppe."

The semidesert zone is another transition area. Whereas the steppe has a continuous cover of grass and in the true desert it is wholly absent, the semidesert has spotty vegetation. Rainfall is six to ten inches, and July temperature averages exceed 75°F. Characteristic plant forms are wormwood and cereal grass. Salt marshes are present.

The temperate deserts of the U.S.S.R. have hot and nearly rainless summers, with July averages to 85°F., and frosty winters. Annual evaporation from free water surfaces is ten times the precipitation, but soil moisture is locally maintained by rivers from the snow-clad Pamirs. The deserts

vegetation grows throughout the year, and precipitation makes possible a luxuriant growth of broadleaf trees, with an admix-

The southern coast of the Crimea has a subtropical Mediterranean climate, as shown by the vegetation in this view near Yalta. (*Courtesy Intourist.*)

from the Caspian Sea to beyond Lake Balkhash are underlain by shifting sands and alkali soils. Vegetation is zoned according to rainfall, ground water, and salinity of the soil. Wormwood or sage is common in the north. All plants are especially adapted to reduce transpiration. Thickets of saxaul bushes have developed locally. During spring rains, ephemeral grasses and flowers rapidly come to life. Poplar and tamarisk grow in some valleys. The marmot is the chief animal, especially adapted to the desert by summer hibernation.

Subtropical Mediterranean forests are confined to the eastern and western valleys of Transcaucasia. Winters are so mild that

ture of conifers. Oak, hornbeam, and beech are typical at the lower elevations. Alder thickets are found in marshy areas.

Mountains introduce vertical zones in addition to the lowland conditions just described, in some cases with successive vegetation types from deserts at their base through meadows, deciduous and then coniferous forests, and finally to alpine tundra at the summits. Thus altitude is reflected by vegetation in replica of latitude. This is especially noticeable in the Caucasus and Pamirs which are capped by permanent snow fields.

Mountain grasslands range from alpine meadows with abundant rainfall on windward slopes to steppe or semidesert in the rain shadow. Forests of the Caucasus are especially rich and varied. In the Altai, steppe vegetation covers the lower slopes to around 3,000 feet, above which is a taiga forest to 6,000 feet, followed by alpine meadows. The snow line lies at 9,000 feet. In the mountains of northeastern Siberia, Daurian larch is dominant, but east of the Kolyma River mountain tundra covers much of the highlands. Drainage and soils differentiate this mountain tundra from the low-level tundra along the coast.

Soils

Russian soil scientists have led the world in the classification of soils on the basis of environmental differences which place their stamp on the soil. Thus the parent material, whether stream alluvium, glacial deposits, or rock weathered *in situ*, acquires a definite profile through the action of ground water and vegetation.

In areas of abundant rainfall, soluble minerals are leached and removed in solution, while in arid regions such minerals remain in the soil. Where they are present to excess as in deserts, the soil becomes alkaline. Grass roots contribute more organic material to the soil than do the leaves of trees. Coniferous forests give rise to more acid soils than deciduous forests.

Across the Soviet Union, the major soil types reflect climatic and vegetation zones, as well as recent geologic history. Tundra vegetation is associated with tundra soils, the taiga is roughly coextensive with podsol soils, mixed forests coincide with brown forest soils, the steppe area has produced rich chernozem soils, the semiarid lands have chestnut-brown soil, and the desert corresponds with saline or alkaline soils.

Tundra soils are unfrozen for so little of the year, and then have such limited drainage, that they seldom develop a mature profile. Decaying vegetation overlies the mineral soil and renders it so acid that cultivated crops can be raised only with special treatment.

Podsols cover nearly half of the Soviet Union. The typical profile shows a surface organic layer derived from coniferous trees, below it a sandy ash-colored horizon which gives the podsols their name, then a dark brownish clay-enriched zone, and below these the unaltered parent material. In the north, podsol formation is retarded by marshes, in the south by deficient moisture. Despite their acid character these podsols provide the soil for a third of the cultivated area.

The most productive soil in the world is the chernozem, more extensively developed in the U.S.S.R. than in any other country. It is a grassland soil, black with organic matter and high in lime and soluble plant foods. Some of it is developed on loess. But the very climatic factors that make this soil so fertile also make its agricultural utilization precarious, for rainfall is low and erratic. Were the rainfall heavier, forests would replace the steppe and there would be no chernozem soil. Chernozems occupy half the cultivated land; so long as the natural sod is not destroyed, wind erosion is seldom serious but, once the soil is cultivated, extensive deflation may take place. Dust-bowl erosion has long been critical in the Eurasian steppes.

In dry lands where water plays a diminished role in soil formation, the parent material has added importance.

Irrigation may make the dry soils usable, but care must be taken for adequate subsurface drainage so that excess water does not evaporate to form a salty crust, known as an artificial solonchak.

CHAPTER 17

MINERAL RESOURCES IN THE SOVIET UNION

There are few Soviet achievements of which Russians are prouder than the charting of their vast mineral wealth, and deservedly so. It is now clear that the Union is one of the richest nations in the world, and that its coal, oil, iron, gold, potassium salts, and phosphate are of vast extent. However, not all their mineral deposits are of high grade, or are easily accessible, or lie near the requisite fuel. Under a socialist or nationalistic regime it may be feasible to develop minerals with little regard to costs, but although the major picture is one of exceptional abundance, overoptimistic conclusions should not be drawn from a mere tabulation.

Geological studies date from the days of Peter the Great who established state mines in the Urals in 1699. With the development of the five-year plans came a great increase in field work, especially with relation to mineral deposits. In 1936, the Central Institute of Geology and Prospecting had a staff of 500 geologists and a budget of $2,300,000. Research has yielded large dividends, for many new mineral localities have been discovered and the boundaries of known deposits enlarged. During the period between the First and Second World Wars, the known reserves of coal increased sevenfold, of petroleum sevenfold, of zinc tenfold, of lead ninefold, of iron ore including ferriferous quartzites one hundred and thirty times, of copper twenty-eight times. Furthermore, vast resources of potassium, phosphate, and aluminum have been newly discovered.[1]

[1] MIKHAILOV, NICHOLAS, "The Land of the Soviets," 22–24.

Power

Coal is the most important source of power, but in the Soviet Union wood for fuel comes ahead of petroleum. Even in 1925, many railway locomotives burned wood. From 1913 to 1937, the place occupied by coal rose from 60 to 70 per cent of all fuels, wood dropped from 22 to 12 per cent, petroleum declined from 17 to 12 per cent, and peat increased from 1 to 6 per cent.

In 1913 when the Twelfth International Geological Congress collected data on the coal reserves of the world, Russia was credited with 230,000,000,000 metric tons. At the Seventeenth Congress in 1937, Soviet reserves were placed at 1,654,361,-000,000 tons, easily second to the United States. These reserves are distributed through 83 fields from Moscow to Kamchatka, with nine-tenths of the tonnage in the Asiatic area. Bituminous coal amounts to 87 per cent.

In the accompanying table, the reserves are bituminous except as listed, and the areas where at least some of the coal is of coking quality are so indicated.

Mining Areas	Reserves in Millions of Metric Tons
Donets Coal Basin (Upper Carboniferous, anthracite and coking)	88,872
North Slope Caucasus (Jurassic)	4,068
Georgia (Jurassic)	309
South Moscow (Lower Carboniferous, lignite)	12,400
Pechora (Permian)	±3,000
Western Urals (Lower Carboniferous)	4,777
Eastern Urals (Triassic, lignite)	2,872
Karaganda (Lower Carboniferous, coking)	52,696

Kuznets (Permian, coking)............	450,658
Minusinsk (Permian)................	20,612
Chulym-Yenisei (Jurassic, lignite).....	43,000
Kansk (Jurassic, lignite).............	42,000
Irkutsk and Transbaikalia (Jurassic)...	81,397
Bureya...........................	26,116
Suchan (coking)....................	42,000
Tunguska (Lower Carboniferous)......	±400,000
Lena (Mesozoic)...................	±60,000
Total for U.S.S.R.................	1,654,361

Coal production has steadily increased so that the Union occupies third place in Eurasia. Not only has tonnage increased but its distribution has also changed.

Year	Total Soviet output, tons	Donets area		Kuznets area	
		Tonnage	Per Cent	Tonnage	Per Cent
1913	29,100,000	25,288,000	87	799,000	3
1928	35,500,000	27,330,000	77	2,743,000	8
1932	64,400,000	45,044,000	70	7,544,000	12
1934	93,500,000	61,496,000	65	11,974,000	13
1936	125,957,000	82,000,000	60	17,300,000	14
				(1937)	
1938	132,900,000			(20,000,000	
				plan)	
1940	164,600,000				

The Donets Coal Basin, whose name is often shortened to Donbas, lies north of the Black Sea and has always been the country's leading producer but, despite a threefold increase since 1913, its proportion of the national output has declined by a third, due to the rise of Kuznets and numerous new fields. The Donets coal fields have an area of 10,000 square miles, about three-quarters of which lies within the Ukrainian S.S.R. There are two thousand shafts. Nearly half the coal is anthracite, and there are large amounts of bituminous coal suitable for metallurgical coke or chemical uses and gasification. The output supplies the blast furnaces based on the Krivoi Rog iron deposits, 200 miles to the west, as well as most railway and industrial needs west of the Urals.

Both north and south of Moscow are lignite areas which now rank third in production, with a 1937 yield of 7,750,000 tons. Much of the coal is used in central heat and power stations. Both here and in the Donets area, there is some underground gasification of coal *in situ*. The air supply is controlled so that either high calorie gas may be obtained for boilers, or "process" gas for synthetic benzine and ammonia.

The newly developed Pechora fields are near the Arctic Circle just west of the Urals. Production in the Vorkuta district supplies coal to Leningrad via a new railway. An annual output of 2,000,000 tons was planned by 1942. Farther south are deposits on the eastern and western slopes of the Urals. The western coals are high in sulphur and do not make suitable coke for blast furnaces, but are usable for locomotives, electrical power, and for reducing sulphide copper ores. The principal mine is at Kizel, with an output of 3,000,000 tons. Much of the coal on the eastern side is lignite, such as deposits near Chelyabinsk, where production increased from 390,000 tons in 1925 to 3,519,000 tons in 1936. The combined output of the western and eastern Ural fields was 8,080,000 tons in 1937.

The development of the Kuznets Basin, sometimes called Kuzbas, has transformed a mid-Siberian steppe, south of the Trans-Siberian Railway, into a great industrial center. Reserves once estimated at 13,000,-000,000 tons have been increased to 450,-658,000,000 tons, and the annual capacity of the 50 operating collieries in 1937 was 17,300,000 tons. The output of the field is equal to nearly all that of India, or half of Japan. Great expansion occurred during the Second World War. With a high calorie content, combined with low ash and sulphur, the coals are the best in the Union. Anthracite accounts for 54 billion tons of the total reserve. Much of the output is

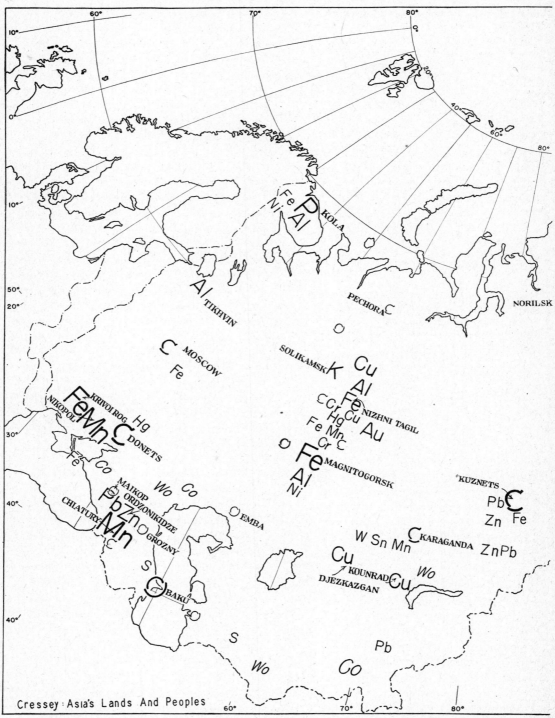

Cressey: Asia's Lands And Peoples

The Soviet Union undoubtedly stands next to the United States as the most highly mineralized nation. C—coal, O—oil. Minerals are in vertical letters: Al—aluminum, Au—gold, Cr—chromium, Cu—copper, Hg—agricultural products, in italics, include Co—cotton and Wo—wool.

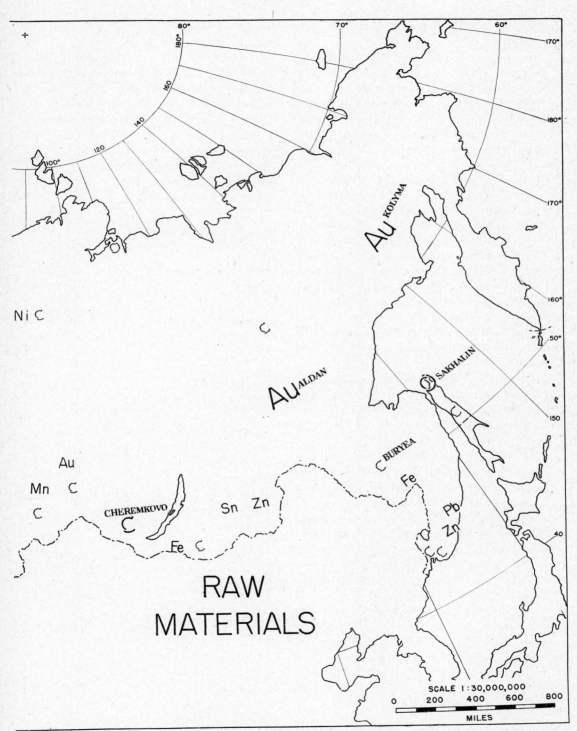

RAW
MATERIALS

The symbols suggest the relative world rank of the respective resources. Fuels are shown in shadow letters:
mercury, K—potash, Mn—manganese, Ni—nickel, Pb—lead, S—sulphur, Sn—tin, Zn—zinc. Industrial

used in the Ural-Kuznets metallurgical combine.

Between Kuznets and the Urals lie the newly surveyed and very important Karaganda coal fields. Their proximity to the Urals has caused them partly to replace Kuznets coal in the Magnitogorsk blast furnaces. The 1937 production reached 3,937,200 tons.

East of Kuznets are a number of partly developed coal fields. The Minusinsk Basin, where a few mines operate at Chernogorsk, lies on the Yenisei south of the Trans-Siberian Railway. The Chulym-Yenisei brown coal field extends north of Krasnoyarsk to the junction of the Angara and west along the railway to Mariinsk, but is undeveloped. East of the Yenisei is the Kansk brown coal area, also along the railway. West of Irkutsk, 3,000,000 tons of coal were mined in 1937 at Cheremkhovo, and the deposits continue east of Lake Baikal.

Important coal fields are present in the Amur Valley, especially along its tributary, the Bureya. Near Vladivostok, coking coal is mined at Artem, 2,110,000 tons in 1937, and at Suchan, 590,000 tons.

In the Yenisei and Lena valleys lie two vast coal regions, largely undeveloped. Deposits east of the Yenisei, at present worked only at Norilsk, are called the Tunguska Coal Field, after the three tributary Tunguska rivers. Deposits along the Lena are worked on a small scale at Sangar Khai. Sakhalin also produces coal. Coal is mined along the borders of the Caucasus and Pamirs.

Not only are Soviet reserves exceedingly large, they are also well distributed. The Urals lack proper metallurgical coke, but new developments at Karaganda will make it unnecessary to bring fuel from Kuznets. Moscow, once dependent on Donets coal, now produces almost enough local lignite. Leningrad once used British or German coal

but has developed large central plants for burning near-by peat.

The geology of oil and gas is more complicated than that of coal, so that reserves can only be generalizations. Soviet production has long been a poor second to the American, but her reserves may approach or exceed those of the United States. Data on petroleum resources in the U.S.S.R. as presented to the Seventeenth International Geological Congress are given in the accompanying table.

	Metric Tons[1]
Apsheron Peninsula (Baku)	781,300,000
Other areas in Azerbaidzhan	1,771,000,000
Grozny	174,800,000
Maikop and vicinity	156,900,000
Georgia	176,200,000
Daghestan	146,000,000
Emba	1,190,400,000
Bashkiria (Sterlitamak)	365,200,000
Perm-Kama	354,000,000
Other West Urals and Volga	471,500,000
Sakhalin	339,800,000
Middle Asia	427,100,000
Total for U.S.S.R.	6,376,300,000

[1] One metric ton of petroleum is equal to 5 to 10 barrels of 42 gallons according to specific gravity,

This vast total may be divided into various categories of probability, of which "proved and prospected" amount to 230,-700,000 tons, and "visible" an additional 652,000,000 tons. The remainder is little more than an optimistic geological estimate. The comparative figure in the United States for these first two categories is 1,765,000,000 tons. Intensive geological and geophysical prospecting has located new fields and spread production widely from the prerevolutionary center at Baku. Production figures are as follows:

	Metric Tons
1901	11,000,000
1913	7,627,000
1920	2,915,000
1928	11,625,400
1932	21,413,200
1936	27,337,700 (from 45 operating fields)

In contrast to coal, oil deposits are largely in a single zone, from the Caucasus and Caspian Sea north to the central Urals.

pipe line from the Caspian Sea to the Black Sea also continues northwest to the Donets Basin.

The Volga above Kuibyshev. Preliminary work at the new dam site is shown on the far bank.

Elsewhere, the far eastern island of Sakhalin is important; oil is produced in the Pechora Basin; and there is a small output at Nordvyk along the Siberian Arctic coast, and in Kamchatka.

Baku in Azerbaidzhan has always been far in the lead as a producer, and production dates from 1869. In 1901 it supplied half the world's output. Most of the production comes from Pliocene sands on the Apsheron Peninsula, but there are numerous horizons down to the Lower Cretaceous. Wells go to a depth of 8,648 feet. Two pipe lines lead south of the Caucasus to. Batumi on the Black Sea.

The second producing district is along the northern slopes of the Caucasus at Grozny and Maikop. Large reserves of natural gas also occur in these areas. A

Northeast of the Caspian along the Emba River are at least 300 salt domes. In 1937 there was a production of 466,000 tons from 20 developed domes. Oil occurs in formations from the Permian to Paleocene. A pipe line from the Caspian Sea leads through the Emba fields northwest to Orsk and eastward across Siberia, probably to Omsk.

The oil fields between the Volga and the southern Urals have been developed since 1928. Reserves here appear to be so extensive that the area is termed a "second Baku." Proved fields extend from the Caspian depression north to the Kama River.

Sakhalin is the chief producing area in the Far East. The 1936 yield in the Okha field amounted to 470,000 tons, of which a third was obtained by Japanese concessionaires.

The third source of power is hydroelectric, and Soviet plans in this field are as ambitious as elsewhere. Only in the Caucasus, Pamirs, Tien Shan, and eastern Siberia are there swift streams fed by melting snow. Elsewhere gradients are gentle and the flow seasonal, but rivers as large as the Volga and Yenisei make the potential power impressive.

Estimates of water power based on stream flow available 50 per cent of the time amount to 280,690,000 kilowatts, while that available 95 per cent of the time is 58,000,000 kilowatts. The Lena system leads in potentialities, followed by the Yenisei and its tributary the Angara, the Far East, Soviet Middle Asia, the Ob, the Volga, the Caucasus, and Kola-Karelia. Most of these localities are remote from the present market for electricity.

An extensive program, initiated in 1920 under the direction of Lenin, calls for a series of coordinated stations on the Volga, the Dnieper, and in the Caucasus, supplemented by steam-operated plants in the Donets, Moscow, Leningrad, and Ural areas. Subsequent plans provide for vast installations on the Yenisei south of Krasnoyarsk and especially on the Angara near Lake Baikal. Several projects are comparable to the Grand Coulee Dam on the Columbia River.

The largest hydroelectric installation in Europe, and when built the largest in the world, was on the Dnieper River where it cuts through the Ukrainian Uplands at Zaporozhe. This had an installed capacity of 900,000 kilowatts when destroyed by the retreating Russians during the Second World War. The aggregate hydroelectric capacity of the Union in 1940 amounted to 2,500,000 kilowatts.

The proposed program is on a truly gigantic scale. Two dams under construction near Kuibyshev on the Volga will each generate over 1,000,000 kilowatts. On the Angara River, fed by the constant flow from Lake Baikal, there are eventually to be eight principal stations with a total capacity of 9,000,000 kilowatts. Four stations on the upper Yenisei will produce 4,000,000 kilowatts. Decades may elapse before these Siberian developments are completed, but the presence of near-by coal and iron makes large-scale industry possible.

Metals

Iron is the indispensable material for construction. Reserves of iron ore were estimated in 1933 at 16,447,000,000 metric tons, of which actual reserves amounted to 9,238,000,000 tons. These latter are further classified as brown limonite ore, 5,484 million; magnetite ore, 2,392 million; and red hematite ore, 1,571 million tons. Deposits are grouped in a few localities: the high-grade Krivoi Rog and inferior Kerch areas in the Ukraine and Crimea, the problematical ores of the Kursk magnetic anomaly, the brown ores south and east of Moscow, numerous occurrences in the Urals notably the magnetite at Magnitogorsk and Nizhni Tagil, newly found deposits south of the Kuznets Basin and near Karaganda, undeveloped reserves along the Angara, and scattered deposits in the Far East. Large-scale production is more localized.

Krivoi Rog has long been the leading center of iron mining, although the Urals were discovered earlier. The ore is in preCambrian ferruginous chert and jaspellite, and is a banded mixture of hematite, altered martite, and magnetite, concentrated by hydrothermal weathering. In origin and problems it resembles the deposits near Lake Superior. The iron percentage in the martite averages 63 per cent, and in the hematite 51 per cent; these two make up three-quarters of the deposit. The magnetite and brown ores both carry 58 per cent iron. In 1937 there were 25 operating mines, one with a capacity of 6,000,000 tons and four others designed for 2,000,000 tons each. Reserves at Krivoi Rog aggregate 1,142,000,000 tons.

Ural iron has been known since 1702, and there are scores of localities. The largest development is at Magnitogorsk in the south, where large-scale operations started in 1931. The annual production is 6,000,000 tons of ore. The ore is magnetite and secondary martite, formed by contact metamorphism, with a metallic content from 55 to 66 per cent. The oldest and second most important center is Nizhni Tagil. Total Ural reserves are placed at 1,390,607,000 tons, of which a third is limonite. Magnitogorsk accounts for 450,-000,000 tons.

South and east of Moscow, notably at Lipetsk and Tula, are sedimentary brown hematite ores of lacustrine and lagoon origin. Reserves total 424,000,000 tons.

Near Kerch at the eastern end of Crimea are deposits consisting of brown oolitic, manganiferous, and phosphatic ores of Pliocene age. Reserves are placed at 2,726,-000,000 tons, but the metallic content is only 35 per cent iron.

When the Kuznets coal field was developed, no near-by iron was known, but since 1930 sizable deposits of magnetite have been developed in the Gornaya Shoria to the south. The ore is formed by contact metamorphism and is associated with skarn with an iron content of 45 per cent. Reserves in the Gornaya Shoria may reach 292,412,000 tons. Of similar importance are the ores found near Karaganda during the Second World War.

East of Lake Baikal ore is mined near Petrovsk-Zabaikal, and in the Amur Valley both near the mouth and in the Little Khingan Mountains.

The preceding deposits are all in production. Among undeveloped reserves, the outstanding is the Kursk magnetic anomaly between Moscow and Kharkov. Compass deviations here have been known since 1874, but high-grade hematite and siderite ores comparable in richness to Krivoi Rog were discovered only in 1931. Reserves listed as "actual" and "probable" amount to 250,000,000 tons, while the total may reach 6,000,000,000. This would make it one of the largest ore bodies on earth, but metallurgical difficulties make development problematical. Small but important ore deposits are in process of development on the Kola Peninsula. Iron is also found in the Caucasus. In Eastern Siberia, the most important locality is along the Angara and Ilim Rivers, northwest of Lake Baikal, where reserves are calculated at 420,850,000 tons.

The production of iron ore amounted to 9,300,000 metric tons in 1913; 8,000,000 in 1929; 14,500,000 in 1933; and 26,500,000 tons (estimated) in 1938. Its utilization is considered in the next chapter.

Manganese is the most essential of all other ferrometals, since 14 pounds are required in the manufacture of each ton of steel. The Soviet Union leads the world in reserves, which were estimated at 700,-000,000 tons in 1936, and in production, which exceeds 4,000,000 tons. The largest deposit is that of Nikopol in the southern Ukraine, but the ore at Chiatury in Georgia is of higher grade, largely mined for export. Manganese is also mined in the Urals, in Kazakhstan, and west of Krasnoyarsk. The Nikopol ore is a Tertiary laterite type deposit above pre-Cambrian crystallines, 4 to 12 feet thick and buried by Quaternary sands.

Copper reserves were greatly enlarged by exploration during the five-year plans, but the quality of the ore is poor. Kazakhstan has the chief deposits, exceeding those of the Urals and the Caucasus. Many of the deposits contain less than two per cent copper, and their economic workability is

Aluminum was regarded as a deficit metal in czarist Russia because the known bauxite deposits were limited and too poor

Gold dredging in Siberia. Most production is obtained from placer deposits. (*Sovfoto*.)

questionable. Production in 1930 amounted to 34,105 metric tons, and in 1936 to 83,000 metric tons, still considerably below the country's requirements. The leading mine is at Kounrad near the north shore of Lake Balkhash, where there are porphyritic deposits with 1.1 per cent copper. A new smelter has an annual capacity of 100,000 tons of metal. Farther west are the richer Djezkazgan deposits where the production is to be double that of Kounrad. The Urals were formerly the principal copper area, with numerous deposits of varied types, chiefly pyrite. Ore bodies are found over a distance of 500 miles from the largest mine at Krasnouralsk in the north to Orsk in the south.

Lead and zinc reserves represent 11 and 19 per cent of the world totals, respectively. Important areas are Ordzhonikidze in northern Caucasia, Ridder in the Altai Mountains, Trans-Baikalia, and the Maritime Province. Lead production amounted to 55,000 tons in 1936, and zinc to 63,000 tons.

to work. The metal is now secured from unsatisfactory ores at Tikhvin east of Leningrad, from large deposits in the northern Urals at Kabakovsk, formerly Nadezhdinsk, and in the southern Urals at Kamensk. Huge nepheline deposits in the Kola Peninsula are also worked for aluminum. The oldest reduction plant is at Volkhov near Leningrad. Two plants are located near the Dnieper hydroelectric station, and another is at Kamensk. A larger plant began operation in 1939 near Kandalaksha in the Kola Peninsula. Despite inferior deposits, the Soviet Union is a major producer, ranking fourth in 1939 with an output of 60,000 tons and a much larger yield in sight.

Nickel is mined in the central and southern Urals, at Norilsk near the lower Yenisei, and in the Kola Peninsula. The output of 3,000 metric tons in 1938 was barely adequate for domestic needs, but enabled the Union to rank as a very poor third in world output, following Canada and New Caledonia.

Gold has long been known in Siberia and the Urals, both as placer and lode deposits.[1] No production figures are published, but conservative foreign estimates place the 1939 output at 4,500,000 ounces, as compared with 5,173,000 ounces in 1936. Optimistic estimates are nearly double these figures. The Union holds second place to the Union of South Africa, closely followed by Canada and the United States. The most important areas are along the Aldan and Kolyma Rivers in Yakutia. Other mining centers are scattered through eastern Siberia, Soviet Middle Asia, the Urals, and the Caucasus.

Platinum production provides over a third of the world's supply, largely from ultrabasic rocks near Nizhni Tagil in the Urals, well known for a century. Chromium is obtained from low-grade ores in the Urals, with an annual yield in excess of 200,000 metric tons of chromite. This places the U.S.S.R. in first place, ahead of Turkey and South Africa.

Tin is found east of Baikal and in Kazakhstan, but production is negligible. Tungsten is mined in the same general area.

Nonmetals

In addition to a wide variety of the usual nonmetallic minerals, the Soviet Union has fabulously large deposits of two uncommon substances: apatite and potassium salts. Each has been developed with dramatic rapidity. In both cases resources and production lead the world.

Apatite is a source of phosphate, secured rarely as mineral apatite but most frequently from phosphate limestone rock as in north Africa. Soviet deposits are located north of the Arctic Circle in the Khibin Mountains of the Kola Peninsula, and are a magmatic segregation from nepheline syenite. Near by is the new town of Kirovsk with a population of 40,000. Two million tons are mined yearly, yielding 1,000,000 tons of purified apatite and 500,000 tons of purified nepheline. Ore reserves are established at 2,000,000,000 tons. When visited by the International Geological Congress excursion of 1937, the mine was regarded as one of the industrial wonders of the world. The property was developed in eight years and there were 20 miles of underground galleries, fully electrified. Ordinary freight trains carry out the ore from the heart of the mountain. The high-grade fertilizers obtained from the apatite are of vital importance in Soviet agricultural expansion. From the nepheline is produced soda and aluminum.

Potash is secured at Solikamsk on the western slope of the northern Urals. Salt had been known for three centuries, but potassium and magnesium salts and bromine were not found until 1925. The annual production amounted to 1,800,000 tons in 1937. Reserves of potassium salts are estimated at 15,000,000,000 tons, and those of magnesium salts at 18,000,000,000 tons. In addition there are still larger deposits of common salt, unworked. Germany has previously been the world's leading potash producer.

Asbestos has been secured from Asbest in the Urals near Sverdlovsk since 1889. The fiber occurs in serpentinized peridotite as in Quebec and Rhodesia. Similar deposits are present in the Altai-Sayan Mountains. Ural reserves are estimated at 17,500,000 tons of fiber longer than 0.7 millimeter, and the production is more than adequate for all domestic needs. Much of the fiber is short, but the percentage of long fiber is reported to be greater than in Canada. The Union holds second place in world output, with a yield over 100,000 tons. Talc and

---

[1] See VON BERNEWITZ, M. W., Russia's Gold Production, U.S. Bureau of Mines, Mineral Trade Notes, May 20, 1936.

soapstone deposits in the Urals are also enormous.

Magnesite occurs in large deposits near Sverdlovsk and Chelyabinsk. The annual output of 800,000 tons supplies domestic needs and provides a large export to western Europe. Austria occupies second place in magnesite production.

Industrial salt is available in abundance. There are deposits at Solikamsk, Emba, and the Donets Basin.

Gems and semiprecious stones have been secured from the Urals for centuries, including emerald, beryl, amethyst, topaz, and massive blocks of malachite. Kaolin production is centered in the Ukraine. Fire clays are present in the Moscow Coal Basin and in the Ukraine. Mercury is available in the Donets Basin and in the Urals.

Summary

Mining is concentrated in a few districts, near the more densely settled areas or along the major railways. The Ukraine has coal, iron, and manganese. The Moscow area has inferior coal and iron. In the Kola Peninsula are spectacular deposits of potash and uncommon minerals. The Urals are a tremendous storehouse of natural wealth, perhaps the richest mountain range of their size on earth. Here are iron, gold, asbestos, potassium and magnesium salts, aluminum, chromium, nickel, low-grade

coal, and oil. The Caucasus have oil, manganese, lead, and zinc. Kazakhstan contains coal, copper, lead, and zinc. The Pamirs, Tien Shan, Altai, and Sayan are all mineralized, with conspicuous coal and iron in the Kuznets Basin. Eastern Siberia, still partly unexplored, has coal, gold, iron, and other minerals. Despite this imposing list, large areas are entirely without resources.

The industrial utilization of these resources will be considered in the next chapter, but a mere listing of resources discloses the exceptional natural wealth of this vast area. Intensive geological research has greatly increased the known reserves, even in long-studied areas. No other land has so great a variety of minerals, and only the United States is richer.

At the same time, it is well to note that among these many deposits are some low-grade ores, especially copper and aluminum, which have doubtful value if operated on a basis of strict capitalist accounting. Moreover, reserves and production need to be considered in terms of a country 8 million square miles in area inhabited by 170 million people.

The Soviet mining industry is still engaged in catching up with the rest of the world, but the accelerated developments just before and during the Second World War indicate that the lag will not long persist.

CHAPTER 18

ECONOMIC DEVELOPMENTS IN THE SOVIET UNION

The industrial task of the Soviet Union under the five-year plans was to overtake and surpass the capitalist world, especially the United States. When one considers the limited development of industry in 1913 and the fact that post-war production did not regain this level until 1926, the audacity of such a goal is obvious. Lenin once said that in terms of industry, old Russia was "four times worse than England, five times worse than Germany, ten times worse than America." Owing to the relatively self-contained character of Soviet expansion, it was little retarded by the world-wide depression of the early 1930's.

Any analysis of Soviet economic development must first consider the reliability of Soviet statistics. Unfortunately a complete check is out of the question, for the only figures available are those of the government. Actual production figures are often confused with planned production or are given as percentages of increase without stating the actual quantity involved. This use of percentages reaches a humorous climax in the annual statistics from an Arctic station where it was reported that 2 per cent of the men had married 50 per cent of the women, yet only one marriage was involved.

By 1938, the Soviet Union claimed to hold first place within Europe in total industrial output. This was undoubtedly true in oil, potash, phosphate, peat, trucks, and tractors, but not in electrical power, coal, steel, copper, aluminum, or cement. Immense strides have been made, but decades must pass before the cumulative results give the Soviet landscape an appearance of material abundance resembling western Europe. With the industrial index of 1913 set at 100, that of 1938 was 908.8.

In terms of 1937 output per person, Soviet pig iron amounted to a third that of Germany or half that of England. The per capita coal production was less than a quarter that of Germany or one-seventh that of England. Cement was but one-fifth the German-English average. Cotton textile production equaled a quarter the English output per capita, while paper was but one-eighth that of Germany and England.

Czarist Russia was dominantly agricultural. Half the manufacturing centered in Moscow and Leningrad, where light industries such as textiles were the rule. The Ukraine and Urals accounted for a third of the total industrial output. Under the five-year plans, and particularly during the Second World War, the industrial center of gravity shifted eastward, almost to the Urals.

Heavy Industry

Iron and steel were fundamental in the five-year plans. The output of pig iron rose from 4,200,000 tons in 1913 to 14,900,000 tons in 1940. Whereas the Ukraine was almost the only steel area prior to the First World War, expansion in the interwar period added huge plants in the Urals and central Siberia.

The southern Ukraine is an ideal production area, for in addition to near-by high-grade coking coal and rich iron ore, there is manganese and hydroelectric power. On account of its favorable geography it

magnetic anomaly, 200 miles north of Donets coal, prove workable, still further expansion is possible.

A blast furnace in construction for the Mariupol steel works on the Sea of Azov. This plant utilizes Donets coal and Kerch iron ore. (*Sovfoto.*)

should remain the major metallurgical area. Iron ore from Krivoi Rog is shipped 200 miles east to blast furnaces in the Donets coal field at Makeevka, Stalino, Ordzhonikidze, Voroshilovsk, Konstantinovka, Kramatorsk, and Krasni Sulin. Coal is also carried west to the ore mines at Krivoi Rog, as well as to furnaces en route at Zaporozhe and Dniepropetrovsk. East of the Donets are steel mills at Stalingrad. In addition to this east-west movement, Donets coal is shipped south to Mariupol on the Sea of Azov where it meets iron ore from Kerch in eastern Crimea; there are also blast furnaces at Kerch. The Makeevka plant alone turned out 1,300,000 tons of pig iron in 1936. If the ores of the Kursk

South of Moscow pig iron and steel are produced on a modest scale at Lipetsk and Tula, and to the east are steel mills at Kulebaki and Vyksa. Moscow also has a steel mill without blast furnaces.

No less than 39 localities produce iron or steel in the Urals. Some of these are old plants operating on charcoal, but none of them is comparable in size to new giant furnaces at Magnitogorsk and Nizhni Tagil. Coal is supplied from Kuznets and Karaganda, for the local Kizel coal is high in sulphur and does not make good coke, although a passable fuel is obtained by mixture with Kuznets coke. Chelyabinsk coal is lignite and suitable only for power. When built, Magnitogorsk was equipped with four furnaces of 1,400 tons capacity, but a fifth has since been added. In what was virgin steppe around Magnet Mountain has grown a city of 145,870 people (1939). Magnitogorsk is said to rank next to Gary, Ind., as the second largest individual steel mill in the world. The extensive plant at Nizhni Tagil is closely followed by new works at Sverdlovsk. Other furnaces are at Chelyabinsk, Khalilovo, and Bakal. The Urals, with a vastly increased steel output and abundance of other metals, stand second to the Ukraine in industrial importance. The absence of local metallurgical coke is a problem, but the newly developed Karaganda coal field is only 600 miles distant.

Although the Kuznets coal field lies 1,417 miles east of Magnitogorsk via the Trans-Siberian Railway, the new direct line reduces this distance to 1,200 miles. When the Ural-Kuznets combine was inaugurated, no nearer coal was known, and the expense of the rail haul, the longest in the world, was to be partly offset by constructing duplicate steel plants at each end. The furnaces at Stalinsk, formerly named Kuznets, thus have a capacity equal to those of Magnitogorsk. When visited by the author in 1937, the four blast furnaces were producing a total of 4,000 tons per day. Near-by iron ore in the Gornaya Shoria is gradually replacing that from the Urals, and the lower quality is offset by the cheaper transportation. The Ural-Kuznets metallurgical combine supplied more than a quarter of the nation's iron in 1936 and was to be expanded to a third by 1942.

East of Lake Baikal is an old iron and steel works at Petrovsk-Zabaikal. New mills are in operation at Komsomolsk on the lower Amur, using Buryea coal and Little Khingan ore. A steel mill came into operation at Tashkent in 1942.

Projected iron centers include the Trans-caucasus and Kola Peninsula. Eventual possibilities in Siberia involve Minusinsk coal and near-by Abakan iron ore, and especially Cheremkhovo coal and Angara-Ilim iron ore, to be developed along with Angara water power.

Copper, aluminum, lead, and zinc are also vital in heavy industry. Geographic problems of bringing ore and fuel together are not so difficult in these cases. There has been a continuous effort to open new deposits and spread production widely. Large-scale electrochemical works have developed around the Dnieper Dam in the Ukraine, and around smaller sources of water power in the Kola Peninsula and Caucasus, with plans for industries in the Urals and Tien Shan. Another chemical industry is east of the Caspian Sea on Kara-Bogaz Gulf, where mirabilite, or sodium sulphate, and other chemicals are extracted from sea water.

Railway equipment is produced in the Ukraine and Ural areas, especially locomotives in a huge plant at Voroshilovgrad, formerly Lugansk; and rolling stock at Dnieprodzerzinsk and Nizhni Tagil. The principal centers of general machine production are Moscow, Leningrad, and Kharkov, with mining machinery at Kramatorsk in the Donets area and Sverdlovsk in the Urals.

There are automobile factories at Moscow, Gorki, and Yaroslavl, and motor-truck plants at Leningrad, Chelyabinsk, Kharkov, and Stalingrad. The production in 1939 amounted to 171,100 trucks and 25,700 passenger cars, a slight decrease from the preceding year.

Agricultural machinery has received much emphasis, with tractor plants at Kharkov, Stalingrad, and Chelyabinsk. Harvesters and combines are made at Rostov-on-Don, Saratov, and Kirovo.

Wartime developments brought great changes in the type and location of Soviet industries. Many factories from the German-occupied areas were dismantled and removed to the Urals, to central Siberia, and to Soviet Middle Asia. For reasons of security, and since this eastward trend is in line with pioneering needs, much of this migration will be permanent.

The building of river steamers has long been important, with shops on the Dnieper at Kiev, on the Volga at Gorki, and elsewhere. Ocean-going vessels are built at Nikolaevsk near Odessa and at Leningrad.

Heavy industry is far more developed west of the Volga than elsewhere. Leningrad stands in a corner by itself. The Moscow-Gorki region is very important, but the Donets-Kharkov-Nikolaevsk region is dominant. The Urals from Magnitogorsk through Sverdlovsk to Nizhni Tagil are a growing area, as are the Caucasus, the Tashkent area, the Kuznets Basin, and the Far East. But even more than indicated by population distribution or cultivated land, the industrial core of the Soviet Union has been west of longitude 45°E. The growth of outlying areas is conspicuous and will continue, but so far as heavy manufacturing was concerned prior to June 22, 1941, the essential area was bounded by Rostov-on-Don, Stalingrad, Gorki, and Leningrad; in short, west of the Volga.

Other Industry

Within the wide scope of light industry, it is only possible to speak of wood products, textiles, food, and new synthetic products. Lumbering is almost as widespread as the forests themselves. Wherever a railroad crosses a river flowing out of a forested area, there are sure to be sawmills. There are no large papermaking centers, but the mills are generally north of the Volga and Kama, especially near Gorki and Vologda, or in White Russia.

Cotton textile production is centered chiefly in the area bounded by Moscow, Ivanovo, and Yaroslavl. Leningrad and the Ukraine produce largely for local consumption. This grouping of mills has little geographic justification because they are remote from the cotton fields of Soviet Middle Asia, and the market is more widely spread. New mills have been built in Middle Asia and the Caucasus.

Linen weaving is also concentrated east of Moscow, although in separate towns from those devoted to cotton spinning. Production increased but slightly between 1913 and 1935.

Food industries gained fourfold from 1913 to 1935. Meat packing in the steppe follows the agricultural margin, with important centers at Saratov on the Volga, and in central Siberia at Kurgan, Petropavlovsk, Novosibirsk, Barnaul, and Semipalatinsk. Siberian butter was exported to England extensively before the First World War.

Sugar, refined from sugar beets, is a significant Ukrainian industry southwest of Kiev and northwest of Kharkov. The Caucasus are noted for wine and canned fruits. Flour production conforms to the wheat areas; in the Ukraine and western Siberia along the railway.

Fishing is most important around Astrakhan, where sturgeon and caviar are dominant. Rostov and the Sea of Azov occupy second place, followed by Murmansk, Vladivostok, and Kamchatka.

One of the few essentials not originally available in the U.S.S.R. was natural rubber. Although *Hevea braziliensis* cannot be grown, desert plants such as native kok-zaghiz or the Mexican guayule are cultivated from the Tien Shan west to White Russia. Artificial rubber is obtained from potatoes in plants at Yaroslavl and Kazan, from limestone at Erevan in Armenia, and from petroleum at Baku.

In Vol. I of the Great Soviet World Atlas significant maps compare the industry of 1913 with that of 1935 (Plates 147–152). Both in geographic extent and in quantity, the contrasts are enormous. Siberia developed, but manufacturing in the European areas expanded even more. The industrial production for 1935 is shown below:

Cities with production from 7 to 10,000 million rubles:
Moscow—machine construction, textiles, food, chemicals.
Leningrad—machine construction, chemicals, shoes and clothing, textiles.
Cities with production from 1 to 2,000 million rubles:
Gorki—machine construction, food.
Kharkov—machine construction, food, shoes, and clothing.
Baku—oil, food, machine construction.
Cities with production from 500 to 1,000 million rubles:
Odessa—machine construction, food, shoes, and clothing.
Kiev—machine construction, food, shoes, and clothing.
Dniepropetrovsk—iron and steel, machine construction, chemicals, food.
Rostov-on-Don—machine construction, food, shoes, and clothing.
Stalingrad—machine construction, iron and steel, food, wood industries.
Yaroslavl—chemicals, machine construction, textiles, food.
Cities with production from 250 to 500 million rubles:
Tbilisi—food, machine construction, shoes and clothing, textiles.
Grozny—oil.
Mariupol—iron and steel, machine construction.
Taganrog—machine construction, iron and steel.
Stalino—iron and steel, food, machine construction.
Zaporozhe—iron and steel, machine construction.
Dnieprodzerzinsk—iron and steel, machine construction, chemicals.
Voronezh—machine construction, food, chemicals.
Tula—machine construction, iron and steel.
Kalinin—textiles, machine construction, shoes, and clothing.
Saratov—machine construction, food.
Kazan—shoes and clothing, food.
Ivanovo—textiles.
Magnitogorsk—iron and steel, ore, chemicals.
Chelyabinsk—machine construction, food.

Sverdlovsk—machine construction, food, iron and steel.

All cities with an industrial production in excess of 250 million rubles in 1935 lie in the European area. In Siberia there are 5 cities whose rank is between 100 to 250 million: Omsk, Novosibirsk, Stalinsk, Irkutsk, and Vladivostok, and one in Central Asia, Tashkent. Cities of the same industrial output in the European area total 36. In the U.S.S.R. as a whole, 69 centers had an industrial output exceeding 100 million rubles in 1935. The corresponding total in 1913, with prices measured in 1926 to 1927 rubles, numbered but 5: Moscow, Leningrad, Baku, Ivanovo, and Odessa.

Transport

The transportation facilities of various areas differ widely. In the southwest there are closely spaced railways, while in the northeast, except for air transport, travel is restricted to widely spaced rivers or winter sled roads. Express trains on the Trans-Siberian cross the continent from Leningrad to Vladivostok in nine and a half days, or one may travel from Odessa on the Black Sea to Murmansk on the Arctic Ocean in three and a half days. But to traverse Siberia from Mongolia northward along the Yenisei requires more than two weeks by boat. Here again, continentality is inescapable.

Railways totaled 52,700 miles in 1938, as compared with 36,350 miles in 1913 excluding the areas lost during the First World War. This mileage, although but a quarter that of the United States, holds second place in the world. Freight turnover in the Soviet Union increased from 41 billion metric ton miles in 1913 to 370 billion in 1939. In the latter year, 1,626 locomotives and 49,100 railway cars were built. Soviet railways have a gauge of 5 feet in contrast to the standard gauge

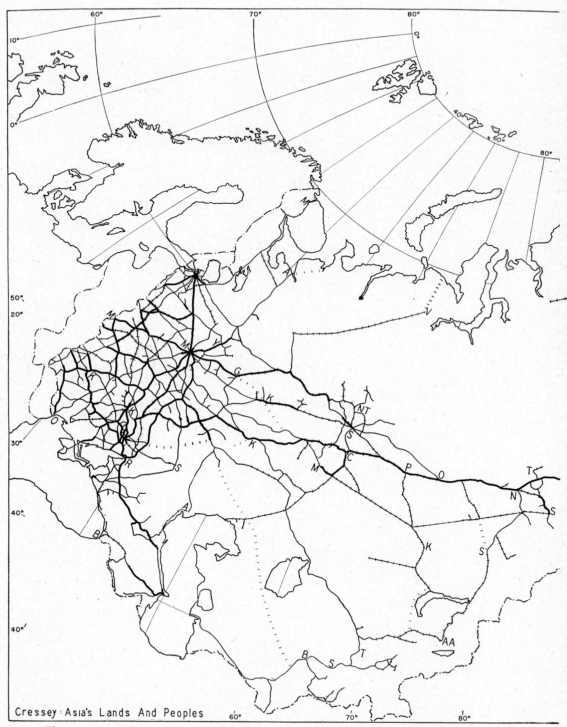

Cressey: Asia's Lands And Peoples

The area west of the Volga is well supplied with railways, but the balance of the country has only a coarse and Middle Asia was one of the noteworthy achievements of the five-year programs.

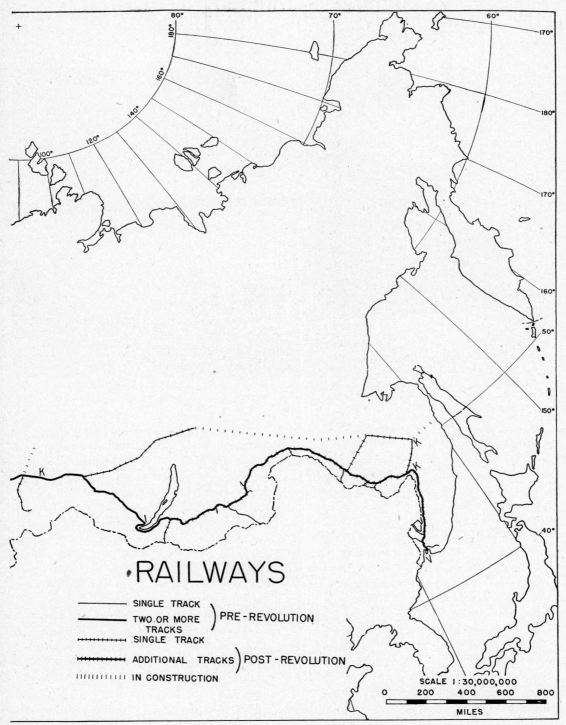

RAILWAYS

——————— SINGLE TRACK	) PRE-REVOLUTION
——————— TWO OR MORE TRACKS	
+++++++++ SINGLE TRACK	
++++++++++ ADDITIONAL TRACKS	) POST-REVOLUTION
‖‖‖‖‖‖‖‖ IN CONSTRUCTION	

SCALE 1:30,000,000

0   200   400   600   800

MILES

network or is entirely without railway facilities. The development of additional transportation lines in Siberia

of 4 feet 8½ inches in western Europe and North America. Most freight cars have four axles as in the United States, around suburban Moscow and Leningrad, in the Urals and Caucasus, and within the Kuznets Basin.

The great expansion of railroad mileage across the plains of the Soviet Union has led to specialized track-laying machines which lay down and advance over complete sections of rails and ties. (*Sovfoto*.)

rather than the two-axle type used in western Europe.

The distribution of railways is shown on the accompanying map. The densest network is in the Donets Coal Basin, with the heaviest traffic moving between there and Kharkov. All the Union west of the Volga and south of Leningrad lies within 35 miles of a railway. The only other area with closely spaced lines is the central Urals. A coarse grid is developing south of the Trans-Siberian. The Union's isolation is shown by the limited railway facilities across the borders. East of the Black Sea, but five railways cross the long frontier: into Turkey, Iran, Mongolia, and two lines to Manchuria.

There are nearly 2,000 miles of electrified railways, operating in the Kola Peninsula,

The utilization of waterways preceded railway construction and has expanded but slowly in recent years. Operating waterways in 1939 totaled 56,170 miles.[1] The freight carried in 1938 was about 23 billion metric ton-miles, or one-sixteenth that of the railways. In 1913 the ratio was nearer one to three. Timber in rafts or barges accounts for over half the total, and minerals and construction materials each represent an eighth. Grain and coal are also important commodities.

The Volga is the leading inland waterway, and its freight accounts for half the total. Its closest competitor is the combined Neva and Svir which link Lakes Ladoga and Onega with Leningrad. The Ob,

[1] Foreign Inland Waterway News, U.S. Bureau of Foreign and Domestic Commerce, November, 1939.

Yenisei, and Lena together account for but one-fourteenth, a fraction that indicates

completed in 1937, diverts water from the upper Volga past the city, thus increasing

The steamer *Kazakstan* in the port of Murmansk. This is one of the vessels used on the Northern Sea Route through the Arctic. (*Sovfoto*.)

the backward character and sparse population of their drainage areas.

The Volga's direction, depth, and economic hinterland make it the country's premier waterway. Baku oil and Donets coal move upstream, while wood floats down-current. Unfortunately the Volga empties into the landlocked Caspian. There have long been plans to build a canal from Stalingrad to the Don, in order that barges and small seagoing steamers might link the Caspian with the Black Sea. In the delta below Astrakhan are sand bars that make transshipment necessary. The headwaters of the Volga system are connected with Lake Ladoga through the Mariinsk Canal, completed in 1808, and frequently enlarged. Moscow lies on a small tributary of the Volga, formerly too shallow for navigation and inadequate for the municipal water supply. The Moscow-Volga Canal,

the water supply and making it possible for barges drawing 8½ feet to reach Moscow from the Caspian.

The Baltic-White Sea Canal links the Gulf of Finland with the White Sea via Lake Onega and is open to vessels of 1,250 tons.

Seagoing ships operate extensively in the Caspian and Black seas, and to a lesser extent in the Baltic, Arctic, and Far East. Freight services link Odessa and Vladivostok via Suez or Panama. This distance of 13,264 miles via Suez or 14,177 via Panama is reduced to 6,835 miles via the Northern Sea Route from Murmansk to Vladivostok. The ton mileage of ocean-borne freight in 1938 was slightly larger than that carried on the rivers.

Highways have never received much attention. Out of a total distance of 840,000 miles in 1938, only 60,000 were surfaced with gravel or cobblestones, and but 2,400 were asphalted. Natural dirt roads predominate—in summer notoriously deep in

The Great Siberian Road where it crosses the low central Urals. Most cart roads are either unsurfaced or covered with gravel.

mud or dust and in winter a series of frozen ruts. The scarcity of crushed rock limits foundation material to sand or river gravel, and handicaps both highways and railroads over much of the country.

Aviation is the most rapidly developing form of Soviet transportation. Scheduled routes covered 71,000 miles in 1938 and linked Moscow with all centers, even across Siberia. Airplanes carried 292,700 passengers.

Agriculture

There are no adequate statistics of land utilization for the country as a whole. According to the best estimate for 1928,[1] arable land amounted to 432,700,000 acres,

[1] TIMOSHENKO, VLADIMIR P., "Agricultural Russia and the Wheat Problem," Stanford: Stanford University Press, (1932).

or 8 per cent of the Union. If meadows, grassland, and permanent pasture are added, the entire agricultural area covered but 13 per cent of the total of 5,392,000,000 acres.

In the area west of the Urals, agricultural land as a whole rises to 43 per cent and, excluding the north of Soviet Europe, the percentage becomes 65, which is even larger than in the settled parts of several western European countries. Little undeveloped good land remains south of Leningrad, where the remaining forest covers 17 per cent. In this area, the rural population ranges from 65 to over 259 per square mile, as against 25 to 65 in the Mississippi Valley. Soviet Asia had but 2 per cent under cultivation, or 6 per cent in any agricultural use.

Tundra covers 1,270,000 square miles, while the taiga forest north of latitude 60°N. accounts for 3,900,000 square miles. Neither area offers important agricultural possibilities on account of climate and soil. Desert and semidesert land in the south occupies 1,000,000 square miles where cultivation seems out of the question. Notable developments have occurred in limited areas but are not capable of indefinite expansion.

373,217,000 acres. This increase was obtained from virgin steppeland in Siberia where 17,297,000 acres were put under

Harvesting wheat in the southern Kirghiz Republic. (*Sovfoto*.)

Optimistic agriculturalists place the limit of feasible cultivation near the Arctic Circle, but there is little expectation that normal agriculture will ever displace the Siberian taiga. Inadequate rainfall is an obstacle in the arid south, and irrigation possibilities are limited.

Climate, natural vegetation, and soil all emphasize the significance of the agricultural wedge from Leningrad to the Black Sea and east to Lake Baikal, with outliers toward the Pacific. This triangle is far from regular, and there are other areas in the Caucasus and Soviet Middle Asia, but its general pattern is obvious. The most important part of the Soviet Union lies toward the Atlantic rather than the Pacific.

During the period from 1913 to 1940, the sown area rose from 262,455,000 to

cultivation during the Second Five-year Plan, by the irrigation of dry lands east of the Volga or in Central Asia, through drainage of marshes in White Russia, and as a result of plowing pasture or forage land no longer needed because of mechanization.

It is doubtful whether there are large possibilities for future expansion of cropland except in the steppe. Despite the country's vast size, much of it must remain agriculturally unproductive. Increased harvests will follow higher crop yields and better utilization rather than added farm acreage. Prior to the Revolution, part of the land always lay idle under the three-crop system of rotating cultivation, pasture, and fallow.

The total of 373,217,000 acres under cultivation (1940) for 170,467,186 people (1939), gives an average of 2.2 acres per person. This compares with 2.8 acres in the United States, or 0.45 in China. The United States and the Union of Soviet Socialist

Republics have nearly the same crop area, but the respective rural populations are 53,820,000 (1940) and 114,557,000 (1939).

changes in industry. Individually owned farms have disappeared. In 1938 there were 242,400 collective farms, with an

An American-designed Rust cotton picker in the Uzbek Republic. (*Sovfoto.*)

Famines have long been the curse of Russia, largely owing to erratic rainfall. Drought and the effects of revolutionary communism in 1921–1922 caused the death of 5,250,000 people. Famine occurred again in 1932–1933 when inadequate rainfall combined with excessive government grain collections and peasant sabotage. Many districts experienced their lowest rainfall in 150 years in 1938, but agricultural organization had developed to the point where extreme distress was avoided.

Soviet agriculture is organized under either state-operated farms or collectives. The latter provide for cooperative share ownership under the active control of the government. On state farms, workers are paid wages; on the collectives they receive a share of the harvest according to their work. Both of these are socialist devices to bring efficiency to farming, parallel to the

average sown area of 1,198 acres, and 3,961 state farms with an average sown area of 6,651 acres, many of which represent pioneering expansion into previously untilled land.

Mechanization has brought increased efficiency in farm practice. Modern tractors and harvesting combines are provided through Machine Tractor Stations on a service contract. In 1938, the country had a total of 483,500 tractors and 153,500 combines.

Wheat and rye are the dominant crops. All grains together covered 253,030,400 acres out of the 338,280,000 plowed acres in 1938, with wheat alone accounting for 102,546,500 acres. Yields of winter wheat were 16.3 bushels per acre and 13.2 for spring wheat. Winter rye averaged 15.5 bushels per acre, spring barley 16.6, oats 26.5, corn 16.0, and rice 16.6.

New varieties of wheat have steadily pushed the area of cultivation to the vicinity of Moscow, Leningrad, Yaroslavl, and Gorki. Grain crops are even grown near the Arctic Circle. Winter wheat predominates in the Ukraine, and spring wheat east of the Don and in Siberia where the autumn is dry and snowfall light.

Although the grain harvest has increased from 80,100,000 metric tons in 1913 to 94,990,000 metric tons in 1938, higher domestic consumption has absorbed the increase. During the five years preceding the First World War, July, 1909, to July, 1914, Russian wheat exports averaged 165,000,000 bushels, in contrast to 52,000,-000 bushels from 1931 to 1936.

Technical crops have received special attention. Cotton production increased three and a half fold between 1913 and 1938; whereas formerly limited to Soviet Middle Asia and a small area in the Transcaucasus, cotton is also grown near Astrakhan on the Volga, along the Kuban River, and in the southern Ukraine as far north as 48°N. The necessity for imports has almost disappeared. Flax has long been important in White Russia, as well as around Moscow and Leningrad. In 1938 the Soviet Union credited itself with 86 per cent of the world total. Sugar beets are grown in great quantity in the Ukraine, around Kursk, and more recently in the Caucasus, Middle Asia, and the Far East.

Subtropical crops such as grapes, tea, oranges, and other citrus fruit are increasing in the Transcaucasus.

The U.S.S.R. appears to lead the world in the total production of rye, barley, oats, potatoes, flax, and sugar beets. Wheat production may also hold first place, with uncertainty due to the statistics for China.

Foreign Intercourse

Between the First and Second World Wars the Union of Soviet Socialist Republics lived more nearly to itself than any other important nation. Few foreigners crossed its borders, and only a handful of Soviet

Grapes grow well in the dry climate in the vicinity of Stalingrad. (*Courtesy of Intourist.*)

citizens left on official business. Internal economy was entirely divorced from international finance. There was no other major country where one might go through the shops and find not a single article of foreign manufacture, or even a magazine or book from abroad.

Foreign trade was a government monopoly, limited to vital imports and the exports with which to pay for them. The fortunate abundance of domestic resources, plus frequent political obstacles to trade imposed by foreign nations, led the Soviets to develop an extreme nationalistic economy.

Imports during the interwar years consisted of complex machinery and tools, even complete factories, metals such as copper and aluminum, oil-well equipment and pipe, raw cotton, and rubber. Exports included timber, manganese, furs and bristles, anthracite, asbestos, and fertilizers, together with some oil and wheat. Political ends have been involved in the export of automobiles and trucks, cotton cloth, and textile and agricultural machinery to peripheral states such as Outer Mongolia, Tannu Tuva, Chinese Sinkiang, Iran, Afghanistan, Rumania, Bulgaria, and the Baltic States of Latvia, Lithuania, and Estonia.

Trade with the United States has shown wide fluctuations, and Soviet imports have always greatly exceeded sales. During the First World War, and again in the First Five-year Plan, imports exceeded $100,-000,000. They then dropped to $9,000,000 in 1933 and rose steadily to $86,943,000 in 1940. Shipments from the United States in that year included machine tools, oil-well equipment, copper, molybdenum, and cotton, plus gasoline and wheat for the Far East. In return, the United States received manganese for its steel industry, anthracite consigned to New England, furs, and gold. American shipments during the years 1941 and 1942 totaled $3,000,000,000.

CHAPTER 19

REGIONS OF SOVIET EUROPE

If Europe starts at the Urals, half of it lies within the Union of Soviet Socialist Republics, but if "Asia begins with Russia," then the real boundary is along the west of the Soviet Union. Traditional Europe is the peninsular area in the west, with historic relations to the penetrating seas. In the continental portion to the east, Slavic peoples and undistinguished topography have long differentiated the landscape from that of Europe proper. More recently socialist ideology has given the Soviet frontier inescapable geographic meaning.

Environmental conditions in Soviet Europe are less favorable than in Germany or even Poland. Rainfall is lower and the variability greater. Farming has been primitive until recently, yet population increase has crowded the land as densely as in more prosperous countries. " . . . the Russians actually utilize their agricultural possibilities much more fully than do the people of the United States. If New England and northern New York, for example, were in Russia, their abandoned farms would undoubtedly be cultivated, and would yield well above the Russian average."[1]

Soviet Europe may be divided into eight geographical regions, each with its characteristic landscape.

The Baltic states of Lithuania, Latvia, Estonia, and Finland have periodically been tied to Russia, but their environment and culture are also related to Germany

[1] VAN VALKENBURG, SAMUEL and ELLSWORTH HUNTINGTON, "Europe," 577.

and the Scandinavian countries. To the Soviet Union, they have strategic significance as a western outlet toward the ocean. Each forms a geographic region.

Ukrainia

Political divisions seldom coincide with geographic regions, but this is nearly the case with the Ukraine. This geographic entity includes all of the Ukrainian Soviet Socialist Republic, the northern part of the Crimea, and the continuation of the Donets Coal Basin beyond the river of the same name. As here used, the Ukraine refers to the political area and Ukrainia to the larger geographic region.

Ukrainia has had a stormy history, marked by numerous invasions of Turks, Mongols, Poles, and Lithuanians, as well as Great Russians. The very word means "on the border." Kiev was the center of a Rus state in the eleventh and twelfth centuries, and is still known as the Mother of Russia. German forces occupied the area at the close of the First World War, and Kiev was again an early objective in 1941.

Although comprising but one-fiftieth of the area of the Union, Ukrainia has one-fifth the population and cultivated land, producing about one-quarter of the wheat and millet as well as two-thirds of the sugar beets. Of the Soviet totals, Ukrainia accounts for half of the coal, two-thirds of the iron, and one-third of the railway traffic. No other area is so fertile, so productive, or so densely populated. Despite the spread of industry during the five-year plans, the

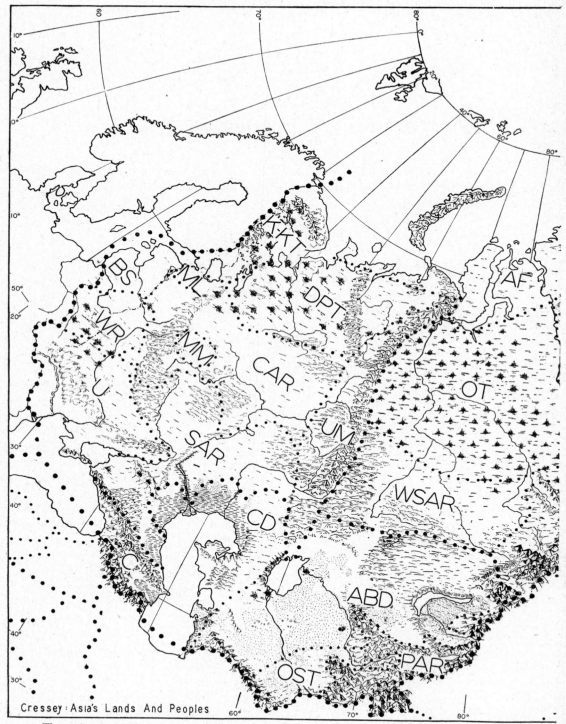

The major geographic provinces and regions of the Soviet Union are as follows: Soviet Europe, divided Pechora Taiga, the Central Agricultural Region, Metropolitan Moscow, the Southern Agricultural Region, and the Cases of Southern Turan, and the Aral-Balkhash Deserts. Soviet Siberia is composed of the West Siberian the Lena Taiga, the Northeastern Mountains, and the Far East.

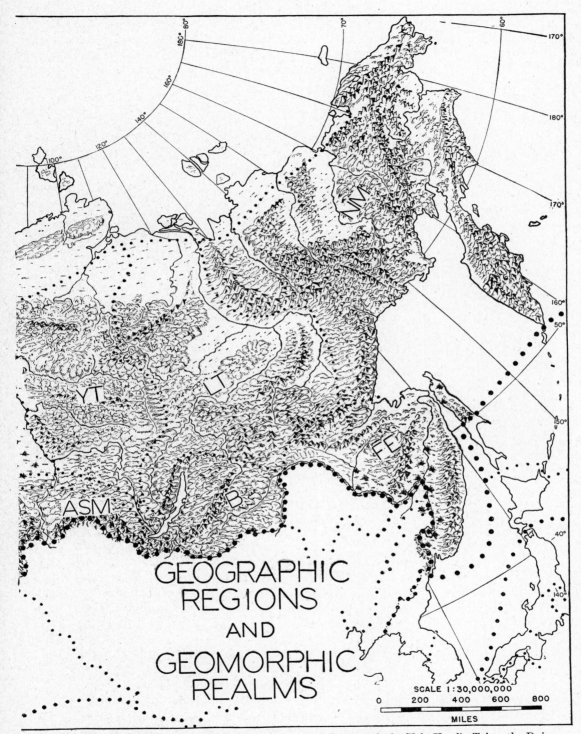

GEOGRAPHIC
REGIONS
AND
GEOMORPHIC
REALMS

SCALE 1:30,000,000

0   200   400   600   800

MILES

into Ukrainia, White Russia, the Baltic States, Metropolitan Leningrad, the Kola-Karelia Taiga, the Dvina-
the Ural Mountains. Soviet Middle Asia, with Caucasia, the Caspian Desert, the Pamirs and associated ranges,
Agricultural Region, the Altai-Sayan Mountains, the Ob Taiga, the Yenisei Taiga, the Arctic Fringe, Baikalia,

Ukraine still retains a unique significance in Soviet economics.

The region has an essential cultural

katchewan. Through the center flows the navigable Dnieper, third longest river in Europe, while in the west are the Bug and

A bridge across the Dnieper at Kiev. Low ground borders the left or eastern bank to the horizon, while the city lies on a high bluff to the west. (*Courtesy of Intourist.*)

unity, but a basic occupational distinction can be drawn between green Ukrainia with its agriculture, and black Ukrainia with its iron and steel. Farm lands may further be divided into the more moist northwest and the semiarid southeast, a division reflecting the transition from the scattered northern forests to the southern open steppe along the Black Sea.

Ukrainia covers nearly 200,000 square miles. If superimposed on the same latitudes in North America, it would bisect the United States-Canadian boundary. Conditions of climate and vegetation resemble the Great Plains of Montana and Sas-

Dniester and in the east the Donets and Don. These rivers wander across featureless country, in most places no more than a few hundred feet above sea level. Hills cross central Ukrainia from west to east, with elevations up to 1,200 feet. Buried crystalline rocks appear in the deeper valleys through this central area. Above them lie young sedimentaries, with a general east-west strike, which form low cuestas or escarpments along the middle courses of the several rivers. In the west, these cuestas are parts of the Volyno-Podolsk Plateau, a continuation of Carpathian foothills; in the east, the Donets

Ridge exposes the deeply eroded roots of ancient mountains.

These structures are reflected in the

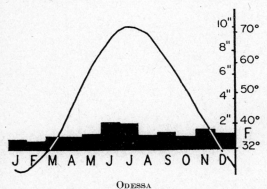

ODESSA

Elevation, 210 feet; average temperature, 49.3°F.; total precipitation, 16.1 inches.

course of the Dnieper, which at Kiev has a flood plain 10 to 12 miles wide on the left or northeast and a 300-foot bluff rising steeply on the right. After following this escarpment 250 miles to the southeast, the river abruptly cuts through the hills with a series of rapids, apparently in an antecedent course, and flows southwest to the sea, 170 miles distant. The Don and Donets have similar courses.

Winters are severe, for cold air masses sweep from the north without obstruction. Even the harbor of Odessa is frozen for several weeks each year. Kiev and Kharkov may experience temperatures of −22°F. In spring and summer, desiccating winds from interior Asia bring dry air and may lift July temperatures as high as 130°F.

Annual precipitation varies from 22 to 24 inches north of the central hills to 14 and 18 inches in the Black Sea steppe. The hills are too low to account for this difference, which seems related to the Carpathian barrier rising to the west across the path of Atlantic moisture. In farming, a constant effort is necessary to conserve the light winter snowfall and critical spring rain.

Although the continental ice sheet covered only the middle valley of the Dnieper, its indirect effects are widespread. Much

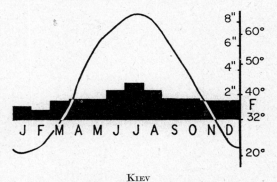

KIEV

Elevation, 590 feet; average temperature, 44.2°F.; total precipitation, 21.1 inches.

of Ukrainia is veneered with wind-laid loess, blown outward from the glaciated regions or derived from outwash flood plains. The resulting black chernozem soil is exceptionally high in organic material and lime, and has maintained its fertility despite centuries of utilization. Chestnut-brown soils prevail in the driest areas to the south, and podsolic types occur in the limited forest section of the north.

Agriculture is important. In 1935, the Ukraine harvested crops on 63,534,500 acres. The area of the Republic is 171,600 square miles, of which 87 per cent may be classed as potentially productive for cultivation, pasture, or forest. Forest land amounted to 12 per cent in 1891, but had dropped to 7 per cent by 1935.

In 1935, grain accounted for 75 per cent of the harvested area, industrial crops such as sugar beets and cotton represented 9 per cent, forage and fodder 8 per cent, and potatoes 5 per cent.

In the limited area north of Kiev, rye, oats, and potatoes are the chief crops. Winter wheat dominates all the central area from the Dniester to the Donets, supplemented by sugar beets, corn, soybeans, sunflower, and barley. Rice is locally raised along the central Dnieper.

1933 as 309,000,000, and in 1934 as 145,000,000 bushels. Prior to the First

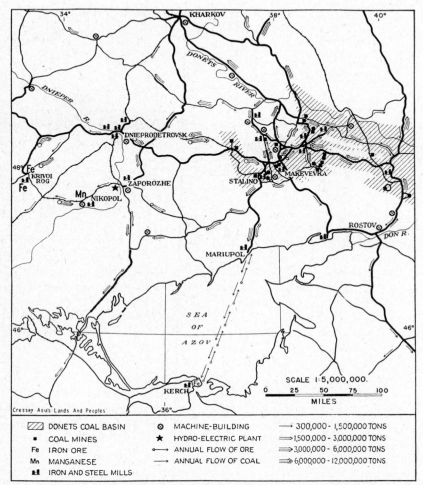

The Donets coal field of the southern Ukraine has long been the major center of heavy industry for the Soviet Union. Iron ore and manganese are available to the west. Railways are shown as on other Soviet maps, with single-track roads in light lines and double-track roads in heavy lines. (*Data from "Great Soviet World Atlas," 1937.*)

The semiarid Black Sea littoral and northern Crimea raise spring wheat, sunflower, rye, oats, and cotton.

Wheat output fluctuates widely with the climate and planned crop diversification, thus the Ukraine yield in 1931 was reported as 237,000,000 bushels, in

World War there was a large surplus for export.

Technical crops include sugar beets, in which this region leads all others by far, sunflower, hemp, flax, 500,000 acres of cotton, and tobacco. Horses, cattle, and pigs are of only local importance.

The industry of Ukrainia exceeds agriculture in importance. Coal, iron ore, manganese, salt, kaolin, and fire clay, plus hydroelectric power, make this a significant area for heavy industry, third in Europe to the lower Rhine and British Midlands. However, Soviet industry has become so nationwide that the proportionate rank of Ukrainia has declined.

The Donets coal fields occupy a structural basin that outcrops as a topographic ridge south of the Donets River. Within this area of 230 miles from east to west and 50 miles width are a dozen important cities and some 200 mines. About an eighth of the production comes from east of the political limits of the Ukraine. Both anthracite and bituminous coals are mined, much of the latter making excellent coke.

Excellent iron ore is produced in the vicinity of Krivoi Rog, 200 miles west of the coal. Since most of the ore moves to the coal, the western part of the coal basin is most developed, with blast furnaces at Makeevka, Stalino, and elsewhere. Iron industries have also arisen near the ore, and at intermediate points where the connecting railways cross the Dnieper at Dniepropetrovsk and Zaporozhe. At the latter, electricity is used in the making of alloy steels. Manganese fortunately lies between coal and ore, and there is adequate fluxing limestone.

In addition to this east-west combine, ore and coal move north and south between the Donets and Kerch at the eastern end of Crimea. Kerch ore is not equal to that of Krivoi Rog, but there are important furnaces at both Mariupol and Kerch.

These basic resources have given rise to a great variety of subsidiary industries, including cement, brick, chinaware, chemicals, aluminum, glass, and machine building. Those which require hydroelectric power are clustered about the dam near Zaporozhe; those which utilize coal are in the Donets area. Where labor supply

A continuous strip steel mill at Zaporozhe, a steel center where Donets coal and Krivoi Rog iron ore meet at the Dnieper River. (*Sovfoto.*)

is vital and fabrication important, industries gravitate toward Kharkov.

The Ukraine is the most urbanized section of the Union. In 1939 the population of the Republic was 30,960,221, of whom 11,195,620 lived in 556 "city points." The population of this region appears to have reached a saturation point, since the estimate for 1931 was 29,042,000 and for 1933 was 31,902,000. Nine-tenths of the people are Ukrainians.

Within the region are 17 cities with a population over 100,000. Kiev, the capital, is the largest with 846,293 people in 1939, placing it after Moscow and Leningrad. The city is beautifully situated on the right bank of the Dnieper near the junction of the Desna. The commercial importance of its site was recognized as early as the eighth century when Greek and Norse traders met here along a major trade

The third city of Ukrainia is Odessa, picturesque seaport on the Black Sea. The population was 604,223 in 1939.

One of the squares in Kiev, capital of the Ukraine. (*Sovfoto*.)

route from the Baltic to the Black Sea. Later on, Kiev became a great religious center. Trade in wheat and sugar, general market functions, and simple industries such as clothing have been supplemented by food and machine industries. Shipbuilding is an old occupation.

Kharkov is the fourth city of the Union, with a population of 833,432 in 1939. Since the Donets coal and steel area is but 125 miles southeast, Kharkov has developed important heavy industries, such as tractors and farm implements, locomotives, machine tools, and electric generators, as well as agricultural products and clothing. Whereas Kiev is old, Kharkov was founded in the seventeenth century. The city lies 461 miles south of Moscow on the direct railway to the Crimea.

Odessa's foreign trade has fluctuated widely with the exportable surplus of wheat and with internal political developments. There are excellent harbor facilities and considerable coastal trade but surprisingly limited foreign service, for passenger facilities to Constantinople and the Mediterranean in 1936–1937 were limited to one Soviet boat every three weeks. This reflects the exceedingly meager contact between the Soviet Union and the outside world. The city increased less than 20 per cent from 1910 to 1935, while Kiev nearly doubled, and Kharkov even more. Industries include food products, agricultural machinery, and the evaporation of sea water for salt.

Rostov-on-Don, 510,253 in 1939, imports steel from the Donets area to the north and is a center of heavy industry much like Kharkov. Agricultural equipment is especially important. The near-by Sea of

Here was the largest hydroelectric station in Europe, with a capacity of 900,000 kilowatts. The dam is 2,500 feet long and

Shevchenko Park and government office buildings in Kharkov. (*Sovfoto.*)

Azov yields large numbers of fish. Commerce in agricultural products includes leather and wheat from the surrounding steppes. This is the traditional center of the Don Cossacks.

The largest city within the Donets Basin is Stalino, 462,395 in 1939. Near by is Makeevka with a population of 240,145. Each is a coal-mining town with great blast furnaces operating on Krivoi Rog ore. Just outside the basin on the north is Voroshilovgrad, formerly Lugansk, with 213,007 in 1939, the leading city for the manufacture of locomotives.

Three cities are grouped around the Dnieper rapids, submerged by the great dam from 1932 until its destruction in 1941.

raises the water level 125 feet. To the north are Dniepropetrovsk, 500,662 in 1939, and Dnieprodzerzinsk, 147,829 in 1939. The new city of Zaporozhe, 289,188 in 1939, is at the dam itself. Abundant electric power and a position midway between Donets coal and Krivoi Rog iron ore have given these cities great industrial importance. All three have blast furnaces and important machine-building works. Zaporozhe has aluminum works and chemical plants.

Mariupol, 222,427 in 1939, and Taganrog are iron centers on the Sea of Azov. Taganrog also serves as a deepwater port for Rostov-on-Don. The ore center of Krivoi Rog, 197,621 in 1939, is the western outpost of steel production in Ukrainia. South of it lies the shipbuilding city of Nikolayev near the Black Sea.

there will probably be great changes in the size and relative importance of given cities. Important though it will be, the Ukraine

Old wooden houses and modern apartments at Minsk, in White Russia. Such contrasts characterize all Soviet cities. (*Sovfoto*.)

At the beginning of the Second World War, the Soviet Union reoccupied parts of eastern Poland ceded to the Union by the Treaty of Brest-Litovsk but lost during the civil war. That part of the area inhabited by Ukrainians was added to the Ukrainian Republic and may be regarded as a continuation of the geographic region here described. The area contains oil, gas, coal, iron, and zinc in modest amounts.

Wartime destruction in the Ukraine was so great, and evacuation, particularly of industrial equipment, so thorough, that restoration of economy to prewar levels will be a matter of years. Although the natural resources of the area make it certain that the type of economy will be similar to that existing before the war,

may not again occupy the dominating place in certain fields of heavy industry that it held before the war. As a matter of fact, the war served to accelerate the planned shift of Soviet economy to the east. Although the U.S.S.R. will probably be in closer economic, cultural, and diplomatic contact with the West then ever before, it will, for the first time, have a really significant proportion of its population and economy in Asia.

White Russia

The Belorussian Soviet Socialist Republic, commonly known as White Russia, is a region of glacially formed swampland along the western border of the Union. Reacquisition of portions of Poland in 1939 extended the Republic westward and increased its original area of 80,000 square miles by more than a third. The population

and rivers are an important source of fish, but the country is too low for much water power.

Harvesting flax in White Russia. (*Sovfoto.*)

in 1939 before the expansion numbered 5,567,976, of whom 1,372,132 were classed as urban. There are 101 "city points," but only three exceeded 100,000 in size. The capital is Minsk, with 238,772 people in 1939.

White Russia includes the hilly swampland at the headwaters of the south-flowing Dnieper and Pripet, and Baltic drainage in the basin of the Western Dvina. A tenth of the region is a bog, much of it in the Pripet or Polesian Marshes. In some areas the extensive lakes and channels make water transport more important than roadways. The Pripet and Bug rivers are connected by an important canal, providing barge service west to Germany. The small villages cluster on sand dunes or natural levees. Even in the more hilly lands to the north there are a great many undrained depressions in the glacial drift. The lakes

The Baltic Sea makes the climate less continental than elsewhere. Rainfall is 22 to 24 inches, which is quite adequate since the evaporation is low. Drought is a rare hazard. Mixed forests of oak, linden, and maple with some spruce and fir cover a quarter of the surface. Hemlock and oak supply tanbark for an important leather industry.

Wet and acid soils limit agriculture to a sown area of 10,000,000 acres, of which 1,740,000 are recently drained swamps. Grain crops are chiefly rye and oats, but local output is below consumption and wheat is imported from the Ukraine. Root vegetables like beets, turnips, and potatoes do well. In the south hemp is grown, in the north flax, which is shipped to Moscow for processing. Pigs are important.

The lack of minerals restricts industry. Peat is used in homes and in central electric generating stations, with a production of 2,500,000 tons in 1937. Lumber, paper, leather, bristles, and meat are notable

from the Tatar invasion in the thirteenth century. Polish influence is important toward the west.

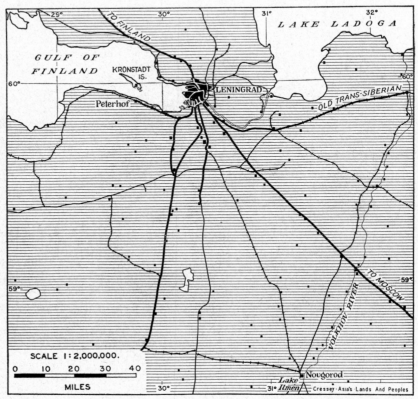

Leningrad was Peter the Great's "Window to Europe." Because of swamp conditions in the delta of the Neva, the first settlement in this area was at Novgorod.

products. The surplus is shipped by waterway north to Riga on the Baltic or south to Kiev.

White Russia is one of the most backward regions of Soviet Europe. Rural areas have been retarded by unfavorable soils and a topography that makes transport difficult, while urban centers have developed slowly for want of a productive countryside and industry. Population distribution is very uneven; some areas have less than 2 people per square mile, others rise to 130. The people represent one of the purest group of Slavs; many of them have lived here without mixture since they fled

Military operations overran the area during both the First and Second World Wars. In each instance the vast Pripet Marshes were of great strategic significance. When Napoleon was retreating from Moscow in November, 1812, many of his remaining troops were drowned when ice gave way on the Berezina River east of Minsk.

Metropolitan Leningrad

When the ancient Varangians from Sweden came into Russia, they found the easiest water passage through the Gulf of Finland up the Neva River to Lake Ladoga, thence south through the Volkhov River to Lake Ilmen and on. The shores of the gulf were exposed to attack and did not offer a suitable site for a city. Instead they built their trading center at Novgorod at the outlet of Lake Ilmen. For several centuries this remained the dominant city in the north, and became a member of the Hanseatic League.

Sweden later recognized the importance of the Neva delta in continental trade and built forts there in 1300 and again in 1600. By defeating the Swedes in 1703, Peter the Great secured for Russia a "window to Europe," and in the same year began construction of St. Petersburg, which was renamed Leningrad in 1924. Partly because the city actually has warmer winters than Moscow, Peter built his Winter Palace on the banks of the Neva. The site of the city was chosen because it provided access to the sea, and with little regard to its suitability for buildings. So many lives were lost in early construction that the city has the reputation of being built on bones. The surrounding delta has numerous distributaries and islands, so that the present city requires 500 bridges. Floods occasionally cause great damage, especially when western winds pile up water in the gulf. During the winter, the Neva is frozen for six months, but icebreakers keep the harbor open except from mid-December to February.

Leningrad owes its importance to the larger setting rather than to its site. Waterways and short canals connect the Neva, via the surrounding Lakes Ladoga, Onega, and Ilmen, with the headwaters of the Volga, Dnieper, and western Dvina. Lake Ladoga is the largest body of water in Europe and nearly the size of Lake Ontario; its southern margin is bordered by a canal to safeguard navigation. The Stalin Canal leads from Lake Onega north to the White Sea. These waterways make Leningrad the natural sea outlet for the trade of the Volga, the Ural and Caspian areas, and even western Siberia. These facilities became

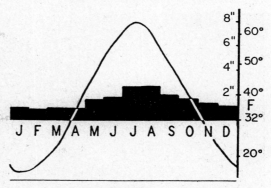

LENINGRAD
Elevation, 30 feet; average temperature, 38.7°F.; total precipitation, 18.8 inches.

important as early as the eighteenth century, giving Leningrad a commercial and industrial advantage never surpassed by any other Russian city. In earlier years Ural metals as well as Volga grain and live-stock found their outlet here.

In exchange for these export shipments, Leningrad early received coal and machinery from England and Germany, cotton from the United States, jute from India, and rubber from the tropics. Foreign capital and engineering skill helped to make the city Russia's leading factory center, especially for technical work. Thus Leningrad acquired an accumulation of skilled and industrial facilities. Riga might provide a better entrepôt on the Baltic, but even with the substitution of rail transport for waterways, Leningrad's historic lead remains.

Industrial facilities in the Leningrad region prior to the war provided 75 per cent of the shipbuilding in the Union, 50 per cent of the electrical equipment, 35 per cent of the paper, 25 per cent of the machine building, 25 per cent of the chemical industry, and important contributions in the field of textiles, furs, shoes, typewriters, rayon, and furniture. Although the five-year programs were designed to spread industry across the Union, the

Moscow, built in 1851. The Red Star Express covers the 403 miles in ten hours.

Few cities in the world are laid out along

A summer evening on the Avenue of the 25th of October in Leningrad, named from the date of the Revolution which started here, Nov. 7, 1917, new style. Long summer evenings characterize this high latitude. (*Sovfoto*.)

products of Leningrad are so indispensable that production has grown over fivefold. Electrical power is obtained from two plants that use peat and from two hydroelectric stations, as well as from coal.

Shipping entering the port in 1933 amounted to but 2,098,000 registered tons, which did not place Leningrad among the 50 leading ports of the world. Lumber was the major export, while machinery was imported. In 1936–1937, passenger service was limited to one Soviet steamer a week to London, plus an additional weekly sailing during the summer, and ten summer calls by the French Line. Rail transport has far surpassed water, with 11 lines radiating from the city. The first line was that to

such handsome lines as was St. Petersburg. Its founder and the succeeding czars built magnificent public buildings, palaces, and churches. As the capital of an empire, the city became the leading cultural center. The museums of the Hermitage and the Winter Palace house one of the greatest art collections in the world.

At the time of Peter's death in 1725, the population numbered 75,000. This increased to 192,000 by 1784, 861,000 in 1881, and 2,075,000 in 1913. After the Revolution, there was acute distress and the population fell to 722,000 in 1920, but in 1939 it reached 3,191,304.

The Leningrad geographic region approximately coincides with the oblast of the same name. Rainfall amounts to 24 inches, and agriculture is more handicapped by excess moisture and a high water table than by drought. January temperatures average 15°F., and the July average is 64°F. Snow falls as late as May. Half the region is covered with forest. Near Leningrad the cleared land is used for market gardens and dairy products; farther away are found potatoes, flax, and pigs. Rye is everywhere less important than hay and fodder crops.

Despite an unattractive site and political changes, Leningrad retains an industrial leadership because of its larger setting and inherited ability. It has well been said that Leningrad stands for skill, Moscow for strength, and Kiev for beauty.

Kola-Karelian Taiga

Karelia and the Kola Peninsula form the eastern margin of the Fenno-Scandian Shield. They resemble Finland, or central Canada, in their complex of ancient crystalline and metamorphic rocks, and in the effects of continental glaciation. Intense ice scour has stripped off the residual soil and smoothed the bedrock; elsewhere glacial debris covers the surface. Deep U-shaped valleys and coastal fiords reveal the intensity of ice action. Innumerable lakes, connected by swift rivers, cover over 10 per cent of the region. Most of the area is hilly and under 1,000 feet in elevation, with isolated mountains to 3,400 feet.

The region covers 105,000 square miles, about equally divided by the Kandalaksha embayment. From Leningrad to Murmansk is just 900 miles by rail, covered by the Polar Arrow Express in 38 hours.

Precipitation decreases from 24 inches in the south to 16 inches in the north. Most of the rain comes in the late summer. Snow falls from October through May, so that the frost-free period is under 100 days except in the south. Temperatures are lowest in the center away from the moderating influence of the ocean.

A taiga forest of pine, spruce, and birch covers 96 per cent of the land of Karelia and continues over much of the Kola Peninsula, bounded by tundra on the higher elevations and along the Arctic Coast. Most of the commercial timber is tributary to Leningrad, with Petrozavodsk as the chief mill town. Fish abound, especially cod and haddock from Arctic waters. The canning industry centers in Murmansk and Kandalaksha. The fur trade goes back to the early days of Novgorod.

Until the First World War, the region was sparsely inhabited except for a small Karelian population near Leningrad and reindeer-herding Lapps in the north. Since 1930 spectacular industrial developments have taken place north of the Arctic Circle. Near the railway and just east of Lake Imandra, is Khibin Mountain. This is an intrusion of nepheline syenite uniquely differentiated into 50 elements and many rare minerals. Apatite reserves total 2,000,-000,000 tons and are mined at a rate of 2,000,000 tons yearly for superphosphate fertilizer. Nepheline is even more abundant and provides a source of aluminum. These are the largest reserves in the world. Here the city of Kirovsk has grown from nothing to 50,000. Electric power is available near Kandalaksha, a few miles to the south.

Another isolated elevation is near Monchegorsk where nickel and copper reserves are second only to those at Norilsk on the Yenisei. Magnetite iron ore is near by.

Murmansk is the Soviet Union's gateway to the open Atlantic, and also the terminus of the Northern Sea Route to the Pacific. It is an important naval base and was the port for Allied supplies during the Second World War. The city lies 20 miles from the sea on the deep Kola fiord, where fresh water and the warmth of the Atlantic drift keep the harbor open the year around, the only ice-free port in the Union. From a population of some 3,000 in 1916, Murmansk grew to 117,054 in 1939. This is

land, although production is but 11 per cent. The area actually forested is 1,527,300,000 acres, of which 370,000,000 lie

Cabbages grow to giant size on the experimental farm near Kirovsk, north of the Arctic Circle, Long hours of sunshine, of low intensity, cause the development of large leaves on all vegetables. (*Sovfoto*.)

much the largest city anywhere within the Arctic Circle. To obtain fuel, the U.S.S.R. has a coal-mining concession in Spitzbergen which supplied 475,000 tons in 1936.

Agricultural conditions are unfavorable except in the extreme south near Petrozavodsk where hay and fodder crops support a small dairy industry. The great expansion of population in the north has brought a need for fresh vegetables, and experimental farms have made it possible to raise vegetables on several hundred acres around Kirovsk, and even at Murmansk.

Dvina-Pechora Taiga

The forest resources of the Soviet Union amount to 21 per cent of the world's timber-

in Soviet Europe. Of this total forest area, 62 per cent is suitable for commercial exploitation. Pine and spruce account for nine-tenths of the conifers, with birch and aspen representing eight-tenths of the deciduous trees.

Forest products are the country's second largest export, normally ranking next to grain. Most of this goes to England, Germany, France, Holland, and Belgium. In normal years, Great Britain receives more timber from the Union than from all the rest of the world combined. In addition to sawn timber, there is a large trade in railroad ties, mine props, and pulpwood, but not in pulp or paper. As supplies diminish in Scandinavia, the reserves of northern Soviet Europe increase in importance.

The increase in importance is also true of internal needs, since commercial forests in the Moscow area are nearly gone.

course in the north. During the summer they carry millions of logs, especially on the Dvina and its tributary the Vichegda.

Greenhouses are widely used in the Arctic for raising fresh vegetables. This scene is south of Murmansk near Kirovsk on the shores of Lake Imandra. (*Sovfoto*.)

From Lake Ladoga to the Urals, and north of latitude 60°N., lies the country's finest coniferous forest, made up of Norway spruce, Scotch pine, larch, and fir, with scattered birch, alder, and willow. Tree growth is slow, for 18-inch logs are often 150 to 170 years old.

Since this forest roughly corresponds with Arctic drainage, it may be called the Dvina-Pechora Taiga, from the names of the two principal rivers. Other rivers of lesser importance are the Onega and the Mezen. Glacial debris and recent marine sediments mask the bedrock except in the low Timan Hills west of the Pechora.

Rivers are frozen from 180 to 200 days and are subject to serious spring floods before ice is cleared from their lower

Along the river banks, clearings extend two to six miles inland. The scattered population lives in drab log houses, raises hay for cattle, and grows a few vegetables such as cabbages and beets. Villages cling to the margin of a river or lake, or lie on the slopes of morainic hills away from the damp lowlands. In the south it is possible to raise fair crops of barley, rye, oats, flax, and hemp.

Arkhangelsk, or Archangel, is the leading city and the Union's largest mill center. The population numbered 281,091 in 1939, yet it lies on the latitude of Nome, Alaska. In 1935, 8⅓ billion board feet were shipped from this port. In the preceding year, 546 vessels called at Arkhangelsk. The White Sea is frozen from November through April, but icebreakers keep the port open for most of the winter except when ice goes out of the rivers. The city

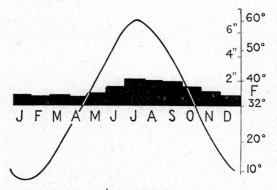

ARKHANGELSK
Elevation, 50 feet; average temperature, 32.5°F.; total precipitation, 15.3 inches.

lies 25 miles from the sea on one of the distributaries, with a 21-foot dredged channel. There is an annual average temperature of 31°F., with 15 inches of precipitation. Four hundred miles upstream is Kotlas, a local commercial center.

The timber of the Pechora Valley has scarcely been touched. Discoveries of oil at Ukhta and coal at Vorkuta are especially important because of the absence of mineral fuel elsewhere in the north.

Central Agricultural Region

Environmental conditions divide the European portion of the Russian Soviet Federated Socialist Republics into three major zones. In the north is the relatively untouched Dvina-Pechora coniferous forest, in the center is the cleared mixed forest, and in the south is the cultivated steppe. Between the first two the boundary roughly follows the limits of Arctic drainage; between the second and third the boundary is determined by climate and vegetation. Whereas the center has over 20 inches of rainfall, the other regions receive less.

The Central Agricultural Region extends from the western frontier to the Urals.

The northern limit lies near 60°N., just beyond the Trans-Siberian Railway from Leningrad to Molotov, formerly Perm, and the region continues south to an irregular line between 52 and 54°N., which bends south in the Kursk and Volga hills, and swings north in the Don and Volga lowlands. Except for industry in the larger cities, this region is dominantly agricultural, the home of millions of peasants who live very near the earth. Metropolitan Leningrad and Moscow are considered separately.

Almost the entire region is drained by the Volga and its tributaries, the Oka and Kama. This is the greatest river in Europe, with a length of 2,309 miles. It carries half the river-borne freight of the Union.

Most of the region is an erosional plain, with gradients so gentle that floods do much damage. Except near the Urals the only elevations over 1,000 feet are in the Valdai, Smolensk-Moscow, and Pre-Volga Hills. Most of the region was glaciated, but strong morainic features are limited to the northwest quarter.

Of the 15 cities of over 100,000 population, 7 lie on the Volga. The westernmost of these is the textile center of Kalinin, at the crossing of the Moscow-Leningrad Railway. Farther downstream is the important city of Yaroslavl, the oldest Russian town on the Volga, and the point where the passenger trains of the Trans-Siberian line cross the river. Its industries include cotton and linen textiles, trucks, and rubber goods. The population was 298,065 in 1939.

Gorki, formerly Nizhni-Novgorod, is at the junction of the Oka. This is the metropolis of the upper Volga, long famous for its great fair which once brought as many as 400,000 visitors; it manufactures automobiles, paper, boats, and a large variety of metal goods, and had 644,116 people in 1939. Kazan, noteworthy for leather, lies near the confluence of the Kazan and Volga Rivers. The population was 401,665 in 1939.

The precipitation is about 20 inches, declining to the east. If rain falls at the proper seasons and the ground receives adequate moisture from melting snow, this is enough for normal agriculture; but unfortunately there are often serious variations. Most of the region has average annual temperatures between 35 and 40°F., with long and severe winters. The frost-free period is 120 to 150 days, exceptionally long for this latitude. The comparable period at the same latitude around Hudson's Bay is but 60 days.

This was a region of mixed conifers and deciduous forests. The largest remaining forest areas are east and north of Gorki, but even around Moscow trees cover two-fifths of the province. Houses are universally built of logs.

Prior to the Revolution, rye was the chief grain, for it is tolerant of podsol soils, cool summers, and the short growing season. The usual black bread is made of rye and molasses. Improvements in spring wheat have pushed its cultivation northward, and it now equals or exceeds the acreage of rye. Considerable land was added to cultivation from 1916 to 1935 through the clearing of forests and the draining of marshland.

Flax and sunflowers each occupy 6 per cent of the cropland. Potatoes and cabbages are widely grown. Livestock includes cattle, sheep, goats, horses, and pigs.

The industries reflect agriculture, for mineral resources are limited. Flour mills operate in many towns, and sugar, leather, felt boots, woolen cloth, and clothing are also important products. Lumber mills and woodworking industries cling to navigable rivers. Peasant handicrafts include lace at Vologda.

The people are largely Great Russians, but toward the east there are islands of Tatars, Bashkirs, and Chuvash, each in their own autonomous soviet socialist republic. Population densities range from 26 to 259 per square mile. In view of the inhospitable climate and poor soil, this represents a moderate crowding. Rural standards of living are low.

Metropolitan Moscow

Few cities in the world and none in the Soviet Union have the glamour that surrounds Moscow, more properly spelled Moskva. Its streets bring together picturesque Cossacks from the lower Volga, tribesmen from Uzbekistan, colorfully dressed visitors from the Transcaucasus, and nomads from the Arctic. Here is the seat of the Soviet government and the heart of Slavic culture. According to an old saying, "There is nothing above Moscow except the Kremlin, and nothing above the Kremlin except heaven." Urban rebuilding has liquidated many of the churches and other architectural monuments, but the Soviets cannot undo the history of the centuries even if they wished. The story of old Russia centers in the Red Square and the Kremlin.

Moscow was first mentioned in 1147 but was not important until after the decline of Kiev when Ivan III became the ruler of all Russia from 1462 to 1505. It remained the capital until Peter the Great removed the government to St. Petersburg in 1711, but several of his successors continued to favor the Kremlin as the proper capital of the country. Much of the city was destroyed in connection with Napoleon's invasion of 1812, but Moscow has always arisen greater from every conflagration.

In 1939, the population of Moscow numbered 4,137,018. This is a great increase from the 1912 figure of 1,617,000, and

Sverdlov Square in the center of Moscow. From left to right is an entrance to the Metro or subway, the Opera House, a department store, a theater, and the Hotel Metropole. (*Sovfoto.*)

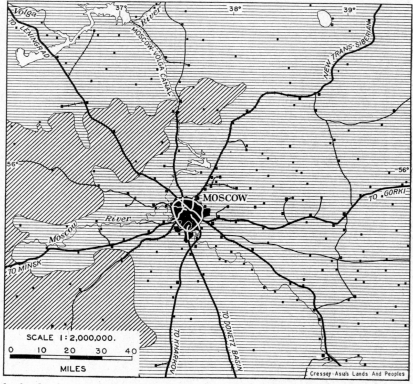

Moscow is the focal point for eleven railway lines. The city surrounds the walled Kremlin on high ground adjoining the Moscow River.

especially from the post-revolutionary low of 800,000 in 1920. The area in 1940 was 114 square miles.

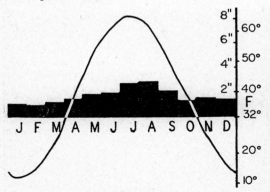

MOSCOW
Elevation, 480 feet; average temperature, 39.0°F.; total precipitation, 21 inches.

The leadership of Moscow reflects its central geographic position. Eleven railways focus on the city, four of them electrified in their suburban sections. Six of these lines are double tracked, two are three tracked, and one is a four-track system. Long before railways, this was the center of trade routes which led northwest to Novogorod, north to Yaroslavl, east to Nizhni-Novgorod, now Gorki, south to the Ukraine, and even brought commerce from Siberia, Middle Asia, and Persia. The city lies in the broad plain of the upper Volga, Oka, and Don. Though Moscow is well to the west of the country as a whole, it is not far from the center of the triangle of population. As a result of the new 80-mile canal to the Volga, Moscow describes itself as the "Port of the Five Seas"—the Baltic, White, Caspian, Azov, and Black—but water-borne freight to such distances is limited. Modern automobile roads radiate to Leningrad, Minsk, Voronezh, Ryazan, Gorki, and Yaroslavl.

Climatic conditions are those of the Central Agricultural Region. With a latitude of 56°N., winter days are but six hours long and temperatures drop as low

as −44°F., with a January mean of 14°F. Snow covers the ground for 150 days, to an average depth of a foot or two. Frost

Few cities have been so extensively rebuilt as Moscow. Modern office buildings and apartment houses are characteristic, but century-old structures and cobblestone streets are just around the corner. (*Courtesy Intourist.*)

hazards require water mains to be laid ten feet deep. During the long summer days the thermometer has reached 97°F., and there is a July average of 66°F.

The city lies on the shallow Moskva River, which flows in a series of broad meanders with undercut bluffs on the outer loops and sand bars on the inside of the bends. The earliest settlement was opposite a narrow island on a 130-foot bluff, where the Kremlin, which in Russian means citadel, was built, originally of wood. The present imposing brick parapets and towers date from Ivan III. This nucleus around which Moscow grew is now a collection of palaces, golden-domed churches, and government offices. In early days the Kremlin was the residence of the aristocracy. Out-

story houses. Magnificent streets with ornate structures alternated with irregular alleys and miserable hovels. The city

The stations of the Moscow subway are attractively finished in ornamental stone from the Urals, stainless steel, and tile. Each station is different. (*Sovfoto*.)

side its eastern gate was a bazaar on the Red Square and beyond it the homes of merchants. To protect this extramural area a second wall was built in 1534, known as the Chinese Wall although it had no connection with Tatars.

As Moscow grew, it expanded farther and a third and fourth wall were built, the latter with a radius of a mile and a half from the Kremlin. These outer two walls have been replaced by circular boulevards, and the built-up city today extends far beyond the limits of the old original nucleus. Streets have a cobweb pattern with radial arteries leading out through old gateways onto intercity highways. Cross streets are more or less concentric with the series of old city walls.

Old Moscow was a city of great contrasts. Most of it was a gigantic village of two-

lacked the metropolitan smartness of Paris or Berlin, and municipal services such as sanitation were of limited development. In 1935, plans were drawn up for ten years of reconstruction, involving magnificent subways, a great extension of housing and office buildings, a new water supply, a notable widening of streets, and sweeping revisions in land use. Expenditures in the first five years amounted to ten billion rubles. No city has ever been so extensively rebuilt in modern times. Some parts have been altered beyond recognition. Housing needs are still urgent, for population continues to grow.

In 1940, there were 135,900 telephones, 27,592 hospital beds, and the daily water consumption was 59.7 gallons per capita. Eighty-two colleges had 94,987 students. There were 40 legitimate theaters and 55 moving-picture theaters. The Soviets have continued Russia's high tradition in the ballet, opera, and drama.

As an industrial area, Moscow produces one-seventh the manufactured goods of the nation. Consumer goods were once dominant, but heavy industry has become very significant. In 1940, the incoming freight of coal, oil, metals, lumber, grain, and raw cotton amounted to 22,900,000 metric tons. Outgoing shipments were only 4,300,000 tons, made up of machinery and other metal products, prepared foodstuffs, textile, and clothing. The industrial area circles the residential city and includes factories for automobiles, agricultural machinery, flour, leather goods, cotton, flax, wool, electrical equipment, and machine tools. Large thermal-electric stations burn near-by lignite or peat, and supply both electricity and steam for heating.

Southern Agricultural Region

In terms of soil the agricultural possibilities of this region are among the most attractive in the entire Union, but if judged by climate the story is very different. Before the arrival of man this was a steppe, treeless except along the streams or in the moister north. For centuries it was the home of nomadic horsemen, the Cossacks of the lower Volga, Don, and Kuban rivers. Into these grasslands came Mongol warriors, and more recently the Russian farmer.

The yearly precipitation decreases from 20 inches in the west to as little as 12 inches in the southeast, with 16 inches a representative figure. Russian agronomists place the agricultural frontier at the 12-inch line, in contrast to American limits of 20 inches. Since low rainfall is associated with high variability, crop failures have been recurrent. In 1892 and 1921, drought reached the proportions of a national calamity.

This is the area of rich black chernozem and almost equally valuable chestnut-brown soils. Both are high in organic matter and soluble minerals, but their very richness is caused by insufficient water to leach the soil.

Successful agriculture depends on building up the soil moisture through careful conservation of winter snow and frequent cultivation to check evaporation. Shelterbelt planting has been used with moderate success for decades. Present irrigation developments are limited to the flood plains of the rivers, but two dams on the Volga near Kuibyshev will supply power to pump water into canals on the eastern Volga steppe.

Some of the largest state farms lie on the drier margins of agriculture in this region. Crop hazards are too uncertain to be risked by the individual, but by specialized techniques the government hopes to obtain a fair harvest in most years. In two decades prior to the First World War, there were three years of complete crop failure at Saratov on the Volga and but five good crops. Drought brings a risk to livestock as well as to grain.

Spring wheat and winter rye are the dominant grains, followed by oats, barley, and millet. The only other crop of importance is sunflower, raised for its oil. Pre-1913 crops of spring wheat averaged but six to seven bushels per acre on the Volga.

Stalingrad is a major industrial center, with a 1939 population of 445,476. It receives coal and steel from the Donets Basin, oil from Baku, and timber down the Volga. For 30 miles, industries line the Volga and include metallurgical works, tractors, shipbuilding, agricultural machinery, oil refining, and lumber yards. Stalingrad's importance will be further increased if a proposed 60-mile canal should link the Don and the Volga. The latter river is frozen 148 days. Although

A horse farm in the Trans-Volga steppes south of Kuibyshev. This is the area that it is proposed to irrigate by the new dam on the Volga. (*Sovfoto.*)

Harvesting winter wheat in the Don steppes. Broad plains and fertile soils have led to extensive mechanized farming. (*Sovfoto.*)

seriously damaged at the height of the German invasion, Stalingrad's location is so important that it will surely be rebuilt.

Kuibyshev, once known as Samara, is near the northern limit of the steppe. It lies on an eastward bend of the Volga and is a local commercial center. Huge hydroelectric projects will irrigate thousands of acres on the trans-Volga steppe. Near-by oil fields form a "Second Baku." The city numbered 390,267 in 1939. Kuibyshev became the temporary capital when Moscow was threatened during the Second World War.

Saratov on the Volga, midway between these preceding cities, had a population of 375,860 in 1939. Other cities include Voronezh on the Don, 326,836 in 1939.

The Ural Mountains

The mineral wealth of the Urals has been known since the fifteenth century. The earliest developments yielded salt, silver, and gold; under Peter the Great, iron was smelted with the use of charcoal. By the nineteenth century, the region was also famous for its gems, semiprecious stones, gold, and platinum.

Developments under the five-year plans have been even more spectacular here than elsewhere. Great metallurgical plants have provided the base for heavy industry. Mining now includes coal, oil, iron, copper, gold, platinum, silver, nickel, aluminum, manganese, asbestos, lead, zinc, magnesium, chromium, potash, salt, and ornamental building stones. No part of the Soviet Union is so richly mineralized. Agriculture is of lesser importance but provides the materials for flour mills and leather tanning. The Urals are now the country's second industrial base, well removed from any frontier. But for their development, the Union might not have been able to carry on in the war against Germany.

Within the Ural region are eight industrial cities which had in excess of 100,000 people in 1939. Sverdlovsk, formerly Ekaterinburg, with 425,544 people and Chelyabinsk, 273,127 people, are key centers for mining and manufacturing on the eastern side of the mountains. The former has a copper smelter, new blast furnaces, and very large works for heavy machines, while the latter mines lignite and manufactures tractors. Molotov, formerly Perm, 255,196, and Ufa, 245,863, are old cities in the western hills, less affected by mining. Nizhni Tagil and Magnitogorsk are giant steel centers in the central mountains, with important railway car shops at the former. The latter grew from nothing in 1929 to 145,870 in 1939.

Railways cross the central Urals at Nizhni Tagil, Sverdlovsk, and Chelyabinsk; and the south Urals at Orsk and Aktiubinsk, with another line west of Magnitogorsk. North-south lines parallel the mountains on either side. Several railroads are electrified.

The Urals are an old range, worn down to rounded hills. In the north the structure continues to the islands of Nova Zemlya, not included in the geographical region; while in the south the Mogudjar Hills extend to the Aral Sea. As here considered, the Urals have an extent of 1,500 miles, with a maximum width of 325 miles in the latitude of Sverdlovsk.

On either side of the central crystalline and metamorphic core are geosynclines of upper Paleozoic sedimentaries. Extensive folding and thrusting from the east have complicated the structure. Volcanic intrusions accompanied the deformation and brought many of the ores. The major folding occurred in the Permian, after which the mountains were worn down to a peneplain and reuplifted in the Tertiary.

In terms of structure, the Urals have a threefold division. Along the east is a

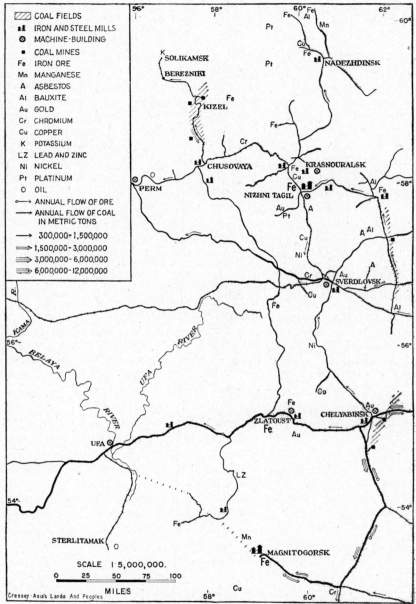

COAL FIELDS
IRON AND STEEL MILLS
MACHINE-BUILDING
COAL MINES
Fe IRON ORE
Mn MANGANESE
A ASBESTOS
Al BAUXITE
Au GOLD
Cr CHROMIUM
Cu COPPER
K POTASSIUM
LZ LEAD AND ZINC
Ni NICKEL
Pt PLATINUM
O OIL
ANNUAL FLOW OF ORE
ANNUAL FLOW OF COAL
IN METRIC TONS
300,000 - 1,500,000
1,500,000 - 3,000,000
3,000,000 - 6,000,000
6,000,000 - 12,000,000

SCALE 1:5,000,000.
0   25   50   75   100
MILES

Cressey · Asia's Lands And Peoples

Few mountain ranges in the world have the mineral wealth of the Urals. This region became the industrial heart of the Union during the Second World War. (*Data from* "*Great Soviet World Atlas,*" 1937.)

peneplained surface which bevels the folded sedimentaries and intrusives at elevations around 750 feet; in the center the crystal-

The author standing at the monument in the central Urals that marks the boundary between Europe and Asia.

line core and intensely overthrust sedimentaries form the main mountain range; while the western section is a dissected plateau from 1,000 to 2,000 feet in elevation, developed on the gently folded rocks of the larger geosyncline. From north to south there is a fourfold division. The northern Urals are the highest and rise to 6,202 feet in Mt. Narodnaya. The central Urals are mere hills, under 1,000 feet where crossed by the railway opposite Sverdlovsk. Farther south elevations reach 5,376 feet in Mt. Yoman-Tau. Beyond the Ural River the Mogudjar Hills lie below 1,800 feet.

Climatic conditions are rigorous. Sverdlovsk has a July average of 63°F. and a January average of 1.7°F., with an annual

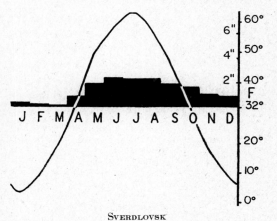

SVERDLOVSK

rainfall of 17 inches. Higher elevations and west slopes receive more precipitation. Yearly averages at Sverdlovsk, Nizhni Tagil, Chelyabinsk, and Perm are all below 35°F. Average temperatures below freezing last 171 days at Sverdlovsk, starting October 19.

Vegetation zones grade from desert and steppe in the south through forest north of Magnitogorsk to tundra in the Arctic and on mountain summits. Where the forest has been cleared, the land is used for hay and pasture.

The Urals lack suitable metallurgical fuel. Charcoal is still used but is inadequate. Noncoking coal is available at Kizel and brown coal at Chelyabinsk. Prewar coal needs amounted to 20 million tons of which half was brought from Kuznets or Karaganda in central Siberia. Oil is produced around Sterlitamak in the west. There are few hydroelectric developments.

Iron ore is the prime resource, with large deposits of magnetite near Nizhni Tagil, Zlatoust, and Magnitogorsk. Blast furnaces of very large dimensions operate at the first and last cities, and at Sverdlovsk. Some of the old charcoal plants are still in production in the western hills. Manganese is present but is too high in phosphorus for satisfactory use. Iron production in the Urals amounted to 2,600,000 tons in 1937.

The problem of the metal industries here as elsewhere is that many exploited deposits are of inferior quality or are remotely located with respect to fuel or markets. For example, Magnitogorsk ore now appears less rich in iron and higher in sulphur than anticipated. Elsewhere the ore is titaniferous. The country urgently needs copper and, although the Urals have large smelters, the ore is unsatisfactory. The same is true of aluminum. Overambitious and overlarge plants, a product of the megalomania expressed in much early planning, have involved management difficulties. The significant fact is that despite all difficulties, socialist enthusiasm has achieved a noteworthy production; whether some ores are of too low grade to justify exploitation is a question that remains to be answered in a closed economy. In nationalistic terms, the war has justified their development.

CHAPTER 20

REGIONS OF SOVIET MIDDLE ASIA

The southern regions of the Soviet Union on either side of the Caspian are areas of young mountains and deserts, so distinct Russian conquests of the nineteenth century, this part of Eurasia, with long-standing oriental contacts, belonged to Persia.

A village in the Caucasus with its ancient watchtowers. Many of the ethnic groups preserve their distinctive architecture. (*Sovfoto*.)

in climate and culture that they deserve separate treatment. Since most of the area lies northwest of the Pamirs, the name Middle Asia is somewhat of a misnomer, but follows Russian usage. The Caucasus are often grouped with the "continent" of Europe, but this is merely a reflection of current political boundaries. Prior to the

Still earlier, Tamerlane ruled both Samarkand and Tbilisi, or Tiflis.

Caucasia

Caucasia is a world in itself. The region between the Black and Caspian seas comprises the alpine mountains and valleys from the Turkish frontier to the Kuban-

Manych Plain. The mountains are geologically young but their human history is old, whereas with the Urals the reverse is

and the same structures reappear in Crimea. In the south the Lesser Caucasus Range includes part of the high Armenian

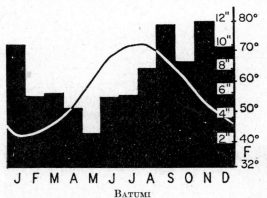

BATUMI
Elevation, 20 feet; average temperature, 57.7°F.; total precipitation, 93.3 inches.

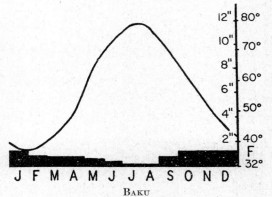

BAKU
Elevation, 0 feet; average temperature, 57.9°F.; total precipitation, 9.5 inches.

true. Serving both as a bridge and a barrier to migration, this region has a long and dramatic history. Across its passes are major trade routes known to Assyrians and Romans. In the mountains cultures have been cradled and found their grave.

Some thirty nationalities live in the region, many of them with picturesque native dress. These include Azerbaidzhanians, Georgians, Armenians, Russians, Ossetians, Abkhazians, Ajarians, Greeks, Kurds, and Jews. Bitter animosities have been the rule. This is the home of Joseph Stalin, a Georgian.

Three union republics lie south of the main range, but the geographic region also includes the north slopes within the Russian Soviet Federated Socialist Republics. From west to east these are the Georgian Soviet Socialist Republic, the Armenian S.S.R., and the Azerbaidzhanian S.S.R. The entire area is about 80,000 square miles, only 1 per cent of the Union, and the population is nearly 10 million.

Caucasia includes three mountain ranges. The Greater Caucasus extends from the Caspian near Baku 685 miles northwest to the Black Sea beyond Novorossisk,

Plateau, largely in Turkey. Connecting these chains in the center are the low Suram Mountains. Between the main ranges are valleys that drain to the Black and Caspian seas. In the west is the Rion Valley and Colchis lowland, while the Kura River drains the eastern Iberian lowland.

In the Greater Caucasus folded Paleozoic formations occur in the center, together with extensive igneous rocks towards the west, but the flanks are made up of Jurassic and Tertiary beds. Folding occurred in the Cenozoic and was accompanied by extensive igneous activity. The highest mountain is volcanic Mt. Elbrus, 18,468 feet, which exceeds anything in Europe. Considerable areas are above the snow line, and there are 1,400 glaciers. The topography is superbly rugged. Serious earthquakes occur several times a century.

The connecting Suram Range is a granite massif which forms the watershed between the Rion and Kura rivers. There are passes as low as 3,280 feet.

The Lesser Caucasus is a block-faulted highland with numerous dormant volcanoes, generally from 6,000 to 10,000 feet. Lake Sevan lies in the center. Just across the border in Turkey is volcanic Mt. Ararat, 16,916 feet.

Climate and vegetation vary abruptly

cultivated area has been expanded by draining swamplands in the Colchis lowland and by irrigation in the Iberian low-

A tea plantation in the Georgian Republic near Batumi. A great expansion of subtropical crops has taken place in this area of Mediterranean climate. (*Sovfoto*.)

with altitude and exposure. The Black Sea littoral has Mediterranean subtropical conditions with 93 inches of rainfall at Batumi. The arid Caspian shore at Baku receives but 9 inches and has an annual temperature of 57°F. with mild winters and hot summers. The Greater Caucasus stop cold northerly winds, while the Suram Range blocks moisture from the west. Snowcapped mountains are seen through palm trees, while deserts and swamps are not far apart. The interior lowlands are similar to the northern Balkans, and along the Black Sea conditions resemble the French Riviera, whereas mountain climates duplicate Nova Zemlya. Deciduous forests cover the lower slopes, followed by conifers and meadows. The flora is exceptionally rich, including 6,000 varieties of flowers. Seifriz has remarked that "plants, like people, seemed to have stopped here in their migratory journeys."

Agriculture is noted for the variety of subtropical products. Corn is an old crop, but the area of cotton, grapes, tobacco, and fruits has been greatly extended, and new crops added such as tea, citrus fruits, tung oil, cork oak, bamboo, and flax. The

land. Wool and hides are produced in the highlands. In western Georgia, the area under tea increased from 2,400 acres in 1917 to 111,640 in 1937, with a production of nearly 5,000,000 pounds. In the same period orange and lemon groves rose from 395 to 25,000 acres. Occasional frosts are a hazard. Caucasian wines have long been famous.

Petroleum has been produced on the Apsheron Peninsula at Baku since 1863. In 1901, Baku supplied half the world output and still accounts for 70 per cent of the Soviet production. There are two pipe lines to Batumi, but most of the oil is shipped by Caspian tankers to the Volga, so that Baku is the first seaport of the entire U.S.S.R. Considerable oil is also produced along the northern foot of the Caucasus near Grozny and Maikop.

Manganese deposits at Chiatury are exceptionally rich, with a production of 1,650,000 metric tons in 1937. Ore is shipped from Poti on the Black Sea to western Europe and the United States.

There are coal mines at Tkvarcheli and Tkvibuli. Hydroelectric possibilities are extensive, especially on the outlet from

Lake Sevan. Small developments include copper, molybdenum, arsenic, and tungsten. Salt is obtained from the Caspian.

In southern Crimea the mountains descend abruptly to the Black Sea and protect the coast from cold northern winds.

The government house in Tbilisi, capital of the Georgian Soviet Socialistic Republic. (*Sovfoto.*)

Mineral waters are bottled along the northern foothills.

Three cities exceeded 100,000 in 1939, each the capital of its republic. Baku dominates Azerbaidzhan, with a 1939 population of 809,347, fifth city of the Union. Oil refining is the chief industry. Tbilisi, formerly spelled Tiflis, lies in the center of Transcaucasia on the upper Kura River, and is the capital of the Georgian S.S.R. Its population in 1939 was 519,175. The city was founded fifteen centuries ago and has numerous light industries. Erevan is the capital of Armenia, with 200,031 people in 1939. On the north slope of the Caucasus are Grozny, Ordzhonikidze, Kislovodsk, and Maikop.

Although at latitude 45°N., the shore is a winter resort of some fame. Charming villas surround the city of Yalta.

Caspian Desert

The Caspian Sea occupies the lowest part of a vast area where no runoff reaches the ocean. Were rainfall more abundant or evaporation less, the basin would be filled to overflowing. During the more humid glacial period, the enlarged Caspian drained westward to the Black Sea with an outlet at an elevation of 150 feet, whereas the surface is now 85 feet below sea level.

Seventy per cent of the water intake of the Caspian comes from the Volga, and 19 per cent from direct precipitation. All of this is lost by evaporation. As conditions vary, the level of the sea fluctuates. In 1306 the surface was 44 feet higher than the summer, dry winds heated to 104°F. come from the east and blow with high velocity.

A Kalmuk yurt in the steppes near Astrakhan, north of the Caspian Sea. Wherever possible, individual nomadism has been replaced by collective farming or grazing.

at present, while in 1845 it was 2 feet lower. Proposed diversions of Volga water near Kuibyshev will further lower the level. To balance this loss, it is possible that part of the Amu Darya may be diverted through an ancient bed from near the Aral Sea to the Caspian.

Attempts to correlate the fluctuating levels of the Caspian and Aral seas with ancient civilizations are confusing. The Caspian level rises with cool wet summers along the Volga, whereas the Aral Sea level depends on melting snow in the Pamirs, with the most runoff during hot dry summers.

Surrounding the Caspian Sea is a desert of limited usability. Much of it is covered with Quaternary sand and clay laid down by the expanded sea and reworked by the wind.

Since the Caspian Desert is invaded during the winter by cold air masses, temperatures drop to −22°F. in the Volga delta and the river is frozen for 112 days. During

Rainfall is from 4 to 12 inches, as compared with annual evaporation from a free-water surface amounting to 48 to 60 inches and from irrigated soil of 34 inches. Even the Volga and Ural diminish in size as they flow southward while in the winter the water of the Emba entirely evaporates before reaching the sea.

Agriculture is limited to strips of irrigation along the rivers. A few wandering nomads, Mongols or Kalmuks, raise sheep and camels. Fishing is very important in the northern Caspian, especially for sturgeon and caviar.

Three minerals are of importance. Oil is produced from salt domes along the Emba River under conditions resembling the Texas and Louisiana Gulf Coast. A pipe line runs 526 miles from Gurev on the coast through the Emba fields to Orsk in the southern Urals, with a probable extension east to Omsk.

Borax and other minerals are secured from rich deposits at Inder Lake, where the production of borax compounds amounts to 30,000 tons and places the U.S.S.R. second to the United States in world output.

At the eastern side of the Caspian is Kara-Bogaz Gulf, enclosed except for a shallow entrance 400 feet wide. This bay receives no rivers, and evaporation is so great that the water contains 29 per cent of salts. Mirabilite, or sodium sulphate, is precipitated naturally and other chemicals are extracted.

The principal city of the region is Astrakhan, on a distributary of the Volga. The population in 1939 numbered 253,655. The city has fish canneries and woodworking industries based on timber rafted down the Volga. Oil is the major import, but extensive sand bars make it necessary for Caspian tankers to unload into barges from which oil is transferred to river steamers at Astrakhan. Extensive dredging is proposed.

Pamirs and Associated Ranges

Soviet frontiers reach into the Pamirs and the great ranges that radiate from the roof of the world. Within the region are the Union's two highest peaks, appropriately named Mt. Stalin, 24,584 feet, and Mt. Lenin, 22,377 feet. The second was originally thought to be the higher, and its name was changed from Kaufmann to Lenin, but corrected elevations showed the former Mt. Garbo to be of greater height and it was then renamed Mt. Stalin. The mountains form a continuous rampart between the Amu Darya and the Dzungarian Gate, a distance of a thousand miles, and also include an outlier near the Caspian.

The structure of the numerous ranges is involved. The Pamirs are a mountainous plateau, mostly over 12,000 feet, with broad valleys five to ten miles wide cut by deep canyons and surrounded by rocky mountains. They lie between the Amu Darya and the Syr Darya.

The Tien Shan, or heavenly mountains, so named from their extension into China, lie north of the Pamirs. Within the Soviet Union the range occupies the area between the Syr Darya and Ili River. Huntington has described the Tien Shan as a plateau, with mountain structures and once with mountain form but long ago reduced to old-age flatness and only recently reuplifted. Erosion has thus been revived, especially around the margins.

This region is the most active earthquake area in the Union. From 1885 to 1932, there were 24 shocks with an intensity over six.

Despite their distance from the sea, enormous glaciers descend from these ranges, notably the 48-mile Fedchenko glacier near the Trans-Alai Range.

The climate is generally dry, with long periods of clear weather. Forests are limited to favored exposures with grass above and below. These upper and lower meadows are used for grazing sheep, horses, and cattle, with seasonal migration up and down the slopes. Lowland villages may be almost deserted during the summer while the flocks are on the upper slopes. While on the move, shepherds live in round felt-covered kibitkas, similar to Mongolian yurts. Agriculture is restricted to the lower valleys and usually depends on irrigation. Many of the canals are very old. Extensive upland areas are a cold desert, in contrast to the hot deserts of the lowlands.

Climatic limitations on agriculture increase with altitude, as shown in the Zeravshan Valley, where rice is cultivated to 4,000 feet, corn to 4,300 feet, peaches to 4,500 feet, grapes to 5,900 feet, millet to 6,400 feet, apricots to 6,900 feet, and barley to 8,200 feet.[1]

[1] Berg, L. S., "The Natural Regions of the U.S.S.R.," Moscow and Leningrad (1937), 132.

Two republics lie in these mountains, the Kirghiz S.S.R. in the east, and the Tadzhik S.S.R. to the south. In 1939, the

New automobile roads make the area more accessible. One leads from Frunze, capital of the Kirghiz Republic, past Lake

Folk dancing in the mountains of the Tadzhik Republic. Soviet policy has encouraged the preservation and development of minority cultures. (*Sorfoto*.)

former had a population of 1,459,301 while the latter had 1,485,091. Many of these people live in lowland valleys or bordering oases, to be considered in the following region.

Ancient caravan routes cross these mountains, though the passes are blocked by snow in winter. One famous route, followed by Marco Polo, leads over the Terek pass to the Tarim Basin in China's westernmost province of Sinkiang, others go to Kashmir in northern India and to Afghanistan. Two historic routes farther north connect the Lake Balkhash area with Dzungaria in northwest China. One follows the Ili Valley, but the more famous is the Dzungarian Gate, a 46-mile gorge only 1,060 feet above sea level.

Issyk Kul and Naryn over the Tien Shan to Osh at the head of the Fergana Valley; passes exceed 12,000 feet. A second extends southward from Osh over a 9,850-foot pass in the Pamirs to Khorog on the Afghan frontier.

Oases of Southern Turan

From the Caspian to the frontiers of China and from the Pamirs to the borders of the agricultural land south of the Trans-Siberian, lie a million square miles of arid and semiarid lowland. Much of it is uninhabitable desert except where mountain-nourished streams turn the waste into a garden. Within this area are two major geomorphic divisions, the Turan

Lowland in the south, and the Kazakh Upland farther north. In terms of land use there are two geographic regions: the midst of unreclaimed desert. Any regional boundary of the Turan Oases must include much barren land. Economic character-

The intake works for the Ferghana Canal which diverts water from the Syr Darya for the cotton fields of the Uzbek and Tadzhik republics. (*Sovfoto.*)

Aral-Balkhash Deserts and the Oases of Southern Turan.

Since the recognized homeland of the Turkmenians is confined to the southwest corner of Turan, the name Turkestan can no longer be applied to all of Soviet Middle Asia. Likewise the Kirghiz live in the mountains rather than in what has been called the Kirghiz Steppe in Kazakhstan.

This is an ancient land of great individuality and unusual history. For thousands of years, the struggle against aridity has dominated all of life and has concentrated settlement in the oases. Rainfall is quite inadequate for agriculture, so that cultivation depends upon irrigation from mountain streams fed by melting snow. Each river has its local settlements in the istics appear more significant than cartographic continuity.

The oases here considered follow the foothills from Mari, formerly Merv, in the west to Tashkent in the east. Other oases are so detached that they are best grouped with the desert region to follow. Mari is the chief settlement along the Murgab Valley, and one of the oldest cities of interior Asia. On the Amu Darya is Chardzhou, famed for the sweetness of its melons, with other towns upstream. Farther east is the historic Zeravshan Valley with the ancient cities of Bukhara and Samarkand, the latter with a population of 134,346 in 1939. Samarkand is especially famous for the monumental buildings that date from Tamerlane. The upper Syr Darya waters the largest oasis of all in the valley of Fergana, surrounded by high mountains except for a six-mile opening on the west. The valley is 180 miles long by 100 miles wide, and supports the cities of Leninabad, formerly Khojent, Fergana, Khokand, and Osh. This is one of the most densely populated areas in the U.S.S.R., with an elaborate irrigation system. Tashkent lies on a tributary of the Syr Darya, the Chirchik; upstream is Chimkent. Tashkent is the industrial metropolis of Soviet Middle Asia with 585,005 people in 1939.

After these streams leave the mountains, they receive no tributaries and grow progressively smaller through seepage, evaporation, and diversion for irrigation. Most of the small streams that enter the Fergana Valley never reach the Syr Darya. Even the sizable Zeravshan withers in the desert without entering the Amu Darya. No progressive climatic change is suggested since the river did not reach the Amu even in the fourth century B.C. Although rainfall is at a minimum in summer, melting snow and glaciers make this the season of maximum flow.

The volume of water and the irrigated area of the chief streams are shown in the accompanying table.[1] Ten acre-feet per acre are needed for satisfactory irrigation.

River	Annual discharge in acre-feet	Irrigated acreage
Amu Darya	53,200,000	1,100,000
Zeravshan	4,160,000	980,000
Syr Darya	15,000,000	2,190,000
Chirchik	7,120,000	480,000

Most oases occupy alluvial fans between the mountains and the desert, at eleva-

[1] DAVIS, ARTHUR P., Irrigation in Turkestan, *Civil Engineering* (1932), II, 2.

tions from 1,000 to 1,500 feet above sea level. Rainfall is slightly higher than on the plains and ground water more abundant,

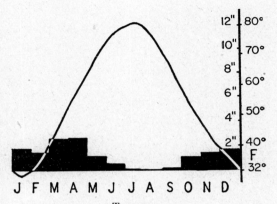

TASHKENT
Elevation, 1610 feet; average temperature, 56.1°F.; total precipitation, 14.7 inches.

so that there is a thin carpet of grass. As dust storms have swept across the desert through the centuries, silt has become trapped among this vegetation. This wind-borne dust is the loess, the basis of extremely fertile soils.

The continentality of the climate is shown in the range between January and July means of over 55°F. for every station except Samarkand. July temperatures at Termez near Bukhara are the highest in the Union, with a maximum of 122°F. and an average of 89.6°F. At Repetek, the sand temperature reached 174°F. on July 20, 1915. Thanks to the dry air, nights are cool. Cloudless summer skies increase the sugar content of grapes, melons, and apricots. Winters are severely cold, with temperatures sometimes near those of Leningrad. Since the edge of invading Siberian air masses is thin, cities on the plain may have lower temperatures than near-by mountains. The snow cover is light but persists for a month.

The precipitation is low and erratic. Tashkent averages 14.7 inches, which is considerably more than many stations. At Bukhara and Chardzhou the rainfall drops to 4 inches. Summers and fall are driest.

are important since their sugar content is greatly increased under conditions of desert irrigation. These oases have long been

A village in the cotton area of the Kazakh Republic. (*Sovfoto*.)

Many irrigation canals are centuries old and have been considerably expanded by new engineering works under the five-year plans. This is especially true in Fergana where water is brought to the dry side of the valley. Some of the ancient canals are underground tunnels, known as karez, or kanats, similar to those in Iran and Sinkiang.

Cotton is the chief crop and has been since the American Civil War when decreased supplies gave Russia the impetus to produce her own needs. The yield did not reach prerevolutionary output until after 1930; of the cultivated acreage cotton now occupies two-thirds. Wheat, rice, and barley are the chief grains. Increasing amounts of cotton and some silk are woven in Middle Asia instead of being shipped to the Moscow textile area. Sugar beets

renowned for their very fine fruit, such as apricots, peaches, cherries, plums, apples, melons, and grapes. The latter are dried as raisins.

Although mining has not been significant, considerable developments are under way. The Fergana Valley contains fair coal and some oil. The near-by mountains have copper, lead, zinc, gold, silver, and arsenic. Hydroelectric power is used to develop phosphate fertilizers. A steel mill was built at Tashkent during the war.

Ancient crafts include the weaving of carpets, preparation of fur and leather, metal work, pottery, and the manufacture of saddles. Keen rivalries between the wandering nomads and sedentary oasis dwellers, as well as between rival oases, have often brought raids and destruction. Each oasis has its own history.

Samarkand lies on the Zeravshan River, whose water is so valuable that the name means "gold spreading." The city's origin turquoise blue. At the beginning of the eighteenth century when there were almost no inhabitants, the city fell under Chinese

The Registan Square in Samarkand with one of the Mohammedan colleges built by Tamerlane, and modern Soviet buildings beyond.

is unknown, but it has been "a sparkling jewel enticing the hearts of Kings through the ages." Alexander the Great plundered the city in 329 B.C. In the eighth century it was the center of Arab culture, and in the thirteenth century was conquered by Genghiz Khan. When Tamerlane made it his capital in 1370, he built the brilliantly decorated mosques, tombs, and other buildings that still stand. Surrounding the central square, or Registan, are the monumental buildings of three ancient colleges, each decorated with enameled tiles of

control. Raiders from the deserts or mountains have often destroyed Samarkand, which has been as often rebuilt.

These oases are steppingstones along the ancient caravan route of inner Asia. This highway from Peking to the Mediterranean followed the foot of the mountains from one river to another and was in use long before the days of Marco Polo and recorded history. Along it flowed silk, tea, and art goods from China and India to Greece and Rome and Roman Britain. At Samarkand, Bukhara, and Merv, merchants of the Orient met traders of the Occident.

The Oases of Southern Turan are in-

places but half that figure. Where it reaches 12 inches in the north, some precarious dry farming is attempted.

The building to the right is a motion-picture theater in Tashkent. (*Sovfoto.*)

habited by a wide variety of races, including Turkomens, Uzbeks, Persians, Tajiks, Kirghiz, Sarts, and Russians. The latter are newcomers, for Tashkent was not occupied until 1866 nor Bukhara till 1873.

It is difficult to evaluate current developments, because few outsiders have been permitted to study the region objectively since before the First World War. Sensitive frontier problems have made this true for a century. Even the 1914 Baedeker states that "Foreigners are not allowed to visit Turkestan except by special permission of the Russian Government. The traveler must send in his request . . . at the latest six months before the beginning of his journey."

Aral-Balkhash Deserts

Here aridity dominates. The annual precipitation averages but 8 inches, in

During the winter when the region is exposed to cold Siberian air, the average January temperature drops below freezing. The delta of the Amu Darya has recorded $-14°F$. In contrast to the imported winter weather, summer temperatures are the result of local insolation. Day and night temperatures in July average 80 to 85°F., which is hotter than the tropics.

Many rivers enter the region, but only a few have enough water to cross the desert and those which do so end in salt lakes or playas. Whereas normal rivers in humid lands gain water from tributaries and flow *in* valleys, these streams lose water, become overloaded with sediment, and flow *on* their flood plain. Sand bars and shifting channels make navigation difficult.

Although northern Kazakhstan has over 5,000 lakes, many of them are ephemeral. The major water bodies are the Aral Sea

Wool is an important product in Middle Asia. These sheep are on a collective farm in the Tadzhik Republic. (*Sovfoto*.)

Salt production on the shores of the Aral Sea in the Kazakh Republic. (*Sovfoto*.)

and Lake Balkhash. The former stands next to the Caspian as the second largest body of water in the Old World. A large part is only 30 to 60 feet deep, and the area fluctuates. Eastern Lake Balkhash is freshened by waters of the Ili River, while the western portion is salt from evaporation.

Within the region are several areas where geologic history, altitude, or climate introduces minor differences. The Kara Kum and Kizil Kum are sandy deserts on either side of the Amu Darya. Some of the shifting sand areas are said to be due to the destruction of the blanket of sparse vegetation by overgrazing or cultivation. Near the Syr Darya is the Golodnaya Steppe, slightly higher and more moist. The Bedpak Dala or Hunger Steppe lies north of the Chu River, while on the south shore of Lake Balkhash is the Semireche Steppe. In the north, the Kazakh Hills are a peneplained mountain range, often incorrectly termed the Kirghiz Steppe.

The soil is generally unleached serozem, a gray desert soil, with local salty or alkaline soils where ground water is close enough to the surface to permit evaporation of capillary moisture. The most prominent vegetation is the bushy saxaul.

Kazakhstan reported nine million cattle in 1936, some of which were in the agricultural region to the north. Most of the people live in oases, similar to those described in the previous region. Most nomads have now been collectivized. Hides, wool, meat, and grain are important exports. Astrakhan sheep are raised in the south. Great agricultural developments took place during the war with labor supplied by farmers evacuated from Soviet Europe.

The discovery of mineral wealth has brought local mining developments, as at Karaganda, now the Union's third most important coal producer. Near the northern shore of Lake Balkhash is a great copper mine at Kounrad, with another development to the west at Djezkazgan. Sulphur is obtained north of Ashkhabad and lead at Chimkent near Tashkent.

The chief cities outside the semicontinuous oases belt are Ashkhabad in the southwest, capital of Turkmenia; Novo Urgench and Khiva on the lower Amu Darya; Frunze and Alma-Ata, capitals of the Kirghiz and Kazakh republics; Kazalinsk on the lower Syr Darya; Kounrad and its smelter town of Balkhash; and the coal city of Karaganda, population 165,937 in 1939.

CHAPTER 21

REGIONS OF SOVIET SIBERIA

Within Siberia are 5 million square miles of northern Asia, much of it mountainous or relatively inaccessible. Permanently frozen ground underlies 3¾ million square miles. Here is the world's greatest forest outside the equatorial selva, and the largest coal deposits outside North America. The Ob, Yenisei, Lena, and Amur are among the world's eight longest rivers.

But these details are only an introduction to Siberia. This is the last great pioneering land outside the tropics, and into it the Russians have gone and are going by the millions. Much of the thrill that characterizes Soviet socialism is associated with the cultivation of virgin land, the development of new mines and industries, the construction of new railways, and the growth of cities in Siberia. The environment places restrictions on the limits to which man may develop this land, but the potentialities are still enormous.

Transport is no longer limited to north-flowing rivers or to a single railway. The Trans-Siberian is double tracked, and the total railway mileage east of the Urals more than doubled in the interwar period. Airplane service has opened the north.

Under the three five-year plans more happened in Siberia than during the entire period since the Cossack leader Yermak crossed the Urals in 1580 and captured the village of Sibir on the Irtysh. Between 1914 and 1933, the population rose from 10,400,000 to 25,636,900, while cultivated land increased from 32,058 to 97,949 square miles. Siberia has 15 per cent of the Union's people and 12 per cent of the cultivated area.

West Siberian Agricultural Region

The surveyors who laid out the Trans-Siberian Railway toward the close of the nineteenth century proved to be practical geographers, for they placed it along what has become the continuation of the agricultural triangle. The railway alternately runs through the rich chernozem steppe and the forest.

The colonization of Siberia dates from 1580. Early settlers kept within the empty forest or along the northern edge of the steppe to avoid conflict with nomadic Mongol tribes.

The West Siberian Agricultural Region is one of the flattest areas on earth. Along the railway one travels 1,200 miles from the Urals to the Yenisei scarcely seeing a hill. For hours the landscape is as monotonous as an ocean voyage. The only vantage points are church spires or grain elevators. Much of the area is covered with Quaternary continental deposits, beneath which are Tertiary marine sediments. Vast glacial lakes left sediments that add to the flatness. Even the folded lands of the Kazakh Hills have been worn down to low relief and gentle slopes. In the steppeland south of the railway are countless thousands of shallow depressions, sometimes filled with lakes, which apparently represent wind scour during a period of greater aridity.

Great annual variations characterize the temperature. Winter snowfall is light, but bitter blizzards pile it into formidable

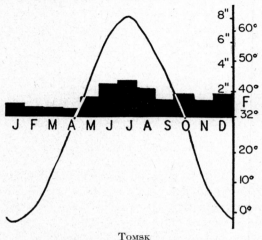

Tomsk
Elevation, 390 feet; average temperature, 30.2°F.; total precipitation, 19.9 inches.

drifts that disrupt railway traffic. Half the year is below freezing, for average temperatures fall below that point in mid-October to remain until mid-April. The short summers have days that are uncomfortably warm, but temperatures exceed 68°F. for only a month. Precipitation is from 12 to 18 inches, chiefly in the summer.

This is the Asiatic equivalent of two areas west of the Urals, the Central Agricultural Region of cleared forest with podsol soils, and the Southern Agricultural Region of cultivated steppe underlain by chernozem soils. Both landscapes are present in western Siberia, although most agricultural development has taken place in the steppe where there are no forests to clear and soils are more fertile. This is the tapering end of the triangle, pinched between limitations of cold on the north and of drought on the south, and limited eastward by the Altai, Sayan, and Baikal mountains.

The great crop of the region is spring wheat, with large amounts of oats, rye,

and barley. Huge grain elevators rise at every railway station and can be seen across the plain long before the town comes in sight. Flour milling is an important industry. This part of Siberia is an important cattle country, long famous for its export of butter. Meat packing is significant.

Siberian villages have surprisingly little in the way of commercial activities. Even settlements of several hundred houses have no store, for people live a nearly self-sufficient existence. Log houses are the rule in the north, replaced by sod houses where timber is not available. Each house has a huge brick stove which occupies nearly a quarter of the kitchen and which often has a platform on top where some of the family may sleep during the winter. Behind each house is usually a vegetable plot, with a barn for the farmer's own cow, pigs, and chickens. The rest of the cultivated land is collectivized and worked cooperatively.

Most of Soviet Siberia has a twofold economic pattern. The rivers provide a north-south orientation, while the railway is an east-west link. The West Siberian Agricultural Region is dominated by the railway, while the regions of the Ob, Yenisei, and Lena Taiga are river-centered.

Where rail and water meet, significant cities develop. Since the Ob and Irtysh are the major rivers, Novosibirsk and Omsk are the leading cities, with populations in 1939 of 405,589 and 280,716, respectively. Krasnoyarsk on the Yenisei and Tomsk near the Ob follow in commercial significance, with 189,999 and 141,215. Industrialization and urban modernization generally decrease with distance from Moscow.

At these latitudes, rivers tend to be deflected to their right by the rotation of the earth; accordingly the eastern bank is often undercut and high, while the other is low and swampy. Approaching the rivers from the west, one finds a ment rising to 50 feet or more in height. Then the river is crossed by a high bridge

Grain from a collective farm awaiting storage in the elevators at Omsk. (*Sovfoto*.)

Modern apartment buildings line the streets of Novosibirsk in central Siberia.

broad swampy flood plain, miles in width, which the railway crosses on an embank- and the train at once enters a city on the right bank.

Altai-Sayan Mountains

South central Siberia is bordered by a continuation of the young mountains

The region is mountainous but is important for mineral wealth rather than topography. Here is a third of the country's coal, lead, and zinc reserves. Deposits

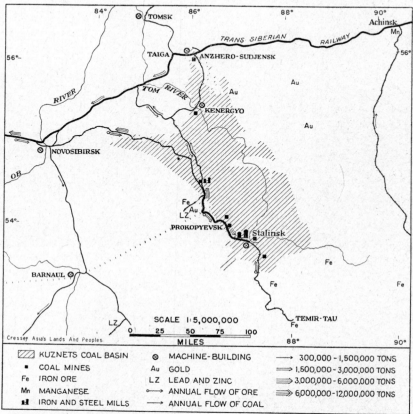

KUZNETS COAL BASIN	⊗ MACHINE-BUILDING	⟶ 300,000 – 1,500,000 TONS
▪ COAL MINES	Au GOLD	⟹ 1,500,000 – 3,000,000 TONS
Fe IRON ORE	LZ LEAD AND ZINC	⟹ 3,000,000 – 6,000,000 TONS
Mn MANGANESE	○⟶ ANNUAL FLOW OF ORE	⟹ 6,000,000 – 12,000,000 TONS
◼ IRON AND STEEL MILLS	⟶ ANNUAL FLOW OF COAL	

The development of the Kuznets coal basin in central Siberia was a major achievement of the First Five-year Plan. Much of the railway mileage within the basin is electrified. (*Data from "Great Soviet World Atlas,"* 1937.)

which begin in the Caucasus, continue through the Pamirs and Tien Shan, and reach to the Arctic. The Altai and Sayan ranges extend for a thousand miles from the Dzungarian Gate to near Lake Baikal. On a purely geologic basis, half the area lies in Mongolia, but no geographically meaningful region can ignore a boundary such as that of the Soviets.

of silver, gold, copper, tin, and manganese are significant. Water-power possibilities along the Yenisei are impressive. Although much of the area is difficult of access, railway lines lead into the mining areas of Ridder, Kuznets, and Minusinsk.

Both the Altai and the Sayan were folded in the middle and late Paleozoic, then after being worn down to essential peneplains, were again uplifted during the late Tertiary. Metamorphic and intrusive rocks make a sequence difficult to un-

10,000 feet. East of the Ob lie the eastern Altai, reaching almost to the Yenisei and formed of two north-south ranges, the

Virgin prairie plowed for the first time in history, in the Minusinsk Basin of the upper Yenisei. (*Courtesy George Bain.*)

scramble. The central portions of the mountains remain rolling uplands above 10,000 feet, comparable to the Pamir and the Tien Shan, with active dissection on the margins.

The Altai system has a general northwest-southeast trend, which continues far into Mongolia. Several divisions may be distinguished within the Soviet Union. The Tarbagatai Range lies between the Dzungarian Gate and Lake Zaisan on the Irtysh. Between the Irtysh and Ob are the Altai Mountains proper, culminating in Mt. Belukha, 15,154 feet. Six glaciers radiate from this peak, one of them five miles long descending to an elevation of 6,400 feet. The snow line is from 8,000 to

Salair and the Kuznets-Alatau, respectively west and east of the Kuznets Basin.

Around the Minusinsk Basin are the two ranges of the Sayan system. The Eastern Sayan, with elevations up to 11,447 feet, is the main range, extending from Lake Baikal to the Yenisei, with a southern branch known as the Western Sayan along the frontier.

Neither the Kuznets nor the Minusinsk basin is level, and the rolling hills give the railways long steep grades. Around the Kuznets Basin is a flat sky line dating from the Mesozoic; the hilly margins carry a Tertiary surface, while the valley of the Tom River is Quaternary.

Steppe vegetation covers the lower slopes of the Altai-Sayan Mountains up to some 3,000 feet, above which there is a splendid

Basin, which receives cold air drainage from the surrounding mountains, has a January average of −5°F., and an extreme low of

The Prokopievsk coal mine in the Kuznets Basin has a capacity of 3,200,000 tons a year. It supplies coke for the Magnitogorsk steel works in the Urals.

taiga forest of Siberian larch, cedar, fir, pine, and birch to 6,000 feet or more, followed by alpine meadows to the snow line around 9,000 feet. Exact heights depend on exposure.

Rainfall at the foot of the mountains and in the basins does not exceed 10 inches but increases notably on the upper slopes. In the western Sayans at 3,840 feet, the Olenya Creek station receives 47 inches, while in the western Altai, the Andobin Mine with an elevation of 1,800 feet has 37 inches. Summer is the rainy season, and the distant Atlantic is the apparent source of the moisture.

Winter temperature inversions, combined with the thinness of the Siberian cold air masses, make the highlands a relatively warm island between the cold plains of Siberia and Middle Asia. The Minusinsk

−65.7°F. July temperatures at Minusinsk average 69°F.

As the steppe grass is usually too short to be harvested, the original inhabitants were nomads. They now live in collectivized villages. Along the upper Tom and Yenisei rivers a quarter of the lowland is in wheat, potatoes, and sunflower. Large areas of virgin prairie are being plowed in the Minusinsk Basin. The chernozem soil is attractive but, with the breaking of the sod, dust-bowl conditions will develop in drier years.

Coal is the great mineral resource, with reserves of 450,658,000,000 metric tons in the Kuznets Basin, and 20,612,000,000 tons in the Minusinsk Basin. Along the northern margins of the region are the Chulym-Yenisei field with 43,000,000,000 tons, and the Kansk field with 42,000,000,000 tons.

The Cheremkhovo mines west of Irkutsk also lie next to the Sayan Mountains, with reserves of 79,000,000,000 tons.

The Kuznets Basin is a closely folded syncline, with many beds dipping 60 to 80°. The carbon ratio is from 80 to 89 per cent, with sulphur at 0.5 per cent. Much of the coal is of coking quality, and some is suitable for gas and chemical use. Production amounted to 774,000 tons in 1913, 2,600,000 tons in 1927, and 16,800,000 tons in 1938. One mine at Prokopyevsk, completely electrified and mechanized, has a capacity of 3,200,000 tons annually. Other mining centers are Stalinsk, formerly named Kuznets, Leninsk-Kuznets, Kemerovo, and Anzhero-Sudzhensk.

Coal for urban and railway use is also mined on a small scale at Chernogorsk near Minusinsk, and at Cheremkhovo west of Irkutsk.

Surrounding the Kuznets Basin are several metal mines. Zinc, gold, and lead are obtained at Salair. Magnetite iron ore is mined in the Gornaya Shoria to the south, formed by metasomatic replacement of limestone, with an iron content of 45 per cent, but the high sulphur must be removed before smelting. Across the mountains in the Minusinsk Basin is excellent undeveloped ore 120 miles southwest of Abakan, which some day may be utilized with local coal.

In the metalliferous Altai at Ridder, southeast of Barnaul, are large lead and zinc plants, handling 1,000 tons of ore daily. This area, among the country's oldest mining districts, also yields silver, gold, copper, and tin. Prehistoric people used bronze tools in their mining operations here.

Manganese occurs near Achinsk, but the ore contains only 20 to 25 per cent manganese in comparison with 50 per cent at Chiatury and 40 per cent at Nikopol. The annual output is 100,000 tons of ore.

The development of great steel works and associated industries in the midst of the empty Kuznets steppe is one of the major achievements of the Soviet Union. In 1937, 30 per cent of the iron ore was mined locally, with the rest from the Urals. Increasing development of near-by ore, plus the availability of Karaganda coal for the Ural plants, tends to make Kuznets an independent unit rather than part of the Ural-Kuznets combine as originally planned.

Cities with smoking factories rise in the Kuznets Basin as abrupt and exotic intrusions in a treeless land scarcely inhabited even by nomads before the First World War. The city of Stalinsk, whose railway station is still named Kuznets, had 169,538 people in 1939. Near-by Prokopyevsk reported 107,227, while Kemerovo had 132,978. The urban population of the Kuznets area and near-by Novosibirsk exceeds 1,000,000.

Ob Taiga

The history of Siberia is the history of her rivers, modified by railroads during the present century. Although the major streams flow across the main line of travel to the east, early travelers used a series of portages to link the tributaries into a water route to the Pacific. The headwaters of the Kama, a Volga tributary, cross the Urals; from there it is a short portage to the tributaries of the Tobol in the Ob system. The Chulym, which enters the Ob from the east, flows within six miles of the Yenisei. By following up a Yenisei tributary, the Angara, to near Lake Baikal, one may either cross to the Amur system or travel via the Lena on toward the Sea of Okhotsk. The Ob was the first Siberian river to be developed and still has better steamers and more freight than the others.

The flatness of the West Siberian Plain is shown in the gradient of the Ob. At a distance of 1,850 miles from its mouth, the winter ice is 30 to 40 inches thick; at Salekhard 40 to 60 inches.

The Ob Taiga has a typical boreal cli-

A village landing on the Yenisei between Krasnoyarsk and Minusinsk. The line of small boats supports the cable for the characteristic Siberian swing ferry. (*Courtesy George Bain.*)

elevation is only 308 feet, a slope of only two inches per mile. Although the plain continues from the Urals eastward beyond the Yenisei to the edge of the Central Siberian Uplands, the geographic region ends near the left bank of the Yenisei.

The Ob has a length of 3,200 miles and is joined by the Irtysh which in turn receives the Ishim and Tobol. The length of rivers navigable at high water in the Ob system totals 19,200 miles, of which two-thirds are in use. Nearly half the freight, chiefly grain and timber, is carried on the Irtysh, navigable into Mongolia. The river is free from ice 175 days at Tobolsk and 153 days at Salekhard, formerly Obdorsk, near the gulf. Near Tobolsk,

mate, *Dc* in Koeppen symbols. Winters are long with a considerable snow cover. The annual precipitation is about 18 inches, decreasing to 14 inches near the Arctic.

The coniferous forest resembles that of the Dvina-Pechora Taiga in general, but lower rainfall, a more severe winter, and poor drainage change many species. Siberian fir predominates, mixed with white-barked trees such as birch and aspen. The Vasyugan Swamp covers 100,000 square miles near the junction of the Ob and Irtysh. Timber is shipped from Salekhard, usually consigned to Arkhangelsk rather than abroad. Very large amounts move upstream to the Trans-Siberian Railway for urban and industrial needs.

There are few cities of significance, and many place names shown on maps are riverside clearings of a few dozen houses.

with over a million square miles. The river lies at the latitude of the Mackenzie in Canada, placing Krasnoyarsk on the paral-

Many of the natives of the Arctic live in birch-bark wigwams during the summer. These are Evenki near Turukhansk on the Yenisei. (*Courtesy Northern Sea Route Administration.*)

Large areas are completely without settlement, inaccessible in summer because of swamps and mosquitoes. Contact with the rest of the Union is chiefly through cities to the south where the railway taps the Ob, Irtysh, or other tributaries.

Yenisei Taiga

From the source of the Yenisei to the ocean is 2,619 miles, but, if the distance be measured along its major tributary, the Angara, and its extensions beyond Lake Baikal, the length is 3,553 miles. Fourth among the world's rivers in length, the Yenisei ranks seventh in drainage area

lel of Edmonton, and Igarka at the same distance beyond the Arctic Circle as Aklavik.

Most of the Yenisei Taiga is within the Central Siberian Upland, particularly the Tunguska Platform where hills gradually rise to an elevation of 4,500 feet along the Lena divide. From these uplands the Yenisei receives three major tributaries. In the south the Verkhne or Upper Tunguska, commonly called the Angara, flows out of Lake Baikal. In the middle is the Podkamena or Stony Tunguska, while the northern tributary is the Nizhni or Lower Tunguska.

Virgin forest extends from south of the Angara 750 miles northward to beyond Igarka. This taiga is a trackless expanse an overseas export from the latter city of 90 million board feet in 1937. In addition to 18 shiploads sent to England, Holland,

Trucks for loading timber at Igarka, the port of the Yenisei. (*Courtesy Northern Sea Route Administration.*)

of conifers and whitewoods. Toward the south, and especially along the Angara, are splendid stands of commercial pine, but adverse conditions in the north reduce the trees to less than a foot in diameter. These forests are so vast that only preliminary studies have been possible, but estimates in the Yeniseisk-Igarka area run to 167 billion board feet of lumber. Conifer reserves along the Angara are three times this figure.

The taiga is usually described as a coniferous forest of fir and pine, but airplane flights over the Yenisei reveal that birch and deciduous softwoods cover a third of the area.

Sawmills are in operation at Krasnoyarsk, Maklakova, Yeniseisk, and Igarka, with

and Germany, three vessels carried lumber from the Yenisei to southeastern Africa.

Permanently frozen ground underlies almost the entire region. Summer heat thaws the ground to a depth of two or three feet beneath the insulating forest, or as deep as ten feet on cleared ground.

The Tunguska Platform contains enormous reserves of coal, known along the rivers and thought to continue between them. Tentative estimates reach 400 billion tons. Local intrusions of trap sheets have altered the coal to graphite, mined since 1862. At Norilsk in the Arctic, nickel, copper, lead, zinc, and coal are mined.

The Yenisei system is the great unifier of the region, for all settlement is along waterways. Four dozen boats operate on the river, a quarter of them with passenger accommodations. Regular steamboat lines operate from the railway at Krasnoyarsk; going south in three days to Minusinsk, north in six days to Igarka, and in eight days to Dudinka. Through most of the region the river is over a mile in width; depths exceed 50 feet except in the estuary.

Russians reached the lower Yenisei via the Arctic in 1610, whereas overland travelers from Tomsk did not see the Yenisei until Yeniseisk was established in 1618.

The most interesting city of the Yenisei Taiga is also the newest, Igarka, which provides a sheltered anchorage where cargoes can be transferred between river and ocean vessels. Though within the Arctic Circle, it lies 400 miles inland from the shallow and stormy estuary. In 1929 Igarka was a settlement with one house and three people; by 1937 its population numbered 15,000. The largest lumber mills east of the Urals cut logs floated down from the Angara for shipment during the two-month navigation period in August and September when the Kara Sea is open. To keep people healthy, fresh vegetables are raised in greenhouses and on open fields. Root crops do well, and leafy vegetables are reasonably successful, but grain does not ripen. Four hundred cows supply fresh dairy products and animal manure.

Arctic Fringe

Although the Arctic might not appear the most attractive part of the Soviet Union, there are few other regions whose development has met with equal enthusiasm. Nearly half the arctic lands of the earth lie within the U.S.S.R., and no other country has given so much attention to the development of northern latitudes.

Interest in northern Siberia and a possible northeast passage to China dates from the middle of the sixteenth century when the Spanish and Portuguese dominated the route around Africa so that the Dutch and English tried to sail via the north of Asia. Sebastian Cabot sent out an expedition in 1553 with instructions to "use all wayes and meanes possible to learn how men may passe from Russia either by land or by sea to Cathaia." Henry Hudson was another who explored this route, but neither expedition was able to sail east of Nova Zemlya.

Russian merchant adventurers sailed to the mouth of the Ob and founded a trading post in 1608, but the fear of foreign penetration led the Czar to forbid all Arctic navigation in 1624. Modern commerce reached the Yenisei again under Nordenskjöld in 1875, and in 1878–1879 he made the first voyage to the Pacific. During the Russo-Japanese War, 22 ships were sent to the mouth of the Yenisei to relieve traffic on the railway.

Soviet activities on an extensive scale date from 1932 when the icebreaker *Sibiriakov* made the first voyage from Arkhangelsk to Vladivostok in a single season. Under the Northern Sea Route Administration, regular services operate to the various rivers and a dozen or more vessels made the complete transit each summer. Icebreakers and airplanes are used in the most difficult areas. Freight through Kara Sea ports, chiefly Igarka, increased from 10,000 tons in 1920 to 137,460 in 1935. Lena freight in 1935 amounted to 13,000 tons. Service to the Kolyma River and points eastward is usually routed via Vladivostok, with 16,000 tons of freight in 1935. Except for exports of Yenisei lumber, most goods are consigned inward. The 1937 total Arctic freight amounted to 250,000 tons.

Four groups of islands divide the Soviet Arctic into five seas. The chief ports of reaching its maximum thickness and extent at the end of April. The Murmansk coast

The radio station on the Arctic island of Dickson at the mouth of the Yenisei. (*Courtesy Northern Sea Route Administration.*)

Reindeer sleds are used for winter travel across the wooded tundra of the northern Yenisei Valley. (*Courtesy Northern Sea Route Administration.*)

the Barents Sea are Murmansk and Arkhangelsk. Ice forms early in October, remains ice free owing to the Atlantic drift. To the east of the Barents Sea are the two islands of Nova Zemlya or new land, separated by the narrow Matochkin Strait, ice-free for four months but fog-bound for 19 days each month. Alternate passages lead north or south of the islands.

The Kara Sea is bounded on the east by Severnaya Zemlya or north land. Ice forms a month earlier and persists a month longer than in the Barents Sea. Both the Ob and the Yenisei have broad estuaries with sand bars where the depth of water is 16 and 23 feet, respectively. On the Ob, the chief river port is Salekhard, but most ocean vessels must unload at Novi Port in the estuary, where there is a floating wharf two miles from the shore. At the mouth of the Yenisei, barren Dickson Island has a good harbor but cannot be reached by river boats, so that transshipment takes place at Igarka. Dudinka is also developing a port for near-by Norilsk coal and nickel.

The Laptev or Nordenskjöld Sea occupies the section from Severnaya Zemlya to the New Siberian Islands. Its chief port is Tiksi Bay in the Lena Delta, where a ten-foot sand bar blocks ocean vessels. Shipping also calls at Nordvyk on the Khatanga River where there is a small production of salt and petroleum.

The East Siberian Sea is so shallow that navigation is difficult. Sand bars at the mouths of the Kolyma and Indigirka necessitate transshipment in the open sea. On the east the sea terminates at Wrangel Island, around which ice conditions are the worst of the entire passage. The Chukchee Sea continues to Bering Strait.

To supplement the steamer services, an air line was inaugurated in 1940 from Moscow to Arkhangelsk, Igarka, Tiksi, and the Chukotsk Peninsula, 4,500 miles distant.

Even though the navigation period is short and the hazards considerable, there is strategic value in a protected route from

Murmansk to Vladivostok. The naval significance is uncertain, but in comparison the Russian fleet was obliged to sail

Nentsi Young Pioneers, the Siberian equivalent of Eskimo Boy Scouts, in the Taimyr Peninsula near the lower Yenisei River. (*Courtesy Northern Sea Route Administration.*)

around Africa in 1905 and arrived in Japanese waters quite unprepared for combat. Like the United States, the Union of Soviet Socialist Republics is a two-ocean country and the Northern Sea Route may even become the Soviets' Panama Canal.

The Soviet Union claims ownership of all land in the sector north to the Pole. In 1937–1938, a scientific station occupied the North Pole, where the ocean depth was found to be 14,075 feet.

Wandering hunters and fishermen spend the summers in birch-bark wigwams along the streams where they catch and dry fish, while the winter months are devoted to trapping. Many Mongoloid peoples are represented, some of them similar to nomads who also keep reindeer in the Sayan Mountains in the south. The names Samoyed and Tungus were formerly used for groups who should now be termed Nentsi and Evenki. Formerly without a written language, they have been given an alphabet. Schools, medical centers, and reindeer-breeding stations have been provided.

Surface travel across the tundra is difficult during the brief summer, for there are innumerable swamps and lakes. According to a native saying, "there are as many lakes as there are stars in the sky."

Normal agriculture is almost impossible, but most Russian commercial and scientific outposts have experimental gardens and greenhouses. On Dickson Island electricity generated by the wind is used to light and heat underground greenhouses.

Conditions near the southern margin of the tundra are illustrated by Dudinka, an old settlement of 2,500 and the administrative and commercial center for the Taimyr Okrug. In 1936, the fur catch was valued at 4,800,000 rubles, and two tons of mammoth ivory were shipped. The frost-free period averages less than 60 days; in 1937, from June 24 to August 18. The temperature dropped to −42°F. on Feb. 28, 1937, and the monthly average was −9°F. Every month has from 64 to 87 per cent cloudiness. Precipitation amounts to 9 inches, almost entirely in the late summer.

Baikalia

Lake Baikal imposes a barrier to all east-west travel in southern Siberia. High mountains along the near-by Mongolian frontier force the railway to blast a shelf at the edge of the water. Farther north the Stanovoi Mountains continue to the Lena Valley. When approaching Baikalia from the west, the Yenisei Ridge and Eastern Sayan Mountains restrict travel to the Krasnoyarsk gateway, so that the only feasible route is by way of Irkutsk.

The lake occupies a graben that makes it the deepest lake in the world, 5,712 feet. Surrounding mountains are over a mile high, so that the fault displacement is 10,700 feet. A severe earthquake in 1861 indicates the sensitive nature of the geology. In area, Lake Baikal is in eighth place among the world's lakes, but in volume it ranks first. The Selenga is the chief of its tributaries, while the Angara forms the only outlet.

The geographic region of Baikalia lies largely to the east of the lake. Confused mountain structures trend northeast-southwest, and include the Pre-Baikal, Trans-Baikal, Yablonovi, and Olekminsk-Stanovik ranges. Much of the region is formed of crystalline and metamorphic rocks, with an elevation over a mile.

The climate appears to represent the furthermost penetration of summer monsoon winds from the Pacific. The maximum temperature of the water in Lake Baikal is delayed until August, and freezing does not occur until January. As a result, the shores have but 90 days below 14°F., while there are 140 such days elsewhere nearby. In summer, the vicinity of Baikal has 70 days with an average of 50° or over, as compared with 100 such days elsewhere. Fishing is important.

Most of Baikalia is covered by a pine forest, with Mongolian-type steppe in the drier lowlands. Cultivated land totals 1½ million acres. Many of the people are Buriats, who specialize in cattle raising.

East of Lake Baikal is coal, and iron is produced in an enlarged plant at Petrovsk. The region also has numerous occurrences of tin, tungsten, zinc, gold, arsenic, and molybdenum. Prospective developments center around water power, coal, and iron

Timber on the way to market in Buriat-Mongolia, near Lake Baikal. (*Sovfoto.*)

Russian villages often extend for a mile or more along a single street, with monotonous unpainted log houses. This scene in Eastern Siberia might be duplicated in many areas. (*Sovfoto.*)

ore west of Irkutsk under the project known as Angarastroi.

The Trans-Siberian Railway links the

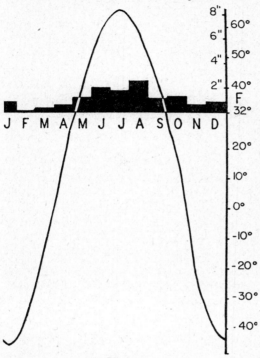

YAKUTSK
Elevation, 330 feet; average temperature, 12.2°F.; total precipitation, 13.7 inches.

three major cities. Irkutsk lies on the swift-flowing Angara, 44 miles from Lake Baikal, and had a population of 243,380 in 1939. Ulan-Ude, formerly Verkhne Udinsk, is at the crossing of the Selenga, the junction for a railway south to the Mongolian People's Republic, and has a large meat-packing plant. Chita lies near the railway junction to Manchuria.

Lena Taiga

Two features of the Lena Valley are of special interest: great gold production and the new railway north of Lake Baikal.

Gold has been obtained from the rivers of the northwest for many decades, and early in the twentieth century was ex-ploited by a large British concession named Lena Goldfields. Production greatly expanded with the discovery of the Aldan fields in 1923 where placer and lode deposits contribute a fifth of the country's gold. The new town of Aldan, formerly Nezametny, has a population of 4,000 and near-by mining camps raise the number of people in the Aldan district to 40,000. An automobile road leads south to the Trans-Siberian Railway at Bolshoi Niever. Bodaibo is also an important producer.

The Lena River has long been handicapped because its headwaters were not reached by the Trans-Siberian. Although the river runs within six miles of Lake Baikal, rugged mountains intervene. This has been changed by the construction of a new railway around the north of Lake Baikal to the Pacific. Much secrecy surrounded the construction of this Baikal-Amur Railway because of its military significance in case of a Far Eastern war.

The climate is the driest and coldest of any Siberian region yet considered. Precipitation is from 6 to 12 inches, and snowfall amounts to little over a foot. Yearly temperature averages are below freezing, so that a continental ice sheet might develop were there enough snowfall. There is no evidence of Pleistocene glaciation. The Lena is frozen at Yakutsk for 210 days.

On account of the low rainfall, grasslands replace the taiga in the lowland plains of the central Lena and Viloui, with resulting black soils. Cultivation is only moderately successful, but 225,000 acres were sown in 1935. Barley and wheat can be raised, but hay and vegetables are the chief crops. Most of the native population live by fishing, gathering furs, and raising reindeer.

Navigation on the Lena began when a steamer was brought from Norway in 1878. There are now a hundred steamships and launches. In order to appreciate the size of this region, it is well to remember that it is a thousand miles from Kirensk on the new railway down river to Yakutsk, and another thousand from there to Tiksi Bay on the Arctic Ocean. Coal is supplied from mines at Sangarkhai north of Yakutsk and at Kangalass. Production amounted to 30,000 tons in 1932 and was to reach 250,000 tons by 1942. Reserves are unprospected but probably large.

Yakutsk, the one city of importance, serves as the capital for the million square miles of the Yakut Autonomous Soviet Socialist Republic. Founded in 1632, it had a population of 27,000 in 1935. Like other Siberian towns, it has broad muddy streets, plank sidewalks, and one-story log houses, plus a few old brick buildings. The city is poorly located on a low terrace at the inside of a bend on a shallow branch of the Lena. The river, here full of islands and 15 miles wide, is shifting away from the town so that boats must unload four miles away at low water. Floods frequently inundate the city.

Northeastern Mountains

This region continues the system of young mountains that cross central Eurasia from the Alps to Kamchatka. This corner of the Union is so inaccessible that the Cherski Range, rising to 9,843 feet, was not discovered until 1926. Kamchatka has the greatest group of volcanoes on the continent, with 127 cones of which 19 are active. The highest is Mt. Kliuchevskaya, 15,950 feet, which has erupted 19 times in two centuries. In 1907, the volcano Shtiubelia ejected four billion cubic yards of ashes, and some of the dust fell in Europe.

The Northeastern Mountains have long been known as the icebox of the world. No inhabited place has observed as low minima as Verkhoyansk and Oimekon. Extreme low temperatures are not related to the winter high pressure over Siberia but are due to intense radiation in calm air and local air drainage into enclosed basins. Verkhoyansk has a January average of −59°F. and an absolute minimum of −90°F. Observations at Oimekon since 1928 show that winters are consistently colder, so that it may replace Verkhoyansk as the coldest station. The unattractive character of the Oimekon district is indicated by its population of 565 households or 2,400 people in an area of 27,000 square miles.

In 1916, all of this region was regarded as outside the limits of possible cultivation. Agricultural experiment stations have shown that some vegetables may be grown in the southern half, especially in the central valley of Kamchatka. Most of the region has as little precipitation as the Aral-Balkhash Desert, but monsoon winds bring 40 inches to the southeastern part of Kamchatka. Mountain tundra replaces taiga forest.

The Okhotsk Sea and the waters around Kamchatka have long been important fishing grounds. Since the catch must be sun dried, the cloudy and foggy weather of summer presents problems. From 1847 to 1871, American whalers secured whale oil and bone here to the value of $87,500,-000; and whales are still caught. Under the Treaty of Portsmouth which ended the Russo-Japanese War of 1904–1905, Japanese fishermen were given special concessions in this area, and the gradual restriction of these arrangements has been the source of much political friction. Salmon, cod, herring, and crab are caught. The chief port on Kamchatka is Petropavlovsk, founded in 1741 and located on one of the world's finest harbors. The port is the most important Soviet harbor on the open Pacific.

The mining of gold on the upper Kolyma started in 1929, and an automobile road leads south to the new town of Magadan at Nagaevo Bay on the Sea of Okhotsk.

One of the shafts of the Artimovo coal mine in Sakhalin. (*Sovfoto.*)

The Far East

Southeastern Siberia borders the Pacific and is significant as the frontier toward Japan. The Third Five-year Plan emphasized the military importance of agricultural and industrial developments, and assigned four billion rubles or 4 per cent of its funds to the political units known as the Khabarovsk and Maritime territories, which include all of the Pacific margin to the Arctic. The geographic region here considered is essentially the Amur Basin, plus Sakhalin.

The decade prior to the Second World War was marked by a great increase in cultivated land, the beginnings of heavy industry, the growth of cities, and active immigration which brought the population to over two million. With the empty spaces coming into use, the Far East is now self-sufficient in its food and industrial needs.

The Amur is the great river of the east, comparable to the three north-flowing rivers. The chief tributaries on the left bank are the Zeya and Bureya, while on the right the Sungari comes from Manchuria, and the Ussuri forms the eastern Manchurian border. Along the central Amur around Khabarovsk is a broad plain which continues up the Ussuri to Lake Khanka. On the east, the plain is enclosed by the Sikhota Alin Mountains, while on the west are the Little Khingan Mountains. West of this is the Bureya-Zeya plain, limited by the extension of the Great Khingan Mountains.

The Far East has a continental climate modified by the Pacific monsoons. Strong dry winter winds blow from the interior, with temperatures far below freezing. In summer, relatively warm oceanic air

Irtysh have such good agricultural possibilities. Korean farmers even raise rice north of Vladivostok. Wheat, rye, oats,

Karl Marx Street in Khabarovsk, the leading city of the Soviet Far East. (*Sovfoto.*)

imports moisture, bringing an annual rainfall of 25 inches to Vladivostok. Although Vladivostok lies in the latitude of southern Crimea, its east coast position gives winter temperatures 45° colder, resembling Halifax.

The flora is of the Manchurian type, with magnificent stands of Korean pine, spruce, fir, and larch, mixed with 10 per cent of deciduous forms such as oak. Timber not only supplies the expanding internal market but is shipped to Japan, China, and Australia. Meadows cover the drier interior basins.

Few other parts of Siberia east of the

and barley are the chief grains; sugar beets are extensively grown. Spring planting is delayed since the ground freezes to ten feet or more under the thin snow cover, and thawing takes place slowly under the cloudy skies of June.

Since the Far East did not raise enough food to supply itself, agricultural colonists from overcrowded parts of Soviet Europe have been offered free transportation, credits, and tax exemption. The Jewish colony of Birobidjan, west of Khabarovsk, is especially interesting. Jews receive full rights throughout the U.S.S.R. but have heretofore had no district that was exclusively their own. This Soviet Palestine provides such a haven and at the same time strengthens the regional economy.

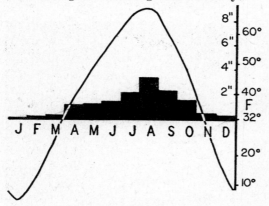

VLADIVOSTOK
Elevation, 50 feet; average temperature, 39.7°F.; total precipitation, 14.7 inches.

The Far East has mineral resources for a growing industry. Steel mills have been built at Komsomolsk to use Buryea coal and iron ore from either the Little Khingan or lower Amur, both of low grade. Lead and zinc have long been secured along the Japan Sea. The chief oil production east of the Urals is in Sakhalin.

Komsomolsk is the magic city of the east. Although founded only in 1932, its population reached 70,000 by 1939. This is the "city of youth," the lodestone of enthusiastic workers from all over the Union. Situated on the lower Amur, it has the largest steel mills and shipyards in the Soviet Far East.

Khabarovsk has developed where the Trans-Siberian Railway spans the Amur. It is the political and commercial center of the area, with a population of 199,364 in 1939.

Vladivostok has a picturesque setting on Peter the Great Bay. The city's trade increased greatly during the First and Second World Wars and during periods of favorable political relations with Manchuria. The harbor is kept open throughout the year by icebreakers. Coal is secured from near-by bituminous deposits. The population numbered 206,432 in 1939.

The Far East offers considerable promise. Soils and climate make agriculture relatively attractive. Timber reserves are excellent, minerals fairly abundant, and transportation rapidly improving. Many of the people are pioneers, and this "new east" resembles Canada's "great west." But neither Canada nor the Soviet Union is primarily a Pacific power.

CHAPTER 22

THE SOUTHWESTERN REALM

The term "Near East" is an indefinite geographical expression which is frequently used but seldom defined. To some it loosely refers to all the lands between Libya and India; to others it is limited to the countries within Asia bordering the Mediterranean; and some would even include India. The words "Middle East" and "Levant" are sometimes introduced for Palestine, Iraq, and near-by areas, but the Middle East is also used variously for North Africa or even India. Like the Far East, the phrase Near East stands for no clearly defined place on the map and it is well to use it sparingly. This chapter is an introduction to the eight major countries of Southwestern Asia, between India and the Mediterranean: Turkey, Syria, Palestine, Trans-Jordan, Arabia, Iraq, Iran, and Afghanistan.

Southwestern Asia spreads over two and a half million square miles, so that it is nearly as large as all the United States. In a certain sense this is a great peninsula, or an isthmus. To the south are the Arabian Sea and the Persian Gulf, on the west are the Red Sea and the Mediterranean, northward are the Black and Caspian seas and the equally limiting Caucasian mountains and Turanian deserts. Only across Suez and the Bosporus is there a link with Africa and Europe. Geographic barriers also enclose the realm to the east where the Sulaiman and Kirthar ranges bar access from India, while the Hindu Kush, Khorassam, and Elburz mountains are a rampart fronting Soviet Middle Asia.

Whatever name is used, this area has physical, cultural, and historical coherence. Much of European civilization had its rise here. Three of the world's great religions, and the only monotheistic faiths, arose in this corner of Asia. In contrast to the Southeast with its abundant summer monsoon rainfall, the Southwest is a land of sparse winter rain. Again in contrast, this is a pastoral land with extensive deserts and a sparse population in comparison to dense populations and intensive rice culture. This is the Mohammedan world, largely Arab in its population. Great changes have taken place within recent decades; here today meets yesterday.

The most striking landscape contrasts are those between the green fields, often irrigated, and the brown desert. Only in a few places is there a continuous expanse of cultivation; elsewhere relatively small oases stand out sharply against the enveloping aridity. Barren mountains, except where high enough to capture rain, and rocky hills are unusually prominent. Semiarid lands lack sufficient rainfall to enable vegetation to carpet the surface and thus hold the soil in rounded slopes, but there is enough running water at times to erode the surface and develop sharp profiles.

The contrast between the desert and the sown, between the tent and the town, has led the city of Damascus to be described as a "great and splendid Arab city set in a girdle of fruit trees and filled with the murmur of running water." The productivity of such irrigated oases ends abruptly across the outermost irrigation ditch. Only a few areas have sufficient rainfall for normal field crops. The largest of these is known as the fertile crescent, a discontinuous belt of cultivation which extends up the Tigris

pastures of the Twenty-third Psalm are vital elements in the human economy. The problem of agriculture is inadequate water

Place map of Southwestern Asia.

and Euphrates, across northern Syria, and southward through Palestine.

Water is the key to life, and the green

rather than infertile soils, although the latter are seriously eroded in many areas. The rainfall is entirely confined to the winter months, with scattered showers from October to May. Large areas receive but ten inches of rain. Summers are dry and the natural vegetation withers under the parching heat. Vegetation zones are matters of elevation and exposure rather than latitude. Thus many shepherds practice transhumance by taking their flocks up the mountains to high level pastures that have summer rain. Since few mountains receive snow, most rivers tend to dry up during the rainless summer. This is a distinct handicap to irrigation.

The concentration of rainfall during the winter months is a characteristic of the western margins of continents in latitudes roughly 30 to 40 degrees on either side of the equator. This regime in the Mediterranean area has given its name to similar conditions in southern California, central Chile, and small areas in southwestern Africa and Australia. During winter months when the sun is vertical in the Southern Hemisphere, the northern belt of cyclonic storms shifts equatorward from central Europe and the Soviet Union. Occasional rain-producing low pressure areas thus invade Southwestern Asia. More properly, a secondary storm path develops south of the Alps and Caucasus and continues eastward with decreasing intensity south of The Himalaya. Since the time, size, and rain-producing capacity of these cyclonic storms are highly variable, agriculture is hazardous. During summer months the path of cyclonic storms lies well to the north of the realm and in its place is a semipermanent belt of high pressure. This gives rise to dry descending air movements and, along the southern margin, to equally dry trade-wind conditions.

With increasing distance into Asia from the Mediterranean, less and less rain occurs. This aridity reaches a climax in the deserts of eastern Iran and northwest India. In the former the meager rainfall comes in winter,

in the latter the wet season is the summer. Between these climatic regimes lie the Sulaiman and Kirthar ranges along the borders of Afghanistan and Baluchistan.

Continental aridity usually brings pronounced temperature contrasts, both annual and daily. This is the case here, with the added influence of different altitudes. Within a given week in summer, temperature readings at one place or another within the realm may range from freezing to 130°F.

Aridity gives the topography a certain sameness in the angularity and association of land forms. Many mountains are geologically young, so that fault scarps and sharp features are common. Earthquakes are recurrent. Abrupt contrasts in elevation, plus limited stream flow, have led to the development of extensive alluvial fans. Some of these face interior playa basins where withering rivers fail to carry their debris to the sea. Much of Turkey and Iran is composed of tectonic basins. Although most of Arabia slopes eastward to the Persian Gulf, large areas contribute no runoff adequate to continue to the sea.

Two extensive mountain systems enclose much of Southwestern Asia, while between them is a series of plateau basins. These same chains continue eastward into China and form the backbone of Asiatic structure. In Turkey the two mountains are the Pontus in the north and the Taurus in the south. Between them is the plateau of Anatolia. Eastward is the smaller plateau of Armenia, on either side of which are mountainous continuations of the Pontus and Taurus, known, respectively, as the Karabagh and Kurdistan. In Iran and Afghanistan, the northern ranges are the Elburz, Khorassan, and Hindu Kush, while the southern edge of the plateau is formed by the Zagros, Fars, and Makran mountains. These systems again converge in the Pamir knot, from which the topographic continuations eastward around Tibet are the Altyn Tagh and The Himalaya.

is the low alluvial plain of Mesopotamia. Fertile soil and adequate water for irriga-

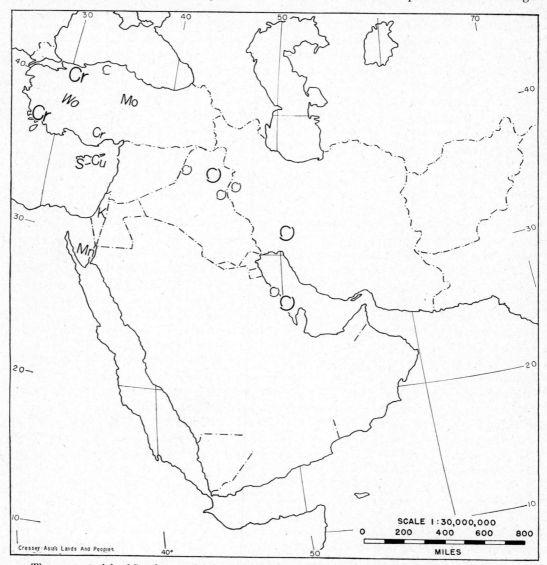

The raw materials of Southwestern Asia are very limited. Oil (O, shadow letter) is important in Iran, Iraq, and eastern Arabia. Chromium (Cr), molybdenum (Mo), coal (C, shadow letter), and wool (*Wo*) are present in Turkey; potassium (K) is secured from the Dead Sea, and manganese (Mn) from the Sinai Peninsula.

Elevations in the mountains reach one to three miles, while the enclosed uplands have a height of half a mile or more.

Between the plateau of Iran and Arabia

tion have made this the most attractive agricultural area in the realm.

Although these countries have nearly the size of the United States, the total population numbers but 57 million. This is nevertheless a dynamic area, for from its peoples have come ideas that have changed the world. If their place in modern times appears small, one has but to recall the empires of the past and the aspects of European culture that arose here.

This is an old land, probably the oldest in Asia in terms of human occupance. In the beginnings of history we find Semitic Assyrians, Babylonians, Canaanites, Hebrews, Phoenicians, and Hittites. Later came Aryan Persians and Kurds, and still later Arabs, Mongols, Turks, Greeks, and Romans. These successive innundations have given a complex racial picture to present-day Southwestern Asia. Three major groups now stand out. Arabs dominate Syria, Palestine, Trans-Jordan, Iraq, and Arabia. Turks and Persians have their own countries. Many minority groups persist in local areas such as the Jews, Kurds, Turkomans, and Afghans.

Despite the great extent of the areas devoted to grazing, nomads number but a small fraction of the total population. City dwellers are likewise limited in number, so that three-quarters of the people are peasant farmers, many of them depending upon irrigation.

Although many racial groups are represented, there is an underlying cultural unity. Part of this is political, an outgrowth of ancient empires. Thus the Moslem world once exceeded that of imperial Rome. Arab culture had a brilliant development in medieval times, as witnessed in the achievements of Damascus and Bagdad. Mathematics was highly developed, and there was a rich and extensive literature on philosophy, law, medicine, travel, and science of which most westerners are still unaware. Modern nationalism appears to have ended the possibility of Pan-Islamic political unity, but a cultural awareness remains.

Mohammedanism binds all of Southwestern Asia into a single unit, whether the people are Arab, Turk, or Persian. Few other factors are so unifying. Mohammedans spread entirely across Africa and Asia, with some ten million in China, seventeen million in the Soviet Union, nearly eighty million in India, and fifty million in the Netherlands Indies.

These Moslems form a self-conscious bloc, for Islam is more than a religious belief; it is a legal code, a social order, and a cultural pattern. All this has its center of gravity in Southwestern Asia.

This realm also has world significance in its resources. Although not so rich as other parts of Asia, oil in Iraq and Iran and chromium in Turkey are major factors in world mineral trade. Iraq could grow as much cotton as Egypt. Turkish tobacco and wool are of the best.

Trade between eastern Asia and Europe must pass through or near this realm, or else detour around Africa. So long as the Soviet Union remains closed, Southwestern Asia commands the highways by water, land, and air. Thus the Suez Canal has changed history and remains a key point for the British Empire. In order to checkmate Suez, Germany sought an overland route in the Berlin to Bagdad Railway, designed to connect the Bosporus with the Persian Gulf. Construction started in 1888, but through service was not available until 1940. It is thus possible to travel entirely across Asia by rail, from Murmansk to Basra. Connections will some day be made with the Indian railways, but freight from Europe to India can move cheaper by water, while passengers and mail will follow the airways. Air service dates from 1921 when the Royal Air Force operated from Cairo to Bagdad. Before the Second World War, planes of the British Overseas Airways, Air France, the Dutch K.L.M., and German Junkers all met in Bagdad.

During the second and third decades of the twentieth century the nations of this realm underwent such rapid changes that Empire of Turkey which covered a maximum of 1,700,000 square miles and ruled 40,000,000 people. Since the history of this

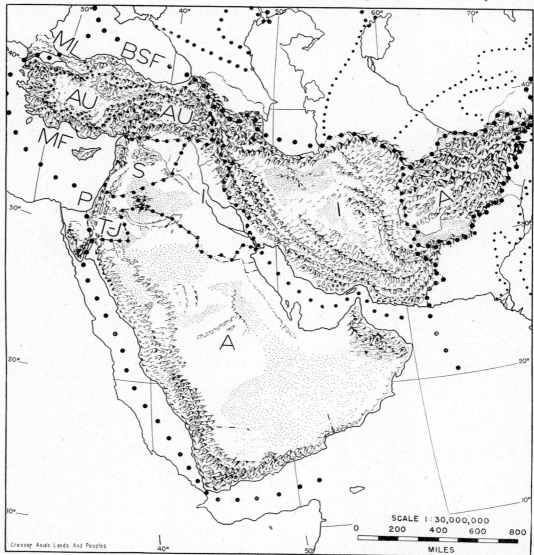

The geographic regions and land forms of the Southwestern Realm. Within Turkey are the Marmara Lowlands (ML), the Black Sea Fringe (BSF), the Anatolian Uplands (AU), the Armenian Highlands (AU), and the Mediterranean Fringe (MF). The other countries of the Southwestern Realm are Syria (S), Palestine (P), Trans-Jordan (T-J), Arabia (A), Iraq (I), Iran (I), and Afghanistan (A). (*Base map by Erwin Raisz, Courtesy Harvard-Yenching Institute, adapted by Rowland Illick.*)

the pace was described as a century in a decade. This process began long ago with the disintegration of the old Ottoman realm is so interwoven, it seems appropriate to sketch these historic changes here as well as in the subsequent chapters.

The rebirth of Turkey under Mustafa Kemal revealed an unsuspected vigor, first demonstrated by the expulsion of the Greeks in 1922. The old foreign extra-territorial restrictions were abrogated and a modern democratic state was set up. The entire economic and cultural system was permeated by new life. Agriculture and industry were modernized under a nation-alistic program which greatly enlarged the cultivated land and crop return. Turkey also set up factories to produce the textiles and simple manufactured goods formerly imported. Laws were passed abolishing the fez and the veil, forbidding polygamy, and ending Mohammedanism as a state religion. One of the most sig-nificant changes was the official adoption of the Latin alphabet. Turkey has become modern but it is determined to remain Turkish.

Syria and Palestine, unlike Turkey, had no earlier political independence. During the First World War, the Arabs were promised that their independence and unity would be upheld if they would revolt against Turkey and thus against Germany, but at the Peace Conferences French and British rivalries prevented this unity. As a result, Syria and Palestine became man-dates, along with Iraq. French occupation of Syria did not prove very successful, for there were 18 rebellions between 1919 and 1941.

Palestine's problems are many and deep, as this is the scene of a head-on conflict between two national interests: the Arab renaissance and Jewish Zionism. Palestine is not only the home of the Jewish religion; Jerusalem ranks after Mecca and Medina as the third most sacred city of Islam. Abraham, Moses, David, and Jesus are all Mohammedan prophets. Arabs have lived in Palestine for thirteen centuries since they drove out the Romans and feel that this constitutes adequate territorial claim.

British interests in the security of Suez are also involved. These rival Arab, Hebrew, and British claims have proved impossible of solution. The Arabs complain that the new Jewish communities have bought up the best land and, although Arabs have shared in the general increase of prosperity, the deeper problem is political. In 1918 there were 55,000 Jews in Palestine; this grew to 435,000 in 1941, an increase from 8 to 31 per cent of the total. The Arabs might agree to a national *home* for the Jews, but the latter aim at a national *state*. Schemes of partition have satisfied no one. It is doubtful whether the Arabs will surrender political control except under continuing force, and that involves explosion throughout the Moslem world.

Arabian developments, like those of Turkey, have been the product of a strong leader, ibn-Saud, King of Saudi Arabia. Much of the peninsula has been unified and tribal warfare reduced. Economic modernization is limited by geographic handicaps.

Iraq was set up as a British mandate but in 1921 it became an independent kingdom and the mandate ended in 1932. Extensive irrigation projects and other agricultural aids have restored some of the ancient productivity. Railways now lead from the Persian Gulf to Europe.

Persia became Iran in 1925, and the change to the ancient name is an indication of the rebirth of national consciousness. For centuries this country has been the scene of rival Russian and British imperial-isms. The Russian bear has sought a warm-water port on the Persian Gulf, while the British lion has been concerned with the security of the route to India. These con-flicting interests have actively remained but have been overshadowed by the devel-opment of internal reforms. Iran has fol-lowed Turkey's lead in many ways. There has been a notable increase in education, communications, and political organization.

Important problems remain in each country, for the settlements of the First World War have never been accepted with enthusiasm. External geostrategic interests of Britain, France, and the Soviet Union are still paramount and refuse to leave the area to its own devices. The Second World War interrupted the development of national reforms but failed to arouse any real enthusiasm for either Allied or Axis powers. Southwestern Asia has not yet found political stability.

CHAPTER 23

TURKEY

Turkey is a miniature continent in itself. On three sides the country is bounded by seas, within which it is still further enclosed by mountains. Continentality is emphasized by seasonal pressure changes which produce, alternately, inward and outward winds. Coastal accessibility and interior inaccessibility are as true of Asia Minor as of Asia as a whole. As a peninsula Turkey is European like Portugal; as a plateau it is as dry as Soviet Middle Asia and almost as cold in winter.

For thousands of years the plateau of Anatolia has been a link between Europe and Asia, while at right angles to it the Dardanelles and the Bosporus have served as an avenue from the Aegean to the Black Sea. Rugged topography and arid climate do not make overland travel easy, but movement has ever been characteristic. No railway or modern road leads directly from northern to southern Turkey across the mountains; instead the grain of the country is from east to west. The bordering mountains have kept out emigrants from Europe and maintained the Asiatic character of the country; only along the Aegean did Hellenic culture secure a foothold.

Innumerable struggles have occurred here, usually between the alien nations of the East and the West. Almost every important country in Europe and in western Asia has fought in this area, either for control of the Straits, to command the through route by land, or for the small patches of fertile soil. Here are many province and city names famous in Greek and Roman

history and in the New Testament, such as Troy, Ephesus, Miletus, and Tarsus.

Turkey dates from the thirteenth century when the Ottoman Turks were nomads in the Anatolian uplands. During the period of its greatest extent in 1566, Turkey reached from Hungary to southern Arabia and from Egypt to the Sea of Azov. Successive losses of land followed until the end of the First World War when the country was deprived of all of its territory except that in Asia Minor and a small area around Istanbul, formerly Constantinople.

In 1922 occurred the Turkish Revolution under Mustafa Kemal Pasha, and the capital was removed to Ankara (pronounced An' kara) in the interior in order to make independence more secure. No part of Turkish history is more dramatic then the events that followed. The old Oriental Turkey has become modernized and Europeanized at a rate that scarcely seemed possible. Despite limited mineral resources and a nonagricultural climate over much of the country, Turkey has established a significant place for herself as the leading nation in Southwestern Asia. Resilience seems to be a characteristic of the Turkish people.

The nearness of the Aegean shore to Greece and the attractiveness of its possibilities led to a very early colonization by Greeks, who dominated the economic life. One of the noteworthy events of the revolution in 1922 was the transfer of all Greeks from Turkey, except Istanbul, to Greece and the repatriation from that

country of all Turks. This deprived
Turkey of some of its most industrious

Geographic strategy is of vital concern to
Turkey, for her position, between two

A modern street in Ankara, the new capital of Turkey in central Anatolia. (*Alice Schalek, from Three Lions.*)

people but was part of the program of
nationalization.

Prior to the establishment of the Republic, most foreigners enjoyed extraterritorial rights which gave special privileges to
foreign investments. These rights gradually
threatened the political and economic
freedom of the country, for most railways,
banks, and public utilities were in foreign
hands; even the customs was under foreign
administration. The recovery of complete
sovereignty and the development of nationalism served as a pattern for China where
extraterritoriality prevailed until 1943.

continents and near a third, is of great
importance in peace and war. Czarist
Russia repeatedly sought an outlet through
the Straits, and as often was blocked by a
coalition of Western powers. During the
First World War Germany brought Turkey
to its side in order to secure a route from
Berlin to Bagdad. In the Second World War
the Allies succeeded in keeping Turkey
neutral and a barrier to further German
advance by agreeing to purchase the bulk
of her exports, previously shipped to
Germany.

Modern Turkey has an area of 294,492 square miles, of which 9,895 square miles are in the European section. The population in 1935 was 16,201,000, equal to an average density of 55 persons per square mile. The country is divided into 58 vilayets, or districts, including Alexandretta, or Hatay, which was returned by France in 1939. Over three-quarters of the people are rural. Agriculture and grazing are the predominant occupations, accounting for 70 per cent of the national income and 90 per cent of the exports. Yet less than 10 per cent of Turkey is under cultivation.

Three major physical divisions characterize Turkey in Asia: the Pontus Mountains along the Black Sea in the north, the central basins of Anatolia and Armenia, and the Taurus Mountains with their continuation in the Anti-Taurus along the Mediterranean to the south. Limited areas of level land fringe each sea. Next to the Aegean and the Sea of Marmara in the west is a hill country that gives relatively free access to the interior plateau. Irregular embayments are partly filled with delta plains.

A cross section from north to south shows a narrow fringe of coastal plain along the Black Sea, an abrupt rise to the rugged one- to two-mile-high Pontus Mountains, a slight descent to the broad undulating Anatolian plateau with its playa lakes, another rise to the high Taurus, and a steep descent to the Mediterranean with little or no coastal plain.

Anatolia is bordered by a complex series of ranges; neither the Pontus nor Taurus are simple mountains. Heights reach about 10,000 feet in each system, somewhat higher in the Taurus. The area is a continuation of Alpine folding, with sediments laid down in an ancient geosyncline cut by volcanic formations. Toward the east, the Pontus and Taurus systems meet in the Armenian knot or crown, with an elevation

of over a mile in the plateau and twice to three times that in the mountains. Mt. Ararat in the extreme east is an active volcano, 16,916 feet high.

Within this mountain enclosure lies the plateau of Anatolia, covering more than a third of Turkey. This is a rolling steppeland of withering rivers and barren plains. Salt lakes and playa flats are interrupted by low ranges a few hundred or a thousand feet above the plain. The general altitude is over 2,000 feet in the west and 4,000 feet in the east.

Most of the usable coastal areas are next to the Aegean and the Sea of Marmara in the west. The Black Sea coast has more level land than along the Mediterranean, where the chief level land is in the Cilician Plain.

Climatic conditions divide the country into two parts: the coastal sections with a Mediterranean type of climate with 20 or more inches of winter rain, and the semiarid plateau also with winter precipitation but with less than 10 inches a year.

Along the Aegean and Mediterranean coasts conditions resemble Greece, with warm dry summers and cool rainy winters. During the latter season occasional cold winds sweep out of the interior through gaps in the mountains. The Black Sea coast has much more rainfall than elsewhere, even 100 inches toward the east, and it occurs during the fall as well as in winter. Vegetation follows altitude, with dry maqui brush on the lower slopes followed by splendid deciduous and then coniferous forests up to the tree line at 6,000 feet, above which are alpine meadows.

Conditions within Anatolia resemble southeastern Soviet Europe, with bitterly cold northeast winds during winter and spring which bring freezing temperatures. Summers are very hot and are accompanied by severe dust storms. The precipitation is under ten inches, with snow on the surface for three months. Moisture from the surrounding seas is lost on the outward slopes of the intervening mountains. Sum-

cally classed as arable, though only 10 per cent was in use, and prior to 1927 less than 5 per cent was cultivated. Pastures

The modernization of agriculture has been one of the objectives of the Turkish government. This combine is harvesting rice on the Cilician Plain (*Ewing Galloway.*)

mers are entirely dry. This is a treeless steppe with many saline wastes.

The mountains of Armenia in eastern Turkey are even colder, with six months of winter. This is sometimes known as the Siberia of Turkey.

The soils of Turkey are thin and seriously eroded. In the steppe, overgrazing has led to the destruction of the soil cover with extensive subsequent deflation. In the more humid areas, deforestation or careless cultivation has brought excessive erosion by the concentrated rainfall. The few alluvial plains now contain much of the soil from the interior which has not been carried out to sea.

Agriculture and grazing are the chief occupations. Out of the total area of the country in 1936, 30 per cent was optimisti-

and meadows cover 35 per cent, mountains and wasteland 13 per cent, and forests 13 per cent.

Wheat is by far the most important crop, accounting for 45 per cent of all field crops. Barley occupies half that area, with corn, rye, and oats as minor cereals. These are all fall planted. Cotton has risen to 3 per cent and tobacco utilizes 1 per cent. Olives, grapes, and filberts are the chief tree and vine crops. Olive trees manage to grow with as little as eight inches of rainfall. Summer rain is a disadvantage.

As a result of government efforts since the Revolution, wheat production has increased so much that Turkey has changed from a wheat-importing to a wheat-exporting country. Yields averaged 16.3 bushels per acre in 1938. Wheat growing is evenly spread through all but a few of the districts, with a tendency to be more important in the drier interior.

Tobacco is a distinctive Turkish export, but the plant is an American variety introduced in 1602 which has acquired unique properties in its new environment. Most of the tobacco is grown in two districts, one in the far west and the other in the north center. It is usually raised on the southern side of hills, protected from high winds; where raised in flat country, straw mats are erected for its shelter. Two-thirds of the crop is exported.

Cotton is grown in the west and south and supplies the raw material for a rapidly growing textile industry. As with wheat, there has been extensive government research and support. Production trebled in the 15 years prior to 1940, and it is estimated that the 700,000 acres now in cotton production might be increased by 2,000,000 additional acres.

Turkey is the world's leading producer of filbert nuts, shipped largely to Europe.

Raisins rate third in the export trade, sometimes second, and the country is in the same export rank as the United States. Production was much more extensive prior to the phylloxera damage in 1900.

Figs apparently originated here and are a major export from Smyrna, now known as Izmir. Turkey is by far the world's largest exporter.

Mohair is a distinctive product of the interior, and the raising of angora goats is an important occupation in central Anatolia. The wool combines softness and durability, and Turkish mohair is the finest in the world.

Turkey's export trade is predominantly made up of agricultural products. Only through the sale of these items is the country able to import the industrial materials that she needs. The chief exports, in normal order, are tobacco, filberts, raisins, cotton, mohair, wheat, wool, figs, hides and skins, and barley. During the decade before the Second World War, Germany increased her purchases through trade agreements until she took more than all other countries combined. The United States held second place, owing to its purchases of tobacco. Only limited exports are consigned to near-by countries in the Balkans or Southwestern Asia.

Mineral resources appear to be limited to a few items, but the production is increasing. Chromium ore is mined at Gutteman in the northwest, at Fethiye in the southeast, and elsewhere to a total of 192,000 metric tons, enough to place Turkey in second place in the world. Molybdenum is obtained near Ankara. Silver, lead, and zinc ore are produced near Balikesir. Turkish meerschaum monopolizes the world market as is true of emery. Increasing amounts of coal are mined at Eregli on the Black Sea.

The geographic regions of Turkey have been variously defined. Merriam divides the country into four regions: those of Mediterranean agriculture chiefly in the west but with narrow belts along the northern and southern coasts, the northern and southern forests, and the area of pastoral nomadism in the interior. Stamp further divides the agricultural region into the northeastern, Marmara, Smyrna, and southern coastal regions; and the area of pastoral nomadism into Inner Anatolia and Inner Armenia. Lyde recognizes essentially the same areas but groups the northern and southern coastal lowlands with the respective mountains. The most detailed classification is that of Banse who lists five provinces and 21 regions in Anatolia, and two provinces and ten regions in Armenia.

Five geographic regions are here considered: the Marmara Lowlands, the Black Sea Fringe, the Mediterranean Fringe including the Aegean, the Anatolian Uplands, and the Armenian Highlands.

Marmara Lowlands

The Sea of Marmara, together with the Dardanelles at the west and the Bosporus at the east, is the traditional boundary between Europe and Asia. North of these waterways on the European side is the plain of Thrace, while to the south are the picturesque hills and plains of Troy, Bursa, and Bithynia.

The annual rainfall is about 25 inches so that a great variety of agricultural products is grown, notably wheat, barley, oats, olives, grapes, tobacco, and silk. Olive trees are especially important in a region where butter is rare and the religion forbids the use of lard. Summers bring clear skies, high temperatures, and a long drought. Winter is the rainy season with occasional snow. Most of the precipitation comes from cyclonic storms that move toward the semi-permanent low over the Black Sea. On account of this seasonal distribution of moisture, the natural vegetation shows drought-resistant features. Differences in elevation introduce sharp contrasts in vegetation, with olives along the seacoast and meadows near the snow line. Miss Newbigin[1] has pointed out that " . . . Mediterranean man's greatest achievement is that he has, wherever possible, replaced the natural vegetation by a series of crops which make use of every drop of water, every square foot of soil, and yield him a complete dietary."

Throughout this corner of Turkey the landscape has an east-west alignment, with an old mature topography cut by young valleys eroded since the early Pleistocene epoch of folding, vulcanism, and uplift. The uplands are thus gently rolling mature areas while the lower slopes are in

[1] NEWBIGIN, MARION, "The Mediterranean Lands," 63.

youth. Elevations reach 8,366 feet in Ulu Dag or the Bithynian Mt. Olympus.

This is a long-settled land so that the cultural landscape is the result of successive human occupance. Agriculture is the occupation for most of the people, with most cultivation below the 750-foot contour line. Many peasants plow their land with a wooden plow, perhaps with an iron tip, although modern steel plows are increasingly in use. Seed is sown broadcast and the harvest is gathered by hand. The grain is threshed by driving a mule or ox over it and is winnowed in the air.

Istanbul, Turkey's great city, lies on a hilly promontory at the southern end of the Bosporus and at the point where a long bay known as the Golden Horn provides an excellent harbor. Only Athens, Rome, and Jerusalem had greater influence in the ancient Occidental world. The Straits are a sea-river, nowhere more than five miles in width and in some places but half a mile; their current is swift. The weather is subject to sudden changes, for winds from the north and south are in conflict, even in the course of the same day. Rainfall amounts to 28 inches a year and falls on 112 days. The population of Istanbul numbers 883,-599. The city of Scutari, renamed Üsküdar, lies on the Asiatic side of the Straits opposite Istanbul.

Black Sea Fringe

The Black Sea coast of Turkey has a rugged littoral where steep-sided block mountains rise directly from the coast. There are few ports and only difficult access to the interior. Settlement is confined to three zones. The maritime belt is largely a mountainous country where people are limited to the accessible coast. There is wilderness within a few miles. Rainfall is abundant, especially to the east, and, although there is a winter maximum, some rain falls at all seasons. Hence typical

Mediterranean trees such as the olive do not grow well. Dense forests of pine, oak, east, and the annual production is over three million metric tons (1941).

A Turkish farmer and his son on the way to market their wool. (*Ewing Galloway.*)

box, and chestnut provide for a lumber industry, although the topography is so unfavorable that many forest areas are inaccessible. Filbert nuts and tobacco are important crops. The second zone lies within the Pontus Mountains, an area of east-west linear basins and upland peneplains which either have a poor forest or are covered with steppe. Farther inland is an uplifted and warped peneplain at elevations of 3,000 to 6,000 feet, with semiarid vegetation and a sparse population.

The port of Eregli, the ancient Heraclea, is the rail outlet for Ankara. Some two billion tons of good coal are available to the

Mediterranean Fringe

The lowland of eastern and southern Turkey is by far the most important part of the country for agriculture. Here too is the best developed Mediterranean type climate with a summer drought that lasts three to six months and some 20 inches of winter rain. Settlement is particularly dense along the Aegean Sea where numerous drowned valleys, partly filled with alluvium, provide a hospitable habitat.

Three lowlands are of special importance: that behind Izmir, formerly Smyrna, in the west, the Pamphylian Plain around

Antalaya in the center, and the Cilician Plain near Adana at the extreme northeastern corner of the Mediterranean. The route of the Bagdad Railway crosses the Taurus by a difficult pass near Adana.

Wheat and barley are the chief crops. Cotton is grown in each area, but especially in the Cilician Plain where climatic conditions resemble those of Egypt. Grapes for sultana raisins, figs, olives, and opium are famous in the hinterland of Izmir. Some irrigated rice is grown.

Summer day and night temperatures average between 75 and 85°F. in July, with maximum readings to over 100°F. Winters are cool but generally above 50°F. in January; occasionally very strong cold winds sweep out down the plateau.

The natural vegetation of the Taurus Mountains is less luxuriant than along the Black Sea, but excellent deciduous and coniferous forests remain. The tree line is near 8,500 feet, and the lowlands have thorny dry brush up to 2,000 feet. Heavy snow falls in the mountains. In many places along the rugged south coast the forested area is near the shore. Much agricultural land depends either upon the irrigation of dry fields, or the drainage of swamplands. Additional land can be reclaimed but the expense may be uneconomic.

Anatolian Uplands

Inner Turkey is a high basin, in places somewhat mountainous. On three sides lofty ranges keep out moisture-bearing winds. Much of the region has interior drainage into shallow reed-lined lakes or salty playas, but a few streams break through the encircling mountains in antecedent canyons. Toward the west the upland gradually descends to the Aegean hills.

The microcontinental character of Turkey is shown in the wind systems. High summer temperatures cause a semipermanent low pressure area to develop over Anatolia with inblowing winds. Since these lose much of their moisture on the encircling mountains and are further heated on reaching the interior, no rainfall results. Winter brings high pressure with dry outblowing winds, but occasional cyclonic storms contribute a little moisture. The rainfall in most areas is under ten inches. The ground has a light snow cover in winter while in summer the dry winds are accompanied by dust storms. Much of the drier surface has lost its soil cover by deflation and is covered with a desert pavement of pebbles.

These semiarid steppes are the home of nomads who keep sheep and goats. Solidified sour milk, or yoghurt, is a staple item in the diet, made from the milk of sheep, buffaloes, goats, and cows. Wool is the basis of the domestic rug industry, while the angora variety is exported. The nomads move with their flocks into the mountain pasture in summer, and in winter descend to the plains where the sheep and goats are kept in enclosures except when the snow cover permits some grazing. Wheat is grown only in the more moist areas such as alluvial fans and irrigated oases. In places the volcanic soils conserve the limited moisture. On the uplands the wheat is of the hard variety as used for macaroni, while that raised in the coastal lowlands is soft wheat.

Although less important economically than the preceding regions, the Anatolian Uplands are the home of the Turkish race. Although the Anatolian steppe has much less economic significance than the surrounding lowlands, it nevertheless dominates all of Turkey by the quality of the men that it produces. It was thus appropriate that, when the country sought to be independent of foreign pressure, the capital was moved from Constantinople to Ankara.

The city occupies a commanding position on an old volcanic plug.

Armenian Highlands

In easternmost Turkey the Pontus and Taurus systems unite to form the Armenian Highlands, also known as a knot or a crown. The region is an eastward extension of Anatolia but has a different orientation since it contains the headwaters of the Tigris and Euphrates. Mountain systems on both north and south surround a central plateau. To the south are the Kurdistan Mountains, a continuation of the Taurus, while extensions of the Pontus system such as the Karabagh enclose the north. Thus Armenia is a small replica of Anatolia. Elevations are higher and the climate more severe than to the west. Volcanoes and extensive lava flows complicate the configuration. Many passes are snowbound for eight months. In the extreme east is the semiactive volcano Mt. Ararat, 16,916 feet high, near the point where the boundaries of Turkey, Iran, and the Soviet Union join.

Nomadic stock raising is more important than agriculture, with extensive seasonal migration up and down the slopes according to the season.

Chapter 24

SYRIA AND PALESTINE

The eastern shores of the Mediterranean have made a cultural contribution to the western world out of all proportion to their as well as to its hinterland in Southwestern Asia. The name Syria is sometimes applied to the entire region, but the importance of

A desert road in Syria near the Iraq border. (*Pasi, from Three Lions.*)

size or productivity. Jerusalem is a holy city to the Jews, Christians, and Mohammedans. The three great monotheistic religions all arose in the same land. Syria and particularly Palestine have been a focal area from which people and ideas radiated to all of the Mediterranean area, the area south of Lebanon and Mt. Hermon makes it appropriate to add the name of Palestine.

Syria was a province of the old Turkish Empire but, following the First World War, it became a French mandate. The area is 57,900 square miles and the population numbered only 3,630,000 in 1935. Palestine, a British mandate, covers 10,429 square miles and had 1,568,664 people in 1941, of whom two-thirds were Moslems and one-fourth Jews. To the east of the Jordan is the Arab state of Trans-Jordan with an area of roughly 34,740 square miles and an estimated population of 300,000.

The ancient lands of Egypt and Mesopotamia were separated by the barren extension of the Arabian Desert which projects northward through interior Syria almost to the present boundaries of Turkey. Travel across this waste was almost impossible, both on account of aridity and owing to the hostile nomads. The one feasible route led up the Euphrates to its headwaters and thence to the delta of the Nile through Palestine and Syria near the Mediterranean. Thus the journey of Abraham from Ur at the head of the Persian Gulf to Palestine followed a roundabout course to the north through the crescent of grasslands which encircles the northern desert.

Syria and Palestine are small lands, with limited rainfall and without important raw materials. Their population has always been scanty. Much of the importance was due to this corridor position between two historic valleys. Trade routes along the coastal avenue date back to the beginnings of history. The migrations of the Children of Israel are not the only movement of people in this avenue between the desert and the sea. Before them came the Amorites and the Philistines. Other invaders were the Assyrians, Babylonians, Persians, Macedonians, Egyptians, Romans, Saracens, Crusaders, Turks, British, and French.

The general structure and configuration of Syria and Palestine are simple. Next to the Mediterranean is a discontinuous coastal lowland, nowhere more than a few tens of miles in width and in places entirely absent. Sand dunes fringe much of the

shore. On the landward side is a series of hills and mountains from one end of the region to the other. Farther east and still

A Syrian water wheel and the ancient Roman aqueduct at Hama on the Orontes River. (*Decherd, courtesy Presbyterian Board of Foreign Missions.*)

parallel to the coast there is an almost continuous lowland, drained by the Jordan River in the south and by the Orontes River in the north. The uplands of Trans-Jordan and interior Syria lie farther east.

The central valley of the Jordan and Orontes is a rift, probably a downfaulted graben which represents, at least in the topography, a dropped keystone in the elongated arch whose eroded flanks form the hill country on either side of the linear depression. This rift structure continues southward through the Red Sea and

Ethiopia to the linear lakes of central Africa. The faulted structure has been

Orontes to Antioch. Since the rift valley dies out in the north and there is no

The port of Haifa has the best harbor facilities along the coast of Palestine. This is the terminus of pipe lines from the oil fields of Iraq. (*Alice Schalek, from Three Lions.*)

questioned, but the topographic continuity remains.

Two lowland gaps cut around the mountainous barrier of these eastern and western uplands: one is in the south across the desert at the end of the Red Sea, the other is the breach in the north where the Gulf of Alexandretta is the terminus for three overland routes to the Euphrates. One is essentially the path of Alexander the Great via the Syrian Gate east of Alexandretta. Another is followed by the modern Bagdad Railway between the Cilician Plain and Aleppo over the Amanus Mountains, and the third leads up the gorge of the

eastern hill country, the northern passes lead directly to the Mesopotamia plains.

These northern routes cross what is known as the Syrian Saddle, the one low level corridor between the mountains of Turkey to the north and those of Syria on the south. More important than the low elevation of the passes is the fact that some moisture from the Mediterranean can penetrate inland to provide a grassland avenue for nomadic migration to the upper Euphrates. Farther south the intervening desert is increasingly formidable and unsuited for caravans.

The western uplands between the rift valleys of the Orontes and Jordan and the coast have several subdivisions. In the of hills: the narrow valley of the Orontes in the north, the valleys near Latakia and Tropoli, the Litani River, and the fertile

The shore of the Sea of Galilee near Capernaum, with characteristic sparse Mediterranean vegetation on the hillsides. (*Ewing Galloway.*)

north there is the Amanus Range, with heights of over a mile; to the south and bounded by the Orontes River and the Latakia gap are the desolate limestone hills of the Cassius Range. Next come the lower and more important Djebel Ansarije. The rugged mountains of Lebanon rise to 10,000 feet and extend from north of Tripoli to the mouth of the Litani River. Only a few groves of the famed cedars remain. The Palestine section to the south includes the rolling hill lands of Galilee with good soils, the low country of Samaria, and the rugged upland of Judea around Jerusalem. Only a few gaps cross this line

vale of Esdraelon around Nazareth. The width of the uplands is less than 40 miles in most areas.

These uplands lie so close to the sea that coastal plains are narrow or absent. None borders the Amanus, Cassius, or Djebel Ansarije ranges, and the few coastal towns are all river-mouth settlements; Seleucia on the Orontes and Latakia.

The plains of Lebanon are narrow but intensively cultivated and constitute one of the most important agricultural areas along the eastern Mediterranean. Here are Tripoli, Beyrouth, and Sidon, with Tyre just to the south in Galilee. Haifa, the best port along the entire coast, lies in the small Plain of Acre. South of Mt. Carmel is the important Plain of Sharon with the port of

feet below sea level. No major cities lie in the rift valley.

If all the salt in the Dead Sea might be

Street bazaars in the city of Damascus. (*Ewing Galloway*.)

Jaffa, ancient Joppa; and still farther south is the Plain of Philistia.

The central rift valley is bounded by bold escarpments on both east and west. Thus Jerusalem is 4,000 feet above the Dead Sea, 15 miles to the east. Various names apply to specific sections: the linear valley of the Orontes is known as the Chab, the south-flowing Litani occupies the Belka, while the depression occupied by the Jordan is known as El Ghor. The Dead Sea is the lowest part of this depression, 1,297 feet below sea level, but even the Lake of Tiberias or Sea of Galilee is 686

assembled in a mass, it would be four cubic miles in volume.[1] The average salinity is 24 per cent, largely magnesium and sodium chlorides. Assuming that the flow of the Jordan has remained constant, this accumulation would have required 50,000 years. There is considerable evidence that the sea was once larger, and it may have once been a fresh-water lake overflowing to the Mediterranean. Potash and bromine are extracted in two modern plants, based

[1] IRWIN, WILFRED, The Salts of the Dead Sea and River Jordan, *Geographical Journal* (1923), LXI, 428–440.

on solar evaporation. The sea covers 400 square miles and has a depth of 1,310 feet. Sheer precipices border much of the shore.

To the east of the rift are the Kurd Dag, the Anti-Lebanon, and Mt. Hermon, 9,700 feet high, all in Syria, and Gilead and Moab in Trans-Jordan. These mountains have a bold face to the west but merge eastward into the desert plains of northern Arabia. The oases of Aleppo and Damascus are the chief settlements.

Most of Syria and Palestine is dry. Abundant rain falls on the higher west-facing slopes but the amount rapidly declines to the east and south. Thus the coastal Lebanon Mountains receive 45 inches while interior Damascus has 12 inches. Proceeding southward along the coast, Beyrouth has 36 inches, Haifa receives 27 inches, Jaffa 21, and Gaza but 17 inches. All stations in the lee, that is to the east, of elevations are dry. Rainfall penetrates into the interior only where there are gaps in the mountains. This is a Mediterranean area with winter rain from weak cyclonic storms between October and April. Summers are dry and very hot. The natural vegetation is so sparse and the land so overgrazed and carelessly cultivated that the torrential rains have led to serious soil erosion which has laid bare many hillsides.

The ruins of ancient towns in what is now desert, such as Palmyra, and the evidence of former agriculture in areas now desolate suggest cyclic changes in rainfall, but there is no positive evidence to demonstrate that the average temperature and rainfall throughout biblical times were materially different from today. It is probable that some of the glowing accounts of agriculture in early Hebrew days were merely in contrast to the surrounding desert. All the ruined cities of the interior were provided with large reservoirs which demonstrate the need for water then as now. Their importance may have been related to

transit trade along routes later abandoned in favor of others, rather than to local agricultural settlement or a large nomadic

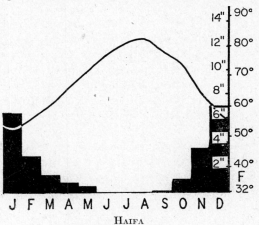

HAIFA
Elevation 30 feet.

population based on notably higher rainfall. Minor changes, lasting even a century, have occurred, but the long-time average probably has remained within narrow limits. Rough correlations between the growth rate of the sequoias and modern rainfall in Jerusalem and in central California suggest that both areas of Mediterranean climate underwent parallel fluctuations. Thus the aridity which sent Joseph into Egypt is recorded in the California sequoias.

Agriculture and grazing are the chief means of livelihood. Spectacular developments have occurred around the Zionist settlements, notably in the Plain of Sharon and the Vale of Esdraelon, but at great expense for drainage of swamps and irrigation. Where water is available "the desert blossoms as the rose." The absence of high mountains with permanent streams makes irrigation a limited possibility. As many hillsides have been entirely denuded of their original vegetation by excessive grazing, soils are thin and stony. The Jordan River might supply water locally, but summer temperatures in the valley are excessively high and the river water is exceptionally high in salts. Rainfall in the plains is almost everywhere marginal for crops, although it fortunately occurs during the winter when evaporation is less.

A great variety of crops is grown. Wheat is the chief grain; olives, figs, grapes, and citrus fruits are widespread; tobacco and cotton are local specialties; and wool is produced in the drier areas. Agricultural imports in Palestine exceed agricultural exports, for the country does not feed itself.

No important minerals are produced other than the salts from the Dead Sea. Hydroelectric power is generated on the Jordan River. An oil pipe line from Iraq has its terminus at the port of Haifa.

The largest city in Palestine is the new Jewish settlement of Tel Aviv, adjoining Jaffa, with 110,000 people in 1935. Other cities in order are Jerusalem, with nearly 100,000, Jaffa, and Haifa.

Palestine presents serious political problems. The Arab world is naturally opposed to any Jewish state, for it would take over what they have regarded as their own land since its conquest from the Romans thirteen hundred years ago. There is also opposition to extensive colonization, for it involves the purchase of considerable parts of the limited agricultural land. On the other hand the Arabs have not developed cultivation to its maximum.

CHAPTER 25

ARABIA

The peninsula of Arabia spreads over an area as large as all of the United States east of the Mississippi, about a million square miles in extent. The country is so dry that there is not a single permanent river. It has been said that, up to the First World War, Arabia contained the largest unexplored and unmapped area in the world outside polar lands. Much has since been done, but someting of this condition may still be true.

Arabia is dry, but not all of it is lifeless desert. Poor grazing grounds alternate with sandy wastes. Higher elevations in the southern corners have a good rainfall. Almost none of the plains has enough moisture for unirrigated crops. Although there are no permanent streams, an extensive system of wadies carries water after the occasional rains. Even though the surface is dry for much of the year, these watercourses usually have an underground flow at shallow depths. Many of the oases are along such wadies, with small irrigated fields supplied from wells.

The total population of Arabia is unknown, but out of a possible seven million people, actual nomads or Bedouins probably number less than a million. Despite their small numbers, grazing is the only use for the great bulk of the region. Most of the remaining people live around the margins of the peninsula where rainfall is slightly higher and irrigated crops may be raised. Conflict between the free wanderers of the desert and fixed settlers in the oases has been characteristic since the earliest times, as was the warfare between the dwellers of Arabia as a whole and the people of the more favored lands of Palestine, Syria, and Iraq.

In general terms, Arabia is a gently tilted plateau which slopes eastward from a divide near the western edge where elevations average 5,000 feet. Numerous irregularities in the interior interrupt this simplicity, in part lava flows and granite peaks to 6,000 feet. It is thus more correct to speak of two general slopes, one to the northeast and the other to the southeast. High mountains rise in the southeastern and southwestern corners.

Much of the geology resembles that of Egypt, as does the climate. Were it not for the presence of the Red Sea, Arabia might be grouped with the Sahara. Asia would thus begin with the Persian Gulf which marks a more distinctive geographic boundary than does the Red Sea.

A number of regional names need to be kept in mind. Along the western coast is the narrow Tehama, or lowland. East of it is the hilly divide or Hejaz which includes a long and important area with Mecca in the center. The central plateau is the Nejd, the fountainhead of the Arab race. Interior Arabia has two great areas of sandy desert: the Rub al Khali in the southeast and the Nefud in the center, connected by a narrow strip of sand through the east, known as the Dahna. These are areas of deflation hollows, wind-scoured in the underlying sandstone, and exceptionally large dunes. Following the winter rains there is usually enough vegetation for some grazing. The Syrian Desert is a northward continuation of geographical Arabia. In the southwest are the highlands of Yemen, up to 8,924 feet, while in the southeast are

Hot seas and gulfs border Arabia on three sides. Temperatures along the Red Sea are so high that they have been de-

The arid mountains of the Hadhramaut contain surprisingly modernistic cities. This is a view of Gattam, unknown to the western world until recent years. (*Helfritz, from Black Star.*)

those of Oman, with a maximum elevation of 9,902 feet. Between them and back from the coast is Hadhramaut. Two other distinctions are between Arabia Deserta in the center, and Arabia Felix, the "happy" area with more water, in the south including the highlands of Yemen.

Arabia has had a diverse political history. Since the end of Turkish rule during the First World War the bulk of the peninsula has been a part of the Kingdom of Saudi Arabia with its capital in the interior at Riyadh or Riad. Yemen and Oman are independent countries. Aden is a British Crown colony and includes a vaguely defined area in the hinterland.

scribed as "hell with the sun blazing down." Although these bodies of water might be expected to yield some moisture despite their relatively narrow width, summer temperatures in the interior are even higher so that rainfall occurs only with local convectional storms or on windward mountain slopes. The monsoon circulation of southern Asia touches southern Arabia in summer, but moist winds never come to the peninsula from the Indian Ocean; instead there are dry winds from Ethiopia. Aden has only two inches of rainfall a year. Occasional cyclonic storms from the Mediterranean cross the north in winter but have been robbed of most of this moisture by the uplands of Syria and Palestine. Winter temperatures drop below freezing when Polar Continental air masses from the

goats, horses, and camels. Wool and hides are thus major exports.

The city of Mecca is the shrine of

The central shrine of Mohammedanism in Mecca is the ancient building known as the Kaaba, always covered with carpet, in one corner of which is the Black Stone which is kissed by all pilgrims. (*Black Star.*)

Soviet Union occasionally extend to Arabia, especially when drawn southward in the rear of passing cyclonic storms. Summer temperatures of over 100°F. are common, with a record of 114°F. along the coast of Oman.

Fixed settlement, which depends upon agriculture, in turn rests on local water supplies, either from springs, wells, or reservoirs. A few wadies have ground water sufficiently close to the surface to permit crops to grow. The highlands of Yemen and Oman are exceptions, for they have passable rainfall. Wheat, barley, and millet are grown in the larger oases; tobacco and dates are widespread. Coffee is raised in Yemen behind Mocha. Grazing is the principal means of livelihood, with sheep,

Mohammedanism, and the surrounding 100 square miles are closed to all who are not followers of the prophet. Five times a day the 220,000,000 Mohammedans of Asia and Africa turn toward the city in prayer. Every year a quarter of a million people make a pilgrimage to the ancient stone building known as the Kaaba with its Black Stone. Mecca lies 45 miles from its Red Sea port of Jidda, and about 250 miles south of Medina, Arabia's second sacred city. Medina is the terminus of the Hejaz Railway north to Trans-Jordan and Damascus.

Two key cities command the entrance to the Red Sea, French Djibouti on the African side and British Aden near the corner of Arabia. Aden receives little trade from its immediate hinterland but is an entrepôt for commerce along the coast. Salt is evaporated from sea water for export.

Spectacular petroleum operations have brought eastern Arabia into prominence, especially the island of Bahrein. The oil field concession is held by the Standard Oil Company of California. The production on Bahrein reached 7,000,000 barrels a year just before the Second World War, while at the near-by Dammar field on the mainland the output was nearly 6,000,000 barrels.

CHAPTER 26

IRAQ

Mesopotamia occupies a structural basin between the plateau of Iran and the table-land of Arabia. As recently as the glacial period, the Persian Gulf extended to the north of Bagdad, some 400 miles inland from the present shore line. The southern half of the area is thus a delta plain. Farther north the sediments are older and the topography is hilly. In the extreme north are the rugged hills and mountains of the Taurus and Kurdistan systems, drained by the upper Tigris, while to the east are parts of the Zagros Mountains of Iran.

Modern Iraq, essentially the valley of the Tigris and the Euphrates, also spreads westward into the Syrian Desert beyond the limits of lowland Mesopotamia. Most of the people and activity cluster around the waterways, especially in the south where the two main rivers unite 100 miles from the gulf to form the Shatt al Arab.

The Tigris and Euphrates may be likened to the Amu Darya and Syr Darya, or to the Nile. Each rises in well-watered mountains and flows across a desert to a growing delta. In southern Iraq, the Tigris and Euphrates have a low gradient, lose more water by evaporation and diversion for irrigation than they receive from tributaries, and are overloaded with silt. Although Bagdad is 500 miles from the sea by river, its elevation is only 113 feet. Forty miles to the west, the Euphrates is only 25 feet higher.

As a result of this low gradient, the rivers have inadequate carrying power and deposition chokes the channel. Natural levees have been built and in many areas

the rivers flow slightly above the level of the surrounding land. Artificial levees further protect the countryside from all

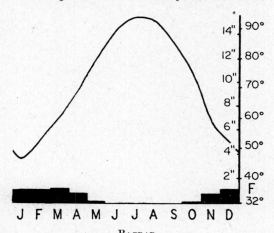

BAGDAD
Elevation, 220 feet; average temperature, 71.9°F.; total precipitation, 6.6 inches.

but the highest floods, and it is simple to construct irrigation canals by which to lead the water away from the rivers. The land between the rivers, that is, the true "Mesopotamia," is thus capable of easy irrigation from either side.

In northern Iraq the rivers flow in normal valleys, rather than on a plain. Diversion canals are less easily constructed and irrigation is on a small scale. Limited strips of flood plain in the north replace the broad lowlands of the south.

Climatic conditions resemble those elsewhere in Southwestern Asia. Rain occurs only during the winter months and is largely the result of passing cyclonic storms. June to October are rainless. Since the elevations of northern Syria are lower than farther south, there is a pathway across the Syrian Saddle for some moisture from the taries in contrast to the Euphrates which follows a desert course farther west with no near-by mountains. The Iranian tributaries

The Tigris River at Bagdad, with a native kurfa in the foreground. (*Ewing Galloway*.)

Mediterranean. The lowlands of northern Iraq thus receive 10 to 15 inches of precipitation a year and the mountains twice that, while the south, cut off from moisture-bearing winds, has half those figures or less.

Much of the water in the rivers comes not from local rainfall over the plains but from the more abundant orographic precipitation in the Taurus and Kurdistan mountains of Armenian Turkey, and the Zagros and other mountains of western Iran. Since the Tigris flows near the base of the Zagros, it receives numerous tribu-

of the Tigris have built great alluvial fans somewhat comparable to those at the foot of The Himalaya along the Ganges and Indus, but the rainfall is too low to permit agricultural utilization.

The Tigris is the more important river for navigation and can be used by small steamships to above Bagdad. The Euphrates has a shifting sand-choked course and is too shallow for modern navigation. Since it receives few tributaries from across the plain and loses water by evaporation, its volume diminishes toward its mouth. Despite its unsuitability for traffic, the

Euphrates forms a direct route from Bagdad to Aleppo and has been an important trade route for centuries. The adjust themselves to scanty and periodic moisture. Trees are entirely absent except along the streams or in the more humid

The holy city of Kazemain near Bagdad with the domes of its minarets covered with leaf gold. Earthquake effects are visible in many of the buildings. (*Ewing Galloway*.)

Tigris is more subject to floods; its length is about 1,150 miles while the Euphrates measures 1,800 miles. So great is the load of the combined rivers that the delta is growing seaward at the rate of a mile and a half per century.

Summer temperatures are frequently above 100°F. and have reached 123°F. in Bagdad where the August average is 93°F. Since the humidity is low, the sensible heat is slightly less than these figures imply. In contrast, January at Bagdad has a mean of 49°F. and a low of 19°F. The average rainfall is 7 inches, with a range of 1 to 22 inches.

Amid such aridity, natural vegetation is limited to the few specialized forms that can upper mountains. Where Mediterranean moisture reaches the north there is a steppe grassland. Elsewhere the natural cover is that of the desert.

Evaporation from the soil into the thirsty air removes moisture from the surface layer where it has been lifted by capillary action. The water evaporates but its dissolved mineral water remains behind to form a crust of salts and alkali. Large areas are thus unsuited for cultivation. Irrigation often intensifies this condition, especially where the added water rises to the surface and evaporates rather than draining into the subsoil. Little natural drainage is possible where the river flows above the level of the adjoining plains. Swamps occupy extensive areas in the lower part of each valley.

Wandering nomads find a meager exist-

The west wall of ancient Ninevah looking toward the traditional tomb of Jonah. The city lies on the left bank of the Tigris and was the capital of the Assyrian Empire. (*Ewing Galloway.*)

ence in the moister plains, but their life is usually anchored to some oasis, possibly a mountainous area that receives more rain. Such is the case with the Sinjar Range which rises to 4,000 feet. The present political boundaries of Iraq exclude parts of the mountains on the east and north which once furnished summer pasture grounds, so that traditional migrations are altered.

The desert itself is brown and lifeless for most of the year and becomes green for only a few weeks after the winter rains. Nomads from the Arabian plains and from the mountains of Iran and Armenia have invaded the oases of Mesopotamia repeatedly throughout history. Desert wells are valuable property, and their control

has often led to warfare. Nomadism is on the decline, for the government policy here as elsewhere throughout Asia is to encourage fixed settlements.

Settled agriculturalists require dependable water supplies for their fields, so that they are confined to the vicinity of rivers and canals. In the north the rainfall permits some unirrigated crops.

The green land of the farmer is in striking contrast to the brown land of the shepherd. The sharp line between the outermost irrigated field and the desert separates two distinct cultures. About 90 per cent of the people live along rivers or canals, so that the cultivated area occupies but a small fraction of the country as a whole. The 100-mile course of the Shatt al Arab around Basra has by far the densest population.

Although Mesopotamia has many climatic disadvantages, it is on the whole more attractive than the neighboring lands of Arabia or Iran. Since the beginnings of recorded history, the valley has been important. Egypt is older but scarcely more significant. Three thousand years before the Christian era this was the home of the Sumerians. Later came the Semites and then the Hittites. Arab peoples now occupy the land.

This history is long and complicated. In general, two areas stand out: Assyria in the north and Babylonia in the south. Assyria occupied the arid and largely unirrigated land in the foothills of the Kurdistan Mountains. Ninevah, on the upper Tigris and near modern Mosul, was its ancient capital, important as the starting point for the caravan route through the grasslands to the Mediterranean and Egypt. Babylonia or Chaldea in the south centered either around the city of Babylon or at Ur. Its livelihood was based upon irrigation in the rich alluvial plains of the Tigris and Euphrates. It is possible that Ur is the oldest city in the world, for archaeological discoveries appear to push its date back to 6,000 years ago. Babylonia probably includes the legendary site of the Garden of Eden. The topography of the north provided good townsites, free from flood, while in the south there were few high sites for cities along the rivers, and large areas are inundated after each flood. Since extensive irrigation works call for effective government supervision, it seems probable that this need for cooperation was a factor in the rise of ancient civilizations.

Iraq's modern history began in 1920 when the three former Turkish vilayets of Basra, Bagdad, and Mosul were made a British mandate. Seven years later Great Britain renounced its mandatory rights and recognized the country as an independent kingdom. The area is about 143,250 square miles and the population in 1942 was estimated at 5,000,000.

Agriculture has always been the basis of the general economy. The alluvial soil is exceptionally fertile and, where irrigation is available, crops are dependable. Unirrigated fields, limited to the more humid north or areas where ground water lies close to the surface, commonly experience drought and crop failure at least one year in four or five. The irrigation system is complex and requires extensive government supervision. Many of the projects, both ancient and modern, involve elaborate canal systems. Where these become useless, large areas must be abandoned. Widespread ruins of canals and towns in what is now desert do not necessarily imply climate changes. Irrigation systems may fail to operate through such causes as the destruction of diversion works in the rivers, the erosion of river beds below the intake level of the canals, breaks in the canal systems where carried on aqueducts or hillsides, accumulation of silt in the canals so that their capacity is reduced, or any one of many political causes. Excess silting was apparently a common reason for abandonment.

Modern irrigation works have greatly added to the cultivable area. Unlike the ancient canals which were filled only during the flood stage of the rivers, these works involve a dam which raises the water level so that there is a dependable supply at all seasons. It has been estimated that the area which it may be possible to irrigate is as much as 6,000,000 acres, of which less than 1,000,000 are now supplied with water.

Dates are the most important crop with an estimated 30,000,000 trees, one-third of all the date palms in the world. These form the country's chief agricultural export, second only to oil. The chief date area is along the Shatt al Arab, especially in the vicinity of Basra where there is a continuous oasis for 100 miles, one to two miles in width. This area leads the world in the export trade in dates, for it furnishes three-fourths of the supply. There is an old saying that date palms grow with their heads in the fire and their feet in the water.

Barley is the safest winter cereal, usually raised on unirrigated fields as it grows in a short season and demands a minimum of rainfall, but wheat is also grown. These dry crops of northern Iraq are harvested in April and May. Irrigated rice and corn are grown in the south and harvested in the fall. Opium is an important crop in the south.

A million acres are suitable for cotton, which is as large an area as utilized in Egypt. The quality is equally high. The original stimulus for the growth came from German interests when that country was interested in the Berlin to Bagdad Railway and its associated economic and political implications.

Iraq's wool is among the best. It is the chief item in the economy of unirrigated areas with less than 10 inches of rainfall.

The exploitation of petroleum has materially influenced the life of Iraq and has provided a large revenue to the government. Production dates from 1927. Much of the production is obtained in the vicinity of Mosul, near ancient Ninevah in the north, especially from the Kirkuk, Naft Khaneh, and Quiarah fields. The normal production just prior to the Second World War amounted to 30,000,000 barrels. A pipe line extends eastward 1,150 miles to the Mediterranean, with terminals at Haifa in Palestine and at Tripoli in Syria. Oil seepages and burning gas jets have been known since early centuries and may account for Biblical references to the "burning firey furnace."

Two cities dominate Iraq: the ancient trade center of Bagdad on the central Tigris and the modern seaport of Basra. Mosul in the oil fields is third in importance.

Geographic regions closely parallel natural conditions, with the major contrasts between the alluvial plain or ancient delta in the south, with its irrigation possibilities, and the dry-farming hilly land of the south. The mountainous areas of Kurdistan and Zagros in the extreme north and east provide still other environments.

CHAPTER 27

IRAN

Among the countries of Southwestern Asia, Iran, formerly known as Persia, ranks second to Arabia in size and second to Turkey in importance. Like the latter, it is in the midst of transition. Many of the cultural changes are associated with the development of improved communications such as the 865-mile Trans-Iranian Railway from the Persian Gulf to the Caspian Sea. This route was completed in 1938 and became a major supply line for military shipments from the United States to the Soviet Union during the Second World War.

Iran and Turkey have further parallels in their surface configuration. Each has encircling mountains on the north and south which close to the east but provide easier access from the west. In both cases there is little room for a coastal plain, and high plateau basins occupy the arid interior. The mountains of northern Iran are the Elburz and Khorassan, a continuation of the Pontus to the west and the Hindu Kush system on the east. Western and southern Iran is bordered by the Zagros, Fars, and Makran mountains.

All these ranges are part of the dual system that extends from the Aegean Sea to the Pamirs and eastward around Tibet. Enclosed within the mountains are successively the plateaus of Anatolia, Armenia, and Iran. The pattern is somewhat like a giant compound hourglass, on its side, with its constrictions corresponding to the Armenian and Pamir knots. Iran is part of the great Alpine-Himalaya fold system, with a series of Paleozoic and Mesozoic sedimentary formations laid down in an ancient sea known as Tethys.

The Elburz are a formidable barrier. They almost bar access from the Caspian littoral to interior Iran except at the west where a road leads to the port of Pahlevi near Resht, and in the east where the railway crosses to Bandar Shah. The highest summit is Mt. Demavend, 18,549 feet. The Elburz are continued eastward in the lower and wider Khorassan Mountains which become the Hindu Kush in Afghanistan. Where level land and irrigation water are available, as around Meshed, there is a dense population; elsewhere the land forms restrict settlement.

The Zagros Mountains along the southwest of the Iranian plateau are a series of high parallel ranges and longitudinal valleys which are the continuation of the Kurdistan in upper Iraq. One elevation reaches 12,850 feet, but 8,000 is the general height of the ridge crests. These mountains are a succession of anticlines and synclines, somewhat in Appalachian style. The streams flow in a trellis pattern, with broad valleys along the axis of the folds and narrow antecedent canyons at right angles. Belts of high mountain meadows and forests alternate with dry lowland valleys. For centuries, shepherds have moved up and down the slopes with the season. This vertical nomadism is known as transhumance. The humid Zagros are succeeded by the drier Fars and equally arid Makran next to India.

The interior is by no means a single basin, for low ranges divide it into a series

407

of enclosures, tectonic in origin. Occasional violent earthquakes indicate that movement is still in process. Several volcanoes

Indus is a coherent natural region although it is not a political unit. During occasional torrential rains and when the snows in the

A mud-walled village amid the barren uplands of Iran. (*Alice Schalek, from Three Lions.*)

are semiactive. Within the enclosing mountain rims, slopes lead inward rather than outward. Each basin has its terminal salt lake or playa flat toward which the withering streams make their way. The largest of the interior basins is Seistan, on the Afghanistan and Baluchistan border. The elevation here is 2,000 feet whereas most other parts of the plateau are twice or three times that height. Two large lakes lie at the extreme east and west of Iran, Lakes Helmand and Urumlyeh, each of them a hundred miles in length. Since runoff is usually inadequate, the load of the streams is deposited en route so that huge alluvial fans encircle the dissected mountains. These gravel slopes are exceptionally large and where they merge they form a continuous piedmont. The interrupted character of the plateau is especially pronounced toward the east. The entire area between the Tigris and the

mountains melt, thousands of dry watercourses are filled with water and fill the innumerable shallow depressions of inner Iran. Few rivers on the plateau have a year-round flow to a terminal lake, so that they are not a dependable source of water for summer irrigation.

The deserts of Iran are among the world's driest. In the eastern area known as Lut are exceptionally large dunes, some of them with a height of 700 feet, as compared with the maximum of 600 feet in the Taklamakan and 500 feet in the Sahara. The Desert of Lut is so dry that in parts there are almost no erosion channels to indicate that water ever runs over the surface. Great deposits of wind-blown silt are associated with these dunes, but since they are stratified and hence laid down in an ancient lake, they cannot be called true loess. In July a temperature of 110°F. was recorded with a relative humidity of 4.2 per cent. Seistan is noted for its "Wind of 120 days" which blows from the north and northwest starting in May; velocities reach 70 miles per hour.

Most of Iran is a boulder-strewn and wind-swept desert. Nearly two-thirds of it is so dry that no drainage escapes to the sea. After the winter rains there may be a carpet of short grass and bright flowers, but this soon withers and there is little steppe grass for pasturage. Much of the interior has but 4 or 5 inches of rain a year, for example Isfahan with 5 inches. Even Bushire on the Persian Gulf receives only 11 inches. The rainfall at Teheran is 9.3 inches.

All of this moisture comes from weak cyclonic storms that invade the plateau from the west several times a month in winter. The amount and distribution are very erratic. Along the Persian Gulf half the annual precipitation may fall in a single day. Mountain slopes in the path of moisture-bearing winds have a snow cover, but there is enough rain for forests in only a few locations. The one exception is the north slope of the Elburz opposite the Caspian whence north winds bring moisture from the sea. Here the precipitation is 50 inches and more, and there is a luxuriant forest. In striking contrast, the south slopes are barren. The Caspian coastal plain is too wet, and, although fertile and productive, parts of it are unhealthy on account of the swamps and malaria. Immediately to the south, in the lee of the Elburz range, the plateau plain is an arid waste where all cultivation depends upon irrigation.

Temperatures are lowered by the altitude, but the bright sun keeps thermometer readings comparable to those in Iraq. Thus Teheran has a July average of 85°F. and a maximum of 110°F. Skies are clear most of the year. Strong winds, usually from the north in winter and south in summer, carry clouds of dust and make travel impossible. It is possible that the highest temperatures on earth may occur

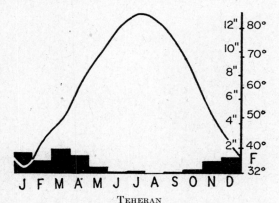

TEHERAN
Elevation, 4,002 feet; average temperature, 61.7°F.; total precipitation, 9.3 inches.

in the deserts of Iran, particularly in Lut, although no observations yet exceed the record 136.4°F. of Azizia in north Africa.

Agriculture depends upon irrigation, and this in turn involves a unique system of tunnels, even ten or twenty miles in length, which bring water from distant sources. These aqueducts are known as kanats, or karez, widely copied through Southwestern Asia and even in Sinkiang. Many of them date back for centuries. The construction of a kanat usually begins on a gentle slope and gradually works underground in the direction of the dry river bed or alluvial fan where it is hoped to find water. The tunnel is only two or three feet in dimensions and has a slope just sufficient to carry water. At necessary intervals a shaft leads to the surface through which the debris is removed. When the source of water is reached, lateral tunnels are dug to increase the collection.

Many villages are lined up along these underground streams, with wells every 20 yards. As many as a thousand wells may tap the same tunnel. Where the kanat comes to the surface the stream is divided

The courtyard of a caravansary with its stables for camels on the ground floor and rooms for travelers above. (*Ewing Galloway.*)

One of the principal streets of Teheran, with the Elburz Mountains in the background. (*S. F. Mack, courtesy Presbyterian Board of Foreign Missions.*)

into irrigation ditches. These elaborate systems are expensive and require frequent attention. Where they fall into disrepair, several villages and extensive fields may have to be abandoned.

Cereals and other crops raised in winter are irrigated after the rains, from March till June, while summer crops require water from May till September. Dry farming is possible only at elevations over 6,000 feet where precipitation is greater and evaporation less. Yields on dry fields are usually only tenfold but may be double that amount if the late rains are abundant. Wheat, barley, and rye are sown after the first rains, which usually fall between November and January. Summer crops are millet, corn, cotton, and rice, with most of the latter grown along the Caspian plain. Tobacco is widely grown, and opium is an important cash crop and export. Persian silk was famous three and four centuries ago but is unimportant today. All crop yields are low, and methods might be improved. The ten million date palms grow largely along the Persian Gulf, and the dates are raised for export to England. Vineyards are chiefly located in the interior.

Persian carpets are world famous but rank only a poor second to oil in the export trade. They are made on hand looms in small shops or homes.

Automobile roads and railways have provided avenues for the modernization of ancient Persia. These include new roads from Bagdad through Hamadan to Teheran, from Teheran across the Elburz to Pahlevi, and eastward to Meshed, plus a network in the interior. The pride of Iran is the rail line from Bandar Shapur on the Persian Gulf to Bandar Shah on the Caspian. Other lines at right angles to this lead entirely across the north of the country, from the Soviet Union to the Afghan frontier.

The oil fields of Iran are even more productive than those of Iraq. The normal prewar yield reached 86,250,000 barrels. Most of this was obtained from the Haft Kel and Mesjid-i-sulaiman fields near the head of the Persian Gulf. There is also an important yield at Naft-i-shah opposite the Iraq fields. The production is controlled by the Anglo-Iranian Oil Company. No other natural resources are produced in quantity, although a variety of minerals are known to be present at least in small amounts. A poor grade of coal is mined in the Elburz Mountains north of Teheran.

Teheran, the capital, has over 200,000 people and is a relatively modern city. It has a splendid winter climate with clear skies and exhilarating frosty air; summers are hot but the air is dry. In contrast is Isfahan whose ancient splendors are such that the Persians write "This is half the world." Its population numbers about 100,000. In the northwest is Tabriz with some 200,000. The population of all Iran was estimated as 15,055,155 in 1942, in an area of 628,000 square miles.

CHAPTER 28

AFGHANISTAN

Afghanistan has close relations with both India and the Soviet Union and so might with some justice be grouped with either Russia. The country has little to invite conquest for itself but it is a potential highway from India to northern Asia and

The capital city of Kabul lies amid the barren highlands of Afghanistan. (*Pix.*)

realm, but its climatic and cultural ties with Iran are such that it is placed with Southwestern Asia. This is the easternmost limit of Mediterranean type winter rain, although the amount is very low. Elevations are higher than in Iran, but land forms and land use are similar.

The world significance of Afghanistan has been as a buffer between Britain and Europe. On its two borders are rival imperialisms and ideologies. Thus the wise and cruel Amir Abdur Rahman, who ruled this country in the last two decades of the nineteenth century, wrote in his autobiography, "This poor goat, Afghanistan, is a victim at which a lion on one side and a terrible bear from the other side are staring and ready to swallow at the first opportunity afforded to them." Despite this fact, the Afghans have maintained their independence with reckless courage. The tribes along India's northwest frontier have given Britain more trouble for a century than any other people along the Indian border. Over the centuries the Afghans have emerged from their mountain fortress to conquer Iran, Bokhara, and Baluchistan, as well as parts of India. The threat to Afghanistan's freedom has been greatest on the north, for the country offers easier access on that side.

Afghanistan has an area of 250,000 square miles, about the size of Texas, and the population exceeds 12,000,000. Several racial divisions are represented, Mongol, Turkish, Indo-Iranian, and others, but nearly all the people are Mohammedans. Different customs, traditions, languages, and ways of life, such as the agriculturalist and pastoralist, all make national unity difficult.

The Hindu Kush extend westward from the Pamirs through central Afghanistan and form a mountainous backbone some 150 miles in width. These magnificent mountains rise to three miles and more. Most passes are closed by snow in winter. Vegetation tends to be more luxuriant on north slopes. To the north are the plains of Bactria with one of the ancient highways from China to Europe. This is an excellent grazing ground, traditionally visited in summer by Uzbek and Khirgiz shepherds with their sheep and horses. Prior to the war, over a million fine karakul lambskins were exported each year. Even locally they sell for $10 each. Conditions resemble the piedmont lowlands of Soviet Middle Asia. In the southwest of Afghanistan are the desert basins of Registan and Seistan, which cover a quarter of the country. In the east are fertile valleys around Kabul and Kandahar, famous for their fruit,

wheat, and rice. This is the most densely inhabited region. Most of the region lies above 4,000 feet. The rainfall is below 15 inches in all settled areas.

Where irrigation is possible, two crops a year may be grown. Wheat and barley are raised in the winter, while millet, corn, sorghum, rice, and tobacco are summer crops. Fruit is an important part of the diet and includes apples, pears, peaches, apricots, cherries, grapes, and figs. Grazing is widespread, with fat-tailed sheep as a large source of wealth.

The lack of topographic coherence makes political unity difficult. There is a large measure of cultural conservatism, but industries and social reforms are making headway. It is a measure of Afghanistan's isolation that foreigners are known as "feringi," the name used by the Turks to characterize the Crusaders. Indian railways on the southern border and Soviet lines in the north compete for the limited foreign trade. The leading exports are wool and skins including karakul lamb, while imports consist of textiles and other manufactured goods.

Automobile roads lead into the capital of Kabul from Iran via Herat and Kandahar with connections from Baluchistan, from Peshwar in India by way of the 40-mile Khyber Pass, and from Termez in the Soviet Union by two roads over the Hindu Kush, one of which crosses the Shibar Pass at 10,500 feet. Kabul has a population of about 200,000, while Herat numbers over 100,000.

Oil occurs near the northern and western borders; other minerals appear unimportant.

Archaeological explorations are just beginning but give promise of striking discoveries. Many of the ancient art objects are of great beauty.

CHAPTER 29

INDIA'S PHYSICAL FOUNDATIONS

In official British parlance, the Indian Empire is often described as the subcontinent of India. In many ways it is an island

Three girls of Travancore, south India. (*Courtesy Indian State Railways.*)

by itself. So far as effective intercourse is concerned, The Himalaya might almost as well be the frozen Arctic Ocean. No part of Eurasia is so detached as this realm. India is as big and as populous as all of western Europe, and its claim to continentality is better than that of Europe. Devoid of good harbors or important near neighbors, India remained isolated until modern times. Even today, no railway crosses its borders.

Extraordinary physical contrasts characterize India. It contains one of the wettest spots on earth as well as one of the driest; the highest and largest of all mountain ranges border vast river lowlands; dense rain forests contrast with lifeless desert; in some areas the problem of agriculture is too much water while elsewhere there is too little. All of these are India. Unlike Japan, with its pattern of microscopic detail, the topographic features of India group themselves into simple major units. Local contrasts exist but are subordinate.

India has charm and glamour, but it also has poverty and problems. The cultural landscape everywhere reflects the intensity of man's quest for livelihood in a land of uncertain rainfall. Wherever the environment permits, crops are grown to the limit. Here is monsoon Asia at its climax, with a seasonal rhythm of rainfall which affects all of man's activities. Although the average rainfall is generally high, its effectiveness is restricted by high temperatures and high evaporation. Surprisingly large parts of the subcontinent are semiarid and even desert.

One of the great problems of India is that it appears to have too many people; it scarcely seems possible that so many can live on so little and have much opportunity for the obviously needed increase in standards of living. The population increased between 1931 and 1941 by 50 million, to reach a total of 388 million in all India. How long can this continue?

India, like China, is not merely a place on the map; here is a rich culture, the product of centuries of contemplative living. Whatever the political future of this land, it has a notable contribution to the trade and civilization of the rest of the world.

Within India are 1,808,679 square miles of mountains, hills, and plains. From the

Geology and Land Forms

Within the Indian Realm are three entirely different areas, unlike in geological

The tomb of Itmaduddaula at Agra is one of the finest examples of Mogul architecture. (*Courtesy Indian State Railways*.)

borders of Iran eastward to the frontier of China is about 2,300 miles, while from the southern tip of the peninsula to northern Kashmir is 2,000 miles. The Tropic of Cancer cuts midway between north and south, but all of India south of the mountain wall is essentially tropical.

The Indian Realm as here considered includes Ceylon but not Burma, which has been separated from the Indian Empire since 1935 and is placed with Southeastern Asia.

history, surface configuration, and utilization. These are the mountain wall of The Himalaya and other encircling ranges; the plains of Hindustan drained by the Indus, Ganges, and Brahmaputra; and the dissected plateau in the peninsula to the south.

In the whole of peninsular India there is not a single marine fossil, except in marginal strips that show local sea invasions. Much of the country is underlain by a basement complex of highly metamorphic schist and gneiss, with some granitic intrusions. Preserved within long troughs or depressions among these crystallines are

Despite their vast antiquity, these sediments are undisturbed and testify to the stability of much of India since the Pre-

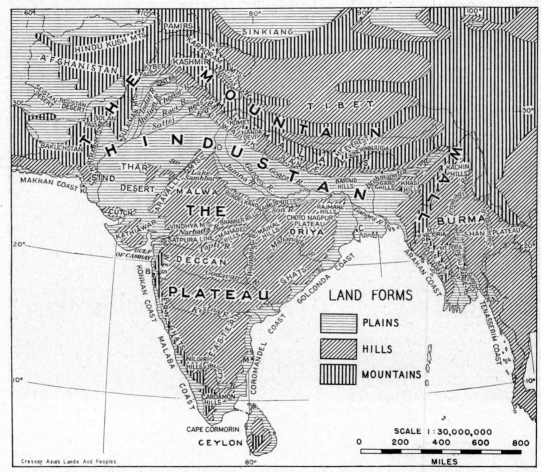

India's plains are chiefly in the lowlands of the Indus, Ganges, and Brahmaputra. Most of the peninsula is hilly, while mountains enclose the country on the north.

altered sediments, now phyllites, slates, and marbles. From the latter is secured beautiful building stone, such as used by the Moguls in the Taj Mahal. All of these are Archeozoic in age. Overlying them, and apparently Proterozoic, are great thicknesses of limestone, shale, and sandstone.

Cambrian. Thus the peninsula is one of the great positive areas of Asia, a massif which has remained undeformed and above sea level.

Near the close of the Paleozoic, sandstones and shales accumulated in freshwater basins. Along with these were beds of coal, especially in the northeast. Permian glacial evidences in latitude 17°N., and in the Salt Range, latitude 33°N., present un-

90 feet thick. Basalt and andesite are typical, with rhyolite in some places. Associated ash and tuff are present, as well

The railway from Bombay to Poona climbs a 3 per cent grade to rise up the escarpment of the Western Ghats. *(Courtesy Indian State Railways.)*

solved problems, for the tillite in the latter area contains boulders whose sources lay 750 miles to the south.

The latest important episode in peninsular geology began in the Cretaceous and continued into the Tertiary when enormous lava flows buried much of the western area. Despite much erosion around the margins, the area still covered is 200,000 square miles. The maximum thickness is unknown, but near Bombay are exposures of at least 6,000 feet. Separate layers of these fissure flows are from 6 to

as interbedded sediments. These horizontal flows are responsible for many flat-topped hills and dissected escarpments.

No satisfactory term describes the area south of the Indus and Ganges lowland. Not all of it is actually peninsular, nor is it all a dissected plateau. The term Deccan is variously used; by some it is restricted to the area of lava flows in the west; by others the term is applied to all the upland south of the Satpura line, to be described later; again it may embrace the entire area below Hindustan. It will here be used for the triangular plateau part of the peninsula, as bounded on the north by the Satpura line.

continuation in the Cardamom Hills at the tip of the Deccan.

The Deccan slopes eastward, so that the

The Gersoppa or Jog Falls, near Shimoga in Mysore, have a height of 860 feet. (*Courtesy Indian State Railways.*)

Escarpments border each side of the Deccan. On the west are the Western Ghats with elevations of half a mile and more. These one-sided mountains rise abruptly from the Arabian Sea, but descend gradually to the plateau on the east. The steep-sided valleys facing the ocean are in the same stage of development as the much deeper valleys of The Himalaya, suggesting that the elevation of the Western Ghats was simultaneous with the uplift of the great mountain wall of Tibet. The Eastern Ghats are a discontinuous line of hills which mark the inner margin of the coastal plain; most elevations are under 3,000 feet. These bordering mountains meet in the south to form the Nilgiri Hills, with their

three main rivers have their source in the Western Ghats. From south to north these are the Cauvery, Kistna, and Godavari. Where they cross the Eastern Ghats the valleys are narrow and the current swift; elsewhere the rivers are near base level and flow through broad open valleys in late maturity. The most noticeable topographic features are the flat-topped hills and scarped edges of the lava flows or horizontal sandstones. Otherwise structure does not notably influence configuration.

The northern margin of the Deccan is less definite. The principal break is the Satpura line between the westward-flowing Narbada and Tapti rivers. This elevation continues eastward into the Maikal Range and the uplands of Chota Nagpur. North and south of the Satpura Range are the Vindhya and Ajanta lines, so that the northern edge of the Deccan is a threefold zone.

Besides the Deccan there are two other hilly sections in the peninsular upland: Malwa in the northwest and Oriya in the east. The former drains north to the Ganges and is limited on the west by the very ancient Aravalli Range which nearly reaches Delhi. Oriya includes the rugged hills and valleys in the basin of the Mahanadi River, including the Chota Nagpur highlands. Although close to Calcutta and well supplied with coal and iron, Oriya is one of the least populous and most backward areas south of the mountains.

Coastal plains border both the Arabian Sea and the Bay of Bengal. On the west, level land is narrow and discontinuous, for in places the Ghats come to the sea as cliffs. The east coast plain continues from the Ganges to Cape Comorin, and around Ceylon. The width is 75 miles or less, and conditions of land use and settlement somewhat resemble the Ganges Delta. South of Bombay the littoral is known as the Konkan and Malabar coasts, whereas on the east are the Coromandel and Galconda coasts.

Both eastern and western margins of peninsular India are almost devoid of natural harbors. Bare rock walls on the west are matched by mangrove swamps in the east. River mouths are particularly unsatisfactory. At many smaller ports it is necessary for steamers to discharge cargo into lighters several miles offshore. The few port cities owe their importance to access to their hinterland rather than to natural harbor advantages.

Between the peninsular plateau and the Himalayan mountain wall lies Hindustan, most of it a great alluvial plain but including the erosional surface of the Thar Desert in the west. This is the heart of Indian life and history. Here are India's greatest rivers, the Ganges and Brahmaputra in the east and the Indus in the west. These rivers and most of their tributaries rise amid the snow-covered ranges to the north. Since their flow does not depend entirely upon the summer monsoon, they never run dry and are thus of great value for irrigation in the plains. In contrast, the rivers to the south in the peninsula are fed only by the summer rain and are often nearly dry during the winter.

Few areas of flat alluvium are so extensive. Scarcely a hill or mound is to be seen. Nearly 1,000 miles from its mouth, the Ganges is only 500 feet above sea level. Deposits of sand and clay extend to depths of thousands of feet, and few pebbles are found on the surface. The only distinction is between the older and slightly higher alluvium with concretions and alkaline soils, and the newer alluvium without nodules.

In the northwest, the lowland of the Indus and the adjoining Thar Desert is 300 to 400 miles wide; along the Ganges the width is half these figures. Where the plain is narrowest lies Delhi, the natural gateway between the crowded ricelands to the east and the drier wheat country of the Punjab.

Although topographically similar, the eastern half with its greater precipitation has five times the population of western Hindustan. The Ganges Delta lies in the province of Bengal, while the Brahmaputra flows across Assam. Two regional names are used in the Indus Valley; the lower portion is the Sind while that near the mountains is Punjab. The latter derives its name from the fact that it is drained by five tributaries of the Indus: the Jhelum, Chenab, Ravi, Beas, and Sutlej.

The ancient geography of southern Asia was once very unlike the present. Where now rise The Himalaya was once a long sea that extended westward to Europe. This ancient Mediterranean is known as Tethys, a subsiding geosyncline which received vast quantities of marine deposits from the Cambrian to the mid-Cenozoic. From the end of the Eocene into the late Pliocene, this trough of sediments was subjected to powerful compression from the north against the peninsula. Most of the orogeny was in the Miocene·; the sea was obliterated, and the towering Himalaya took its place. Beds that were once horizontal are now powerfully faulted, folded, and overturned on a grand scale, and flank a central igneous core. Structure guides topography, with linear ranges following the direction of folding.

Fringing the main rampart which extends 1,500 miles from the Indus to the Brahmaputra are lower mountains, known as foothills even though they rise to 5,000 feet. The chief of these are the Siwaliks, which give their name to the great system of ancient river deposits of which they are composed. These beds resemble those now accumulating in Hindustan and are from 16,000 to 20,000 feet in thickness. The Miocene and Pliocene fauna is famous for its variety of mammalian remains. Apparently these beds accumulated as ancient alluvial fans in a foredeep much as the present sediments of the Ganges and Indus. North of the Siwaliks are still other deformed geosynclines.

Occasional earthquakes in Assam and the Punjab indicate that movement is still under way.

On the northwest, north, and northeast of Hindustan the mountains rise abruptly from the plain. From one end to another the rampart is continuous, although a variety of ranges marks both ends. The chief mountains in the west are the Sulaiman and Kirthar ranges, which extend from the Makran coast toward the Pamirs.

No single name can be given the Assam mountains in the east, nor is their structural relation to The Himalaya entirely clear. The general trend is north-south, but there is a western offshoot in the Khasi Hills. The main range is The Himalaya, but behind its western end lie other ranges, including the Karakorum. In this inner range rises K^2, the second highest mountain on earth, 28,250 feet, while in the eastern Himalaya is Mt. Everest, 29,141 feet.

Behind the mountain wall are two areas of the Indian Empire: Baluchistan and Kashmir; beyond them are Iran and Afghanistan. To the north are Tibet, Nepal, and Bhutan. Few passes cross the front ranges. No roads lead from India to Burma so that all contact is by the sea. The same was true of Iran until the Second World War. North to Tibet are several passes near Darjeeling and others from the Punjab. From Kashmir several passes connect with Chinese Sinkiang, including the 18,550-foot Karakorum Pass and the main trail by way of Gilgit.

Even before the conquests by Alexander the Great in 326 B.C. the northwestern frontier was the avenue of invaders. The Khyber Pass leads to Kabul in Afghanistan and the Bolan Pass to Quetta in Baluchistan; between them is the Gomal Pass. These and other gateways have been of great historical significance to India and to the capital at Delhi, comparable to the relations in China between the Nankow Pass and Peiping. There is a coastal avenue to Iran along the Makran coast in southern Baluchistan.

Climate

It has well been said that although every schoolboy understands the Indian monsoon, the official meteorological department is still in doubt as to its origin. Nowhere else are so many people so intimately dependent upon rainfall rhythms; the whole prosperity of India is tied up with the eccentricities of its seasonal winds. Other lands have their climatic personality, but in few is it so prominent or meaningful. Alternately India is lush and green, or a dreary brown; supersaturated atmosphere gives way to extreme aridity. Seasonality thus dominates all life.

The conventional explanation has been that the monsoon circulation is the result of thermal relations between land and sea. Thus a heated continent means that the air is expanding, rising, and overflowing with resulting low pressure above the land and high pressures on the encircling sea. Surface winds would thus blow landward during the summer and seaward in winter. The winds from the sea bring rain, while the descending and outblowing air is dry.

This oversimplification cannot be quite true. We now know that the Indian circulation is independent of temperatures and pressures in central Asia, because of the Himalaya barrier. Furthermore, heat alone is not enough explanation. India is hotter in May before the summer monsoon than in July when the circulation is at its height; temperatures also remain high after the end of the monsoon. If heat and low pressure alone were the answer, the area of heaviest rainfall would correspond with rising air, whereas the hottest part of India is actually the driest. The monsoon fluctuates from year to year, but the highest summer temperatures are correlated with years of low monsoon precipitation.

In the tropical oceans there are no monsoons, and none would exist in India were it not for the climatic conditions that arise because of the proximity of land and sea. These latitudes lie in the zone of the trade winds, and, if the earth were all water or all land, there would be a steady circulation due to lower pressure and rising air at the thermal equator. In the Northern Hemisphere the equatorward winds are turned to their right, according to Ferrel's law, and become northeast and progressively easterly winds as they approach the low pressure doldrums; below the equator are the southeast trades.

Since the axis of the earth is tilted, the vertical rays of the sun shift with the season 23½° alternately toward the respective pole, causing the thermal equator to move to a lesser degree with them. Thus the trade-wind belts migrate north and south. If this were all, the northeast trades over India would shift southward in the winter, bringing their associated subtropical high pressure with them. In summer the southeast trades would cross the geographical equator and invade southern India.

Apparently the monsoons represent a modification of these conditions. As the sun advances northward during the spring, the equatorial low pressure belt moves also, though with a lag. Over the Bay of Bengal and the Arabian Sea, weak high pressure anticyclones feed the northeast trade winds, but this flow of equatorward air is not so strong as the southeast trades developed over the uninterrupted Indian Ocean.

Land heats faster than water, and, coincident with the Arabian Sea and Bay of Bengal highs, low pressure circulation develops over Indo-China and strong lows form over India and Arabia. The normal northward retreat of subtropical high pressure is blocked by the low pressure belt over these lands north of the triangular-shaped seas, so that, in turn, the migration of the thermal equator is checked in spite of its unbalanced predominance of southerly trades.

During late May and early June, this unbalanced low pressure belt, on reaching the tip of India, cuts the connection between the two restraining anticyclones over the sea, and the belt abruptly shifts northward to central and northern India and southeastern Asia generally to join the local lows already developed there. Thus the southeast trades rush north to join the cyclonic circulation over the land. This soon is therefore an accentuated and diverted trade wind shifted from the Southern to the Northern Hemisphere. One arm of the

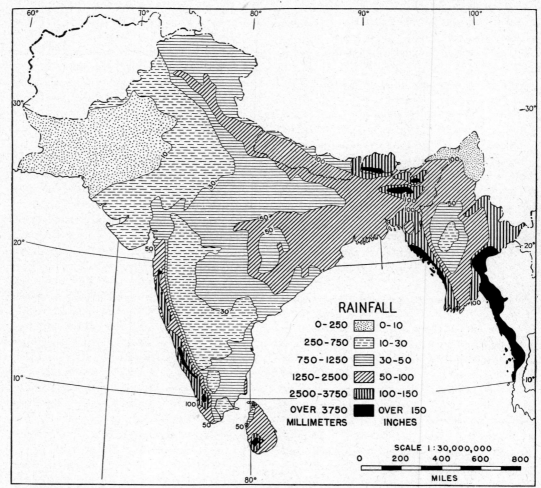

RAINFALL

0– 250	0– 10
250– 750	10– 30
750– 1250	30– 50
1250– 2500	50– 100
2500– 3750	100– 150
OVER 3750 MILLIMETERS	OVER 150 INCHES

SCALE 1:30,000,000

0   200   400   600   800

MILES

The rainfall of India ranges from less than 5 inches per year in the northwest to more than 400 inches in the hills along the Western Coast and at the head of the Bay of Bengal. (*After H. G. Champion, "Indian Forest Records," and E. K. Cook, "Geography of Ceylon."*)

change occurs with such suddenness that the monsoon is said to break. During July, the mean monsoon velocity at Bombay is 14 miles per hour.

As the southeast trades cross the geographical equator, the rotation of the earth turns them to their right, and they become the southwest monsoon. The summer monsoon from the Arabian Sea strikes the western mountainous coast of the peninsula of India nearly at right angles. Over the Bay of Bengal the movement is more from the south, but upon reaching the mountains the circulation is deflected upward over the Khasi Hills and to the right and left, up the Brahmaputra and Ganges valleys.

Since the trade winds have crossed several thousand miles of warm Indian Ocean, they arrive in India with a high moisture content. However, the land is even warmer than the sea so that sufficient cooling for condensation requires uplift of about 500 feet. This is admirably illustrated by the heavy rainfall on the Western Ghats and northern mountains. Within the plateau, convectional storms account for much of the rain. This is also true over Hindustan, but here a third cause of rising air is produced by the crowding and convergence of air streams next to the mountains.

Just before the monsoon breaks, the instability of the frontal atmosphere develops local thundershowers on land and even tropical cyclones in the Arabian Sea and Bay of Bengal that bring what are often known as the mango rains, since this fruit is just maturing. Similar storms continue, but with less intensity, throughout the period of the southern monsoon and yield considerable rain. Cyclones are especially active at the end of the summer, when their onshore winds may develop the so-called tidal waves that inundate east coast deltas. The sea may rise 10 to 30 feet in half an hour, as in 1876 when 200,000 were drowned at Backergunge near the head of the Bay of Bengal. On Oct. 7, 1937, a storm wave 40 feet high, accompanying a hurricane, swept up the mouth of the Hooghly River causing the loss of some 300,000 lives.

The monsoon arrives in the far south first in Ceylon in early June, then at Travancore and the tip of Burma by the beginning of June, and reaches Bombay about June 5. The Bengal branch arrives in Calcutta by June 15 and progresses up the Ganges Valley to the Punjab by July 1. The southerly monsoon continues until mid-September in the Punjab, mid-October in Bombay, late October in Calcutta, and early November in the south. In Calcutta the monsoon proper lasts from June 15 to September 15, with intermittent showers and high humidity through October. By that time the sun has shifted southward beyond the geographical equator, although the thermal equator lags behind it. The mechanics necessary for pulling the southeast trade winds into India are no longer present, so that the southerly winds gradually weaken and withdraw before the developing northeast trades.

Variations in the arrival, duration, distribution, and intensity of the monsoon are of profound importance but have largely eluded explanation. We know little about the causes for trade-wind fluctuations, although there appear to be interesting correlations between such items as pressures over the Australian deserts and subsequent Indian rainfall. Other studies show parallelism between Indian drought and low Nile floods due to diminished Ethiopian rainfall. Seasonal forecasts are made with considerable success.

During winter months, monsoon wind directions are reversed. Northwest winds move down the Ganges Valley and turn southward and southwestward over the peninsula. These appear to be modified northeast trade winds. Their velocity is but half that of the summer monsoon. Normal winter subtropical high pressure over the Tropic of Cancer is augmented by local anticyclonic conditions in northern India. These winds blow from October to the end of February and represent India's cool season.

Since the winter monsoon air is descending and directed seaward, it is dry and rainless over India. Since Ceylon receives the northern monsoon off the ocean, its highlands have ample rain. The Madras coast also has winter rain, either from cyclones or the northeast monsoon which strikes the Madras coast from the ocean.

From December to March northwest India has a procession of weak cyclonic storms which move across the Punjab from Iran. This is a branch of the cyclonic path that divides in western Europe and moves through the Mediterranean and Asia Minor, in contrast to the main route through Germany and the Soviet Union. Presumably the Indian storms continue into China, where they are well known, but almost no lows are recorded in the lower Ganges Valley and their influence does not reach the Deccan. From December to March these shallow depressions bring variable winds and a few inches of rain to the wheat fields of the upper Indus. The total rainfall is low but significant. Much of the Karakorum snow cover is derived from these winds. Winter is a dry season of clear skies except in Madras, and in the Punjab and Northwest Frontier where winter is a slightly rainy season.

Air travel has called for increased information as to winds aloft, so that something is known of the thickness of the monsoons.[1] In June, southwesterly winds prevail at one and two kilometers, but from three to six kilometers the wind is from the northwest, veering to the northeast in the peninsula. In July and August the monsoon thickens to four kilometers, but throughout the summer, east winds prevail at six and eight kilometers. The northerly monsoon is three kilometers thick in October, with strong west winds aloft all during the winter. At no season does monsoon circulation cross far beyond the mountain wall. Above four kilometers the winds are steadily from the west from December through March.

The Indian Realm has the widest possible variations in rainfall. The heaviest precipitation is orographic, as on the slopes of the Western Ghats, the Assam Hills, or the Outer Himalaya. In each of these the amount exceeds 200 inches. The wettest spot is Cherrapunji in the Khasi Hills of Assam. This station stands at the edge of the hills where great masses of air crowd against the 4,000-foot cliffs. For the 72-year period ending in 1930, the average rainfall was 451.6 inches, almost all of it concentrated in half the year.[1] Annual totals vary from 283 inches in 1908 to an 11-month record of 905 inches in 1861. The rainfall in the single month of July, 1861, reached 366 inches. Some localities in the Western Ghats may even be wetter.

Most of the rainfall on the lowlands is associated with cyclonic storms that move westward from the Bay of Bengal. An inch may fall in ten minutes, and 40 inches has been recorded in 24 hours. The rainy season is not continuous and there may be days or weeks of clear skies in the drier areas. Parts of the Sind have almost no rainfall, and yet Doorbaji, with an annual average of 5 inches, once received 34 inches in two days.

Rain shadows are pronounced. Thus in the Deccan, southern Madras, and Tibet the yearly total drops to 20 inches or less. When the winds move down slope, foehn warming and evaporation occur.

Not only is the monsoon eccentric in the total amount of precipitation, but variations in its beginning or end or concentration may be even more serious. When periods of lessened rainfall or other irregularities occur two years in succession, widespread disaster may result.

---

[1] RAMANATHAN, K. R., and K. P. RAMAKRISHNAN, The General Circulation of the Atmosphere over India and Its Neighbourhood, *Memoirs of the India Meteorological Department*, Part X (1939), XXVI, 189–245.

[1] The world's heaviest known rainfall is on the slopes of Mt. Waialeale on the island of Hawaii in the path of the trade winds. The average for the 20-year period ending 1938 was 460.2 inches. See Chap. 1.

India has three seasons. The arrival of the monsoon in June inaugurates the wet season. This is really India's spring, for

Following the cessation of the rains, temperatures decrease; the cool season extends from late November, or December

The hill station of Simla is the hot-weather capital for Delhi. (*Courtesy Indian State Railways.*)

nature then comes to life. Despite the high sun, the ocean air and clouds keep the day temperature in the nineties. The heat increases from south to north as the winds lose their effect. Humidity is high, but breezes make it bearable. In Bombay, June to September temperatures average 82°F. for day and night, while in Calcutta the figure is 84°F. Conditions are even more unpleasant just after the rains, for the humidity is high and, although the thermometer is lower, sensible temperatures increase. During the rainy period, it is difficult to dry one's clothing except over a fire. Furniture put together with glue is apt to come apart. Books and shoes mildew overnight.

in the south, through February. Light frosts occur in the Ganges Valley, and the clear skies make the climate attractive to the European although poorly clad Indians may complain bitterly of the cold.

The hot season begins in March. Temperatures rise to 100°F. or more in the daytime, but the nights are cooler. The sun is nearly vertical in April and May and the air relatively still. All work is suspended at mid-day, for heat and glare are intense as the molten sun shines from a cloudless sky. Dust storms and tornadoes are locally destructive.

Despite marked variations in rainfall, Indian climate is essentially a unit. Although only half the country is actually within the tropics, the mountain wall is so effective a barrier that northern India is 3 to 5°F. warmer than corresponding latitudes in the United States. It therefore seems a mistake to divide India as is done by Koeppen, with an *Aw* type of climate in the south and *Cw* in the north; both seem really tropical, with dry winters. The contrast between the bulk of India and the desert and steppe, *BS* and *BW*, of the northwest is valid.

As average annual rainfall diminishes from place to place and as it becomes more concentrated in one season, variations from year to year increase.[1] When the normal total is under 20 inches, no agriculture is attempted without irrigation, and rainfall fluctuations are expected and planned for. Where the total exceeds 80 inches, there is almost always a surplus of moisture. Forty inches of rain is normally adequate but, when it fails, famine is threatened. Thus, the most seriously affected areas are those where there is usually almost enough water. In most of India some 30 inches of rain are needed to allow for evaporation, and only the precipitation above that figure is meaningful for agriculture.

Long experience with rainfall fluctuations has brought population distribution into close agreement with climatic possibilities, but so great is the pressure of people that too many have occupied the marginal lands where drought is certain to recur.

Natural Vegetation

India has a rich and diversified flora, but little of it is distinctive to the country. Every type of climax vegetation is repre-

sented except natural grasslands and savanna. Most vegetation reflects monsoon alternations of rainfall. There are some differences north and south of the Tropic of Cancer, but resemblances are far more important. Large areas of original forest have been cleared for agriculture, and many hill lands are periodically burned over to ensure a better crop of grass for grazing. About a fifth of greater India is officially classed as forest, but much of it is in the Assam Hills or other inaccessible areas. Where cultivation has been allowed to lapse, extensive tracts have grown up to jungle and bamboo thickets. Within the settled parts of India commercial timber is so scarce that farm buildings are usually built of mud.

Throughout India, altitude is more important than latitude in determining floristic regions. The Himalayan zone is especially interesting ecologically. Within a horizontal distance of 60 miles are reproduced essentially all the vegetation types found in a 3,000-mile traverse of North America from the tip of Florida to Labrador. On the lower slopes of The Himalaya, dense tropical forests pass at successively higher elevations into pine, oak and maple, birch and fir, mountain meadows, and bare rock.

Much of the peninsula is by nature a great monsoon forest land of teak, banyan, palms, and bamboo. Planted trees such as the mango replace part of the original cover. The plains of Hindustan are so extensively cultivated that portions are now nearly treeless.

The major factors in the distribution of forest types are climatic. Soil, drainage, exposure, and history are locally significant but do not alter the general picture. The pattern of natural vegetation thus reflects the distribution of rainfall, and at the same time forecasts possibilities of agricultural utilization.

[1] WILLIAMSON, A. V. and K. G. T. CLARK, The Variability of the Annual Rainfall of India, *Quarterly Journal of the Royal Meteorological Society* (1931), LVII, 43–56. See review with map in *Geographical Review* (1931), XXI, 676.

Four major forest types are defined by Champion.[1] These are the tropical forests with six associations based largely on types from wet to dry; the temperate forests, which also have three moisture associations; and the alpine forms. There

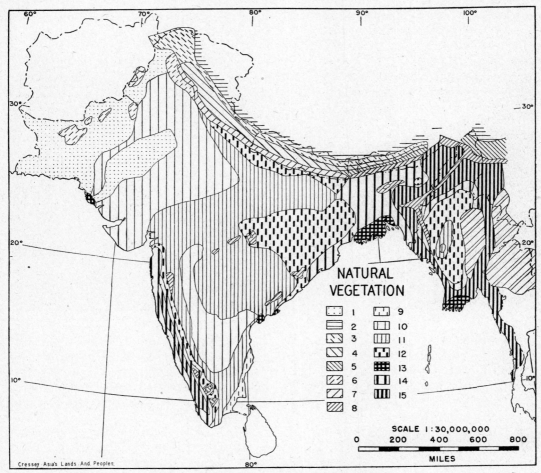

NATURAL
VEGETATION

SCALE 1:30,000,000

0 200 400 600 800

MILES

Cressey *Asia's Lands And Peoples*

India's varied flora may be generalized as follows:

1. Tropical wet evergreen
2. Tropical semievergreen
3. Tidal
4. Tropical moist deciduous
5. Tropical dry deciduous
6. Tropical thorn forest
7. Tropical dry evergreen
8. Subtropical wet forest

9. Subtropical pine forest
10. Subtropical dry forest
11. Wet temperate
12. Moist temperate
13. Dry alpine
14. Alpine
15. Desert

(*After H. G. Champion, "Indian Forest Records."*)

moisture; the subtropical forests with three

[1] CHAMPION, H. G., Preliminary Survey of the Forest Types of India and Burma, *Indian Forest Records*, new series I, No. 1 (1936).

are, in addition, tidal forests, the steppe, and the desert. Not all areas have reached climax conditions, either on account of man's interference or through other causes.

The tropical wet evergreen forest is composed of a large number of species without local dominants. Most trees are plains, threaded with distributaries. Large areas are flooded with each high tide. Salt water covers the sea margins of such

Tiger hunting in the tall grass of Nepal. (*Ewing Galloway.*)

150 feet tall, often with straight trunks for 100 feet. The canopy is very dense and is laced together by vines. Ground vegetation is nearly absent, or there may be an undergrowth of canes. Temperature means are near 80°F., and the rainfall is 80 inches, or even 120 inches for optimum conditions. The longer the dry season, the heavier must be the total rainfall. These forests reach their greatest development in Assam, the foothills of the eastern Himalaya, and the Western Ghats.

Tropical semievergreen forests border the evergreen types on the lowlands, where rainfall is somewhat less or where the soil is porous. The forest is dense and from 80 to 120 feet tall. Evergreens predominate in the lower canopy with deciduous forms rising above them.

The Ganges, Mahanadi, and various east coast rivers meet the sea in low delta deltas, but blocked river water inundates the interior areas. In such situations there are tropical tidal forests, as in the Sundarbans southeast of Calcutta. Dense stands of mangroves rising to 100 feet are characteristic.

The tropical moist deciduous forest is more open and has purer stands. Trees reach 100 feet, with a bamboo undergrowth. Climbing vines are large and abundant. This is the representative monsoon forest, although the term may also be applied to drier groups. During the rainless period the trees lose their leaves. Drought comes in March and April rather than the cooler season, and new leaves may arrive before the monsoon rains. Mean temperatures average above 75°F., and the rainfall is 60 to 80 inches with a dry season of four to six months. These forests are the typical home of the important teak tree. A variant of this type is the sal forest which flourishes with rainfall down to 40 inches; this is an important commercial timber. Soil variations produce local subsidiary types, among them impenetrable thickets of bamboo.

Tropical dry deciduous forests have a continuous but uneven canopy. Many of the same species present in the moist forests also grow here but are reduced to 50 feet. Single species cover wide areas. The lower rainfall limit is 30 inches, and the undergrowth is drought resistant, or xerophytic. There is a striking contrast between the entirely leafless period with exposed soil, and the luxuriant growth after the rains.

Thorn forests with acacia, mimosa, and euphorbia growing 15 to 30 feet high occur in the drier Deccan and around the Thar Desert with a rainfall of 10 to 30 inches.

Special conditions of winter rain along the Madras coast and in Ceylon account for the tropical dry evergreen forests. Hard-leaved trees predominate, 30 to 40 feet high.

Subtropical montane forests are found on the Nilgiri and Cardamom hills, the higher mountains of the Assam frontier, the Himalayan foothills, and in Baluchistan. Those in the south and northeast are of the wet type. Along the central Himalaya pine forests prevail, while in the northwest are subtropical dry forests. The subtropical wet forests have average temperatures of 65 to 75°F. and a wide range of rainfall, always in excess of 65 inches and up to that of Cherrapunji. Trees generally rise 70 to 100 feet with a shrubby undergrowth and many vines. Elevations range from 3,000 to 6,000 feet. Oaks and chestnuts are usually present. Subtropical pine forests characteristically have a pure stand of hard pine. The rainfall is 40 to 50 inches, and the formation extends continuously on the southern slopes of the Siwalik Range. Annual fires, started by natives to drive out wild animals, or in order that the ash may fertilize the soil, prevent the development of undergrowth but favor the growth of grass for grazing. Dry evergreen subtropical forest is found in the Punjab foothills and elsewhere in the northwest.

Temperate mountain forests are restricted by temperature requirements to higher elevations. Rainfall may be 60 to 250 inches. There are considerable floristic differences between the main area in The Himalaya and the mountain summits at the end of the peninsula. As elevations increase, the wet evergreen forests of laurel, oak, and chestnut but without conifers change to moist temperate forests with pine and beautiful Himalayan cedar. Heights of 150 feet are not uncommon. These are comparable to the forests of the temperate zone in Europe and North America. Altitudes range from 5,000 to 11,000 feet. The dry temperate forest is present on the inner ranges of The Himalaya where rainfall is under 40 inches. Winter snow covers the ground to a depth of 7 feet at 6,000 feet elevation, 14 feet at 8,000 feet, and 18 feet at 10,000 feet.

Alpine vegetation of stunted trees and rhododendron prevails between 9,000 and 11,500 feet. Larch and birch are the principal trees. Xerophytic plants requiring but 10 inches of rainfall live at even higher elevations. Mountain meadows with buttercups and primroses grow up to 18,000 feet.

The Indus Valley and Baluchistan have the sparsest vegetation, partly true desert and in part marginal steppe. The Thar Desert is actually somewhat more humid than areas nearer the Indus now irrigated. Only specialized xerophytic forms can survive the aridity and extremely high temperatures.

The term jungle is an Indian word for a rank growth of brush, vines, and tall grass, often growing on abandoned land.

of the Ganges, Indus, and smaller rivers exemplify the newer alluvium, while the older alluvium occupies interstream areas

The arid landscape of Sind, two miles east of Karachi. Where the lower Indus Valley is unirrigated the landscape is that of the adjoining Thar Desert. (*Courtesy Indian State Railways.*)

Soils

Four major soil types are present in India: the alluvial soils of Hindustan, some of them with steppe or desert characteristics; the black regur soils of the Deccan; the red soils of the southern and eastern peninsula; and the soils with lateritic characteristics.[1]

The older Pleistocene alluvium is reddish brown in color with lime concretions from one to four inches in diameter which are known as kunkur. This soil is the bhangar, in contrast to the modern alluvium or khadar. Present-day alluvial soils are more sandy and seldom contain concretions. The deltas and flood plains

with elevations up to 180 feet above the rivers. Rajputana and the Thar are covered with soils that show steppe and desert features including a veneer of wind-blown loess. Some of these grassland soils extend well down the Ganges Valley into regions now naturally covered with forest.

The black soils, or regur, range from deep black to brown and gray. The upper horizon is three to six feet thick, and has a high content of clay which gives it water-holding capacity, unusual stickiness, and also rapid desiccation. The soils have a fairly large iron and aluminum content, adequate lime and magnesium, and some organic matter. In many respects, these tropical black soils are similar to temperate chernozems. They differ from lateritic soils in that the latter develop with heavier rainfall and a forest cover, while regur has

[1] SCHOKALSKY, Z. J., The Natural Conditions of Soil Formation in India, Contributions to the Knowledge of the Soils of Asia—2, *Dokuchaiev Institute of Soil Science*, Academy of Sciences of the U.S.S.R., Leningrad (1932), 53–152.

something of a steppe environment. Most of the regur overlies basaltic lava flows. It was once assumed that the distinctive color resulted from the weathering of this rock, but typical regur is also known to overlie metamorphic rocks. The nature of the coloring matter is still uncertain but may be a mineral constituent rather than organic carbon. These soils spread over Bombay, Hyderabad, the Central Provinces, and the Central India Agency.

Reddish soils may be divided into the red soils proper, best developed on metamorphic rocks in the southern part of the peninsula, and lateritic soils formed exclusively on laterite. True laterite was first described in India, and as a geological formation is a residual product developed exclusively on flat surfaces, often of peneplain characteristics. The underlying bedrock may be of various types, usually crystalline. As a result of long-continued tropical leaching, laterite is a rock of porous and slaglike structure, unequally permeated with iron oxides and varying in color from reddish brown to yellow. White kaolinized spots may occur. Iron and aluminum oxides are abundant, often forming 90 per cent of the whole. The development of such laterite may require one or more geological epochs, possibly since the Eocene.

Where modern soils develop on these laterites, they are termed lateritic. Since the parent material is already highly weathered, environmental factors can modify it but slightly. Two types of lateritic soils may be distinguished, those formed at high levels on original laterite, and those developed at low levels or on slopes over redeposited laterite. True lateritic soils are confined to relatively small areas in Ceylon, northeastern Madras, the Western Ghats, and Chota Nagpur. High temperature, abundant rainfall, and tropical forest cover are conditioning factors.

Red soil types grade from black to brown. They are usually deficient in organic matter but contain lime and magnesia. Iron and aluminum compounds are abundant. Such tropical soils cover large areas in Madras and Mysore, Bihar and Orissa, and the northern part of the Central Provinces.

This summary omits the bog and coastal soils, the extreme alkaline types in the northwest, and areas of bare rock. Vertical zonations introduce many soil types on the slopes of The Himalaya. These mountain soils are likewise present in the Vindhya and Satpura ranges, the Nilgiri and Cardamom hills, and central Ceylon.

Mineral Resources

The mineral wealth of India is strikingly concentrated in the uplands 200 miles west of Calcutta. Coal, iron ore, limestone, manganese, copper, and mica are in fair proximity, out of which has grown a large iron and steel industry. Elsewhere mineral deposits are widely scattered. Taken as a whole, the Empire is not an important mineral producer. Extensive geological studies under British direction make it unlikely that significant reserves remain undiscovered. In terms of both area and population, the known reserves are exceptionally low. Only a tenth of one per cent of the people are engaged in mining.

To medieval Europe, India was synonymous with gold and precious stones. Pliny referred to Indian gold in A.D. 77. It is now evident that the concentration of mineral wealth in the hands of a few did not imply rich mineral resources. Thus many of the gold placers now worked yield such a low return that only the cheapest labor can operate them. Production figures reflect human poverty rather than mineral wealth. Ancient India knew the arts of smelting and made use of iron, copper, and bronze. Primitive slag heaps are widespread.

Coal reserves are variously estimated suitable for metallurgical coke. Largely undeveloped Tertiary lignite reserves are present in Assam and the Punjab. Produc-

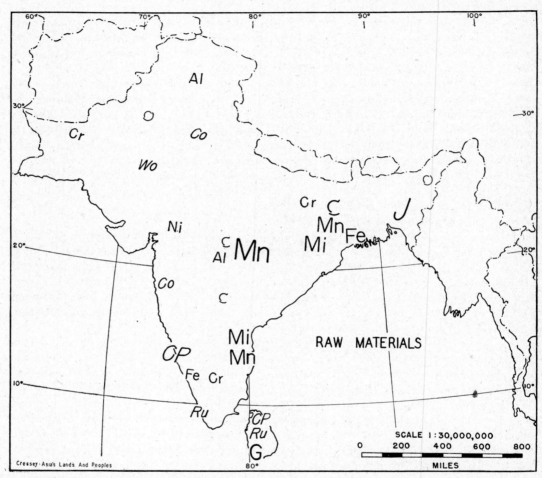

India has large amounts of a few raw materials. The symbols suggest relative world rank: C—coal and O—oil are shown in shadow letters. Minerals, in vertical letters, are as follows: Al—aluminum, Cr—chromium, Fe—iron, G—graphite, Mn—manganese, Mi—mica, Ni—nickel. Agricultural products of industrial importance are *Co*—cotton, *CP*—cocoanut products, *J*—jute, *Ru*—rubber, *Wo*—wool.

from 54 to 79 billion tons. Most of this is good bituminous coal of Permo-Carboniferous age in the Damodar Valley in Bengal and Bihar, and in the valleys of the Mahanadi and Godavari. These occurrences are down-faulted remains of fresh-water basins. One seam in the Bokaro field is 126 feet thick. Only limited amounts are tion in 1938 reached 28,000,000 long tons, including a small export to Japan. The supply is adequate for the local needs of transportation, textile factories, and smelting. Household consumption in all India totals only two million tons annually. After the United Kingdom, India is the largest coal producer in the British Empire.

Petroleum is entirely lacking in Hindustan and the plateau, but there is a small output in the Punjab and in Assam.

Archean rocks are found widely in the plateau but are not commercially workable. Hematite ore of exceptionally high

The great fuel supply of India is cow dung, molded into cakes and plastered on the rocks or courtyard walls to dry. (*Courtesy Paul F. Cressey.*)

The small oil production in the Punjab and Baluchistan represents the eastern margin of the Mesopotamian and Iran district.

The wide distribution of the native iron industry suggests a similarly extensive occurrence of iron ore. Such is the case, although most deposits are not of modern economic significance.[1] At the time of the invasion of Alexander the Great, 326 B.C., India was as familiar with iron and steel as was Greece. One of the largest iron ore bodies of the world is in the Salem district southwest of Madras. The ore is a rich magnetite but is not suited for modern blast-furnace treatment, and there is no near-by coal. Similar magnetite ores in

quality is present in the northeastern plateau, chiefly in the Singhbhum district in Bihar and Orissa. The chief outcrop is a range 30 miles long in the native state of Bonai where it is mined cheaply by open-cut methods. The ore is associated with banded jasper, and the average iron content exceeds 60 per cent. Both quality and tonnage are said to equal those of Lake Superior, with conservative estimates of a billion tons of "actual" ore and another billion of "potential" ore. Indian statistics give the reserves of the district as 3,600,-000,000 tons, and for the entire country at several billion more. This iron belt is by far the largest and best reserve in all Asia,[1] with the possible exception of those in the Soviet Union.

[1] KALYONASUNDARAM, V., The Geographical Basis of the Indian Iron and Steel Industry, *Journal Madras Geographical Association* (1934), VIII, 233–263, with maps.

[1] LEITH, C. K., *Proceedings World Engineering Congress* (1931), XXXIII, I, 14–15.

Iron ore is widely distributed in Mysore, with hematite schist and limonite mined in the Bababudan hills. Other high-grade ores are present in Portuguese Goa, within four miles of a harbor. Gwalior has several ore deposits but they are remote from coal. Lateritic ores with 30 per cent iron are widespread in the peninsula. The 1937 production of iron ore was 2,870,832 tons.

Three-quarters of the world's manganese is mined in the Soviet Union and India. Production of this ferroalloy fluctuates with the world output of steel, in which it is used to remove oxygen and sulphur, or in some cases as a toughening alloy. India's yield in 1937 was 1,051,594 long tons, somewhat below the average, and about a third that of the U.S.S.R. Deposits are widely scattered, with the largest reserves in the Central Provinces, Bihar and Orissa, and Madras. Deposits of manganese represent residual concentrations from the long-continued weathering of rocks, such as those in the Indian peninsula. The local steel industry uses a tenth of the supply, and the rest goes to England and France.

The import and export of gold bullion has no relation to production or actual use. It represents rather speculation and the movement of wealth. In the nineteenth century, India was one of the largest buyers of gold and silver in the world. When Great Britain went off the gold standard in 1931, shipments of gold from India exceeded a billion dollars in eight years. There is a prosperous mining area at Kolar in Mysore west of Madras, and numerous native operations elsewhere which report no statistics. The Kolar production in 1938 amounted to 320,000 fine ounces, which is a large decrease from the peak yield of 616,758 ounces in 1905.

Two characteristic Indian minerals are mica and graphite. Over three quarters of the world's sheet mica comes from India. Excellent supplies in Bihar and Madras, plus cheap labor, make split sheets of muscovite available at low prices. Trimmed sheets are produced up to 80 square inches. Ceylon has long been noted for natural graphite. There is a large export to Japan, but artificial graphite has reduced the demand elsewhere.

Copper, chromite, and bauxite are minor products. Salt is mined in the Salt Range of the Punjab and is evaporated from sea water along the coasts of Bombay and Madras. India is deficient in nonferrous minerals, with no zinc, little lead, and no tin.

The unproductive state of the mineral industry in the Indian Empire is indicated by the following figures of production, the rough annual average for the decade of 1930 in millions of United States dollars: coal 23, gold 11, lead 5, manganese 5, silver 4, tin 3, salt 3, and tungsten, iron ore, and mica 1 each. Note that these represent the yield for 1,800,000 square miles and over 350 million people.

CHAPTER 30

INDIA'S PEOPLE AND THEIR ACTIVITIES

People and Politics

In all of Asia there is nowhere else the cultural heterogeneity found in India. The political unity imposed by Great Britain tends to obscure the internal diversity in race, language, religion, and material civilization. India is a land of widest contrasts; congestion and poverty are countered by wealth and spiritual insight. The system of caste has compartmentalized social and economic activities among Hindus, although Mohammedans and the other sects tend to be democratic.

Few generalizations apply everywhere. The Sikhs of the Punjab with their splendid physique and casteless society have little in common with the impoverished outcastes of Madras. Primitive hill tribes in Assam and educated Mohammedans, city students and illiterate peasants or ryots, wealthy Parsees in Bombay; all these make national coherence difficult.

More than elsewhere in monsoon Asia outside of Japan, India has accepted the material culture and veneer of European civilization. But despite the long exposure there has been little modification of the nonmaterial aspects of social organization and ideas. In the industrial cities there is a slight modification of minor aspects of caste, but the basic provisions against intermarriage and social intercourse in general remain.

The political structure of India is as complex as the social. Two-thirds of the country is included in the 12 provinces of British India. Since 1935 Burma has been set apart as a separate country. Ceylon has always been a crown colony. Several small Portuguese and French possessions remain along the coast as souvenirs of earlier conquests. The rest of India is divided into some 560 Indian states, some of them very large, others but a few square miles in size. Each state is more or less sovereign in internal affairs but has been bound by a variety of treaties to the old British East India Company, or to the British government, or to the King of England ruling as Emperor of India. They are thus under varying degrees of British supervision.

Under the constitution of 1935, the British provinces were Assam, Bengal, Bihar, United Provinces, Punjab, Northwest Frontier, and Sind, forming a tier across Hindustan; with Bombay, Central Provinces, Orissa, and Madras in the peninsula. Sind has since been separated from Bombay.

The Indian states, largely in the interior, include Hyderabad, Mysore, and Travancore in the south; Rajputana with its 18 states, Central India Agency with 148 states, Gwalior, and 354 states near Bombay under the oversight of the Western States Agency, plus the outlying areas of Kashmir and Baluchistan. Nepal and Bhutan in the north are independent kingdoms entirely free from British protection, and outside of India. Since many of these states enjoy different degrees of autonomy, the constitutional problem of an All-India Federation is exceedingly complicated. Some of the native rulers cling to ancient customs and refuse to cooperate in any scheme for unification. Added to this is the more serious problem of bringing together the Hindus and the

administration, coinage, army, and customs regulations.

The political pattern of present-day

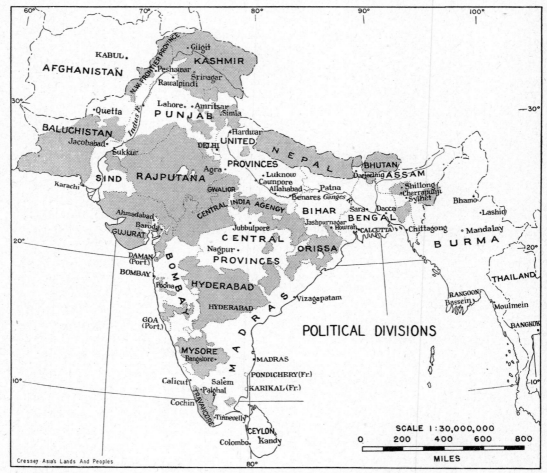

India's political structure with its 12 provinces and approximately 560 native states is too complex to be mapped at this scale but the major divisions are shown. Nepal and Bhutan are independent kingdoms. The other shaded areas are Indian states while the unshaded areas within India are provinces.

Mohammedans. In most independent districts there is a British Resident, as representative of the Viceroy, whose unofficial authority usually increases as the area of states diminishes. A few of the larger states have their own railway systems with a distinctive gauge, independent postal

India represents a crystallization of the chaos that England found, and produced, when the East India Company carried on its operations in the seventeenth and eighteenth centuries. The Mogul dynasty reached its peak under Akbar, who ruled from 1556 to 1605. Even then the southern

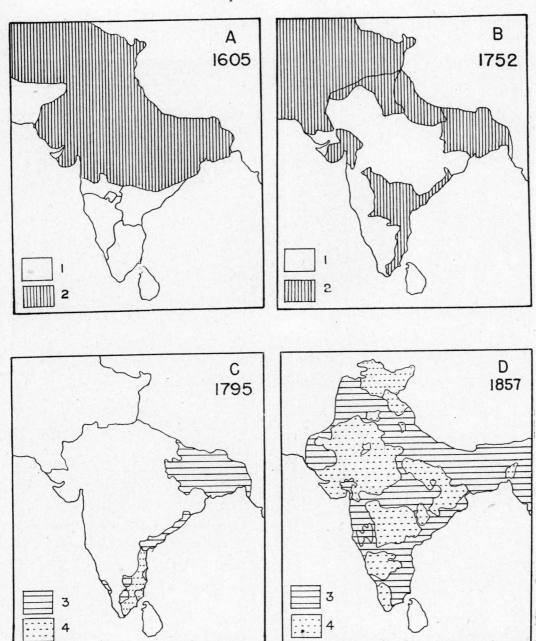

India has not experienced unified control for many centuries. In 1605 independent Mohammedan states (1) controlled the south whereas the Mogul Empire (2) dominated the north. In 1752 the same divisions remained but with very different territorial distribution. By 1795 the East India Company (3) had acquired considerable areas in the east while other areas (4) were under British protection. The map for 1857 represents the situation prior to the Sepoy Rebellion and the transfer of the East India Company's political control to the British Government.

peninsula was divided among independent Mohammedan and Hindu states. The

the penetration of European traders, but the collapse of India was due as much to

The entrance to the caves at Ajanta. (*Courtesy Indian State Railways.*)

arrival of Vasco da Gama's three small vessels at Calicut in May, 1498, forecast

internal as to external factors. These involved petty jealousies and ambitions of many native rulers which could easily be fanned into sectional warfare.

The British came originally for trade rather than conquest. As warehouses were established along the coast, the East India Company entered into political relations with whoever ruled the region. In most areas these were the local governors, and in some cases even rebel chieftans. When civil difficulties arose, the British found it necessary to employ police to guard their possessions, and from this they expanded to militia and to the aid of their political favorites. Successive events, in part accidental, in part manipulated, gave the East India Company and its militarily supported native rulers increased political control. In places, this expansion was piecemeal, the frontier advancing as it was expedient to quell disturbances in bordering territory; elsewhere whole provinces were transferred to British administration, either under their official Mogul governor or under rebellious leaders.

A part of the present pattern was changed from flux to fixation by Hastings in 1817–1818. In some areas, widespread consolidation of petty kingdoms had just occurred; elsewhere territorial chaos was still the rule; hence the diversity in the present protected areas. After the Sepoy Rebellion, in 1858, control of British India was transferred from the East India Company to the British Crown. Since the British advanced from the sea, modern political geography is quite unlike that of ancient times where invaders came from the northwest. Present boundaries largely disregard those of Akbar.

In all the history and prehistory of India, there had never been an invasion from the sea till the arrival of the Dutch, Portuguese, French, and English. Although there are no records of overseas political conquests by Indians themselves, there was a considerable migration to the East

Indies. Thus Hinduism spread to Java a thousand years ago. India's chief gateways were the northwest passes toward Iran and central Asia. Even Chinese pilgrims came this way. Prior to the arrival of Europeans, India had no seaports of importance, and the chief ocean-borne trade was that carried on by the Arabs between Bombay and Zanzibar. Today, conditions are reversed and the seaports form the front doors. The passes have become the postern gate, little used but still a continual threat for penetration. Beyond them lay first czarist territorial expansion and now Soviet communism.

Any understanding of racial complexity must go back thousands of years and depends on relationships still little understood. The two main strains today are the Dravidians in the south and the Aryans in the north. Before either arrived, there were dark-skinned peoples akin to early negroid stocks of Africa and Melanesia, some of whom still live as aborigines in the central part of the peninsula. All known migrations have come as waves from the northwest, each pushing aside or partly mingling with its predecessor. Within historic times these have included Greeks, Scythians, Huns, Afghans, known as Moguls when they came into India, and Persians.

The most recent conquest was that of the Mohammedans who spread eastward down the Ganges Valley to Bengal in the twelfth century, but who have never penetrated the peninsula in large numbers.

The major cultural clash in present-day India is between the Hindus, who represent two-thirds of the population, and the Mohammedans, who comprise one-fifth. The former give to India such cultural and religious unity as it has, but there is no common language, race, or history for the more than two hundred million who make up the caste-stratified society of Hinduism. Hindus comprise at least three-quarters of the population almost everywhere in Hindustan and the plateau except in Assam in Bengal, Telegu and Tamil in Madras, and Punjabi in the Indus lowland. This

An open-air village shop operated by Mohammedans. (*Courtesy Paul F. Cressey.*)

where they are but half, and in the Punjab and Bengal where Mohammedans number three-fourths. It is quite impossible to redraw boundaries so that different racial groups might be in separate political areas. Proposals to create a Moslem state under the name of Pakistan cannot be based on any valid boundary.

The nearly 400 million people of India have 9 great religions, and over 200 languages of which 20 are spoken by at least a million people each. Even the name India was not applied to all of the country until modern times. There has never been a common tongue throughout the realm until the introduction of English, which is spoken by less than three million. Hindustani is widely used in the Ganges Plain, Bengali language distribution has little relation to provincial boundaries or to religion.

There are more than 2,000 castes in Hindu society, with the Brahmans at the top and the "untouchables" or depressed classes, which are outside the caste system, at the base. These latter number over 50 million people. These differences are in part ethnographic, for the higher castes tend to have fairer skin, higher foreheads, and rounder faces. Aryans, who represent the latest invasions, in general are fairer and have thin noses while Dravidians are dark skinned and broad nosed. The class stratification of Hindu society is a serious barrier to modernization.

The restrictions of language and religion divide people into isolated cultural communities which make government and business difficult. In social, linguistic, and political structure, the peninsula of India is more complex than anything the peninsula of Europe has ever known. Without external guidance, national coherence is very difficult.

Toward the end of the sixteenth century, the total population of India was approximately 100 millions; by the first census of 1872 the number rose to 206 millions. The population of India, including both British India and the Indian States, at the 1941 census was 388,800,000, an increase of 13 per cent in a decade. The Northwestern Frontier and Bombay increased by 25 and 20 per cent, respectively, while Baluchistan declined by 12 per cent. Half these people live in Hindustan, which occupies but one-fifth the area. In the lower Ganges Valley, population densities exceed 1,000 per square mile, while parts of the desert and delta jungles are essentially empty. Only a tenth of the total live in cities of 5,000 or over, for India is the most rural of all the large countries of the world. Literacy in 1939 was 12 per cent, with the largest numbers in Bengal and Madras. With a birth rate of 34 and a death rate of 24, the average expectation of life is but 27 years, as compared with 58 in Great Britain.

The results of the 1939 census are shown in the accompanying table.

Provinces

Assam	10,205,000
Bengal	60,314,000
Bihar	36,340,000
Bombay	20,858,000
Central Provinces	16,822,000
Madras	49,342,000
Northwest Frontier	3,038,000
Orissa	8,729,000
Punjab	28,419,000
United Provinces	55,021,000
Sind	4,537,000
	295,827,000

States and Agencies

Assam	725,000
Baluchistan	356,000
Baroda	2,855,000
Bengal	2,142,000
Central India	7,502,000
Chattisgarh	4,054,000
Cochin	1,423,000
Deccan	2,786,000
Gujarat	1,457,000
Gwalior	3,992,000
Hyderabad	16,184,000
Kashmir	4,021,000
Mysore	7,329,000
Northwest Frontier	2,378,000
Orissa	3,025,000
Punjab	6,553,000
Rajputana	13,670,000
Travancore	6,070,000
	92,973,000

Totals

India (1939)	388,800,000
Portuguese India (1931)	579,970
French India (1936)	299,000

Indian agricultural economy is based on rice, except in the northwest or specialized areas such as those devoted to cotton or jute. Since flooded fields require level land, hills are often sparsely populated. One of the least occupied and most backward parts of the country is the Chota Nagpur Plateau near the bend of the Ganges, northwest of Calcutta.

Two factors guide population distributions in India: level alluvium and adequate water. Densities are high in the Ganges lowland and along both coasts. The Indus lowland has good soil but is too dry for agriculture, except where irrigated. The blankest areas on the population map are the arid lands of Rajputana and Baluchistan in the northwest, and the mountains of Kashmir. India's problem, like China's, is agricultural overpopulation. Famines once took a tremendous toll, but railways and efficient grain distribution under government supervision have eliminated starvation in the twentieth century. Disease is still serious, and the influenza epidemic of 1918–1919 is estimated to have caused the loss of over 12,000,000 lives.

the marginal livelihood of the overcrowded land.

India is a land of villages, over two-thirds

A village street of the better type, near Cape Comorin in Travancore. (*Courtesy Indian State Railways.*)

Agriculture

The world of the average Indian farmer ends at his horizon. His interest is centered in the village where he lives except for an occasional journey of a few miles to a bazaar or fair. Within this circle, life follows a routine round of simple stereotyped activities. With an eye on the sky for the monsoon and with his hands in the earth for food, man lives close to nature.

The agricultural landscape differs with the season and from north to south, but everywhere below The Himalaya it has a characteristic Indian touch. The foliage is tropical and luxuriant, cultivated fields are tiny and of irregular shape as the result of generations of repeated subdivision, and livestock is abundant. The poverty of the people and houses of mud and straw reflect

of a million in number. Most of them are located away from paved roads or railways and are but little affected by the tides of nationalism that sweep the cities. Each settlement is nearly self-sufficient with its own artisans, carpenters, and blacksmiths who furnish all needed tools. A shop or two supply the few material wants, and a temple or mosque cares for the religious needs. Traditional practices still suffice, and the high percentage of illiteracy makes changes difficult. Outside markets for farm produce are limited, so that increased labor brings few rewards. Recurrent years of poor crops pile up indebtedness to the local moneylender.

Despite extensive government efforts for agricultural improvement, the sheer magnitude of the reform problem means that for most farmers cultivation is still rudimentary. Plows are simple iron-tipped sticks which stir but do not overturn the soil. In most areas they are light enough but the area is only one-tenth and one-fifth of the respective crop totals. Cooperative societies are locally an aid.

A seed drill. Simple farm tools made from local materials are characteristic. (*Courtesy Indian State Railways.*)

to be carried to the fields on the farmer's back, but in the black soils of the Deccan the plows are heavier and require up to six yoke of oxen. Crops are reaped with a sickle, threshed by the feet of cattle, and winnowed in the wind. The mattock is used in place of a spade.

Some progress has been made in consolidating scattered holdings, but many farmers with no more than three or four acres in all till one or two dozen farm plots.

Each province has its agricultural department, and considerable acreages are now sown with improved seeds, especially in the case of irrigated wheat and cotton,

The Indian income needs desperately to be raised, but there is little hope of this through mining, lumbering, fishing, animal husbandry, or industry. Agriculture remains the dominant occupation, yet the cultivated area can scarcely be enlarged further without prohibitive expense. The crop area rose 14 per cent during the first quarter of the century, but population increased nearly as much. Only one-seventh of the land is double-cropped, but only modest increases are feasible here. Probably the most hopeful prospect is through better seed selection and increased returns per acre. Present acre yields are much below world averages.

Fertilization would materially increase the harvest, but farmers are too poor to purchase commercial preparations. Unfortunately for the future, India does not appear to have phosphates or other raw materials for the manufacture of mineral fertilizers. The large number of farm animals suggests the availability of manure, but in the absence of other fuel for domestic needs, cattle and buffalo dung is made into cakes and burned. Compost piles are used somewhat, and there is a limited plowing under of legumes for green fertilizer. Rotation and fallowing are common practices, and the interplanting of legumes and grains also helps to maintain fertility.

Without irrigation India would be a different country. Seasonal rainfall, often irregular, leaves much of the land a semi-desert for half the year. In the northwest there is never enough precipitation. Irrigation is an old practice, greatly expanded under the British. Water is supplied by wells, reservoirs, and canals, and the irrigated area amounts to over 20 per cent of the total under cultivation. The total area served by canals is 35,000,000 acres.

About 15,000,000 acres are irrigated by wells, chiefly in the United Provinces, Punjab, Madras, and Bombay. Many devices are used to lift the water, but the most common is a leather bag at the end of a rope which runs over a pulley above the well and is pulled by a pair of oxen. The oxen usually walk down an incline when the well is deep. Elsewhere the Persian water wheel is used with earthen jars attached to the rim of the wheel; here again oxen are used. Still more simply, water is lifted by manual labor by means of a long pivoted lever. Since well water is difficult to secure, it is used sparingly and only on high-value crops.

The construction of reservoirs, usually known as tanks, goes back to very ancient times. Some are shallow ponds dug to catch rain water, others are made by a dam across a stream; some tanks hold several billion cubic feet of water, others cover less than an acre. South India is the most characteristic region for reservoirs. In Madras there are tanks known to be 1,100 years old. Except in the Indus lowland, these reservoirs are a conspicuous feature of the landscape. About 10,000,000 acres are irrigated in this manner.

Most villages in the Deccan have their tank, perhaps the gift of some former rich resident. To it come the cattle for water, in it are washed the clothes and vegetables, into it is dumped the refuse, from it are obtained fish, and the water is often the only source for domestic use. Toward the end of the dry season when the pond shrinks to a fraction of its normal size, the odors become excessive. Small wonder that cholera, malaria, and other diseases are widespread.

India has the longest mileage of modern irrigation canals in the world, some 75,000 miles in all. Most of these are in the northwest where engineering skill has turned the wastelands of the Punjab and Sind into a great oasis which produces wheat and cotton in what was formerly an empty desert. Canal irrigation in the peninsular plateau must depend on stored seasonal rain, but the rivers of Hindustan are fed by melting snows and do not run dry. The Punjab has long been famed for the diversion weirs across its streams near the mountains, which take irrigation water from the rivers so that the interstream areas, or doabs, are made available for wheat growing.

Under British direction, the irrigated area has been greatly enlarged, and more than 10,000,000 additional settlers have been provided for. The most important factor in population redistribution has been this reclamation of wasteland. Egypt has long been famed for its Assouan Dam, but it was the lessons learned on the Indus that made modern Egyptian irrigation possible. The mile-long Sukkar Barrage on the lower Indus irrigates an area in the Sind larger than the whole of cultivated Egypt. This project is equaled by works in the Sutlej Valley in the Punjab. Both irrigation schemes were completed in 1932, and each provides water for over 5,000,000 acres.

Along the east coast it has been customary to construct diversion canals at the head of the deltas in order to bring water to the areas between the streams. Such canals usually operate only when the river is in flood stage. A large irrigation project on the Cauvery River at Mettur stores water for 1,300,000 acres and generates considerable electric power. On the west coast there is even a canal under the Western Ghats to bring irrigation water from the wet coastal slopes to the drier interior near Tinnevelly.

India is credited with nearly half the world's cattle. Humped cows or oxen and water buffalo are found everywhere, with camels in the dry northwest and elephants in the wetter east. Hindus hold the cow in religious esteem and, since the taking of life is forbidden, the animals are never killed no matter how feeble or diseased. Working bullocks must be fed, but cows are usually left to pick up what they can find. Millions of useless cattle compete for food urgently needed for work animals.

India provides a contrast to China in its source of farm power. In the former, oxen or buffaloes do the work; in the latter there is greater dependence upon human labor. Not all the draft animals in India are efficient, but their abundance is significant.

The dairy industry is but little developed, and water buffalo milk is preferred to cow's milk as it is richer in fat. A few areas specialize in cattle breeding, with fine strains in Gujarat and Nellore. Good pasture is limited. Hindus and many Mohammedans eat no meat, but hides constitute a valuable export.

All statistics in India, agriculture included, are complicated by the lack of political uniformity. Reliable census data are available from most British provinces, but from only a third of the Indian states. Since the 560 states include two-fifths of the total area and represent somewhat different geographical conditions, the total picture is obscure. The generalizations here given are selected with care, but many of them lack full statistical accuracy.

In 1931, the reported crop area[1] amounted to 333,500,000 acres, equal to 40 per cent of the total region covered by census data. This is slightly over an acre per capita. Land normally cultivated but fallow at the time of the census would raise the per capita farm acreage. Rice covers about 25 per cent of the crop area; the grain sorghums jowar, bajra, and ragi account for 30 per cent; wheat covers 10 per cent; while oil seeds and cotton each represent 7 per cent; millet is also important. Within British India alone, 34 per cent is cultivated, 7 per cent fallow, 13 per cent forest, and 45 per cent waste or not available for cultivation (1927). Much of the forest is in Assam, and the wasteland is in the Thar Desert.

Rice is the staple crop in all the wetter areas, but it is too expensive for the poorer classes who live on grain sorghums and millet. Rice culture follows the rainfall lines. Where the rainfall exceeds 80 inches, rice is dominant; with 40 to 80 inches it is still important; under 40 inches it is grown only with irrigation. The principal areas are the lower Ganges and the east coast deltas. The total area is about 80 million acres. Two crops a year are grown near Madras, but elsewhere one is the rule succeeded by a fallow period or a legume.

[1] Agricultural Statistics of India, Calcutta (annual), I British India, II Native States.

Imports of about 2 million tons a year are essential, chiefly from Rangoon.

Some rice is sown broadcast, but trans-

seedbeds. Unhusked rice is known as paddy, and the flooded fields where it is grown are commonly called paddy fields.

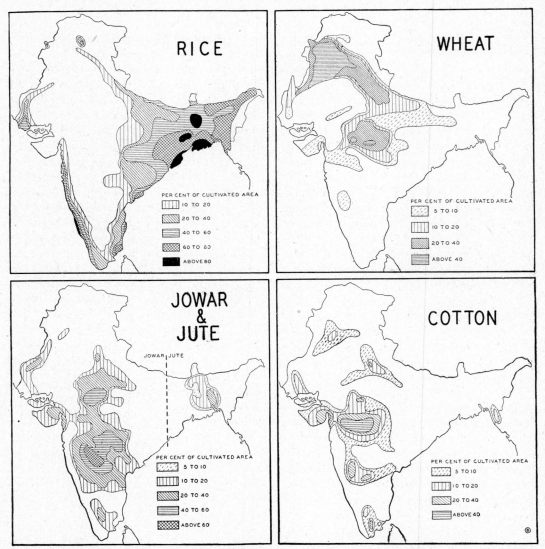

Rice, wheat, and the grain sorghums, chiefly jowar, are the three major food crops of India. Each has its distinct area. Jute in the east and cotton in the west are the principal commercial fibers. (*After Van Valkenburg in Economic Geography.*)

planting is customary. An acre of seedlings will suffice for six to ten times the field area, and the young rice is ready to be transplanted after four to five weeks in

Three varieties of grain sorghums are widespread. Jowar is comparable to Chinese kaoliang and resembles American broom corn. It grows 8 to 12 feet tall with an appearance that resembles corn, except that it has a cluster of grain at the top. Jowar covers 40,000,000 acres, chiefly in pends upon stored ground moisture and the scanty precipitation from winter cyclonic storms. New irrigation projects in the Sind

Harvesting grain sorghums in Palitana (Kathiawar). (*Courtesy Indian State Railways.*)

Malwa and the western Deccan, where the rainfall is 20 to 40 inches. It is usually a summer crop but may be grown in the winter in the south. Jowar is grown for both food and fodder. Bajra is more tolerant and hence planted on poorer soils, and is not so tall. It covers 20,000,000 acres with much the same regional distribution as jowar, although in any particular area it takes the poorer sites. Both of these sorghums are rotated with cotton. Ragi requires a rice climate but will grow on poorer soils; its locale is the southern Deccan.

Wheat is the third crop of India, with western Hindustan and the Malwa Plateau as the principal areas. Karachi has an export surplus in some years. The crop area is about 30,000,000 acres. Nearly half of this is irrigated, for wheat is planted after the summer rains and otherwise de-

and Punjab have materially increased wheat production. The yield is only ten to eleven bushels per acre, but India ranks fourth in world acreage.

Other food crops are barley, millet, corn, legumes, sugar cane, and many vegetables. Barley competes with wheat but is crowded onto the poorer soils in the drier areas, such as the United Provinces. In the absence of a meat diet, legumes are significant. Gram or chick-pea accounts for 15,000,000 acres. It is always a winter crop and provides a valuable rotation for soil fertility. India's acreage of sugar cane is the second largest in the world, but the yield per acre is but a quarter that of Java so that imports are necessary. Cane is raised in Hindustan, with the best yields in the United Provinces. Great improvements are possible in varieties of cane and in cultivation practices.

Raw cotton, peanut oil and other oil seeds, jute, and tea are important export crops.

Cotton is grown very widely in India,

provided work for the slack season and offered a modicum of income. Factory-made cloth is better, but the peasant has little cash with which to buy it.

Reeling cotton yarn in a Kathiawar farmyard. The man in the background is preparing a loom. (*Courtesy Indian State Railways.*)

but the black-soil zone with under 50 inches of rainfall in the Deccan behind Bombay leads in the total of 25,000,000 acres. The Indian acreage is second to the United States, but the production is only a quarter and acre yields are the lowest in the world. The fiber is coarse and too short for the best cloth, but meets the needs of Japanese mills which purchased nearly half the export prior to the Second World War. Most of the balance is used by Indian mills, but some cotton is still spun in the homes. One of the complaints of Indian nationalists is that modern industry has displaced the old household looms which

Oil seeds in India have commonly meant sesame, linseed from flax grown for its oil rather than its fiber, rape, mustard, and castor bean. Peanuts were not reported prior to 1911, but by 1931 were grown on over 5,000,000 acres in British India alone. They now form the chief vegetable oil export and make the country the leading world source. Many parts of the plateau share in the production, chiefly the drier areas. Indian linseed once dominated the world market but is now surpassed by the Argentine product. Cocoanut oil is an important export from the west coast and Ceylon.

Jute is the coarse fiber used for making burlap and gunny sacks, and India has practically a monopoly on the supply. Its 3,500,000 acres contribute a sixth of India's export trade. One area dominates production, the wet delta lands of Bengal where fall floods inundate wide areas and make it necessary to cut the crop under three or four feet of water. After the plant is gathered, it is soaked or retted until the fiber is loosened.

Tea was introduced from China about 1850, although it is now known that varieties are indigenous in Assam. The hills of central Ceylon form the largest single area, followed by the Brahmaputra Valley and the district south of the Khasi Hills in Assam. Tea is also grown near Darjeeling and elsewhere in the Himalaya foothills, and in the Cardamom and Nilgiri hills at the extreme end of the peninsula.

Some of the earliest exports of India were her spices, such as curry, chilies, pepper, ginger, nutmeg, and cloves. Coffee and quinine are raised in the southernmost hills, and tobacco grows in the foothills of The Himalaya. Indian indigo was known to the Greeks and Romans but the synthetic dye has nearly eliminated the native product.

India has a wide variety of tropical fruits. The cultivated mango has a delicious flavor, when one learns to like it, and in the summer is the chief fruit for the poorer classes. Other fruits are pumeloes, limes and other citrus fruits, custard apples, bananas, guava, and papaya. In the northwest apples, peaches, and pears are raised.

Crop seasons are divided between the summer-planted and autumn-harvested kharif crops, and the winter-grown rabi crops. The distinction is not entirely seasonal, since kharif crops may be grown in the far south during the winter, thanks to its rain. The planting of kharif crops is delayed until after the first monsoon rains; if these arrive unusually late, difficulty follows. The chief rabi crops are wheat, barley, oats, and legumes; typical kharif crops are early rice, grain sorghums, most cotton, and jute.

The soil directly supports two-thirds of the people, and indirectly all but a small fraction. Cultivated land amounts to only 2.51 acres per family in the United Provinces and 12.15 acres in Bombay. For all of census India the per capita average is slightly over an acre. Hindustan is thus more congested than the plateau, but these figures represent available food possibilities rather than relative prosperity. It is probable that each region is filled to its capacity. As population increases, the pressure for food becomes more acute. Since harvests depend on rain and since agriculture supplies most of the national income, it may well be said that the government's budget is a gamble against the monsoon.

Many problems account for the serious status of agriculture and make the solution uncertain. Economic factors of a poor land system and staggering debt combine with very low market prices. Religious prohibitions on the elimination of unproductive livestock as well as the absence of a meat diet are serious barriers. Lack of fertilizer is especially unfortunate in a land of poor tropical soils, naturally low in organic matter due to rapid oxidation in a tropical climate.

British rule has reduced famine, brought internal stability and external markets, opened vast tracts by irrigation, and provided scientific agricultural advice. Instead of appreciating these supposed contributions, Indian nationalists point to the elimination of former rural incomes from cotton weaving and salt production, the financial drain of supporting a handsomely paid foreign supervisory staff, and the impoverishment of the country by excess exports and the shipments of needed food-stuffs such as oil seeds.

lack of modernization, the sheer bulk of the production is so great that the

Winnowing grain. (*Courtesy Indian State Railways.*)

Behind all these problems lies the tremendous total of 388,800,000 people. With such numbers and with such social and political problems, the best agricultural plans are difficult to put in operation.

Industry

Five primary activities contribute to the wealth of a nation: agriculture, animal husbandry, forestry, mining, and fishing. Only the first is of major significance in India. Secondary production involves the manufacture of these primary materials, but modern Indian industry is restricted to the products of agriculture and the few mines. The arrival of a significant industrial era for India has long been forecast, but its appearance seems to be gradual and its future problematical. Despite the

League of Nations listed India as the twelfth industrial nation of the world.

Long before the arrival of Europeans, certain arts and crafts attained a considerable measure of development. Indigenous architecture developed under the Hindus, while the Mohammedans introduced Arabian styles in the twelfth century. Few countries have matched Indian textile skills in cotton, wool, and silk. Cotton cloth was woven from long-staple varieties of cotton no longer cultivated and was prized by the Greeks. Artistic temple and household vessels were made of copper and brass. Superior steel was exported several centuries before Christ, some of it to be worked into "Damascus" swords. When the British arrived, they eagerly sought the muslin from Dacca, the carpets and shawls from Kashmir, the marble inlay from Agra, dyes such as indigo, and a variety of spices.

Village handicrafts, many of them still more important than factory production, provided simple household pottery, iron plows, sickles and hoes for agriculture, coarse cotton cloth, vegetable oils, and leather. There are wide contrasts between the luxury items produced for court use and export, and the simple peasant needs. The lack of an intermediate market and the cost of transport restricted traditional industry to the village and its requirements.

The march of world events has profoundly altered all this. Whether deliberate or not, the effect of British rule has been to destroy many Indian crafts and to make the country an exporter of raw materials and an importer of manufactured goods. The shipping, fabricating, and reselling of these products have brought large profit to British firms. British investments at the beginning of the Second World War amounted to 250 million pounds of government loans plus nearly the same amount in private securities.

In 1936 there were only 10,000 modern factories in all India, with a daily average of 1,652,147 workers. These are strikingly localized,[1] largely in or near Calcutta, which is far in the lead, Bombay, Ahmedabad, Cawnpore, Jamshedpur, Madras, and Sholapur. No other city had more than 20,000 factory workers in 1936. The highly uneven distribution of modern industry and its concentration on cotton and jute are noteworthy features of India today. Conspicuous developments occurred during both the First and Second World Wars.

Industrial developments will be considered under the headings of heavy

[1] LOKANATHAN, P. S., Localization of Industry in India, *Journal Madras Geographical Association* (1932), VII, 16–35, with map.

industries, chemicals, textiles, and miscellaneous manufactures.

Coal production is localized in the Chota

A Hindu carpenter using a simple drill. The use of the feet in this type of work is common. (*Courtesy Paul F. Cressey.*)

Nagpur Plateau of Bengal and Bihar. The principal mines are at Raniganj, Jherria, Karanpura, and Bokaro, and the output is barely sufficient for Indian needs so that the west coast imports South African coal. Despite cheap labor and shallow workings, the coal industry is not prosperous. Many of the miners are part-time farmers who work intermittently, staying away from the mines when they have earned enough for the next few days.

Hydroelectricity is a new development. The largest installation is in the Western Ghats near Bombay where pipes descend 1,725 feet and develop a pressure of 750 pounds per square inch against the turbines. Railways near Bombay are mostly electrified. Electric power is also developed on the Jhelum in Kashmir, the Cauvery in

Madras, and elsewhere. All these sources may be enlarged to a limited extent, but their distribution is highly regional. On

Jamshedpur, 155 miles west of Calcutta.[1] Production started in 1911 and the plant represents an investment of $100,000,000.

The Tatanagar Iron and Steel Works at Jamshedpur represent the climax of industrialization in India. Blast furnaces are shown to the right while the smokestacks on the left are above the open-hearth furnaces. (*Black Star.*)

account of seasonal rainfall, expensive reservoirs are needed. Most of the country has no prospective source of industrial power.

Pig iron is produced at Burnpur near Asansol, at Kulti in Bengal, and at Badravati in Mysore; and both pig and steel at the new center of Jamshedpur.[1] The location of raw materials is the dominating factor, and few other Indian centers seem feasible.

The greatest steel plant is that of the Tata Iron and Steel Company, Ltd., at

All of this is Indian capital, and the industry is the pride of the Nationalists. Jamshedpur holds thirtieth place among world steel centers. Rich 60 per cent hematite ore comes 45 miles from Gurumaishini in the Singhbhum district; coal is brought 115 miles from Jherria; and dolomite flux is transported 40 miles. Manganese is near by. Assembly costs are less than half those in the United States or England, and the Tata plant is the cheapest producer of pig iron in the world. Steel costs are high since there is little scrap for melting.

[1] KALYONASUNDARAM, V., The Geographic Basis of the Indian Iron and Steel Industry, *Journal Madras Geographical Association*, (1934), VIII, 233–263, with maps.

[1] ANSTEY, VERA, "The Economic Development of India," London: Longmans, Green (1931), 242–508.

To produce one ton of pig iron at Jamshedpur requires 1¾ tons ore, 1⅔ tons coking coal, plus about ½ ton of dolomite flux. The five blast furnaces produced nearly two million tons of pig iron in 1940, and the steel output from seven open-hearth furnaces was about one million tons. This is three-fourths of India's production of pig, and nearly all its steel. This is said to be the largest iron and steel works in the British Empire.

Although the capacity of the Tata works has been enlarged several times and there is a protective tariff, production still fails to meet the needs or to keep out steel imports. There is normally an annual importation of 300,000 to 400,000 tons of steel from England, and an export of iron ore and pig iron to Japan. Some Jamshedpur steel is profitably shipped to California.

The Kulti plant of the Bengal Iron Company has five furnaces with a capacity of 300,000 tons; no steel is produced. There are also two blast furnaces at Burnpure and one in Mysore.

Aluminum was not produced until 1939 when a plant was opened in Bengal with a capacity of 3,000 tons annually. Copper ores from the Singhbhum district are smelted at Mandhandar in Bihar. There is little refining of other metals. Suitable raw materials for cement are widespread, but transportation costs for coal are high since none of the plants is near the mines. Bombay and Calcutta are the chief markets, yet there are no cement works within 300 miles of either city. The total production could meet nearly all needs, but rail costs to the seaboard counterbalance ocean freight so that imported cement is used along the coast. Railway industries are one of the largest of all employers.

Chemicals are an essential part of modern industry and are so interdependent that the absence of one link may handicap many others. Most of the raw materials are available in India, but they are seldom near to both power and markets. Adequate supplies of sulphuric acid are produced from imported materials, but in the case of most other chemicals the output is on an experimental basis. The necessary skilled workers are few in number.

Textiles are India's characteristic industries, chiefly cotton mills around Bombay and jute mills near Calcutta. Out of 295 cotton mills, 203 are in Bombay province, 22 in the United Provinces, 21 in Madras, and 15 in the Central Provinces. A part of Bombay's leadership is due to the initiative of Parsi industrialists, but the localization also reflects the concentration of cotton growing on the black regur soils of the Deccan. Short-staple varieties predominate here, with improved long-staple cotton on the irrigated lands of the Indus. The growth of cotton was stimulated by the American Civil War, and the first successful mill started operations in 1853. Production is increasing but has met stiff competition from Japan.

Jute production goes back a century. It is the cheapest of all fibers, and India dominates the world market. The material is used for gunny sacks, burlap, coarse carpets, and cordage. The industry is highly centralized, with 90 out of 95 factories along the banks of the Hooghly River near Calcutta. The industry employs nearly as many workers as all the cotton mills.

A similar concentration characterizes the other industries. Leather preparation is centered in Madras province on account of suitable bark for tanning purposes. Excellent cowhide as well as goat- and sheepskin is exported to Europe and the United States. Hides and skins rank sixth in the export trade. Sugar factories must lie close to the cane, so there are 13 in the United Provinces and 11 in Bihar and

Orissa, out of a total of 29 mills. The chief paper mills are close to the Calcutta market and to coal, but their raw material is sabi grass which comes 900 miles down the Ganges. At another mill bamboo pulp is used. This appears the most desirable material for the future, provided that the power may be secured cheaply. Lac, a resin secreted by an insect, is used in shellac and sealing wax, in lithographic ink, and as a stiffener in hats. Bengal and the United Provinces lead in its production. India has no good kaolin for a high-grade pottery industry. There are 32 flour mills, 5 woolen mills, numerous match factories, and local plants for crushing oil seeds and the manufacture of brick or tile.

Indian industry enjoys a natural advantage with respect to competing imports. On the other hand, the chief markets are the coastal seaports, and in the case of interior industries the rail freight to seaboard may equalize the sea-borne charges. India has no shortage of essentials for industry. Coal, iron, and many other minerals are adequate for present needs, although probably not for a vast expansion comparable to that of Europe. The great problem is geographic, for the essential raw materials are concentrated in a few localities. Vast consuming areas are either without raw materials, as Hindustan, or do not have the power to develop what they possess. Bombay has hydroelectric power, a market, and a port, but no minerals. Calcutta has both port and market, and within 200 miles has the best association of coal and iron ore. This would seem to be the most promising area for heavy industry. Technical and financial aid are still other problems.

The bulk of India's present industry is made up of consumers' goods rather than machines or tools or producers' goods. It may be a long while before India becomes a great primary manufacturing region.

Communications

Since the Europeans approached India from the sea, coastwise shipping was developed before internal communications. Unfortunately the country has few harbors. Coral reefs, delta shoals, and monsoon winds make it necessary at many ports for vessels to discharge cargo into lighters several miles offshore. Several of the few good harbors along the coast of the peninsula are cut off from their hinterland by the Ghats.

Internal communications have been equally unsatisfactory. Rivers are alternately in flood or reduced to a mere trickle and are unfit for dependable transportation. The plains of Hindustan are entirely without road-making materials, and local travel is difficult during the muddy season. Neighboring villages are even now cut off from each other during the rains, so that trade is limited.

Railway construction began in 1853. Unfortunately, several rail gauges have been used so that passengers must sometimes change cars, and freight must break bulk en route. Half the mileage is the Indian broad gauge, 5 feet 6 inches as compared with the United States standard of 4 feet 8½ inches. There are many different broad-gauge rail systems, but most are interconnected. Two unconnected regions of meter gauge occur in the north and in the south. Narrow-gauge feeder or hill lines use either 2 feet 6 inch or 2 feet track. In 1937 the broad-gauge systems totaled 21,197 miles, the meter-gauge 17,773 miles, and the narrow-gauge 4,158 miles, a total of 43,128 miles. India thus ranks third in mileage, preceded by the United States with 238,539 miles (1937) and the Soviet Union with 52,425 miles (1936).

Passenger revenues amount to 30 per cent of the whole. Railway coal and materials account for nearly half the freight, emphasizing the undeveloped state of commerce. Agricultural products are the the port of Vizagapatam and Madras, 1,030 miles or 37 hours distant.

A canal in Travancore where waterways play an important role. (*Courtesy Indian State Railways.*)

dominant revenue freight. Freight charges per mile are very low.

When railways were first laid out they naturally radiated from Calcutta and Bombay, and to a lesser extent from the other ports of Madras and Karachi.

From Bombay, the chief western gateway, it is 861 miles north to Delhi. Another route northeast via Jubbulpore and Allahabad is the main line to Calcutta, 1,223 miles or 40 hours away. A third route runs through the cotton area to Nagpur, and another provides connections with Madras, 794 miles to the southeast.

Four main railway lines radiate from Calcutta; north and east into Assam; northwest to the coal fields and up the Ganges Valley 950 miles to Delhi; west to the important rail center of Nagpur in the central Deccan; and southwest along the coast to

Madras is the focus of lines north to Vizagapatam, south to the port of Ceylon, and for two lines into the southern Deccan.

Nagpur lies at the intersection of the commercial hinterlands of Madras, Calcutta, and Bombay. The trade boundary between the two latter ports continues north to Delhi. Thus each seaport has approximately the same tributary area.

There is still no line connecting Burma with India, although surveys have been made both along the coast as well as via the Hukong Valley in the north. Ceylon is but 22 miles by boat from India, and there are intervening islands and sand bars known as Adam's Bridge which might make railway construction feasible. Proposals to link up the Indian system with Europe involve the politically undesirable route through Afghanistan to Soviet Middle Asia, or a line by way of the deserts of Iran to Bagdad.

The present rail net provides adequate coverage for most of the country. The closest spacing follows the concentration of population in the Ganges Valley. The sparsely inhabited areas of Baluchistan, the Thar Desert and western Rajputana, the eastern Deccan, and Oriya in the northeast of the plateau are correspondingly low in rail mileage. The Western Ghats fringe the sea so closely that no coastal railway extends south from Bombay. The Himalaya impose an abrupt barrier, although mountain lines reach the summer resorts or hill stations of Simla north of Delhi and Darjeeling north of Calcutta.

India has four major automobile highways, following a framework that dates back into the remote past. The most famous is the Grand Trunk road, from the Khyber pass via Delhi to Calcutta. The others connect Calcutta with Madras, Madras with Bombay, and Bombay with Delhi. It has proved very difficult to provide a satisfactory system of improved automobile roads; in many areas they cost almost as much as railways. Only 200 miles of the Grand Trunk highway are paved with asphalt; elsewhere water-bound macadam is the rule. Numerous rivers are unbridged, and sections of many important roads are liable to be inundated.

The total length of all highways in 1938 was 319,131 miles, of which 66,000 miles were water-bound macadam and 122,000 miles good-weather roads. The best subsidiary roads are in south India. In 1941, there were 123,400 motor vehicles of which 77,000 were passenger cars.

The lack of good roads has always been one of India's handicaps, whether in trade, social coherence, or political unity. Nor has there been well-developed water transportation by river, canal, or coastwise vessels to take its place. Cultural stagnation was inevitable. The country has never had an important north-south highway across the Satpura line from Hindustan into the peninsula; Jubbulpore commands the best gap. Regional isolation has been the rule. Each invading monarchy has found India relatively easy to subdue but difficult to organize.

CHAPTER 31

REGIONS OF NORTHERN INDIA

Within the Indian Realm are many diverse environments, here grouped into 14 geographic regions. Five of these are in Hindustan and three in the encircling mountains; these make up Northern India. Six regions are in the plateau to the south with Ceylon, and form the geographic province of Peninsular India. The regions of Northern India are the Bengal and Orissa Lowland, the Ganges Valley, the Brahmaputra Valley, the Indus Valley, the Thar Desert, the Western Frontier, the Himalayan Highlands, and the Assam Hills.

Bengal and Orissa Lowland

The Ganges and Brahmaputra deltas form a fitting approach to the regions of India. No other area is more homogeneous in land forms, climate, utilization, race, or language. Mohammedans are somewhat more numerous than Hindus, but the difference is religious rather than racial. The bulk of the region lies in the province of Bengal, but it also includes the Mahanadi delta and the coastal part of Orissa, plus a small section of Assam in the Surma Valley.

From the Bay of Bengal to The Himalaya is 350 miles. In an east-west direction the region narrows to 140 miles between the Garo and Rajmahal hills and widens to 300 miles in the latitude of Calcutta. Bengal itself covers 82,955 square miles, most of it level. The adjoining areas raise the total for the region to 90,000 square miles.

Within this delta plain live some 55,000,- 000 people. Nowhere else in India, and in few other places in Asia, are there so many per square mile. The average for the province was 616 in 1931, and in some rural areas that figure is trebled. In contrast, the delta of the Mississippi has 45 per square mile (1930). Despite the presence of Calcutta, the rural population is 96 per cent of the whole. Bengali is spoken by 9 out of 10 people.

This region is the flood plain of the two great river systems of the northeast. Large areas are inundated by the October and November floods, and hundreds of thousands of people have been drowned in these months. Countless natural distributaries and artificial canals intersect the plain, especially near the coast. Three sections around the margins are slightly higher: next to Chota Nagpur in the west, the Barind Hills in the north, and the Madhupur area in the Surma Valley. Each upland is covered with scrub jungle and the hilltops are little used. Elsewhere the river plains are less than 50 feet above sea level. The old delta in the west is less apt to be flooded than the new and actively growing delta in the east. In the eighteenth century the Ganges and Brahmaputra had separate mouths, and changes are still frequent. The seaward margin of the Ganges delta, known as the Sundarbans, is intricately cut by tidal channels and covered with mangrove forest. Conditions in the Mahanadi delta are similar, while between the two are coastal sand dunes.

The climate of the Bengal and Orissa lowland is excellent for rice and jute but

457

ill-suited for man, at least for Europeans and probably for the natives as well. The monsoon breaks in mid-June, bringing

from mid-March until the break of the monsoon. The winter cool period is short. Rainfall amounts to 50 inches in the

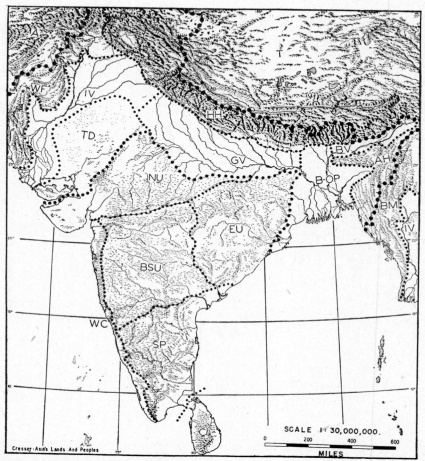

The geographic regions and land forms of India. This map clearly shows the isolation of India on the north. Within Northern India are the Bengal-Orissa Lowland, the Ganges Valley, the Brahmaputra Valley, the Indus Valley, the Thar Desert, the Northwestern Frontier, the Himalayan Highlands, and the Assam Mountains. Peninsular India includes the following geographic regions: the West Coast, the Black Soil Region, the Northern Uplands, the Eastern Uplands, the Southern Peninsula, and Ceylon. (*Base map by Erwin Raisz, courtesy Harvard-Yenching Institute, adapted by Rowland Illick.*)

copious rain from a warm sea, and provides some coolness and relief after the sultry spring. September and October have intermittent showers and are very trying, as temperatures rise and the humidity is still high; at this season Europeans go to the hill station of Darjeeling, as is also the case

Mahanadi delta and increases eastward with 60 inches in Calcutta, 74 inches in Dacca, and 157 inches at Sylhet. Despite the almost complete absence of winter rain, the ground is so moist that the landscape remains green throughout the year. Malaria is especially serious here.

Rice covers 87 per cent of the cultivated land in Bengal, some 25,000,000 acres in all; in coastal Orissa the percentage is 82. favors the acid soils that are deficient in lime, and the crop covers 2,000,000 acres.

Calcutta dominates eastern India and

Calcutta is India's premier city, the major port at the head of the Bay of Bengal. Jute is the leading industry.

Dry crops such as wheat or millet are absent, but vegetables and oil seeds are grown. Jute is the great cash crop, especially on the new delta where each flood brings a layer of fertilizing silt. Jute was the second largest city in the British Empire in 1941, when the population numbered 2,488,183, including the suburb of Howrah with 379,292. The city lies on the outside of a bend on the eastern bank of the Hooghly River, 120 miles from where ships take on a pilot outside the mouth. The port extends for 20 miles along

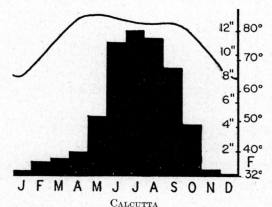

CALCUTTA

Elevation, 21 feet; average temperature, 77.9°F.; total precipitation, 58.8 inches.

the river, here at a depth of 27 feet. Spring tides average 11 feet and keep the shifting channel of the Hooghly scoured; otherwise silting would block the river as it is no longer an important distributary of the Ganges.

The location of Calcutta is significant. The Hooghly gives deep water; no other rivers block railway access to the west; canals bring raw jute from the east; coal and iron are near by; natural levee accumulations permit the drainage of sewage away from the city into other streams; and in the economic hinterland live some 200,000,000 people. It is around the corner from Europe but closer to the newer markets of the Far East. As a result of these geographic advantages, Calcutta is one of the leading ports of the Orient. In 1936–1937, the net tonnage of ships entering the port was 4,082,572.

Calcutta was the British capital until 1912 and is still the commercial and financial metropolis of India. Bombay has the advantage of proximity to Europe, but Calcutta is nearer domestic markets. Scores of great British firms have splendid

office buildings here, and the metropolitan area extends beyond the political limits to include numerous residential and industrial suburbs on both sides of the river. So many workers have come from elsewhere that in 1941 the sex ratio was 1,000 men to 452 women. The European population numbers some 15,000, and there are about the same number of Anglo-Indians, or those of mixed percentage.

The only other port of the region is Chittagong in the east, terminus of a narrow-gauge railway to the jute and tea districts. Interior cities are few and small; the largest is the old provincial capital of Dacca, 213,218 in 1941, in the center of the jute area.

On most sides, the Bengal and Orissa Lowland is clearly limited by hills or the sea. To the southwest, the Chilka Lake at the southern edge of the Mahanadi delta is a historic boundary. On the northeast and northwest, the main valleys of the Ganges and Brahmaputra are set off by slight climatic differences.

Ganges Valley

The Ganges is the life of India. The river rises behind the snow-crowned Himalaya and flows 1,500 miles through eastern Hindustan. Along its banks are the classical cities of Hindu history. The Ganges landscape typifies the agricultural regime and population density made possible by the monsoon.

The region is sharply bounded by hills to the north and south, but grades imperceptibly east and west where rainfall changes bring transitions in crops. Within the area lie most of the United Provinces and the northern half of Bihar, a total of about 120,000 square miles and 75,000,000 people.

Beneath the valley is an accumulation of sand and clay to unplumbed depths, ancient alluvial deposits spread by Tertiary and Quaternary rivers in a vast geosyncline. The relief is almost featureless, with an elevation of only 700 feet at Delhi. The plain surfaces are named the khadar, while the older are the bhangar. Although the summer rain is heavy, capillary action

A village near Jhansi, United Provinces, with its unirrigated fields. (*Courtesy Indian State Railways.*)

Ganges has two main tributaries: the Jumna which joins it from the west and south, and the Gogra from the north.

The rivers carry great quantities of silt in their flood stage, and its accumulation has built extensive natural levees, often capped by artificial embankments. When these are overtopped, widespread inundation results, often with the formation of a new channel and the development of lakes or swamps along the old course. Between the valleys, higher ground prevents flooding. These areas of older and higher alluvium contain early Pleistocene and Pliocene fossils and calcium carbonate nodules which are used for making lime or surfacing roads. The present flood-

in the dry winter brings water to the surface when its evaporation concentrates soluble salts and alkalis in the upper soil horizon. Overirrigation and poor subsurface drainage aggravate the situation in the United Provinces where three million acres have thus been ruined.

The summer monsoon from the Bay of Bengal is turned to the west up the valley by the mountain barrier. Thus, precipitation decreases westward away from the sea. At the same time, maximum summer temperatures increase so that the drier west is also hotter. Patna in Bihar has 44 inches of rain and maximum temperatures of 88°F. For Benares to the west the figures are 41 inches and 91°F.; Cawnpore has 32 inches and 93°F.; Agra has 29 inches and 95°F.; while Delhi near the western edge receives only 25 inches. throughout. Jowar, bajra, barley, sugar cane, oil seeds, and corn are widely distributed. Cotton predominates in the west.

A bazaar street in Muttra, United Provinces. (*Courtesy Indian State Railways.*)

Maximum temperatures come in May except in the west where June is hotter.

The rainfall occurs during the growing season and is normally adequate, but in drier seasons irrigation is available from wells and canals which distribute river water. Irrigation is regularly used for such crops as cotton and sugar cane. Cultivated land exceeds 70 per cent of the total, and double cropping is common. The prevalence of large landholdings has led to serious agrarian problems.

The Ganges Valley grows almost every kind of crop produced in India. Summer rice in the east interfingers with winter wheat in the west, although each is grown

The region leads in sugar cane and lac and in the density of cattle. Some writers divide the valley into upper and middle regions, for the two extremes differ in crop combinations, irrigation practices, natural vegetation, and soil, but there is only a gradational change between the dominance of such wet and dry crops as rice and wheat and their respective climates.

The chief cities are Patna, Benares, Allahabad, and Cawnpore on the Ganges, Agra and Delhi on the Jumna, and Lucknow. Patna is the modernized capital of Bihar, celebrated for its rice. Benares, 263,100 in 1941, is a sacred city for both Hindus and Buddhists, and its history goes back long before the Christian era. The many pilgrims provide a market for fine craft work. It is reached by river steamers

A low hill within the walls forms an acropolis. Delhi commands the narrowest gap between the Ganges and Indus Valleys.

The sacred Ganges is lined with bathing ghats at Benares. (*Courtesy Indian State Railways.*)

and has the first railway bridge over the Ganges above Sara, north of Calcutta. Allahabad, 260,630 in 1941, is a commercial center at the junction of the Jumna. Cawnpore is the most important industrial city of northern India, a creation of modern cotton, wool, leather, oil seed, and sugar industries. The population of 487,324 in 1941 has doubled in ten years. Agra, 284,149 in 1941, is the site of the exquisite Taj Mahal. The third largest city in the region is Lucknow, with 387,177 in 1941, capital of the United Provinces.

The position of Delhi (pronounced Del'hi) is unique in both site and situation. It lies on the Jumna and was at the head of navigation until irrigation withdrawals reduced the flow of the river. Here was the place where water travel from the east changed to overland routes westward to the rivers of the Punjab. Immediately west of the city is the Ridge, northernmost continuation of the Aravalli Range.

Communications farther south are blocked by the Thar Desert, while to the north

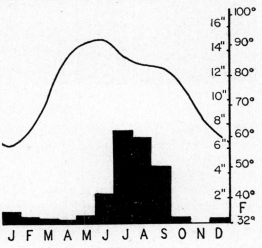

DELHI
Elevation, 718 feet; average temperature, 77.1°F.; total precipitation, 26.2 inches.

rise The Himalaya. From Delhi to Hardwar where the Ganges leaves the mountains is just over 100 miles. Delhi's strategic location is thus the most logical place for the political control of both dry Mohammedan western Hindustan, and the wet

Brahmaputra Valley

The Brahmaputra is even longer than the Ganges, and for the first half of its 1,800-

The women of Assam show many of the racial traits that characterize the aborigines of Burma and southwestern China. (*Courtesy Indian State Railways.*)

eastern Hindu part. Delhi is 950 miles from Calcutta, and 861 and 940 miles from Bombay and Karachi, respectively. Railways lead in half a dozen directions. At least six other capitals had been built on the site before the British moved the government of India here from Calcutta in 1912. The government offices are in a suburb known as New Delhi. The 1941 population of 675,812 makes it India's fourth city. The hill station of Simla, at an elevation of 7,116 feet in the mountains to the north, is the hot weather capital.

mile course it flows eastward parallel to the latter but behind the mountains. In this section through Tibet it is variously known as the Nari Chu or Tsangpo. Parts of its course were unsurveyed until the twentieth century. When it enters the Assam lowland, the river carries a tremendous burden of sediment so that the channel is braided and shifting, although navigable. During the rainy season the water rises 30 to 40 feet and floods vast areas, eliminating the necessity for irrigation.

The Brahmaputra Valley as a geographical region is here limited to the lowland within Assam. It opens to Bengal on the west, but on the other three sides is hemmed in by mountain walls, lofty on the north and east but low to the south. The Brahmaputra Valley is thus in contrast to the Ganges Valley where there is access from three sides. The valley is some 500 miles long but nowhere much more than 50 miles wide, one of the smallest of all Indian regions.

The Garo and Khasi hills on the south partly keep out the monsoon rains, but a strong current moves up the valley and gives an average rainfall in excess of 80 inches. Where the monsoon crosses the hills, there are dry foehn effects on the north slopes.

Rice throughout, jute in the west, and tea in the foothills are the chief crops. Assam is one of the world's leading tea producers for export. The valley still contains large forests of teak and sal. Elephant ivory and rhinoceros horn are secured in the forest zones. Large areas of land are unused, partly jungle marsh along the river banks, so that cropland is generally under 20 per cent.

Assam is different from the rest of India in race and history. It forms a separate cultural area with many primitive tribes; conditions resemble those of Burma. Unlike the Ganges Valley, population densities average but 150 per square mile; hence there is a large migration into Assam, especially for seasonal labor in the tea plantations.

Lignite coal and oil are obtained in the bordering hills. River steamers carry most of the freight, although there are narrow-gauge railways. No bridge spans the Brahmaputra.

Indus Valley

Western Hindustan includes the plains and low hills from the Aravalli Range west to the Sulaiman Mountains, and from the Salt Range and Siwaliks south to the Arabian Sea. Much of it is the alluvial

Punjabi moneylenders wander over Northern India and are one of the economic parasites of the country. Interest rates may reach 75 per cent a year. (*Courtesy Paul F. Cressey.*)

valley of the Indus, but the southeastern half lies in the Thar Desert where there is an erosional and aeolian rather than river-deposited surface. Each half forms a geographic region.

The tributaries of the Indus extend along the base of The Himalaya for 400 miles west of Delhi, and the main river flows south across the plain for 600 miles before reaching the sea. About 140,000 square miles are included within the region, with a population of some 30,000,000. Two distinct subregions are present, the Punjab in the north with two-thirds the area and nine-tenths the people, and the Sind[1] south of the constriction made by the Sulaiman Mountains and the Thar Desert.

The word Punjab is of Persian origin and refers to the area drained by the five tributaries of the Indus: the Jhelum, Chenab, Ravi, Beas, and Sutlej. Each rises in The Himalaya and follows a shifting course across vast alluvial fans until it joins the Indus halfway to the sea. Since the outer Himalayan hills or Siwaliks are composed of easily eroded sedimentary rocks, each river is overloaded with sediment whose deposition en route across the plain continually raises the stream beds. This aggradation has built the bed of the lower Indus 70 feet above the surrounding country. Irrigation by diversion canals is made easy, but flood hazards are acute.

Each of the rivers frequently changes its course, often by tens of miles. In the third century B.C. the course of the Indus was 80 miles to the east of the present channel, and it emptied into the Rann of Cutch. The Jumna, now a Ganges tributary, once flowed to the west, and several hundred miles of abandoned river channels through the Thar Desert may represent its old course. Dead cities date back to 3000 B.C.

Interstream areas are known in India as doabs, originally from the country between the Ganges and the Jumna. For the most part they are slightly higher and the sediments are mid-Pleistocene rather than Recent. Differences between older and younger alluvium as referred to in eastern Hindustan are slightly more emphasized here, such as the presence of lime nodules or kunkur, but nowhere reach the contrasts exhibited in Japan.

Three surfaces may be recognized in both east and west: the modern deltas, the newer alluvium or khadar, and the older alluvium

or bhangar. The material of each is essentially similar, and the topographic differences are only gradational. Part of the contrast may relate to glaciation in The Himalaya; in part it may merely represent normal stream planation.[1]

The Indus Valley is hot, even for India. Jacobabad in the northern Sind has June temperatures consistently reaching 120° and with a maximum of 127°F.; and the monthly day and night mean is 98°F.:[2] rainfall is but 4 inches per year. The eastern Punjab is somewhat more humid, with precipitation up to 20 inches. Winters are cool, with frost in the north.

During the winter small cyclonic storms moving across Hindustan from Iran produce a little rain, but most of the limited precipitation is in the summer. The Indus Valley is exposed to both arms of the monsoon; but the one which moves up the Ganges is nearly dry upon arrival, while the Arabian Sea division is rainless since it here moves nearly overland from Iran and Arabia.

Irrigation is essential for successful agriculture in most of the valley, although some crops may be grown without it in the north and east where rainfall is higher or ground water is available from the hills. Canals are an ancient development but have been greatly expanded by the British. There are 75,000 miles of canals and 35,000,000 million acres of canal-irrigated land in all India, of which half are in the Indus Valley. Each of the major streams has its system of distributaries, with their

[1] PITHAWALLA, MANECK B., Settlements in the Lower Indus Basin (Sind), *Journal Madras Geographical Association* (1938), XIII, 323–357.

[1] WADIA, D. N., "Geology of India," 282–293.

DeTERRA, HELMUT, and T. T. PATTERSON, "Studies on the Ice Age of India and Associated Human Cultures," Carnegie Institution of Washington (1939).

DeTERRA, HELMUT, The Quaternary Terrace System of Southern Asia and the Age of Man, *Geographical Review* (1939), XXIX, 101–118.

[2] The highest official air temperature on earth is at Azizia in northern Africa, 136.4°F.

inverted dendritic pattern. Colonization started in 1886, and the 1891 population density of 7 per square mile in the Punjab money is required to get rid of surplus water due to subsoil saturation as is spent on irrigation supply.

The Sukkar Barrage or dam across the Indus controls irrigation over a million acres of agricultural land in Sind. (*Courtesy Indian State Railways.*)

Irrigated land near the Sukkar Barrage in the Sind. The cattle and wooden plows are characteristic. (*Courtesy Indian State Railways.*)

rose to 272 in 1911. The sequence of problems that follow irrigation of dry lands is shown by the fact that almost as much

Wheat is the most important crop, but only half is irrigated. Yields in the Punjab average 12.2 bushels per acre which is slightly above the all-Indian average of 11.2. Barley and oil seeds are other spring-harvested crops, while millet and corn are

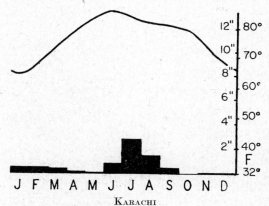

KARACHI
Elevation, 13 feet; average temperature, 77.6°F.; total precipitation, 7.6 inches.

autumn crops. Cotton is an important cash crop during the summer on irrigated land.

The people of the Punjab are predominantly Mohammedans. The Punjabi themselves are tall and well built and have a long military tradition. Many of them travel throughout India as salesmen and as moneylenders, for the uncertainties of the monsoon and the general lack of capital often make it necessary for farmers to borrow money.

Among the various peoples of the Punjab are the Sikhs, with a religion somewhat intermediate between the Hindus and Mohammedans. The men are tall with a splendid physique and make good soldiers. A quarter of the Indian army in India are Sikhs, who also serve as policemen in British cities throughout the Far East. Although they number but an eighth of the people in the Punjab, they own a quarter of the irrigated land.

The three cities of importance are Lahore, with 671,659 people in 1941, Amritsar with 391,010 in 1941, both in the Punjab, and Karachi, 359,492 in 1941, in Sind. Karachi is India's fourth port and ships wheat and raw cotton, but its humidity is too low for cotton mills. The city has been developed during the twentieth century as an outlet for the northwest. Since Karachi is 200 miles closer to Aden than is Bombay, it is the nearest port to Europe, and also the terminus for air services.

Thar Desert

Between the Indus Valley and the Aravalli Range at the edge of the plateau is an arid region, nearly empty in its northern and more desert area, and only sparsely inhabited in the south near the sea. It includes a large number of native states in western Rajputana and northern Bombay. In the north is the Thar Desert proper, while in the south is Cutch.

The summer aridity of northwest India presents several problems. Low pressures and proximity to the sea would suggest rain, but instead there are cloudless skies. Winds from the east are dry since the monsoon has lost all of its moisture coming up the Ganges Valley, while on the north and west are mountain barriers that keep out surface winds. From the south, winds enter the Sind with a relative humidity of 80 per cent, but high surface temperatures reduce this figure to 55 per cent in the interior. A convectional rise to 3,000 feet would give rain, but before this elevation is reached, surface air mixes with dry air masses from the west so that cloud formation is prevented. Thus the sun, directly overhead, shines without interruption and heats the surface, still further lowering the relative humidity.

The rainfall is generally under ten inches and, since there is little possibility of irrigation, most of the area is a desolate waste, covered with shifting sands or scattered brush. Older rock hills here and

A small village in the Sind Desert west of Karachi. (*Courtesy Indian State Railways.*)

The evaporation of sea water in large salt pans is an important industry in Kathiawar. (*Courtesy Indian State Railways.*)

there project above the undulating surface. Camel caravans link the few oases.

Here and there are shallow playa lakes. The most important is Lake Sambhar, which covers 90 square miles with a maximum depth of four feet after occasional rains; at other seasons it is a largely dry salt flat.

The Rann of Cutch, to the south, was an arm of the sea in early historic times, but is now nearly filled with sediments alternately wet and dry with the season. From its salt-incrusted surface and from sea spray, the southern monsoon annually carries 130,000 tons of salt into Rajputana.[1]

In 1819, 200,000 square miles in the western Rann sank 12 to 15 feet, while a near-by area of 600 square miles rose several feet.

Western Frontier

Northwestern India is not only a place, it is a problem. Nowhere else does the British Empire have a land frontier of such military significance. Through these mountains came all previous invasions of India; beyond them today is the communist Soviet Union and the restless Mohammedan world.

Across the Indus tower the 11,000-foot Sulaiman and the 7,000-foot Kirthar ranges. What lies in their immediate hinterland is not so significant as the fact that they are a rampart bounding India on the west. This 600-mile length of mountain wall is about the same distance as the boundary next to Burma, but in the east there are climatic as well as topographic barriers to penetration. The history of the two frontiers is entirely different.

Six significant routes lead westward: the Khyber Pass to Kabul in Afghanistan, the important Bolan Pass to Quetta in Baluchistan, the arid Makran coastal

[1] HOLLAND and CHRISTIE, *Records* Geological Survey of India, XXXVIII, part 2 (1909).

strip, and the lesser Gomal, Kurram, and Tochi passes. These are paths of history. In addition there are 350 trails usable for camels. All these tend to be one-way roads in terms of defense, easy for the descent of warlike tribesmen who wish to raid the plains but difficult for the British to penetrate and to police. Road building has become the key to the pacification of this frontier.

From Istanbul to the Indus, Asia is a succession of high arid plateaus, surrounded by mountains. Anatolia is the westernmost; Baluchistan, the easternmost. Nowhere in this succession is there much rain, but such precipitation as occurs follows the Mediterranean sequence of summer drought when subtropical high pressure moves northward, and of winter rain which occurs with the displaced belt of cyclonic storms. The Sulaiman Mountains mark the boundary between winter-Mediterranean and summer-monsoon rainfall.

In topography, climate, race, and ways of livelihood, both Baluchistan and Afghanistan might properly be grouped with Southwestern Asia, but in trade and history they are related to India. The Western Frontier region as here considered includes Baluchistan, most of the Northwest Frontier Province, and part of the Punjab behind the Salt Range. The area is some 170,000 square miles, and population densities range from nearly zero in some deserts and mountains, to 6 for Baluchistan as a whole, 100 for the Northwest Frontier Province; and a few hundred per square mile in the fertile valleys of the Punjab.

Climatic conditions improve from south to north, although level land unfortunately diminishes. Quetta with ten inches of rain represents the mean. Thus Makran is a desolate coastal strip where people and their cattle alike subsist on fish. Baluchistan is a land of interior drainage and withering rivers which descend from barren mile-high mountains. Great gravel fans testify to the aridity of the country. Into them,

The Salt Range has long attracted geological attention. At its base are immense beds of Eocene salt, and the

The excavation of the ancient Dharmrajika stupa at Taxila, near Rawalpindi, has revealed much about India's early history centuries before the Christian era. (*Courtesy Indian State Railways.*)

Persian-style tunnels or karez have been driven for water to irrigate lower flood plains. Sorghum is the chief grain, with some wheat and barley. Excellent fruits are raised. In the corner of the Punjab, wheat leads and is followed by millet, barley, and corn.

This is the land of the nomadic pastoralist rather than the settled farmer. Transhumance is common; as summer comes the shepherds move their flocks and herds to the cooler mountain slopes; in the winter they descend to the lowlands or even to the Sind.

Baluchistan produced 21,428 tons of chromite in 1936–1937, as well as a small amount of coal.

overthrust structure reveals an excellent stratigraphic record.

The three most important cities are Quetta, the capital of Baluchistan; the great arsenal and military post of Rawalpindi, the gate to Kashmir, with 181,169 people in 1941; and Peshawar on the railway to the Khyber Pass, population 130,967 in 1941.

Himalayan Highlands

Himalayan structure and topography are complex, increasingly so toward the west. In general there are three parallel zones. The Outer Himalaya includes the mile-high Siwaliks with a series of Appalachian-type anticlines and synclines, dissected into a series of escarpments and dip slopes and separated by linear valleys called duns. At the southern limit is a

in Tibet, but flow in opposite directions and cross the mountains 1,500 miles apart. Numerous rivers with headwaters on the

The Himalayan sky line towers above the foothills of Nepal near Sandakphu. (*Ewing Galloway.*)

great overthrust directed from the north. The Lesser Himalaya, in the middle, rises 7,000 to 15,000 feet and is marked by recumbent folds and strong thrusting. On the north is the Great Himalaya Range with an average crest line of 20,000 feet. Its geological structures are imperfectly known but appear to resemble Scottish Highland faults rather than Alpine nappes. Igneous intrusions make the structure complex.

The Himalayan Highlands present many geological problems, not the least of which are the river systems. Thus the Indus and Brahmaputra rise near each other in the area of the Manasarowar Lakes

north slopes, such as the Sutlej which rises in the same lake region, break through the ranges at right angles in antecedent valleys, the rivers being older than the mountains.

Some of these valleys are the deepest canyons on earth. "The most remarkable example is the Indus Valley in Gilgit Agency where at one place the river flows through a narrow defile, between enormous precipices nearly 20,000 feet in altitude, while the bed of the valley is only 3,000 feet above its level at Haiderabad (the head of its delta). This gives to the gorge the stupendous depth of 17,000 feet, yet the fact that every inch of this chasm is carved by the river is clear from the fact that small patches or 'terraces' of river gravel and sand beds are observed at heaps of moraine at elevations of 6,000 feet and lower. Although the peninsula was not glaciated at this time, parallel

A street in Leh along the upper Indus in the western Himalaya. (*Courtesy Indian State Railways.*)

various elevations."[1] It is but 12 miles from the Indus to the peak of Nanga Parbat, 26,629 feet high. At a point on the Kali Gandak where the stream is at 9,000 feet, near-by elevations on either side rise to 26,810 and 26,504 feet. The Sutlej and Brahmaputra have comparable gorges.

The youthful character of these valleys is indicated by their gradients. Thus, the Brahmaputra descends 7,200 feet in 25 miles through the main range. Few of these chasms can be traversed, so that access to Tibet is over lofty divides, snow-blocked for many months.

Pleistocene glaciers have left enormous

[1] WADIA, D. N., "Geology of India," 19.

climatic changes brought widespread alterations in the fauna and flora.

The giant peaks are in the Great Himalaya; Nanga Parbat in Kashmir; Nanda Devi in the United Provinces, 25,645 feet; Mt. Everest in Nepal, 29,141 feet; and Kangchenjunga at the edge of Nepal, 28,146 feet.

Between the Punjab and Chinese Sinkiang is a complex of mountains, the whitest, snowiest, iciest ranges outside of polar regions. In the midst of them lies the Karakorum Pass with an elevation of 18,550 feet. This name has been variously applied to some of the snowy mountains, but it is now recognized that the Karakorum Pass is not in the Karakorum

Range. The range lies between the Indus and Shaksgam, and includes the world's second highest peak, K², with an elevation

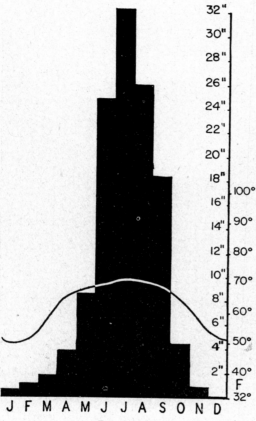

DARJEELING
Elevation, 7,376 feet; average temperature, 52.70°F.;
total precipitation, 122.7 inches.

of 28,250.[1] Within this area are numerous glaciers 30 and 40 miles long.[2]

Within the Himalaya and Karakorum area there are fifty summits over 25,000 feet of which only two have been climbed, Kamet and Nanda Devi.

Mt. Everest stands supreme, because of both its height and the difficulty of ascent. Serious attempts to climb it date from 1920 and involve an approach from the

[1] MASON, KENNETH, Karakorum Nomenclature, *Geographical Journal* (1938), XCI, 123–152.
[2] CRESSEY, GEORGE B., Glaciation on the Roof of the World, *Geographical Review* (1931), XXI, 157–160.

north just before the arrival of the monsoon in May.

Between the Indo-Gangetic Plain and the Himalayan Highlands is a line of swamps and undulating topography, continuous for most of the distance except in the drier west. In the east this forested strip is known as the duars, elsewhere it is the terai. Where the terai has not been drained, this marginal zone has a sparse population. North of it lie the first foothills, actually mile-high mountains but termed hills because of what lies beyond.

Vegetation height limits are influenced by rainfall as well as altitude, with the heaviest precipitation in the east. Dense subtropical forests extend as high as 6,000 feet. Deciduous forests are typical between 5,000 and 11,000 feet, and in this zone are the hill stations of Darjeeling, 7,135 feet, and Simla to the west, 7,116 feet. The former has 122.7 inches of rain while the latter receives but 72 inches. Coniferous trees are present from 9,000 to 12,000 feet. Here the air has lost most of its moisture and rainfall is under 40 inches. Rhododendron grows from 9,000 to 13,500 feet, while stunted alpine growths, seldom over two feet in height, prevail above this, according to exposure. Beyond is barren rock and snow. On the south slopes, the snow line descends to 14,000 feet in the east and 19,000 feet in the west. On the dry Tibetan side elevations are higher.

Between the Outer and Lesser Himalaya and north of the Punjab is the famed Vale of Kashmir in the Jhelum Valley. At an elevation of 5,250 feet lies Srinagar, surrounded by cultivated fields and glorious mountains, the capital of the Indian state of Kashmir. The people of Kashmir are noted for their art and industry. Shawls made of goats' wool, carpets, woolen cloth, and wood carving are world famous. Houseboat trips on the Jhelum and the Dal Lake provide some of the most beautiful views in the world.

Indian cultural influences do not extend far into the mountains, but British political influence is effective even in Lhasa. Most where the winds are forced to rise over mountains. The second heaviest rainfall station in the world is at Cherrapunji,

The Dal Lake at Srinagar in the Vale of Kashmir. This is a justly famous tourist center in the western Himalayan Highlands. (*Courtesy Indian State Railways.*)

of Tibet has already been considered in the chapters on China.

Assam Mountains

The region includes the east-west Garo and Khasi hills and the north-south ranges near the Burma border. The lowlands of Assam have already been considered. Although the area is small, the rainfall is noteworthy and the lack of roads into Burma makes this an effective barrier for the eastern frontier.

The Assam Mountains receive the full force of the monsoon from the Bay of Bengal, and the rainfall is especially heavy where the average total is 451.6 inches. This station lies at 4,309 feet next to the steep southern face of the Khasi Hills; in contrast Shillong within the mountains but back from the edge of the range at 4,920 feet receives but 84 inches, while Sylhet in the lowlands to the south has 157 inches.

Natural vegetation reflects the rainfall, with a dense tropical rain forest with little agriculture or lumbering in the wetter areas. Agriculture is limited to fire clearings where the ash supplies fertilization, and to the few areas of alluvium along the streams. Corn, millet, and rice are grown.

CHAPTER 32

REGIONS OF PENINSULAR INDIA

The contrasts between northern and southern India are largely in matters of surface configuration. Rainfall is slightly the Northern Uplands, the Eastern Uplands, the Southern Peninsula, and Ceylon.

The West Coast is sharply defined by the

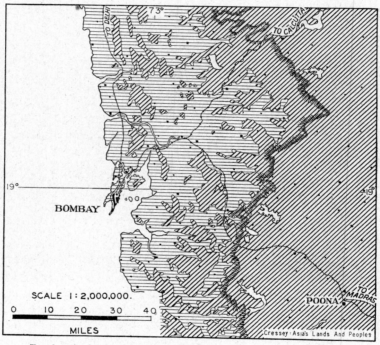

Bombay is the cotton mill center and chief port of western India.

lower in the southern farm lands, and crops are therefore different. Many of the inhabitants are Dravidians rather than the Hindu peoples of the north. Hindu religion predominates with only small areas of Mohammedans. None of these contrasts is at all comparable to the striking differences between North and South China.

Within Peninsular India are five major regions, while near-by Ceylon adds a sixth: the West Coast, the Black Soil region,

line of the Western Ghats, but elsewhere other boundaries are less clear. The Vindhya Range sets off the Northern Uplands. East of Bombay there is the famous area of Deccan lava flows with its Black Soil region. The Eastern Uplands from the Godavari River to the Chota Nagpur Plateau include a variety of topographic and geographic conditions, different from their surroundings and sufficiently homogeneous to be grouped together. This leaves the Southern Peninsula of Madras and Mysore. Some regional classifications define an East Coast comparable to the West Coast, but the Eastern Ghats are much lower and do not isolate the southern interior from the coastal lowlands.

West Coast

The West Coast region is a narrow strip of lowland and escarpment from Cape Comarin at the tip of the peninsula to the Gulf of Cambay, a thousand miles to the north. Little uniformity and less coherence can be expected in such an attenuated area, yet certain factors entitle the region to be considered as a unit.

The Arabian Sea is bordered by fault escarpments on three sides, perhaps as recent as the Pliocene; these mark the margins of a down-dropped block. One of these dislocations forms the Western Ghats at the edge of the Deccan Plateau. Viewed from the sea, these are 3,000-foot mountains; seen from the east they are a line of hills. The topographic contrast of this asymmetrical divide is striking; youthful canyons on the west are actively gnawing into eastward-draining open valleys in late maturity.

The northern half of the escarpment is cut in horizontal lava flows, so that slopes have a steplike development. Farther south, granitic rocks prevail and the land forms are more rounded.

Toward the south, the Eastern and Western Ghats meet in the Nilgiri Hills, which rise to 8,700 feet. South of them is the 800-foot Palghat Gap, and farther south are the high Cardamom Hills.

The Western Ghats receive the full effect of the summer monsoon off the Arabian Sea. Throughout most of the region, precipitation at sea-level stations exceeds 100 inches, diminishing to the north. Bombay has only 74 inches and

southern Gujarat but 40 inches. As the moist winds rise over the mountains, rainfall increases to 200 and even 300 inches at

A village street in British Cochin, south India. (*Courtesy Indian State Railways.*)

hill stations. In the basin of the hydroelectric installation near Bombay, as much as 540 inches has been recorded in 90 days.[1]

In the extreme north are the only westward-flowing rivers of importance in all India, the Narbada and Tapti. South of these valleys the Western Ghats present a barrier which is crossed by only three railways until the Palghat Gap is reached. Along the Konkan coast in the north the mountains come close to the sea and restrict level land to discontinuous strips a few miles in width. Farther south the Malabar coast widens to 70 miles. Barrier beaches with sand dunes and lagoons fringed with mangrove swamp are characteristic.

In general there are three linear subregions: a sandy coastal strip intensively

[1] LYDE, L. W., "The Continent of Asia," 445.

used for cocoanut palms; a cultivated zone of alluvium, half of it in rice; and the heavily forested mountain slopes. Large only Indian area for the commercial production of coir, the fiber from cocoanut husks. Copra and cocoanut oil form impor-

The crowded city of Bombay, whose name means "good bay." (*Courtesy Indian State Railways.*)

supplies of bamboo, teak, ebony, and sandalwood are rafted down the turbulent rivers in flood stage. Despite the extensive area of unproductive land, the population density exceeds 400 per square mile.

Overland communications are limited and have always tended to isolate the region from the rest of India. Access to the sea is not much easier, for harbors are few and most navigation must be suspended for three months at the height of the monsoon. Trade dates back to early times when Arab merchants made regular voyages to Zanzibar and the African coast, back and forth with the monsoons. Most of the Indian sailors or lascars employed on British boats trading with Asia come from this region. Coastal fishing is important.

Several special products are obtained here. The oldest and most famous are pepper, ginger, and other spices. This is the

tant exports. Coffee acreage has declined but is replaced by tea. Rubber is gradually expanding. Quinine is produced on government cinchona plantations in the Nilgiri Hills at altitudes over 3,000 feet and is sold at low prices at every post office in India in order to check malaria.[1]

Bombay is the one good natural harbor, not only of the West Coast but almost for all India. The city lies on a hilly island which protects a large bay, sheltered at all seasons. Behind the city two passes give access for railway lines to the interior. Hydroelectric power is available in the mountains and is supplemented by coal brought from Calcutta by boat. The hinterland grows cotton, India's most important commercial crop and the basis

[1] PASUPATHI, K. N., Chinchona Cultivation in India, *Journal Madras Geographical Association* (1939), XIV, 410–414.

of the city's chief industry. Bombay's development coincides with the completion of rail connections in 1861, just in time to profit from the cotton shortage that arose with the United States Civil War. After this emergency passed, the opening of the Suez Canal in 1869 established Bombay as the principal western gateway to India. Although second to Calcutta as a port, Bombay is of major importance for communications with Europe. It is the center of Indian finance and industrial management, whereas Calcutta is dominated by British capital.

The population of Bombay was 1,489,883 in 1941, second to Calcutta. The city is particularly congested, and high labor costs are driving cotton mills to the interior. Social contrasts are striking. On the one hand Bombay has some of the worst industrial slums in the world; on the other hand there are splendid boulevards and wealthy Parsee and European merchants. There is a constant flow of factory workers back and forth to their family homes in the villages, so that the ratio of women to men in Bombay is 547,000 to 942,000. Linguistic and racial groupings are much more heterogeneous than in New York City. In public places, caste is an almost forgotten phenomenon, although in some aspects it is rigid. Housing conditions are so serious that one-third of the population live in single rooms occupied by six persons or more.

The second most important port on the West Coast is the Portuguese city of Goa, terminus for the only rail line across the Ghats between Bombay and the Palghat Pass. Other cities of historic interest are Calicut and Cochin, the latter with a newly developed port that rivals Madras.

Black Soil Region

The most distinctive and one of the most puzzling soils of India is the black regur

soil of the western Deccan. In color, clay content, abundance of lime, and fertility it somewhat resembles the chernozems of

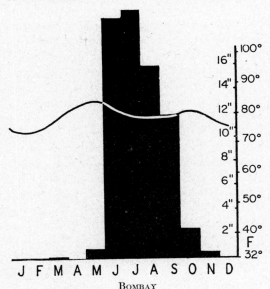

BOMBAY
Elevation, 37 feet; average temperature, 79.3°F.; total precipitation, 79.4 inches.

temperate grasslands, but it is low in organic matter and the color is not a result of carbonaceous material. The distribution of black soil is more or less coextensive with the great flows of basalt, and it was once regarded as a normal product of weathering *in situ*. It is now clear that representative regur is also found on metamorphic rocks and alluvium, and that not all areas underlain by lava have typical black soil.

Black soil is best developed on level to undulating upland or valley areas where soil-forming processes have reached maturity. On slopes where erosion intervenes, the color is more reddish and the soil more sandy. Where most mature, the regur is a heavy clay, high in calcium carbonate, iron oxides, and alumina, but low in humus. Even without fertilizers it produces excellent crops, and the texture is especially favorable for the retention of summer moisture for winter agriculture. The black color may be due to dark mineral constituents.

The best environmental conditions for the regur appear to be 20 to 40 inches of rainfall, concentrated in a brief wet season, with high temperatures at other times of the year. Natural vegetation is of the dry savanna type. Only a part of the geographic region has fully developed deep black soil; elsewhere it is medium to reddish black and more sandy.

Most of the Black Soil region is underlain by great fissure eruptions of basaltic lava, poured out at an uncertain date between the late Cretaceous and early Eocene. Despite erosion, more than 200,000 square miles are still covered. The term "trap" as sometimes applied to the area is used in the Swedish meaning of stairs or steps, referring to the surface form of the outcrops, rather than as a geologic term for the rock itself. To avoid confusion it is better to describe the material as basalt and the topography as a scarped tableland.

Individual flows are a few tens of feet in thickness and may be separated by ash or sedimentary layers. Columnar jointing is so well developed that the water table is at considerable depths, often beyond the reach of the native wells. The material is a uniform augite basalt, grayish green to purple or red in color. There is a maximum thickness of 6,000 feet in the west, but the flows thin rapidly in all directions. No trace remains of ancient volcanoes, and the material all appears to be derived from fissures.

The Black Soil region is limited on the west by the crest of the Western Ghats with their heavier rainfall, although basalt locally reaches the sea. The geographic boundary on the north is near the Narbada Valley, which in turn is bounded on the south by the Satpura and Mahadeo hills and on the north by the Vindhya Range. Eastward and southward the limits of the region are not so clear. In general, the region reaches the Waingange Valley along the eightieth meridian, and extends to the southern limits of Bombay and Hyderabad. Within the area is all of interior Bombay, all of Hyderabad, and the western half of the Central Provinces. Two westward-flowing rivers drain the north: the Narbada and Tapti, while the Godavari and Kistna flow to the east.

Throughout the region, jowar is the dominant food crop, both for man and beast. It is grown on the black soil and accommodates itself to rainfall variations. Bajra replaces jowar as a supplementary food crop on lighter soils. Legumes are often interplanted. These are rainy crops and are rotated with wheat and linseed which will grow during the dry season. Rice is rarely raised.

Cotton is the chief commercial crop, but conditions are not too favorable. The short rainy period requires that quick-maturing short-staple varieties be grown. Planting occurs as soon as the rains moisten the ground in June, and the growing season is somewhat lengthened by irrigation. Fortunately, the regur soils retain moisture into the maturing period. American varieties do not do well here, although they are suited to the Indus Valley. Most of the fiber is under one inch. The chief areas are the deep black soils of the Tapti and upper Godavari valleys.

The interior Deccan is one of India's traditional famine zones. It lies in the rain shadow of the Western Ghats, so that rainfall is from 20 to 40 inches; the variability is 25 per cent. Not only does the total vary, but the duration and intensity fluctuate. When it does rain, an average of $\frac{1}{2}$ inch per day is common. Since the surface regur soil is tight, much of the water runs off. Tanks are widespread, and numerous large reservoirs, many of them modern engineering works, store rainfall in the areas of heavier precipitation near the Western Ghats. The fortunate moisture-retaining

Marathas, whose distribution closely corresponds with the extent of the lava

A village sugar mill in southern India. The cane is crushed between rollers turned by the oxen at the right, while the sirup is evaporated over a fire in the background. (*Courtesy Paul F. Cressey.*)

capacity of the soil does not necessitate as much irrigation as elsewhere.

Until the introduction of railways and an export market for cotton, wheat, and linseed, the Deccan remained backward and isolated. Few of the invasions into Hindustan from the northwestern passes effectively penetrated the Vindhyan forests and mountains. Cultural conditions changed but little for centuries, and in the absence of stimulating intercourse there could be little progress. Each village was self-sufficient. The blacksmith, carpenter, and potter worked for the village as a whole and were paid by it at harvesttime. There were few outside needs and little money with which to buy them.

Population densities now average 200 per square mile, with about 10 acres per farm family. Most of the people are

flows. Only a few cities are outstanding. Hyderabad is a capital city with 739,159

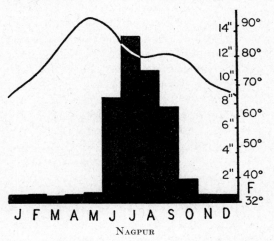

NAGPUR

in 1941; Poona had a 1941 population of 258,197; midway between them is Sholapur with 212,620 in 1941; and near the edge of the Eastern Uplands is the important rail center of Nagpur, 301,957 in 1941.

Son River. In the southwest, the peninsula of Kathiawar is a subregion. In political terms, the Northern Uplands include

The palace of the rajah on the hilltop at Amber. Much of the wealth of India is concentrated in the hands of the rulers. (*Courtesy Indian State Railways.*)

Other cities serve as local commercial towns. The area of the region approximates 170,000 square miles, and the population exceeds 30,000,000.

Northern Uplands

The Northern Uplands form a triangular region in the northwest corner of the Plateau, within the curve of Hindustan. The region is well bounded but somewhat complex internally. Two exposures of Archean gneiss buttress either end, the ancient Aravalli Range in the west and the Bundelkand Massif in the east. On the south are the Vindhya, Bhanrer, and Kaimur ranges. The Ganges Lowland borders the north as far eastward as the

eastern Rajputana, Gujurat, and other Indian states under Bombay, Gwalior, and the Central India Agency.

The geology and resulting surface are equally varied. Overlying the Archean complex are early Paleozoic formations, while burying both in the southern half is an extension of Deccan basalt flows with some black soils. This lava area is the Malwa Plateau. Elevations rise from the Ganges lowland to 2,500 and 4,000 feet in the bold Vindhya escarpment overlooking the Narbada Valley. Portions of the Aravalli reach 5,000 feet.

Rainfall decreases from 40 inches in the east, under the influence of the Ganges Valley monsoon, to 20 inches in the west where the Arabian Sea monsoon is dominant. High temperatures reduce the agricultural effectiveness of this precipita-

the rail center of Jubblepore, 178,339 in 1941, which commands the gap for a railroad southward through the Satpura line,

A village street of the poorer class in south India. Large numbers of people live in conditions even poorer than this. (*Courtesy Paul F. Cressey.*)

tion. Wheat, jowar, and cotton are grown. Population is sparse for India, and there are substantial areas in forest or otherwise not in cultivation.

The state of Gujurat on the west is a drier continuation of the West Coast with some rice but more millet and cotton. Central Kathiawar has forest-clad hills that contain India's only lions; elsewhere the peninsula is dry and barren.

The region has two cities of interest. Ahmadabad in Gujurat with 591,267 in 1941 is a highly industrialized city, second to Bombay in cotton milling and at one time the home of Mohandas Gandhi. It was once the capital of the Mogul Kingdom and has more than trebled in size since 1900. In the extreme east is

as well as a route westward to Bombay via the Narbada Valley. It is also a cotton manufacturing center.

Eastern Uplands

No part of India south of the mountain wall is so much dissected and so unusable for agriculture as the Eastern Uplands. Dense forests and primitive tribes go together. Fortunately there is great mineral wealth.

The Eastern Uplands lie in parts of Bihar and Orissa, the eastern Central Provinces, and northernmost Madras. Like the Northern Highlands, they are surrounded on two sides by the lowland of Hindustan. Along the north are the Maikal and Mahadeo Hills, a continuation of the Satpura line; westward the area merges with the Black Soil region. The southern limit is less well defined but is drawn near the Godavari River, excluding the delta. Between the Eastern Ghats and the sea is a narrow coastal plain, which may be included for convenience.

Over large areas, cultivated land drops below 10 per cent, and nowhere is it much over 50 per cent. This is not due to inadequate or fluctuating rainfall, for precipitation is from 40 to 60 inches and is as dependable as anywhere in the country. Most hillsides are still in forest and too steep for cultivation if cleared. Rice and ragi millet are the dominant crops, but irrigation is difficult on account of the extent of stream dissection. Only locally is it possible to irrigate interstream areas with canals to divert river water. Wheat, cotton, jowar, and bajra are absent. Corn, oil seeds, and legumes are grown for local consumption.

Within the region are practically all the Permo-Carboniferous rocks of the Deccan, and in them there is excellent bituminous coal. The principal fields are in Bihar, Hyderabad, and the Central Provinces. Reserves in the Raniganj, Jherria, Bokaro, and Karanpura fields account for the bulk of India's coal, particularly that of coking quality. The near-by iron range of Singhbhum has provided a basis for spectacular metallurgical developments in the new city of Jamshedpur. Mica and manganese deposits are extensive.

The eastern coast is as poorly supplied with harbors as the western. With the completion of a railroad from Nagpur over the Eastern Ghats to Vizagapatam, this city has become an important port for the region, with the best harbor on the entire east coast. Shipments of second-grade manganese ore are important. The backward nature of the Eastern Uplands is suggested by the absence of any city with 100,000 people.

Southern Peninsula

The Southern Peninsula has high temperatures and high humidity throughout the year. There is never a cool season except in the highlands, so that the terms summer and winter become meaningless. The thermometer rarely exceeds 100°F., but the climate is enervating and fully tropical. Palm trees flourish. Most of the area is sheltered from the southwest monsoon by the Western Ghats, but beginning in October there are three months of heavy rain brought by tropical hurricanes off the Bay of Bengal during the "retreating" monsoon. The annual rainfall declines from 50 inches at Madras to half that figure in the shadow of the Western Ghats, but there higher and cooler elevations increase the rainfall effectiveness. The area receives but little moisture from the northeast monsoon winds.

Within the geographic region are three topographic subregions: the Carnatic coastal plains and deltas of the Godavari, Kistna, and Cauvery Rivers; a succession of low hills up to 500 feet; and the tableland of Mysore in the west. Population densities vary accordingly, from an average of 400 per square mile and a maximum of four times that figure along the coast to 150 per square mile in the northwest plateaus. The total population is about 50,000,000 in an area of 125,000 square miles.

This is one of the most progressive parts of all India. The people speak Tamil and Telegu and are unusually literate since a third of the people in Madras are able to read and write. Hindus comprise 88 per cent of the total and there are only a few Moslems. Many cultural contrasts set off this southern region from the rest of India, such as the bright-colored clothes and old-style Hindu architecture.

Rice and ragi millet are the staple crops,

The total irrigated area in Madras province covers 7,500,000 acres. A considerable part of this is the result of modern

The Meenakshi Temple and Golden Lily Tank at Madura represent the Hindu architecture of south India.
(*Courtesy Indian State Railways.*)

the former where fields may be flooded, the latter on drier upland soil. Cultivation is more difficult than for dry crops such as jowar, since irrigation is imperative. Since rainfall is uncertain, the Southern Peninsula has often been a famine zone. Precipitation records indicate that in the stations where the average is 25 to 30 inches per year, during 50 years there are 11 to 13 which are dry and 6 to 8 with severe drought. With 30 to 40 inches, 7 to 11 years are dry of which 2 to 5 are serious. Where the rainfall exceeds 40 inches in the northern Deccan, only 4 to 7 years are dry in 50, of which from none to 2 are severely dry. Tanks and wells are widely used.

engineering works. In the Cauvery delta, 1,000,000 acres have long had an uncertain supply from local irrigation canals. With the building of a huge dam upstream at Mettur, this area now has dependable water and 300,000 additional acres are available for raising rice.

Cotton is grown on 2,000,000 acres, partly for export. The big cash crop is peanuts, raised for their oil, especially in the area northwest of Madras. Sugar cane, cocoanuts, and tobacco are also grown. Teak and sandalwood come from the higher hills in the west. Commercial crops are not so important as in the Black Soil region.

Laterite is widespread in the plateau but reaches its climax in the south. Where fully developed, it is a brick-red porous the residual bricklike product of long-continued weathering on a peneplain; from this parent material may be developed a

A bird's-eye view of the city of Srirangam with its Hindu temples. (*Courtesy Indian State Railways.*)

residual formation, high in hydrated oxides of iron and aluminum and low in clay and silica. Extreme compositions range from limonite to bauxite. Underlying bedrock is apparently less important as a determining factor than a rainfall of over 50 inches, a wet and dry season, the absence of erosion, and tropical vegetation. The development of true laterite may require a time as long as that since the Eocene. When freshly quarried, laterite may be cut with a shovel, but on exposure to the air it becomes indurated and makes a good building material. The word is from the Latin meaning a brick. Laterite is equally well developed on the high basalt hills of Bombay and the low areas of Madras. The term laterite should be restricted to

lateritic soil. The agricultural value is low. Older buried laterites are found at various horizons in the stratigraphic column.

Madras is India's third city, 777,481 in 1941, and her fourth port.[1] The site has nothing to recommend it and was chosen accidentally when an English ship unloaded cargo on an open sandy beach. The present harbor is an artificial enclosure

[1] ARMSTRONG, C. C., The Port of Madras, *Journal Madras Geographical Association* (1939), XIV, 146–154.

LOGANATHAN, P. S., The Industries of Madras, *Journal Madras Geographical Association* (1939), XIV, 155–163.

DOWIE, P. G., The Physical Aspects and the Geology of the Neighborhood of Madras, *Journal Madras Geographical Association* (1939), XIV, 319–401.

about a half mile square. The hinterland requires some port, and in the absence of possible competition, Madras has grown. The vicinity lacks coal or important industrial minerals, but hydroelectric power may be brought from the Western Ghats.

The city of Madras has long had foreign contacts, and its hinterland is one of the most advanced parts of the Indian Realm. A higher percentage of people speak English there than elsewhere, and the city is more Europeanized. This progressiveness of southern India resembles the situation in Canton and South China.

Leather preparation is a significant industry, with the bark of the avaram shrub used for tanning. Sheepskins are exported in tanned form; goatskins commonly are untanned. Cowhide is shipped in both forms. Hides and skins account for 54 per cent of the outgoing trade of Madras, with peanut oil 16 per cent. Raw cotton and tobacco are also shipped. The number of cotton mills is declining within the city, but those which remain are among the largest and best. Cotton mills are important throughout Madras province.

Bangalore in the Mysore upland has a population of 406,760 in 1941, and its elevation gives it a healthy and pleasant aspect. The 1941 population of Madura was 239,144.

Ceylon

The island of Ceylon has long been a port of call halfway across the Indian Ocean for ships between the East and the West. Chinese junks here met Arab vessels 2,000 years ago, and trade between the Orient and Europe by this route supplemented the overland commerce through central Asia. Ceylon is shown on Ptolemy's maps of the second century A.D. and was visited by the Chinese Buddhist pilgrim Fa Hsien in the fourth century. In the thirteenth century, Marco Polo on his way home

described Ceylon as "the best island of its size in the world."

Ceylon has been a British Crown Colony

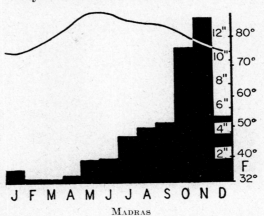

MADRAS
Elevation, 22 feet; average temperature 81.8°F.; total precipitation, 49.6 inches.

since 1802, and so its administration is separate from that of India. Before that time it was Portuguese and later Dutch.

Geologically, Ceylon is a slightly detached part of the Western Ghats, separated by a submerged gap comparable to that of Palghat. The strait is 22 miles wide, full of sand banks and low islands, and through it there is only one navigable passage. In its geography Ceylon resembles India, with increased emphasis on low latitude.

The core of the island is a mass of Pre-Cambrian crystalline rocks which form a central mountain area, rising to 8,292 feet. Encircling these hills and mountains are lowlands and a coastal plain. Mineral resources in the interior include graphite, gem stones such as sapphires and rubies, and iron ore for which there is no coal.

As Ceylon is nearly on the equator, the temperature is uniform throughout the year. Thus Colombo has monthly averages between 79 and 82° for the year. Both monsoons bring rain, first to one side of the island and then to the other. On the slopes precipitation amounts to 100 and 200 inches, and the total everywhere exceeds 50 inches except in the extreme southeast and northwest where there are no hills to

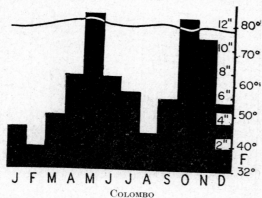

COLOMBO
Elevation, 24 feet; average temperature, 80.2°F.; total precipitation, 83.1 inches.

lift and cool the monsoon winds. The climatic division between the east and west coasts, conditioned by seasonal rains, is as geographically important as the topographic difference based on altitude. Drainage is more significant than irrigation for most crops.

Within an area of 23,232 square miles, the 1940 population numbered 5,981,000. Only a fifth of the land is productive, although more than half might be cultivated. A dependable tropical climate prevents distress. The rice production does not meet local needs, but the export of commercial crops pays for imported food.

Around the sandy coast are extensive cocoanut plantations, hence copra is a large export. Rice is grown on the plains, and its acreage is nearly as large as that in cocoanuts. Other lowland crops are cinnamon, cloves, and citronella oil. Ceylon is a typical tropical island, with warm but not oppressive temperatures which favor agriculture.

The interior hills were once covered with splendid forests, of which only small areas remain. Many areas were cleared by fire to secure suitable soils for raising coffee. This crop has now declined and is replaced by tea. Ceylon tea is superior to most of the Assam product, and there is a large export to England and the United States. Tea is Ceylon's most valuable export. Rubber now exceeds tea in acreage, but the value is only half. Cacao and quinine are also produced. Some of the mountain people carry on migratory cultivation in fire clearings. The mountain core has always had greater economic significance than the lowlands.

Colombo is the chief city, 284,155 in 1931, and the leading port of the Indian Ocean. The harbor is partly artificial and adequate for the extensive transit traffic. Kandy in the hills is an important center for Buddhism, which has entirely disappeared from India proper. On the east coast is the splendid natural harbor of Trincomalee, chief British naval base in the Indian Ocean.

CHAPTER 33

INDIA'S PLACE IN THE WORLD

Foreign Trade

The early trade of India was limited by inadequate internal communications and the difficult routes to Europe either around Africa by sea or overland via Iran. Muslins and gems were traded for gold. The Suez Canal changed part of the picture in 1869 when bulky agricultural products of low value could reach Europe. Until 1931 India was the world's greatest market for the precious metals. Most of these were hoarded and taken out of circulation. Lyde states that, since the days of the Roman Empire, India has consumed 60 per cent of the world's gold production and 40 per cent of its silver.[1]

Two trade avenues led outward from pre-British India, neither very significant. One crossed the northwestern frontier to inner Asia and China; the other contact was provided by Arab sailors who traded along the coasts westward to Africa and eastward sometimes as far as Canton. It is a commentary on India's isolation that her most important export was not goods but a religion, Buddhism, which traveled to China with the lightest of baggage.

The individual purchasing power of the Indian peasant is low, but the aggregate bulk is so large that the country ranks as one of the major foreign-trade areas. Measured in the pre-devaluation gold dollars of 1932, the United Kingdom led the world with a total foreign trade of 4,677 million dollars in 1937, followed by the United States with 3,797 million dollars. Next in order were Germany, France, Japan, Canada, Belgium, the Netherlands, and India in ninth place with 827 million dollars' worth of trade.[1]

India's overseas trade has fluctuated widely. Imports reached their maximum in 1920–1921 when the total was $1,143,700,000, in contrast to $280,100,000 in the depression year of 1933–1934. Exports have ranged from $1,368,500,000 in 1925–1926 to $336,000,000 in 1934–1935. In any case, the per capita trade total is low, only $4.05 in 1937. Ceylon statistics are separate, and amount to $35.65 per person.

Until the First World War, England dominated Indian trade, particularly imports. Since the war, England's share has steadily fallen, amounting to 39 per cent of the imports and 33 per cent of the exports in 1937. In terms of total trade, Japan had 15 per cent and the United States 9 per cent, respectively. Two-thirds of the shipping is in British boats. India is still Britain's best customer, with even more trade than with the United States.

Exports are dominantly agricultural. Raw and manufactured cotton made up 25 per cent, while jute and burlap comprised 22 per cent of the whole in 1936–1937. Tea constituted 10 per cent and would be more if Ceylon were included. Peanuts and other oil seeds accounted for 9 per cent. Leather and manganese are also significant. Raw cotton exports doubled from 1932 to 1937, with about half the

[1] Lyde, L. W., "The Continent of Asia," 473.

[1] Foreign Commerce Yearbook, U.S. Department of Commerce (1938), 419.

shipment going to Japan. Wheat is a diminishing and erratic export. Iron and steel shipments are increasingly important.

machinery, lubricating oil, raw cotton, and electrical goods; in all with a value of $98,162,000. On the other hand, Indian

Loading cotton grown in the Deccan on the modern docks at Bombay. (*Courtesy Indian State Railways.*)

Imports include decreasing amounts of cotton cloth, 19 per cent of the total in 1936–1937, machinery 11 per cent, pig iron and other metals 8 per cent, automobiles 6 per cent, and petroleum 5 per cent. India is thus a standard example of an undeveloped land with agricultural exports and manufactured imports, gradually working toward a balance. Few of her products are indispensable, but the world secures substantial parts of its jute, manganese, mica, graphite, and tea from the Indian Realm.

United States trade with India in 1941 included Indian imports of automobiles,

exports to the United States totaled $131,510,000, half of it jute and burlap with important quantities of raw cotton, goatskins, shellac, mica, manganese, and agricultural products. Each of these figures is double that for 1939.

The greatest transit port of the Indian Realm is Colombo in Ceylon, a point of call for every boat traveling from Suez to Singapore. The net register of ships entering in 1937 amounted to 20,425,000 tons, as much as all the ports of India and Burma together. Most of these vessels took on or discharged very little cargo but stopped for supplies. Bombay and Calcutta are rivals for first place among Indian ports. If shipments of bullion are included, Bombay usually leads in value; for merchandise only, or in tonnage, Calcutta is ahead. The tonnage of vessels entering Bombay in 1941 was six million tons while Calcutta had nine million tons. Karachi is third with two million, followed by Madras with one million tons and Cochin with about the same.

Imports at each port are similar, but exports reflect local production: cotton from Bombay, jute from Calcutta, cotton and wheat from Karachi, and hides from Madras.

Most of India's trade has been westward, but eastern Asia is playing a larger role. Japan captured much of Britain's textile business and replaced Germany for miscellaneous manufactures prior to the Second World War. The United States has found an enlarging market in India. Railways to China and the Soviet Union may someday involve extensive commerce, but the centers of population of India's neighbors are remote from the border.

India will assuredly produce a larger share of her own industrial needs, certainly of textiles, and this will somewhat disrupt present trade relations. But as internal prosperity increases, purchasing power will rise, and a rich India will be a better world customer than a poor India.

Political Relations

To find solutions for India's political problems is extraordinarily difficult, and to administer them may be even more so. Until 1919, British India was a dependency ruled by the government of the United Kingdom. In that year, a considerable measure of internal autonomy was granted the British provinces, although vital items of defense and finance were reserved to the Viceroy. The protected Indian states retain their individual and complex treaty relations to the crown, and for the most part are not subject to any action by Britain that might affect their independence.

In 1935 there were further extensions of provincial autonomy with elected legislatures, and a central government was set up which provided for an All-India Federation uniting the democratically organized provinces and the autocratic Indian states. The Government of India Act of that year contains the longest and most complex constitution in the world, and its workability is still uncertain. Although not expressly stated, some sort of Dominion status within the Empire was the goal. The scheme involved dual authority and reserved rights by which England retained control of foreign affairs, the army, and finance.

Will India remain within the British Commonwealth? All the present dominions have the tradition of English parliamentary government, and it is an open question as to whether this will work in India. Is nationalist India able to defend itself and maintain internal order? Wide differences of opinion exist on these problems. Many British and some Indians, including most of the Princes, consider that the end of external rule would bring civil anarchy. The Nationalists believe that India can achieve political coherence despite her lack of cultural unity, but the evidence is not clear. Any weakening of governmental authority would be especially serious because of the dependence of so much agriculture on government-supervised irrigation, and on account of the potential cultural antagonisms now held in check.

Internal fragmentation has permitted British rule, for no group resents England quite so much as it fears other groups. The removal of the capital from Calcutta to interior Delhi away from possible naval protection represented a large measure of maturity and points the way to diminishing external authority.

Only about 4,000 Englishmen are actually in the civil or administrative services. Others are engaged in railway or other technical occupations, and there were about 60,000 in the army during the interwar years, but the total of all Britishers in India is quite inadequate to hold the country by force. When India is ready for independence, it is probable that she will have it. What her place in the world will then be, only time can tell.

The Indian Ocean has been essentially a British lake, economically tributary to commercial England. From Cape Town to Singapore, British trade in British ships bound for British ports has dominated all activity. The only important exception was the Netherlands Indies with its rubber and tin. India is the most significant of the lands bordering this ocean, both in population and productivity. It may be half a century before industrial developments make the country reasonably self-sufficient and the center of a commercial sphere of its own. When that time comes, the Indian Realm should be one of the half-dozen major economic units of the world. If it is not, it will be a reflection on the people and their climatic handicaps.

But can India work out its own destiny in the meantime? Expanding Japan is only around the corner, and European imperialistic struggles hold other dangers. India is without adequate military defense of her own, but the spirit of nationalism has gone so far that it is doubtful whether India can again be conquered and subdued by an outside power. Even if this should temporarily be the case, the ultimate emergence of an independent India is reasonably assured. India will never dominate the world in industrial or political authority, but its leading place in the affairs of southern Asia and the Indian Ocean is certain.

Cultural Contributions

Amid the contrasts and confusion of India, one must be careful to give proper values to the many aspects of Indian life. No single generalization nor observation gained from a casual tour can embrace them all. Why is India so confusing? Why are the realities of poverty in such contrast to the material resources and the spiritual achievements?

"India must not be judged by its great ports and other industrial areas. These latter are the scene of striking anachronisms, symptomatic of the direct impingement of the modern on the medieval. In Bombay, for instance, the motorcar—driven possibly by a Parsee lady—dodges in and out between foot-passengers and bullock-carts; the latest product of the universities jostles with the fakir, and broad and beautiful streets look out to the narrow alleys of an Eastern bazaar. In a few moments one may pass from the luxurious dancing hall of the Taj Mahal Hotel to dimly lighted back-streets whose pavements are covered with the sleeping figures of the inhabitants of the chawls, *i.e.*, working-class dwellings, or from the operating theater of an up-to-date hospital to the haunts of emaciated, disabled beggars, who drag their possibly self-mutilated limbs through the noisome dust and dirt of the gutters. Mechanical inventions and the materialistic outlook have begun to leaven India, but it is necessary to realize the immense size and importance of what still remains unleavened. The crumbling of the authority of caste, the loosened bands of religion, the adoption of the Western 'economic' outlook, and acceptance of Western methods and ideals have as yet affected only a tiny percentage of the people. The masses undoubtedly still live in the material surroundings and retain the social outlook of medievalism.[1]"

An evaluation of the Indian way of life

The Jain temple at Balabhais in Kathiawar is a fairyland of domes and spires, representative of the exotic beauty of India. (*Courtesy Indian State Railways.*)

should not be based on the extent to which it differs from or resembles our own. Cultural differences among people reflect their history and environment rather than innate biological differences. The importance of a civilization is in proportion to its past, present, and potential world influence, and here the case for India is secure.

India has one of the world's few great historic cultures. The others are the Chinese and Japanese, and the Egyptian and Babylonian which developed in two lines: the Greek, Roman, and European on the one hand and the Islamic civilization on

[1] ANSTEY, VERA, "The Economic Development of India," 1–2.

the other. Each has made major contributions to our world. Because India has had limited relations with North America, the United States is just beginning to appreciate the tradition of that country. The Occident has too exclusively studied its own cultural heritage and has considered that of others merely where there has been a clash of ideas. As world intercourse increases, contacts with Indian civilizations are bound to enlarge.

More than elsewhere, Hindu life revolves around philosophy and religion, man's relations to the universe. Materialism is held in abeyance. Systematic introspection has been practiced in India for thousands of years. Certain attitudes of mind and ethical ideas are unique, one of which is intellectual tolerance. To each person only a facet of the truth is visible. We see the universe only in terms that our minds are capable of understanding; hence no one is wholly right, no one wholly wrong. Truth in its larger aspects is understandable only to a few individuals, and tolerance is implicit. Indian literature is one of the world's oldest and richest. Architecture and the arts date back to the third millennium B.C. Hindu culture is not alone, for there are 90 million Mohammedans, 50 million of the depressed classes and other entirely different groups.

Certain unique qualities have kept the Indian point of view from wider acceptance in other civilizations, in addition to its geographic isolation. The exaltation of the quiet life has prevented it from dealing with obvious evils about it. Other parts of the world have developed more active philosophies, but in a hectic world the west increasingly looks with tolerance and interest upon Oriental concepts of peace. The philosopher, Will Durant, has summarized these relations as follows.

"As invention, industry and trade bind the continents together, or as they fling us into conflict with Asia, we shall study its civilizations more closely, and shall absorb, even in enmity, some of its ways and thoughts. Perhaps, in return for conquest, arrogance and spoliation, India will teach us the tolerance and gentleness of the mature mind, the quiet content of the unacquisitive soul, the calm of the understanding spirit, and a unifying, pacifying love for all living things."[1]

Indian civilization is a continuous and mature stream. The present century of cultural change involves not the discarding of the traditional, but rather a modifying of the inherited to meet the needs of the modern world. India's culture is bound to persist, and we need increasingly to understand the wealth of its resources. To this task geography merely provides the preface.[2]

[1] DURANT, WILL, "The Story of Civilization," 633.
[2] BROWN, W. NORMAN, India and Humanistic Studies in America, American Council of Learned Societies, *Bulletin* 28 (1939), 1–26.

CHAPTER 34

THE SOUTHEASTERN REALM

Southeastern Asia lies between India and China, but it differs from them in climate, topography, people, and most geographic essentials. The realm includes two distinct geographic provinces: the peninsular Farther India and the insular lands of the East Indies. The name Indo-China should not indicate any transitional or intermediate character. Lyde has suggested that the proper term would be "Indo-Pacific" from the adjoining oceans. The northern part of the realm in Burma, Thailand, and Indo-China is semicontinental and predominantly Buddhist. The southeast including peninsular Thailand, Malaya, the Netherlands Indies, and the Philippines is maritime, and Mohammedan with the exception of the Philippines.

No other part of Asia has had such divided political imperialism, with contests since the sixteenth century. The British and French have squeezed Thailand on either side. To the south is the Dutch Empire, while to the east lie the Philippines with Spanish and American backgrounds. This is the area which the Japanese conquered during the Second World War and which added so greatly to their resources and strategic position. Never before had it been under unified rule.

The importance of Southeastern Asia arises both from its intrinsic assets and from its position athwart the shipping lanes which pass through the Strait of Malacca at Singapore. All vessels bound from Europe to China or Japan must pass here. Airways equally focus on this realm. Before the Second World War, Rangoon, Bangkok, and Singapore were regular points of call for British Overseas Airways from London to Australia and Dutch K.L.M. service from Amsterdam to Batavia. Air France planes from Paris to Saïgon also called at the first two cities. Dai Nippon Airways operated to Bangkok for at least a year prior to Pearl Harbor. Manila and Singapore were on the Pan-American route from San Francisco to the Orient.

This is a tropical land, lying across the equator and influenced by the great land masses of Asia with its monsoons and of desert Australia, in part by trade winds blowing over the warm encircling seas, and by typhoons. Winter winds blow from the northeast, either as northeast trade winds or as monsoon circulation which originated in the heart of Asia. They are thus relatively cool and somewhat moist. Summer winds blow from the southwest from May to October, or in the Southern Hemisphere from the southeast, and bring heavy rainfall and humidity. Seasons are best defined as wet or dry rather than as summer or winter. Much of the seasonal variation in temperature is due to the degree of cloudiness. Hence March, April, and May are usually hotter than June, July, and August. To an extent not appreciated by dwellers outside the tropics, temperature is influenced by elevation. Noticeably cooler conditions prevail above two or three thousand feet.

Rainfall is a matter of exposure and topography, with nearly 100 inches in the plains and even heavier precipitation on windward slopes. Thus, Burma and the western sides of the Malay peninsula are dominated by the Indian Ocean southwest rainy season from October to January with the northeast monsoon and trade winds. The eastern sides of the Philippines

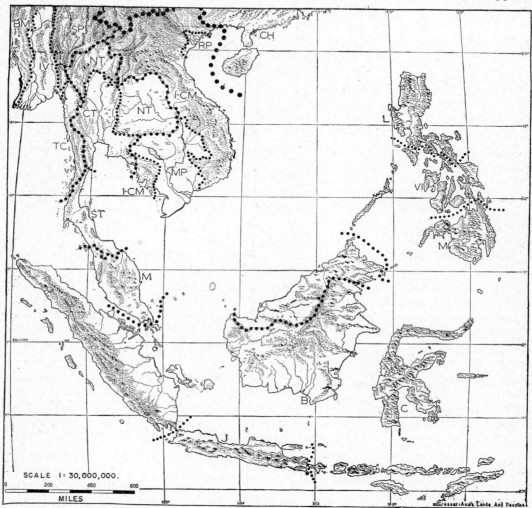

The geographic regions and land forms of Southeastern Asia. Political boundaries and other geographic conditions divide the realm as follows. Burma includes the Irrawaddy Valley, the Burma Mountains, the Shan Plateau, and the Tenasserim Coast. Thailand is divided into four regions; Central, Northern, Northeastern, and Southern. The regions of Indo-China are the Red Plain, the Indo-China Mountains, and the Mekong Plain. Malaya is a region by itself. The Netherlands Indies include Java and the Outer Provinces of Sumatra, Borneo, and the other islands. Within the Philippines there are Luzon, the Visayan Islands, and Mindanao. (*Base map from Erwin Raisz, courtesy Harvard-Yenching Institute, adapted by Rowland Illick.*)

summer monsoon which brings rain from mid-May to mid-October. The eastern sides of the Thailand-Malay peninsula and the Annam coast of Indo-China have their have rain throughout the year, while the western sides of the islands receive most of their rain from summer typhoons and southwest winds. Singapore near the equator has rain throughout the year. Java has most of its rain from October to April with less precipitation at the opposite season when dry southeast trade winds blow from Australia.

Natural vegetation closely follows rainfall and temperature. On well-drained soils at low and intermediate elevations, tropical rain forests occur where the precipitation exceeds 80 inches. With less rain and a seasonal dry period the dominant trees are deciduous, a monsoon forest with teak. Scrub growth occurs with less than 40 inches. Great plantations of rubber, cocoanut, sugar cane, kapok, and cinchona (for quinine) are locally important. The first four require lowland positions. Coffee and tea grow on mountain sides up to 4,000 feet, while cinchona is found at higher elevations.

The realm as a whole is characterized by an incomplete development of cropland. If the natural vegetation were cleared, drainage and irrigation arranged, public health administered, and transportation provided, the various lands might easily provide a home for millions of people on subsistence agriculture and for great quantities of plantation crops. Whether the world would be any better off merely to pack this corner of Asia and the adjoining islands with people, as in Java, is another question. And the future market for tropical products is also uncertain. Still other grave problems arise in the field of political control. Until the distant time when the various areas can govern themselves, separately or in some federation, a considerable measure of international supervision will be necessary.

Most tropical soils are infertile or at best only moderately fertile. Java is an exception; but it is clear that vast areas of Sumatra, Borneo, and New Guinea never can be productive for agriculture and that considerable parts of Indo-China and Thailand

are equally hopeless. It is thus unlikely that the realm as a whole can ever have the population densities of India, eastern China, or Java.

Land utilization includes forestry with crops such as wild rubber and cocoanuts, plantation crops of tea, coffee, rubber, cocoanuts, oil palms, tobacco, and sugar cane, and subsistence agriculture.

Two methods of crop production are characteristic: wet-field rice in the plains and migratory fire-cleared plots in the hills. Lowland rice is generally transplanted from seedbeds into puddled paddy fields. It may be sown broadcast in which case the fields are merely plowed and the seed scattered before the land is flooded.

In the caiñgin type on well-drained upland soils, forest clearings are made by cutting the brush and accessible branches and girdling the trees at the beginning of the dry season; when these are dry, the area is burned and the ash fertilizes the poor tropical soil. The soil need not be plowed; instead the seed is planted in holes an inch deep made by a stick. After one crop, or at most two or three, weeds choke out planted crops and the clearing is abandoned. The land then reverts to forest and is not again cleared for several years until the weeds have been killed by shade trees. This practice is named caiñgin from its development in the Philippines; in Thailand it is called tam rai cultivation; in Burma, taungya; in Assam, jhum; in Ceylon, cheena; and in the Netherlands Indies, ladang. At least one mountain tribe in far northern Burma attempts systematic reforestation of abandoned caiñgins. In parts of the Netherlands Indies rubber trees are set out, but this is uncommon. In many areas the fields grow up to cogon grass rather than forest; this is because the cogon is burned annually and only a few dwarf trees can get started. Once the land is covered with cogon grass, it cannot be recultivated except by modern plows and becomes a grassy desert or artificial savanna.

This type of upland cultivation does not encourage erosion. The ash provides a temporary fertilizer on soils otherwise unable to produce an annual crop. Neither tools nor animals are needed, and good crops are often raised. On the other hand, the method requires excessive labor and large areas per person, much valuable timber is destroyed, and relatively useless grasslands often result.

Geological conditions vary too widely to offer many generalizations, but a belt of young petroleum-rich formations extends in a long arc from Burma south and east through the East Indies. Outside of it is a line of active volcanoes, while inside the crescent are large deposits of tin, iron, aluminum, manganese, chromium, and other minerals.

Laterite is widely developed, the product of long-continued leaching under stable geological conditions on a peneplain with a wet tropical climate. The more soluble minerals have been removed leaving a residue of concretionary reddish iron and aluminum oxides. Laterite develops in the subsoil near the fluctuating water table and hardens into rock on exposure. It has long been quarried for building purposes, as shown in the ruins of ancient cities in several areas—many of them a thousand years old. The presence of laterite usually means that the surface soils are very infertile. The tectonic stability of eastern Thailand, southern Indo-China, Borneo, and parts of Sumatra accounts for the abundance of laterite in these countries in contrast to the Philippines and Java where changes in elevation have been frequent and erosion is accelerated.

In spite of relatively luxuriant vegetation, it is well to emphasize the sterile character of almost all tropical soils where formed under a continuously rainy climate by weathering *in situ*. Alluvial plains and soils in alternating wet and dry climates are more fertile. Pendleton has pointed out that many flat areas suffer from too little erosion to remove the leached and worn-out surface accumulation. Termite mounds are often six to eight feet high with a diameter of 15 to 20 feet. Their better drained and more productive soils are frequently used for garden crops.

The continental portion in the north is dominated by six great rivers, each flowing from the southeastern corner of Tibet. From west to east they are as follows: the Irrawaddy drains central Burma and reaches the sea near Rangoon; it is paralleled by the Sittang. Farther east is the Salween whose mouth is at Moulmein. The shorter Menam flows to the sea past Bangkok. Part of the Thailand—Indo-China frontier lies along the Mekong whose mouth is near Saïgon. North and east at Haiphong is the Red River. Each stream has its delta plain which dominates its respective hinterland.

No part of Asia contributes more to the export trade in raw materials. Among metals there are tin and aluminum from Malaya and the Netherlands Indies, manganese and chromium from the Philippines and elsewhere, tungsten from Burma, Thailand, and Indo-China, iron ore from Malaya and the Philippines, nickel from Celebes and Burma, zinc and lead from Burma, and gold from the Philippines. In the field of fuel, coal is widespread but of limited quantity and poor quality. This is an important reason why practically all of the ores, except tin and gold, are exported from the realm without smelting. Oil is the great source of power, with major production in Sumatra and Borneo. Agricultural exports are even more impressive and include rubber from Malaya, Sumatra,

Borneo, and Thailand, cocoanut products from the Philippines and the Netherlands Indies, palm oil from Malaya and Sumatra, rice surplus in Asia at Rangoon, Bangkok, and Saïgon. Teak and other tropical hardwoods are an increasing export. If

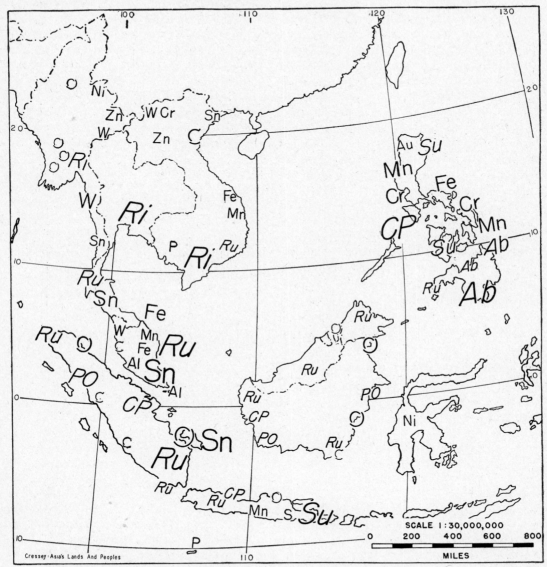

Southeastern Asia is extraordinarily rich in raw materials. These include the fuels coal (C) and oil (O) in shadow letters; the minerals chromium (Cr), iron (Fe), manganese (Mn), nickel (Ni), phosphate rock (P), sulphur (S), tin (Sn), tungsten (W), and zinc (Zn); and the agricultural products abaća (*Ab*), cocoanut products (*CP*), palm oil (*PO*), rubber (*Ru*), and sugar (*Su*).

abaća or Manila hemp from Mindanao, sugar from Java and Luzon, and the largest the market demands, the output of each of these agricultural products can be greatly increased. On the other hand, if the industrial nations go in for synthetic rubber and domestic supplies of sugar and vegetable oils, these tropical areas must prepare for a very uncertain future.

It is well to distinguish between native subsistence agriculture with an exportable surplus produced at an unknown cost and sold at the market price, and plantation agriculture which has a high overhead, must pay dividends, and depends upon special processing as in the case of sugar, tea, or quinine. Vegetable oils and carbohydrates can be produced much more cheaply in equatorial regions than in temperate zones.

Many different peoples have crowded into this realm, some of them Mongoloids from Tibet or people from China of pre-Chinese stock, some Dravidians and Hindus from India, others who brought Buddhism from Ceylon, and Arabs with Mohammedanism. Only within recent years has the story begun to unfold. Impressive ruins as at Angkor in Indo-China and Borobudur in Java betray a notable measure of civilization a thousand years ago. Numerous races now live here, among them Mon, Khmer, Cambodian, Annamese, Burmese, Shan, Lao, Thai, Malay, and the great variety of peoples in the islands.

The area and population of the various countries are shown in the accompanying table. Except for Java, the density is much lower than in the adjoining lands of India, China, and Japan. Population figures obviously need to be interpreted in terms of the carrying capacity of the land and the rate of increase. These problems are considered separately for each country.

Country	Populations in thousands, and year	Area in square miles	Density per square mile
Burma	14,667 (1931)	262,732	57
Thailand	14,465 (1937)	200,000	72
French Indo-China	23,030 (1936)	285,800	81
British Malaya	5,174 (1937–1938)	51,200	100
Netherlands Indies	70,476 (1940)	735,267	96
Java	48,416 (1940)	51,035	948
Philippine Islands	16,000 (1939)	114,000	140

CHAPTER 35

BURMA

Although Burma might be considered a part of the Indian Realm, its culture and geography bear many resemblances to Thailand and the rest of Southeastern Asia. In place of Aryans are Mongols; instead of Hindus the people are Buddhists. Monsoon conditions resemble those of India so that many of the same crops are grown. In the absence of easy overland access either to India or to Thailand, the economic life of Burma moves through its chief seaport of Rangoon. The country lies to one side of the main routes of travel and, in terms of modern exploitation, is an undeveloped new land.

Since 1937 Burma has been separate from Indian jurisdiction and is ruled directly by the Emperor in London through his governor and a native legislature. It is neither a colony nor a dominion, but rather a semiself-governing unit of the British Empire. The area is 262,732 square miles, but a third of this is more or less independent under local rulers.

The population numbered about 16,000,-000 in 1941. In 1931 it was 14,667,146, of whom nine million were Burmese, one and a third million Karens, one million Shans, another million Indians, and the rest divided among scores of racial groups, including 200,000 Chinese. Most of these people migrated from the north in prehistoric times. Despite Burma's position between India and China, the topographic barriers on each side are so formidable that no military conqueror has ever passed from one country to another, and transit trade has been negligible. Military opera-

tions, however, have developed along the Thai frontier.

The Burmese are an attractive people,

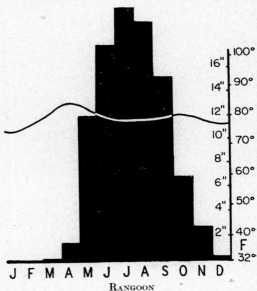

RANGOON
Elevation, 18 feet; average temperature, 79.2°F.; total precipitation 99.0 inches.

and scarcely a boy does not attend school except in the remoter areas. Literacy is thus far higher than elsewhere in Southeastern Asia. The women are graceful and well dressed, and live a free and open life. Eighty per cent of the people are rural. The population density is only 57 per square mile, so that even allowing for the large area of mountains, Burma is an underpopulated land. One writer has described Burma as the "happiest land in Asia" because of this lack of population pressure. A great variety of non-Burmese people live in the mountains of the north

501

and east. There is a large seasonal migration of workers from Madras for work in the rice fields.

Grain is threshed by the trampling of water buffalo and later winnowed in the wind. (*Ewing Galloway.*)

The southern monsoon from the Bay of Bengal is guided by the north-south alignment of the topography. The time of rainfall is of great importance; heavy rains continue from mid-May until mid-October, while the rest of the year is dry. Where the monsoon strikes the coastal mountains on either side of the Irrawaddy delta, the rainfall is 200 inches or more. Rangoon has 99 inches. In this wet area rice is the universal crop. In the upper valley near Mandalay there is a region with less than 40 inches of rain and a pronounced dry season; here the crops are millet, sesame, peanuts, cotton, and beans.

Cultivated land is reported as 11 per cent of the total area, and 38 per cent more is listed as cultivable. Some 16,000,000 acres are cultivated, of which rice occupies about 70 per cent. Only a sixteenth of the cultivated land of Burma is planted to a second crop. Wherever rainfall or irrigation permits, rice is the preferred crop. Burma has an annual production of some 7,000,000 tons, and an exportable surplus, which averaged 3,500,000 tons from 1930 to 1940. Rangoon is one of the three great export centers of Asia for rice. Rubber is a newer crop, with 100,000 acres in plantations around Mergui. Small humped oxen and water buffalo are the usual farm animals. Work elephants are still used, especially in the forest industries, but the number is declining.

A significant production of petroleum, tin, tungsten, lead, zinc, silver, and precious stones makes Burma an important mining area. Oil and teak are the second and third exports.

Irrawaddy Valley

The Irrawaddy Valley and the adjoining Sittang lowland are the heart of Burma, with most of the agricultural land and population. During Tertiary times this was an arm of the sea, in which accumulated a great thickness of sediments, now

veneered with the alluvium of the Irrawaddy and its associate the Sittang. The

automobile roads across the border are
the famous Burma Road eastward to

Elephants are used to transport teak logs at Rangoon. (*Ewing Galloway*.)

region is 200 miles wide in the delta but
narrows northward till it reaches the limit
of navigation at Bhamo, 600 miles from the
sea. Between the Irrawaddy and the
Sittang lowland is the Pegu Range, which
culminates in the 5,000-foot volcano of
Mt. Popa near the northern end. The
seaward margin of the delta ends in a maze
of low islands with tidal mangrove forests
not unlike the Sundarbans of the Ganges.
Extensive dike systems are necessary in the
delta. Soils are fertile, although easily ex-
hausted, and the land is intensively utilized.
The dry region of central Burma around
Mandalay forms a separate subregion.

Although Burma has 2,000 miles of
meter-gauge railway, the Irrawaddy remains the main highway. No railway leads
to the outside world, and the only two
China and one through the Shan States
into northern Thailand.

The central Irrawaddy contains important oil wells, with production from
Oligocene formations in the Yenangyaung
and Chauk fields, 300 miles north of
Rangoon. These areas are declining in
yield, but newer fields at Singu have
maintained the production for decades
near the 1938 level of 260,000,000 gallons.
Part of the oil goes to Rangoon refineries
by pipe line; the rest is shipped on the
river. Largely undeveloped Tertiary coal
is present.

Rangoon is Burma's one great city, with
a population in 1931 of 400,415 and a
provisional total of 498,369 in 1941.
Immigrants who were born in India made
up over half of the 1931 population, and

present a clash in culture. The migrant character of Rangoon's population was shown by the ratio of males to females

Rangoon is a city with thousands of pagodas. Here are those around the Shwe Dagon Temple. (*Ewing Galloway.*)

which was 13 to 7 in 1941. The city is 20 miles from the sea at the junction of several streams and near a southern spur of the Pegu Range. Rangoon does not lie on the Irrawaddy itself but is connected with a navigable distributary through a canal. Rangoon handles 86 per cent of Burma's foreign trade. Exports are rice, oil, teak and other timber, rice bran, metals and ores, hides and skins, with rice equal to the value of all others together. Two-thirds of the rice and teak and almost all of the petroleum go to India. Imports are made up of cotton goods, machinery, and miscellaneous manufactured articles.

The city lies to one side of the steamship lanes connecting Europe with Singapore, but it is on the main air routes between Europe and Southeastern Asia. The chief industries are the rice mills, and the primary business is commerce. Bassein is the principal port on the Irrawaddy itself.

Mandalay in the interior dry zone is an ancient capital city and the heart of inner Burma. It is reached by river steamer, by road, or by an 18-hour rail trip from Rangoon, 386 miles to the south. The population was 163,527 in 1941.

Burma Mountains

Between the Irrawaddy and the Brahmaputra is a series of more or less parallel mountain ranges, little known geologically, wet and densely forested, and but sparsely populated. The western area, within Assam and Bengal, has already been considered under India, but two-thirds of these mountains are in Burma. The region includes the embayed Arakan coast and bordering Arakan Yoma range in the south, and the Kachin and other hills in the north.

The Burma Mountains form an effective barrier to travel. A few cart roads lead over difficult passes, but there is no trade. In structural terms, a core of old crystalline rocks is flanked by closely folded sedimentaries on either side. Elevations reach 10,085 feet in Mt. Victoria and 12,553 feet in Mt. Sarametti on the Indo-Burma border.

The absence of roads across the border made it impossible to reinforce Allied troops during the Japanese invasion and rendered the recapture of Burma especially difficult. British policy in India has apparently been to isolate the country by not developing external land communications. Burma has thus remained apart from Indian life, except as trade moved by sea.

This region receives the full impact of the southwest monsoon off the Bay of Bengal and, where this is augmented by orographic influences, precipitation becomes very heavy. The Arakan coast has a few stations that report 200 inches, but records are not available for the mountains. The highest precipitation is presumably at intermediate elevations.

Natural vegetation follows climate and altitude. Where rainfall exceeds 80 inches, there is a dense tropical evergreen rain forest with little agriculture or lumbering. With 40 to 80 inches of rainfall and a longer dry season, the trees lose their leaves in the dry season. This is the home of many excellent types of trees, of which teak is the chief timber now exploited. Burma has no natural grassland, but where rainfall is under 40 inches the forest is replaced by scrub. Frosts may occur above 3,000 feet in the north.

Traditional agriculture has been a matter of clearing the forests by cutting the brush and girdling and burning the trees. The ash then supplies some of the much-needed fertilization. Within a few years weeds crowd out cultivated plants and the plot is abandoned in favor of another. The introduction of government forest preserves now restricts this waste. Corn, millet, and some rice are the crops. Large areas might be developed, although malaria must first be controlled.

Jade and amber are secured in limited amounts.

The people of these mountains include a wide variety of non-Burmese races, some of them known as Chins and Kachins. Considerable areas are classed as "non-administered" where the government does not attempt to exercise jurisdiction. Slavery was permitted until early in the century, and some tribes in the far north are still warlike.

The most developed section is the Arakan coast, a discontinuous strip of coastal plain and small deltas with offshore islands and rocky peninsulas. Most of the population live in the northern half, but the entire coast accounts for only a million people. No estimates are available for the region as a whole, but the density is much below the optimum. The Burma Mountains are so rainy, so hilly, and so malarial that the future is limited. Development must await effective administration, education, transportation, markets for lumber, and agricultural planning.

Shan Plateau

Eastern Burma is a plateau averaging 3,000 to 4,000 feet, largely inhabited by Shan tribesmen. It resembles western Yunnan and northern Thailand in ethnic diversity. The elevation moderates the climate, so that this is a temperate land within the tropics. Part of the country is a dissected upland, but there are extensive areas in which agriculture might expand. The region is drained by the deep valley of the Salween River and to the east by the Mekong.

Beneath the Shan Plateau is a block of old gneiss and ancient limestones, sharply bounded along the Irrawaddy lowland by a 3,000-foot fault scarp. Within this complex is one of the world's best sources of lapis lazuli. Rubies have long been of importance, with a yield of 141,490 carats in 1937. Sapphires and jade are also famous. Rich silver, lead, zinc, and copper deposits are mined at Bawdwin. In 1933, lead production amounted to 72,000 tons, enough to place Burma eighth in world output, and silver totaled 5,000,000 ounces. The mines at Bawdwin were worked by the Chinese in the fourteenth century and are one of the richest deposits of their type in the world. Only rock with over 20 per cent lead and zinc combined is now considered as ore.

Two railroads climb onto the Shan Plateau, the meter-gauge lines to Shwenyaung and the important line to Lashio. At the turn of the century, British and French interests were both seeking a rail route into southwestern China. The French line from Indo-China to Yunnan was completed first, but on account of the formidable character of the topography on the Burma frontier the British railway was not continued beyond Lashio. With the blockade of the China coast during the Second World War, China opened in 1939 a spectacular automobile route from Kunming in Yunnan to Burma, with twin terminals at the railhead of Lashio and at Bhamo on the navigable Irrawaddy. This new back door to China will be of increasing importance in peacetime trade with Europe.

Tenasserim Coast

Burma projects 500 miles southward along the Malay peninsula in a strip averaging but 50 miles in width. This is the Tenasserim Coast, comparable to the Arakan lowland and mountains in both configuration and monsoon rainfall. The one city of importance is Moulmein in the north, where the Salween delta is virtually a continuation of the Irrawaddy delta lands. Elsewhere mountains prevail. The north-south alignment of the topography is shown in the course of the Tenasserim River which follows a valley within 20 to 40 miles of the sea for 150 miles.

Tungsten and tin are important, with production at Mergui and Tavoy. Tungsten production began in 1910 and for a few years prior to the First World War, Burma led the world, but since then has consistently been second to China. The tin output amounted to 6,623 tons in 1937. The long wet season with 200 inches of rain is favorable for rubber and cocoanut plantations.

CHAPTER 36

THAILAND

Thailand was the only independent kingdom in Southeastern Asia never conquered until its submission to the Japanese in 1941. The country has well been called a buffer state, for in 1896 France and Britain agreed by treaty to preserve it as an independent nation between their expanding territories in Burma and Indo-China. The country was known as Siam until 1939 when the name was changed to Thailand, land of the Thai (free) people.

Foreign pressure by Britain and France has several times changed the boundaries, particularly in the east next to Indo-China and in the South next to Malaya. In 1941 Thailand regained part of Cambodia and part of the right bank of the Mekong which were lost in 1907. This area covered 21,000 square miles with a population of over 1,000,000. In 1943, Japan returned the lost areas in Malaya.

Little is known about the early dwellers of Thailand, but they appear to have been Negritos who were later driven out by successive waves of Mongoloid people who made their way down the river valleys from the north and west. Their descendants are now the Mon, Cambodians, and Annamese. Still later, but before the Christian era, another population wave of Tibeto-Burman people moved south along the Irrawaddy and entered Thailand. Peoples and cultures of India came in the sixth century, both directly and via Sumatra and Java. Another group of immigrants from the Yangtze Valley were the Lao-Tai who arrived in strength after their defeat by Kublai Khan in the thirteenth century. Their principal descendants are the present-day Thai.

Although the Thai are the chief inhabitants, the Chinese population is also considerable with some 800,000 who are still Chinese citizens and over 2,000,000 with some degree of Chinese parentage. Much of the retail and import and export business is in Chinese hands; no other group is willing to work so hard for so little remuneration. Chinese shops are found even in small remote villages. Serious racial antagonisms have developed on several occasions.

The country has an area of 200,198 square miles and a population that numbered 14,464,489 in 1937. This is an average density of 72 per square mile but the distribution varies widely, with many of the people concentrated in the plains around Bangkok. One province in the north has but 13 persons per square mile while a southern province counts 362. Seventy per cent of the population live in agricultural villages. Only in a few mountain valleys of the north is there any serious pressure of the people on the land. This situation is reflected in the availability of surplus rice for export.

Mountains close off Thailand on the west, north, and northeast; to the east the boundary is chiefly along the Mekong River. Only one major stream is entirely within the country, the so-called Menam. Actually the name is Menam Chao Bhraya (or Phya), and menam simply means river. To the west is the shorter Meklohng, while the northeast is drained by tributaries of the Mekong.

The mountains of Thailand are a con-

Alluvial plains are limited to the vicinity of the three rivers. Around Bangkok the Menam-Meklohng lowland has a maximum

Siamese architecture is typified by this Buddhist temple at Chiengmai. (*Courtesy Presbyterian Board of Foreign Missions.*)

tinuation of the complex that extends southward from the corner of Tibet through western Yunnan and Burma. Farther south these form the backbone of the Malay Peninsula. A few peaks reach 8,000 feet in northern Thailand, but elevations are under a mile in most sections. The north is a country of parallel ridges and valleys, all trending north and south. The limestone mountains rise abruptly from the valley floors, but others usually have lower foothills and intermediate slopes. The northern boundary with Burma lies along the Tanen Taung Gyi Range; farther south and extending down the peninsula this is known as the Tenasserim Range. The northeastern part of the country is enclosed on the west and south by low linear mountains which meet at a right angle near the town of Korat. Together these mountainous sections cover about one-third of Thailand.

width of 175 miles and extends upriver some 250 miles. A narrow belt of alluvium follows the Nam Mun in the northeast, while east central Thailand extends into the low plains of Cambodia.

Most of the remainder of the country consists of rolling hills, chiefly old peneplains. The most important of these areas is the Korat Plateau in the northeast. This is a slightly dissected area with an elevation of only a few hundred feet, underlain by horizontal red sandstones and other sedimentary rocks of Triassic age. Soils of low productivity limit the population.

Most of the central part of Thailand has been geologically stable for a considerable period, so that erosion is normal. Thick alluvial deposits obscure the underlying rocks, which include Pre-Cambrian, and Carboniferous to Pleistocene. Igneous intrusions are widespread in the western mountains. Granite batholiths form the core of all the main mountains.

The climate over most of Thailand may be divided into two seasons. The rainy period occurs during the southwest monsoon from the end of April until late in October; the dry winter season wind from the northeast lasts from November until mid-February and is followed by the hottest weather.

This has been called a monsoon climate, but such a classification is an oversimplification. The migration of the heat equator north and south across Thailand twice annually means the passage of the doldrum belt, with its quiet air and the sky full of magnificent cumulus clouds, often thunderheads. Thus, much of the rainfall is in localized thundershowers. The northeast and southeast trade winds, which theoretically blow on opposite sides of the doldrums, are considerably modified by the monsoonal conditions in the west. Local land and sea breezes are often mistaken for "monsoon" winds. Occasionally a typhoon will come directly across the South China Sea; fading out over Thailand, such depressions bring general rain over wide areas. For a week or so, between November and February, north winds from a high pressure area over Asia accompany an overcast sky and bring markedly lower temperatures in interior Thailand.

Temperatures in Thailand are moderate to high. The prevailing seasonal temperatures, particularly in the central portion, are determined largely by the degree of cloudiness, or its absence. Thus it is that the season of highest temperatures is in late March, April, and early May. Once the rains are well started, *i.e.*, once the sky is overcast much of the time, temperatures are considerably lower. On the other hand, because of the high humidity, bright sunny days after local showers seem very hot. In central, peninsular, and south-

eastern Thailand maximum temperatures seldom reach 100°F., while minimum temperatures are seldom lower than 65°F.

Because of the greater distance from the sea, the increased elevation of the interior valleys, and the mountains which cut off much of the wind, the range of temperatures is much greater in northern Thailand. Houses have fireplaces for warmth which are used nightly much of the winter, and warm clothing is desirable. Only on the highest mountains have frosts been reported.

The total annual rainfall in Thailand varies from about 30 to 120 inches. In southern peninsular Thailand there is seldom a long dry season. In this area the monsoon winds from the Bay of Bengal bring heavy rains to the western coast and slopes during the months of May to September. The eastern coast of the peninsula receives most of its rain between October and January from the northeast trade winds which sweep in off the South China Sea and the Gulf of Siam. The rainfall quantities and regime in southeastern Thailand much resemble those of western peninsular Thailand.

Much of the rain which falls in central Thailand is from convectional showers and from squalls from the southwest. The average rainfall in this plain is about 40 inches. Around Bangkok gentle sea breezes are frequent during the summer months. During the almost rainless winter months northeast breezes are common. Both in the western part of the central plain and in western Korat there are very pronounced rain shadows, with inadequate moisture for the growth of rice.

Since ancient times the civilization of the country has been founded on rice. It now supports nine-tenths of the people, either with its production, milling, or export. The crop acreage amounts to 95 per cent of all planted land. Although Thailand produces but 5 per cent of the world's rice, it is the third largest exporter. One-third or more of the crop is shipped, and this accounts for 70 per cent of the nation's foreign income. The principal customer before 1914 was Europe. Since then the market has been China, Singapore, India, and Cuba. Farming methods are still primitive, but mechanical pumps have been introduced under cooperative credit arrangements. Lowland rice requires a constant supply of water, and many areas lack adequate amounts of summer rainfall in dry years. At times half the crop may be ruined by too much or too little water; even so, famine is rare. Only one crop is raised a year, except in the Chiengmai Valley. The agricultural unsuitability of much of the land is unfortunate. Thailand has overspecialized on rice and depends on a fluctuating market. It must import cotton and other needs, a large part of which might be grown locally.

Other crops hold a decidedly inferior position, for they occupy but 500,000 acres of which rubber and cocoanuts account for 300,000 and 127,000 acres, respectively. Tobacco, cotton, corn, and beans are the chief upland or unirrigated field crops.

Cultivated land is estimated at 12,355,000 acres, or 10 per cent of the total area. Even in the delta around Bangkok only 40 per cent is utilized, so that expansion is probably possible, particularly for dry crops. Farms average four acres, but there are wide regional differences. The economic status of the individual farmer is complicated by large debt, tenancy, and marketing problems. Water buffaloes are the principal draft animals in the wet rice areas, with considerable numbers of bullocks in the drier farm areas. Work elephants are employed in the teak forests and in the Kra Isthmus.

Forest resources are still large although the valuable teak forests have been considerably exploited. Seventy per cent of the country is covered by some type of forest, much of it very slow-growing hardwood types.

Tin comes between rice and rubber as Thailand's second export resource. The production is from the peninsula and amounted to 16,998 tons in 1939, 9 per cent of the world total. Many types of mining are employed, from primitive shaft mines to hydraulic mining and the use of enormous dredges. Tungsten is also produced.

The scarcity of fuel is a major obstacle to industrialization. There is no petroleum and such coal as exists is lignite. Rice husks are a common fuel for power plants in Bangkok.

One of the nation's international assets is that she owns the narrowest part of the Malay Peninsula at the Kra Isthmus. The possibility of constructing a canal at this point has been discussed for a century by rival British, French, and Japanese interests. Such a waterway would reduce the journey between Europe and East Asia by 600 miles and end the dominance of Singapore. The engineering problems would involve the use of winding rivers with steep banks, and cutting through a 250-foot ridge.

The railways are of meter gauge and radiate from Bangkok. One line leads west and south to Singapore, one line extends eastward to form a link with Indo-China, a bifurcated branch penetrates the northeast, and another runs north with a road connection into Burma. The railways total about 2,000 miles, but there are only 1,000 miles of paved highways.

Within Thailand are four geographic regions, conventionally named Central, Northern, Northeastern, and Southern.

Central Thailand

Central Thailand is the heart of the country, with the bulk of the people and the best riceland. It has been described as 68,000 square miles of almost unbroken monotonous scenery.[1] Through the middle extends the Menam-Meklohng plain. The rainfall varies from 30 to 60 inches and is approximately 11 acres, twice that of any other region. Annual floods cause many of the people near the waterways to live in

Many farmers along the Menam River above Bangkok build their homes on high stilts for protection against flood. (*Burton Holmes, from Ewing Galloway.*)

well distributed during the rice season. Only 15 per cent of the region is cultivated, of which wet rice occupies 75 per cent. Nevertheless this region accounts for more than half of the country's total cultivated area. Much of this is sown broadcast after plowing the moist soil rather than transplanted into paddies from seedbeds. With the progress of the rainy season the fields become deeply flooded, often as much as 10 or 12 feet; this rice is called "floating rice." The utilized land per farm family is

[1] The areas for the four regions are those of Zimmerman for the land surface alone. These add up to 193,000 square miles rather than the usual total of 200,198 square miles for the country as a whole.

compact villages along the natural levees. The rivers and canals are almost the only means of communication across the plain. Practically all houses in rural Thailand are elevated on poles. Considerable areas which are not easily flooded are left in wild jungle. Bullock carts are used in the dry season across areas where one must travel by boat during the rains.

Boats on the rivers and canals are the principal means of transportation in the Bangkok plain. Many houses float on pontoons along the river banks. It is only within the past decade that any highways have led out from Bangkok, even to the international airport about 20 miles distant.

Highway development in the Bangkok plain has been greatly retarded not only by the heavy clay soil, flooded for many months annually for rice growing, and the numerous rivers and canals which have to be bridged, but by the absence of suitable surfacing materials near by and a reluctance to facilitate further competition with the state-owned railways.

Such a large portion of the Bangkok plain is now used to produce rice that most of the natural vegetation has been completely altered. Judging by the magnificent groups of towering *yang* (dipterocarp) trees growing about some of the older Buddhist temples along the river banks and a few relics of similar forests near the head of the plain, such forests probably lined the river banks for much of the distance through this plain. Nearer the sea, where the land is lower and brackish water comes in with the tides, mangroves are important. Back from the river channels grasses so tall that "even a man on elephant back could not see out over them," comprised the principal type of vegetation. The lower slopes of the hills around the plain are still covered with forest which varies from a relatively luxuriant rain forest to low, open hardwood forests, depending upon the soil and rainfall conditions of the locality. Since almost all of the rain falls during the southwest monsoon period, between June and October, there are striking differences in the vegetation between that in the dry rain shadow along the western side of the valley and that in the especially heavy rain area near the mountains along the border of the Korat Plateau.

Toward the southeast and southwest, hills introduce a different landscape, with more forest and less rice. The hills to the east have heavy rainfall, but those to the west lie in a rain shadow and are drier than the plain.

Bangkok is Thailand's one important city, with a population of over 800,000. The city lies 15 miles from the sea on the Menam Chao Bhraya in the midst of a tidal flat intersected with numerous canals. The old port extends along the river and near it are the larger commercial establishments; the new port is some miles below the city. Since there is a troublesome bar with a normal depth of 13 feet at the mouth of the river, larger steamers anchor outside and transfer their cargo to lighters. The bar is being dredged to 26 feet. About a thousand steamers call each year. The modern city is laid out along spacious lines, with western buildings and innumerable Buddhist temples in Siamese architecture; elsewhere there are narrow streets with the shops of Chinese traders. The royal palace and associated buildings are in strikingly beautiful Thai architecture, with brilliantly colored tile roofs. Rice milling, teak sawmills, cement works, and match factories are the chief industries.

Northern Thailand

Northern Thailand is a mountainous area between the Salween and the Mekong. Half a dozen streams, tributaries of the latter or of the Menam, follow parallel courses through north-south valleys which lie at elevations of about 1,000 feet. Mountains rise steeply to heights of over a mile. Many of the rivers are graded, and have developed open valleys where rice is grown; elsewhere cultivation is of the migratory hillside type. In parts of the Chiengmai Valley where irrigation water is available, two crops of rice are raised. Cotton, tobacco, and opium are specialized crops.

The long dry season and the relatively low rainfall, little more than 35 inches annually, have been important factors in the development of the native vegetation. The most important forest types are (1) the more or less deciduous "monsoon" forests, of which teak is a component if the soils are sufficiently good; (2) the evergreen forests, more on the northern slopes and at higher elevations; (3) on the highest ridges and peaks, the limited forests in which pine and dwarf oaks are conspicuous; and (4) on intermediate slopes on poor sandy soils, some development of the low, slow-growing, relatively open forests so much more extensively developed in the Korat region.

This region covers 35,000 square miles, and has 16 per cent of the total population outside Bangkok. Only 7 per cent is in cultivation. Many of the hill tribes are Shans or other non-Thai people.

Teak is the distinctive export, but the quality is not quite so good as in Burma.

The principal city is Chiengmai (Jieng Hmai) at the rail head, 410 miles or 20 hours north from Bangkok.

Northeastern Thailand

The landscape of the Northeast has three components: extensive open forests which near the villages grade into dry scrub jungles growing on soils often too infertile to be cultivated; alluvial lowlands with small diked rice fields; and grassy plains too deeply flooded after the rains and too dry at other seasons to be used for crops. This is a flat to rolling region where erosion is so slight that the thoroughly leached soils have not been eroded, hence their content of plant foods is low. Some areas of less infertile soil have a denser and better forest, often utilized for migratory caiñgin agriculture.

This region is known as the Korat Plateau, from the name of the chief town. It lies east and north of the low Dong Phya Yen Mountains which rise abruptly from Central Thailand to heights of 5,000 feet. The region as a whole is underlain by horizontal sandstones and shales, purplish red in color. The mountains represent igneous uplifts. Elevations in the Korat Plateau are under 600 feet, decreasing to the south-

east. The Korat Plateau is drained by tributaries of the Mekong, the Lam Moon (Nam Mun) and Lam Chi.

Northern Thailand has many of the same tribespeople who live in eastern Burma and southwestern China. These are Kaws. (*Henry O'Brien, courtesy Presbyterian Board of Foreign Missions.*)

The climate reflects the interior location, with greater seasonal variations than at Bangkok. Rainfall is erratic in time and uncertain in distribution, and the underlying sandstones are very permeable; agriculture is thus handicapped. Rice occupies 99 per cent of the cropped area, but there is only a small surplus for export. Cattle and pigs are also shipped out of the region. Their presence accounts for the superior fertility of the soil near the villages. Small plots of tobacco, mulberry, and cotton are grown by many farmers. On account of rapids in the Mekong, trade flows to Bangkok.

Northeastern Thailand covers 62,000 square miles and has a population of some

5,000,000. Seven per cent of the land is under cultivation, which accounts for 22 per cent of the country's cropland.

Southern Thailand

Southern Thailand lies in the long Malay Peninsula. The region is nowhere more than 70 miles wide and, in places where it borders Burma, only 10 miles in width. This is an attractive region with palm-lined beaches, beautiful offshore islands, and verdure-clad mountains. In the south the people are of Malay types, Mohammedan in religion. The area is 28,000 square miles. Seven per cent is cultivated, with four acres per farm family. Elevations reach 4,520 feet but are under 3,000 feet in most areas.

Proximity to the sea makes the climate delightful, without excessive temperatures. The western side of the peninsula has its rainiest season between May and October, while the eastern is wettest from October to February. As a result of this exposure to both monsoons, there are about 100 inches of rainfall and high humidity. Temperatures are moderated by the sea.

From the latitude of Bangkok south to the isthmus of Kra the international boundary between Burma and Thailand follows the crest of the mountains. The isthmus of Kra is a relatively low pass between the Gulf of Siam and the Indian Ocean. South of this locality and on most of the way to Singapore, the higher mountains are *en échelon*. Between the many more or less separated ranges there are a number of relatively low and wide valleys, through which pass railways and highways that make easy the crossing of the peninsula. Some of the river valleys are quite well developed, with considerable areas of lowland plain. There are also coastal plains which have been formed more by degradation than from alluvial deposits. Notable monadnocks are the towering and sometimes fantastically shaped lime-stone bluffs which stand isolated in the plains, as islands off the coast, or in inland lakes. These hills are important because of the phosphatic bat guano found in the caves, and as the nesting place for the birds which build the edible nests.

The granitic batholiths which form the cores of the main mountain ranges in peninsular Thailand are for the most part tin-bearing. The very deep weathering and the subsequent erosion of the overlying rocks and of the granites themselves have liberated the tin ore which is mined on an extensive scale by placer, hydraulic, shaft, and dredger methods.

The natural vegetation of the region may be divided as follows: (1) tropical rain forest; (2) evergreen forests on less rainy mountain slopes; (3) mangrove swamps, especially in the muddy estuaries along the seacoasts; (4) grassy plains here and there at low elevations; and (5) fresh-water swamps. In the extreme northern part of the region is an extension of vegetation types from dry western Central Thailand. These are (6a) bamboo thorn scrub in the drier rain-shadow region and (6b) dwarf open hardwood forests on poor sandy soils on the lower slopes of the mountains, west of the thorn scrub.

As in all other regions of Thailand, rice is the most important and most generally raised crop. But there is relatively less of it produced than in other regions, for many of the people here have other and easier ways to make a living. At times rice is even imported. Hevea rubber is produced in great quantities; a considerable part of it by natives who have only small plots. Tin-mining companies employ large numbers of laborers, and there are also individuals who wash tin on their own in the rivers. The long coast line provides ample opportunity for fishing; in normal times the export of salt fish to Singapore is considerable.

CHAPTER 37

INDO-CHINA

Indo-China, officially written as French Indochine, is the largest and most populous of the continental countries in Southeastern Asia. Most of the people and agriculture are in the fertile deltas of the Mekong in the south and the Red River in the north; between them is a mountainous backbone with only scattered settlements along the coast and the valley of the Mekong in the west. Its shape may be likened to a coolie carrying pole with a basket of rice hung at either end. Sharp contrasts characterize the mountains and plains, and the north versus the south.

Five political units make up French Indo-China, each with its geographic personality. Tonkin next to China in the north is drained by the Red River. Hanoi is its capital and also the administrative center for the entire country; Haiphong is the principal seaport. Annam includes a long strip of mountains and isolated coastal plains. Its capital is Hué. To the west is Laos in the mountains and the central hill country of the Mekong with the capital in Vientiane. Cochin-China occupies the lower Mekong and is dominated by its capital city of Saïgon. Cambodia covers the broad plain of the central Mekong, under the administration of Pnom-Penh. The combined area of French Indo-China is 285,800 square miles, larger than Texas, and in 1936 the population was 23,030,000. Chinese numbered 326,000, and Europeans but 43,000.

Much of the country was under Chinese rule from 213 B.C. to A.D. 931, and many cultural traits survive. French penetration dates from the seventeenth century but political control is the result of wars and negotiations between 1858 and 1907. Several areas are still protectorates rather than fully colonial. Indo-China has been the most prosperous and most populous of all French colonies. The position of the French in this part of the world differs in its recency from the British or Dutch, each of whom has a long tradition of political relations with its subjects. The development of colonial self-government has no place in French policy.

In 1941 as the result of a Japanese-instigated war with Thailand, Indo-China ceded 21,750 square miles to Thailand, largely in western Cambodia with additional area in Laos.

Indo-China shows wide differences in the character and distribution of her people. In the Tonkin Delta there are 1,500 people per square mile, the small scattered plains of Annam average 550, central Cochin-China has about 375, while in the lake region of Cambodia there are but 175 people per square mile. So inhospitable is much of the country that in an area of 230,000 square miles, out of 285,800, the density is only some 15 per square mile. Population congestion is particularly acute in the Tonkin Delta where some districts report as many as 6,000 rural people per square mile of rice fields. More than 90 per cent of the people in the country are rural.

Annamese are the most numerous of the various peoples, since they comprise about 70 per cent of the total. They live from the far north of Tonkin to the far south of Cochin-China. They have copied the Chinese in their customs, arts, political

from northwest to southeast. Along the Chinese frontier adjoining Kwangsi and Yunnan are the mountains of northern

A native meal in Saïgon, with food and utensils that reflect strong Chinese influences. (*Ewing Galloway*.)

organization, religion, literature, and writing. Cambodians, the second group with 6 per cent, have an Indian background in their culture and language but are Buddhist in religion and have many similarities to the Thai. The Cambodians are the descendants of the Khmers whose brilliant and artistic civilization reached its zenith about eight centuries ago. Thai people occupy the mountains of Laos and Tonkin, and share the area with numerous other primitive tribes.

Mountains cover more than half of Indo-China, with three systems each trending

Tonkin. They are carved from great masses of limestone and have steep-walled canyons and spires which terminate in a series of islands in the Gulf of Tonkin. The highest peak is 7,879 feet. The Annam Cordillera consists of a series of ranges and half a dozen plateaus which reach from one corner of the country to another. Elevations rise to 10,306 feet. The widest developments of the system are in the north and the south. Almost everywhere the mountains handicap communications between the hill country near the Mekong and the coast. The mountains of southwestern Cambodia rise to 4,149 feet but are of limited extent.

There are two types of plains: those along the coast and those in the interior. The latter lie entirely along the Mekong, partly in Laos but largely in central Cambodia in the area around the Tonle Sap. This basin becomes a vast lake after the rains when the Mekong is high and backs up into the lake. In the dry season it shrinks to a third of its maximum size. Fishing is very important here. In Tonkin is the delta of the Red River (Song-koi) and its tributary the Black (Song-bo), with an area of 5,400 square miles. The course of the Red is so straight that it must have tectonic control. Since Hanoi at the head of the delta has an elevation of only 15 feet and the flood crest may reach 35 feet, dikes are necessary to protect much of the lowland. The coast of Annam has a series of small deltas and coastal plains, separated from one another where the mountains reach the sea. Their combined area is about 7,700 square miles. Much of the shore line is inhospitable and without shelter; an important exception is the magnificent harbor of Cam Ranh Bay, a partly developed naval base near the extreme east. The delta of the Mekong begins at Pnom Penh where the river divides into distributaries. Most of it lies in Cochin-China, but it reaches into Cambodia. The area of the delta is roughly 26,000 square miles. So much sediment is brought into the sea that the coast line to the south is advancing as much as 250 feet per year. This plain is the largest in Indo-China.

Almost all of Indo-China is within the tropics, so that lowland temperatures and humidity are always high. Two major climatic provinces are formed by the Annam Cordillera which lies at right angles to the seasonal winds. To the west there is the monsoon regime from the Indian

Ocean with summer rain from May to October, modified by occasional typhoons from the China Sea. Areas in the lee of

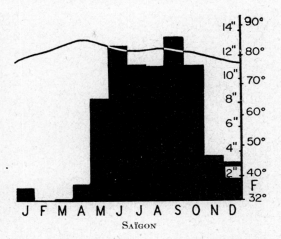

SAÏGON

mountains tend to be drier. In Saïgon April is the warmest month, 86°F., and December the coolest, 80°F. Rainfall amounts to 78 inches, with September as the wettest month, 14 inches, and February the driest, 0.1 inch. Some mountain stations report 220 inches.

Eastern Indo-China has an opposite regime, dominated by the South China Sea. In the southern half, the rainy season occurs with typhoons and the northeast monsoon in the fall, from September to January. Tonkin has its distinctive climate, related to relief and location, with cooler weather and only a brief dry period. Monthly average temperatures everywhere exceed 63°F. Wide fluctuations in rainfall occur from year to year, often in a ratio of 2:1. Agriculture is affected accordingly. These are in part related to typhoons which strike all sections of the east coast but especially north of Hué. May to December are the most common months. In addition to destructive winds, typhoons may bring as much as 25 inches of rain in 24 hours.

Indo-China is a land of primary production, from fields and mines, similar to the other lands of the peninsula. Intensive small-scale rice culture stands in contrast to modern plantations of rubber, tea,

Coal output in 1937 amounted to 2,308,000 metric tons. Other metals include tin, zinc, tungsten, chromium, antimony, iron,

Saïgon is one of the finest cities of Southeastern Asia. This is one of the principal business streets. (*De Cou, from Ewing Galloway.*)

and coffee. Cultivated land occupies about 13 per cent of the country, almost entirely in the plains. Rice accounts for two-thirds of the nation's export, much of it consigned to China. France also bought rice. Tonkin is so densely populated that there is no export surplus. In contrast, the Mekong Valley ships in large amounts from Saïgon. The yield is the lowest per acre of any country in Eastern Asia, a result of insufficient fertilization and primitive methods.

Mining is concentrated in the north. Excellent coal, much of it anthracite, is obtained near Honggay east of Haiphong.

and manganese. Phosphate rock is mined in the south. The reserves are extensive and a considerable increase in production is possible. At present most minerals are exported. Hydroelectric power is also available. Indo-China has the basic raw materials of heavy industry in abundance and can also supply textile fibers, rubber, vegetable oils, timber, and other require-ments for light industry. Of all the lands of Southeastern Asia and of all French colonies anywhere, Indo-China is best endowed for industrial developments. Mod-ern industry is now limited to rice milling, textiles, sugar production, public utilities in the few cities, and railway shops. French capital has been interested in the production of raw materials for export,

Delta with which it is connected by a canal known as L'Arroyo Chinois. The city resembles a French provincial town. Bor-

The temples of Angkor are the finest examples of ancient architecture in Southeastern Asia. In the foreground is a modern village occupied by the temple priests. (*Ewing Galloway*.)

especially to France, rather than the development of large-scale industry within the colony.

A railway follows along the coast from north to south, with two lines to the Chinese frontier in the north, one of which continues to Kunming. A newly constructed railway in the southwest connects Pnom Penh with Thailand. There is considerable navigation on the lower 350 miles of the Mekong but rapids on the central river handicap traffic. The Red River is navigable for 275 miles.

Saïgon is the premier city. It lies 40 miles from the sea on the narrow and winding Donai River, just to one side of the Mekong

dering Saïgon is its twin industrial city of Cholon. The 1931 census credits Saïgon with 123,298, of whom 11,115 were Europeans. Cholon then had 134,060 people, half of them Chinese. French steamship lines make the run to Marseilles in 25 days.

Hanoi and Haiphong in the north are each cities of over 100,000, which is also the population of Pnom Penh.

The most remarkable architectural ruins of Southeastern Asia are those at Angkor in Cambodia. This ruined city once rivaled Rome or Carthage. Most of the temples and palaces were built of laterite faced with sandstone and are still well preserved. These ruins were lost in the jungle until discovered in 1858. They represent the climax of Khmer civilization 800 years ago. The chief temple area is a step pyramid rising to five towers, 213 feet in height.

Three geographic regions stand out: the Red Plain, the Indo-China Mountains, and the Mekong Plain. The first and last are delta ricelands with intensive utiliza-tion; the second is a wilderness of forest where cultivated land is limited to fragments of coastal plain, rough country along the central Mekong, or plateau remnants. In these mountains stock raising and European plantations of rubber are of increasing importance. Many of the people are backward.

CHAPTER 38

MALAYA

Rubber, tin, and Singapore describe British Malaya. This southernmost tip of Asia has an importance out of all proportion to its area or population. It is one of the most advanced agricultural lands of the Orient, largely owing to the initiative of commercial plantations. Foreign investments in rubber plantations alone amount to $275,000,000. The export of rubber and tin became so profitable and wages paid to workers on plantations and in mines were so high that domestic food production has been neglected and two-thirds of the requirements were imported.

The British Empire has been fortunate in having men of great vision, among them Sir Stanford Raffles, who foresaw the strategic importance of the Strait of Malacca and secured Singapore for England in 1819. Through the strait passes all the shipping between Europe or India and Eastern Asia, so that Singapore is one of the world's busiest ports of call and the logical center for the collection, grading, and export of many tropical products such as rattan, rubber, spices, gums, and resins.

In common with many other British areas, the political structure is complex. The four Federated Malay States of Perak, Pahang, Selangor, and Negri Sembilan are governed by native rajahs under a British High Commissioner. The five Non-federated Malay States are protectorates: Johore in the south since 1885, Perlis, Kedah, Kelantun, and Trengganu to the north since 1909 when they were obtained from Thailand. During Japanese occupa-

tion in 1943, the last four were returned to Thailand. The Straits Settlements are crown colonies: Penang, Wellesley, and

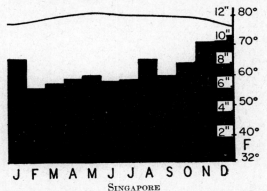

SINGAPORE
Elevation, 10 feet; average temperature, 80.1°F.; total precipitation, 92.9 inches.

Dindings in the north, Malacca and Singapore in the south, as well as some outlying islands. British North Borneo, Brunei, and Sarawak are also related to British Malaya.

Singapore lies 75 miles north of the equator, but the climate of the peninsula is moderated by the surrounding seas. Daytime temperatures seldom exceed 88°F. and may drop as low as 70°F. at night. Rain amounts to nearly 100 inches a year at most lowland stations, or double that amount in the hills, and falls on 200 days. Relative humidity is always uncomfortably high, seldom below 75 per cent during the day and frequently over 90 per cent at night. Actual rainfall departs widely from the average. The doldrums or intertropical front moves north and south with the sun and brings large cumulus clouds and showery weather, especially in the early afternoon. The northeast winds prevail during December, January, February, and to 1,080 people per square mile. Malays and Chinese each account for over 40 per cent of the population, followed by Indians

A rubber plantation in the Straits Settlement north of Singapore. Sap is gathered as shown in the foreground. (*Ewing Galloway.*)

March, and southeasterly trades from May through September. It is not correct to speak of these seasonal shifts as monsoonal. No typhoons touch Singapore.

Malaya is mountainous, with a framework of north-south ranges *en échelon*. Elevations reach 7,186 feet, but much of the peninsula is a low-lying plain from which mountains and hills rise abruptly. Dense rain forest covers the mountains and uncleared lowlands of the interior. Mangrove swamps occupy extensive mud flats particularly along the western coast.

The population in 1937–1938 amounted to 5,174,000 in an area of 50,880 square miles, so that the average density was 100. In the Straits Settlements this rises at 15 per cent. Most of the Malays are still conservative rice farmers although many also have small rubber groves, while the Chinese and Indians work for wages in rubber and tin. In most cities the Chinese outnumber all other races together and include many people of considerable wealth. The entire European population in 1938 was but 24,000, including plantation and mine managers, merchants, professional men, and officials.

Rubber outranks tin as Malaya's most important product. Out of a total crop area of 5,074,000 acres in 1939, or 13 per cent of the entire country, rubber plantations accounted for 3,442,649 or 65 per cent, rice fields covered 14 per cent, and cocoanuts 12 per cent. Since the rubber has been exported at widely fluctuating market prices, the economic life of the colony has been subject to extremes. Prior to the Second World War, Malaya produced 38 to 54 per cent of the total supply, but as late as 1905 the plantation production was only 150 tons.

Low prices led to the Stevenson control plan in 1922 which raised prices from $0.29 to $1.23 per pound, in comparison with production costs of $0.19. The resulting high prices stimulated planting in the Netherlands Indies and elsewhere, and the plan was abandoned in 1928. Rubber dropped to $0.03 per pound in 1933, and a new agreement, this time international, again attempted to control production and prices. The maximum output in Malaya came in 1930 to 1934 and averaged 436,516 long tons. In 1939 the figure was 376,755 tons. By 1937 the annual world potential production was 1,800,000 tons in comparison with consumption needs of 1,000,000 tons. Since the synthetic plant capacity developed during the Second World War in the United States alone amounted to 813,000 long tons and thus nearly equaled prewar world needs, the future of natural plantation rubber is not promising. Natural rubber has been sold for $0.15 a pound with profit, whereas synthetic costs in 1943 in cents per pound were as follows: Buna S, 36; Butyl, 33; and Neoprene, 45.[1]

The trees of *Hevea brasiliensis* grow best below elevations of 1,000 feet on the west side of the peninsula. Rainfall is a critical factor, with the highest yield following a high rainfall, well distributed throughout the year. On the plantations about 100 trees are grown per acre, whereas native groves have many more trees per acre but lower yields. Yields vary from 200 to

1,000 pounds per acre, according to the soil, the climate, the number of trees, and the variety. About one-third of the rubber was produced on small native holdings.

The Asiatic maritime tropics have proved to be an ideal place to grow rubber. This area includes Ceylon and the southern west coast of India, peninsular Burma and Thailand, southern Indo-China, Malaya, Sumatra, Borneo, and Mindanao. Year-around temperatures are high, rainfall is about 100 inches, soils are suitable, and cheap labor is easily imported. Although South America and Africa have equatorial areas, they lack the labor supply and have more of a continental climate, as well as very serious leaf diseases.

Rice is the staple food, but only 727,000 acres are devoted to its cultivation, largely in the Nonfederated Malay States where rubber cultivation is less extensive. Government irrigation projects have considerably increased the yields. Natives usually prefer to raise rubber as it requires less work and brings a higher return in good years. Only Malays are permitted to own land suitable for raising rice. Additional good land is available but the cost of clearing forest and swamp is formidable.

Cocoanuts are the third crop. Cocoanut palms begin to bear after six or seven years, and continue for 60 years. On fertile soil, an average tree will yield 40 to 60 nuts a year, or 2,500 per acre, enough for over half a ton of copra. Most of the acreage is on the low coastal plain and near rivers. Oil palms are also important.

Malayan pineapples rank next to Hawaiian in export value, with shipments largely to the British Empire.

Prior to the First World War, the economy of Malaya rested on tin mining, as carried on by the Chinese. Although rubber is now more important, the 1939 production of tin amounting to 55,950 tons was 30 per cent of the world production.

[1] *Chemical and Engineering News*, May 25, 1943, 743.

For centuries, alluvial tin has been washed out by primitive methods, but most of the mining is now done by large dredges.

extreme south, with the naval base in the north near the town of Johore Bahru on the mainland. The city accounted for

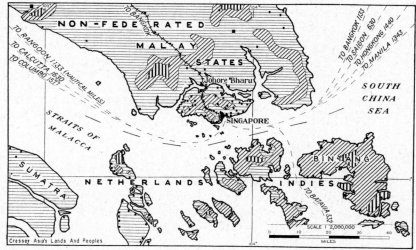

Singapore was designed to be one of the key points along the life line of the British Empire.

Lode mining is small but will increase as the gravels are worked out. Smelters at Singapore and Penang handle not only the tin from Malaya but that from Burma, Thailand, and Indo-China as well.

Japanese interests have greatly expanded the production of iron ore, manganese, and bauxite, with the entire production going to Japan. Iron ore from the states of Kelantan, Trengganu, and Johore amounted to 1,944,701 tons in 1939. Manganese comes from the first two of these areas and bauxite from the third. Very large amounts of bauxite are also obtained from the Dutch island of Bintan just across the Singapore Strait.

Local coal is of poor quality but is used in the tin industry and on the railways.

Singapore is the crossroads of the East. The island measures some 24 by 14 miles and is separated from the mainland by a channel a mile wide. The city lies at the

445,719 people in 1931, of whom 340,614 were Chinese. By 1941 the total had increased to 727,000. Commerce rather than industry provides the main occupation, and Singapore is the great trade center of the realm. When the British Empire made Singapore a military base, they overlooked the problem of air power and defense in depth. The naval base was of value only so long as it was in the center of a protected area. The strategic location of Singapore remains, but it needs to be reinterpreted.

North Borneo, Brunei, and Sarawak are other British possessions in Southeastern Asia, but call for little attention. They cover coastal plains and low hills, rising to mountains that reach 13,455 feet. The tropical climate, evergreen forest, and products resemble the other parts of Borneo. Rubber, sugar, petroleum, and copra are important exports.

CHAPTER 39

NETHERLANDS INDIES

The following figures provide an appropriate preface to the Netherlands Indies:

Area	Population in 1940	Area in square miles	Density per square mile
Java and Madura....	48,416,000	51,035	948
Outer Provinces.....	22,060,000	702,232	30
Netherlands Indies...	70,476,000	753,267	94

No other country in the world supports such a density of agricultural population as Java. By contrast, few lands are more empty than interior Borneo or New Guinea. The Dutch have been in the East Indies since before the founding of the United East India Company in 1602, but effective political administration is only a matter of a century. A census in 1816 during the brief period of British control gave the population of Java as 5 million. By 1845 it reached 9.4 million, and in 1880, 19.5 million. The 1900 figure was 28.4 million and in 1930 the total reached 40.9 million. No wonder Ellsworth Huntington has written about "Java, the Despair of Malthus." And yet the land supports these people in reasonable comfort. Perhaps nowhere are there brighter and more cheerful native people.

The Dutch have been the most successful of all colonial administrators, and the development of the islands has been greatly to the mutual advantage of the natives and the people of the Netherlands alike. No other European race has been willing to settle in colonial lands for a lifetime, as have the Dutch. Racial prejudice is lacking and children of mixed parentage have full status with Dutch. Thus out of the 242,372 (1931) "Europeans," from two-thirds to three-fourths are Eurasians. Since 1922 the Netherlands Indies have ceased to be a colony and have become an integral part of the Kingdom of the Netherlands.

Most of the native people are Malays in the broad sense, an intelligent and cheerful folk who work hard when they must, but who prize their leisure as they do their property. About 250 languages are spoken in the islands, grouped into Indonesian, Melanesian, and Polynesian types. Mohammedanism is the prevailing religion, brought by Arabs in the thirteenth century. Arabs numbered 71,000 in 1930. In the same year there were 1,234,000 Chinese, mostly shopkeepers and merchants.

The Netherlands Indies lie across the equator and extend one-eighth of the way around the earth, no less than 3,100 miles. From north to south the distance is more than a third of that figure. The total area is a quarter that of the United States. In some respects they belong to Asiatic geography, but in other regards they are linked with Australia and Melanesia. Cultural contrasts range from the Dutch civilization of Batavia to the recent headhunters of the outer islands. Java has appropriately received the most attention, but the contrasts in development between the center and periphery are diminishing.

The largest island is Dutch Borneo with 213,589 square miles. Sumatra follows with an area of 162,268, then comes Dutch New Guinea with 153,321, and Celebes with 71,763. The conventional grouping cently uplifted marine formations, as in the north coasts of Java and Sumatra, and by alluvial coastal plains. The Lesser

The typical Javanese landscape is composed of rice fields, cocoanut palm trees, and towering volcanoes. (*Satake*.)

is into the Greater Sunda Islands of Java, Sumatra, Borneo, Celebes, and adjoining smaller islands that lie on the Sunda continental shelf of Asia; the Lesser Sunda Islands from Bali to beyond Timor; and the Moluccas and Dutch New Guinea which are on the Australian continental shelf.

The islands may also be divided geologically into these three parts. The first and last are relatively stable and are characterized by erosional land forms. The surrounding seas are shallow and the islands were connected with Asia and with Australia in fairly recent geological time. Considerable areas are underlain by re-

Sunda group has deep sea basins and steep-sided islands; here mountain building is in full swing, with frequent earthquakes as well as volcanic action. A volcanic arc borders the Java, Sumatra, and Borneo block and then circles around the New Guinea block to reach the Philippine Islands.

Java has more than a hundred volcanoes many of which are active, while Sumatra and the other islands of the outer arc are only slightly less volcanic. The eruption of Javanese volcanoes, including destructive mud flows, has cost the lives of thousands of people. Many of these volcanoes exceed a mile in elevation, and there are mountains over 10,000 feet on half a dozen islands. Supercraters or caldera are numerous.

The most famous of these volcanoes is

Although the islands are equatorial, temperatures are moderated by the sea and never become excessive. The hot

Coral reefs and mangrove swamps fringe much of the coast of Java, here shown south of Garoet. (*Courtesy Netherlands Airforce.*)

Krakatao, an island in the middle of the Sunda Strait between Java and Sumatra. During its eruption of 1883, two-thirds of the island was blown away. Some of the ejected material was thrown to a height of 17 miles and carried completely around the world, producing brilliant sunsets. This has become the type example of explosive eruptions. The sound was heard in Singapore and Australia, and tidal waves drowned 36,000 people on near-by islands. Renewed activity in 1927 resulted in the appearance of a new island of ash called Anak Krakatao, "the child of Krakatao," reported to be 400 feet high in 1942. The eruption of Tambora in 1815 was of comparable violence.

nights and high humidity, however, combine to make lowland climates very enervating for Europeans. Everyone who can possibly do so spends some weeks each year in the mountains. Temperature is largely a matter of elevation rather than of season; thus in Batavia at sea level the warmest and coolest monthly averages differ by only 1°, with the yearly average 78.6°F. In contrast, Bandoeng at 2,395 feet has a yearly average of 71.2°, while Tosari at 5,588 feet averages 60.6°F., and Gede at 9,914 feet has 48°F. Frost occurs only on high sheltered plateaus.

The so-called monsoon circulation is a result of the location between Asia and Australia with their alternating high and low pressures, plus the shifting of the northeast and southeast trade-wind belts. Because of the position astride the equator, southwest, heavy rainfall results. Dry rain-shadow conditions prevail behind the mountains. Local convectional rain is

The eruption of Anak Krakatao, here shown on Feb. 9, 1929, resulted in the formation of an ash island over the spot where the explosion of 1883 had left water a thousand feet deep. (*Neumann van Padang.*)

rainy seasons vary from north to south. In January, air blows outward from Asia and reaches the Indies as a northeast wind, merging with the trades. It is relatively dry at sea level but yields heavy rain on mountain slopes. After crossing the equator, the winds curve to blow from the northwest, and bring rain to Java and the other islands to the east. July has opposite conditions, with dry southeast trade winds which since they come from arid Australia yield little rain except where forced to rise over mountains. With increasing distance from their desert source region, and especially after crossing the equator and turning to blow from the

important at all seasons. Thunderstorms are numerous near the equator, with a world record average of 322 thunderstorm days a year at Buitenzorg, south of Batavia.

Rainfall is nearly everywhere adequate for agriculture, except in eastern Java, Madura, and the eastern islands near Australia. Where the rainfall drops below 60 inches, corn replaces rice; elsewhere there is a rice harvest every week in the year, provided that irrigation water is available for the short dry periods.

Luxuriant tropical rain forests generally prevail where the land has not been cleared, except in the swamps of Sumatra.

Almost no forests remain in Java except on high mountains or steep slopes. Pure stands of trees are rare, and the economic value of the forest is restricted by transportation problems. Great diversity of all life, both plant and animal, is characteristic of all humid tropical regions. Commercially useful timber is surprisingly limited, although Java has teak forests. Many trees are damaged by parasites, and decay is rapid in the humid tropics. Mangrove swamps border the lower coasts and are often succeeded inland by nipa palm. Where the forest has been cleared for migratory agriculture, rank grasses sometimes recapture the land as elsewhere in Southeastern Asia.

The soils of Java are unusually fertile for the tropics, largely owing to their content of volcanic ash of basic rather than acidic composition. On account of long cultivation and intensive agricultural practices, fertilizers are now desirable, but the quality of the soil is still good. Large areas in Sumatra, Borneo, Celebes, and New Guinea are devoid of volcanoes; there some of the soils are strikingly infertile.

Agriculture is of two types: small-scale subsistence cultivation and large-scale estate or plantation agriculture. Almost the entire output of the latter is for export, plus an increasing share of native production in the Outer Provinces. Since no aliens, including the Dutch, are allowed to purchase land already in native use, the natives are protected in their holdings and food supply. This is one of the outstanding aspects of Dutch administration. Foreign sugar producers in the settled areas, for example, may only rent land for fixed periods and even then are permitted to grow but one crop in three years on any one tract. Anyone can lease uncleared forest.

Irrigated rice fields, here known as sawahs, similar to the paddy fields of India, represent the most intensive utilization of the landscape. Although largely

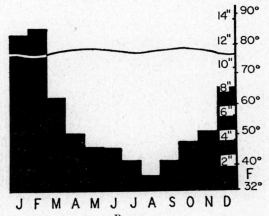

BATAVIA
Average temperature 78.8°F.; total precipitation, 70.9 inches.

confined to the lowlands in Java, spectacular terraces extend well up the volcanic slopes. In favored localities one crop succeeds another the year around.

Other native food crops include corn, sweet potatoes, cassava (in part for tapioca), peanuts, and soybeans. Fruit trees and vegetable gardens surround every house. Water buffaloes are used in the rice areas with the heaviest rain, oxen in the drier sections. In backward areas, many farmers practice migratory ladang or fire cultivation, similar to the caiñgin clearings already described. In areas of better soils, the land is used again after a few years of fallow so that villages are more or less fixed. Still another type of land use is found in permanently occupied areas that are incapable of irrigation; here corn is more important than rice. Among native commerical crops are cocoanuts, kapok, pepper and other spices, rubber, cassava, and coffee.

Plantation agriculture has reached a high development in the Netherlands Indies. Foreign capital directed with skill by intensive scientific research, combined with cheap labor and a favorable environment, has transformed large areas of wilderness

is grown on rented native farms, the supervision is entirely under foreign control. Sumatra ranks next to Java as an

A bamboo suspension bridge in central Java.

into productive sources of commodities for the world market. Unfortunately so much good land is available that oversupply has brought repeated economic distress. In 1937 there were 2,389 estates with a total area of 6,090,000 acres, 45 per cent of which was under cultivation. Half the number were in Java. Although the planted area was but 0.6 per cent of the entire land surface of the Indies, the estates contributed 54 per cent of the total agricultural exports.

Whereas most estates specialize in one product, notably rubber or copra, many combine several products, such as rubber and coffee or tea, or cinchona (for quinine) and tea. Other plantation products are sugar, tobacco, kapok, sisal, and palm oil. Although most of the sugar cane

area of estates, with tobacco plantations dating from the 1860's. Dutch investments of all types in 1938 amounted to 2,300,-000,000 guilders, as compared with total foreign investments including Dutch of 3,500,000,000 guilders. (One guilder is normally worth $0.40.)

As a result of this agricultural productivity the islands contributed 90 per cent of the world's quinine, 85 per cent of the pepper, 65 per cent of the kapok, a third of the rubber and sisal, a quarter of the palm oil and copra, and a fifth of the tea. Sugar and coffee are also important agricultural exports, although the former declined from 11 per cent of the world supply in 1929 to 5 per cent in 1939, especially because of greatly increased production in British India. Despite these exports, the domestic food supply has been maintained, and famines are unknown. Java practically feeds itself. The Outer Provinces have concentrated so much on export crops that some importation of rice was necessary until 1938 when the Indies were self-supporting for the first time.

Large agricultural possibilities still await development in the Outer Provinces, even though the soil is usually less fertile than in Java. Colonization is under way, with considerable supervised migration from overcrowded Java.

Mineral deposits are few in number but large in value. Important amounts of petroleum are produced in Sumatra near Palembang and Djambi in the south, and Medan in the north. Borneo yields oil at Balikpapan and Tarakan. Java has a small output near Rembang, and there is oil on the island of Ceram. The 1940 production was 7,938,000 metric tons. This provides the largest yield between California and Iran. Low-grade coal produced in west-central Sumatra and Borneo amounted to 1,456,647 tons in 1938.

Tin from the islands of Banka and Billiton supplies a third of the Asiatic production, to the extent of 43,900 tons in 1940. Bauxite on the island of Bintan, opposite Singapore, has been mined for Japanese interests, with an output of 275,000 tons in 1940, one-sixth of the world production. Sulphur and manganese from Java and nickel from Celebes complete the list of significant minerals.

The export of various commodities amounted to 743 million guilders in 1939, with rubber, oil, sugar, tin, and tea as the leading products in order. One-quarter of the shipments came to the United States. Since the total of all imports amounted to but 470 million guilders, the Netherlands Indies had a large export surplus with considerable profit to the Netherlands. The chief imports are cotton goods from Japan, machinery from the United States and the Netherlands, iron and steel products, and foodstuffs.

Java

Nowhere in the tropics, of either the Old World or the New, is there a land like Java. Its population increase is almost without parallel, as is the intensity of its land use. The combination of luxuriant vegetation, picturesque volcanoes, cheerful people, and intelligent administration makes Java an unusually attractive island. Arable land in 1938 amounted to 19,400,000 acres. This is so close to the maximum that no more than an additional 4 per cent can be made suitable for agriculture. Rice fields already climb the slopes of volcanoes wherever land can be terraced. For administrative purposes Java is always linked with the small near-by island of Madura.

Along the northern shore is a low coastal plain of alluvium across which the silt-laden rivers follow diked channels. This is intensively devoted to sawahs for rice or to sugar cane. Farther south is a zone of low hills where the soils are less fertile, usually marl and limestone. The central mountain backbone has numerous volcanoes, rising above a base of folded sedimentary rocks. Eighty-five peaks exceed 6,000 feet, and the highest volcano reaches 12,200 feet. Here and there are intermontane basins, nearly level, which are covered with rice sawahs. The original forest mantle is preserved only on the higher slopes. A hilly coastal zone parallels the south shore, with but little level land.

Rain comes chiefly with the west monsoon, though convectional showers occur at all seasons. Only in the extreme northeast is the amount under 40 inches; most of the lowlands have 60 to 100 inches. One mountain station reports nearly 400 inches a year.

A prodigious amount of work has gone into irrigation, chiefly for rice but also for sugar cane and other crops. Irrigated

fragments of broken mirrors on the hillsides, freshly planted fields, all shades of green in growing fields, ripe brown rice,

Terraced rice fields spread over the hills near Bandoeng wherever water may be obtained for irrigation. Elsewhere the land is devoted to dry crops or to tea, coffee, and cocoanuts. (*Courtesy Netherlands Airforce.*)

land accounts for 42 per cent of the total in Java. Whereas in extratropical Asia it is necessary to use great care to prevent erosion where water flows from one terrace level to another, Javanese soils are so nonerosive that little is needed in the way of stones or broken crocks to line the spillways.

Rice and corn account for two-thirds of the acreage. Corn, peanuts, and cassava are raised as second crops after the rice harvest on drained sawahs, or where irrigation is not available. Both early- and late-maturing rice are raised, with the harvest in 70 to 140 days. As rice is grown the year around in rainy western Java, one may see side by side bright green seedbeds, flooded fields glistening like

and elsewhere the harvest in process. Thus the same plot may yield two crops of rice and another crop within the year. Both acreage and production have been increasing, especially under government encouragement since the depression of the 1930's reduced exports of sugar and made it necessary to curtail imports. The yield is about 30 bushels per acre per crop. Java practically supplies its own rice, with a small surplus from 1936 to 1939, but the Outer Provinces are importers. Corn is usually grown on less fertile land and without irrigation. The yield averages 15 bushels per acre.

The chief root crop is cassava, with a large export to the United States for tapioca. Both sweet and white potatoes are grown. Peanuts and soybeans are other food crops.

Fish supply an important item in the

owned by the natives but rented to estates. Sugar cane is harvested 13 or 14 months after planting, and is rotated with other

The ancient Buddhist stupa of Borobudur in central Java is one of the finest souvenirs of Java's rich cultural history. (*Satake*.)

diet and are raised in ponds throughout the island, both inland and along the seashore. In some places, the sawahs are reflooded after the rice harvest and fish become a secondary "crop."

Rubber in Java is grown at elevations of 300 to 1,500 feet, while in Sumatra most estates are below 300 feet. In Java this is due to the lack of available lowlands not already in cultivation.

Sugar is one of the best known exports from Java, and the most important until the 1920's when the production reached 3,000,000 tons. Practically all of the Javanese output is grown on irrigated land

crops so that the same land is planted to cane once in three years. No second or ratoon crop is grown. Extensive research work has enabled the Dutch to develop some of the most productive varieties of cane in the world, now also raised in Hawaii, Cuba, and Louisiana where the cooler climate requires a growing season up to 22 months. The average yield per acre in Java is three times that in the Philippine Islands. At the peak of the industry in 1930 the acreage was 489,000; from this it dropped to 68,000 acres in 1935. This is an example of how seriously tropical products are affected by world economic conditions. Even the Netherlands subsidized the production of beet sugar in the homeland.

inhabit the island: the Sundanese in the west, the Javanese in the center, and the Madurese in the east. During the eighth

The city of Bandoeng in the cooler uplands of western Java bears many resemblances to the homeland of the Dutch.

Quinine is a unique product, an alkaloid made from the bark of the cinchona tree. No other remedy for malaria is so satisfactory. Seeds were brought to Java from South America in 1854. Most cinchona is grown at an elevation of 5,000 feet in western Java on fertile porous soils, rich in organic matter. Here, as with sugar, the yield has been greatly increased through research. Although once a government monopoly, it is now chiefly raised on private plantations.

For all this the Dutch deserve great credit, but so too do the native peoples. Java has an able population, with a tradition of progress for more than a thousand years. Three ethnographic groups of Malays

and ninth centuries the people were Buddhists and later on Hindus. Among their architectural achievements is a giant stupa or monument known as the Borobudur in central Java. The ornamentation of the four sculptured terraces is particularly rich, comparable in artistry to the ruins at Angkor in Indo-China. With the arrival of Mohammedanism, this monument was covered with earth and trees to prevent its desecration and was unearthed only a century ago.

Most Europeans who have gone to Asia as businessmen or administrators have little thought of making it their fixed home. In marked contrast, many Dutch have setted in Java with considerable permanence, sending their children to the homeland only because adequate higher education is not fully available in the

The city was founded in 1619. There are really four towns: the artificial port of Tandjong Priok, six miles away, the old

A rubber estate in Sumatra with its homes for the laborers. Large areas of rain forest in the outer islands have been cleared for plantations whereas little such undeveloped land is available in Java. (*Courtesy Netherlands Airforce.*)

Indies. This established type of settlement is particularly noticeable in the hills at Bandoeng where a little bit of Holland has been transplanted.

Java is noted as the first place where remains were found of very early man. The discovery of *Pithecanthropus erectus* at Trinil in 1891 has been followed by the finding of three additional skulls by 1940. *Pithecanthropus* is of approximately the same early Pleistocene age as *Sinanthropus* in China; no other human fossil material is so old.

In Java there are half a dozen cities with over 100,000 people. Batavia is the capital and chief seaport, with a 1940 population of 470,700, of whom 40,100 were Europeans.

town of Batavia, the adjoining settlement of Meester Cornelis, and the new section known as Weltevredan. Owing to the oppressive heat, many government offices have been moved to Buitenzorg in the foothills, home of the famous botanical gardens, and some bureaus even to Bandoeng in the mountains. Batavia remains the great commercial center of the Netherlands Indies, with 2,400 ships entering the harbor in 1939. It is 532 nautical miles from Singapore.

Surabaya is the second city and port, with 311,300 people in 1940 among whom were 28,900 Europeans. Surabaya is a modern city and the port for the sugar trade of eastern Java and commerce with the islands beyond.

Semarang is the port of north central

Colonization of these islands from over-crowded Java has been a definite government policy for several decades. Where

Balinese women sorting coffee beans in a farm courtyard.

Java. Bandoeng, Surakarta, and Djokjakarta are interior towns, each with well over 100,000 people.

Outer Provinces

The Outer Provinces include the large islands of Sumatra, Dutch Borneo, Celebes, and Dutch New Guinea, plus scores of smaller islands. Although they contain but half the population of Java, they already surpass that island in the value of exports. Rubber is by far the most important estate crop, with the east coast of Sumatra overwhelmingly in the lead in acreage. Here there are 266 estates, with an average size of 8,000 acres; American, British, Belgian, and French capital is invested along with Dutch.

plantations have secured and developed new land through lease, the problem of securing coolies is relatively simple; but where groups of colonists are to be settled on new land, much preliminary work is required by the government. The Javanese are wet rice farmers, and irrigation systems are not easy for the individual pioneer to arrange. Migratory ladang, or caiñgin, cultivation offers no attractions for the immigrant.

The people of these islands vary widely in culture. Those in the west belong to Malay groups, while to the east are Papuans. Some tribes such as the Kubus of interior Sumatra and the Dayaks of Borneo represent low-level ethnographic groups; others compare with the inhabitants of Java in civilization, notably the people of Bali and Lombok directly east of Java, where there is much the same intensity of agriculture.

On Sumatra, the principal cities are Medan and its port of Belawan-Deli in the northern rubber area, the oil center of Palembang in the south, and Padang on the west coast.

The cities of Borneo include the oil towns of Balikpapan and Tarakan on the east coast.

On Celebes the chief city is Macassar at the south.

CHAPTER 40

THE PHILIPPINE ISLANDS

An understanding of Philippine geography should be preceded by a glimpse of its history. In no other part of Southeastern Asia has European penetration had the same effects. Magellan reached the islands in 1521, and Spain took possession in 1565. Although the islands were diverse in language, they were already knit together in culture, and the Filipinos had an extensive trade with China and other parts of the Orient.

Spanish interests centered in trade and Christianity. Commerce came to be of great importance and, for generations, the Manila galleon from the Philippines to Acapulco in Mexico, en route to Spain, was one of the most tempting and romantic prizes ever set before a privateer. In return came supplies of Mexican silver dollars for the China trade, widely current in the Far East until the 1930's. A unique heritage from Spanish rule is that 95 per cent of the people are Christians, largely Roman Catholic. Spanish is still widely spoken among the wealthy class, and the three centuries of colonial rule have left a deep impress. In some particulars this is but a surface covering for the basic Malay culture.

In 1898 Admiral Dewey won the Battle of Manila Bay and introduced a period of American control which has resulted in a veneer of Anglo-Saxon civilization. Thus English is used in the larger cities and by the younger generation, but smaller towns and rural settlements have been less affected. American rule has been unique in the history of European imperialism. Elsewhere colonies have been justified solely for their benefits to the mother country, notably so with the French. By contrast, in his instructions to the commission that set up a civilian government, U.S. Secretary of State Elihu Root wrote as follows:

"In all forms of government and administrative provisions which they are authorized to prescribe, the commission should bear in mind that the government they are establishing is designed not for our satisfaction or for the expression of our political views, but for the happiness, peace and prosperity of the people of the Philippine Islands, and the measures adopted should be made to conform to their customs, their habits and even their prejudices to the fullest extent consistent with the accomplishment of the indispensable requisites of just and effective government."

This was followed in 1934 by the Tydings-McDuffie Act which provided for the full independence of a Philippine Commonwealth in 1946. Never before had a Western power voluntarily given up its richest colony.

With American administration came free access to the world's richest market. Sugar, cocoanut oil, copra, abacá or Manila hemp, and tobacco were shipped to the United States in large amounts without the tariff restrictions imposed on adjoining tropical lands. This enriched the average Filipino and provided funds for education and public works, but it did not compel agriculture to be efficient. As a result, the yield of sugar per acre was only one-third that of near-by Java. The American administration of the Philippines was seriously negligent in its lack of an adequate policy for scientific agriculture and forestry, in contrast to the strong support of research elsewhere by Dutch, French, and British governments. High-cost Philippine products could scarcely compete in the general world market. This was not admitted when political independence was first sought and has resulted in agitation for continued economic reciprocity with the United States.

The Japanese invasion in 1941 showed how weak an independent Philippines would be, and how vulnerable the United States was in the Western Pacific. The islands have a longer coast line than that of the United States, and it is impossible to defend it all. The question of military security, added to economic problems and the uncertain prospects of stable internal authority, makes independence a serious venture. Government will probably follow South American patterns of democracy rather than those of North America.

The Tydings-McDuffie Act provided that the United States shall surrender all army posts upon the attainment of full independence, but that the matter of naval bases shall be considered at that time. Since it is very doubtful whether the latter could be protected without the former or whether the United States could effectively defend either in case of a subsequent war, it may be wiser for the United States to withdraw entirely. The alternative is effective military control of the entire Western Pacific.

A glance at the globe will show that the great-circle route from Seattle to Manila passes directly through Tokyo. If America is to maintain a military interest in the Philippines, she must carefully weigh matters of grand strategy. It was once hoped that the Philippines would furnish a great base for United States trade with Orient, with Manila as a rival to British Hongkong,

but the position is unsuitable as a basis for relations with China and Japan.

A striking illustration of American geographic illiteracy in 1898 is shown in the treaty with Spain by which the United States bought the islands for $20,000,000. The commissioners had no suitable map and hence incorrectly defined the boundary of what they wished to secure. This resulted in uncertainty concerning a 150-mile string of islands next to Formosa in the north, and the omission of the Sulu Archipelago in the south. A subsequent payment of $100,000 was necessary to include the latter, and two other treaties were needed before all the Philippines were transferred. The United States also neglected to take over the Caroline, Marshall, and Mariana islands, then Spanish. These later came into German hands and were transferred to Japan after the First World War. It was from bases in these islands that Pearl Harbor was bombed on Dec. 7, 1941.

An attractive economic future potentially awaits the Philippines. They have soil, minerals, location, and room for four times the present population. But many problems must be solved before the Philippines become one of the ranking nations of Eastern Asia.

Except for minor tribes, the various people of the Philippines are essentially Mongoloids with a Malaysian culture, but the detailed ethnographic background is uncertain. The census records only the very unscientific racial differentiation of Christian and non-Christian people. Whereas the former include those who speak various languages such as Visayan, Tagalog, and Ilocano, they are all related as a racial group. Among non-Christians are the Mohammedan Moros, the Negritos, and the "pagan" Igorots; among the latter are such groups as the Ifugao and the Bontoc. No less than 87 different languages are spoken. Tagalog has been proclaimed the national language but is used by only a quarter of the people.

In 1940 the population numbered 16,-

more to Hawaii. The American population was 8,739, exclusive of military personnel and their families. It is not impossible that

Filipino farmhouses are usually raised above the ground so that animals may find shelter beneath. Sliding windows and steeply pitched thatch roofs reflect the tropical climate. Shocks of rice are drying in the foreground. (*Fenno Jacobs, from Three Lions.*)

000,313, as compared with 12,588,066 in 1930 and 7,635,426 in 1903. Since the total land area is 115,600 square miles (1939 data), there is a density of 139 per square mile. In the island of Cebu this rises to 628 while in Mindanao it drops to 34. Chinese account for 117,461, and there are 750,000 more with some Chinese blood. More than three-fourths of the retail trade is in their hands. Japanese numbered 29,272, half of them in Davao to the south. About 50,000 Filipinos have come to the United States mainland, and as many

the islands may come to have as many people as Japan.

Among American contributions have been good roads, elementary schools, and public health. Where the infant mortality in Manila was once 80 per 100, it had fallen in 1940 to 6 per 100.

If the 7,083 islands of the Philippines were in the New World, they would extend from Cuba to the Guianas, a distance equal to that from upper Lake Michigan to the Gulf. Two-thirds of the area is in Luzon and Mindanao, which cover 40,814 and

36,906 square miles, respectively. Among other islands of importance are Mindoro, Panay, Negros, Cebu, Bohol, Leyte, and enough to have names, and only 1,095 are inhabited.

The mountain system of the Philippines

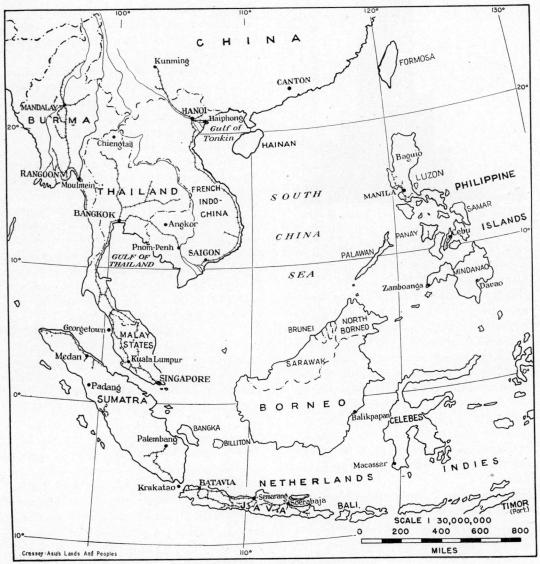

Communications map.

Samar, all of them part of the central Visayan group, and Palawan to the west. Only a third of the islands are large is a succession of north-south trending folds, fault blocks, and volcanic ranges. In the central area many of the synclinal basins are below sea level and account for the embayed and insular character of the archipelago. There are at least 20 active

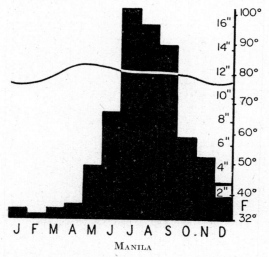

MANILA

craters. One of the most symmetrical cones in the world is that of Mayon in Luzon. The highest elevation is Mt. Apo in Mindanao, 9,450 feet. Earthquakes are also frequent but have seldom been destructive, partly owing to the type of house construction. Like the central islands of the Netherlands Indies and Japan, the islands are mountains in the process of rising from the sea, with most formations of Cenozoic age. To the southeast is the greatest depth in the ocean, the Mindanao Deep at 35,410 feet. Extensive areas are mountainous, and level land is largely in interior valleys rather than on coastal plains.

Rainfall seasons rather than temperature differences determine the climatic regions of the islands. Only in the extreme north is there noticeably cooler weather in winter. Along the west coast the dry season lasts from November till mid-March, with temperatures in the lower seventies, and continues until mid-June with considerably warmer days though temperatures rarely reach 100°F. The rainy season lasts from June through October and is accompanied by cloudy weather and high relative humidity. This rainfall regime is modified where mountains lie in the path of moisture-bearing winds. The east coasts have a fall and winter maximum but no dry season in summer. In the south rain is distributed throughout the year. Interior valleys more or less surrounded by mountains are much drier than the coasts. Conditions are everywhere suitable for crops of one type or another, although irrigation may be necessary for a few months.

No part of Asia has so many or such destructive typhoons. They rarely visit Mindanao, but the central and northern islands experience these violent storms from April to December. Typhoons first appear in the vicinity of the Caroline, Marshall, and Mariana Islands and move west and then north. Their high winds and torrential rainfall bring serious destruction to cocoanut plantations, fields of sugar cane and abacá, and the irrigation arrangements for rice fields. Shipping likewise suffers.

Forests cover 58 per cent of the islands (1938), with man-made artificial grasslands or cogonals accounting for 18 per cent. Twenty-two per cent is in farms, but only two-thirds of this is actually cropped. The potentially arable land is placed at 54 per cent. Excellent tropical hardwoods are present in abundance, and there is a considerable export, especially of lauan, incorrectly termed Philippine mahogany, to the United States, Japan, and China. Much of the best timber is relatively inaccessible. Experimental plantings of true mahogany grow to a diameter of 20 inches in 20 years.

Agriculture is characterized by subsistence rice, export sugar, cocoanut products, abacá or manila hemp, tobacco, and other crops. There are few large foreign-managed plantations, for the Filipinos have discouraged foreign investments in the belief that "every additional dollar of American capital is another nail in the coffin of Philippine independence." Rice and to-

Cebu, western Negros, and Leyte where more than half the area is in crops. In most of Mindanao, Palawan, and the northern

Igorot rice terraces form a striking note in the mountain landscape of northern Luzon. (*Fenno Jacobs, from Three Lions.*)

bacco are the usual crops in the fertile valleys. Cocoanuts are grown on the sandy coastal plains and up the hillsides to elevations of 1,000 feet and more. Abacá is raised on the moist eastern slopes especially in Mindanao. Corn and sweet potatoes occupy the drier and unirrigated soils. Rubber production is not important although there is a Goodyear plantation in Mindanao. Pineapples are canned by Del Monte on the same island.

Cultivated land is concentrated in central and southern Luzon, southern Panay,

mountains of Luzon, cropland averages less than 10 per cent. The fact that only 8 per cent of the farm land appears to be double-cropped is an indication that no land shortage exists. Only a quarter of the farmers irrigate their land.

Rice is raised on nearly half the total crop area. Four methods of cultivation are used: flooded fields in which the rice is transplanted from seedbeds, the sabog method of broadcast sowing on wet or flooded fields, dry upland rice grown on plowed fields known as secano cultivation, and caiñgin rice planted in fire-cleared forest openings where the individual seeds are placed in small holes made by a stick or other sharp-

Cocoanut palms line most village streets in Luzon.
(*Courtesy Robert L. Pendleton.*)

pointed tool. Corn is the second great food crop, generally raised on drier land. On Cebu and Bohol, where the soils are derived from coral formations and are largely unirrigable, corn almost entirely replaces rice.

Too much of the agriculture is designed for export markets in the United States. It has been estimated that over half the population obtain their livelihood from cocoanut products, sugar, abacá, tobacco, and embroidery. As a result, the islands do not feed themselves, and nearly a fifth of their imports are foodstuffs.

The acreage in cocoanut palms, amounting to 15 per cent, is third only to that of rice and corn. Production occurs along the shores of most islands except in northeastern Luzon where typhoons are too destructive. The Philippines have usually led

the world in the export of cocoanut oil and are second to the Netherlands Indies in copra. The area southeast of Manila has been called one of the largest artificial forests in the world. Ground-water supply and elevation are as important as rainfall and soil in determining the location for cocoanut cultivation. Thus coastal plains are suitable, even though sandy, since ground water from the hilly interior here comes near the surface. Trees begin to bear at the age of six or seven years and continue for 40 to 60 years. To form copra, the cocoanut meat is dried over a fire made from the outer husk. Aside from its export value, the tree supplies food, clothing, and shelter. The chief use of cocoanut oil, now one of the principal vegetable oils of commerce, is in soap and margarine. Some American steamers on the run from the United States start with enough fuel oil for the round trip; when they reach Manila, half their tanks are empty and these are cleaned and filled with cocoanut oil for the return trip.

Sugar production had a spectacular rise from 1920 to 1934, following the removal of United States import duties and ending with the imposition of quotas. From 2 per cent of the world's total, the islands rose to 16 per cent, with 44 "centrals" or modern steam sugar mills producing "centrifugal" sugar. Cane is raised by peasants and sold to the refining companies, whereas in Java the entire process is in the hands of the same concern; hence in part the difference in yields. The volcanic soils of Negros and central Luzon provide ideal conditions, with just the right length of dry season. Yields are lower than in most countries but have increased considerably. The importance of sugar as a cash crop is shown in the fact that it accounts for over half of all exports. In the peak year of 1934, shipments amounted to 1,275,000 tons, valued at $65,450,000. Independence without access to the American market may bring the end of the industry, for Philippine sugar cannot yet compete on the world market the United States, and so the market should remain. Another fiber is Philippine sisal.

Abacá or manila hemp supplies marine cordage for the entire world. Most of the production is around Davao in Mindanao. (*Ewing Galloway.*)

market. Since the industry has provided tax revenue to the extent of $10,000,000, the political results are serious.

Abacá is one of the unique crops of the Philippines, grown nowhere else so widely. Abacá belongs to the banana family, with fibers 8 to 10 feet in length. This fiber is very strong and elastic, and exceptionally resistant to salt water, hence its use for marine cordage. The trade name is Manila hemp. It is chiefly grown on Mindanao and is southern Luzon where there is a wet tropical climate without strong winds. The production around Davao was largely developed by the Japanese. In acreage, but not in value, it exceeds sugar cane. In this case only 25 per cent of the export is to

Tobacco was one of the chief products under Spanish rule but now accounts for only 2 per cent of the crop area. The principal district is the Cagayan valley in northern Luzon.

The Philippines are able to produce at least small quantities of such crops as cotton, cassava, coffee, fruits, forest products, kapok, and rubber. But these are the very items of which surplus supplies are available elsewhere. Careful agricultural research and a study of foreign markets will be essential. If the market for the present export crops is curtailed and the islands are not to sink into economic chaos, a considerable period of American preferential tariffs may be necessary.

The mining industry has had a spectacular growth. The Philippines now produce more gold than Alaska or any American state except California. The output in 1941 amounted to 1,109,000 ounces, five times that of 1931. Silver is usually associated in equal amounts by weight. Most of the yield is from the Benguet district near Baguio in northern Luzon.

Iron ore production has developed rapidly, with 1,191,641 metric tons shipped to Japan in 1941. Camarines Norte in eastern Luzon, the island of Samar, and Surigao in eastern Mindanao are the producers, with an estimated reserve of 500 million tons at Surigao. These are lateritic ores with low silica, sulphur, and phosphorus, and an iron content of 48 per cent, easily mined and near tidewater.

Chromium was not discovered until 1935, but by 1939 the Philippines produced 164,000 metric tons and ranked fifth with 11 per cent of the world output. The Zambales deposit in western Luzon is among the largest in the world, with 10 million tons of ore, much of it averaging 50 per cent chromium oxide.

Manganese is very extensive but of medium quality. Shipments to the United States started in 1935, and the 1940 output was 58,038 metric tons.

Copper, lead, and zinc are present, but not in sufficient quantities to make export to the United States attractive.

Petroleum is lacking and coal almost so. The coal is lignite of Oligocene age and not suitable for smelting. Unfortunately there appears to be no basis for a domestic metallurgical industry, so that coke must be imported or the ores exported.

Luzon

Within the Philippines are many divergent environments and types of land utilization. A critical delineation of regions should consider the climatic contrasts between the east and west coasts, the distribution of cocoanuts and abacá, or topography. The simplest scheme is to deal separately with Luzon, the Visayan Islands in the center, and Mindanao.

Luzon is the largest, best known, and most important of the islands. Even here wide contrasts exist between the highly developed central agricultural plains and the backward lands in the mountains. Primitive negritos using bows and arrows live but 50 miles from Manila.

Two mountain ranges extend into northern Luzon. Between them is the Cagayan Valley, longest in the Philippines. The subregion drains northward and is cut off from Manila by rough terrain. Its rich river-bank soils have made it the leading tobacco district. Because of the intermontane position, there is a considerable dry period.

West of the Cagayan Valley lies the Mountain Province. The elevation averages 4,000 feet, so that the climate is temperate. Here is the highest peak in Luzon, Mt. Pulog which rises to 9,400 feet. The city of Baguio has become the principal summer resort of the islands, frequented during the hot dry season from mid-March through May. Within the province is the Bontoc area, famous for the rice terraces of the Igorots which cling to the steep rainy side of the valleys. Here too is the major gold mining district of the islands. The northeast coast of Luzon is also mountainous and backward.

Most of the cropland of Luzon lies in the central lowland around Manila Bay and northward to Lingayen Gulf; over 40 per cent of the land is under cultivation. Rice is the great crop, with cocoanuts in the southern part and sugar to the north.

Along the west coast is the rugged and densely forested Zambales area, which terminates to the south in the Bataan peninsula and the island of Corregidor, famous for the heroic stand of the Filipino and

The southern peninsulas of Luzon are a mixture of mountains, volcanoes, and in-

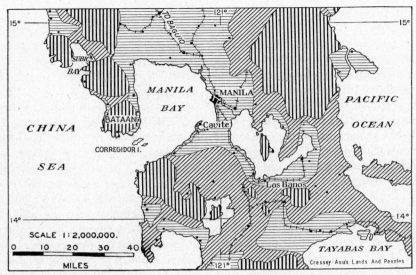

Manila is the first city of the Philippines. America's naval bases are at Cavite and Olongopo, while Corregidor is an army post.

The Americanized city of Manila lies to the right of the Pasig River, while the ancient walled Spanish town is on the left. (*Ewing Galloway*.)

American troops against the Japanese in 1942.

terior plains. The commercial crops are cocoanuts and abacá.

Manila is the chief city of the Philippines, with a population in 1939 of 623,493, four times that of its nearest rival, Cebu. Manila is situated on the delta of Pasig River where it enters the broad but shallow Manila Bay. The modern port has been developed behind breakwaters at one side of the river, with an extensive area built up by dredged mud from the harbor. Interisland vessels dock along the river. An old walled city known as Intramuros is a relic of Spanish days, in contrast to the conspicuous penetration of American cultural forms. Manila's chief industries relate to the export and import trades, and to shipping.

Visayan Islands

Although these numerous islands have but half the area of Luzon, their population is nearly as large. In several districts the land is over 50 per cent cultivated, and population densities are higher than anywhere else in the Philippines. Mountains and plains are roughly in the proportion of two to one.

The small island of Cebu dominates the Visayans. The black clay coral soil of the island is mostly incapable of irrigation and too dry for rice, so that corn is the staple food, and cocoanuts the export. The climate is healthy and drier than elsewhere, the rainfall is about 40 inches, and the people very industrious. Cebu has the densest population, and its port of Cebu city recorded a 1939 population of 146,817. The adjoining island of Negros has fertile volcanic soils which have helped it to become the major sugar producer.

Mindanao

Much of Mindanao is undeveloped and unmapped, and the sparse population of the interior is in sharp contrast to Luzon. Most of the 1,997,304 people live along the coast and near the few towns, although land not too steep to plow is most abundant inland. Extensive plains with relatively extensive swamps occur in Cotabato and the Agusan Valley on either side of the north-south mountain axis. Settlement possibilities are considerable and include upland areas from 1,000 to 5,000 feet above sea level climatically suitable for Europeans. Soils in the vicinity of the numerous volcanoes have been enriched by falls of ash so that their fertility is good. Alluvial soils are also rich, but elsewhere leaching has markedly reduced the fertility.

The extensive forests provide large and excellent timber reserves, except where they have been burned over by caiñgin cultivation and replaced by cogon grass. These grasslands supply the food for a considerable cattle industry. Iron ore, gold, and some coal are the mineral resources now in production.

Abacá and ramie have been extensively cultivated by the Japanese around Davao in the south. Rubber is grown in limited amounts near Zamboanga. Excellent pineapples and bananas are raised. Copra forms an important export.

SUGGESTED READINGS

These references are limited to the more readily accessible literature and do not give proper credit to the great volume of material from Asiatic sources or in European languages other than English.

A more complete bibliography may be assembled by consulting *Current Geographical Publications* issued by the AMERICAN GEOGRAPHICAL SOCIETY, *Recent Geographical Literature* prepared by the ROYAL GEOGRAPHIC SOCIETY, and the *Bibliographie géographique* formerly published by the ASSOCIATION OF FRENCH GEOGRAPHERS.

CHAPTER 1. THE PACIFIC BASIN

America Faces the Orient

Two excellent volumes present the historical aspects of trade with Asia: MARJORIE and SYDNEY GREENBIE: "Gold of Ophir," New York: Doubleday (1925); and J. M. CALLAHAN: America in the Pacific and the Far East, Johns Hopkins University, *Studies in History and Political Science*, XIX (1901), 1–177. The discoveries of the whaling trade are summarized by S. WHITTEMORE BOGGS: American Contributions to Geographical Knowledge of the Central Pacific, *Geographical Review*, XXVIII (1938), 177–192.

General aspects of Pacific geography may be found in NICHOLAS ROOSEVELT: "The Restless Pacific," New York: Scribner (1928); FELIX RIESENBERG: "The Pacific Ocean," New York: Whittlesey (1940); and HAWTHORNE DANIEL: "Islands of the Pacific," New York: Putnam (1943). The *Proceedings* of the Pacific Science Congress contain numerous articles on the Far East in the volumes from Japan in 1926, Java 1929, Canada 1933, and California 1939.

Trans-Pacific Contacts

The American Council of the Institute of Pacific Relations has sponsored a number of volumes dealing with eastern Asia, such as KATE MITCHELL: "Industrialization of the Western Pacific" (1942); PELZER, GREENE, and PHILLIPS: "Economic Survey of the Pacific Area," 2 vols. (1941–1942); current data are published in the fortnightly *Far Eastern Survey*. An excellent summary of commerce is in ETHEL B. DIETRICH: "Far Eastern Trade of the United States," New York: Institute of Pacific Relations (1940). Current trade statistics may be secured from the U.S. DEPARTMENT OF COMMERCE: *Foreign Commerce Yearbook*, Washington (annual). ROBERT B. HALL:

American Raw Material Deficiencies and Regional Dependence, *Geographical Review*, XXX (1940), 177–186, deals with our trans-Pacific trade in strategic and critical materials.

Hawaii

The best geographic literature on the Hawaiian Islands has been written by three former geographers at the University of Hawaii, OTIS W. FREEMAN, JOHN WESLEY COULTER, and STEPHEN B. JONES. FREEMAN's contributions are The Peopling of Hawaii, *Journal of Geography*, XXVII (1928), 125–144; Economic Geography of the Hawaiian Islands, *Economic Geography*, V (1929), 260–276; and The Economic Geography of Hawaii, University of Hawaii *Research Publication* No. 2 (1927), reviewed in the *Geographical Review*, XVIII (1928), 330–333. Among COULTER's extensive writings are The Island of Hawaii, *Journal of Geography*, XXXI (1932), 225–236; Land Utilization in the Hawaiian Islands, University of Hawaii *Research Publication* No. 8 (1933); Pineapple Industry in Hawaii, *Economic Geography*, X (1934), 288–296; The Oahu Sugar Cane Plantation, *Economic Geography*, IX (1933), 60–71; and his especially valuable chapter on The Territory of Hawaii, in WILLIAM H. HAAS: "The American Empire," Chicago: University of Chicago Press (1940), 216–305. The work of JONES covers both climatology and political geography, as in The Classification of Hawaiian Climates, written with ROLAND BELLAIRE, *Geographical Review*, XXVII (1937), 112–119; The Weather Element in the Hawaiian Climate, *Annals* Association of American Geographers, XXIX (1939), 29–57; Geography and Politics in the Hawaiian Islands, *Geographical Review*, XXVIII (1938), 193–213; and Hawaii and the Pacific, written with KLAUS MEHNERT, *Geographical Review*, XXX (1940), 358–375. An additional reference is in *Fortune*, Hawaii, Sugar-coated Fort, XXII (1940), 31–37, 78–82.

Geostrategy in the Pacific

For a review of German geopolitical thinking on Japan, see HANS W. WEIGERT: Haushofer and the Pacific, *Foreign Affairs*, XX (1942), 732–742. EARL B. SHAW has contributed a chapter entitled United States Pacific Defense to the volume edited by SAMUEL VAN VALKENBURG: "America at War," New York: Prentice-Hall (1942).

CHAPTER 2. ASIA'S CONTINENTAL PATTERNS

The Geographic Personality

British geographers have written two standard volumes on the continent: L. DUDLEY STAMP: "Asia," New York: Dutton, 3d ed. (1935); and LIONEL W. LYDE: "The Continent of Asia," London: Macmillan (1933). The outstanding French volumes are those in the series entitled "Géographic universelle," Paris: Librairie Armand Colin (1928–1932), with the following volumes devoted to parts of Asia: "Asie occidentale" by RAOUL BLANCHARD; "Haute Asie" by FERNAND GRENARD; "Asie des moussons" by JULES SION, Part 1, "Généralités—Chine—Japon"; Part 2, "Inde—Indochine—Insulinde"; and "Etats de la Baltique, Russie" by P. CAMENA D'ALMEIDA. The chief German series is in the "Klute Handbuch der Geographischen Wissenschaft," Potsdam Akademische Verlagsgesellschaft Athenaion (1931–1937), with two volumes entitled "Nordasien, Zentral-und Ostasien" and "Vorder-und Sudasien." A volume in Russian which deals with Asia outside the U.S.S.R. is V. M. STEIN: "Economic Geography of Asia," Leningrad: Geographic-Economic Scientific Research Institute (1940), reviewed by GEORGE B. CRESSEY in the *Far Eastern Quarterly*, I (1942), 180–184. Only one other volume has been written by an American, namely, DANIEL R. BERGSMARK: "Economic Geography of Asia," New York: Prentice-Hall (1935), but the series of articles by VAN VALKENBURG, CRESSEY, and HALL entitled Agricultural Regions of Asia, *Economic Geography*, VII (1931–1936), supplies a comprehensive picture of land forms, climate, and land use. Three volumes, old but still useful, are A. H. KEANE: "Asia," London: Stanford (1906), 2 vols.; ARCHIBALD LITTLE: "The Far East," Oxford: Clarendon Press (1905); and D G. HOGARTH: "The Nearer East," Oxford: Clarendon Press (1905). For an anthropological survey see L. H. D. BUXTON: "The Peoples of Asia," New York: Knopf (1925). The geology is described by KURL LEUCHS: "Geologie von Asien," Berlin: Borntraeger (1937), 2 vols.

The best set of maps covering all of the continent except the extreme north is the 1:4,000,000 series of the British General Staff.

Configuration and Drainage

The classic account of Asiatic geology is that of EDUARD SUESS: "The Face of the Earth," Oxford: Clarendon Press (1904–1924), 5 vols.; summarized by J. W. GREGORY: Suess's Classification of Eurasian Mountains, *Geographical Journal*, XLV (1915), 497–513. The synthesis of E. ARGAND entitled La Tectonique de l'Asie is presented in the *Comptes rendues*, Thirteenth International Geological Congress, Brussels, (1924), I, 171–372. A summary volume dealing with various parts of the continent is edited by J. W. GREGORY: "The Structure of Asia," London: Methuen (1929).

Climate and Vegetation

The best descriptions of regional climates are those by various authors in the "Koeppen-Geiger Handbuch der Klimatologie," Berlin: Borntraeger (1931). Somewhat older descriptions may be found in W. G. KENDREW: "The Climates of the Continents," Oxford: Clarendon Press (1927). Meteorological data are available in H. HELM CLAYTON: "World Weather Records," Smithsonian Miscellaneous Collections, LXXIX (1927) and XV (1934).

People

GRIFFITH TAYLOR has contributed many stimulating ideas in his "Environment, Race, and Migration," Chicago: University of Chicago Press (1937).

Geostrategy in Asia

The classic volume on geopolitics is HALFORD J. MACKINDER: "Democratic Ideals and Reality," New York: Holt (1942). ISAIAH BOWMAN has surveyed the political geography of the world following the First World War in "The New World," Yonkers-on-Hudson: World Book (1928), 4th ed.

CHINA

General References on China

An extensive bibliography may be found in GEORGE B. CRESSEY: "China's Geographic Foundations," New York: McGraw-Hill (1934), also published in a French edition under the title of "Géographie humaine et économique de la Chine," Paris (1939); and in Chinese, Commercial Press (in press). Some of this information is summarized in his Agricultural Regions of Asia: China, *Economic Geography*, X (1934), 109–142. Other standard volumes are ARCHIBALD LITTLE: "The Far East," Oxford: Clarendon Press (1905); L. H. D. BUXTON: "China, the Land and the People; a Human Geography," Oxford: Clarendon Press (1929); JULES SION: "Asie des moussons," Chine-Japon, Paris: Librairie Armand Colin (1928); and JULEAN ARNOLD: "China, a Commercial and Industrial Handbook," Washington: Bureau of Foreign and Domestic Commerce (1926). The annual volumes of the *China Yearbook*, Chicago: University of Chicago Press, and the *Chinese Yearbook* (in Chinese) contain a large amount of statistical data. The various publications of the INSTITUTE OF PACIFIC RELATIONS are invaluable, notably the fortnightly *Far Eastern Survey* of the American Council. The *Journal* of the Geographical Society of China has been published since 1934. Considerable material on physical geography may be obtained from the *Journal* of the Association of Chinese and American Engineers. Two excellent volumes whose scope is much wider than their titles are J. Lossing Buck: "Land Utilization in China," Chicago: University of Chicago Press (1937), 3 vols.; and James Thorp: "Geography of the Soils of China," Nanking: National Geological Survey (1936). Aerial photographs are available in Hans Koester: Four Thousand Hours over China, *National Geographic Magazine*, LXXIII (1938), 571–598.

The outstanding atlases are those prepared by V. K. Ting, Wong Wen-hao, and S. T. Tseng of the Geological Survey, and published by the *Shun Pao*, a newspaper in Shanghai. The larger "New Atlas of China" was issued in 1933, while a smaller "New Maps of the Chinese Provinces" has appeared in its third edition; both are entirely in Chinese. The best atlases in English, though limited to place geography, are the "Atlas of the Chinese Empire" published by the China Inland Mission, London (1908); and the "Postal Atlas of China," Nanking (1936). Two timely volumes are Marthe Rajchman: "New Atlas of China," New York: Day (1941), dealing with transportation; and G. F. Hudson and Marthe Rajchman: "An Atlas of Far Eastern Politics," New York: Institute of Pacific Relations (1942). The most useful wall map, now old, is that by Alexander Hosie: "Commercial Map of China," London: Philip.

CHAPTER 3. THE CHINESE LANDSCAPE

The best histories are those of Kenneth S. Latourette: "The Chinese, Their History and Culture," New York: Macmillan (1934), 2 vols.; and "The Development of China," Boston: Houghton, 5th ed. (1937). J. G. Andersson has described his archaeological studies in "Children of the Yellow Earth," London: Kegan Paul, Trench, Trubner (1934). The early work on *Sinanthropus* is summarized by Davidson Black and others: Fossil Man in China, *Memoirs* Geological Survey of China, Series A, No. 11 (1933). Carl W. Bishop has written extensively on the beginnings of Chinese culture: The Geographic Factor in the Development of Chinese Civilization, *Geographical Review*, XII (1922), 19–41; The Rise of Civilization in China with Reference to its Geographical Aspects, *Geographical Review*, XXII (1932), 617–631; The Beginnings of Civilization in Eastern Asia, *Annual Report* Smithsonian Institution (1940), 431–445; and Origin of the Far Eastern Civilizations, Smithsonian Institution (1942). Among the various

articles of Percy M. Roxby are The Expansion of China, *Scottish Geographical Magazine*, XLVI (1930), 65–79; and The Terrain of Early Chinese Civilization, *Geography*, XXIII (1938), 225–236. The meaning of place names is described by Joseph E. Spencer: Chinese Place Names and the Appreciation of Geographic Realities, *Geographical Review*, XXXI (1941), 79–94.

CHAPTER 4. CHINA'S PHYSICAL ENVIRONMENT

Geological studies will be found in the publications of the National Geological Survey and the Geological Society of China. The best summary of historical geology is J. S. Lee: "The Geology of China," London: Thomas Murby (1939). The Tokyo Geographical Society has published a "Geological Atlas of Eastern Asia" in 17 sheets, scale 1:2,000,000, Tokyo (1929).

Climatic material is largely restricted to the publications of the Jesuits at Zikawei Observatory near Shanghai, and the National Research Institute of Meteorology at Nanking and Chungking. Among the former publications are H. Gauthier: "La température en Chine," (1918); and E. Gherzi: "Etude sur la pluie en Chine," (1928); "Atlas de l'humidité relative en Chine," (1934); and "Atlas thermométrique de la Chine," (1934). The publications of the Institute include "The Chinese Rainfall" by Coching Chu and others, (1936), and his "A Brief Survey on the Climate of China," (1936); also Chang-wang Tu: Climatic Provinces of China, *Journal* Geographical Society of China, III (1936), in Chinese with English abstract; and Chinese Air Mass Properties, *Quarterly Journal* Royal Meteorological Society, LXV (1939), 33–51. W. J. Kendrew has prepared a chapter on climate for L. H. D. Buxton: "China, the Land and the People."

Soil characteristics are described in James Thorp's "Geography of the Soils of China," and the numerous *Soil Bulletins* of the National Geological Survey many of which describe regional geography. Environmental aspects of agriculture are presented by T. Min Tieh: Soil Erosion in China, *Geographical Review*, XXXI (1941), 570–590. See also W. C. Lowdermilk and D. R. Wickes: China and America against Soil Erosion, *Scientific Monthly*, LVI (1943), 393–413, 505–520; and Ancient Irrigation in China Brought up to Date, *Scientific Monthly*, LV (1942), 209–225.

Mineral resources are evaluated in H. Foster Bain: "Ores and Industry in the Far East," New York: Council on Foreign Relations, rev. ed. (1933); Wilfred Smith: "A Geographical Study of Coal and Iron in China," Liverpool: University Press (1926); and Thomas T. Read: "Economic—Geographic

Aspects of China's Iron Industry, *Geographical Review*, XXXIII (1943), 42–55. The unusual importance of salt is described by JOSEPH E. SPENCER: Salt in China, *Geographical Review*, XXV (1935), 353–366. In addition to the production figures of the *China Yearbook*, wartime developments are described by A. VIOLA SMITH in Mineral Resources, Production and Trade of China, *Foreign Minerals Quarterly*, IV (1941), 1–31.

CHAPTER 5. FARMING IN CHINA

The outstanding study of agriculture is J.L. BUCK's "Land Utilization in China," summarized in GEORGE B. CRESSEY: Foundations of Chinese Life, *Economic Geography*, XV (1939), 95–104. Many of the travel observations of F. H. KING in "Farmers of Forty Centuries," New York: Harcourt (1926) are still valid. The standard German source is WILHELM WAGNER: "Die Chinesische Landwirtshaft," Berlin: Paul Parey (1926). Source materials from Chinese authors collected by the INSTITUTE OF PACIFIC RELATIONS are published in "Agrarian China," Chicago: University of Chicago Press (1940). Regional crop distributions are mapped in GLENN T. TREWARTHA: Ratio Maps of China's Farms and Crops, *Geographical Review*, XXVIII (1938), 102–111. Economic aspects are considered by FRED J. ROSSITER: in *Foreign Agriculture*, issued by the U. S. Bureau of Agricultural Economics: Agriculture in China, III (1939), 431–498.

CHAPTER 6. REGIONS OF NORTH CHINA

General material on regions may be found in J. L. BUCK's "Land Utilization in China"; THORP's "Geography of the Soils of China"; LITTLE's "The Far East"; and LYDE's "The Continent of Asia." The feel of North China has been well captured by HERMAN KEYSERLING: "The Travel Diary of a Philosopher," London: J. Cape; New York: Harcourt (1925). Problems of flood and drought are considered in WALTER H. MALLORY: "China: Land of Famine," New York: American Geographical Society (1926). One of the best travel accounts is HARRY A. FRANCK: "Wandering in Northern China," New York: Century (1923).

Yellow Plain

The problem of the Yellow River has been considered by O. J. TODD in various articles, particularly in The Yellow River Problem, *Transactions* American Society of Civil Engineers, CV (1940), 346–453; and Taming "Flood Dragons" Along China's Hwang Ho, *National Geographic Magazine*, LXXXI (1942), 205–234. Other aspects are described by FREDERICK G. CLAPP: Along and Across the Great Wall of China, *Geographical Review*, IX (1920), 221–249; The

Hwang Ho, Yellow River, *Geographical Review*, XII (1922), 1–18; and GEORGE B. BARBOUR: Pleistocene History of the Huangho, *Bulletin* Geological Society of America, XLIV (1933), 1143–1160. Two of the principal cities are described in articles by MARGARET HITCH: The Port of Tientsin and Its Problems, *Geographical Review*, XXV (1935), 367–381; W. ROBERT MOORE: The Glory That Was Imperial Peking, *National Geographic Magazine*, LXIII (1933), 745–780; and JOHN W. COULTER: Peiping, *Journal of Geography*, XXXIII (1934), 161–171.

Shantung Peninsula

CHARLES K. EDMUNDS: Shantung, China's Holy Land, *National Geographic Magazine*, XXXVI (1919), 231–252.

Loessland

The origin and characteristics of the loess are described by GEORGE B. BARBOUR: The Loess of China, *China Journal of Arts and Sciences*, III (1925), 454–463, 509–519; and Recent Observations on the Loess of North China, *Geographical Journal*, LXXXVI (1935), 54–65; and MYRON L. FULLER: Some Unusual Erosion Features in the Loess of China, *Geographical Review*, XII (1922), 570–584. Farming possibilities in Shansi are described in two articles by RAYMOND T. MOYER: Agricultural Practices in Semi-arid North China, *Scientific Monthly*, LV (1942), 301–316; and Agricultural Soils in a Loess Region of North China, *Geographical Review*, XXVI (1936), 414–425.

Manchurian Plain

A large amount of information from Japanese sources is available in the reports of the SOUTH MANCHURIAN RAILWAY, the *Manchurian Year Books*, replaced by the *Far East Year Book* in 1941, and the magazine *Contemporary Manchuria* (from 1937 on). OWEN LATTIMORE has contributed numerous articles particularly his "Manchuria, Cradle of Conflict," New York: Macmillan (1932); and Chinese Colonization in Manchuria, *Geographical Review*, XXII (1932), 177–195. Articles by E. E. AHNERT and C. WALTER YOUNG are included in the symposium entitled "Pioneer Settlement," New York: American Geographical Society (1932). Three studies by GEORGE F. DEASY are as follows: The Future of Manchurian Agriculture, *Journal of Geography*, XXXVII (1938), 20–27; The Soya Bean in Manchuria, *Economic Geography*, XV (1935), 303–310; and Recent Trends in Manchoukuoan Trade, *Economic Geography*, XVI (1940), 162–170. Two general articles are ROBERT B. HALL: The Geography of Manchuria, *Annals* American Academy of Political and Social Science, CLII (1930), 278–292; and JOHN

B. Appleton: The Economic and Commercial Development of Manchuria, *Bulletin* Geographical Society of Philadelphia, XXXII (1934), 75–87. The metropolis of the north is covered by Shannon McCune: Harbin, Manchoukuo, *Journal of Geography*, XXXIX (1940), 187–196. The details of expanding cultivation are considered by W. Ladejinsky: Agriculture in Manchuria, *Foreign Agriculture*, I (1937), 157–182.

Khingan Mountains

Bruno Plaetschke: "Das Bergland der nordwestlichen Mandschurei," Petermann's Mitteilungen, Erganzungscheft 232 (1937).

CHAPTER 7. REGIONS OF SOUTH CHINA

General information may be obtained from each of the general references listed at the beginning of the preceding chapter. Harry A. Franck's volume for this area is entitled "Roving through Southern China," New York: Century (1925).

Yangtze Plain

The classic account of intensive agriculture is that of F. H. King: "Farmers of Forty Centuries." Details in a small area of the delta south of Shanghai are described by George B. Cressey: The Fenghsien Landscape, *Geographical Review*, XXVI (1936), 396–413. A sociological study farther west is Hsiaotung Fei: "Peasant Life in China," New York: Dutton (1939). The development of transportation facilities is considered by Joseph E. Spencer: Trade and Transshipment in the Yangtze Valley, *Geographical Review*, XXVIII (1938), 112–123. Shanghai's port problems are analyzed in the publications of the Whangpoo Conservancy Board, notably "The Port of Shanghai," 9th ed. (1936), revised frequently. Geographical details may be obtained from John E. Orchard: Shanghai, *Geographical Review*, XXVI (1936), 1–31. Pictures and description are presented in Robert W. Moore: Cosmopolitan Shanghai, Key Seaport of China, *National Geographic Magazine*, LXII (1932), 311–335. China's southern capital is the subject of an article by Julius Eigner: The Rise and Fall of Nanking, *National Geographic Magazine*, LXXIII (1938), 189–224.

The Szechwan Basin

The standard volume is Alexander Hosie: "Szechwan, Its Products, Industries, and Resources," Shanghai: Kelly and Walsh (1922). Further details are available in Joseph Beech: The Eden of the Flowery Republic, *National Geographic Magazine*, XXXVIII (1920), 355–390. Developments in the new capital are described by Joseph E. Spencer: Chang-

ing Chungking—the Rebuilding of an Old Chinese City, *Geographical Review*, XXIX (1939), 46–60. The geography of Chengtu is covered in George D. Hubbard: The Geographic Setting of Chengtu, *Bulletin* Geographic Society of Philadelphia, XXI (1923), 109–139. Rural life is portrayed by Joseph E. Spencer: The Szechwan Village Fair, *Economic Geography*, XVI (1940), 48–58.

Southeastern Coast

Two old but excellent travel accounts are those of Robert Fortune: "Three Years' Wanderings in the Northern Provinces of China," London: J. Murray (1847); and "Two Visits to the Tea Country of China," London: J. Murray (1853). Conditions in Fukien are described by Floy Hurlbut: "The Fukienese; a Study in Human Geography," Muncie (1939). Topographic conditions in the northern end of the region and the adjoining South Yangtze Hills are described by George B. Cressey in The Land Forms of Chekiang, *Annals* Association of American Geographers, XXVIII (1938), 259–276.

Canton Hinterland

The geography of the West River Valley is the subject of a study by Gustav Hauke-Fochler: "Die Natur des Si Kiang-Stromgebietes (Sudchina)," *Mitteilungen Geographische Gesellschaft*, München, XXVII (1934), 143–266. Agricultural conditions are described by T. Y. Tang: Land Utilization in South China, *Proceedings* Sixth Pacific Science Congress, California (1939), IV, 933–940; and Chen Han-seng: "Landlord and Peasant in China," New York: International Publishers (1936). For photographic details of the western area see G. Weidman Groff and T. C. Lau: Landscaped Kwangsi, China's Province of Pictorial Art, *National Geographic Magazine*, LXXII (1937), 671–726. British interests are presented in Hong Kong—Britain's Far-flung Outpost in China, *National Geographic Magazine*, LXXIII (1938), 349–360. Conditions of intensive agriculture in the West River delta are described by Glenn T. Trewartha: Field Observations on the Canton Delta of South China, *Economic Geography*, XV (1939), 1–1

Southwestern Uplands

The standard volume is H. R. Davies: "Yunnan, the Link between India and the Yangtze," Cambridge: University Press (1909). A collection of essays by Chinese authors has been translated by J. Siguret: "Territoires et populations des confins du Yunnan," Peiping: Henry Vetch (1937). Conditions among the tribespeople of western Yunnan are the subject of "The Tower of Five Glories: A Study of the Min Chia of Ta Li, Yunnan," London: Cresset Press (1941); and The Tali District of Western Yunnan, *Geographical Journal*, XCIX (1942), 50–60, both by C. P. FITZ-GERALD. ARNOLD HEIM has described the Earthquake Region of Taofu in *Bulletin* Geological Society of America, XLV (1934), 1035–1050. Observations of a geographer are contained in Kweichou: an Internal Chinese Colony, *Pacific Affairs*, XIII (1940), 162–172, by JOSEPH E. SPENCER. Two articles on the highway to Burma are PATRICK FITZGERALD: The Yunnan-Burma Road, *Geographical Journal*, XCV (1940), 161–174; and HENRY CRAW: The Burma Road, *Geographical Journal*, XCIX (1942), 238–246. Political geography is the subject of OWEN LATTIMORE: Yunnan, Pivot of Southeast Asia, *Foreign Affairs*, XXI (1943), 476–493.

CHAPTER 8. REGIONS OF OUTER CHINA

OWEN LATTIMORE has presented a detailed analysis of these regions and the adjoining areas of North China in his "Inner Asian Frontiers of China," with bibliography, New York: American Geographical Society (1940).

Mongolia

The best American studies are those of the American Museum of Natural History, notably CHARLES P. BERKEY and FREDERICK K. MORRIS: "Geology of Mongolia," New York (1927); ROY CHAPMAN ANDREWS: "The New Conquest of Central Asia," New York (1933); and also his Explorations in the Gobi Desert, *National Geographic Magazine*, LXIII (1933), 653–716. A geographical evaluation of conditions in Suiyuan province may be found in GEORGE B. CRESSEY: The Ordos Desert of Inner Mongolia, *Journal of the Scientific Laboratories*, Denison University, XXVIII (1933), 155–248. Some of the finest descriptions of Mongolian life are those in the classic volumes by EVARISTE REGIS HUC: "Travels in Tartary, Thibet and China, 1844–46." OWEN LATTIMORE has summarized some of his observations in The Geographical Factor in Mongol History, *Geographical Journal*, XCI (1938), 1–20. Colonization possibilities are considered by GEORGE B. CRESSEY and by OWEN LATTIMORE in the volume "Pioneer Settlement," New York: American Geographical Society (1932).

Sinkiang

Much of our knowledge of Chinese Turkestan grows out of the explorations of SIR M. AUREL STEIN, summarized in his "On Ancient Central-Asian Trails," London: Macmillan (1933); and Innermost Asia, Its Geography as a Factor in History, *Geographical Journal*, LXV (1925), 377–403, 473–501. Of only slightly less importance is the work of SVEN HEDIN: "The Silk Road," London: Routledge (1938); "The Wandering Lake (Lop-nor)," New York: Dutton (1940); and "Through Asia," New York: Harper (1899) 2 vols. ELLSWORTH HUNTINGTON's "The Pulse of Asia," Boston: Houghton (1919) provides stimulating ideas, but his comments on climatic changes should be read in connection with the articles of REGINALD C. F. SCHONBERG entitled The Climatic Conditions of the Tarim Basin, *Geographical Journal*, LXXV (1930), 313–323; The Habitability of Chinese Turkestan, *Geographical Journal*, LXXX (1932), 505–511; and "Peaks and Plains of Central Asia," London: Martin Hopkinson (1933). Delightful travel accounts are provided in the volumes of MILDRED CABLE and FRANCESCA FRENCH entitled "Through Jade Gate and Central Asia," London: Constable (1927); "A Desert Journal: Letters from Central Asia," London: Constable (1934); and "The Gobi Desert," London: Hodder and Stoughton (1943). OWEN LATTIMORE's contributions include "The Desert Road to Turkestan," London: Methuen (1928); China Opens Her Wild West, *National Geographic Magazine*, LXXXII (1942), 337–367; Caravan Routes of Inner Asia, *Geographical Journal*, LXXII (1928); and Origins of the Great Wall of China: A Frontier Concept in Theory and Practice, *Geographical Review*, XXVII (1937), 529–549. Reports of an experienced traveler are contained in ERIC TEICHMAN's The Motor Road from Peking to Kashgar, *Geographical Journal*, LXXXIX (1937), 297–308; and in his "Journey to Turkistan," London: Hodder (1937).

Tibet

The plateau of Tibet has been the object of more exploration than any other part of the continent, and there is a voluminous literature including many articles in the *Geographical Journal* and an extensive series by JOSEPH F. ROCK in the *National Geographic Magazine* since 1924. Detailed studies in southeastern Tibet have been carried on by F. KINGDON WARD, largely published in the *Geographical Journal*, and by J. W. and C. J. GREGORY. SVEN HEDIN's explorations are the subject of numerous volumes. Conditions in the northwest are described by ROBERT B. EKVALL: "Cultural Relations on the Kansu-Tibetan Border," University of Chicago Publications in Anthropology, *Occasional Papers*, No. 1 (1939). The area adjoining Szechwan is covered by J. HANSON-LOWE: A Journey along the Chinese Tibetan Border, *Geographical Journal*, XCV (1940), 357–367; and Notes on the Climate of the South Chinese-Tibetan

Borderland," *Geographical Review*, XXXI (1941), 444–453. This area is also described by P. H. STEVENSON: Notes on the Human Geography of the Chinese-Tibetan Borderland, *Geographical Review*, XXII (1932), 599–616. The city of Lhasa has been described repeatedly. Two of the more recent articles, beautifully illustrated, are those by C. SUYDAM CUTTING: In Lhasa, the Forbidden, *Natural History*, XXXVII (1936), 102–126; and F. SPENCER CHAPMAN: Lhasa in 1937, *Geographical Journal*, XCI (1938), 497–507; who has also written "Lhasa; the Holy City," London: Chatto (1938). Travel through the desolate north is graphically portrayed by PETER FLEMING: "News From Tartary," New York: Scribner (1936). Two general volumes are those of SIR CHARLES BELL, temporary British resident in Lhasa, entitled "Tibet, Past and Present," Oxford: Clarendon Press (1924); and "The People of Tibet," Oxford: Clarendon Press (1928). An American expedition in eastern Tibet is pictured by RICHARD L. BURDSALL and TERRIS MOORE: Climbing Mighty Minya Konka, *National Geographic Magazine*, LXXXIII (1943), 625–650.

CHAPTER 9. CHINA IN THE NEW WORLD

Problems of industrial development are considered in SUN YAT-SEN: "The International Development of China," New York: Putnam (1929); and H. D. FONG: "The Post-war Industrialization of China," New York: National Planning Association (1942). Conditions before the Japanese invasion are dealt with in the "Report of the American Economic Mission to the Far East," New York: National Foreign Trade Council (1935); and KATE L. MITCHELL: "Industrialization in the Western Pacific," New York: Institute of Pacific Relations (1942). The various publications of the INSTITUTE OF PACIFIC RELATIONS contain numerous articles.

Details of foreign trade may be found in the annual and decennial reports of the CHINESE MARITIME CUSTOMS, or in the *China Year Book*. See also CHARLES K. MOSER: "Where China Buys and Sells," Washington: Bureau of Foreign and Domestic Commerce (1935).

THE JAPANESE EMPIRE

General References on Japan

The annual *Japan Yearbook* published in 1941 as the *East Asia Yearbook*, Tokyo, includes a thousand pages of statistics on commerce, agriculture, cities, mining, and industry. Information on specific places, in Baedeker style, will be found in "An Official Guide to Japan," Tokyo: The Japanese Government Railways (1933). The THIRD PACIFIC SCIENCE CONGRESS, meeting in Tokyo in 1926, published a set of *Guide Books*, three volumes of *Proceedings*, and a summary on "Scientific Japan."

Current material on many economic aspects is prepared by the INSTITUTE OF PACIFIC RELATIONS, either in the indispensable *Far Eastern Survey*, published fortnightly in New York, the quarterly *Pacific Affairs*, or the biannual *Problems of the Pacific*. *Asia Magazine*, the *National Geographic Magazine*, and *Amerasia* are useful. The September, 1936, issue of *Fortune* is devoted to Japan. Several Japanese newspapers issue large annual supplements in English, notably the *Tokyo Nichi-Nichi* and the *Osaka Mainichi*. Problems of population, agriculture, industry, and trade are considered by E. B. SCHUMPETER: "The Industrialization of Japan and Manchukuo, 1930–1940," New York: Macmillan (1940).

The two best American studies are GLENN T. TREWARTHA: A Reconnaissance Geography of Japan, University of Wisconsin *Studies in the Social Sciences and History*, No. 22 (1934); GUY-HAROLD SMITH and DOROTHY GOOD with SHANNON McCUNE: "Japan, A Geographical View," New York: American Geographical Society (1943). A more general study is JOHN F. EMBREE: The Japanese, *Smithsonian Institution War Background Studies*, VII (1943).

An excellent geographic analysis is that by JULES SION in the Géographie universelle series, "Asie des moussons," Paris: Librairie Armand Colin (1928) I, 189–266. The observations of a former British Consular officer in the Orient are in ARCHIBALD LITTLE: "The Far East," Oxford: Clarendon Press (1905), 279–317. K. OSEKI has written The Economic Geography of Japan, *Scottish Geographical Magazine*, XXXI (1915), 449–465, 519–531. Interesting books of travel are HARRY FRANCK: "Glimpses of Japan and Formosa," New York: Century (1924); and W. H. MURRAY WALTON: "Scrambles in Japan and Formosa," London: E. Arnold & Co. (1934). Two thoughtful contributions by INAZO NITOBE are "Japan, Some Phases of Her Problems and Development," London: Benn (1931); and "Lectures on Japan: An Outline of the Development of Japanese People and Their Culture," London: Benn (1937). Historical references include G. B. SANSOM: "Japan, A Short Cultural History," London: The Cresset Press (1931); JOSEPH H. LONGFORD: "The Evolution of New Japan," New York: Putnam (1913); and HELEN PRATT: "Japan, Where Ancient Loyalties Survive," New York: American Council, Institute of Pacific Relations (1937).

The following lists do not include references to the many excellent studies in Japanese, often with English summaries, in the *Geographical Review of Japan* and the *Japanese Journal of Geology and Geography*, or to less accessible foreign literature.

CHAPTER 10. JAPAN'S NATURAL FOUNDATIONS

Maps

The best physical map of the Japanese Empire is published by the Kokusai Bunka Shinkokai (The Society for International Cultural Relations) in Tokyo (1937), on a scale of 1:2,000,000. An earlier wall map was issued in 1931 by the Land Survey Department, on a scale of 1:2,000,000. An exceptionally fine "Map of Land Utilization" has been prepared by Kan-Ichi Uchida, Tokyo: The Kobunsha Co., scale 1:8,000,000. Detailed topographic maps showing contours and culture are available on several scales.

Land Forms

The most detailed analysis of Japanese topography is that by Robert Burnett Hall and Akira Watanabe: "Landforms of Japan," *Papers* Michigan Academy of Science, Arts, and Letters, XVIII (1932), 157–207. Glenn T. Trewartha has published a brief article accompanied by an excellent geomorphic map by Guy-Harold Smith under the title of Notes on a Physiographic Diagram of Japan, *Geographical Review*, XXIV (1934), 400–403. This map is reproduced together with additional descriptions in Trewartha: A Reconnaissance Geography of Japan, University of Wisconsin *Studies in the Social Sciences and History*, No. 22 (1934). On the basis of his field studies in Japan, Sumner W. Cushing has written on Coastal Plains and Block Mountains in Japan, *Annals* Association of American Geographers, III (1913), 43–61. Geological details may be supplied by various maps, especially the "Geological Map of the Japanese Empire" published by the Imperial Geological Survey of Japan (1926), scale 1:4,000,000; and the "Geological Atlas of Eastern Asia," scale 1:2,000,000, issued by the Tokyo Geographical Society (1929). The Imperial Geological Survey has published a bulletin on The Geology and Mineral Resources of the Japanese Empire (1926). Charles Davison: "The Japanese Earthquake of 1923," London: Thomas Murby (1931) is an excellent treatment. Davison has also written an article entitled The Japanese Earthquake of 1 September, 1923, *Geographical Journal*, LXV (1925), 41–61.

Climate

The standard reference on climate is T. Okada: The Climate of Japan, *Bulletin* Central Meteorological Observatory of Japan, IV (1931), 89–416. C. Warren Thornthwaite has applied his classification in The Climates of Japan, *Geographical Review*, XXIV (1934),

494–496. "World Weather Records" by H. Helm Clayton, Smithsonian Miscellaneous Collections, LXXIX and XC (1927 and 1934), is an additional source of data.

Forests and Soils

Little has been written in English concerning the geographic aspects of vegetation and soils in Japan. Conditions are summarized in Trewartha's A Reconnaissance Geography of Japan.

Mineral Resources

A comprehensive picture of mineral resources in eastern Asia is contained in H. Foster Bain: "Ores and Industry in the Far East," New York: Council on Foreign Relations (1933), rev. ed. John E. Orchard's "Japan's Economic Position," New York: Whittlesey (1930), is based on a year's field study. See also his article Can Japan Develop Industrially? *Geographical Review*, XIX (1929), 177–200. Statistical information may be found in the United States Department of the Interior: *Minerals Yearbook*; likewise in *The Mineral Industry*, an annual edited by G. A. Roush and published by McGraw-Hill, New York.

CHAPTER 11. THE HUMAN RESPONSE IN JAPAN

Population Problems

A detailed evaluation of population principles and conditions in Japan may be found in E. F. Penrose: "Population Theories and Their Application," Stanford University: Food Research Institute (1934); and in W. R. Crocker: "The Japanese Population Problem: the Coming Crisis," London: Allen & Unwin (1931). Another approach is Shiroshi Nasu: The Problem of Population and Food Supply in Japan, "Problems of the Pacific," Chicago: University of Chicago Press (1928), 339–360. Population movements are described by T. W. Freeman: Recent and Contemporary Japanese Migration, *Scottish Geographical Magazine*, LIII (1937), 323–325; and Ellen C. Semple: Japanese Colonial Methods, *Bulletin* American Geographical Society, XLV (1913), 255–275.

Discussions of population distributions are contained in the following: Mark Jefferson: The Distribution of People in Japan in 1913, *Geographical Review*, II (1916), 368–373; Wesley Coulter: A Dot Map of Distribution of Population in Japan, *Geographical Review*, XVI (1926), 283–284; and John E. Orchard: The Pressure of Population in Japan, *Geographical Review*, XVIII (1928), 374–401. The best analysis of geographical evolution is Carl W. Bishop: The Historical Geography of Early Japan, *Geographical Review*, XIII (1923), 40–62.

Agriculture

Picturesque descriptions of farm conditions during the first decade of the century will be found in F. H. KING: "Farmers of Forty Centuries," New York: Harcourt (1926). Current conditions are described by DOROTHY J. ORCHARD: Agrarian Problems of Modern Japan, *Journal of Political Economy*, XXXVII (1929), 129–149, 285–311. See also ELLEN C. SEMPLE: Influence of Geographical Conditions upon Japanese Agriculture, *Geographical Journal*, XL (1912), 589–607. GLENN TREWARTHA'S A Reconnaissance Geography of Japan contains a large amount of regional material, as does also ROBERT BURNETT HALL: Agricultural Regions of Asia, Part VII—The Japanese Empire, *Economic Geography*, X (1934), 323–347; XI (1935), 33–52, 130–147. Statistics on production and population make up E. F. PENROSE'S "Food Supply and Raw Materials in Japan," Chicago: University of Chicago Press (1929). Three articles by United States government agriculturalists are O. L. DAWSON and W. LADEJINSKY: Recent Japanese Agricultural Policies, *Foreign Agriculture*, III (1939), 263–274; W. LADEJINSKY: Agrarian Unrest in Japan, *Foreign Affairs*, XVII (1939), 426–433; and W. LADEJINSKY: Japan's Food Self-sufficiency, *Foreign Agriculture*, IV (1940), 355–376. Numerous articles in the *Far Eastern Survey* deal with the economic and political aspects of agriculture. Statistical material is available in the annual *Japan-Manchoukuo Yearbook*.

Fishing

The *Japan-Manchoukuo Yearbook* contains statistical information. No satisfactory geographic descriptions are available. KATHLEEN BARNES has written Fisheries, Mainstay of Soviet-Japanese Friction, *Far Eastern Survey*, IX (1940), 75–81.

Industry

There are two outstanding volumes on industrial and economic conditions, both of them based on extensive field work. The more geographic is JOHN E. ORCHARD: "Japan's Economic Position." HAROLD EUGENE MOULTON: "Japan, an Economic and Financial Appraisal," Washington: Brookings (1931), is chiefly concerned with economic organization. Much material will be found in the *Far Eastern Survey*. Statistical reports may be found in the *Japan-Manchoukuo Yearbook* and in *Foreign Commerce Yearbook*, United States Department of Commerce (1938). The MITSUBISHI ECONOMIC RESEARCH BUREAU has issued a volume on "Japanese Trade and Industry, Present and Future," London: Macmillan (1936).

Communications

An excellent evaluation of old highways is found in ROBERT BURNETT HALL: Tokaido: Road and Region, *Geographical Review*, XXVII (1937), 353–377.

The Japanese Landscape

Rural conditions are described in two articles by ROBERT BURNETT HALL: Some Rural Settlement Forms in Japan, *Geographical Review*, XXI (1931), 93–123; and A Map of Settlement Agglomeration and Dissemination in Japan, *Papers* Michigan Academy of Science, Arts, and Letters, XXII (1937), 365–367. Urban conditions are considered by HALL in The Cities of Japan—Notes on Distribution and Inherited Form, *Annals* Association of American Geographers, XXIV (1934), 175–200; by GLENN T. TREWARTHA in Japanese Cities, Distribution and Morphology, *Geographical Review*, XXIV (1934), 404–422; and by DARRELL H. DAVIS: Some Aspects of Urbanization in Japan, *Journal of Geography*, XXXIII (1934), 205–221.

CHAPTER 12. REGIONS OF OLD JAPAN

There are three particularly valuable studies of regional geography. The most detailed is GLENN T. TREWARTHA: A Reconnaissance Geography of Japan. ROBERT BURNETT HALL's articles on Agricultural Regions of Asia are also valuable; so too is the article on climate by OKADA. A wealth of local information may be secured from "An Official Guide to Japan." Only those areas for which specific articles are available are here listed.

Central Honshu

GLENN T. TREWARTHA has prepared two detailed field studies on representative silk and tea areas, respectively, The Suwa Basin, a Specialized Sericulture District in the Japanese Alps, *Geographical Review*, XX (1930), 224–244; and A Geographic Study in Shizuoka Prefecture, Japan, *Annals* Association of American Geographers, XVIII (1928), 127–259.

Western Honshu and the Inland Sea

Conditions in the vicinity of Kyoto are considered by ROBERT BURNETT HALL: The Yamato Basin, Japan, *Annals* Association of American Geographers, XXII (1932), 243–290; and by JOSEPH A. RUSSELL: The Teas of Uji, *Economic Geography*, XVI (1940), 211–224.

Northern Honshu

A study of a small area may be found in GLENN T. TREWARTHA: The Iwaki Basin: Reconnaissance Field

Study of a Specialized Apple District in Northern Honshu, Japan, *Annals* Association of American Geographers, XX (1930), 196–223.

CHAPTER 13. REGIONS OF OUTER JAPAN

Hokkaido

Several articles by DARRELL H. DAVIS are the result of his field work: Type Occupance Patterns in Hokkaido, *Annals* Association of American Geographers, XXIV (1934), 201–223; Present Status of Settlement in Hokkaido, *Geographical Review*, XXIV (1934), 386–399; and Agricultural Occupation of Hokkaido, *Economic Geography*, X (1934), 348–367. Conditions in 1920 are considered by WELLINGTON D. JONES: Hokkaido, the Northland of Japan, *Geographical Review*, XI (1921), 16–30.

Karafuto

The following article covers both Japanese and Soviet parts of Sakhalin: HERMAN R. FRIIS: Pioneer Economy of Sakhalin Island, *Economic Geography*, XV (1939), 55–79. A special chapter in the *Japan-Manchoukuo Yearbook* is devoted to Karafuto.

Korea

HOON K. LEE has a detailed volume entitled "Land Utilization and Rural Economy in Korea," published under the auspices of the Institute of Pacific Relations, Shanghai: Kelly and Walsh (1936). General geographic descriptions are provided by J. WRIGHT BAYLOR: The Geography of Chosen, *Economic Geography*, VII (1931), 238–251; JOHN WESLEY COULTER and BERNICE BONG HEE KIM: Land Utilization Maps of Korea, *Geographical Review*, XXIV (1934), 418–422; and In the Diamond Mountains: Adventures among the Buddhist Monasteries of Eastern Korea, by LORD CURZON; *National Geographic Magazine*, XLVI (1924), 353–374. Another reference is W. LADEJINSKY: Chosen's Agriculture and Its Problems, *Foreign Agriculture*, IV (1940), 95–122. See also the various annual reports of the GOVERNMENT GENERAL OF CHOSEN. SHANNON McCUNE has contributed a number of articles on Korea including Chosen, Japan's Continental Possession, *Journal of Geography*, XXXIV (1935), 305–317; Climatic Regions of Korea and Their Economy, *Geographical Review*, XXXI (1941), 95–99; Recent Development of P'yongyang, Korea, *Economic Geography*, XLX (1943), 148–155; Notes on a Physiographic Diagram of Tyosen (Korea), with ARTHUR H. ROBINSON, *Geographical Review*, XXXI (1941), 653–658; and three bulletins on the Climate of Korea, Research Monographs on Korea (1941).

Formosa

No adequate literature is available, but descriptive material is in E. H. DE BUNSEN: Formosa, *Geographical Journal*, LXX (1927), 266–287; W. CAMPBELL: Formosa under the Japanese, *Scottish Geographical Magazine*, XVIII (1902), 561–576; and the *Japan Manchoukuo Yearbook*.

South Seas

Two studies are YUKUO UYEHARA: Ryukyu Islands, Japan, *Economic Geography*, IX (1933), 395–405; and B. H. CHAMBERLIN: The Luchu Islands and Their Inhabitants, *Geographical Journal*, V (1895), 289–319, 446–462, 534–545. Three volumes that describe conditions in the Mandated Islands are PAUL H. CLYDE: "Japan's Pacific Mandate," New York: Macmillan (1935); TADAO YANAIHARA: "Pacific Islands under Japanese Mandate," New York: Institute of Pacific Relations (1939); and GERALD SAMSON: "Warning Lights of Asia," London: R. Hale (1940).

CHAPTER 14. JAPAN'S WORLD POSITION

International relations and foreign trade are described in the following references: JOHN C. LE CLAIR: Japan's Trade with the Netherlands Indies, *Foreign Affairs*, XV (1937), 381–383; EMIL LEDERER: Japan in World Economics, *Social Research*, IV (1937), 1–32; and JOHN ORCHARD: Economic Consequences of Japan's Asiatic Policy, *Foreign Affairs*, XII (1933), 71–85. An evaluation of Japan's economic status is A. E. PARKINS: How Big Is Japan? *Economic Geography*, XI (1935), 338–346; and FREDA UTLEY: "Japan's Feet of Clay," London: Faber (1936). Much valuable material is in the *Far Eastern Survey*. An excellent cultural evaluation of Japan is contained in WILL DURANT: "The Story of Civilization," New York: Simon & Schuster (1935), 826–938.

THE UNION OF SOVIET SOCIALIST REPUBLICS

CHAPTER 15. THE SOVIET REALM

General References on the Soviet Union

The preparation of the Soviet chapters involved an extensive bibliography in Russian but, since the material is not easily available, the following notations are largely limited to references in English.

Few texts on Europe or Asia give adequate attention to the U.S.S.R. Two thoughtful chapters are in SAMUEL VAN VALKENBURG and ELLSWORTH HUNTINGTON: "Europe," New York: Wiley (1935); and a somewhat longer treatment may be found in GEORGE D. HUBBARD: "Geography of Europe," New York:

Appleton-Century (1937). An excellent analysis is that by P. CAMENA D'ALMEIDA: "Etats de la Baltique, Russie" (1932), in the French series entitled "Géographie universelle." A similar survey is provided in four sections of the "Klute Handbuch." In "Mitteleuropa, Osteuropa," Potsdam (1933), are articles by MAX FRIEDERICHSEN: Das Europäische Russland, 321–434; and BRUNO PLAETSCHKE: Die Kaukasuslander, 435–464. The volume "Nordasien, Zentral-und Ostasien," Potsdam (1937), contains HELMUT ANGER: Siberien, 125–210; and ARVED SCHULTZ: Russisch Turkestan, 211–244.

The best geographical material from the Soviet viewpoint are the volumes by NICHOLAS MIKHAILOV entitled "Soviet Geography," London: Methuen (1935); and "Land of the Soviets," New York: Furman (1939). Geographic ideology is presented in a chapter by VLADIMIR ROMM entitled Geographic Tendencies in the Soviet Union, in SAMUEL N. HARPER: "The Soviet Union and World-problems," Chicago: University Press (1935). There is a short but very worth-while article with maps by BENJAMIN SEMENOV-TIAN-SHANSKY: Russia: Territory and Population, *Geographical Review*, XVII (1928), 616–640.

Unsurpassed cartographic information dealing with all aspects of geography is available in the first and second volumes of the "Great Soviet World Atlas," Moscow (1938 and 1940), with a translation volume by GEORGE B. CRESSEY. A convenient reference for place names is the LITERARY DIGEST "Map of the U.S.S.R.," New York: Funk (1934). Current Russian literature and maps may be obtained from the Four Continent Book Corporation, 255 Fifth Avenue, New York City. The AMERICAN RUSSIAN INSTITUTE published a useful map in 1942 which indicates changes in place names together with new rivers and industrial developments. Two small convenient atlases of economic information with supplementary text are "Soviet Russia in Maps," Chicago: Denoyer-Geppert (1942); and JASPER H. STEMBRIDGE: "An Atlas of the U.S.S.R.," New York: Oxford University Press (1942).

Among the many histories of Russia, one of the best is D. S. MIRSKY: "Russia, A Social History," New York: Appleton-Century (1932). Recent boundary changes are described by J. A. MORRISON: Territorial-administrative Structure of the U.S.S.R., *American Quarterly on the Soviet Union*, I (1938), 25–58. The quest of the Russian bear for warm water is described in ROBERT J. KERNER: "The Urge to the Sea: the Course of Russian History," Berkeley: University of California Press (1942).

A comprehensive review is provided by P. MELEVSKY-MALEVITCH: "Russia U.S.S.R.," New York: W.

F. Payson (1933). KARL BAEDEKER'S "Russia," Leipzig: Baedeker (1914) is old but indispensable for detailed travel information. Current information is available from the AMERICAN RUSSIAN INSTITUTE, particularly their publication entitled *The American Review on the Soviet Union*.

CHAPTER 16. ENVIRONMENTAL FACTORS IN THE SOVIET UNION

The best reference in Russian on environmental conditions is L. S. BERG: "Priroda S.S.S.R." (The Natural Regions of the U.S.S.R.), Moscow and Leningrad (1937). Among PROFESSOR BERG'S other volumes is one entitled "Geographical Zones of the U.S.S.R., Part I, Introduction, Tundra, The Forest Zone," Leningrad (1930). There is a vast amount of comprehensive material in the series entitled "Reference Books on the Water Resources of the U.S.S.R.," issued for various regions by the HYDROLOGICAL SERVICE since 1936.

Geology

The extensive literature on Soviet geology is well summarized in the various guidebooks, reports, and other publications of the SEVENTEENTH INTERNATIONAL GEOLOGICAL CONGRESS, Moscow (1937); especially in the article by A. D. ARKHANGUELSKY: Structure géologique et histoire géologique de l'URSS in Vol. II of the *Report*, 285–304. ARKHANGUELSKY has also written a guidebook for the Second International Congress of Soil Science, Moscow (1930), entitled "Outline of the Structure and History of the Russian Platform." V. A. OBRUCHEV: "Geology of Siberia" is available in a German edition (1926) and in Russian (1935–1936). The first volume of KURT LEUCHS: "Géologie von Asien" is devoted to northern Asia. The best summary of glaciation is I. P. GERASIMOV and K. K. MARKOV: "The Glacial Period in the Territory of the U.S.S.R." (in Russian with a 20-page English summary); see review in *Geographical Review*, XXXI (1941), 343–345. Permanently frozen ground is described in GEORGE B. CRESSEY: Frozen Ground in Siberia, *Journal of Geology*, XLVII (1939), 103–169. Volumes II and III of "The Face of the Earth" by EDUARD SUESS contain old but significant comments on Russia.

Land Form Regions

Only scattered material is available on regional geomorphology, but the following articles clear up the structure of northeastern Siberia: S. V. OBRUCHEV and K. A. SALISHCHEV: The Mountain Systems of Northeastern Asia, *Geographical Review*, XXV (1935), 625–642; and V. A. OBRUCHEV: The Yablonovi and

Stanovoi Ranges in the Light of New Data, *Geographical Journal*, LXXXVI (1935), 422–440. The most authoritative statement in Russian is by B. TH. DOBRYNIN: Geomorphological Divisions of European U.S.S.R., presented to the International Geographical Congress, Warsaw (1934).

Climate

The most detailed climatic study is A. V. VOZNESENSKY: "Map of the Climates of the U.S.S.R.," (in Russian with English summary), Leningrad: *Transactions* Bureau of Agro-Meteorology, XXI (1930). The section of the "Koeppen-Geiger Handbuch" on Klimakunde von Russland (in Europa und Asien) contains tables and a map of climatic regions. KENDREW's "Climates of the Continents" has a chapter on the Russian Empire. Two articles by STANISLAUS NOVAKOVSKY deal with the human climatology: The Effect of Climate on the Efficiency of the People of the Russian Far East, *Ecology*, III (1922), 275–283; and Arctic or Siberian Hysteria as a Reflex of the Geographic Environment, *Ecology*, V (1924), 113–127. A brief summary of the environment is in L. I. PRASOLOV: The Climate and Soils of Northern Eurasia as Conditions of Colonization, in "Pioneer Settlement" issued by the American Geographical Society, New York (1932), 240–260.

Natural Vegetation

WILLIAM SEIFRIZ has written a series of articles entitled Sketches of the Vegetation of Some Southern Provinces of Soviet Russia, in the *Journal of Ecology*, XIX (1931), 360–371, 372–382; XX (1932), 53–68, 69–77, 78–88; XXIII (1935), 140–146, 147–160. See also BORIS A. KELLER: Distribution of Vegetation on the Plains of Southern Russia, *Journal of Ecology*, XV (1927), 189–233. There is a good description of European forests in RAPHAEL ZON and W. N. SPARHAWK: "Forest Resources of the World," I, New York: McGraw-Hill (1923). Descriptions of dry-land forests may be found in G. N. VYSSOTSKY: Shelterbelts in the Steppes of Russia, *Journal of Forestry*, XXXIII (1935), 781–788; and N. T. MIROV: Two Centuries of Afforestation and Shelterbelt Planting on the Russian Steppes, *Journal of Forestry*, XXXIII (1935), 971–973.

Soils

"The Great Soil Groups of the World and Their Development" written in Russian by J. D. GLINKA has been translated by CURTIS F. MARBUT, Ann Arbor: Edwards Bros. (1927). Numerous articles on soils and related geographic problems were published in the *Proceedings* and *Guidebooks* of the Second

International Congress of Soil Science, Moscow (1930).

CHAPTER 17. MINERAL RESOURCES IN THE SOVIET UNION

Some of the best material is that issued in connection with the Seventeenth International Geological Congress, including an expected volume on "Petroleum Resources of the World." A bulletin prepared by M. M. PRIGOROVSKY is entitled "The Coal Resources of the U.S.S.R." Three of the delegates subsequently wrote of their observations: CYRIL FOX: Mineral Development in Soviet Russia, *Transactions* Mining, Geological, and Metallurgical Institute of India, XXXIV (1938) part 2, 100–201; E. L. BRUCE: Mineral Deposits of the Southern Ukraine and of the Ural Mountains, *Canadian Mining and Metallurgical Bulletin*, CCCXIX (1938), 505–523; and TOM EDWARDS: The Mineral Deposits of the U.S.S.R., *The Mining Magazine*, LVIII (1938), 265–279, 335–343.

The UNITED GEOLOGICAL AND PROSPECTING SERVICE OF THE U.S.S.R. issued two bulletins in 1933, Mineral Resources of the U.S.S.R. and Power Resources of the U.S.S.R. A comprehensive volume entitled "Electric Power Development in the U.S.S.R.," which includes both coal and water resources, was prepared by the KRZIZHANOVSKY POWER INSTITUTE of the Academy of Sciences in 1936.

The latest information on various products is available in *The Minerals Industry*, McGraw-Hill (annual). There is an excellent series on lead and zinc in The Metalliferous Altai of Soviet Russia by ANDREW and EDITH MEYER in the *Engineering and Mining Journal*, CXXXVII (1936), 275–278, 348–353, 468–472, 476, 515–520. A comprehensive article on Russian aluminum is R. J. ANDERSON: Russian Aluminum, *The Mining Magazine*, LVIII (1938), 73–86. The UNITED STATES BUREAU OF MINES has prepared an article on Mineral Production and Trade of the U.S.S.R. (Russia), *Foreign Minerals Quarterly*, I, No. 2 (1938), 1–72. A comprehensive report now somewhat out of date is The Petroleum Resources of Russia by ARTHUR HUBER REDFIELD, *Bulletin* American Association of Petroleum Geologists, II (1927), 493–513.

CHAPTER 18. ECONOMIC DEVELOPMENTS IN THE SOVIET UNION

Interesting accounts of economic developments during the early five-year plans are contained in the volume by the former *Christian Science Monitor* correspondent, WILLIAM H. CHAMBERLIN: "Russia's Iron Age," Boston: Little (1934); the report of an engineer, ALCAN HIRSCH: "Industrialized Russia,"

New York: Chemical Catalogue Co. (1934); and CALVIN B. HOOVER: "The Economic Life of Soviet Russia," New York: Macmillan (1931). Current developments are reported in the U.S. BUREAU OF FOREIGN COMMERCE *Foreign Commerce Weekly* and its predecessor, *Russian Economic Notes*. The AMERICAN-RUSSIAN CHAMBER OF COMMERCE published a "Handbook of the Soviet Union" in 1935. WILLIAM MANDEL has written on Soviet Transport, Today and Tomorrow in *The American Review on the Soviet Union*, III (1941), 28–45.

Agriculture

Specialized material on agriculture is contained in two publications by VLADIMIR P. TIMOSHENKO: "Agricultural Russia and the Wheat Problem," Stanford University: Food Research Institute (1932); and "Russia as a Producer and Exporter of Wheat," Stanford University: Food Research Institute (1932). Changes in farming are described by W. LADEJINSKY: Collectivization of Agriculture in the Soviet Union, *Political Science Quarterly*, XLIX (1934), 1–43, 207–252; and Soviet State Farms, *Political Science Quarterly*, LIII (1938), 60–82, 207–232. Critical conditions in the south are presented by N. M. TULAIKOV: Agriculture in the Dry Region of the U.S.S.R., *Economic Geography*, VI (1930), 54–80. CURTIS F. MARBUT, former Chief of the U.S. Bureau of Soils, has written two articles growing out of his visit to the Second International Soil Congress, Russia and the United States in the World's Wheat Market, *Geographical Review*, XXI (1931), 1–21; and Agriculture in the United States and Russia, *Geographical Review*, XXI (1931), 598–612. In this connection there is a valuable comment by V. P. TIMOSHENKO: The Expansion of the Wheat Area in Arid Russia, *Geographical Review*, XXIII (1933), 479–481. Conditions in the late 1930's are described by LAZAR VOLIN: Recent Developments in Soviet Agriculture, *Foreign Agriculture*, I (1937), 3–28; Effects of the Drought and Purge on the Agriculture of the Soviet Union, III (1939), 175–196; The Russian Peasant Household under the Mir and the Collective Farm System, IV (1940), 133–146.

CHAPTER 19. REGIONS OF SOVIET EUROPE

Regional references on Soviet Europe, which will not be repeated under the various regions, include MIKHAILOV, HUBBARD, D'ALMEIDA, and FRIEDERICHSEN. Another excellent source is L. S. BERG: "The Natural Regions of the U.S.S.R.," in Russian. BAEDEKER's "Russia" is invaluable for city maps and travel information. Excursion guidebooks for the Seventeenth International Geological Congress deal with the Caucasus, the Urals, Kola-Karelia, Moscow, the Petroleum Areas, the Ukraine and Crimea, Nova Zemlya, and Siberia.

Ukrainia

Farming conditions are described in LOUIS G. MICHAEL: The Soviet Ukraine—Its People and Agriculture, *Foreign Agriculture*, III (1939), 281–306. Two articles on mineral wealth are those by STANISLAUS NOVAKOVSKI: Natural Resources of Ukraine, *Journal of Geography*, XXIII (1924), 293–300; and E. L. BRUCE: Mineral Deposits of the Southern Ukraine and of the Ural Mountains, *Canadian Mining and Metallurgical Bulletin*, CCCXIX (1938), 505–523. Historical and political aspects are provided in "The Ukraine" by W. E. D. ALLEN, Cambridge: University Press (1940); and in A. S. ELWELL-SUTTON: The Ukraine, *Contemporary Review*, CLV (1939), 681–690.

Kola-Karelian Taiga

Conditions of vegetation are considered by WILLIAM SEIFRIZ: The Plant Life of Russian Lapland, *Ecology*, XV (1934), 306–318; and R. RUGGLES GATES: Notes on the Tundra of Russian Lapland, *Journal of Ecology*, XVI (1928), 150–160. The exploitation of the potash deposits is described in the small volume by A. E. FERSMAN: "The Scientific Study of Soviet Mineral Resources," Moscow (1935). Economic developments are considered by WILLIAM O. FIELD, JR.: The Kola Peninsula, *American Quarterly on the Soviet Union*, I (1938), 3–21.

Dvina-Pechora Taiga

Forest and lumbering possibilities are dealt with by JOHN D. GUTHERIE: Some Notes on the Forests of Northern Russia, *Journal of Forestry*, XXII (1924), 197–204; and EDWARD P. STEBBING: The Forest Region of North East Russia and Its Importance to Great Britain, *Geographical Journal*, LI (1918), 359–374. An interesting account of travel from Leningrad to the Dvina River is DAVID R. BUXTON: A Journey in Northern Russia, *Blackwood's Magazine*, CCXXXIV (1933), 149–174.

Central Agricultural Region

M. MELVINA SVEC has written a travel account entitled Voyaging down the Volga, *Journal of Geography*, XXXVIII (1939), 297–304. For a general survey see ST. KOLUPAILA and M. PARDE: La Volga, étude hydrologique, *Annales de géographie*, XLIII (1934), 32–48.

Southern Agricultural Region

Problems in cultivating the steppe regions of the lower Volga are covered in N. M. TULAIKOV:

Agriculture in the Dry Region of the U.S.S.R., *Economic Geography*, VI (1930), 54–80.

The Ural Mountains

The geological history of the Urals is outlined by ANATOLE SAFONOV: Orogeny of the Urals, *Bulletin* American Association of Petroleum Geologists, XXI (1937), 1439–1463. The development of Magnitogorsk is described by JOHN SCOTT in "Beyond the Urals," Boston: Houghton (1942); and Magnetic City, Core of Valiant Russia's Industrial Might, *National Geographic Magazine*, LXXXIII (1943), 525–556.

CHAPTER 20. REGIONS OF SOVIET MIDDLE ASIA

In addition to general references such as MIKHAILOV, D'ALMEIDA, and BERG, suggestive material will be found in LIONEL W. LYDE: "The Continent of Asia," London: MacMillan (1933). One of the best sources is the volume by A. WOEIKOF of St. Petersburg entitled "Le Turkestan Russe," Paris (1914). The best references in German are ARVED SCHULTZ: "Die Naturlichen Landschaften von Russisch-Turkestan," Hamburg: Friederichsen (1920); and his section in the "Klute Handbuch" on "Russisch Turkestan"; and FRITZ MACHATSCHEK: "Landeskunde von Russisch Turkistan," Stuttgart (1921).

Caucasia

Two excellently illustrated articles dealing with modern conditions are those by JOHN LEHMAN: Change in the Caucasus, *Geographical Magazine*, II (1935), 125–141; and JOHN R. JENKINS: Climbing in the Caucasus, *Geographical Magazine*, VII (1938), 55–72. One of the excellent series of botanical studies by WILLIAM SEIFRIZ is entitled Vegetation Zones in the Caucasus, *Geographical Review*, XXVI (1936), 59–66. The history of political complications is considered by WILLIAM O. FIELD, JR.: The International Struggle for Transcaucasia, *American Quarterly on the Soviet Union*, II (1939), 21–44. A journey in 1925 is described by FRIDTJOF NANSEN: "Through the Caucasus to the Volga," New York: Norton (1931). The "Klute Handbuch" has a section on "Die Kaukasuslander" by BRUNO PLAETSCHKE; and *Petermann's Mitteilungen*, Erganzungscheft 189 (1926), is on Transkaukasien by ANTON BÜDEL.

Caspian Desert

ELLSWORTH HUNTINGTON reviews the problem of climatic changes in an article entitled Fluctuations in the Caspian Sea, *Bulletin* American Geographical Society, XXXIX (1907), 577–596. The problem of agriculture in the lower Volga is considered briefly by W. C. LOWDERMILK and N. MIROV: Irrigation in the Caspian Lowlands, *Geographical Review*, XXIII (1933), 336–337. Petroleum production northeast of the Caspian is described by C. W. SANDERS: Emba Salt Dome Region, *Bulletin* American Association of Petroleum Geologists, XXIII (1939), 492–516. Conditions in the northeast are pictured by IRVINE C. GARDNER: Observing an Eclipse in Asiatic Russia, *National Geographic Magazine*, LXXI (1937), 179–197.

Pamirs and Associated Ranges.

In 1903 the Carnegie Institution sent an expedition to the mountains and deserts of Central Asia under RAPHAEL PUMPELLY, WILLIAM M. DAVIS, and ELLSWORTH HUNTINGTON, whose report is "Explorations in Turkestan," Washington (1905). ELLSWORTH HUNTINGTON has also written The Mountains of Turkestan, *Geographical Journal*, XXV (1905), 22–40, 139–158; and The Mountains and Kibitkas of Tian Shan, *Bulletin* American Geographical Society, XXXVII (1905), 513–530. WILLIAM M. DAVIS has further described his travel in A Summer in Turkestan, *Bulletin* American Geographical Society, XXXVI (1904), 217–218. An expedition under W. RICKMER RICKMERS is described in The Alai-Pamirs in 1913 and 1928, *Geographical Journal*, LXXIV (1929), 209–231.

Turan Oases and Deserts

Geographic conditions in the deserts and oases of Turan are described by ALBRECHT PENCK: Central Asia, *Geographical Journal*, LXXVI (1930), 477–487; and W. RICKMER RICKMERS: "The Duab of Turkestan," London: Cambridge University Press (1913). Agricultural developments are considered by VALENTINE V. TCHIKOFF; The Cotton Empire of the U.S.S.R., *Asia*, XXXII (1932), 255–263; LYMAN D. WILBUR: Surveying through Khoresm, *National Geographic Magazine*, LXI (1932), 753–780; and ARTHUR P. DAVIS: Irrigation in Turkestan, *Civil Engineering*, II (1932), 1–5. Other agricultural developments are reported in ROBERT K. NABOURS: The Land of Lambskins, *National Geographic Magazine*, XXXVI (1919), 77–88. Animal life is described by DANIEL KASHKAROV and VICTOR KURBATOV: Preliminary Ecological Survey of the Vertebrate Fauna of the Central Kara-Kum Desert in West Turkestan, *Ecology*, XI (1930), 35–60. Conditions in Kazakhstan are dealt with by ALLAN MOZLEY: The Ponds, Lakes, and Streams of the Kirghiz Steppe, *Scottish Geographical Magazine*, LIII (January 1937), 1–10. ELIZABETH W. CLARK has written a brief article entitled Golden Samarkand, *Home Geographic Monthly* (November, 1932), 37–42. General travel accounts may be found in BOSWORTH GOLDMAN: "Red Road through Asia," London: Methuen (1934); ELLA K. MAILLART: "Turkestan

Solo," New York: Putnam (1935); ELLA R. CHRISTIE: "Through Khiva to Golden Samarkand," London: Seeley Service (1925); and EGON ERWIN KISCH: "Changing Asia," New York: Knopf (1935).

CHAPTER 21. REGIONS OF SOVIET SIBERIA

Developments during the first two five-year plans are described in articles by GEORGE B. CRESSEY: News From Siberia, *Harper's Magazine*, CLXXVII (1938), 148–157; and Pioneering in Yeniseiland, (incorrectly spelled "Yeneseiland"), *Journal of the Scientific Laboratories*, Denison University, XXIV (1939), 103–169. An earlier account is GEORGE FREDERICK WRIGHT: "Asiatic Russia," New York: McClure, Phillips (1902). BORIS BAIEVSKY has a general article entitled Siberia—The Storehouse of the Future, *Economic Geography*, III (1927), 167–192. Economic developments are covered in numerous short articles in the fortnightly *Far Eastern Survey* published by the INSTITUTE OF PACIFIC RELATIONS. The mineral wealth of Siberia is described by P. P. GOUDKOFF: Economic Geography of the Coal Resources of Asiatic Russia, *Geographical Review*, XIII (1923), 283–293. Conditions under czarist rule are described by GEORGE KENNAN in Siberia—The Exiles' Abode, *Journal* American Geographical Society, XIV (1882), 13–68.

Standard German sources are ARVED SCHULTZ: "Siberien," Breslau: Ferdinand Hirt (1923); ERICH THIEL: "Verkehrsgeographie von Russisch-Asien," Berlin: Ost-Europa-verlag (1934); and HELMUT ANGER: "Siberien" in the "Klute Handbuch."

Two volumes that describe Siberia just prior to the Second World War are R. A. DAVIES and ANDREW J. STEIGER: "Soviet Asia," New York: Dial Press (1942); and EMIL LENGYEL: "Siberia," New York: Random House (1943).

Yenisei Taiga

FRIDTJOF NANSEN's trip up the Yenisei in 1913 is described in "Through Siberia, The Land of the Future," London: Heinemann (1914). Volumes by modern travelers are BOSWORTH GOLDMAN: "Red Road through Asia," London: Methuen (1934); H. P. SMOLKA: "Forty Thousand against the Arctic," London: Hutchinson (1937); and RUTH GRUBER: "I Went to the Soviet Arctic," New York: Simon & Schuster (1939). A detailed study of the entire Yenisei Valley is presented by GEORGE B. CRESSEY in Pioneering in Yeniseiland. Life among the Nentsi is described by H. U. HALL: A Siberian Wilderness: Native Life on the Lower Yenisei, *Geographical Review*, V (1918), 1–21. A trip to Igarka and up the Yenisei is described by BOSWORTH GOLDMAN: The

Arctic Gateway to Siberia, *Geographical Magazine*, II (1936), 231–245; and a brief description of a trip down the Yenisei is provided by A. J. STEIGER: The Mighty Yenesei, *Asia*, XXXVII (1937), 510–513.

Arctic Fringe

In addition to "Forty Thousand against the Arctic," H. P. SMOLKA has written two other studies entitled The Economic Development of the Soviet Arctic, *Geographical Journal*, LXXXIX (1937), 327–343; and Soviet Strategy in the Arctic, *Foreign Affairs*, XVI (1938), 272–278. RUTH GRUBER's "I Went to the Soviet Arctic" contains extensive travel information. Another travel volume is LEONARD MATTERS: "Through the Kara Sea," Sheffington (1932). The U.S.S.R. COUNCIL OF THE INSTITUTE OF PACIFIC RELATIONS has published a report by SEMION JOFFE entitled "The Northern Sea Route as a Transport Problem," (1936). The Soviet Conquest of the Far North is the title of an article by BRUCE HOPPER in *Foreign Affairs*, XIV (1936), 499–505. Abstracts of papers presented at the Seventeenth International Geological Congress on the Geology of Arctic Regions of Eurasia are reprinted in the *Pan-American Geologist*, LXXII (1939), 273–292.

Lena Taiga

The most recent account of the Lena Valley will be found in RUTH GRUBER's "I Went to the Soviet Arctic." Conditions among the native tribes are described by WALDEMAR JOCHELSON: The Yakut, *Anthropological Papers* American Museum of Natural History, XXXIII (1933), 35–225.

Northeastern Mountains

The discovery of the Cherski Range is described by SERGEI OBRUCHEV: Discovery of a Great Range in Northeast Siberia, *Geographical Journal*, LXX (1927), 464–470. N. KRIJANOVSKY has listed the Volcanoes of Kamchatka in the *Bulletin* Geological Society of America, XLV (1934), 529–549. Problems of fishing in the northwestern Pacific are covered in two articles by STANISLAUS NOVAKOVSKY: Geographic Regions of the Fisheries in Asiatic Russia, *Journal of Geography*, XXII (1932), 1–15; and by BORIS BAIEVSKY: Fisheries of Siberia, U.S. Bureau of Fisheries *Document* 1006, (1926), 37–64.

The Far East

Three reports by the U.S.S.R. COUNCIL OF THE INSTITUTE OF PACIFIC RELATIONS in 1936 provide a comprehensive picture of the Amur Basin: "Nature and Natural Resources of the Soviet Far East"; A. TSYMEK: "The Forest Wealth of the Soviet Far East and its Exploitation"; and E. RAIKHMAN and

B. VVEDENSKY: "The Economic Development of the Soviet Far East." STANISLAUS NOVAKOVSKY has written three articles on climatic conditions: Climatic Provinces of the Russian Far East in Relation to Human Activities, *Geographical Review*, XII (1922), 100–115; The Probable Effect of the Climate of the Russian Far East on Human Life and Activity, *Ecology*, III (1922), 181–201; and The Effect of Climate on the Efficiency of the People of the Russian Far East, *Ecology*, III (1922), 275–283. FRIDTJOF NANSEN: "Through Siberia, the Land of the Future" describes conditions in 1913. Material on Sakhalin includes articles by H. R. FRIIS: Pioneer Economy of Sakhalin Island, *Economic Geography*, XV (1939), 55–79; GIICHIRO KOBAYASHI: Preliminary Report on the Geology of the Oil Fields in North Sakhalin, *Bulletin* American Association of Petroleum Geologists, X (1926), 1150–1162; and I. P. TOLMACHOFF: The Results of Oil Prospecting on Sakhalin Island by Japan in 1919–25, *Bulletin* American Association of Petroleum Geologists, X (1926), 1163–1170. A comprehensive analysis of economic and cultural developments is provided in WILLIAM MANDEL: "The Soviets in the Far East," New York: Institute of Pacific Relations (1943).

SOUTHWESTERN ASIA

CHAPTER 22. THE SOUTHWESTERN REALM

The best description of the realm is R. BLANCHARD: "Asie occidentale," Paris: Librairie Armand Colin (1929); a brief but usable summary is that of SAMUEL VAN VALKENBURG: Agricultural Regions of Asia, part 2—The Near East, *Economic Geography*, VIII (1932), 109–133. Portions of two volumes on the Mediterranean Basin deal with southwestern Asia: ELLEN CHURCHILL SEMPLE: "The Geography of the Mediterranean Region," New York: Holt (1931); and MARION ISABEL NEWBIGIN: "Mediterranean Lands," New York: Crofts (1924). ISAIAH BOWMAN has written a stimulating article entitled The Mohammedan World, *Geographical Review*, XIV (1924), 62–74.

CHAPTER 23. TURKEY

The best regional geography of what is now Turkey, Syria, Palestine, Iraq, and Arabia is that of EWALD BANSE: "Die Türkei: Eine Moderne Geographie," Brunswick: Westermann (1919), 3d ed.; reviewed by ELLEN CHURCHILL SEMPLE: The Regional Geography of Turkey: A Review of Banse's Work, *Geographical Review*, XI (1921), 338–350; a shorter but excellent treatment is by G. P. MERRIAM: The Regional Geography of Anatolia, *Economic Geography*, II (1926), 90. CARL L. STOTZ has contributed studies

of two areas in the vicinity of Constantinople: Life in the Communities along the Bosphorus, *Journal of Geography*, XXXI (1932), 181–192; and The Bursa Region of Turkey, *Geographical Review*, XXIX (1939), 81–100. A further geographic study of a limited area is the volume by JOHN A. MORRISON: "Alisar: a Unit of Land Occupance in the Kanak Su Basin of Central Anatolia," Chicago: University of Chicago Libraries (1939). The Black Sea fringe is described in ERNEST NOWACK: Journeys in Northern Anatolia, *Geographical Review*, XXI (1931), 70–92. LEON DOMINIAN has written The Peoples of Northern and Central Asiatic Turkey, *Bulletin* American Geographical Society, XLVII (1915), 832–871. Two articles summarize agricultural conditions, G. STRATIL-SAUER: Cereal Production in Turkey, *Economic Geography*, IX (1933), 325–336; and N. WILLIAM HAZEN: Turkish Agriculture—Changing Agro-economic Policy, *Foreign Agriculture*, IV (1940), 221–272. A general volume is G. BIE RAVNDAHL: "Turkey, Commercial and Industrial Handbook," Washington: U.S. Department of Commerce (1926).

CHAPTER 24. SYRIA AND PALESTINE

Two excellent articles on the regional geography of the northern and southern areas are BESSIE L. ASHTON: The Geography of Syria, *Journal of Geography*, XXVII (1928), 167–180; and D. H. KALLNER and E. ROSENAU: The Geographical Regions of Palestine, *Geographical Review*, XXIX (1939), 61–80. The Syrian Landscape is the subject of an article by GERMAINE MERLANGE in the *Geographical Magazine*, XII (1940–41), 153–167. Conditions in the interior are described by ELLEN CHURCHILL SEMPLE: The Ancient Piedmont Route of Northern Mesopotamia, *Geographical Review*, VIII (1919), 153–179; E. RAY CASTO and OSCAR W. DOTSON: Economic Geography of Trans-Jordan, *Economic Geography*, XIV (1938), 121–130; and HOWARD CROSBY BUTLER: Desert Syria, the Land of a Lost Civilization, *Geographical Review*, IX (1920), 77–108. An American forester, W. C. LOWDERMILK, has written The Cedars of Lebanon, Then and Now, *American Forests*, XLVII (1941), 16–20; a further study of this area is H. E. VOKES: Geological Observations in the Lebanon Mountains of Western Asia, *Bulletin* Geological Society of America, LII (1941), 1715–1731.

The standard works on historical Palestine are GEORGE ADAM SMITH: "The Historical Geography of the Holy Land," New York: Harper (1932), 25th ed.; and his "Atlas of the Historical Geography of the Holy Land," London: Hodder (1915). The question of climatic changes is considered by ELLSWORTH HUNTINGTON: "Palestine and Its Transformation,"

Boston: Houghton (1911); and J. W. GREGORY: Palestine and the Stability of Climate in Historic Times, *Geographical Journal*, LXXVI (1930), 487–494. Political and economic developments are discussed by ELLSWORTH HUNTINGTON: The Future of Palestine, *Geographical Review*, VII (1919), 24–35; ANDRÉE CHOVEAUX: The New Palestine, *Geographical Review*, XVII (1927), 75–88; K. H. HUGGINS: Problems of Palestine, *Scottish Geographical Magazine*, LV (1939), 85–97; ARCHER CUST: The Palestine Report: Its Geographical Background, *Scottish Geographical Magazine*, LIII (1937), 380–387; and E. RAY CASTO: Economic Geography of Palestine, *Economic Geography*, XIII (1937), 235–259; with illustrations in FREDERICK SIMPICH: Change Comes to Bible Lands, *National Geographic Magazine*, LXXIV (1938), 695–750; and JOHN D. WHITING: Canoeing down the River Jordan, *National Geographic Magazine*, LXXVIII (1940), 781–808. Crop possibilities are summarized by A. T. STRAHORN: Agriculture and Soils of Palestine, *Geographical Review*, XIX (1929), 581–602; N. W. HAZEN: Agriculture in Palestine and the Development of Jewish Colonization, *Foreign Agriculture*, I (1937), 119–148; and A. BONNÉ: Natural Resources of Palestine, *Geographical Journal*, XCII (1938), 259–266. BAILEY WILLIS has presented a new interpretation in his Dead Sea Problem: Rift Valley or Ramp Valley?, *Bulletin* Geological Society of America, XXXIX (1928), 490–542.

CHAPTER 25. ARABIA

Although there is an extensive literature on exploration and travel, very few articles deal with the systematic aspects of Arabian geography. Among explorers the outstanding names are Charles M. Doughty, Alois Musil, H. St. J. Philby, T. H. Lawrence, and Bertram Thomas. Since most of this work has been done by Englishmen, there are numerous articles in the files of the *Geographical Journal* and *Geographical Magazine*. Explorations up to 1921 are summarized by D. G. HOGARTH: Some Recent Arabian Explorations, *Geographical Review*, XI (1921), 321–337. Work in the north is the subject of an article by JOHN KIRTLAND WRIGHT: Northern Arabia, the Explorations of Alois Musil, *Geographical Review*, XVII (1927), 177–206. Conditions in the extreme south are described by W. H. INGRAMS: The Hadhramaut: Present and Future, *Geographical Journal*, XCII (1938), 289–312; G. CATON-THOMPSON and E. W. GARDNER: Climate, Irrigation, and Early Man in the Hadhramaut, *Geographical Journal*, XCIII (1939), 18–38; and RUTHVEN W. PIKE: Land and Peoples of the Hadhramaut, Aden Protectorate, *Geographical Review*, XXX (1940), 627–648.

CHAPTER 26. IRAQ

Four useful references are SIR WILLIAM WILL-COCKS: Mesopotamia—Past, Present, and Future, *Annual Report* Smithsonian Institution (1910), 401–416: O. G. S. CRAWFORD: The Birthplace of Civilization, *Geographical Review*, XVI (1926), 73–81; R. J. D. GRAHAM: The Future of Iraq, *Scottish Geographical Magazine*, XLIII (1927), 281–287; and J. C. A. JOHNSON: The Kurds of Iraq, *Geographical Magazine*, X (1940), 382–393; XI (1940), 50–59.

CHAPTER 27. IRAN

The notable changes between the early years of the twentieth century and the period shortly before the Second World War are strikingly contrasted in the two following articles: E. SYKES: Life and Travel in Persia, *Scottish Geographical Magazine*, XX (1904), 403–415; and BARONESS RAVENSDALE: Old and New in Persia, *National Geographic Magazine*, LXXVI (1939), 325–355. The ingenious development of underground water supply is described by COMMODORE B. FISHER: Irrigation Systems of Persia, *Geographical Review*, XVIII (1928), 302–306. Conditions of topography and travel in the desolate interior deserts are described by ELLSWORTH HUNTINGTON: The Basins of Eastern Persia and Seistan, Washington: Carnegie Institution, *Publication 26*, (1905), 219–317; HENRY McMAHON: Recent Survey and Exploration in Seistan, *Geographical Journal*, XXVIII (1906), 333–352; and ALFONS GABRIEL: The Southern Lut and Iranian Baluchistan, *Geographical Journal*, XCII (1938), 193–210. FREDERICK G. CLAPP, an American geologist, has contributed two articles based upon extensive field work: Geology of Eastern Iran, *Bulletin* Geological Society of America, LI (1940), 1–101; and Teheran and the Elburz, *Geographical Review*, XX (1930), 69–85. The humid Elburz area is described by J. B. L. NOEL: A Reconnaissance in the Caspian Provinces of Persia, *Geographical Journal*, LVII (1921), 401–418. Conditions of British and German strategy are considered in THOMAS H. HOLDICH: Between the Tigris and the Indus, *Geographical Review*, IV (1917), 161–170. MOUSTAFA KHAN FATCH has prepared an excellent survey in his "The Economic Position of Persia," London: King (1926).

CHAPTER 28. AFGHANISTAN

Accounts of travel in Afghanistan are given in the following references: EVERT BARGER: Exploration of Ancient Sites in Northern Afghanistan, *Geographical Journal*, XCIII (1939), 377–391; and CHRISTOPHER SYKES: Some Notes on a Recent Journey in Afghanistan, *Geographical Journal*, LXXIV (1934), 327–336. Two articles which present developments up to 1942 are ANNEMARIE CLARAC-SCHWARZENBACH: Afghanistan in Transition, *Geographical Magazine*, XI (1904), 326–341; and W. K. FRASER-TYTLER: Afghanistan, *Scottish Geographical Magazine*, LIX (1943), 1–6. The experiences of a geologist are recorded in ERNEST F. FOX: "Travels in Afghanistan," New York: Macmillan (1943).

THE INDIAN REALM

General References on India

A general treatment of the Indian Realm will be found in each of the standard textbooks on Asia: L. DUDLEY STAMP: "Asia," New York: Dutton (1935), 3d ed., 173–390; L. W. LYDE: "The Continent of Asia," London: Macmillan (1933), 356–491; and DANIEL R. BERGSMARK: "Economic Geography of Asia," New York: Prentice-Hall (1935), 171–261. In addition L. DUDLEY STAMP has written a useful elementary textbook called "The Indian Empire, Part IV, India, Burma, and Ceylon," New York: Longmans (1929). A wide variety of information is contained in the first four volumes of *The Imperial Gazetteer* entitled "The Indian Empire," Oxford: Clarendon Press (1908–1909); the annual *Indian Year Book and Who's Who*, Bombay: Times of India Press; JOHN MURRAY: "A Handbook for Travellers in India, Burma, and Ceylon," London: J. Murray (1933); and the volume on Asia of the "Oxford Survey of the British Empire" edited by A. J. HERBERTSON and O. J. R. HOWARTH, Oxford: Clarendon Press (1914). One of the best geographic evaluations of Indian problems, internal and external, may be found in C. B. FAWCETT's "A Political Geography of the British Empire," Boston: Ginn (1933). The standard French reference is JULES SION: "Asie des moussons," II, Paris: Librairie Armand Colin (1929). VERA ANSTEY: "The Economic Development of India," London: Longmans (1929) is particularly valuable in its field. A useful Indian treatment is that by B. B. MUKHERJEE: London: Thacker (1931), entitled "An Economic and Commercial Geography of India."

CHAPTER 29. INDIA'S PHYSICAL FOUNDATIONS

Geology and Land Forms

The standard volume is D. N. WADIA: "Geology of India," London: Macmillan, 2d ed. (1939).

Maps

A useful series of wall maps published by GEORGE PHILIP & SON on the Indian Empire is included in their series of "Comparative Wall Atlas Maps,"

scale 1 inch = 64 miles. The best large wall map is "India and Adjacent Countries," scale 1 inch = 32 miles. The standard atlas is that published as Vol. XXVI of the "Imperial Gazetteer of India," Oxford: Clarendon Press, rev. ed. (1931).

Climate

A simple summary of climate may be found in W. G. KENDREW: "The Climates of the Continents," Oxford: Clarendon Press (1927), 95–132. Monsoon conditions are described by G. C. SIMPSON: The South-west Monsoon, *Quarterly Journal* Royal Meteorological Society, XLVII (1921), 151–172; and upper air movements are covered by K. R. RAMANATHAN and K. P. RAMAKRISHNAN: The General Circulation of the Atmosphere over India and Its Neighbourhood, *Memoirs* India Meteorological Department, XXVI, Part X (1939), 189–245. Rainfall problems are described in two articles by A. V. WILLIAMSON: The Variability of the Annual Rainfall of India, *Quarterly Journal* Royal Meteorological Society, LVII (1931), 43–56; and an article prepared with K. G. T. CLARK entitled The Rainfall Regions of India, *Geography*, XVI (1931), 98–108; and in a study by H. A. MATTHEWS: A New View of Some Familiar Indian Rainfalls, *Scottish Geographical Magazine*, LXII (1936), 84–97, with a note by P. R. CROWE on pages 187–188. Another source is LEONARD O. PACKARD: Response to Rainfall in India, *Bulletin* American Geographical Society, XLVII (1915), 81–99. The standard map source is the "Climatological Atlas of India," Edinburgh (1906).

Natural Vegetation

The best ecological analysis of vegetation is H. G. CHAMPION: A Preliminary Survey of the Forest Types of India and Burma, *Indian Forest Records*, I, No. 1 (1936). A simple summary is provided by L. A. KENOYER: Plant Life of British India, *Scientific Monthly*, XVIII (1924), 48–65.

Mineral Resources

A comprehensive treatment is provided by J. COGGIN BROWN: "India's Mineral Wealth," London: Oxford University Press (1936). There are also valuable chapters in D. N. WADIA: "Geology of India,"; and H. FOSTER BAIN: "Ores and Industry in the Far East," New York: Council on Foreign Relations (1933). Current production statistics will be found in G. A. ROUSH, editor: *The Mineral Industry*, New York: McGraw-Hill (1938); and in *The Minerals Yearbook* published by the UNITED STATES DEPARTMENT OF THE INTERIOR. A summary article is LEWIS FERMOR: India's Mineral Resources and the War, *Asiatic Review*, December, 1940.

CHAPTER 30. INDIA'S PEOPLE AND THEIR ACTIVITIES

People and Politics

The languages, religions, and population of India are described in Vol. I of "The Indian Empire," IMPERIAL GAZETTEER OF INDIA. For an analysis of city developments see HENRY F. JAMES: The Urban Geography of India, *Bulletin* Geographical Society of Philadelphia, XXVIII (1930), 101–122. Conditions in 1931 are described by G. FINDLAY SHIRRAS: The Census of India, 1931, *Geographical Review*, XXV (1935), 434–448. General evaluation will be found in J. T. DEASY: The Problems of India, *Social Science*, XIV (1939), 197–217.

Agriculture

An excellent summary of Indian agriculture may be found in three installments of SAMUEL VAN VALKEN-BURG's Agricultural Regions of Asia: India, *Economic Geography*, IX (1933), 109–136; X (1934), 14–34; and Farther India, *Economic Geography*, IX (1933), 1–19. An extensive analysis of land-use statistics is presented in L. DUDLEY STAMP's "Asia." General descriptions of agricultural problems are available in A. and G. L. C. HOWARD: "The Development of Indian Agriculture," Oxford: University Press (1927); Vol. III of "The Indian Empire"; and the "Linlith-gow Report" of the ROYAL COMMISSION ON AGRI-CULTURE IN INDIA. *Command Paper* 3132 (1928); as well as in Chap. 4 of the "Asia" volume of the "Oxford Survey of the British Empire." A report which includes much more than its title suggests is "India as a Producer and Exporter of Wheat," Stanford University, *Food Research Institute*, III, No. 8 (1927), 317–412. The most detailed analysis is that by TH. H. ENGELBRECHT: "Die Feldfruchte Indiens in ihrer geographischen Verbreitung," Ham-burg Colonial Institute, Hamburg, XIX (1914). A useful map which indicates the extent of cultivated land has been made by WELLINGTON D. JONES: An Isopleth Map of Land under Crops in India, *Geographical Review*, XIX (1939), 495–496. Economic aspects are considered by W. LADEJINSKY: Agricul-tural Problems of India, in *Foreign Agriculture*, III (1939), 321–346; and The Food Supply of India, *Foreign Agriculture*, VI (1942), 265–281.

Industry and Communications

The standard treatment is VERA ANSTEY: "The Economic Development of India."

CHAPTER 31. REGIONS OF NORTHERN INDIA

In addition to the specific material on various regions listed below, a large amount of valuable material is contained in the textbooks on Asia by L. DUDLEY STAMP, L. W. LYDE, and DANIEL R. BERGSMARK. The Indian installments on the Agri-cultural Regions of Asia by SAMUEL VAN VALKENBURG are especially useful. Other schemes of regional division are described by J. N. L. BAKER: Notes on the Natural Regions of India, *Geography*, XIV (1928), 447–455; F. J. RICHARD: Cultural Regions in India, *Geography*, XV (1929), 20–29; and DANIEL R. BERGSMARK: The Geographic Regions of India, *Journal of Geography*, XXVIII (1929), 108–122. An Indian analysis of physiographic regions has been prepared by M. B. PITHAWALLA: The Need of Uniformity in the Geographic Divisions of India, *Journal* Madras Geographical Association, XIV (1939), 213–228; and Physiographic Divisions of India, *Journal* Madras Geographical Association, XIV (1939), 423–434.

Bengal and Orissa Lowland

There is no satisfactory treatment of the region as such, but pertinent material will be found in the following references: HUGH McPHERSON: The Indian Province of Bihar and Orissa, *Scottish Geographical Magazine*, XLVII (1931), 1–19; A. V. WILLIAMSON: Irrigation in the Indo-Gangetic Plain, *Geographical Journal*, LXV (1925), 141–153; and W. H. WOOD: Rivers and Man in the Indus-Ganges Alluvial Plain, *Scottish Geographical Magazine*, XL (1924), 1–16.

Ganges Valley

This area is covered in the articles by McPHERSON, WILLIAMSON, and WOOD listed under the Bengal and Orissa Lowland. The capital is described in W. J. GRANT: Delhi, the Flower of India, *Geographical Magazine*, XII (1940), 132–145.

Brahmaputra Valley

Consult C. F. JONES: Tea in Assam, India, *Journal of Geography*, XXIII (1924), 181–188.

Indus Valley

Geographic conditions in the Punjab are described in two articles by R. MACLAGAN GORRIE: Pressure of Population and Misuse of Land in the Punjab, *Scottish Geographical Magazine*, LIV (1938), 284–295; and Soil and Water Conservation in the Punjab, *Geographical Review*, XXVIII (1938), 20–31. Addi-tional information may be obtained from the articles by WILLIAMSON and WOOD listed under Bengal and Orissa Lowland. See also F. F. FERGUSSON: Famine and Water Supply in Western Rajputana, *Geograph-ical Journal*, XCIII (1939), 39–53.

Western Frontier

A brief note in the *Geographical Review*, XVI (1926), 318–319 suggests the strategic significance of this area.

Himalayan Highlands

The literature on The Himalaya is very extensive, particularly for the less accessible areas. Almost every volume of the *Geographical Journal* contains accounts of explorations. Illustrated articles are available in the *National Geographic Magazine*. The difficulty of normal travel is pointed out by KENNETH MASON: The Himalayas as a Barrier to Modern Communications, *Geographical Journal*, LXXXVI (1936), 1–16. Accounts of the various Mt. Everest expeditions will be found in the following volumes: C. G. BRUCE: "The Assault on Mt. Everest, 1922," London: E. Arnold & Co. (1923); HUGH RUTTLEDGE: "Everest 1933," London: Hodder (1934); SIR FRANCIS YOUNGHUSBAND: "Everest: the Challenge," London: Nelson (1936); and HUGH RUTTLEDGE: "Everest: the Unfinished Adventure," London: Hodder (1937). The account of a Swiss expedition is ARNOLD HEIM and AUGUST GANSSER: "The Throne of the Gods," New York: Macmillan (1939).

CHAPTER 32. REGIONS OF PENINSULAR INDIA

West Coast

The best geographic analyses of the West Coast have been prepared by WARREN STRAIN: The West Coast of India, *Journal of Geography*, XXXI (1932), 1–20; and ETHEL SIMKINS: The Coast Plains of South India, *Economic Geography*, IX (1933), 19–50, 136–159.

Black Soil Region

ETHEL SIMKINS has written a detailed study in "The Agricultural Geography of the Deccan Plateau of India," London: Philip (1926). Two other useful articles are A. V. WILLIAMSON: Indigenous Irrigation Works in Peninsular India, *Geographical Review*, XXI (1931), 613–626; and K. I. G. SUNDARAM: A Deccan Village in India, *Journal of Geography*, XXX (1931), 49–57.

Southern Peninsula

In addition to the articles by ETHEL SIMKINS on "The Agricultural Geography of the Deccan Plateau of India," The Coast Plains of South India, and A. V. WILLIAMSON: Indigenous Irrigation Works in Peninsular India, previously listed, there are two studies by SUMNER CUSHING: The Geography of Godavari—a District in India, *Bulletin* Geographical

Society of Philadelphia, IX (1911), 169–187; and The East Coast of India, *Bulletin* American Geographical Society, XLV (1913), 81–92. The eastern margin of the peninsula is well described by J. RILEY STAATS: India East Coast, *Journal of Geography*, XXI (1932), 93–111.

Ceylon

The standard reference on Ceylon is ELSIE K. COOK: "A Geography of Ceylon," London: Macmillan (1931). Detailed information is presented by JOHN R. BAKER who describes The Sinharaja Rain-Forest, Ceylon, *Geographical Journal*, LXXXIX (1937), 539–549.

CHAPTER 33. INDIA'S PLACE IN THE WORLD

Foreign Trade

Current statistics will be found in the *Indian Year Book and Who's Who*, and the *Foreign Commerce Yearbook* of the UNITED STATES DEPARTMENT OF COMMERCE. General economic information is in VERA ANSTEY's volumes on "The Economic Development of India" and on "The Trade of the Indian Ocean."

Political Relations

India's internal and external problems are well summarized by C. B. FAWCETT: "A Political Geography of the British Empire."

Cultural Contributions

An able evaluation may be found in WILL DURANT: "The Story of Civilization," New York: Simon & Schuster (1935). See also H. G. RAWLINSON: "India, a Short Cultural History," New York: Appleton-Century (1938).

SOUTHEASTERN ASIA

CHAPTER 34. THE SOUTHEASTERN REALM

Summarized material may be found in the general volumes on Asia such as BERGSMARK: "Economic Geography of Asia"; STAMP: "Asia"; LYDE: "The Continent of Asia"; and SION: "Asie des moussons." The Institute of Pacific Relations has sponsored a number of volumes dealing with this part of Asia, such as KATE MITCHELL: "Industrialization of the Western Pacific"; PELZER, GREENE and PHILLIPS: "Economic Survey of the Pacific Area" in two volumes; KARL G. PELZER: "Agriculture and Settlement in Southeastern Asia"; and JACK SHEPHERD: "Industry in Southeast Asia." Current data are published in the fortnightly *Far Eastern Survey.* The *Annals* of the American Academy of Political and Social Science for March, 1943, CCXXVI, is devoted to Southeastern Asia and the Philippines; as is the November, 1942, issue, II, of *The Far Eastern Quarterly.* Four installments of SAMUEL VAN VALKENBURG'S series on the Agricultural Regions of Asia relate to this area, principally Part III, Farther India, *Economic Geography,* IX (1933), 1–18, which deals with the continental portion. An excellent evaluation of mineral resources may be found in H. FOSTER BAIN: "Ores and Industry in the Far East." The importance of rice is described by V. D. WICKIZER and M. K. BENNETT: "The Rice Economy of Monsoon Asia," Stanford University: Food Research Institute (1941). JOHN L. CHRISTIAN has contributed two articles: Recent Literature Relating to Southeast Asia, *Far Eastern Quarterly,* I (1942), 378–386; and Anglo-French Rivalry in Southeast Asia, *Geographical Review,* XXXI (1941), 272–282. The stimulating impressions of a *New York Times* correspondent may be found in ROBERT A. SMITH: "Our Future in Asia," New York: Viking (1940).

CHAPTER 35. BURMA

The best material on Burma is in the articles by L. DUDLEY STAMP who served in the country for several years as petroleum geologist. See especially his articles: Burma, An Undeveloped Monsoon Country, *Geographical Review,* XX (1930), 86–109; The Irrawaddy River, *Geographical Journal,* XCV (1940), 329–356; Notes on the Vegetation of Burma, *Geographical Journal,* LXIV (1924), 231–237; and the detailed analysis prepared jointly with LESLEY LORD: The Ecology of Part of the Riverine Tract of Burma, *Journal of Ecology,* II (1923), 129–159. Another useful summary is The Geography of Burma, by MARION MURPHY, *Journal of Geography,* XXX (1931), 17–33. Three useful general volumes are J. S. FURNIVALL: "Introduction to the Political Economy of Burma," rev. by J. R. ANDRUS, Rangoon: Burma Book Club (1938); W. J. GRANT: "The New Burma," New York: Macmillan (1941); and JOHN L. CHRISTIAN: "Modern Burma," Berkeley: University of California Press (1942). The transition from agriculture to industry is covered in O. H. SPATE: Beginnings of Industrialization in Burma, *Economic Geography,* XVII (1941), 75–92. Production figures are given in LEWIS FERMOR: Burma's Mineral Resources and the War, *Asiatic Review,* January, 1941. Burma's largest city is the subject of an article by O. H. K. SPATE and L. W. TRUEBLOOD: Rangoon: A Study in Urban Geography, *Geographical Review,* XXXII (1942), 56–73.

CHAPTER 36. THAILAND

The most detailed geographical study is that of WILHELM CREDNER: "Siam, das Land der Tai," Stuttgart: Engelhorns (1935). Conditions under the absolute monarchy are best described by WALTER A. GRAHAM: "Siam," London: Moring, 3d ed. (1924). Later developments are covered in VIRGINIA THOMPSON: "Thailand, the New Siam," New York: Macmillan (1941); an older survey may be found in a chapter in "The Far East" by ARCHIBALD LITTLE; a brief study of people and history is provided in a bulletin by the Smithsonian Institution entitled Siam—Land of Free Men, by H. G. DEIGNAN (1943). ROBERT L. PENDLETON has contributed numerous excellent articles from the standpoint of a soils scientist of wide experience in the Asiatic tropics, particularly in Laterite and Its Structural Uses in Thailand and Cambodia, *Geographical Review,* XXXI (1941), 177–202; Land Use in Northeastern Thailand, *Geographical Review,* XXXIII (1943), 15–41; Some Interrelations between Agriculture and Forestry, Particularly in Thailand, *Journal* Thailand Research Society, XII (1939), 33–52; and Soils of Thailand, *Journal* Thailand Research Society, XII (1940), 235–260. The results of field studies of regional land use are in CARLE C. ZIMMERMAN: "Siam, Rural Economic Survey," Bangkok: Bangkok Times Press (1931), summarized in Some Phases of Land Utilization in Siam, *Geographical Review,* XXVII (1937), 378–393; and J. M. ANDREWS: "Siam, Second Rural Economic Survey," Bangkok: Bangkok Times Press (1935). Farm conditions are covered by W. LADEJINSKY: Thailand's Agricultural Economy, *Foreign Agriculture,* VI (1942), 165–184. The account of a visit in 1938 may be found in L. DUDLEY STAMP: Siam before the War, *Geographical Journal,* XCIX (1942), 209–224. The political aspects of a canal across the Malay Peninsula are considered by WILLIAM J. RONAN: The Kra Canal: A Suez for Japan? *Pacific Affairs,* IX (1936), 406–415.

CHAPTER 37. INDO-CHINA

The two best references in French are P. GOUROU: "L'Indochine française," Hanoi (1929); and JULES SION: "Asie des moussons," part 4, L'Indochine. A series of regional monographs bears the title "Indochine française," Hanoi: Imprimerie d'extrême Orient (1931); "L'Atlas de l'Indo-chine," Hanoi (1936?) contains maps of land use and resources. English-speaking geographers have given surprisingly little attention to the country. The best treatment of culture, economy, and administration is VIRGINIA THOMPSON: "French Indo-China," New York: Macmillan (1937). A general description is contained in ARCHIBALD LITTLE: "The Far East." The most important city of the country is described by SHANNON McCUNE: Saïgon, French Indo-China, *Journal of Geography*, XXXVI (1937), 24–33. Pictures of the ruins of Angkor may be found in the *National Geographic Magazine*, XXIII (1912), 209–272; and LIV (1928), 303–332.

CHAPTER 38. MALAYA

The geological foundations of Malaya are presented by J. B. SCRIVENOR: The Physical Geography of the Southern Part of the Malay Peninsula, *Geographical Review*, XI (1921), 351–371, who has also written "Geology of Malaya," London: Macmillan (1931); while the equally basic problems of people are described by C. A. VLIELAND: The Population of the Malay Peninsula, *Geographical Review*, XXIV (1934), 61–78. Agricultural production is considered in two articles by W. I. LADEJINSKY: Agriculture in British Malaya, *Foreign Agriculture*, V (1941), 103–125; and Agricultural Policies of British Malaya, *Foreign Agriculture*, V (1941), 159–164; and also in an article by GEORGE F. DEASY: The Oil Palm in Malaya, *Journal of Geography*, XLI (1942), 21–32. The political background is the subject of RUPERT EMERSON: "Malaysia;" New York: Macmillan (1937); and L. A. MILLS: "British Rule in Eastern Asia," Minneapolis: University of Minnesota Press (1942). There are three excellent articles by E. H. G. DOBBY: Settlement and Land Utilization, Malacca, *Geographical Journal*, XCIV (1939), 466–478; Singapore: Town and Country, *Geographical Review*, XXX (1940), 84–109; and Settlement Patterns in Malaya, *Geographical Review*, XXXII (1942), 211–232.

Three articles on Sarawak are T. H. HARRISSON: The Oxford University Expedition to Sarawak, 1932, *Geographical Journal*, LXXXII (1933), 385–410; D. L. LEACH: The Survey of Sarawak, *Geographical Journal*, C (1942), 98–106; and J. C. SWAYNE: Sarawak, *Scottish Geographical Magazine*, LVIII (1942), 59–63.

CHAPTER 39. NETHERLANDS INDIES

General information on government and economic problems may be found in AMRY VANDENBOSCH: "The Dutch East Indies," Berkeley: University of California Press, 3d ed. (1942); JAN O. M. BROEK: "Economic Development of the Netherlands Indies," New York: Institute of Pacific Relations (1942); and in the "Handbook of the Netherlands East-Indies," Buitenzorg, Java: Department of Agriculture, Industry, and Commerce (1930). Two sources on geology are H. ALBERT BROUWER: "Geology of the Netherlands East Indies," New York: Macmillan

(1925); and J. H. F. UMBGROVE: Geological History of the East Indies, *Bulletin* American Association of Petroleum Geologists, XXII (1938), 1–70. Excellent maps are available in the "Atlas van Tropisch Nederland," Amsterdam (1938). Excellent geographical surveys are provided in three articles by SAMUEL VAN VALKENBURG: Agricultural Regions of Asia, Part VIII, Malaysia, *Economic Geography*, XI (1935), 227–246, 325–337; Part IX, Java, XII (1936), 27–44; and Java: The Economic Geography of a Tropical Island, *Geographical Review*, XV (1925), 563–583. His article entitled Java: A Study of Population, *Papers* Michigan Academy of Science, Arts, and Letters, XIV (1930), 399–415, deals with one of the island's most pressing problems. An excellent summary of agricultural economics may be found in the article entitled Agriculture of the Netherlands Indies, *Foreign Agriculture*, IV (1940), 511–574, by W. LADEJINSKY. Conditions shortly before the arrival of the Japanese are described in a lecture by G. H. C. HART: Recent Development in the Netherlands-Indies, *Geographical Journal*, XCIX (1942), 81–102.

Publications issued at the time of the Fourth Pacific Science Congress in 1929 contain much material of value, notably in the volume edited by L. M. R. RUTTEN: "Science in the Netherlands East Indies," Amsterdam (1929); in the 35 Excursion Guides; in the four volumes of *Proceedings;* and in "Krakatau" the subject of a volume by CH. E. STEHN, W. M. DOCTERS VAN LEEUWEN, and K. W. DAMMERMAN, Batavia (1929).

The outer islands are the subject of articles by JAN O. M. BROEK: The Economic Development of the Outer Provinces of the Netherlands Indies, *Geographical Review*, XXX (1940), 187–200; GEORGE F. DEASY: Localization of Sumatra's Oil Palm Industry, *Economic Geography*, XVIII (1942), 153–158; and HENDRIK DE LEEUW: Sumatra, Economic and Geographic, *Bulletin* Geographical Society of Philadelphia, XXVIII (1930), 16–35. Excellent photographs are available in MAYNARD OWEN WILLIAMS: Bali and Points East, *National Geographic Magazine*, LXXV (1939), 313–352. The geology and climate as they have interacted to develop the soils and so influence the land-use pattern are best described by E. C. JUL. MOHR: "Soils of Equatorial Regions, with Particular Reference to the Netherlands East Indies," trans. by ROBERT L. PENDLETON, Ann Arbor: Edwards Bros. (1943).

CHAPTER 40. THE PHILIPPINE ISLANDS

General surveys of Philippine geography may be found in the volume edited by WILLIAM H. HAAS: "The American Empire," Chicago: University of Chicago Press (1940); and in articles by WARREN D.

SMITH: The Philippine Question, *Economic Geography*, IX (1933), 303–320; ALDEN CUTSHALL: The Philippine Islands and Their People, *Journal of Geography*, XLI (1942), 201–211; and THEODORE ROOSEVELT: Land Problems in Puerto Rico and the Philippine Islands, *Geographical Review*, XXIV (1934), 182–204. The observations of a geologist long resident in the islands are in the article by WARREN D. SMITH: Geologic and Physiographic Influences in the Philippines, *Bulletin* Geological Society of America, XXVIII (1917), 515–542; and his "Geology and Mineral Resources of the Philippine Islands," Manila: Bureau of Science (1924). The "Census Atlas of the Philippines," V (1939), provides maps of topography, transportation, population, climate, agriculture, forests, and mining. A splendidly illustrated article is that by FAY COOPER COLE: Peoples of the Philippines, *Natural History*, XXXIV (1934), 507–522. The SMITHSONIAN INSTITUTION has published a useful bulletin by HERBERT W. KRIEGER: "Peoples of the Philippines," Washington (1942). One of the most complete geographic treatments is provided in an elementary textbook prepared for use in the Philippines by HUGO H. MILLER and MARY E. POLLEY: "Intermediate Geography," Boston: Ginn (1932). *Fortune Magazine* contains an article with excellent pictures in its issue for June, 1940, XXI, 47–57, 146–158.

Studies of specific products form the subject of the following articles. Agricultural conditions are reported by SAMUEL VAN VALKENBURG in Agricultural Regions of Asia, Part X, Philippine Islands, *Economic Geography*, XII (1936), 231–249; and OWEN L. DAWSON: Philippine Agriculture, a Problem of Adjustment, *Foreign Agriculture*, IV (1940), 383–456. The geographic aspects of sugar, cocoanuts, and lumber are considered by ALDEN CUTSHALL: Trends of Philippine Sugar Production, *Economic Geography*, XIV (1938), 154–158; LUIS J. BORJA: The Philippine Coconut Industry, *Economic Geography*, III (1927), 382–390; and his The Philippine Lumber Industry, *Economic Geography*, V (1929), 194–202. The *Proceedings* of the Pacific Science Congress held in California contain two items on raw materials: RAMÓN ABARQUEZ: Mineral Resources of the Philippines, II (1939), 895–904; and JOSÉ B. BARCELON and ELPIDIO C. VERA: Fuel Resources of the Philippines, II (1939), 909–914. These commodities are summarized by ALDEN CUTSHALL in Mineral Resources of the Philippine Islands, *Scientific Monthly*, LIV (1942), 295–302.

Two contributions to regional geography are GEORGE S. CASE: The Geographic Regions of the Philippine Islands, *Journal of Geography*, XXVI (1927), 41–52; and ROBERT L. PENDLETON: Land Utilization and Agriculture of Mindanao, Philippine Islands, *Geographical Review*, XXXII (1942), 180–210

Index